THE PENGUIN RHYMING DICTIONARY

Rosalind Fergusson was born in Liverpool in 1953 and obtained her degree in French from Exeter University. From there she took a teaching certificate and became an assistant teacher at a school in West Sussex. From 1978 to 1984 she worked for Market House Books where she trained as an assistant editor and lexicographer and rose to the position of Senior Editor. During this time she worked on a range of reference books. Since leaving Market House Books she has worked as a freelance editor.

Her other publications include Pan's *English–French Companion Dictionary* (1982), *The Penguin Dictionary of Proverbs* (1983), *Choose Your Baby's Name* (1987), *The Hamlyn Dictionary of Quotations* (1989) and *The Penguin Dictionary of English Synonyms and Antonyms* (1992). Rosalind Fergusson has also edited and co-edited a number of dictionaries and reference books and has contributed to Longman's *Dictionary of Twentieth-Century Biography* (1985) and *The Bloomsbury Good Word Guide* (1988) among others.

Rosalind Fergusson is married and lives in Littlehampton. Her leisure interests include walking, sailing, photography and music.

THE PENGUIN
RHYMING DICTIONARY

ROSALIND FERGUSON

MARKET HOUSE BOOKS LIMITED

PENGUIN BOOKS

PENGUIN BOOKS

Published by the Penguin Group
Penguin Books Ltd, 27 Wrights Lane, London W8 5TZ, England
Penguin Books USA Inc., 375 Hudson Street, New York, New York 10014, USA
Penguin Books Australia Ltd, Ringwood, Victoria, Australia
Penguin Books Canada Ltd, 10 Alcorn Avenue, Toronto, Ontario, Canada M4V 3B2
Penguin Books (NZ) Ltd, 182–190 Wairau Road, Auckland 10, New Zealand

Penguin Books Ltd, Registered Offices: Harmondsworth, Middlesex, England

First published by Viking 1985
Published in Penguin Books 1985
13 15 17 19 20 18 16 14 12

Copyright © Market House Books Ltd, 1985
All rights reserved

Printed in England by Clays Ltd, St Ives plc
Set in Times

PREFACE

Milton, in his preface to *Paradise Lost*, complained of the 'troublesome and modern bondage of rhyming . . . the invention of a barbarous age, to set off wretched matter and lame metre'. Yet many creators of superb matter and lilting metre, both before and since 1668 (when these words were written), have felt it necessary to make their verses rhyme. Some poets have relied on their heads to satisfy this need, others have resorted to rhyming dictionaries. *Walker's Rhyming Dictionary*, for example, has been in continuous publication for 150 years. According to its preface, it has 'been a friend in need to generations of poets and rhymesters from Byron downwards'. But when John Walker, a retired schoolmaster, compiled his *Rhyming Dictionary* in 1775, he had to do so without the benefit of a computer.

Had he had access to modern technology, the main part of his *Rhyming Dictionary*, in which the words are listed in reverse alphabetical order (working from the last letter of each word back to the first), would have been relatively simple to produce from the headword list of any standard dictionary. However, this list alone does not provide the poet seeking a rhyme for, say, *trite*, with any of the perfect rhymes: *sight, indict, Fahrenheit, acolyte* or *apartheid*. On the other hand, it throws together as if they rhymed those classic examples of English spelling inconsistency: *bough, cough, though, rough* and *through*.

To compile the *Penguin Rhyming Dictionary*, a list of words together with their phonetic transcriptions was extracted from a standard dictionary data base. The computer was programmed to sort these words, working from the end of the phonetic transcription back to the beginning, into phonetic order. Unsuitable and unrhymable words were then discarded and the remainder of the list was sorted into rhyming groups. The result it that homophones (phonetically identical words of different meaning), such as *sight, cite* and *site*, are now grouped together, and such rhymes as *stipulation* and *manipulation*, rather than being buried in an alphabetical list of *-ation* words, appear side by side.

With its ability to scan through a complete list of phonetic transcriptions in a matter of minutes, the computer is an incomparably more versatile rhymester than the live poet with his dying brain cells and deteriorating memory. This dictionary offers to the poet the fruits of the computer's labour, providing him or her with all the words that one would expect to find in a standard English dictionary, including a selection of proper names. There is only one condition of entry for a word: that there should be at least one other word that rhymes with it. Because poetry is not only a question of rhymes – and because poets may wish to know what their verses mean – a short gloss is provided for the more obscure words.

R F
1984

HOW TO USE THE DICTIONARY

1. To find the rhymes for any particular word, first look in the index, which forms roughly the second half of the book.

2. The index will refer the user either to a group number (e.g. 15) or a subgroup number (e.g. 15.3) in the first part of the book.

3. Find the word you have looked up in the group or subgroup to which you have been referred. The words closest to this word will be its closest rhymes.

4. If you have been directed to a group rather than to a subgroup, you will find several separate paragraphs under the group heading. The first paragraph contains monosyllabic words, the second paragraph disyllabic words, and so on.
   Example: To find the closest rhymes to **ballet**, look this word up in the index. The reference **2** means that it will be found in the group headed **2**. Because it has two syllables it will be found in the second paragraph. The words that follow it – **Calais, callais, palais, chalet**, etc. – are its closest rhymes.

5. Note that **ballet** can be made to rhyme, with varying degrees of closeness, with all the words in group **2** and its subgroups. This applies to all the words in all the groups (see note (b), below).

6. Within each paragraph, whether in a main group or in a subgroup, the words given are listed in phonetic order, working from the end of the word to the beginning. The basis of the phonetic order is given on page ix. However, in most cases, paragraphs are short enough for a word to be located by quickly scanning it, rather than by trying to work out its position in the phonetic order.

7. If the index directs you to a subgroup rather than to a group, you will find a list of close rhymes that have been picked out and placed in a subgroup because it would not have been possible to place them next to each other in a main group. (This usually means that some of the words in the subgroup contain different numbers of syllables.)

   Example: To find the closest rhymes to **atmosphere**, go as directed by the index to subgroup **6.1**, where all the words ending in **-osphere** are listed – from **biosphere** to **magnetosphere**.

The following points should be noted:

(a) All the words in the lists contained in the first part of the book are included in the alphabetical index in the second part of the book.

(b) The rhyming words are arranged in the numbered groups under one-syllable headings, such as *-ite*, *-ank*, and *-oe*. These headings are broad guides to the final sound of the words in the groups. For example, the *-oe* groups contains **potato**, **although**, and **show** as well as **hoe** and **roe**.

(c) Some group headings are followed by a guide to further rhyming possibilities, often in the form of a cross-reference. Unless otherwise stated, these cross-references apply to all the subgroups of both the group in which they appear and the group to which they refer. For example, the cross reference from group **5** to group **16** applies also to the subgroups **5.1** to **5.24** and subgroups **16.1** to **16.406**.

(d) The glosses that follow difficult words are intended as brief guides to their meanings or to the field in which they are used; they do not constitute full dictionary definitions. The italicized labels – *US, Scot, Austral*, etc. – indicate that the word is an American, Scottish or Australian synonym, often informal, for the given gloss. Thus (*Welsh* mountain) means 'a Welsh word for mountain'. However, (Welsh mountain) means 'a mountain in Wales'.

PHONETIC ORDER

a as in *sat*
ar as in *card, half*
ay as in *day, rail*
e as in *bed*
err as in *err, fern*
air as in *pair, rare*
ee as in *meet, teach*
ear as in *veer, fear*
i as in *win*
ie as in *tie, bite*
ire as in *fire*
o as in *pot*
or as in *form, talk*
oor as in *moor*
oy as in *boy, coil*
oe as in *toe, boat*
ow as in *town, foul*
our as in *hour*
u as in *mug*
oo as in *foot*
ue as in *true, tool*
er as in *water* and other unstressed vowel sounds
b as in *big*
k as in *kite, car*

ch as in *chip*
d as in day
f as in *fall, phone*
g as in *gate*
j as in *job, page*
h as in *hat*
l as in *lean*
m as in *mope*
n as in *neat*
ng as in *sing*
p as in *pearl*
qu as in *quick*
r as in *ripe*
s as in *soon*
sh as in *sheep, nation*
zh as in *treasure*
t as in *team*
th as in *thing*
dh as in *bathe*
v as in *vase*
w as in *wool*
x as in *box, works*
y as in *yoke*
z as in *zoo, reason*

RHYMING DICTIONARY

1 -ar

are, ah, bar, baa, Ba (soul in Egyptian mythology), car, scar, char, dah (sound in Morse code), fa, far, Ga (African people), gar (freshwater fish), jar, ha, haar (North Sea fog), lah, blah (silly talk), mar, ma, maar (volcanic crater), knar (knot in wood), parr, par, pa, spar, spa, Kwa (language group), Ra, bra, Kra (isthmus of Thailand), Fra (title of Italian monk), Saar (European river), shah, ta, tar, tahr (goatlike mammal), Ptah (Egyptian god), star, var (unit of power), moire, schwa (unstressed vowel sound), pya (Burmese coin), tsar.

aa (volcanic rock), toea (Papua New Guinea coin), baba, Sabah (Malaysian state), durbar (native ruler's court), oba (African chief), drawbar (metal bar on tractor), crowbar, towbar, Pooh-Bah, subah (province in Mogul empire), Akbar (Mogul emperor of India), rollbar, unbar, Dunbar, facebar (wrestling hold), disbar, crossbar, kasbah, busbar (electrical conductor), fracas, markka (Finnish currency), taka (Bangladeshi currency), Neckar (West German river), shikar (big-game hunting), trocar (surgical instrument), chukar (partridge), sidecar, calcar (spurlike projection), railcar, Shankar, eschar (dry scab on skin), streetcar, boxcar (US closed railway van), cha-cha, kwacha (Zambian currency), morcha (Indian anti-government demonstration), Dada, radar, sirdar, numdah (coarse Indian felt), Gondar (Ethiopian city), sofar (marine location system), shofar (ancient Jewish horn), afar, sol-fa, gaga, Degas, Hagar (Old Testament character), durgah (tomb of Muslim saint), nougat, Elgar, kanga (African woman's cotton garment), koftgar (Indian goldsmith), ajar, nightjar, Lehár, Doha (capital of Qatar), Zohar (Jewish mystical work), hoo-ha, belah (Australian tree), nullah (Indian stream or drain), moolah (Slang money), kiblah (direction of Mecca), dobla (medieval Spanish coin), éclat (brilliant success), verglas (thin film of ice), hoopla, Omagh, summa (medieval scholastic compendium), grandma, Sennar (region of the Sudan), dinar, thenar (palm of the hand), Donar (Germanic god), sonar, Dahna (Arabian desert), faux pas, papa, culpa (act of neglect), oompah, grandpa, COSPAR (Committee on Space Research), feldspar, Berar (region of India), Kura (Asian river), hurrah, Accra, Biskra (Algerian town), mudra (Hindu religious dancing movement), Stranraer, presa (musical term), paisa (Indian coin), pulsar, orgeat (drink made from barley), Qatar, ta-ta, guitar, sitar, hectare, kantar (unit of weight), qintar (Albanian coin), daystar (the sun), lodestar (star used in navigation), Telstar, instar (stage in insect development), sunstar (starfish), earthstar (woodland fungus), navar (aircraft-navigation system), Avar (former European people), louvar (whale-like fish), dvandva (compound word), halvah (Middle Eastern sweet), boulevard, boudoir, couloir (mountain gully), armoire, memoir, Renoir, mirepoix (mixture of sautéed vegetables), octroi (duty on goods), voussoir (wedge-shaped stone), bourgeois, patois, Magyar, cholla (spiny cactus), Konya (Turkish city), gunyah (*Austral* bush hut), quasar, Isar (European river), bizarre, Mizar (multiple star), beaux-arts, hussar.

antiar (Javan tree), caviar, Cantuar. (of Canterbury), handlebar, turbocar, judoka (judo expert), Halakah (traditional Jewish literature), motorcar, advocaat, la-di-da, deodar (Himalayan cedar), tahsildar (Indian tax collector), havildar (Indian noncommissioned officer), zamindar (Indian landowner), Kandahar (Afghan city), Omaha, almemar (raised platform in synagogue), Tsushima (Japanese islands), Charminar (16th-century Indian monument), seminar, Achernar (star), Tanana (Alaskan river), jaçana (long-legged bird), grandpapa, Peckinpah, fluorspar, akhara (Indian gymnasium), Amen-Ra (Egyptian sun-god), registrar, commissar, Manisa (Turkish city), collapsar (black hole), Aisha (Mohammed's favourite wife), langue de chat, Parashah (reading in synagogue), coup d'état, pietà, Bogotá, Janata (Indian political party), avatar (manifestation of Hindu deity), superstar, colcothar (jeweller's rouge), bolivar (Venezuelan currency), cultivar (cultivated plant), chihuahua, pesewa (Ghanaian coin), Aduwa (Ethiopian town), tous-les-mois (plant with edible tubers), peau de soie (silk or rayon fabric), escritoire, remontoir (device in a watch), polynya (water surrounded by ice).

Mauna Kea (extinct Hawaiian volcano), justiciar (medieval king's deputy), Mauna Loa (active Hawaiian volcano), Jogjakarta (Indonesian city), Kathiawar (large Indian peninsula), petit bourgeois.

1.1
debar, millibar (unit of atmospheric pressure), Zanzibar.

1.2
Calabar (Nigerian port), Malabar (Indian coastal region), coolabah, cinnabar (chief ore of mercury), isobar, isallobar (line on map).

1.3
doodah, Üsküdar (Turkish town).

1.4
cigar, Chandigarh (Indian city), budgerigar.

1.5
aha, ha-ha, brouhaha.

1.6
Bihar (Indian state), Cooch Behar (Indian city), pakeha (non-Maori).

1.7
à la, fa-la, Lala (Indian form of address), tra-la, Haleakala (Hawaiian volcano).

1.8
zila (Indian administrative district), Shangri-la.

1.9
galah (Australian cockatoo), escolar (spiny-finned fish), Agartala (Indian city).

1.10
Armagh, Hama (Syrian city), Toyama (Japanese city).

1.11
cymar (woman's short jacket), Waldemar (Danish king), Kohima (Indian city).

1.12
mama, Shema (basic Jewish doctrine), jacamar (tropical bird), Palomar (Californian mountain observatory), Beach-la-Mar (Pacific trading language), grandmama, Panama.

1.13
hoorah, tempura (Japanese food).

1.14

mara (South American rodent), Pará (Brazilian state), Tambora (Indonesian volcano), baccarat, agora (Israeli coin), Aymara (South American Indian people).

1.15

Navarre, baklava (rich cake), samovar (Russian tea urn).

1.16

peignoir, rouge et noir (card game).

1.17

abattoir, repertoire, conservatoire.

1.18

devoirs (compliments), reservoir.

1.19

bazaar, alcazar (Moorish palace in Spain), Balthazar, kala-azar (tropical disease), superbazaar (Indian department store).

2 -ay

eh, ay, bay, bey (Turkish form of address), Kay, cay (low island or bank), day, dey, fay, fey, gay, jay, hey, hay, hae (*Scot* have), lay, clay, flay, fley (*Dialect* be afraid), gley (bluish-grey soil), play, splay, slay, sleigh, May, may, neigh, nay, née, nae (*Scot* no), Neagh (Northern Irish lake), pay, Spey, spay, spae (*Scot* foretell), qua (in the capacity of), re, ray, bray, brae, cray (*Austral* crayfish), dray, fray, Frey (Norse god), frae (*Scot* from), grey, Gray, spray, tray, trey, stray, say, Tay, tay (*Irish* tea), stay, they, weigh, whey, way, wae (*Dialect* woe), ngwee (Zambian coin), sway, yea.

plié (ballet posture), mouillé (phonetics term), foyer, abbé, Torbay, cube (tropical plant), sickbay, Bombay, bombé (having projecting swollen shape), rosebay (type of rhododendron), parquet, Les Cayes (Haitian port), okay, croquet, tokay (small lizard), bouquet, Biscay, risqué, heyday, Mayday, pay-

day, urdé (heraldic term), bidet, Friday, coudé (describing type of telescope), workday, weekday, midday, half-day, someday, Mande (language group), Monday, sundae, Sunday, noonday, washday, birthday, Thursday, Tuesday, doomsday, café, parfait (frozen dessert), au fait, Hofei (Chinese city), buffet, margay (catlike mammal), reggae, nosegay, deejay, Mahé (island in Seychelles), ballet, Calais, callais (Neolithic ornamental stone), palais, chalet, Male (capital of the Maldives), vale (farewell), waylay, melee, Pelé, relay, Islay, au lait, olé, piolet (type of ice-axe), coulee (flow of molten lava), bouclé, bouclée (support for billiard cue), pipeclay, soufflé, reflet (lustre), agley (*Scot* awry), inlay, unlay (untwist), replay, foreplay, wordplay, swordplay, endplay, screenplay, gunplay, display, misplay (play badly), horseplay, mislay, bobsleigh, outlay, lamé, Niamey (capital of Niger), semé (heraldic term), gourmet, dismay, nene (Hawaiian goose), fine (musical term), chiné (mottled), mornay, pince-nez, frappé, épée, prepay, repay, Taipei (capital of Taiwan), Hopeh (Chinese province), coupé, Hupeh (Chinese province), Nupe (Nigerian people), toupee, Gaspé (peninsula in Quebec), jaspé (variegated), strathspey (Scottish reel), parkway, walkway, beret, ciré, Shiré (African river), foray, moray, Fauré, Kure (Japanese port), hooray, chambray (fine woven cloth), hombre (*US* man), defray, affray (noisy fight or disturbance), passé, Tigré (Ethiopian province), in re (in the matter of), sunray, stingray, cy pres (legal term), respray, betray, portray, entrée, estray (stray domestic animal), distrait, astray, ashtray, Vouvray (dry white wine), x-ray, essay, per se, lycée, plissé, hearsay, assay, gainsay, unsay, soothsay, cliché, broché (woven with raised design), crochet, bouchée (vol-au-vent), touché, dragée, Roget, projet (draft of proposed treaty), congé, satai (spiced barbecued meat), pâté, pattée (describing type of cross), Leyte (Philippine island), jeté, conté (artist's hard crayon), Changteh (Chinese port), Chengteh (Chinese city), mainstay, outstay, backstay (nautical term), jackstay (nautical term), Cathay, pavé (paved surface), névé (mass of ice), survey, corvée (forced labour), duvet, purvey, chevet (part of church), inveigh, convey, airway, fairway, stairway, leeway, freeway, seaway, clearway, doorway, Norway, throughway (*US* motorway), subway, hatchway, archway, headway, Medway, speedway, skidway (*US* platform for logs), midway, tideway (strong tidal current), Broadway, roadway, halfway, maguey (fibre-yielding plant), railway, spillway (channel carrying surplus water), Solway, Galway, hallway, tramway, someway, Anhwei (Chinese province), sternway (ship's movement), Conway, runway, gangway, slipway, shipway (shipbuilding structure), paceway (*Austral* racecourse), Kweisui (Chinese town), gateway, outweigh, footway (pedestrian path), beltway (*US* ring road), pathway, driveway, causeway, cruiseway (canal for recreational purposes), soignée, passepied (17th-century minuet), blasé, Laotze (ancient Chinese philosopher).

holiday, everyday, unbirthday, Wednesday, coryphée (leading ballet dancer), merengue (Caribbean dance), popinjay, cassoulet, underclay, cor anglais, teleplay, underplay, interplay, overplay, animé, consommé, résumé, Dubonnet (*Trademark*), cloisonné (type of enamel work), Hogmanay, Massenet (French composer), underpay, overpay, Kol Nidre (Jewish prayer), émigré, Castlereagh (British statesman), divorcé, fiancé, Colonsay (Hebridean island), recherché, écorché (anatomical figure), ricochet, negligee, protégé,

Fabergé, décolleté, overstay, naiveté, Milky Way, alleyway, anyway, taxiway, Camagüey (Cuban city), cableway, Hemingway, expressway (*US* urban motorway), Rambouillet (breed of sheep), sommelier, atelier, Parmentier (cookery term).

Marinduque (Philippine island), Hiroshige (Japanese artist), Tenzing Norgay, Oriente (Cuban province), companionway (stairway on ship), ukiyoe (school of Japanese painting), summa cum laude (highest achievement in examination).

2.1
Rainier, Fourier, dossier, métier, boulevardier, Du Maurier, couturier, Olivier.

2.2
Douai (French city), roué, Niue (Pacific island).

2.3
Benue (Nigerian state), tatouay (large armadillo), habitué.

2.4
obey, mangabey (monkey), disobey, Iskander Bey (Albanian patriot).

2.5
flambé, harambee (East African work chant).

2.6
piqué, appliqué.

2.7
decay, tourniquet, sobriquet, communiqué.

2.8
today, workaday, Faraday, Saturday, yesterday, alackaday.

2.9
Santa Fe, auto-da-fé (ceremony of Spanish Inquisition), Morgan le Fay.

2.10
Haringey, Fotheringhay.

2.11

belay (make secure), delay, gilet (bodice resembling waistcoat), Millais, relay, roundelay (medieval dance), virelay (old French poem).

2.12

allay, Malay, Pelée (volcano in Martinique), Rabelais, Mandalay (Burmese city), Charollais (breed of cattle), brise-soleil (structure protecting window), underlay, beaujolais, interlay, overlay, cabriolet.

2.13

roble (oak tree), paso doble.

2.14

carnet, KaNgwane (South African homeland).

2.15

matinée, ratiné (coarse cloth), in nomine (musical term).

2.16

barré (guitar-playing procedure), Le Carré.

2.17

mare (plain on moon's surface), moiré, soirée, Whangarei (New Zealand port), ricercare (musical term).

2.18

bourrée, purée, de jure (according to law).

2.19

array, cabaret, disarray, Monterey (Californian city), Monterrey (Mexican city).

2.20

assay, chassé (ballet step), bio-assay (biology term), immunoassay (immunology technique).

2.21

Ruse (Bulgarian city), repoussé (raised design), retroussé.

2.22

cachet, sachet, attaché, papier-mâché.

2.23

maté (tree cultivated for caffeine), écarté (card game), Hakodate (Japanese port).

2.24

sauté, Obote, cenote (natural well in limestone), chayote (tropical climbing plant), chicalote (type of poppy).

2.25

velouté, kachang puteh (Malaysian roasted nuts).

2.26

byway, highway, superhighway (US fast dual carriageway).

2.27

noway, Ogooué (African river).

2.28

aweigh, away, flyaway, throwaway, stowaway, breakaway, takeaway, hideaway, foldaway, Alloway, Galloway, rollaway (mounted on rollers), mulloway (Australian fish), Stornoway, caraway, faraway, straightaway, waterway, motorway, cutaway, counterweigh, castaway, Hathaway, overweigh, areaway (passageway between buildings).

2.29

ridgeway, carriageway, steerageway (nautical term), passageway.

2.30

Bizet, frisé (fabric with long nap), Champs Elysées.

2.31

rosé, San Jose (Californian city), exposé.

3 -err

err, Ur, burr, bur, birr (make whirring sound), cur, Kerr, skirr (move rapidly), chirr (make shrill sound), fur, fir, her, blur, slur, myrrh, murre (type of guillemot), knur (knot in tree trunk), per, purr, spur, br'er, sir, shirr, stir, were, whirr, 'twere.

voyeur, recur, occur, incur, concur, Frondeur (French rebel), coiffeur, defer, refer, prefer, infer, confer, transfer, millefleurs (floral design in textiles), demur, longspur (songbird), hotspur (impetuous person), Hotspur, larkspur, cockspur (type of grass), masseur, chasseur, douceur (a tip or bribe), deter, hauteur, inter, bestir, astir, aver, prie-dieu, milieu, seigneur, poseur.

butterbur (flowering plant), cocklebur (coarse weed), underfur, connoisseur, force majeure, voyageur (Canadian woodsman), rapporteur (person who prepares report), disinter, raconteur, Richelieu, écraseur (surgical cutting device).

entrepreneur, carillonneur (bell-ringer).

3.1
saboteur, littérateur (professional writer), restaurateur.

4 -air
air, heir, e'er, Ayr, ere, bare, bear, care, scare, chair, dare, fare, fair, hair, hare, lair, blare, Clare, flair, flare, glare, glair (egg-white), mare, mayor, Khmer (former Cambodian civilization), ne'er, snare, pear, pare, pair, spare, quare (*Irish* remarkable), square, rare, prayer, share, tear, tare, stair, stare, there, their, they're, vair (medieval fur trimming), wear, ware, where, swear.

tuyère (nozzle in blast-furnace), howe'er, forebear, forbear, Flaubert, threadbare, Rambert, highchair, wheelchair, armchair, pushchair, midair, Kildare, Mayfair, warfare, fieldfare, welfare, fanfare, infare (*Dialect* wedding reception), unfair, funfair, mohair, unhair (remove hair from hide), horsehair, éclair, declare, Sinclair, commère (female compere), nightmare, plein-air (art term), whene'er, Bonaire (West Indian island), ensnare, au pair, ampere, impair, compere, compare, despair,

foursquare (firmly), headsquare, where'er, confrère (fellow member of profession), corsair, torchère (stand for holding candelabrum), ploughshare, parterre (formally-patterned garden), Altair (star), Voltaire, Basse-Terre (West Indian island), Astaire, Lothair (German king), trouvère (medieval French poet), seaware (large seaweed), nowhere, neckwear, hardware, redware (seaweed), stemware (stemmed glasses), firmware (computer term), somewhere, treenware (wooden utensils), tinware, stoneware, glassware, forswear (reject with determination), elsewhere, unswear (retract), sportswear, nightwear, footwear, software, liveware (personnel working with computers), menswear, Gruyère, meunière (cookery term), Robespierre, misère.

overbear, Medicare (*US* health insurance programme), aftercare, Aberdare, nom de guerre, maidenhair (tropical fern), De la Mare, doctrinaire (theoretical and impractical), abampere, porte-cochere (covered entrance for vehicles), fourragère (ornamental cord on uniform), solitaire, Finisterre (Spanish headland), Finistère (French department), tableware, kitchenware, ironware, earthenware, ovenware, basaltware (black stoneware), chargé d'affaires.

4.1
premiere, derrière (buttocks), portière (curtain hung in doorway), rivière, jardinière, boutonniere (flowers worn in buttonhole), son et lumière.

4.2
carfare (*US* bus fare), savoir-faire.

4.3
affair, thoroughfare, chemin de fer.

4.4
bêche-de-mer (marine organism), coco de mer (palm tree), Weston-super-Mare.

4.5

debonair, questionnaire, legionnaire, billionaire, millionaire, concessionaire, commissionaire, multimillionaire.

4.6

repair, prepare, disrepair.

4.7

beware, anywhere, everywhere.

4.8

aware, underwear, Delaware, well-aware, chinaware, unaware, lustreware (pottery with lustre decoration), otherwhere, silverware.

4.9

knitwear, agateware (ceramic ware resembling agate), graniteware (enamel-coated iron vessels).

5 -ee [see also **16**]

be, bee, quay, key, ski, Dee, fee, ghee (clarified butter), gie (*Scot* give), gee, he, lea, Leigh, lee, li (Chinese unit of length), ley (line of prehistoric track), flea, flee, glee, plea, mi, me, mee (Malaysian noodles), knee, pea, pee, re, Bric, bree (*Scot* thin soup), Cree, scree, dree (*Scot* endure), free, spree, tree, three, see, sea, Hsi (Chinese river), she, tee, te, tea, thee, wee, we, twee, Twi (Negroid people), ye, zee (*US* zed).

drawee, cooee, bawbee (former Scottish coin), Frisbee (*Trademark*), ackee (tropical fruit tree), Bacchae (priestesses of Bacchus), Torquay, trochee (metrical foot), latchkey, turnkey, passkey, Volsci (ancient Latin people), ashkey, lychee, Kochi (Japanese port), Penchi (Chinese city), Chaldee, grandee, standee (person who stands), vendee, spondee, Dundee, fundi (East African mechanic), thuggee (practices of Indian thugs), lungi (Indian loincloth or turban), Meiji (period in Japanese history), burgee (ship's identification flag), gee-gee, squeegee, ogee (architectural moulding), Fuji, algae, Belgae (ancient Celtic people), pongee (silk

fabric), mallee (shrubby eucalyptus tree), bailee, Philae (island in Upper Egypt), Orly, Thule, Eastleigh, mamey (tropical fruit tree), thermae (ancient Roman public baths), gimme, Cannae (ancient Italian city), Pawnee, Shawnee, koine (a common language), donee (receiver of gift), townee, whangee (bamboo grass), rappee (English snuff), tapis (tapestry or carpet), tepee, cowpea (tropical climbing plant), rupee, Tupi (South American Indian people), yippee, chickpea, boree (Australian acacia tree), Horae (Roman goddesses), Puri (Indian port), decree, machree (*Irish* my dear), carefree, grigri (African talisman), agree, Capri, esprit, shoetree, ridgetree (timber along roof ridge), gumtree, crosstree (nautical term), farci (stuffed), Parsee (member of religious sect), precis, sycee (silver ingots), emcee (master of ceremonies), Shansi (Chinese province), Shensi (Chinese province), Kiangsi (Chinese province), sightsee, Clichy (industrial Parisian suburb), specie, chichi, buckshee, banshee, shoji (Japanese rice-paper screen), bougie (catheter), settee, titi (South American monkey), coatee, goatee, suttee (Hindu custom), bootee, tutee, stacte (Old Testament incense spice), draftee, Santee (US river), grantee, mustee (person of mixed parentage), trustee, moolvie (Muslim learned man), peewee, ennui, étui, razee (sailing ship), fusee (spindle in watch).

Savaii (island in Western Samoa), employee, diploë (bone in skull), Meroë (ancient Sudanese city), honeybee, bumblebee, heitiki (Maori neck ornament), Waikiki, Didache (early Christian treatise), Cherokee, après-ski, hydroski (hydrofoil on seaplane), debauchee, Tweedledee, Sekondi (Ghanaian port), refugee, takahe (New Zealand bird), appellee (accused person), parolee, infulae (ribbons on bishop's mitre), internee, Mycenae, calipee (edible part of turtle), Principe (island west of Africa), cap-a-pie (from head to foot), Kayseri (Turkish city), conferee (conference participant), disagree, doubletree (horizontal bar on vehicle), saddletree (frame of saddle), whiffletree (crossbar in harness), trestletree (ship's timber), manteltree (lintel over fireplace), axletree (carriage axle), Sadducee, fricassee, undersea, oversee, Marshalsea (former English court), licensee, garnishee (legal term), repartee, allottee, deportee, picotee (type of carnation), legatee (recipient of legacy), manatee (whale-like mammal), devotee, inductee (*US* military conscript), appointee, El Misti (Peruvian volcano), peccavi, vis-à-vis, ach-y-fi (Welsh expression of disgust), eau de vie, ratatouille, fedayee (Arab commando), cuir-bouilli (hardened leather), bourgeoisie, devisee (legal term), jalousie, Zuider Zee, chimpanzee.

Kauai (Hawaiian island), evacuee, interviewee, Wu-lu-mu-ch'i (Chinese city), chincherinchee (South African plant), fiddle-de-dee, bahuvrihi (linguistics term), satyagrahi (exponent of nonviolent resistance), Maebashi (Japanese city), recognizee (legal term).

5.1
lei, payee, Danaë (Greek mythological character), Pompeii.

5.2
torii (gateway to Japanese temple), reliquiae (fossil remains), facetiae (witty sayings), minutiae, exuviae (layers of shed skin), amicus curiae (legal adviser to court).

5.3
marquee, maquis (Mediterranean shrubby vegetation), raki (strong aromatic drink), bidarkee (Eskimo canoe).

5.4
chickadee (small songbird), Pasargadae (ancient Persian city).

5.5
pledgee, Himeji (Japanese city).

5.6
gidgee (small acacia tree), mortgagee, obligee (creditor), perigee.

5.7
agee (*Scot* awry), apogee.

5.8
pili (Philippine tree), jubilee, Galilee, galilee (medieval church porch), Rosie Lee.

5.9
alee, Tralee, libellee, fleur-de-lis, Omphale (Greek mythological queen), shiralee (*Austral* swagman's bundle), Peterlee, Trincomalee (Sri Lankan port), Thermopylae.

5.10
Wad Medani (Sudanese town), bouquet garni, maharani, Liliuokalani (queen of Hawaiian islands).

5.11
trainee, distrainee (legal term), detainee.

5.12
jinni (Muslim mythological spirit), nominee, examinee, Mnemosyne (Greek goddess), Euphrosyne (Greek goddess).

5.13
Chinee, assignee (legal term), consignee.

5.14
Guarani (Paraguayan currency), Kootenay (US river), alienee (legal term), abandonee (legal term).

5.15
kepi, escapee.

5.16
topee, épopée (epic poem).

5.17
Marie, sirree, jamboree, chickaree (red squirrel), referee, transferee, sangaree (spiced drink), dungaree, kedgeree,

rapparee (17th-century Irish soldier), camporee (local Scout meeting), gaucherie, Sault Sainte Marie (Canadian inland port), chinoiserie.

5.18
degree, pedigree, filigree, mistigris (joker in poker game).

5.19
lessee, addressee.

5.20
promisee, Tennessee, Pharisee, felo de se (person who commits suicide).

5.21
foresee, endorsee, divorcee.

5.22
remittee, Hippolyte (queen of the Amazons), typothetae (*US* printers collectively).

5.23
amputee, distributee (legal term).

5.24
guarantee, warrantee, absentee, patentee, covenantee.

6 -eer
ear, bier, beer, kier (vat in bleaching process), cheer, deer, dear, fear, sphere, gear, jeer, here, hear, leer, Lear, Leah, clear, mere, smear, near, sneer, peer, pier, spear, queer, rear, sear, sere, cere (swelling on bird's beak), ser (Indian unit of weight), sheer, shear, tear, tier, steer, stere (unit for measuring timber), veer, weir, Wear, we're, year.

Aïr (region in the Sahara), Zaïre, Meir, gambier (astringent obtained from plant), fakir, Bashkir (Mongoloid people), voir dire (legal term), nadir, mudir (local governor), killdeer (US plover), reindeer, endear, mandir (Hindu temple), ensphere, headgear, footgear, Aegir (Norse god), Tangier, cohere, adhere, menhir, inhere, mishear, unclear, emir, Vermeer, Mimir (Norse

mythological giant), Ajmer (Indian city), Thirlmere, Grasmere, besmear, Kashmir, cashmere, Izmir (Turkish port), compeer (person of equal status), Shakespeare, lequear (ceiling with sunken panels), eyrir (Icelandic coin), career, Fenrir (Norse mythological wolf), uprear, Asir (region of Saudi Arabia), Aesir (chief Norse gods), Landseer, sincere, cashier, Ayrshire, Cheshire, Berkshire, Yorkshire, Shropshire, Hampshire, Wiltshire, Flintshire, wheatear (small songbird), haltere (insect's modified hind wing), frontier, austere, wasteweir (channel carrying surplus water), Goodyear, vizier.

Aboukir, belvedere, bayadere (Hindu dancing girl), bombardier, Agadir, brigadier, balladeer, grenadier, commandeer, interfere, hemisphere, barysphere (central portion of earth), bathysphere, overhear, Cordelier (Franciscan friar), chandelier, cameleer, fusilier, bandoleer (soldier's shoulder belt), gondolier, gasolier (fitting for gaslights), pistoleer (soldier armed with pistol), cavalier, chanticleer, Tirich Mir (Pakistani mountain), insincere, Derbyshire, Denbighshire, Lancashire, Radnorshire, Leicestershire, Gloucestershire, Worcestershire, Warwickshire, Brecknockshire, Pembrokeshire, Staffordshire, Bedfordshire, Hertfordshire, Oxfordshire, Cambridgeshire, Monmouthshire, racketeer, rocketeer (rocket engineer), musketeer, profiteer, gadgeteer (lover of gadgetry), muleteer, pamphleteer, sonneteer, puppeteer, corsetier, gazetteer, volunteer, oversteer.

Diyarbakir (Turkish city), Buckinghamshire, Nottinghamshire.

isodiaphere (type of atomic nucleus), Merionethshire.

6.1
biosphere, ecosphere, thermosphere (atmospheric layer), atmosphere, troposphere (lowest atmospheric layer),

aerosphere (earth's entire atmosphere), hydrosphere (earth's watery regions), centrosphere (central part of earth), mesosphere (atmospheric layer), stratosphere, photosphere (visible surface of sun), lithosphere (earth's crust), exosphere (highest atmospheric layer), rhizosphere (soil around plant's roots), ionosphere, ozonosphere (region of stratosphere), magnetosphere.

6.2
chimere (bishop's sleeveless gown), Vladimir, epimere (part of embryo), cassimere (woollen cloth), antimere (biology term), kerseymere (woollen cloth).

6.3
amir (former ruler of Afghanistan), Windermere, centromere (part of chromosome), metamere (animal's body segment), Buttermere, blastomere (embryonic cell), Rothermere (British newspaper magnate), actinomere (biology term).

6.4
veneer, engineer, domineer, scrutineer, mutineer, mountaineer, carabineer (soldier armed with carbine).

6.5
pioneer, Bikaner (Indian city), buccaneer, chiffonier (tall chest of drawers), sloganeer, cannoneer, auctioneer, pontonier (military bridge builder), souvenir, gonfalonier (medieval Italian magistrate), electioneer.

6.6
appear, reappear, diapir (geological fold), disappear.

6.7
cuirassier (16th-century mounted soldier), xerosere (ecology term), adipocere (waxy substance from corpses).

6.8
Breconshire, Lincolnshire, Huntingdonshire, Cardiganshire, Northampton-

shire, Carmarthenshire, Caernarvonshire.

6.9
privateer, charioteer.

6.10
megathere (extinct sloth), dinothere (extinct elephant-like mammal), isothere (line on map), chalicothere (extinct horse-like mammal), titanothere (extinct horse-like mammal), uintathere (extinct rhinoceros-like mammal).

6.11
revers, revere, severe, Bedivere, Guinevere, persevere, Guadalquivir (Spanish river).

7 -ie
I, ay, aye, eye, bye, buy, by, Skye, sky, die, dye, fie, guy, hi, high, hie (to hurry), lie, lye (alkaline solution), Bligh, fly, ply, sly, my, nigh, nye (flock of pheasants), snye (side channel of river), pie, pi, spy, wry, rye, cry, scry (divine by crystal-gazing), dry, fry, pry, spry, try, sigh, shy, tie, Thai, taille (former French tax), sty, thigh, thy, vie, why, Wye, swy (*Austral* gambling game).

shiai (judo contest), aye-aye, kowhai (New Zealand tree), rabbi, thereby, whereby, hereby, nearby, flyby (flight past), forby (*Scot* besides), Dubai, goodbye, Sakai (Japanese port), cockeye (squinting eye), rocaille (decorative rock work), sockeye, Tokay (Hungarian sweet wine), buckeye (US tree), pinkeye (acute conjunctivitis), bronchi, deadeye (nautical term), redeye, goldeye (US fish), Sendai (Japanese city), hi-fi, sci-fi, bigeye (tropical fish), gilgai (*Austral* natural water hole), nilgai (Indian antelope), Songhai (West African people), magi, fungi, Weihai (Chinese port), Pohai (inlet of Yellow Sea), Shanghai, shanghai, Tsinghai (Chinese province), ally, Alai (Russian mountain range), Eli, walleye (divergent squint), mayfly, firefly, blowfly, shoofly, blackfly, catchfly (plant with sticky parts), gadfly, sandfly, gallfly, greenfly, horsefly, housefly, botfly, imply, comply, demy (size of paper), Katmai (Alaskan volcano), Panay (Philippine island), Menai, mooneye (US freshwater fish), Brunei, Sinai, charpai (type of bedstead), porkpie, magpie, espy, potpie (meat and vegetable stew), decry, descry, retry, assai (musical term), asci (botany term), Kasai (African river), Masai (African people), Pasay (Philippine city), Versailles, nisi, loci, bonsai, workshy, cockshy (target in throwing games), shuteye, necktie, recti (straight muscles), hogtie (*US* tie limbs together), untie, pigsty, Levi (Old Testament character), oxeye, cocci (bacteria), Veii (ancient Etruscan city), banzai (Japanese patriotic cheer).

Haggai (Old Testament prophet), alibi, syllabi, lullaby, passer-by, overdye, argufy, satisfy, ultrahigh, jai alai (Spanish game), jus soli (legal term), butterfly, overfly, damselfly, dragonfly, dobsonfly (large insect), haeremai (Maori expression of welcome), decani (musical term), Iceni (ancient British tribe), goldeneye (diving duck), Philippi, occupy, counterspy, samurai, Madurai (Indian city), prophesy, lex loci (law of the place), Hokusai, chigetai (Asian wild ass), Paraguay, Uruguay, tiger's-eye.

locus standi (legal term), dissatisfy, preoccupy, decree nisi.

certiorari (legal term), corpus delicti (facts constituting an offence), dramatis personae.

7.1
radii, bindi-eye (Australian plant), nuclei, genii, Falerii (ancient Italian city), Helvetii (Celtic tribe), pons Varolii (nerve fibres in brain).

7.2
Mackay, Malachi.

7.3
defy, deify, reify (make real), rubefy (make red), speechify, preachify, Frenchify, ladyfy, edify, modify, codify, dandify, salify (mix with salt), jellify, stellify (change into a star), vilify, nullify, uglify, amplify, simplify, ramify, mummify, tumefy (swell up), carnify (medical term), unify, cockneyfy, magnify, damnify (injure), tepefy (make tepid), typify, stupefy, liquefy, aerify (change into a gas), scarify, rarefy, horrify, torrefy (dry with intense heat), scorify (refine by smelting), glorify, purify, chondrify (change into cartilage), metrify (translate into poetic metre), petrify, vitrify, nitrify (treat with nitrogen), putrefy, countrify, basify (make basic), casefy (become cheese-like), specify, versify, ossify, crucify, calcify, falsify, Nazify, certify, prettify, citify, fortify, mortify, notify, brutify (brutalize), beautify, fructify (bear fruit), sanctify, stultify, quantify, testify, mystify, justify, vivify (bring to life).

syllabify, alkalify, exemplify, saponify (change into soap), personify, reunify, indemnify, solemnify, transmogrify, electrify, diversify, intensify, denazify, acetify (convert into vinegar), identify, demystify, revivify, detoxify, oversimplify.

7.3.1
nidify (build a nest), rigidify, solidify, humidify, lapidify (change into stone), acidify, dehumidify.

7.3.2
jollify, mollify, qualify, disqualify.

7.3.3
dignify, lignify (make woody), signify, presignify.

7.3.4
clarify, saccharify (convert into sugar).

7.3.5
terrify, verify, esterify (chemistry term).

7.3.6
gasify, classify, pacify, declassify.

7.3.7
dulcify (sweeten), demulsify (separate an emulsion), emulsify.

7.3.8
ratify, gratify, stratify, beatify, interstratify (geology term).

7.3.9
rectify, objectify (represent concretely), subjectify (interpret subjectively).

7.4
assegai (sharp light spear), anthropophagi (cannibals).

7.5
belie, quillai (South American tree), rely, villi (finger-like projections), morbilli (measles), locus sigilli (position of document seal).

7.6
July, vox populi, lapis lazuli.

7.7
ally, alkali, underlie, Lorelei, overlie, antalkali.

7.8
reply, multiply.

7.9
apply, supply, misapply.

7.10
deny, Gemini, anno Domini.

7.11
sori (spore-producing structures), tori (*plural of* torus), a priori, a fortiori, memento mori, a posteriori.

7.12
awry, serail (harem), Terai (Indian marshland), caravanserai.

7.13
Mira Ceti (star), arbor vitae (coniferous tree), aqua vitae, curriculum vitae.

8 -ire [see also **17.4**]
ire, byre, dire, fire, gyre (circular movement), hire, lyre, mire, pyre, spire, quire, choir, squire, sire, shire, tire, Tyre, tyre, wire.

sapphire, backfire, wildfire, hellfire, shellfire, camphire (henna), samphire (Eurasian plant), bonfire, gunfire, misfire, crossfire, spitfire, portfire (device for firing rockets), foxfire (glow emitted by fungi), bemire, admire, quagmire, pismire (*Dialect* ant), vampire, empire, umpire, respire, transpire, inspire, conspire, expire, acquire, inquire, enquire, esquire, Bushire (Iranian port), satire, retire, attire, saltire (heraldic term), entire, haywire, rewire, tripwire, desire.

retrofire (firing of retrorocket), retrochoir (space behind cathedral altar), Molly Maguire (Irish secret society member).

8.1
afire, melaphyre (type of basalt), granophyre (granitic rock), lamprophyre (igneous rock).

8.2
aspire, perspire, suspire (to sigh), acrospire (botany term).

8.3
require, antechoir (part of church).

9 -or
or, oar, ore, o'er, awe, boar, bore, caw, corps, core, score, chore, chaw (*Dialect* chew without swallowing), door, daw (jackdaw), dor (dung beetle), four, for, fore, gore, jaw, hoar, whore, haw, lore, law, lor (exclamation of dismay), claw, flaw, floor, splore (*Scot* a revel), more, maw, mor (acidic humus), nor, gnaw, snore, paw, pore, pour, spore, squaw, roar, raw, braw (*Scot* excellent), craw, draw, drawer, straw, soar, saw, sore, shore, Shaw, pshaw, tor, tore, taw (large marble), torr (unit of pressure),

store, thaw, Thor, Waugh, war, wore, swore, yaw, your, yore.

forbore, Gabor, chokebore (shotgun), smoothbore, markhor (Himalayan goat), décor, ichor (blood-like fluid), encore, threescore, fourscore, stridor (high-pitched breathing sound), moidore (former Portuguese coin), sudor (sweat), jackdaw, bandore (16th-century stringed instrument), landau, vendor, indoor, Indore (Indian city), condor, outdoor, ephor (ancient Greek magistrate), therefore, wherefore, guffaw, Roquefort, Balfour, nagor (African antelope), rigor (medical term), Bogor (Indonesian city), gewgaw (showy trinket), algor (chill), nylghau (Indian antelope), pledgor, crackjaw (difficult to pronounce), lockjaw, Tanjore (Indian city), heehaw, Hawhaw, Johore (Malaysian state), Lahore (Pakistani city), abhor, bylaw, folklore, dewclaw, scofflaw (*US* habitual lawbreaker), Danelaw, deplore, implore, explore, coleslaw, outlaw, claymore (two-edged sword), Seymour, Timor, Broadmoor, ignore, rapport, forepaw, pawpaw, Cawnpore (Indian city), downpour, southpaw, furor, withdraw, uproar, bedstraw, lessor, Esau, seesaw, eyesore, Mysore, foresaw, Warsaw, bowsaw, tussore (Indian silk), bedsore, handsaw, jigsaw, whipsaw (saw with flexible blade), footsore, seashore, foreshore, ashore, bashaw (important person), kickshaw (worthless trinket), rickshaw, Bradshaw, offshore, scrimshaw (shell or ivory carving), cumshaw (tip or gift), inshore, onshore, longshore, Utah, lector (university lecturer), Choctaw (American Indian people), cantor (leading singer in synagogue), grantor, Nestor (Greek mythological character), restore, drugstore, prewar, postwar, hacksaw, bucksaw (woodcutting saw), Luxor (Egyptian town), señor, signor, bezoar (hairball).

hellebore (poisonous plant), usquebaugh (Irish liqueur), Maribor (Yugoslavian city), underscore (to stress), overscore (cross out), battledore (former racket game), theretofore, heretofore, obligor (debtor), underfloor, son-in-law, overslaugh (military term), Barrymore, Baltimore, Aviemore, Mount Rushmore, Mackinaw (US short coat), Tengri Nor (Chinese salt lake), assignor (legal term), Elsinore, Koko Nor (Chinese lake), millepore (coral-like organism), nullipore (red seaweed), madrepore (coral), Singapore, blastopore (embryology term), archespore (spore-making cell), overawe, overdraw, windlestraw (*Dialect* dried grass stalks), promisor, Arkansas, wappenshaw (gathering of Scottish clansmen), alongshore, Wichita, Ouachita (US river), legator (person making bequest), Minotaur, guarantor, warrantor, patentor, williwaw (*US* state of turmoil), man-of-war.

daughter-in-law, sister-in-law, father-in-law, mother-in-law, brother-in-law, imperator, recognizor (legal term), caveat emptor.

9.1
Dior, Melchior, Gwalior (Indian city), excelsior, Confiteor (Catholic prayer).

9.2
macaw, zoochore (botany term), albacore (variety of tunny), isochor (line on graph), esprit de corps, anemochore (botany term).

9.3
louis d'or (former French coin), humidor (humid tobacco-storing container), cuspidor (spittoon), corridor, stevedore, Corregidor (Philippine island), lobster thermidor.

9.4
adore, picador, Mogador (Moroccan port), commodore, Ecuador, mirador (balcony or turret), Labrador, comprador (agent of foreign enterprise), mata-

dor, Salvador, toreador, conquistador, El Salvador, San Salvador.

9.5
before, petit four, hereinbefore.

9.6
afore, trochophore (invertebrate's larva), lophophore (minute organism's tentacles), semaphore, ctenophore (marine invertebrate), pinafore, gonophore (biology term), carpophore (botany term), carrefour, sporophore (spore-bearing organ), photophore (light-producing organ), siphonophore (marine invertebrate), ommatophore (eye-bearing stalk), chromatophore (zoology term), pneumatophore (biology term), gametophore (plant part).

9.7
Tagore (Indian poet), Chandernagore (Indian port).

9.8
galore, Vellore (Indian town), roquelaure (man's hooded cloak), Bangalore, Mangalore (Indian port).

9.9
hackamore (*US* rope halter), sycamore, sophomore, sagamore (American Indian chief), mattamore (subterranean storehouse), furthermore, evermore, nevermore, forevermore.

9.10
diaspore (mineral), zoospore, endospore, megaspore (botany term), microspore (botany term), tetraspore, exospore (outer layer of spore), teliospore, aeciospore, chlamydospore, aplanospore.

9.11
Chickasaw (American Indian people), stegosaur, dinosaur, pterosaur, hadrosaur, vavasor (baron's vassal), plesiosaur, ichthyosaur, ankylosaur, megalosaur, elasmosaur, tyrannosaur, titanosaur.

9.12
mentor, centaur, stentor (loud-voiced person), bucentaur (Venetian state barge).

9.13
herbivore, carnivore, omnivore, insectivore.

10 -oor
boor, Boer, dour, Gur (language group), lur (Bronze Age musical horn), Moore, Moor, moor, poor, spoor, Ruhr, sure, tour, you're, cure, lure, Muir, pure.

Niebuhr (German historian), tambour, pandour (18th-century Croatian soldier), Darfur (Sudanese province), Uigur (Mongoloid people), Kungur (Chinese mountain), langur (monkey), adjure, abjure, conjure, velours, Namur (Belgian province), Sedgemoor, unmoor, Dartmoor, Exmoor, Nippur (ancient Babylonian city), Jaipur (Indian city), Nagpur (Indian city), Kanpur (Indian city), parure (set of jewels), hachure (lines drawn for shading), brochure, assure, cocksure, unsure, detour, contour, Guntur (Indian city), procure, obscure, ordure (excrement), bordure (outer edge of shield), endure, rondure (curvature), ligure (Old Testament precious stone), doublure (decorative lining inside book), armure (silk or wool fabric), immure, demure, tenure, inure, conure (small parrot), manure, purpure (heraldic purple), guipure, impure, couture, nervure (biology term), gravure (method of printing).

troubadour, pompadour (18th-century women's hairstyle), kieselguhr (type of rock), Damanhûr (Egyptian city), Kohinoor, Nishapur (birthplace of Omar Khayyám), Jamshedpur (Indian city), Lyallpur (Pakistani city), Jabalpur (Indian city), Bhagalpur (Indian city), commissure (tissue linking two organs), embouchure, reassure, plat du jour, Thanjavur (Indian city), dasyure (small marsupial), clair-obscure (art term), Réaumur, confiture (fruit preserve), prefecture, calenture (mild tropical fever), cynosure (centre of attraction).

somatopleure (embryonic tissue), Chota Nagpur (East Indian plateau), Kuala Lumpur, photogravure, rotogravure.

10.1
amour (love affair), Amur (Asian river), paramour.

10.2
ensure, insure, reinsure, coinsure.

10.3
liqueur, secure, pedicure, manicure, sinecure, epicure, insecure.

10.4
allure, colure (circle on celestial sphere), velure, craquelure (cracks on old paintings), cannelure (groove around bullet).

10.5
mature, armature (moving electrical part), premature, immature, crenature (notch in scalloped edge), overture, caricature, magistrature.

11 -oy
boy, buoy, coy, Fowey, joy, hoy (freight barge), cloy, ploy, poi (Hawaiian food), Roy, Troy, soy, toy.

carboy (bottle for corrosive liquids), dayboy, playboy, highboy (*US* tallboy), choirboy, hautboy (strawberry), doughboy (boiled dumpling), lowboy (*US* table with drawers), cowboy, ploughboy, linkboy (torch carrier in streets), pageboy, bellboy, callboy, smallboy (steward's assistant), tallboy, schoolboy, tomboy, houseboy, potboy (employee in public house), footboy (boy servant), liftboy, postboy, kikoi (African banded cloth), decoy, Khoikhoi (language group), McCoy, Sainte Foy (suburb of Quebec), enjoy, ahoy,

Namhoi (Chinese city), alloy, deploy, employ, Amoy (Chinese port), Hanoi, annoy, charpoy, sepoy (Indian soldier serving British), teapoy (table with tripod base), Rob Roy, viceroy, destroy, Tolstoy, travois (American Indian sled), savoy, Savoy, envoy, renvoi (legal term), convoy, borzoi.

maccaboy (rose-scented snuff), sonobuoy (buoy detecting underwater noises), paperboy, attaboy, stableboy, didicoy (type of gypsy), overjoy, permalloy (iron–nickel alloy), redeploy, Illinois, Iroquois, corduroy, cunjevoi (tropical plant).

hobbledehoy, paduasoy (silk fabric).

11.1
alloy, kumbaloi (worry beads), hoi polloi, saveloy.

12 -oe
owe, oh, beau, bow, Chou (Chinese dynasty), dough, doe, doh, foe, go, Joe, ho, hoe, lo, low, blow, flow, floe, glow, slow, sloe, mow, mo (*short for* moment), mot (witty remark), know, no, snow, Poe, po (chamber pot), Po (Italian river), row, roe, crow, fro, froe (cutting tool), grow, pro, throw, sew, sow, so, soh, show, toe, tow, stow, though, whoa, woe, Vaud (region of Switzerland), zo (Tibetan cattle).

Rouault (French artist), duo, Abo (*short for* Aborigine), jabot, Garbo, oboe, hobo (*US* a vagrant), bubo (a swelling), elbow, flambeau (torch), mambo (dance), crambo (word game), combo, rainbow, longbow, crossbow, oxbow (curved lake), psycho, Tycho (crater on moon), bucko (*Irish* young fellow), stucco, milko (*Austral* milkman), wilco, salchow (ice-skating jump), Glencoe, plonko (*Austral* alcoholic), bronco, Moscow, gaucho, poncho, shadow, eddo (Asian plant), meadow, Bordeaux, dildo, rondeau (poem), rondo (musical work), Sappho,

Defoe, UFO, nympho, info, ergo, Virgo, doggo, forego, sorgo (fodder crop), bongo, Congo, mongo (Mongolian currency), drongo (tropical bird), outgo, Glasgow, banjo, heigh-ho, coho (Pacific salmon), Soho, halo, Gwelo (Zimbabwean town), furlough, kyloe (Scottish cattle), Lilo (*Trademark*), silo, Shiloh, rouleau, tableau, pueblo, deathblow, airflow, inflow, outflow, whitlow, Oslo, Hounslow, ammo, demo, memo, trumeau (architectural term), Sumo (Japanese wrestling), Malmö, lino, rhino, wino, mono, tonneau, foreknow, dunno, Gounod (French composer), Juno, capo (guitar attachment), chapeau (hat), hippo, hypo, typo, tempo, burrow, furrow, scarecrow, Velcro (*Trademark*), escrow (legal term), hydro, Afro, aggro, outgrow, hedgerow, Monroe, repro, metro, retro (*short for* retrorocket), de trop (superfluous), Cointreau, intro, Castro, bistro, maestro, Jethro, peso, verso, torso, whoso (whoever), Rousseau, trousseau, CUSO (Canadian voluntary service organization), Tussaud, also, fatso, scherzo, schizo, sideshow, peepshow, ditto, Shinto (Japanese religion), tiptoe, bestow, gusto, although, bravo, servo, Provo, galvo (*short for* galvanometer), salvo, Volvo (*Trademark*), Oyo (Nigerian state), yo-yo, Tokyo, ouzo, muso (*Austral* musician).

Bilbao, cacao, sirocco, Morocco, morocco (leather), Monaco, touraco (African bird), fiasco, Tabasco, gazpacho, quebracho (South American tree), foreshadow, aboideau (Canadian dyke), tournedos, commando, tally-ho, bibelot (trinket), Fontainebleau, overflow, Alamo, dynamo, piano, volcano, Huguenot, pompano (Atlantic fish), Llandudno, Limpopo, status quo, quid pro quo, Diderot (French philosopher), bordereau (insurance invoice), Cicero, allegro, overgrow, semipro, in vitro,

overthrow, Curaçao, oversew, so-and-so, calypso, concerto, undertow, hammertoe, de facto, tick-tack-toe (*US* noughts and crosses), mistletoe, octavo (book size), proviso.

continuo (musical term), La Rochefoucauld (French writer), Acapulco, overshadow, fortepiano (type of piano), Avogadro (Italian physicist).

12.1
K.O., Mayo (Irish county), carabao (water buffalo), Galileo, Bulawayo (Zimbabwean city).

12.2
guyot (submerged mountain), Leo, Cleo, Rio, Krio (African language), trio, con brio (musical term), absente reo (legal term).

12.3
radio, audio, rodeo, studio, cameo, Romeo, Borneo, Scipio (Roman general), Scorpio, stereo, cheerio, curio, vibrio (bacterium), embryo, Lashio (Burmese town), nuncio (papal representative), patio.

Pinocchio, capriccio (lively musical work), adagio, solfeggio (musical term), arpeggio, seraglio (harem), intaglio (engraving), Ontario, etaerio (class of fruit), Ajaccio, pistachio, mustachio.

braggadocio (boasting), oratorio, ex officio.

12.3.1
video, presidio (Spanish military establishment).

12.3.2
billyo, punctilio (strict etiquette).

12.3.3
olio (miscellany), folio, polio, portfolio, imbroglio (confused situation).

12.3.4
Roneo (*Trademark*), Antonio.

12.3.5
Rosario (Argentine port), scenario, Lothario (libertine), impresario.

12.3.6
ratio, fellatio.

12.4
Io (satellite of Jupiter), ngaio (New Zealand tree), noyau (nut liqueur), Ohio.

12.5
Ibo (African people), placebo, gazebo, Essequibo (South American river).

12.6
bimbo (*Slang* fellow), limbo, akimbo.

12.7
umbo (small hump), gumbo (thick stew), jumbo, nelumbo (aquatic plant), Colombo, mumbo jumbo.

12.8
squacco (European heron), shako, whacko (*Slang* exclamation of delight), tobacco.

12.9
echo, dekko, gecko, secco (wall painting), re-echo, Art Deco, El Greco.

12.10
chico (US shrub), Nikko (Japanese town), picot, pekoe, beccafico (European songbird), Puerto Rico.

12.11
tricot (knitted fabric), medico, calico, coquelicot (corn poppy), haricot, Jericho, portico, Mexico, magnifico, simpatico (pleasant), politico.

12.12
cocoa, coco (*short for* coconut), loco, smoko (*Austral* teabreak), poco (musical term), rococo, con fuoco (musical term), Orinoco.

12.13
flamenco, Lysenko (Russian geneticist), Timoshenko (Russian general).

12.14
fresco, Enesco (Rumanian musician), UNESCO, alfresco, Ionesco (French dramatist).

12.15
disco, Frisco (*short for* San Francisco), cisco (fish), Morisco (Spanish Moor), San Francisco.

12.16
mikado, Barnardo, Dorado (constellation), bravado, avocado, El Dorado, Colorado, desperado, muscovado (raw sugar), amontillado, aficionado, incommunicado, Llano Estacado (region of Texas).

12.17
dado, gambado (leather stirrup), Toledo, tornado, strappado (form of torture), bastinado (form of torture), carbonado (industrial diamond).

12.18
lido, speedo, credo, libido, Toledo, torpedo, teredo (mollusc), tuxedo.

12.19
widow, aikido (Japanese self-defence system), comedo (blackhead), do-si-do, Bushido (code of the samurai).

12.20
Dido, Hokkaido.

12.21
dodo, Jodo (Buddhist sect), Komodo (East Indian island), Quasimodo.

12.22
udo (Oriental plant), judo, ludo, Trudeau, pseudo, escudo (Portuguese currency), testudo (Roman military manoeuvre).

12.23
bandeau (headband), Brando, Orlando, glissando (musical term), scherzando (musical term), sforzando (musical term), ritardando, San Fernando, rallentando.

12.24
kendo (Japanese sport), crescendo, innuendo, diminuendo (musical term).

12.25
window, tamarindo (tamarind).

12.26
argot, Argo, cargo, largo, magot (Oriental figurine), embargo, Chicago, galago (bushbaby), virago, farrago (hotchpotch), botargo (fish roe), Santiago.

12.27
sago, Tobago, lumbago, plumbago (graphite), imago (adult insect), San Diego, Winnebago (US lake), solidago (plant genus), pichiciego (Argentine armadillo).

12.28
ego, gigot (leg of mutton), Vigo (Spanish port), amigo, Montego, superego, alter ego.

12.29
chigoe (tropical flea), Bendigo (Australian city), indigo, vertigo, Abednego.

12.30
Sligo, serpigo (skin disease), prurigo (skin disease), lentigo (freckle), intertrigo (chafed skin), impetigo.

12.31
logo, Togo (African republic), à gogo.

12.32
Hugo, colugo (flying lemur), aerugo (verdigris), lanugo (covering of fine hair).

12.33
ago, undergo, sapsago (Swiss cheese), archipelago.

12.34
NALGO, hidalgo (Spanish nobleman).

12.35
mango, quango, tango, fandango, Durango (Mexican state), contango (stock exchange term).

12.36
bingo, dingo, jingo, lingo, gringo, stingo (strong beer), flamingo, eryngo (a plant), Santo Domingo (capital of Dominican Republic).

12.37
Idaho, Navaho, Arapaho.

12.38
aloe, callow, fallow, hallow, mallow, sallow, shallow, tallow, marshmallow.

12.39
Carlow (Irish county), Harlow, Marlowe, Monte Carlo.

12.40
bellow, cello, fellow, felloe (part of wooden wheel), jello (US jelly), hello, mellow, yellow, niello (compound used in engraving), duello (duelling), bordello, bedfellow, Longfellow, morello, Martello, Othello, Novello, Punchinello (clown), ritornello (musical term), saltarello (Italian dance), violoncello.

12.41
kilo, Iloilo (Philippine port).

12.42
below, billow, pillow, willow, furbelow, pomelo (grapefruit), tupelo (tree), Murillo (Spanish painter), peccadillo (trivial misdemeanour), armadillo, cigarillo, Michelangelo.

12.43
follow, hollow, wallow, swallow, Apollo.

12.44
bolo (a knife), kolo (Serbian folk dance), Jolo (Philippine island), polo, solo, criollo (type of cocoa), palolo (marine worm), Marco Polo.

12.45
alow (nautical term), hallo, cembalo (harpsichord), cymbalo (dulcimer), piccolo, pedalo (pedal boat), buffalo, brigalow (Australian acacia tree), gigolo, bungalow, tangelo (tangerine–grapefruit hybrid), tremolo, bummalo

(Bombay duck), cattalo (breed of cattle), diabolo (game with spinning top).

12.46
aglow, afterglow, counterglow (glow in sky).

12.47
Imo (Nigerian state), primo, supremo.

12.48
Eskimo, ultimo (last month), proximo (next month), Geronimo, centesimo (monetary unit), fortissimo, bravissimo, pianissimo, generalissimo.

12.49
Como, Nkomo, homo, duomo (cathedral), major-domo.

12.50
machismo, verismo (type of opera), gran turismo.

12.51
Arno (Italian river), Kano (Nigerian state), Carnot (French physicist), llano (South American grassland), guano (excrement of sea birds), Meccano (*Trademark*), Nagano (Japanese city), Romano (type of cheese), soprano, Cinzano, San Stefano (Turkish village), oregano.

12.52
meno (musical term), tenno (Japanese emperor), steno (*US* shorthand typist), Renault (*Trademark*), ripieno (musical term).

12.53
journo (*Austral* journalist), Pernod (*Trademark*), inferno.

12.54
beano, kino (dark red resin), keno (US game of chance), chino (*US* cotton twill cloth), fino (dry sherry), leno (fabric weave), Reno, vino, albino, bambino, zecchino (gold coin), ladino (white clover), amino, merino, neutrino (elementary particle in physics), casino, Latino (*US* Latin American), Trevino, maraschino, cappuccino, Borodi-

no (Napoleonic battle site), palomino, Filipino, solferino (reddish-purple colour), San Marino (European republic), concertino (musical term), andantino (musical term), Valentino, San Bernardino (Californian city).

12.55
minnow, winnow, domino, topminnow (small fish), Maginot.

12.56
kimono, kakemono (Japanese wall hanging).

12.57
Apo (Philippine mountain), da capo (musical term), Gestapo.

12.58
depot, Aleppo (Syrian city).

12.59
kakapo (parrot), apropos, malapropos.

12.60
arrow, barrow, farrow, Jarrow, Harrow, harrow, marrow, narrow, sparrow, tarot, yarrow, handbarrow, wheelbarrow, restharrow (woody plant).

12.61
claro (cigar), taro (Asian plant), Pissarro (French painter), saguaro (giant cactus), Pizarro (conqueror of Peru), Utamaro, Kilimanjaro.

12.62
Pharaoh, faro (card game), ranchero (*US* rancher), bolero, primero (card game), pampero (South American wind), torero (bullfighter), Herero (African people), sombrero, montero (Spanish hunting cap), cruzeiro (Brazilian currency), caballero (Spanish gentleman), banderillero (bullfighter's assistant).

12.63
hero, Nero, Pierrot (French pantomime clown), cero (Atlantic fish), zero, Pinero (English dramatist), subzero, antihero, superhero, Rio de Janeiro.

12.64
Biro (*Trademark*), Cairo, giro, tyro (novice), autogiro (aircraft).

12.65
borrow, morrow, morro (rounded hill), sorrow, tomorrow.

12.66
duro (silver peso), Douro (Spanish–Portuguese river), Truro, bureau, maduro (cigar), Politburo, chiaroscuro (art term).

12.67
Negro, Montenegro (region of Yugoslavia).

12.68
basso (bass singer), Picasso, sargasso (seaweed), El Paso (Texan city).

12.69
gesso (white plaster), expresso.

12.70
so-so, nitroso (chemistry term), maestoso (musical term), grandioso (musical term), mafioso (member of the Mafia), virtuoso, oloroso (sherry), doloroso (musical term), amoroso, capriccioso (musical term).

12.71
mezzo (musical term), Arezzo (Italian city), intermezzo.

12.72
bateau (flat-bottomed boat), gateau, plateau, chateau, mulatto, annatto (tropical tree).

12.73
dato (Philippine chief), rubato (musical term), spiccato (musical term), Waikato (New Zealand river), staccato, legato, sfumato (art term), tomato, esparto, vibrato, castrato, pizzicato, obbligato (musical term), ostinato (musical term), moderato, inamorato (lover).

12.74
Cato, jato (jet-assisted takeoff), Plato, NATO, potato.

12.75
ghetto, stretto (musical term), zucchetto (skullcap), stiletto, palmetto (small tropical palm tree), libretto, neutretto (hypothetical particle in physics), falsetto, terzetto (vocal trio), cavetto (architectural moulding), amoretto (cupid), vaporetto (Venetian steamboat), Tintoretto, lazaretto (ship's locker), allegretto.

12.76
Quito (capital of Ecuador), keto (chemistry term), Leto (mother of Apollo), Pitot (French physicist), Tito, veto, coquito (palm tree), mosquito, graffito, bonito (small marine fish), magneto, Negrito (member of Asian people), Hirohito, sanbenito (garment worn by heretics), incognito.

12.77
Otto, Giotto, lotto, blotto, motto, potto (short-tailed mammal), grotto, Watteau, ridotto (musical entertainment), risotto.

12.78
auto, quarto, Oporto.

12.79
koto (Japanese musical instrument), photo, Kyoto (Japanese city), con moto (musical term), in toto, telephoto, Kumamoto (Japanese city).

12.80
couteau (a knife), Pluto, Maputo (capital of Mozambique), prosciutto (Italian cured ham), tenuto (musical term), ritenuto (musical term), sostenuto (musical term).

12.81
recto, perfecto (cigar).

12.82
alto, Rialto, contralto.

12.83
canto, manteau (a cloak), panto, portmanteau, Taranto (Italian port), quo warranto (legal term), Esperanto, Espiritu Santo (Pacific island).

12.84

lento, cento (type of poem), memento, pimento, Sorrento, pentimento (art term), Sacramento, Benevento (Italian city), Risorgimento (Italian political movement), divertimento (musical work), pronunciamento (manifesto).

12.85

conto (Portuguese currency), pronto, Toronto.

12.86

presto, manifesto.

13 -ow

ow, bow, bough, cow, scow (boat), chow, ciao (Italian greeting), dhow (Arab sailing boat), Dou (Dutch painter), how, Lao (Asian people), plough, Slough, slough (bog), mow (grimace), now, pow, row, brow, Frau, prow, sow, sough (make sighing sound), thou, vow, wow.

meow, Cracow, Foochow (Chinese port), Soochow (Chinese city), Changchow (Chinese city), Hangchow (Chinese port), Moldau, endow, hoosegow (*US* jail), know-how, somehow, pilau, allow, snowplough, Mau Mau, eyebrow, highbrow, lowbrow, hausfrau, kowtow, Paotow (Chinese city), avow, bow-wow, powwow.

disendow, anyhow, disallow, middlebrow, disavow.

14 -our

our, hour, bower, cower, scour, dower (widow's inheritance), Gower, gaur (Asian wild cattle), lour (look menacing), flour, flower, glower, power, paua (New Zealand shellfish), sour, shower, tower, stour (*Dialect* turmoil).

embower, Glendower (Welsh chieftain), deflower, safflower, Mayflower, wallflower, cornflower, cornflour, sunflower, moonflower (night-blooming plant), willpower, empower, manpower, horsepower, watchtower, devour.

Eisenhower, gillyflower, cauliflower, passionflower, hydropower, superpower, overpower.

15 -oo

ooh, boo, coo, coup, chew, do, goo, Jew, who, loo, blue, blew, clue, clew (ball of yarn), flu, flew, flue, glue, plew (fur trade term), slew, Shluh (North African people), moo, gnu, pooh, rue, roux, roo (*Austral* kangaroo), brew, crew, Crewe, cru (wine-producing region), screw, drew, grew, sprue (tropical disease), shrew, true, strew, through, threw, Sioux, sue, sou (coin), shoe, shoo, choux (type of pastry), chou (type of cabbage), too, to, two, woo, Wu (Chinese dialect group), ewe, you, yew, queue, cue, Kew, kyu (judo grade), skew, due, dew, few, phew, hue, hew, lieu, mew, smew (diving duck), knew, new, pew, spew, stew, thew (muscle), view, zoo.

zebu (type of ox), bamboo, cuckoo, Manchu (Chinese dynasty), eschew (avoid), hairdo, redo, Urdu, kudu (African antelope), hoodoo, voodoo, Hindu, undo, outdo, snafu, Corfu, kung fu, ragout (stew), juju, boohoo, Wuhu (Chinese port), yoo-hoo, yahoo, igloo, canoe, Vishnu (Hindu god), coypu, hoopoe, pooh-pooh, shampoo, Nehru, guru, Hebrew, ecru (yellowish-grey colour), aircrew, accrue, airscrew (propeller), woodscrew, thumbscrew, unscrew, corkscrew, withdrew, Andrew, Renfrew, untrue, bestrew, construe, lasso, shih-tzu (breed of dog), fichu (scarf), cashew, cachou (type of sweet), snowshoe, gumshoe, Honshu, horseshoe, bijou, Attu (island off Alaska), battue (hunting term), tattoo, thereto, whereto, hereto, Hutu (African people), tutu, Bantu, Mantoux (French physician), into, onto, unto, bayou (marshy stream), debut, imbue (instil), fescue (a grass), rescue, miscue, askew, subdue, mildew, vendue (*US* public sale), endue (endow), fondue, undue, sundew, curfew, argue, ague, value, curlew, purlieu (outlying area), emu, genu (knee), menu, venue, non-U, foreknew, anew, issue, tissue, pursue, ensue, statue, virtue, Matthew, nephew, purview (scope), preview, revue, review, Jesu.

caribou, bunraku (Japanese puppet theatre), Katmandu, derring-do, Dien Bien Phu (Vietnamese battle site), kinkajou, sapajou (capuchin monkey), ballyhoo, misconstrue, overthrew, jujitsu, overshoe, acajou, Lissajous (French physicist), passe-partout, cockatoo, thitherto, hitherto, Timbuktu, thereinto, whereinto, hereinto, rendezvous, I.O.U., barbecue, curlicue (decorative curl), autocue, feverfew (medicinal plant), Montague, clerihew (humorous verse), devalue, revalue, ingénue (naive girl), impromptu, interview, overview.

Machu Picchu (ruined city of Incas), Mogadishu (capital of Somali Republic), tu-whit tu-whoo, undervalue, Bartholomew, cock-a-doodle-doo.

15.1
taboo, peekaboo, bugaboo (source of fear), marabou (African stork), marabout (Muslim holy man).

15.2
teledu (Asian badger), billet-doux (love letter), didgeridoo.

15.3
ado, to-do, amadou (fungal tinder), well-to-do, overdo.

15.4
Lulu, Sulu (Philippine archipelago), Zulu, Gazankulu (South African homeland), Honolulu.

15.5
halloo, trou-de-loup (pit dug for defence), toodle-oo, calalu (Caribbean edible leaves), ormolu (gilt decoration), Port-Salut (French cheese), Peterloo, Waterloo, Tuvalu (group of Pacific islands), hullabaloo, Kinabalu (Malaysian mountain).

15.6
buroo (*Dialect* unemployment benefit), Karoo (South African plateau), Peru, jackeroo (*Austral* trainee sheep-station manager), buckaroo (*US* cowboy), switcheroo (*US* unexpected change), wanderoo (Indian monkey), kangaroo, wallaroo (large kangaroo), Timaru (New Zealand port), Brian Boru (medieval Irish king).

15.7
bedew (cover with dew), honeydew, residue.

15.8
adieu, overdue.

15.9
renew, sinew, detinue (legal term), retinue, continue, avenue, revenue, discontinue.

15.10
bazoo (*US* mouth), kazoo, razoo (*Austral* coin), Kalamazoo.

16 -y [This is the unstressed syllable at the end of such words as *baby*, *charity*, and *autonomy*. Rhymes dependent on this syllable alone are unsatisfactory and should be avoided. Further rhymes for **16.112–16.209** may be created by adding *-ly* to appropriate adjectives. See also **5**.]
rugby, busby, Grimsby, Trotsky, hardly, homely, scarcely, costly, lively, paisley, acme, pygmy, chimney, chutney, scampi, debris, laundry, foundry, sundry, belfry, angry, hungry, paltry, poultry, sultry, pastry, Chelsea, Nazi, safety, ninety, empty, sixty, earthy, lengthy, filthy, swarthy, ivy, envy, clumsy, Swansea.

panoply, calumny, industry, bankruptcy, dynasty.

16.1
ai (three-toed sloth), Bahai (member of religious group), Lanai (Hawaiian island), lanai (Hawaiian veranda), Molokai (Hawaiian island).

16.2
Hawaii, Mordecai (Old Testament character).

16.3
doughy, joey, blowy, Chloe, snowy, showy, toey (*Austral* nervous), shadowy, billowy, willowy.

16.4
chewy, phooey, gooey, hooey, louis, Louis, bluey (*Austral* blanket or bundle), gluey, screwy, tui (New Zealand songbird), dewy, Dewey, Brahui (Pakistani language), Drambuie (*Trademark*), Rapa Nui (Easter Island), Wanganui (New Zealand port).

16.5
abbey, cabby, scabby, gabby (talkative), flabby, crabby, shabby, tabby, Newtonabbey.

16.6
Babi (Persian religious heretic), carby (*Austral* carburettor), Derby, Mugabe, Punjabi, Wahhabi (member of Muslim sect), kohlrabi, Abu Dhabi, Hammurabi (ancient Babylonian king).

16.7
baby, gaby (simpleton), maybe, crybaby, bushbaby.

16.8
plebby, webby, Entebbe.

16.9
Kirkby, herby.

16.10
Phoebe, phoebe (US bird), Hebe (Greek goddess), freebie, Galibi (American Indian people).

16.11
bobby, dobby (loom attachment), hobby, lobby.

16.12
obi, Kobe (Japanese port), dhobi, goby, Gobi, Toby, adobe, Nairobi, Okeechobee (lake in Florida).

16.13
chubby, hubby, clubby (sociable), rabi (Indian crop), scrubby, grubby, shrubby, tubby, stubby.

16.14
booby, jube (gallery in church), looby (foolish person), ruby.

16.15
wallaby, Araby, sassaby (African antelope).

16.16
Philby, trilby, astilbe (flowering plant).

16.17
Djambi (Indonesian port), namby-pamby.

16.18
Tshombe (African statesman), zombie.

16.19
baccy, lackey, tacky, wacky.

16.20
khaki, kaki (Asian fruit tree), charqui (dried meat), parky, saki (monkey), sake (Japanese liquor), Saki (Scottish author).

thearchy (government by gods), diarchy, triarchy, malarkey (nonsense), nomarchy (modern Greek province), menarche (first occurrence of menstruation), gynarchy (government by women), eparchy, Iraqi, squirearchy, autarchy (unrestricted rule), autarky (economic self-sufficiency), pentarchy, heptarchy.

hagiarchy (government by saints), matriarchy, patriarchy, oligarchy, hierarchy, trierarchy (Athenians providing state triremes), Nagasaki, Kawasaki, sukiyaki, teriyaki (Japanese cookery term).

16.21

laky (reddish), flaky, snaky, quaky, shaky, headachy.

16.22

checky (heraldic term), recce, Shimonoseki (Japanese port).

16.23

jerky, murky, perky, quirky, turkey, Turkey, Albuquerque.

16.24

cheeky, leaky, cliquey, sneaky, peaky, squeaky, creaky, freaky (*Slang* strange), streaky, tiki (Maori amulet), dashiki (loose-fitting Negro garment), cock-a-leekie.

16.25

dicky, hickey (gadget), quickie, tricky, sticky, garlicky, gimmicky, panicky, finicky, entelechy (philosophy term), parastichy (botany term), orthostichy (botany term).

16.26

spiky, crikey, psyche, Psyche (Greek mythological character), Tyche (Greek goddess).

16.27

cocky, jockey, hockey, gnocchi, rocky, stocky, outjockey (outwit by deception), jabberwocky.

16.28

balky (inclined to stop suddenly), chalky, Gorky, gawky, porky (obese), pawky (*Scot* having dry wit), talkie, stalky, Milwaukee, walkie-talkie.

16.29

Loki (Norse god), smoky, poky, croaky, hokey cokey, okey-dokey.

16.30

ducky, lucky, clucky (*Austral* pregnant), plucky, mucky, truckie (*Austral* truck driver), yukky, unlucky, Kentucky.

16.31

bookie, cookie, hooky, rookie, Gurmukhi (Punjabi script), cleruchy (Athenian colony).

16.32

kooky, fluky, spooky, kabuki (Japanese drama), Saluki, bouzouki.

16.33

stomachy (paunchy), anarchy, synarchy (joint rule), monarchy, schipperke (breed of dog), synecdoche (figure of speech), sciamachy (fight with imaginary enemy), theomachy (battle among the gods), logomachy (argument about words), tauromachy (bullfighting), Andromache, gigantomachy (battle fought by giants).

16.34

milky, silky.

16.35

bulky, sulky.

16.36

hanky, lanky, manky, cranky, swanky, hanky-panky, Killiecrankie (Scottish battle site).

16.37

inky, kinky, dinky, slinky, pinkie, Malinke (African people), Helsinki.

16.38

donkey, wonky.

16.39

chunky, funky, junkie, flunky, monkey, spunky.

16.40

pesky, kromesky (type of croquette).

16.41

risky, frisky, whisky.

16.42

dusky, husky, musky, Russky.

16.43

Dostoevsky, Alexander Nevski (Russian prince).

16.44
Tchaikovsky, Stokowski (US conductor), Malinowski (Polish anthropologist).

16.45
Nijinsky, kolinsky (Asian mink).

16.46
catchy, snatchy (disconnected), patchy, scratchy, fratchy (quarrelsome), Apache.

16.47
starchy, hibachi (portable brazier), Karachi, vivace, mariachi (Mexican street musicians).

16.48
sketchy, stretchy, tetchy.

16.49
itchy, bitchy, pitchy, semplice (musical term).

16.50
botchy, blotchy, veloce (musical term), sotto voce, viva voce.

16.51
Bauchi (Nigerian state), grouchy.

16.52
duchy, touchy, archduchy.

16.53
duce, Baluchi (Muslim people), penuche (coarse Mexican sugar), Vespucci, Mizoguchi (Japanese film director).

16.54
Ranchi (Indian city), Comanche.

16.55
paunchy, raunchy.

16.56
bunchy, punchy, crunchy.

16.57
baddie, caddie, caddy, daddy, laddie, Paddy, paddy, sugar daddy, finnan haddie.

16.58
cadi (Muslim judge), khadi (Indian cotton cloth), hardy, Mahdi (Sudanese military leader), mardy (*Dialect* spoilt or irritable), tardy, foolhardy, Matadi (Zaîrese port), Takoradi (Ghanaian port).

16.59
lady, cedi (Ghanaian currency), shady, charlady, milady, landlady, maravedi (Spanish coin).

16.60
eddy, heady, neddy, Pedi (member of African people), ready, thready, steady, already, unready, unsteady.

16.61
birdie, sturdy, wordy, Makurdi (Nigerian port), hurdy-gurdy.

16.62
beady, needy, speedy, reedy, greedy, seedy, weedy, tweedy.

16.63
biddy, kiddy, giddy, midi, middy (midshipman), Zebedee, perfidy, raggedy, tragedy, remedy, comedy, Kennedy, subsidy, accidie (apathy), chickabiddy (term of endearment), tragicomedy.

16.64
bridie (*Scot* meat pie), tidy, vide, untidy, mala fide, bona fide.

16.65
body, noddy (tropical sea-bird), poddy (*Austral* hand-fed calf), shoddy, toddy, waddy (Aborigine's wooden club), wadi (watercourse), embody, dogsbody, anybody, everybody, antibody, busybody, underbody, afterbody (discarded part of rocket), disembody, Irrawaddy (Burmese river).

16.66
bawdy, gaudy, Geordie, lordy (exclamation of surprise).

16.67
Cody, toady, tody (West Indian bird), petalody (botany term), staminody (botany term), polypody (type of fern).

16.68
dowdy, Gaudi (Spanish architect), howdy, cloudy, rowdy, Saudi, pandowdy (*US* fruit pie), howtowdie (Scottish chicken dish).

16.69
buddy, cuddy (small cabin in boat), bloody, muddy, nuddy, ruddy, study, fuddy-duddy, understudy.

16.70
goody, woody, goody-goody.

16.71
Judy, moody, broody, shrewdie (*Austral* shrewd person), camoodi (anaconda).

16.72
nobody, Lombardy, somebody, Picardy, malady, melody, psalmody, threnody (ode of lamentation), monody (solo in Greek tragedy), hymnody, jeopardy, dipody (metrical unit), tripody (metrical unit), parody, prosody, rhapsody, bastardy, custody, Mahanadi (Indian river), tetrapody (metrical unit), chiropody.

16.73
alcalde (Spanish mayor), Vivaldi, Fittipaldi (Brazilian motor-racing driver).

16.74
wieldy, unwieldy.

16.75
Grimaldi, Garibaldi, garibaldi.

16.76
oldie, mouldy.

16.77
Andy, bandy, candy, Kandy (Sri Lankan city), dandy, Gandhi, handy, pandy (school punishment), randy, brandy, sandy, sandhi (linguistics term), shandy, bandy-bandy (small Australian snake), jaborandi (tropical shrub), onus probandi (burden of proof).

16.78
bendy, trendy, Wendy, effendi (Turkish title of respect).

16.79
bhindi (Indian vegetable), Hindi, Sindhi (inhabitant of Pakistan), shindy, windy, Rawalpindi.

16.80
Fundy (Canadian bay), Lundy, mandi (large Indian market), Grundy (narrow-minded critical person), aliunde (from another source), salmagundi (mixed salad dish), jaguarundi (feline mammal).

16.81
Burgundy, organdie, Ormandy (US conductor), Normandy.

16.82
daffy, NAAFI, Taffy, taffy (*US* chewy sweet).

16.83
furphy (*Austral* rumour), Murphy, surfie (*Austral* male surfer), turfy.

16.84
Ife (Nigerian town), beefy, leafy.

16.85
jiffy, Liffey (Irish river), miffy (easily upset), sniffy (contemptuous), spiffy (*US* smart or stylish), squiffy, salsify.

16.86
coffee, toffee.

16.87
trophy, strophe, Sophie, Sophy (title of Persian kings).

16.88
chuffy (*Scot* chubby), huffy, fluffy, snuffy (unpleasant), puffy, scruffy, toughie, stuffy, dandruffy.

16.89
goofy, Sufi (member of Muslim sect), Newfie (inhabitant of Newfoundland).

16.90
atrophy, exstrophy (medical term), pansophy (universal knowledge), teleg-

raphy, tachygraphy (shorthand), calligraphy, epigraphy (study of ancient inscriptions), stratigraphy (study of geological history), scintigraphy (medical diagnostic technique), lexigraphy (system of writing), hypertrophy, anastrophe (rhetorical device), catastrophe, monostrophe (type of poem), apostrophe, phototelegraphy (telegraphic transmission of photographs), radiotelegraphy.

16.90.1
tenorrhaphy (surgical repair of tendons), herniorrhaphy (surgical repair of hernia), staphylorrhaphy (repair of cleft palate).

16.90.2
biography, zoography (branch of zoology), cacography (bad handwriting or spelling), chalcography (copper or brass engraving), zincography, discography, glyphography (printing process), stylography (engraving with stylus), xylography (printing from wooden blocks), holography, thermography, tomography (x-ray technique), filmography, seismography, cosmography, scenography (depicting in perspective), pornography, phonography (representing sounds by symbols), ethnography (branch of anthropology), typography, topography, cerography (engraving on waxed plate), xerography, pyrography (creating design by burning), orography (mapping mountain relief), chorography (mapping regions), micrography, hydrography (mapping oceans and rivers), reprography, petrography (classification of rocks), nosography (written classification of diseases), cartography, glyptography (engraving gemstones), cryptography (study of codes), lithography, orthography.

lexicography, selenography (mapping moon's surface), iconography.

autobiography, phototypography, palaeontography (description of fossils), chromolithography, photolithography.

16.90.2.1
geography, cardiography, radiography, ideography (using written symbols), hagiography, palaeography (study of ancient handwriting), bibliography, stereography (study of geometrical solids), areography (description of Mars), choreography, physiography (physical geography), biogeography, zoogeography, historiography, electrocardiography.

16.90.2.2
pyelography (x-ray examination of kidneys), metallography (branch of metallurgy), dactylography (study of fingerprints), crystallography, encephalography.

16.90.2.3
demography, anemography (recording wind measurements).

16.90.2.4
planography (printing from flat surface), stenography, organography (description of biological organs), uranography (mapping of stars), oceanography.

16.90.2.5
dittography (unintentional repetition), hyetography (study of rainfall distribution).

16.90.2.6
photography, chromatography (chemistry term), telephotography, astrophotography, cinematography.

16.90.3
dystrophy, epistrophe (rhetorical device), antistrophe (section of choral ode).

16.90.4
theosophy (religious or philosophical system), philosophy, anthroposophy (mystical doctrine).

16.91
baggy, jaggy (jagged), flaggy (limp), quaggy (marshy), ragi (cereal grass), craggy, scraggy, shaggy.

16.92
leggy, dreggy (full of dregs).

16.93
piggy, ciggy, twiggy.

16.94
boggy, doggy, foggy, froggy, groggy, soggy, demagogy.

16.95
corgi, porgy (Atlantic fish).

16.96
bogey, bogie (wheels on railway coach), dogie (*US* motherless calf), fogy, logy (*US* dull or listless), stogy (*US* long cheap cigar), yogi, judogi (judo costume).

16.97
buggy, muggy, shuggy (*Dialect* fairground swing).

16.98
boogie, boogie-woogie.

16.99
romaji (alphabet for transliterating Japanese), argy-bargy.

16.100
cagey, stagy (theatrical).

16.101
edgy, fledgy (feathered).

16.102
clergy, theurgy (divine intervention), chemurgy (branch of chemistry), zymurgy (study of fermentation processes), micrurgy (microscopic technique), dramaturgy.

16.103
widgie (*Austral* unruly young woman), prodigy, effigy, elegy, strategy, syzygy (position of celestial body), Murrumbidgee (Australian river), apophyge (architectural term).

16.104
bodgie (*Austral* unruly young man), dodgy, splodgy, podgy, stodgy, pedagogy (teaching principles and practice).

16.105
orgy, Georgie.

16.106
anagoge (allegorical interpretation), apagoge (logic term), paragoge (linguistics term), isagoge (academic introduction to topic).

16.107
budgie, smudgy, pudgy.

16.108
eulogy, anergy (lack of energy), energy, synergy, liturgy, lethargy.

16.108.1
geophagy (eating soil), theophagy (sacramental eating of god), omophagy (eating raw food), anthropophagy (cannibalism).

16.108.2
allergy, mammalogy (study of mammals), analogy, tetralogy (four related literary works), metallurgy, genealogy, mineralogy, pyrometallurgy, electrometallurgy.

16.108.3
trilogy, brachylogy (concise style), antilogy (contradiction in terms).

16.108.4
ology, symbology, ecology, tocology (obstetrics), oncology (study of tumours), conchology (study of shells), paedology, pedology (study of soils), graphology, psephology (study of elections), nephology (study of clouds), morphology, ufology, algology, typhlology (study of blindness), haplology (omission of syllable), hoplology (study of weapons), gemology, zymology (chemistry of fermentation), pomology (fruit cultivation), homology, nomology (science of law), seismology, cosmology, oenology (study of wine), menology (ecclesiastical calendar), penology

(punishment of crime), rhinology, Sinology (study of Chinese), technology, ichnology (study of fossil footprints), hymnology, limnology (study of lakes), hypnology, ethnology, carpology (branch of botany), typology (theology term), tropology (use of figurative language), aerology (study of the atmosphere), serology, virology, hierology (sacred literature), orology (mapping mountain relief), horology, urology, neurology, necrology (list of dead people), hydrology, dendrology (study of trees), agrology (study of soils), petrology (study of rocks), metrology (study of measurement units), patrology (writings of Church Fathers), gastrology, astrology, misology (hatred of reasoning), nosology (classification of diseases), scatology, cetology (study of whales), tautology, otology, proctology, histology, Christology, pathology, ethology (study of animal behaviour), anthology, sexology, doxology.

amphibology (ambiguity of expression), pteridology (study of ferns), methodology, angelology, enzymology, potamology (study of rivers), entomology, ophthalmology, iconology, immunology, herpetology (study of reptiles), Scientology (religious cult), helminthology (study of parasitic worms).

geomorphology, palaeethnology (study of prehistoric man), dialectology, psychopathology, neuropathology, phytopathology (study of plant diseases).

16.108.4.1
geology, rheology (branch of physics), theology.

archaeology, stoichiology (branch of biology), radiology, ideology, audiology (study of hearing), ophiology (study of snakes), hagiology (writings about saints), teleology, speleology, craniology, balneology (study of therapeutic baths), Mariology, embryology, glaciol-

ogy, sociology, aetiology (study of causes), deltiology (collecting picture postcards), osteology, ichthyology, axiology (study of values), phraseology, physiology, museology (science of museum organization).

astrogeology, dysteleology (philosophy term), venereology, soteriology (doctrine of salvation), bacteriology, ecclesiology (study of Christian Church).

epidemiology, phytosociology (study of plant communities).

16.108.4.2
biology, myology (study of muscle diseases), bryology (study of mosses), cryobiology, psychobiology, microbiology, agrobiology, radiobiology, sociobiology.

16.108.4.3
oology (study of bird's eggs), zoology, protozoology (study of protozoans), palaeozoology (study of fossil animals).

16.108.4.4
trichology (study of hair), codicology (study of manuscripts), myrmecology (study of ants), synecology (ecological study of communities), gynaecology, autecology (ecological study of individuals), lexicology (study of vocabulary), toxicology, musicology.

16.108.4.5
phycology (study of algae), mycology (study of fungi), psychology, parapsychology, metapsychology.

16.108.4.6
cacology (bad choice of words), malacology (study of molluscs), pharmacology.

16.108.4.7
pharyngology, laryngology, otolaryngology.

16.108.4.8
philology, syphilology, dactylology (manual sign language), vexillology (study of flags).

16.108.4.9
anemology (study of winds), etymology, epistemology (theory of knowledge).

16.108.4.10
phenology (study of recurring phenomena), phrenology, palynology (study of pollen), selenology (study of the moon), terminology, criminology, phenomenology, biocenology (branch of ecology).

16.108.4.11
phonology, chronology, lichenology, volcanology, organology, demonology, campanology, oceanology, geochronology (ordering of geological events), dendrochronology.

16.108.4.12
apology, topology, escapology, anthropology, palaeoanthropology.

16.108.4.13
chorology (geography term), acarology (study of mites), futurology, numerology (divination by numbers), martyrology, meteorology, gastroenterology.

16.108.4.14
phytology (botany), cytology, sitology (study of nutrition), parasitology.

16.108.4.15
eschatology (branch of theology), grammatology (study of writing systems), dermatology, haematology, thaumatology (study of miracles), somatology (study of the body), stomatology (study of the mouth), rheumatology, pneumatology (branch of theology), erotology, geratology, teratology (study of monsters), systematology, symptomatology.

16.108.4.15.1
climatology, primatology (branch of zoology), microclimatology, palaeoclimatology (study of past climates).

16.108.4.16
ontology (philosophy term), deontology (branch of ethics), gerontology, palaeontology, micropalaeontology (study of microscopic fossils).

16.108.4.17
cryptology (study of codes), Egyptology.

16.108.4.18
lithology (study of rocks), mythology, ornithology.

16.109
mangy, rangy.

16.110
bingey (*Austral* the stomach), dingy, mingy, stingy, lozengy (heraldic term).

16.111
scungy (*Austral* miserable), gungy, spongy.

16.112
alley, bally, kali (salt-marsh plant), dally, galley, Halley, pally, rally, sally, Sally, sallee (Australian eucalyptus tree), challis (lightweight fabric), tally, valley, wally (*Scot* made of china), tomalley (lobster's liver as food), reveille, trevally (marine fish), teocalli (truncated Aztec pyramid), dilly-dally, soapolallie (Canadian fruit drink), shillyshally, peelie-wally (*Scot* looking unwell).

16.113
Bali, barley, Kali (Hindu goddess), Charlie, Dali, Mali, parley, quale (essential quality), Gurkhali (language of Gurkhas), Somali (African people), tamale (Mexican food), finale, Umtali (Zimbabwean city), triticale (wheat–rye hybrid), Mexicali (Mexican city), Rub' al Khali (Arabian desert).

16.114
Bailey, bailey, bailie (*Scot* municipal magistrate), ceilidh, scaly, daily, gaily, paly (heraldic term), Old Bailey, Bareilly (Indian city), Israeli, Disraeli, ukulele, jus naturale (Roman natural law).

16.115
belly, Kelly, skelly (Lake District fish), Delhi, deli, jelly, smelly, nelly, Shelley, telly, Leadbelly, potbelly, Grappelli, underbelly, vermicelli, tagliatelle, Machiavelli, Tirunelveli (Indian city).

16.116
early, Burghley, burly, burley (thin-leaved tobacco), curly, girlie, hurley (stick used in hurling), pearly, surly, wurley (Aboriginal hut), hurly-burly.

16.117
barely, fairly, squarely, rarely.

16.118
Ely, dele (symbol for deletion), Healey, Lely (Dutch portrait painter), mealy (powdery), freely, Greeley (US political leader), steely, stele (upright stone slab), wheelie, Swahili, sapele, Ismaili (follower of Aga Khan), Matabele (African people), campanile (bell tower), jus civile (Roman civil law).

16.119
dearly, merely, nearly, really, yearly, sincerely, biyearly.

16.120
billy, skilly (thin soup), Chile, chilly, chilli, dilly (*Slang* remarkable person), filly, gillie (*Scot* huntsman's attendant), ghillie (laced shoe), hilly, lily, frilly, Scilly, silly, Tilly.

Cybele (Phrygian goddess), hillbilly, readily, steadily, bodily, Caerphilly, gingili (sesame oil), family, simile, homily, merrily, verily, Sicily, Chantilly.

cantabile, rockabilly (type of rock music), Piccadilly, piccalilli, subfamily, facsimile, willy-nilly, lilly-pilly (Australian tree), willy-willy (*Austral* cyclone or duststorm).

superfamily (biological classification), sal volatile.

16.120.1
primarily, ordinarily, necessarily, momentarily.

16.121
phyle (ancient Greek tribe), highly, Riley, wily, corpus vile (worthless object of experiment), heterostyly (botany term).

16.122
collie, colly (*Dialect* soot or grime), dolly, folly, golly, jolly, holly, lolly, Molly, molly (tropical fish), Polly, poly, brolly, trolley, volley, wally, wolly (*Dialect* pickled cucumber), loblolly (US pine tree), Barbirolli.

16.123
Chorley, Morley, squally, Crawley, sorely, Warley (English town), Macaulay, Bengali, Nepali, creepy-crawly.

16.124
poorly, surely, purely, Kalgoorlie (Australian city).

16.125
oily, doily, roily (cloudy or muddy).

16.126 [see also **16.164**]
coley, choli (short-sleeved bodice), coly (African bird), goalie, holy, holey, lowly, slowly, moly (Greek mythological magic herb), soli (musical term), aïoli (garlic mayonnaise), unholy, pinole (type of flour), ravioli, guacamole (dish using avocados), roly-poly.

16.127
hourly, sourly.

16.128
cully (*Slang* pal), gully, mulley (having no horns), sully.

16.129
bully, fully, pulley, woolly, patchouli (tree yielding fragrant oil), fearfully, awfully, dreadfully, hopefully, frightfully.

16.130
coolie, schoolie (*Austral* schoolteacher), Julie, truly, duly, muley (having no

horns), newly, Grand Coulee (US dam), unruly, guayule (bushy shrub), unduly, douroucouli (monkey).

16.131
neighbourly, emboly (embryology term), Kimberley (South African city), Stromboli (island with active volcano), broccoli, rascally, Wycherley (English dramatist), orderly, elderly, argali (Asian wild sheep), soldierly, gingerly, scholarly, formerly, normally, mannerly, finally, signally, equally, neroli (brown fragrant oil), thoroughly, Thessaly, cicely (aromatic plant), partially, specially, leisurely, Italy, quarterly, utterly, masterly, westerly, easterly, systole, sisterly, fatherly, weatherly (nautical term), northerly, motherly, brotherly, southerly, gravelly, Beverly, Tivoli, overly, miserly.

usually, hyperbole, epiboly (embryology term), melancholy, disorderly, anomaly, unmannerly, naturally, generally, literally, severally, especially, officially, initially, diastole, northwesterly, southwesterly, northeasterly, southeasterly.

materially, macrocephaly (abnormal largeness of skull), microcephaly (abnormal smallness of skull), hydrocephaly, macrencephaly (abnormal largeness of brain), universally, incidentally.

16.131.1
virtually, actually, effectually, eventually.

16.131.2
beggarly, splenomegaly (abnormal enlargement of spleen), acromegaly (chronic disease), cardiomegaly (abnormal enlargement of heart).

16.131.3
marginally, originally.

16.131.4
personally, occasionally.

16.131.5
Tripoli, tripoli (porous rock), Gallipoli.

16.131.6
properly, monopoly, oligopoly (economics term), Trichinopoly (Indian city).

16.131.7
latterly, philately.

16.132
drably, chablis.

16.133
pebbly, trebly.

16.134
ghibli (hot North African wind), glibly, scribbly.

16.135
knobbly, wobbly.

16.136
bubbly, doubly, stubbly.

16.137 [further rhymes may be derived from **228.16**]
probably, terribly, horribly, passably, possibly, presumably.

16.138
trembly, Wembley, assembly, subassembly.

16.139
humbly, crumbly, grumbly.

16.140
darkly, clerkly, Berkeley.

16.141
meekly, treacly, weakly, weekly, biweekly, triweekly.

16.142 [further rhymes may be derived from **228.23**]
quickly, prickly, sickly, thickly, radically, tragically, publicly, typically, basically, drastically, physically, specifically, strategically, emphatically, dramatically, diametrically.

16.143
likely, unlikely.

16.144
blankly, frankly.

16.145
Hinckley (English town), wrinkly, crinkly.

16.146
badly, gladly, madly, Bradley, sadly.

16.147
deadly, medley.

16.148 [further rhymes may be created by adding -ly to the past participle of appropriate verbs]
fiddly, Ridley (English bishop), tiddly, markedly, fixedly, decidedly, allegedly, ashamedly, concernedly, resignedly, assuredly, confessedly, repeatedly, admittedly, reportedly, advisedly, supposedly, confusedly, unashamedly, unconcernedly, unadvisedly.

16.148.1
deservedly, reservedly, unreservedly.

16.149
oddly, godly, ungodly.

16.150
lordly, broadly.

16.151
cuddly, Dudley.

16.152
cowardly, niggardly, dastardly, inwardly, outwardly.

16.153
worldly, unworldly, otherworldly.

16.154
friendly, unfriendly.

16.155
kindly, blindly.

16.156
roundly, soundly, profoundly.

16.157
secondly, jocundly.

16.158
chiefly, briefly.

16.159
snuffly, roughly.

16.160
giggly, niggly, wiggly.

16.161
ugli, ugly, smugly.

16.162
googly, Hooghly (Indian river).

16.163
singly, shingly, tingly.

16.164 [see also **16.126**]
wholly, solely.

16.165
gamely, lamely, namely.

16.166
seemly, extremely, unseemly.

16.167
timely, sublimely, untimely.

16.168
comely, glumly.

16.169
manly, Stanley, unmanly, Osmanli (relating to Ottoman Empire).

16.170
gainly, mainly, vainly, ungainly.

16.171
Henley, cleanly, uncleanly.

16.172
keenly, cleanly, queenly.

16.173
only, lonely.

16.174
christianly, maidenly, seamanly, commonly, womanly, humanly, workmanly, matronly, certainly, heavenly, slovenly, unchristianly, uncommonly, gentlemanly.

16.175 [further rhymes may be created by adding -ly to the present participle of appropriate verbs]
kingly, jokingly, seemingly, swimmingly, exceedingly, accordingly, decreasingly, surprisingly.

16.176
wrongly, strongly.

16.177
ripply, triply.

16.178
amply, damply.

16.179
pimply, simply.

16.180
parsley, sparsely.

16.181
bristly, gristly, Sisley (French painter), thistly.

16.182
closely, jocosely, morosely.

16.183
loosely, sprucely, profusely.

16.184
purposely, seriously, previously, obviously.

16.185
fleshly, freshly.

16.186
Attlee, Batley (English town), flatly, rattly.

16.187
Atli (legendary Norse king), Hartley, partly.

16.188
lately, stately.

16.189
fitly, minutely, alternately, definitely, fortunately, immediately.

16.189.1
ultimately, approximately.

16.190
slightly, knightly, nightly, rightly, sprightly, sightly (attractive), fortnightly, unsightly.

16.191
hotly, motley.

16.192
courtly, portly, shortly.

16.193
minutely, absolutely.

16.194
compactly, exactly.

16.195
directly, correctly.

16.196
faintly, saintly.

16.197
Bentley, gently, intently.

16.198
urgently, patiently, patently, instantly, constantly, presently, evidently, consequently.

16.199
ghastly, lastly.

16.200
beastly, priestly, Priestley.

16.201
istle (fibre from tropical trees), modestly, honestly.

16.202
ghostly, mostly.

16.203
deathly, Llanelli.

16.204
earthly, unearthly.

16.205
monthly, bimonthly, trimonthly.

16.206
actively, positively, effectively, respectively, comparatively.

16.207
lovely, unlovely.

16.208
Lesley, Presley, Wesley.

16.209
drizzly, grisly, grizzly.

16.210
gammy, jammy, hammy, clammy, mammy, ramie (shrub yielding fibre), trammie (*Austral* tram driver), chamois, tammy, tamis (cloth for straining), Miami.

16.211
army, barmy, balmy, kami (Japanese divine spirit), smarmy, palmy (prosperous), swami (Hindu title of respect), Zeami (Japanese dramatist), kirigami (art of paper cutting), salami, tsunami (tidal wave), macramé, pastrami, origami.

16.212
Amy, gamy.

16.213
Emmy (US television award), jemmy, semi.

16.214
Fermi, wormy, taxidermy, diathermy, radiothermy (radiation treatment), aluminothermy (chemical process).

16.215
creamy, dreamy, preemie (*US* premature baby), seamy, steamy, steamie (*Scot* public washhouse), polysemy (having many meanings), monosemy (having only one meaning), Aruwimi (Zaïrese river).

16.216
Jimmy, shimmy, blasphemy, elemi (fragrant resin), Ptolemy, synonymy, eponymy (derivation from person's name), toponymy, metonymy (figure of speech).

16.217
limy, limey, blimey, slimy, rimy, grimy, stymie, cor blimey.

16.218
dormie (golf term), horme (psychology term), stormy.

16.219
Komi (Finnish people), foamy, homy, loamy, cleome (tropical plant), Daho-

mey, Salome, anomie (lack of social standards), polychromy (multicoloured decoration), stereochromy (method of wall painting).

16.220
chummy, dummy, gummy, lumme, plummy, mummy, rummy, Brummie, crummy, crumby, tummy, yummy.

16.221
gloomy, plumy, roomy, rheumy.

16.222
Naomi, alchemy, sodomy, infamy, syngamy (sexual reproduction), enemy, gourami, sesame, bosomy, academy, antinomy (contradiction within a law), anatomy, epitome.

16.222.1
bigamy, digamy (second marriage), polygamy.

16.222.2
oogamy (type of sexual reproduction), dichogamy (botany term), endogamy (marriage within social unit), homogamy (botany term), monogamy, misogamy (hatred of marriage), isogamy (botany term), autogamy (biology term), exogamy (marriage outside social unit), heterogamy (botany term), anisogamy (type of sexual reproduction).

16.222.3
bonhomie, economy, agronomy (science of cultivation), gastronomy, astronomy, isonomy (equality before the law), autonomy, taxonomy, pathognomy (study of the emotions), Deuteronomy, cytotaxonomy (classification by cell structure).

16.222.3.1
theonomy (being governed by God), physiognomy.

16.222.4
zootomy (animal dissection), phlebotomy (incision into vein), lobotomy, dichotomy, trichotomy (division into three categories), leucotomy (brain sur-

gery), colotomy (incision into colon), tenotomy (incision into tendon), sclerotomy (eye surgery), neurotomy (surgical cutting of nerve), necrotomy (dissection of corpse), microtomy (cutting of thin sections), nephrotomy (incision into kidney), gastrotomy, autotomy (shedding of body part), cystotomy (incision into bladder), lithotomy (removal of bladder stone), varicotomy, thoracotomy (incision into chest wall), pharyngotomy, laryngotomy, tonsillotomy, laparotomy (investigative abdominal surgery), enterotomy (incision into intestine), hysterotomy (incision into uterus).

16.222.4.1
tracheotomy, craniotomy, stereotomy (cutting three-dimensional solids), osteotomy (surgical cutting of bone), ovariotomy, episiotomy (incision into perineum).

16.222.5
colectomy (surgical removal of colon), splenectomy (removal of spleen), embrectomy (removal of embryo), nephrectomy (removal of kidney), gastrectomy, vasectomy, glossectomy (removal of tongue), mastectomy, cystectomy (removal of bladder), appendectomy, salpingectomy (removal of Fallopian tube), tonsillectomy, pneumonectomy, adenectomy (removal of gland), prostatectomy, appendicectomy, cholecystectomy (removal of gall bladder).

16.222.5.1
thyroidectomy, adenoidectomy, haemorrhoidectomy.

16.222.5.2
hysterectomy, oophorectomy (removal of ovary).

16.222.6
colostomy, gastrostomy (artificial stomach opening), tracheostomy, ileostomy (abdominal operation), gastroenterostomy (intestinal operation).

16.223
Annie, canny, Danny, fanny, nanny, cranny, granny, trannie, shanny (European fish), kokanee (type of salmon), uncanny, hootenanny.

16.224
ani (tropical bird), barney, carny (coax), blarney, Mani (Persian prophet), rani (Indian queen or princess), Mbabane (capital of Swaziland), afghani (Afghan currency), Killarney, sherwani (Indian man's long coat), biriani, Alemanni (4th-century Germanic people), frangipani (fragrant shrub), Pakistani, Hindustani, chilli con carne, Azerbaijani (Iranian people), Mina Hassan Tani (Moroccan port).

16.225
rainy, brainy, grainy, veiny, zany, Na-Dene (language group), Dunsany (Irish writer).

16.226
any, benne (sesame plant), benny (*Slang* amphetamine tablet), fenny (marshy), jenny, Jenny, blenny, many, penny, Kilkenny, catchpenny (designed for instant appeal), pinchpenny (miserly), Asantehene (Ghanaian ruler).

16.227
Ernie, byrnie (coat of mail), journey, attorney.

16.228
beanie (*US* close-fitting hat), genie, meany, teeny, weeny, sweeny (veterinary term), Syene (ancient Egyptian town), bikini, zucchini, Puccini, Houdini, wahine (Polynesian or Maori woman), Irene, Messene (ancient Greek city), Rossini, martini, linguini (type of pasta), Cherubini, fettucine, fantoccini (marionettes), Toscanini, scaloppine (thin slices of meat), Mistassini (Canadian lake).

16.228.1
Cellini (Italian sculptor), Fellini, Mussolini, tortellini (type of pasta).

16.229

skinny, finny, guinea, Guinea, hinny, Linnhe (Scottish loch), linhay (*Dialect* farm building), blini, Pliny, mini, ninny, pinny, spinney, brinny (*Austral* a stone), cine, tinny, whinny, dominie (*Scot* schoolmaster), hominy (*US* coarsely-ground maize), satiny, scrutiny, mutiny, destiny, ignominy, piccaninny.

16.229.1

polygyny (having many female partners), aborigine.

16.229.2

progeny, philogyny (fondness for women), phylogeny (evolution of species), homogeny (similarity through common ancestry), monogyny (having one female partner), ethnogeny (origin of races), orogeny (mountain formation), misogyny, ontogeny (development of organism), embryogeny (development of embryo), epeirogeny (formation of continents).

16.229.3

Rimini, postliminy (legal term), niminy-piminy.

16.229.4

larceny, coparceny (joint heirship).

16.230

piny, spiny, briny, sine (without), shiny, tiny, winy, sunshiny.

16.231

bonny, Johnny, Swanee, yonnie (*Austral* a stone), gironny (heraldic term), Suwannee (US river).

16.232

corny, horny, brawny, scrawny, tawny, thorny, mulligatawny.

16.233

bony, cony, phoney, pony, crony, Tony, stony, yoni (female genitalia in Hinduism).

Marconi, Bodoni (style of type), kongoni (hartebeest), spumone (Italian ice cream), Oenone (Greek nymph), Benoni (South African city), compony (heraldic term), padrone (Italian innkeeper), Shoshone (American Indian people), tortoni (rich ice cream), canzone (lyrical song).

cannelloni, chitarrone (large lute), Gaborone (capital of Botswana), macaroni, cicerone (tourist guide), minestrone, rigatoni (type of pasta), panettone (Italian spiced bread), zabaglione.

Antonioni (Italian film director), Sierra Leone.

16.233.1

baloney, polony, abalone, provolone (soft cheese).

16.234

downy, brownie, townie.

16.235

bunny, dunny (*Scot* cellar), funny, gunny (*US* coarse fabric), honey, money, runny, sunny, sonny, Sunni (branch of orthodox Islam), tunny, baldmoney (aromatic flowering plant).

16.236

Nguni (language group), loony, Cluny (French town), moony, spoony (foolishly amorous), uni (*short for* university), puny, puisne (of lower rank), Sakyamuni (title of Buddha).

16.237

peony, ebony, Albany, balcony, Gascony, Tuscany, Alderney, euphony, symphony, agony, garganey (Eurasian duck), villainy, colony, scammony, Chamonix, Tammany (US Democratic party organization), harmony, Germany, simony, Romany, fourpenny, twopenny, fivepenny, timpani, tympany (medical term), company, tenpenny, sixpenny, barony, guarani (Paraguayan currency), tyranny, irony, atony, rhatany (South American shrub), betony (Eurasian plant), tetany, dittany (aromatic plant), litany, Brittany, gluttony,

Antony, Bethany, Saxony, saxony (fine yarn), oniony.

chalcedony, diaphony (musical term), telephony, Persephone, telegony (genetics term), Antigone, disharmony, alimony, ceremony, acrimony, agrimony (flowering plant), matrimony, patrimony, parsimony, sanctimony, antimony, testimony, accompany.

16.237.1
irony (resembling iron), bryony, Hesione (Greek mythological princess), Alcyone (Greek mythological character).

16.237.2
tiffany (fine gauzy fabric), polyphony (musical term), epiphany, antiphony (type of choral singing).

16.237.3
Zoffany (British painter), cacophony, colophony (translucent amber substance), homophony (linguistics term), monophony, heterophony (musical term).

16.237.3.1
theophany (manifestation of deity), radiophony (electronic music), stereophony.

16.237.4
theogony (origin of the gods), mahogany, homogony (botany term), cosmogony (origin of universe), schizogony (type of asexual reproduction), heterogony (biology term).

16.237.5
felony, miscellany.

16.237.6
lemony, hegemony (domination by one group), anemone, Gethsemane.

16.237.7
botany, cottony, neoteny (zoology term), monotony, astrobotany, palaeobotany (study of fossil plants).

16.238
acne, hackney, Hackney, chloracne (skin disease), Arachne (Greek mythological character).

16.239
cockney, Hockney, Procne (Greek mythological princess).

16.240
kidney, Sydney, Sidney.

16.241
slangy, tangy.

16.242
dinghy, springy, stringy.

16.243
cappie (*Scot* ice-cream cone), chappie, happy, nappy, snappy, pappy (mushy), crappie (US freshwater fish), scrappy, sappy (full of energy), yappy, unhappy, slaphappy.

16.244
harpy, okapi, syncarpy (botany term), parthenocarpy (fruit development without fertilization).

16.245
peppy, cacoepy (bad pronunciation), orthoepy (study of correct pronunciation).

16.246
chirpy, Euterpe (Greek Muse).

16.247
sleepy, creepy, creepie (*Scot* low stool), weepy, Praesepe (cluster of stars).

16.248
chippy, dippy (*Slang* crazy), gippy, hippie, lippy (*US* insolent), clippie, slippy, nippy, drippy, zippy, recipe, gossipy, Xanthippe (wife of Socrates), Mississippi.

16.249
stripy, stenotypy (form of shorthand), phonotypy (phonetic transcription of speech), stereotypy.

16.250

copy, kopje (small hill), choppy, floppy, sloppy, poppy, stroppy, soppy, jalopy, phenocopy (biology term), microcopy (reduced photographic copy), photocopy.

16.251

dopey, Hopi (American Indian people), ropy, soapy.

16.252

guppy, puppy.

16.253

loopy, droopy, groupie, soupy, NUPE.

16.254

syncope, Agape (Christian love), Alleppey (Indian port), canopy, canapé, therapy, syrupy, satrapy (ancient Persian province), entropy.

calliope (*US* steam-powered organ), apocope (linguistics term), telescopy, Penelope, Parthenope (Greek mythological character), allotropy (chemistry term), lycanthropy (transformation into wolf), philanthropy, misanthropy.

cryotherapy, psychotherapy, chemotherapy, thermotherapy, hypnotherapy, hydrotherapy, massotherapy, phototherapy (medical treatment using light).

radiotherapy, heliotherapy (therapeutic use of sunlight), physiotherapy, immunotherapy, mechanotherapy (treatment using mechanical devices), organotherapy (treatment using gland extracts), roentgenotherapy (therapeutic use of x-rays).

16.254.1

wicopy (US plant), pericope (passage read in church).

16.254.2

cryoscopy (determination of freezing points), endoscopy, rhinoscopy (examination of nasal passages), horoscopy, uroscopy (examination of urine), microscopy, spectroscopy (analysis of spectra), stethoscopy, stereoscopy, ophthalmoscopy, retinoscopy (ophthalmic procedure), ornithoscopy (divination by bird observation).

16.255

impi (Bantu warriors), skimpy, Wimpy (*Trademark*).

16.256

Pompey, swampy.

16.257

bumpy, dumpy, jumpy, humpy (angry or gloomy), lumpy, scrumpy, grumpy, stumpy.

16.258

crispy, wispy.

16.259

colloquy, obloquy (defamatory statement), soliloquy, somniloquy (talking in one's sleep), ventriloquy.

16.260

Barrie, Barry, barye (unit of pressure), carry, Gary, gharry (Indian horsedrawn vehicle), harry, Harry, Larry, marry, parry, tarry, miscarry, glengarry (Scottish woollen cap), remarry, intermarry.

16.261

Bari (Italian port), karri (eucalyptus tree), Chari (African river), sparry (geology term), sari, tarry, starry, ambary (plant yielding fibre), shikari (hunter), safari, Bihari (member of Indian people), Aparri (Philippine port), curare, Ferrari, Vasari (Italian writer and artist), Andvari (Norse mythological character), Cagliari (Sardinian port), zamindari (large Indian agricultural estate), Carbonari (Italian secret political society), Stradivari, charivari.

16.261.1

Pahari (language group), Kalahari, Mata Hari.

16.262

berry, bury, Bury, Kerry (Irish county), skerry (*Scot* small rocky island), cherry, Derry, derry (*Austral* grudge or dislike), ferry, jerry, Jerry, merry, mere (Maori war club), perry, sherry, Terry, terry (towelling fabric), very, wherry (type of boat), knobkerrie (South African tribesman's stick), chokecherry (US species of cherry), flos ferri (deposit from hot springs), equerry, Owerri (Nigerian town), beriberi, Pondicherry, Londonderry.

16.263
burry (prickly), furry, firry (abounding in fir trees), blurry.

16.264
aery, airy, Carey, scary, chary, dairy, fairy, hairy, lairy (*Austral* gaudy), clary (aromatic plant), glary, Mary, nary (*Dialect* not), prairie, vary, wary, scalare (South American freshwater fish), costmary (aromatic plant), canary, unwary, airy-fairy, Tipperary, cassowary, bersagliere (Italian soldier), condottiere (former European mercenary soldier).

16.265
eyrie, eerie, Erie, beery, cheery, deary, sphery (resembling a sphere), leery, bleary, peri, Peary (US arctic explorer), query, dreary, theory, veery (US thrush), weary, Kediri (Indonesian city), Kashmiri, Guarneri (family of violin-makers), bokmakierie (South African songbird), Dhaulagiri (Nepalese mountain), metatheory (critical study of philosophy).

16.266
daiquiri (iced drink containing rum), Valkyrie, porphyry (type of rock), harakiri.

16.267
fiery, miry, spiry, wiry, expiry, enquiry, inquiry, praemunire (former legal term).

16.268
corrie (circular hollow in hillside), lorry, quarry, sorry, whare (Maori hut).

16.269
dory (spiny-finned fish), gory, hoary, lory (small parrot), flory (heraldic term), glory, saury (tropical fish), Tory, storey, story, John Dory (spiny-finned fish), vainglory, outlawry, furore, centaury (Eurasian plant), clerestory (row of church windows), blindstorey (church storey without windows), signori, hunky-dory, con amore, apospory (botany term), Montessori (Italian educational reformer), cacciatore (Italian cookery term), multistorey, Ruwenzori (African mountain range), Alpha Centauri, viola d'amore (former stringed instrument).

16.270
jury, Jewry, houri, Nuri (Indo-European people), Drury, Curie, fury, Tandoori, potpourri, decury (ten Roman soldiers), Venturi (Italian physicist), Missouri.

16.271
cowry, kauri (New Zealand coniferous tree), dowry, Lowry, Maori.

16.272
curry, scurry, hurry, flurry, slurry, Murray, spurry (low-growing plant), Surrey, surrey, worry.

16.273
mercury, augury, strangury, penury.

16.274
diary, friary, priory, flowery, floury, showery, brewery, Barbary, Burberry (*Trademark*), turbary (peat-cutting area), bribery, Albury (Australian city), daubery, strawberry, snowberry, crowberry, blubbery, rubbery, shrubbery, blueberry, dewberry, Newbury, hackberry, blackberry, cloudberry, Sudbury, dogberry, bilberry, Tilbury, tilbury (horse-drawn carriage), mulberry, anbury (veterinary or botany term), Banbury, cranberry, spiceberry, Shaftesbury, Avebury, Tewkesbury, raspberry, Shrewsbury, gooseberry, Dewsbury, Aylesbury, Salisbury,

Bloomsbury, Queensberry, quackery, Thackeray, Zachary, bakery, peccary (pig-like mammal), succory (chicory), cookery, rookery, piscary (location for fishing), hatchery, archery, lechery, treachery, witchery, butchery, century, spidery, doddery, gaudery (cheap finery), powdery, quandary, boundary, thundery, puffery (exaggerated praise), Nagari (type of Indian script), vagary, beggary, Gregory, roguery, sugary, Calgary, angary (legal term), Sungari (Chinese river), forgery, cudgerie (tropical tree), drudgery, soldiery, alary (relating to wings), raillery, hellery (wild behaviour), celery, sealery, Tuileries, coloury (having colour), scullery, foolery, saddlery, chandlery, burglary, jugglery, butlery (butler's room), cutlery, mammary, gramarye (magic), emery, memory, creamery, primary, flummery, plumbery, mummery, nummary (relating to coins), summary, summery, rosemary, cannery, granary, tannery, stannary (tin mine), swannery, joinery, clownery, gunnery, nunnery, apery (imitative behaviour), papery, drapery, peppery, foppery, coopery (barrel-making), dupery, trumpery, orrery (model of solar system), library, contrary, brasserie, glossary, sorcery, grocery, chancery, tertiary, washery, fishery, luxury, treasury, usury, lingerie, battery, cattery, flattery, artery, martyry (martyr's shrine), Tartary, lottery, pottery, cautery, watery, coterie, notary, rotary, votary, buttery, psaltery (ancient stringed instrument), mastery, blustery, lathery, feathery, leathery, carvery, reverie, every, ovary, Calvary, silvery, Mercury, colliery, misery, causerie (informal talk), rosery, rosary.

zedoary (aromatic ginger-like substance), checkerberry, elderberry, syllabary (list of syllables), chinaberry, Canterbury, huckleberry, whortleberry, loganberry, Glastonbury, boysenberry, serviceberry, grotesquery, debauchery,

solidary (marked by common interests), lapidary (dealer in gemstones), embroidery, prebendary, secondary, legendary, periphery, midwifery, housewifery, menagerie, corollary, tomfoolery, diablerie (devilry), exemplary, Montgomery, customary, chicanery (verbal trickery), reliquary, antiquary, arbitrary, patisserie, greengrocery, illusory, adversary, compulsory, secretory, bijouterie (type of jewellery), perfunctory, emunctory (relating to excretory organ), adultery, desultory, effrontery, peremptory, monastery, upholstery, recovery, discovery.

Devanagari (Indian syllabic script), haberdashery, introductory.

jiggery-pokery, noli-me-tangere (warning against touching).

16.274.1
laniary (tooth adapted for tearing), apiary, topiary, vespiary (wasps' nest), farriery, curriery, furriery, bestiary, vestiary (relating to clothes), ostiary (low-ranking Catholic official), aviary, breviary, hosiery, subsidiary, stipendiary, incendiary, pecuniary, fiduciary (trustee), intermediary.

16.274.1.1
biliary (relating to bile), miliary (resembling millet seeds), ciliary, nobiliary (relating to the nobility), auxiliary, domiciliary, superciliary (relating to the eyebrow).

16.274.1.2
judiciary, officiary (body of officials), justiciary, beneficiary.

16.274.2
mortuary, actuary, February, January, ossuary (receptacle for human bones), statuary, sanctuary, sumptuary (relating to extravagance), estuary, textuary (relating to a text), residuary, obituary, electuary (palatable substance containing drug), voluptuary.

16.274.3
bobbery (pack of hunting dogs), jobbery (corruption in public office), slobbery, snobbery, robbery, corroboree (*Austral* noisy gathering).

16.274.4
chicory, hickory (US nut tree), mickery (pool in river bed), trickery, formicary (ant hill), Terpsichore (Greek Muse), apothecary.

16.274.5
mockery, rockery, crockery, comstockery (*US* excessive censorship).

16.274.6
goliardery (ribald Latin verse), camaraderie.

16.274.7
dromedary, hebdomadary (weekly).

16.274.8
grindery (place for sharpening tools), bookbindery.

16.274.9
piggery, amphigory (piece of nonsense writing), allegory, vinegary, category.

16.274.10
buggery, snuggery, thuggery, skulduggery.

16.274.11
Hungary, ironmongery.

16.274.12
doggery (surly behaviour), toggery (clothes), pettifoggery, demagoguery.

16.274.13
perjury, surgery, psychosurgery, neurosurgery, cryosurgery, electrosurgery.

16.274.14
injury, gingery, orangery.

16.274.15
calorie, gallery, Malory, salary, Valerie, kilocalorie.

16.274.16
Hilary, Hillary, pillory, armillary (relating to bracelets), pupillary, capillary, ancillary, artillery, fritillary, tutelary (serving as guardian), distillery, axillary (relating to the armpit), maxillary (relating to upper jaw), submaxillary (relating to lower jaw).

16.274.17
drollery, cajolery.

16.274.18
formulary (book of prescribed formulas), cartulary (collection of legal records), vocabulary, constabulary.

16.274.19
chancellery, intercalary (inserted in the calendar), epistolary (relating to letters).

16.274.20
armoury, gendarmerie.

16.274.21
spermary (sperm-producing organ), infirmary.

16.274.22
bloomery (type of ironworks), perfumery.

16.274.23
hennery (place for keeping poultry), venery, millenary (one thousand years), decennary (decade).

16.274.24
fernery, ternary, turnery (objects made on lathe), quaternary (consisting of four).

16.274.25
beanery (cheap restaurant), deanery, denary (based on ten), plenary (complete), greenery, scenery, senary (relating to six), machinery, catenary (type of geometric curve), centenary, duodenary (relating to twelve), bicentenary, tricentenary, quincentenary, quatercentenary.

16.274.26
ordinary, millinery, culinary, seminary, luminary, urinary, parcenary (joint heirship), mercenary, sanguinary, subordinary (heraldic term), extraordinary, imaginary, disciplinary, preliminary,

coparcenary (joint ownership), veterinary, multidisciplinary, interdisciplinary, genitourinary, eleemosynary (dependent on charity).

16.274.27
binary, finery, pinery, quinary (consisting of five), trinary (consisting of three), vinery (place for growing grapes), winery, refinery.

16.274.28
unary (consisting of single element), buffoonery, sublunary (between moon and earth), festoonery.

16.274.29
legionary, pulmonary, coronary, cautionary, dictionary, functionary, pensionary, visionary, antiphonary (collection of biblical passages), precautionary, reactionary, revolutionary, evolutionary.

16.274.29.1
stationery, stationary, inflationary.

16.274.29.2
cessionary (legal term), discretionary, concessionary.

16.274.29.3
missionary, seditionary, expeditionary.

16.274.29.4
lectionary (book of church readings), confectionery, insurrectionary.

16.274.30
slippery, frippery, polypary (base of coral colony).

16.274.31
empery (dominion), extempore.

16.274.32
numerary (relating to numbers), honorary, funerary, vulnerary (relating to a wound), temporary, literary, itinerary, contemporary, supernumerary.

16.274.33
tracery, embracery (attempt to corrupt jury).

16.274.34
pessary, accessory, possessory (relating to possession).

16.274.35
bursary, cursory, nursery, precursory, anniversary.

16.274.36
emissary, dimissory (granting permission to depart), commissary, promissory, janissary (Turkish sovereign's personal guard), necessary, rescissory (having power to rescind), rotisserie, unnecessary.

16.274.37
spicery, derisory.

16.274.38
sensory, dispensary, suspensory, incensory (incense-burner), ostensory (container for displaying Host), extrasensory.

16.274.39
residentiary (officially resident), penitentiary, obedientiary (holder of monastic office), plenipotentiary.

16.274.40 [some words in 16.274.43 may be pronounced to rhyme with this group]
datary (Catholic official), gyratory, natatory (relating to swimming), condemnatory, celebratory, compensatory, anticipatory.

16.274.40.1
judicatory, applicatory, deprecatory, justificatory.

16.274.40.2
ambulatory (relating to walking), circulatory, adulatory, congratulatory.

16.274.41
jittery, glittery, pituri (Australian shrub).

presbytery, auditory, pellitory (European plant), military, solitary, cemetery, limitary, vomitory (causing vomiting), dormitory, fumitory (European plant), planetary, sanitary, monitory (warning), monetary, unitary, dignitary, feretory (Catholic shrine), territory, transitory.

proprietary, pituitary, hereditary, insanitary, premonitory, depository, repository, suppository, expository, paramilitary.

16.274.42
tributary, salutary, statutory, contributory, distributary (stream draining river), executory (not yet effective), noncontributory, interlocutory, circumlocutory.

16.274.43
dietary, placatory, predatory, laudatory (expressing praise), feudatory (relating to feudalism), mandatory, prefatory, offertory, purgatory, nugatory (of little value), fumatory (relating to smoking), chrismatory (receptacle for consecrated oil), signatory, damnatory, repertory, raspatory (surgeon's rasp), juratory (relating to legal oath), vibratory, secretary, migratory, pulsatory, hortatory (urging), lavatory.

masticatory (relating to chewing), educatory, obligatory, consolatory, undulatory, lacrimatory, reformatory, explanatory, cosignatory, declaratory, preparatory, perspiratory, respiratory, inspiratory (relating to inhalation), expiratory (relating to exhalation), procuratory (legal term), dispensatory, invitatory, salutatory, sternutatory (causing sneezing), conservatory, observatory, accusatory, excusatory.

reverberatory, undersecretary.

16.274.43.1
aleatory (dependent on chance), retaliatory, conciliatory, reconciliatory.

16.274.43.2
amendatory (*US* corrective), recommendatory.

16.274.43.3
rogatory (seeking information), derogatory, interrogatory, supererogatory (superfluous).

16.274.43.4
dilatory (time-wasting), depilatory.

16.274.43.5
amatory, defamatory, declamatory, acclamatory, proclamatory, exclamatory, inflammatory.

16.274.43.6
minatory (threatening), discriminatory, hallucinatory.

16.274.43.7
oratory, laboratory, exploratory.

16.274.44
factory, lactary (relating to milk), olfactory, phylactery (case containing Hebrew texts), refractory, calefactory (giving warmth), satisfactory.

16.274.45
nectary (nectar-secreting structure), rectory, sectary (member of a sect), refectory, trajectory, directory, protectory (institution for destitute children).

16.274.46
victory, valedictory, contradictory.

16.274.47
sedimentary, rudimentary, alimentary, elementary, supplementary, complimentary, complementary, documentary, parliamentary, testamentary (relating to a will), unparliamentary.

16.274.48
lientery (medical term), sedentary, voluntary, commentary, promontory, momentary, fragmentary, mesentery (anatomy term), dysentery, inventory, involuntary.

16.274.49
bistoury (long surgical knife), history, mystery, magistery (alchemical substance), prehistory, consistory (diocesan court), psychohistory (psychology term), protohistory.

16.274.50
slavery, knavery, bravery, savoury, unsavoury, antislavery.

16.274.51
livery, quivery, shivery, delivery, olivary (olive-shaped).

16.274.52
ivory, salivary.

16.274.53
revisory, advisory, supervisory.

16.275
gimmickry, mimicry.

16.276
bawdry (obscene language), Cawdrey (English lexicographer), tawdry.

16.277
balladry, bastardry (*Austral* malicious behaviour), wizardry.

16.278
ribaldry, cuckoldry, heraldry.

16.279
husbandry, legendry.

16.280
orphrey (embroidered border on vestment), gallimaufry (*US* hotchpotch).

16.281
comfrey (Eurasian plant), Humphrey.

16.282
imagery, savagery.

16.283
jewellery, riflery (*US* rifle marksmanship), hostelry, cavalry, devilry, revelry, chivalry, rivalry.

16.284
deaconry, falconry, felonry (felons collectively), almonry (house of alms-giver), cannonry (artillery), canonry (office of canon), weaponry, heronry (colony of herons), masonry, blazonry, archdeaconry, freemasonry, citizenry.

16.285
poetry, rabbitry, marquetry, parquetry, circuitry, rocketry, coquetry (flirtation), basketry, musketry, gadgetry, toiletry, summitry (holding summit conferences), puppetry, corsetry, telemetry (measurement of distant events), photogrammetry (making measurements from photographs).

16.285.1
symmetry, planimetry (measurement of plane areas), asymmetry, dissymmetry, altimetry, bathymetry (measurement of ocean depth), acidimetry, oxidimetry (chemistry term), alkalimetry, dolorimetry (measurement of pain).

16.285.2 [further rhymes may be derived from **17.342.3**]
biometry (statistics applied to biology), zoometry (branch of zoology), psychometry (measurement of mental processes), allometry (biology term), thermometry, astrometry (branch of astronomy), isometry (maths term), hypsometry (measurement of altitude), photometry, optometry, iodometry (chemistry term), anemometry (measurement of wind speed), dynamometry (power measurcment), anthropometry (measurement of human body).

16.285.2.1
geometry, tacheometry (measurement of distance), stoichiometry (branch of chemistry), craniometry, stereometry (measurement of volume), sociometry (study of social relationships).

16.285.2.2
chronometry, trigonometry.

16.286
bigotry, helotry (serfdom), zealotry (excessive zeal), papeterie (box for papers), barratry (legal term).

16.286.1
psychiatry, podiatry (*US* chiropody), antipsychiatry (psychiatric theory), neuropsychiatry.

16.286.2
zoolatry (worship of animals), bardolatry (excessive admiration for Shake-

speare), idolatry, monolatry (worship of one god), necrolatry (worship of the dead), iconolatry, demonolatry.

16.286.2.1
hagiolatry (veneration of saints), heliolatry (sun worship), bibliolatry (excessive devotion to Bible), Mariolatry (veneration of Virgin Mary), ecclesiolatry (devotion to ecclesiastical traditions).

16.287
gantry, pantry.

16.288
entry, gentry, sentry, re-entry, passementerie (decorative trimming).

16.289
wintry, carpentry.

16.290
country, upcountry.

16.291
pedantry, infantry, pageantry, gallantry, tenantry, errantry, Coventry, pleasantry, peasantry.

16.292
vestry, ancestry.

16.293
sophistry, registry, palmistry, chemistry, ministry, tapestry, forestry, artistry, dentistry, baptistry, casuistry, biochemistry.

16.294
dassie (rodent-like mammal), gassy, lassie, glacé, Plassey, Massey, massé (stroke in billiards), massy (massive), rasse (small catlike mammal), brassie, sassy, chassis, Kumasi (Ghanaian city), Manasseh (Old Testament character), Malagasy (inhabitant of Madagascar), Tallahassee, Haile Selassie.

16.295
farcy (veterinary term), classy, glassy, brassy, grassy, Likasi (Zaîrese city), dalasi (Gambian currency), sannyasi (Brahman mendicant), Adivasi (member of Indian people).

16.296
Basie, lacy, racy, Tracy, O'Casey, Sulawesi (Indonesian islands).

16.297
Jesse, messy, Crécy, dressy, in esse (actually existing).

16.298
mercy, Percy, pursy (short-winded), Circe, gramercy, controversy.

16.298.1
reversi (board game), arsy-versy.

16.299
fleecy, Naoise (Irish mythological character), greasy, Tbilisi (Russian city).

16.300
missy, prissy, sissy, prophecy, Gallice (in French), policy, Anglice (in English), pleurisy, secrecy, courtesy, Eurydice, Chalcidice (Greek peninsula), sub judice, impolicy, discourtesy.

16.300.1
Odyssey, geodesy (measurement of earth), theodicy (branch of theology).

16.301
icy, dicey, spicy, pricey, vice (instead of).

16.302
bossy, lossy (dissipating energy), flossy (*US* showy), glossy, mossy, mossie (African sparrow), Mossi (African people), posse, in posse (possible).

16.303
horsy, Glauce (Greek mythological character), saucy.

16.304
mousy, Firdausi (Persian epic poet), housey-housey.

16.305
fussy, hussy, pussy.

16.306
goosy, juicy, Lucy, Senussi (member of Muslim sect), Debussy, acey-deucy (type of backgammon).

16.307
abbacy, embassy, argosy (large merchant ship), legacy, fallacy, jealousy, prelacy (office of prelate), Wallasey, pharmacy, primacy, lunacy, papacy, heresy, piracy, oracy (use of speech), curacy (office of curate), euphrasy (flowering plant), leprosy, fantasy, ecstasy, privacy.

idiocy, celibacy, advocacy, candidacy, delegacy (university committee or department), profligacy, supremacy, diplomacy, contumacy (wilful resistance to authority), Varanasi (Indian city), obstinacy, adequacy, conspiracy, accuracy, magistracy, apostasy, isostasy (geological theory).

episcopacy (church government by bishops), inadequacy, inaccuracy, idiosyncrasy.

16.307.1
efficacy, delicacy, intricacy, inefficacy.

16.307.2
intimacy, legitimacy, illegitimacy.

16.307.3
geognosy (study of earth's structure), pharmacognosy (branch of pharmacology).

16.307.4
numeracy, literacy, confederacy, degeneracy, illiteracy.

16.307.5
mobocracy, ptochocracy (government by the poor), ochlocracy (mob rule), democracy, timocracy (political system), nomocracy (government based on law), monocracy, pornocracy (domination by prostitutes), technocracy, hypocrisy, bureaucracy, isocracy (equality of political power), stratocracy (military rule), squattocracy (*Austral* rich farmers collectively), autocracy, plutocracy, slavocracy (domination by slaveholders), gynaecocracy, hierocracy (government by priests), pantisocracy

(community ruled by all), meritocracy, gerontocracy, aristocracy.

16.307.5.1
theocracy (government by deity), theocrasy (mingling of deities), hagiocracy (government by holy men).

16.308
Anglesey, minstrelsy.

16.309
fancy, Nancy, geomancy (divination from random dots), theomancy (divination through an oracle), sciomancy (divination through ghosts), rhabdomancy (water divining), chiromancy (palmistry), pyromancy (divination by fire), necromancy (black magic), hydromancy (divination by water), cartomancy (fortune-telling with cards), bibliomancy (divination from random texts), ornithomancy (divination from bird behaviour).

16.310
chancy, Jhansi (Indian city).

16.311
wincey (type of cloth), chaplaincy, De Quincey (English essayist), captaincy.

16.312
buoyancy, fluency, truancy, vacancy, piquancy, cadency (heraldic term), pudency (modesty or prudishness), infancy, agency, regency, valency, clemency, tenancy, pregnancy, frequency, errancy (tendency to err), currency, flagrancy, vagrancy, decency, potency, constancy, solvency, poignancy.

incumbency, presidency, redundancy, exigency, Excellency, inclemency, athermancy (nontransmission of radiant heat), subtenancy, permanency, malignancy, discrepancy, occupancy, infrequency, delinquency, transparency, complacency, indecency, militancy, transmittancy (physics term), hesitancy, prepotency (superiority of power), expectancy, consultancy, accountancy, consistency, conservancy, insolvency.

constituency, diathermancy (transmission of radiant heat), eigenfrequency (physics term), belligerency (being at war), itinerancy, inconsistency, electrovalency (chemistry term).

16.312.1
leniency, expediency.

16.312.2
tendency, dependency, ascendancy, superintendency (office of superintendent).

16.312.3
urgency, surgeoncy (office of surgeon), emergency, insurgency, detergency (cleansing power), counterinsurgency.

16.312.4
stringency, contingency.

16.312.5
efficiency, deficiency, proficiency, sufficiency, inefficiency, insufficiency.

16.312.6
blatancy, patency, dilatancy (physics term).

16.313
epilepsy, narcolepsy (medical term), nympholepsy (state of violent emotion), catalepsy (medical term).

16.314
gypsy, tipsy.

16.315
popsy (*Slang* attractive young woman), dropsy, biopsy, autopsy.

16.316
curtsy, Chertsey.

16.317
ritzy, baronetcy.

16.318
footsie, tootsy, Watutsi (member of African people), tootsy-wootsy.

16.319
ashy, flashy, plashy (wet or marshy), splashy, mashie, brashy (loosely fragmented), trashy, Lubumbashi (Zaîrese city).

16.320
marshy, Ustashi (Yugoslav terrorist organization).

16.321
fleshy, meshy.

16.322
dishy, fishy, rubbishy, maharishi.

16.323
squashy, washy (watery), wishy-washy.

16.324
gushy, slushy, mushy, rushy.

16.325
bushy, cushy, pushy.

16.326
sushi (Japanese food), acouchi (South American rodent).

16.327
batty, catty, scatty, chatty, fatty, platy (freshwater fish), natty, patty, ratty, tatty, Scarlatti, chapatti, Hanratty, Togliatti (Russian city), Cincinnati.

16.328
arty, hearty, lathi (Indian policeman's wooden stick), smartie, party, coati, Masbate (Philippine island), Gauhati (Indian city), Komati (African river), nonparty, ex parte (legal term), Astarte (Phoenician goddess), illuminati (enlightened people).

16.328.1
karate, Marathi (Indian language), Gujarati (Indian people), literati (scholarly people).

16.329
eighty, Ate (Greek goddess), Haiti, platy (geology term), slaty, matey, weighty.

16.330
Getty, jetty, netty (*Dialect* lavatory), petty, sweaty, yeti, confetti, spaghetti, machete, Rossetti, spermaceti (white

waxy substance), Donizetti (Italian operatic composer).

16.331
dirty, shirty, thirty.

16.332
Beatty, meaty, peaty, rete (anatomy term), treaty, sweetie, graffiti, Tahiti, entreaty, Cavite (Philippine port), Papeete (capital of Tahiti), Nefertiti.

16.333
bitty, kitty, ditty, nitty, pity, gritty, smriti (Hindu sacred literature), pretty, city, shitty, witty.

laity, moiety (half), probity, rackety (noisy), crotchety, nudity, crudity, fidgety, nullity, comity (courtesy), samiti (Indian political association), committee, enmity, wapiti (large US deer), uppity, self-pity, equity, rarity, varsity, scarcity, paucity, falsity, sanctity, quantity, chastity, velvety, laxity, fixity.

acerbity, improbity, heredity, absurdity, fidelity, credulity, extremity, Yosemite, infirmity, subcommittee, amenity, indemnity, solemnity, inequity, obliquity, iniquity, antiquity, propinquity (nearness), jequirity (tropical climbing plant), entirety, alacrity, integrity, nitty-gritty, lithotrity (crushing of bladder stone), necessity, caducity (perishableness), intercity, perplexity, complexity, convexity.

infidelity, incredulity, serendipity, mediocrity.

16.333.1
deity, velleity (weakest level of desire), aseity (philosophy term), multeity, haecceity (philosophy term), spontaneity, corporeity, homogeneity, erogeneity, incorporeity.

16.333.2
piety, ubiety (being in particular place), dubiety, impiety, sobriety, propriety, society, satiety, anxiety, inebriety, impropriety.

16.333.2.1
variety, contrariety, notoriety.

16.333.3
congruity, vacuity, acuity, circuity (roundabout quality), tenuity, annuity, fortuity, fatuity, gratuity, superfluity, incongruity, perspicuity, promiscuity, assiduity, ambiguity, contiguity, perpetuity.

16.333.3.1
ingenuity, continuity, discontinuity.

16.333.4
rickety, pernickety.

16.333.5
quiddity (essential nature), fluidity, morbidity, rigidity, frigidity, solidity, validity, timidity, humidity, cupidity, stupidity, rapidity, liquidity, viridity (greenness), aridity, acridity, lucidity, avidity, invalidity, superfluidity (physics term).

16.333.5.1
acidity, placidity, hypoacidity, hyperacidity.

16.333.6
oddity, commodity, incommodity, discommodity (economics term).

16.333.7
fecundity, jocundity, profundity, infecundity.

16.333.8 [further rhymes may be derived from **228**]
locality, rascality, modality, sodality (Catholic religious society), feudality, frugality, molality (chemical concentration), venality, finality, tonality, plurality, neutrality, centrality, natality, vitality, mortality, totality, brutality, fatality, frontality, causality, animality, externality, atonality, hospitality, immortality, polytonality, universality, inhospitality.

16.333.8.1
reality, ideality, cordiality, geniality, unreality, partiality, speciality, social-

ity, bestiality, joviality, congeniality, materiality, impartiality, commerciality, provinciality, territoriality, artificiality, superficiality, extraterritoriality.

16.333.8.1.1
potentiality, confidentiality.

16.333.8.1.2
triviality, conviviality.

16.333.8.2
duality, actuality, punctuality, sensuality, mutuality, sexuality, spirituality, eventuality, individuality, pseudomutuality (psychology term), homosexuality, heterosexuality.

16.333.8.3
technicality, topicality, practicality, whimsicality, illogicality, impracticality.

16.333.8.4
regality, legality, prodigality, illegality.

16.333.8.5
formality, normality, informality, abnormality, subnormality.

16.333.8.6
criminality, originality.

16.333.8.7
banality, commonality (commonness), personality, impersonality, conventionality, constitutionality, unconventionality.

16.333.8.7.1
nationality, rationality, irrationality.

16.333.8.8
principality, municipality.

16.333.8.9
morality, liberality, amorality, immorality, generality, temporality, ephemerality.

16.333.8.10
mentality, sentimentality.

16.333.9
agility, fragility, humility, tranquillity, sterility, virility, febrility (feverishness), gracility (slenderness), docility, facility,

fertility, motility, utility, futility, gentility, hostility, servility, civility, solubility, puerility, imbecility, infertility, versatility, infantility, incivility.

16.333.9.1
mobility, nobility, immobility.

16.333.9.2 [further rhymes may be derived from 228.16]
ability, debility, stability, probability, credibility, fallibility, gullibility, inability, capability, disability, possibility, sensibility, notability, suitability, flexibility, instability, permeability, improbability, practicability, availability, desirability, impossibility, responsibility, compatibility, unsuitability, susceptibility, suggestibility, manipulability, incompatibility.

16.333.9.2.1
liability, viability, reliability, unreliability.

16.333.9.2.2
risibility, visibility, divisibility, invisibility.

16.333.9.3
senility, juvenility.

16.333.10
jollity, polity (political organization), quality, equality, frivolity, inequality.

16.333.11
amity, calamity.

16.333.12
dimity (cotton fabric), sublimity, proximity, longanimity (patience), anonymity, synonymity, unanimity, magnanimity, equanimity, pusillanimity.

16.333.13
deformity, conformity, enormity, uniformity, nonconformity, unconformity.

16.333.14
sanity, vanity, urbanity, profanity, humanity, inanity, insanity, Christianity, inhumanity.

16.333.15
lenity, serenity, obscenity.

16.333.16
modernity, maternity, paternity, quaternity (group of four), fraternity, confraternity (organized group of men).

16.333.16.1
eternity, coeternity (eternal coexistence), taciturnity.

16.333.17
trinity, affinity, infinity, virginity, vicinity, Latinity, divinity, masculinity, femininity, asininity, consanguinity.

16.333.17.1
salinity, alkalinity.

16.333.18
unity, immunity, community, impunity, disunity, importunity, opportunity.

16.333.19
dignity, indignity, malignity, benignity.

16.333.20
charity, clarity, parity, barbarity, vulgarity, molarity (chemical concentration), polarity, disparity, solidarity, viviparity, oviparity.

16.333.20.1
familiarity, peculiarity, unfamiliarity, multicollinearity (statistics term).

16.333.20.2
hilarity, similarity, capillarity (surface tension), dissimilarity.

16.333.20.3 [further rhymes may be derived from **17.174**]
secularity, jocularity, muscularity, regularity, angularity, singularity, popularity, insularity, irregularity, unpopularity.

16.333.20.3.1
particularity, perpendicularity.

16.333.21
ferity (wildness), verity, celerity (speed), temerity, asperity, prosperity, sincerity, austerity, posterity, dexterity, severity, insincerity, ambidexterity.

16.333.22
priority, majority, minority, sonority, sorority, authority, seniority, inferiority, superiority.

16.333.23
purity, security, obscurity, impurity, futurity, maturity, insecurity, immaturity.

16.333.24
celebrity, muliebrity (womanhood).

16.333.25
audacity, mordacity, mendacity, fugacity (chemistry term), sagacity, tenacity, pugnacity, opacity, loquacity, veracity, voracity, vivacity, pertinacity, inveracity.

16.333.25.1
capacity, rapacity, incapacity.

16.333.26
diversity, perversity, adversity, university.

16.333.27
cecity (blindness), obesity.

16.333.28
felicity, publicity, duplicity, simplicity, complicity, tonicity, sphericity, lubricity (lewdness), basicity (chemistry term), toxicity, infelicity, catholicity, Catholicity, atomicity, historicity (historical authenticity), eccentricity, concentricity, electricity, chromaticity (quality of a colour), authenticity, domesticity, alcoholicity, thermoelectricity, hydroelectricity, photoelectricity.

16.333.28.1
triplicity (group of three), multiplicity.

16.333.28.2
plasticity, elasticity, inelasticity, homoscedasticity (statistics term), photoelasticity (physics term), heteroscedasticity (statistics term).

16.333.29
nicety, benedicite (blessing).

16.333.30

verbosity, viscosity, velocity, villosity (biology term), callosity, pomposity, porosity, atrocity, monstrosity, schistosity (medical term), nebulosity, animosity, tenebrosity, reciprocity.

16.333.30.1

grandiosity, curiosity, preciosity (affectation), speciosity, religiosity (extreme piety), incuriosity.

16.333.30.2

virtuosity, strenuosity, sinuosity, tortuosity, impetuosity, anfractuosity (state of being convoluted).

16.333.30.3

precocity, bellicosity, varicosity.

16.333.30.4

vinosity (distinctive quality of wine), luminosity, voluminosity.

16.333.30.5

ferocity, tuberosity, generosity.

16.333.31

density, immensity, propensity, intensity, extensity (psychology term).

16.333.32

entity, identity, nonentity.

16.333.33

cavity, gravity, suavity, concavity, depravity.

16.333.34

levity, brevity, longevity.

16.333.35

privity (relationship recognized by law), declivity (downward slope), acclivity (upward slope), proclivity, motivity (power of moving), captivity, festivity, expressivity, creativity, permittivity (electrical property), sensitivity, objectivity, subjectivity, selectivity, collectivity, reflectivity (physics term), receptivity, resistivity (electrical property).

16.333.35.1

nativity, negativity, relativity.

16.333.35.2

activity, reactivity, inactivity, hyperactivity, radioactivity.

16.333.35.3

productivity, conductivity, reluctivity (physics term), superconductivity.

16.334

Blighty, flighty, mighty, nightie, almighty, Venite (95th psalm), Aphrodite, Amphitrite (Greek goddess), pendente lite (legal term).

16.335

Scottie, dotty, hottie (*Austral* hot-water bottle), zloty, knotty, snotty, potty, spotty, Menotti (Italian composer), manicotti (large stuffed noodles).

16.336

dorty (*Scot* sullen or haughty), forte, forty, haughty, naughty, sporty, sortie, shortie, warty, pianoforte.

16.337

surety, Trimurti (three Hindu gods).

16.338

dacoity (armed robbery), hoity-toity.

16.339

dhoti (Indian man's long loincloth), floaty, roti (type of unleavened bread), throaty, peyote (cactus), coyote, Don Quixote.

16.340

doughty, grouty.

16.341

butty, cutty, chuttie (*Austral* chewing gum), gutty (*Irish* urchin), smutty, nutty, putty, puttee (cloth wound around leg), rutty (full of ruts), tutty (impure zinc oxide).

16.342

footy, sooty, tutti (musical term), bobotie (South African curried dish), deputy.

16.343

booty, cootie (*US* body louse), snooty, fruity, beauty, cutie, duty, Djibouti

(African republic), agouti, gomuti (East Indian palm), busuuti (Ugandan woman's long garment), tutti-frutti.

16.344
gaiety, liberty, puberty, Hecate (Greek goddess), maggoty, property, champerty (legal term), carroty, poverty, chocolaty, vanaspati (vegetable fat), Amravati (Indian town), Ross and Cromarty.

16.345
crafty, draughty.

16.346
hefty, lefty.

16.347
fifty, nifty, thrifty, shifty, swiftie (*Austral* a trick).

16.348
lofty, softy, toplofty (haughty).

16.349
mufti, Mufti (Muslim legal adviser), tufty.

16.350
guilty, silty.

16.351
faulty, malty, salty.

16.352
fealty, realty, owelty (legal term), cruelty, faculty, penalty, mayoralty, specialty, subtlety, shrievalty (office of sheriff), novelty, casualty, difficulty, commonalty (ordinary people), personalty (personal property), admiralty, severalty (state of being separate).

16.352.1
loyalty, royalty, disloyalty, viceroyalty.

16.353
anti, ante, canty (*Dialect* lively), scanty, Dante, Fanti (Ghanaian people), shanty, Zante (Greek island), chianti, andante, infante (Spanish prince), Ashanti (region of Ghana), Alicante, vigilante, Ypsilanti (Greek revolutionary), diamanté, Rosinante (worn-out old

horse), dilettante, concertante (musical term), pococurante (indifferent).

16.354
dainty, painty.

16.355
kente (brightly-coloured African cloth), plenty, twenty, aplenty, Mindszenty (Hungarian cardinal), lentamente (musical term), cognoscenti (connoisseurs).

16.356
flinty, minty, shinty (form of hockey), teosinte (Central American grass).

16.357
Monty, monte (gambling card game), Brontë.

16.358
jaunty, flaunty (ostentatious).

16.359
bounty, county, Mountie.

16.360
frumenty (sweetened spiced porridge), guaranty, warranty, certainty, seventy, sovereignty, suzerainty, uncertainty.

16.361
Asti, pasty, epinasty (growth of plant part), nyctinasty (botany term), hyponasty (growth of plant part), photonasty (plant's response to light), pederasty.

16.361.1
neoplasty (surgical repair of tissue), zooplasty (transplantation technique), anaplasty (plastic surgery), rhinoplasty (plastic surgery of nose), autoplasty (transplantation from own body), osteoplasty (bone grafting), heteroplasty (transplantation from another body), dermatoplasty (skin grafting), keratoplasty (plastic surgery of cornea).

16.362
nasty, vasty, contrasty (having sharp contrast).

16.363
hasty, pasty, tasty.

16.364
chesty, testy, Tibesti (African mountain range).

16.365
thirsty, bloodthirsty.

16.366
misty, Christie, twisty, modesty, majesty, honesty, amnesty, touristy, sacristy, travesty, immodesty, lese-majesty, dishonesty, Corpus Christi.

16.367
frosty, Anticosti (Canadian island).

16.368
busty, dusty, fusty, gusty, lusty, musty, rusty, crusty, trusty.

16.369
breathy, abernethy.

16.370
pithy, stichomythy (dialogue in Greek drama).

16.371
bothy (*Scot* small shelter), mothy, frothy.

16.372
couthie (*Scot* friendly), toothy.

16.373
Timothy, apathy, empathy, sympathy, telepathy, antipathy.

16.373.1
psychopathy, allopathy, neuropathy (disease of nervous system), hydropathy (water cure), naturopathy.

16.373.1.1
theopathy (religious emotion after meditation), idiopathy (disease of unknown cause), homeopathy, osteopathy.

16.374
healthy, stealthy, wealthy, unhealthy.

16.375
worthy, airworthy, seaworthy, roadworthy, blameworthy, unworthy, noteworthy, trustworthy, praiseworthy, newsworthy, Galsworthy.

16.376
smithy, prithee, stithy (*Dialect* a forge), withy (willow tree).

16.377
navvy, savvy.

16.378
ave, jarvey (coachman), Harvey, grave (musical term), Mohave (American Indian people).

16.379
cavy, cave, cavie (*Scot* hen coop), Davy, slavey (female servant), navy, gravy, wavy, agave (tropical plant).

16.380
bevy, bevvy (*Dialect* alcoholic drink), chevy, heavy, levee, levy, replevy (legal term).

16.381
curvy, scurvy, nervy, topsy-turvy.

16.382
bivvy (*slang* small tent), skivvy, chivy, divvy (*short for* dividend), Livy, privy, civvy (*slang* civilian), tantivy (at full speed), divi-divi (tropical tree).

16.383
covey, lovey, lovey-dovey.

16.384
movie, groovy.

16.385
Muscovy, anchovy, Pahlavi (Middle Persian language).

16.386
maxi, braxy (disease of sheep), taxi, waxy, chronaxie (physiology term), epitaxy (growth on crystal), anthotaxy (flower arrangement on stem).

16.387
sexy, apoplexy.

16.388
dixie (large metal pot), Dixie (southern states of USA), nixie (female water sprite), pixie, pyxie (evergreen shrub), tricksy (mischievous).

16.389
doxy (opinion or doctrine), foxy, moxie (*US* courage), proxy, epoxy, hydroxy (chemical compound), orthodoxy, heterodoxy.

16.390
galaxy, metagalaxy (the universe).

16.391
jazzy, snazzy.

16.392
carzey, ghazi (Muslim fighter against unbelievers), Swazi (African people), Benghazi (Libyan port), Nastase, kamikaze, Ashkenazi.

16.393
daisy, hazy, lazy, mazy (perplexing), crazy, Bel Paese (creamy Italian cheese), upsy-daisy.

16.394
kersey (woollen cloth), jersey, Jersey, Mersey.

16.395
easy, cheesy, sleazy, queasy, breezy, wheezy, Zambezi, speakeasy, pachisi (Indian board game), uneasy.

16.396
busy, dizzy, fizzy, frizzy, tizzy, poesy, tin lizzie, busy Lizzie.

16.397
gauzy, mawsie (*Scot* woollen jersey), Gagauzi (Russian language).

16.398
Boise (US city), noisy, cramoisy (crimson).

16.399
cosy, dozy, Lozi (Zambian language), mosey, nosy, posy, rosy, prosy.

16.400
lousy, blowzy (slovenly), drowsy, frowzy (shabby), Dalhousie (British statesman).

16.401
fuzzy, muzzy.

16.402
boozy, choosy, floozy, woozy, newsy, Pusey (English ecclesiastic), Brancusi, Watusi (member of African people).

16.403
flimsy, slimsy (*US* frail), whimsy.

16.404
gansey (*Dialect* pullover), pansy, tansy (flowering plant).

16.405
frenzy, Mackenzie.

16.406
Kinsey (US zoologist), quinsy.

17 -er [This is the unstressed syllable at the end of such words as *grocer* and *ancestor*. Rhymes dependent on this syllable alone are unsatisfactory and should be avoided. Further rhymes may be created by adding -*er* to appropriate adjectives and verbs.]
chamber, vodka, polka, Oscar, butcher, scripture, rupture, sculpture, pasture, moisture, Buddha, pilfer, sulphur, Edgar, soldier, chandler, handler, burglar, stapler, sampler, dogma, asthma, Wagner, partner, cobra, extra, pizza, fuchsia, tonsure, azure, sculptor, Ulster, hamster, monster, gangster, youngster, ether, author, premier, Kenya, junior, Windsor, sepulchre.

17.1
layer, player, payer, Freya (Norse goddess), stayer, Malaya, bricklayer, platelayer (railway-track layer), ratepayer, taxpayer, soothsayer, purveyor, surveyor, conveyor, Eritrea (Ethiopian province).

17.2
skier, rhea, Rhea, ria, seer.

Euboea (Greek island), Achaea (region of Greece), trachea, Medea (Greek mythological princess), idea, Judaea, Chaldea (ancient Babylonian region), Hygeia (Greek goddess), Crimea, eupnoea (normal breathing), dyspnoea (difficulty in breathing), spiraea, chorea, sangria, sightseer, tortilla (Mexican pancake), Hosea.

Kampuchea, ratafia, Tanzania, hyperpnoea (increased breathing rate), Nicosia, panacea, overseer, Boadicea, galatea (strong cotton fabric), barathea.

Laodicea, Arimathea.

17.2.1
epopoeia (epic poem), Cassiopeia, pharmacopoeia (list of drugs), prosopopoeia (figure of speech), onomatopoeia.

17.2.2
Korea, Maria, Peraea (ancient Palestinian region), sharia (Islamic doctrines), diarrhoea, pyorrhoea (discharge of pus), leucorrhoea (vaginal discharge), banderilla (bullfighter's assistant), logorrhoea (excessive talkativeness), gonorrhoea, pizzeria, trattoria, Caesarea, Tia Maria (*Trademark*), amenorrhoea, dysmenorrhoea, spermatorrhoea.

17.3
Nubia, hakea (Australian shrub), clarkia, lochia (vaginal discharge), branchia (aquatic animal's gill), bronchia (bronchial tubes), breccia (type of rock), torchier (type of lamp), India, morphia, logia (collection of Christ's sayings), collier, cochlea, trochlea (anatomy term), nuclear, buddleia, Anglia, cattleya (tropical orchid), Antlia (constellation), denier, daphnia, Bosnia (region of Yugoslavia), Napier, rapier, sepia, copier, croupier, barrier, carrier, farrier, garrya (ornamental shrub), harrier, aria, Zaria (Nigerian city), terrier, quarrier (quarryman), warrior, currier, furrier, spurrier (spur maker), fimbria (anatomy term), nutria (coypu fur), Bactria (ancient Asian country), Istria (peninsula in Adriatic Sea), Austria, Mercia, deutzia (flowering shrub), me-

teor, cottier (Irish smallholder), courtier, protea (tropical shrub), Hestia (Greek goddess), Ostia, Parthia, Scythia, clothier, uvea (part of eyeball), clavier, salvia, banksia (Australian shrub), nausea, zoysia (type of grass), woodsia (small fern).

euphorbia (flowering plant), Colombia, Columbia, Slovakia (region of Czechoslovakia), Walachia, rudbeckia (flowering plant), petechia (mark on skin), welwitschia (African desert plant), Cambodia, Hollandia (Indonesian port), montgolfier (hot-air balloon), rauwolfia (tropical tree), Thuringia (region of East Germany), sedilia (group of church seats), saintpaulia (African violet), East Anglia, costumier, arrhythmia, anosmia (inability to smell), petunia, insignia, insomnia, tilapia (African freshwater fish), Olympia, Calabria (region of Italy), anarthria (loss of coherent speech), collinsia (US plant), eupepsia (good digestion), dyspepsia, eclampsia (toxic condition during pregnancy), bilharzia (pathogenic blood fluke), rickettsia (pathogenic microorganism), strelitzia (African plant), opuntia (prickly pear), poinsettia, forsythia, anoxia (lack of oxygen), tillandsia (tropical plant).

Appalachia, Philadelphia, multinuclear, thermonuclear, mononuclear, intranuclear, extranuclear, Ichinomiya (Japanese town), bladder ketmia, pleurodynia (muscular pain between ribs), algolagnia (sexual perversion), photocopier, Alexandria, hypochondria, Cappadocia (ancient Asian region), polydipsia (excessive thirst), pre-eclampsia (toxic condition during pregnancy), differentia (logic term), hydrometeor (meteorology term), Yugoslavia, Andalusia.

Czechoslovakia, hemianopsia (sight defect), intelligentsia, macula lutea (spot on retina), gynaecomastia (abnormal male breast development), anacoluthia (lack of grammatical sequence).

17.3.1
labia, Swabia (former West German duchy), Arabia, Bessarabia (region of Russia).

17.3.2
Serbia (republic of Yugoslavia), suburbia, ytterbia (chemical compound), exurbia (*US* region outside suburbs).

17.3.3
Libya, tibia, Namibia.

17.3.4
obeah (type of witchcraft), cobia (game fish), phobia, theophobia (fear of God), zoophobia, Francophobia, phagophobia (fear of eating), algophobia (fear of pain), ochlophobia (fear of crowds), Anglophobia, xenophobia, monophobia (fear of being alone), aquaphobia (fear of water), aerophobia, acrophobia, necrophobia, hydrophobia, Negrophobia, astraphobia (fear of thunderstorms), claustrophobia, photophobia, nyctophobia (fear of night), Germanophobia, agoraphobia, triskaidekaphobia (fear of number thirteen).

17.3.5
Gambia, Zambia, Senegambia (region of Africa).

17.3.6
gaillardia (flowering plant), La Guardia (US politician), tachycardia (abnormally rapid heartbeat), bradycardia (abnormally slow heartbeat), megalocardia (abnormal enlargement of heart).

17.3.7
stadia, Arcadia, Acadia (Maritime Provinces of Canada).

17.3.8
media, redia (parasitic larva), acedia (apathy), multimedia (combined use of media), cyclopedia, hypnopaedia, encyclopedia.

17.3.9
Lydia, Numidia (ancient African country).

17.3.10
Mafia, raffia, tafia (West Indian rum), agraphia (loss of writing ability), dysgraphia (impaired writing ability), paragraphia (psychiatric term).

17.3.11
Sofia, dystrophia.

17.3.12 [see also 17.146]
aphagia (inability to swallow), dysphagia (difficulty in swallowing), polyphagia (abnormal desire to eat), omophagia (eating of raw food), aerophagia (spasmodic swallowing of air), menorrhagia (excessive bleeding during menstruation), metrorrhagia (abnormal bleeding from uterus).

17.3.13 [see also 17.149]
diplegia, aquilegia (columbine), hemiplegia, quadriplegia, cycloplegia (paralysis of eye muscles), paraplegia, aqua regia (metal-dissolving corrosive mixture).

17.3.14 [see also 17.150]
Phrygia, steatopygia (excessively fat buttocks).

17.3.15
cambogia (gum resin), apologia.

17.3.16
myalgia (muscular pain), analgia (inability to feel pain), neuralgia, nephralgia, metralgia (pain in the uterus), gastralgia, arthralgia, otalgia (earache), nostalgia, coxalgia (pain in hip joint), causalgia (pathology term), cardialgia, hemialgia (pain on one side), cephalalgia (headache), odontalgia (toothache).

17.3.17
Somalia, Charlotte Amalie (capital of Virgin Islands).

17.3.18 [see also **17.433**]
dahlia, galea (helmet-shaped structure), vedalia (Australian ladybird), Westphalia, regalia, psoralea (tropical plant), Australia, azalea, Lupercalia (Roman fertility festival), echolalia (psychiatric term), glossolalia (gift of tongues), marginalia (marginal notes), penetralia (innermost parts), genitalia.

17.3.18.1
bacchanalia, Saturnalia (ancient Roman festival), paraphernalia.

17.3.19
Saint Helier, hotelier, psychedelia.

17.3.20
Elia, lobelia, grindelia (flowering plant), Rumelia (part of Ottoman empire), camellia, stapelia (cactus-like plant), Karelia (region of Russia), phocomelia (congenital deformity of limbs), syringomyelia (disease of spinal cord).

17.3.21
ILEA, cilia, Pamphylia (ancient Asian region), familiar, Cecilia, conciliar (of ecclesiastical councils), Brasília, sensibilia, unfamiliar, juvenilia, bougainvillea.

17.3.21.1
memorabilia, imponderabilia.

17.3.21.2
zoophilia, paedophilia, Anglophilia, haemophilia, necrophilia, coprophilia (abnormal interest in faeces), Germanophilia, ailurophilia (liking for cats).

17.3.22
foliar (relating to leaves), Grolier (denoting decorative bookbinding style), Mongolia, magnolia, Aetolia (mountainous region of Greece), melancholia, Anatolia (Asian part of Turkey).

17.3.23
Julia, dulia (veneration for saints), abulia (loss of willpower), peculiar,

hyperdulia (veneration for Virgin Mary).

17.3.24
lamia (monster in classical mythology), zamia (tropical plant), macadamia (Australian tree), adynamia (weakness), Mesopotamia.

17.3.25
Urmia (Iranian lake), hypothermia, hyperthermia.

17.3.26
pyaemia (blood poisoning), leukaemia, ischaemia (inadequate blood supply), Bohemia, anaemia, uraemia, sapraemia (blood poisoning), academia, tularaemia (infectious disease), hyperaemia (excess blood in organs), bacteraemia (bacteria in the blood), septicaemia, hypoglycaemia (insufficient blood sugar), hyperglycaemia (excessive blood sugar).

17.3.26.1
toxaemia, anoxaemia (oxygen deficiency in blood).

17.3.27
skimmia (ornamental shrub), bulimia (insatiable hunger).

17.3.28
kalmia (evergreen shrub), ophthalmia (inflammation of the eye), xerophthalmia (eye disease).

17.3.29 [see also **17.434**]
pannier (large basket), Hispania, Britannia.

17.3.30
Sarnia (Canadian port), Goiânia (Brazilian city), Titania, Oceania (Pacific islands), Christiania.

17.3.31
mania, Rainier, Albania, Rumania, leishmania (pathogenic protozoan), Tasmania, Campania (region of Italy), Lithuania, Araucania (region of Chile), miscellanea, Pomerania (region of Eu-

rope), collectanea (miscellany), Transylvania, Pennsylvania.

17.3.31.1
theomania (religious mania), nymphomania, phagomania (compulsive desire to eat), egomania, Anglomania, monomania, hypomania (psychiatric term), pyromania, dipsomania, kleptomania, mythomania (psychiatric term), bibliomania, decalcomania (process of transferring designs), megalomania, balletomania, erotomania (abnormally strong sexual desire).

17.3.31.2
Mauritania, Ruritania, Lusitania, Tripolitania (part of Libya).

17.3.32
hernia, vernier (measuring scale), Hibernia.

17.3.33 [see also **17.435**]
taenia (ancient Greek headband), xenia (botany term), gardenia, Armenia, Ruthenia (region of Russia), asthenia, Slovenia (republic of Yugoslavia), catamenia (menstruation), leucopenia (insufficient white blood cells), hebephrenia (form of schizophrenia), schizophrenia, sarracenia (insectivorous plant), myasthenia (muscular weakness), neurasthenia (nervous breakdown).

17.3.34
linear, tinea (fungal skin disease), zinnia (flowering plant), robinia (tree genus), Sardinia, Virginia, bauhinia (ornamental plant), bilinear, trilinear, collinear (on same straight line), Fourdrinier (paper-making machine), actinia (sea anemone), Bithynia (ancient Asian country), vaccinia (cowpox), gloxinia, rectilinear, curvilinear, interlinear, Abyssinia.

17.3.35
cornea, salicornia (salt-marsh plant), California.

17.3.36
Ionia, zirconia (chemical compound), Snowdonia, aphonia (loss of voice), dysphonia (speech impairment), begonia, mahonia (evergreen shrub), paulownia (Japanese tree), pneumonia, ammonia, bignonia (tropical shrub), boronia (aromatic shrub), claytonia (succulent plant), boltonia (flowering plant), houstonia (flowering plant), Livonia, Slavonia (region of Yugoslavia), Caledonia, Macedonia, Babylonia, eudemonia (happiness), myotonia (lack of muscle tone), catatonia (form of schizophrenia), aniseikonia (visual defect), bronchopneumonia, pleuropneumonia.

17.3.36.1
pogonia (orchid), Paphlagonia (ancient Roman province), Patagonia.

17.3.36.2
valonia (acorns used in tanning), escallonia (ornamental shrub), Cephalonia (Greek island), Catalonia.

17.3.37
myopia, diplopia (double vision), photopia (eye's adaptation to light), Utopia, ectopia (displacement of body part), dystopia (worst possible place), presbyopia, amblyopia (impaired vision), Ethiopia, cornucopia, asthenopia (eyestrain).

17.3.37.1
nyctalopia (night blindness), hemeralopia (day blindness).

17.3.37.2
tritanopia (blue blindness), protanopia (red blindness), deuteranopia (green blindness).

17.3.37.3
scotopia (adjustment for night vision), heterotopia (displacement of body part).

17.3.38
area, Caria (ancient Asian region), varia (collection of literary works), Ica-

ria (Greek island), cercaria (larva of parasitic flatworm), Bulgaria, Dzungaria (region of China), filaria (parasitic roundworm), Samaria, Bavaria, calvaria (top of skull), miliaria (heat rash), araucaria (coniferous tree), adularia (mineral), laminaria (brown seaweed), sanguinaria (plant yielding red dye), cineraria, persicaria (red-stemmed plant), urticaria, alfilaria (flowering plant), Carpentaria (gulf in north Australia).

17.3.38.1
malaria, talaria (winged sandals), calceolaria.

17.3.39
feria (Catholic non-feast day), ceria (chemical compound), Iberia, Liberia, Siberia, inferior, Egeria (female adviser), Nigeria, Algeria, krameria (South American shrub), superior, bacteria, ulterior, anterior, interior, hysteria, wisteria, posterior, exterior, gaultheria (aromatic shrub), diphtheria, latimeria (primitive fish), cryptomeria (coniferous tree), cafeteria, echeveria (tropical plant), sansevieria (cultivated plant), nitrobacteria (soil bacteria).

17.3.40
Syria, Styria (province of Austria), porphyria (hereditary metabolic disease), Illyria, Assyria.

17.3.41
scoria (mass of lava), Gloria, gloria, noria (waterwheel with buckets attached), thoria (chemical compound), euphoria, dysphoria (uneasy feeling), peloria (botany term), Pretoria, Vitória (Brazilian port), Victoria, Astoria, phantasmagoria.

17.3.42
courier, urea, curia, Manchuria, Etruria, pyuria (medical term), Liguria (region of Italy), anuria (suppression of urine production), dysuria (painful urination), polyuria (excessive urine production), thiourea (crystalline substance), ketonuria (medical term), phosphaturia (medical term), haematuria, phenylketonuria (congenital metabolic disorder).

17.3.42.1
albuminuria (urine containing albumin), haemoglobinuria (urine containing haemoglobin).

17.3.42.2
Masuria (region of Poland), glycosuria (excess sugar in urine).

17.3.43
Cambria (Latin name for Wales), Salambria (Greek river).

17.3.44
Umbria (mountainous region of Italy), Cumbria, Northumbria.

17.3.45
Andrea, calandria (part of heat-exchanger).

17.3.46
cassia (tropical plant), glacier, brassiere, Circassia (region of Russia).

17.3.47
mahseer (Indian fish), tarsier, intarsia (mosaic of inlaid wood).

17.3.48
fancier, financier, estancia (Spanish-American ranch).

17.3.49 [see also **17.326**]
indicia (distinguishing markings), comitia (Roman legislative assembly), Phoenicia, notitia (register of ecclesiastical districts), adventitia (body organ's external covering).

17.3.50
Numantia (ancient Spanish city), tradescantia, bona vacantia (unclaimed goods).

17.3.51
lithia (chemical compound), Pythia (Greek mythological priestess), stichomythia (dialogue in Greek drama).

17.3.52
Cynthia, Carinthia (Austrian province).

17.3.53 [see also **17.436**]
Xavier (Spanish saint), Moldavia, Moravia, Belgravia, Octavia, Scandinavia.

17.3.54
trivia, Olivia, Bolivia.

17.3.55
fovea (anatomy term), Segovia, synovia (lubricating fluid in joint), Monrovia (capital of Liberia).

17.3.56
apraxia (disorder of nervous system), ataxia (lack of muscular coordination), ataraxia (peace of mind), echopraxia (psychiatric term).

17.3.57
cachexia (weakened condition), alexia (word blindness), dyslexia, anorexia, hyperpyrexia (extremely high fever).

17.3.58
ixia (flowering plant), asphyxia.

17.3.59 [see also **17.332**]
glazier, brazier, grazier, Caucasia, aphasia (disorder of nervous system), dysphasia (impaired coordination of speech), aplasia (congenital absence of organ), dysplasia (abnormal development of organ), Aspasia (ancient Greek courtesan), fantasia, hypoplasia (incomplete development of organ), hyperplasia (enlargement of body part), Anastasia, Australasia, anaplasia (biology term), euthanasia, achondroplasia (skeletal disorder), antonomasia (rhetorical device).

17.3.60 [see also **17.334**]
framboesia (tropical disease), Silesia (central European region), silesia (twill-weave fabric), ecclesia (church congregation), amnesia, aesthesia (normal sensitivity), analgesia, Indonesia, paramnesia (memory disorder), hypermnesia (unusually good memory), telaesthesia (paranormal perception), thermaesthesia (sensitivity to temperature), anaesthesia, kinaesthesia (sensitivity to movement), synaesthesia (medical term), hypaesthesia (reduced sensibility to touch), cryptaesthesia (extrasensory perception), hyperkinesia (excessive movement), hyperaesthesia (increased sensitivity).

17.3.61
Tunisia, Dionysia (ancient Greek festivals).

17.3.62 [see also **17.335**]
osier, hosier, crosier (bishop's crook), ambrosia, afrormosia (hard teak-like wood).

17.4 [see also **8**]
ayah, buyer, dyer, liar, flyer, maya (Hindu concept), Maia (Greek mythological character), briar, crier, dryer, fryer, friar, prior, stria, via.

Aglaia (Greek goddess), inlier (geology term), supplier, outlier (geology term), papaya, Uriah, greenbrier, sweetbrier, latria (Catholic supreme worship), Messiah, Josiah, Isaiah.

Surabaya (Indonesian port), Zedekiah, Hezekiah, Obadiah, lammergeier (rare vulture), jambalaya (Creole savoury dish), multiplier, Nehemiah, Jeremiah, Biedermeier (conventional), stegomyia (mosquito), Zephaniah, occupier, Araguaia (Brazilian river).

peripeteia (abrupt turn of events), photomultiplier (device measuring electromagnetic radiation).

17.4.1
modifier, qualifier, amplifier, magnifier, purifier, pacifier, rectifier, quantifier (indicator of quantity), humidifier, disqualifier, preamplifier, intensifier, dehumidifier.

17.4.2
pariah, Zachariah, Zechariah, Black Maria.

17.5 [see also **17.430**]
oyer (13th-century assize), coir (coconut fibre), Goya, hoya (Australasian plant), soya, caloyer (Greek Orthodox monk), employer, sequoia (giant redwood tree), destroyer, dianoia (philosophy term), paranoia.

17.6
boa, koa (Hawaian tree), goer, goa (Tibetan gazelle), Goa (district of India), lower, blower, mower, moa, Noah, rower, grower, proa (sailing boat), sower, stoa.

Iowa, jerboa, Balboa (port on Panama Canal), balboa (Panamanian currency), widower, playgoer, churchgoer, racegoer, Alloa, follower, aloha, glass-blower, Samoa, genoa, Genoa, anoa (Indonesian cattle), borrower.

Shenandoah, concertgoer, Krakatoa, Mies van der Rohe (US architect).

17.7
Padua, Joshua, vacua (*plural of* vacuum), rescuer, valuer, Capua (Italian town), Papua, decidua (membrane lining pregnant uterus).

17.7.1
jaguar, Nicaragua.

17.7.2
mantua (loose gown), Mantua (Italian city), Gargantua.

17.8
doer, brewer, sewer, ewer, skewer, skua, Dewar, viewer, wrongdoer, pursuer, reviewer, evildoer, tamandua (tree-living mammal), Porirua (New Zealand city), Rotorua, revenuer (*US* revenue officer), interviewer.

17.9
Abba, dabber (printers' ink pad), jabber, blabber, slabber (*Dialect* slobber), crabber (crab fisherman).

17.10
arbour, barber, harbour, Saba (West Indian island), klangfarbe (musical term), casaba (melon), Ali Baba, Orizaba (Mexican city).

17.11
caber, labour, neighbour, sabre, ceiba (tropical tree), tabor (small drum), Weber (German composer), belabour (thrash severely).

17.12
Berber, Djerba (Tunisian island), Thurber (US humorist).

17.13
Sheba, amoeba, Kariba (dam on Zambezi river), zareba (enclosure around African village), Beersheba (Israeli town), Bathsheba, entamoeba (parasitic amoeba).

17.14
bibber (drinker), fibber, gibber, calibre, Excalibur.

17.15
Khyber, fibre, briber, scriber (pointed tool), Tiber, copaiba (yellowish resin), subscriber.

17.16
cobber, jobber, clobber, slobber, robber, swabber (*Slang* uncouth fellow), stockjobber (stock exchange dealer).

17.17
dauber, Micawber, absorber, Catawba (American Indian people).

17.18
lobar, sober, October, araroba (Brazilian tree), Manitoba.

17.19
lubber (clumsy person), blubber, rubber, scrubber, grubber (heavy hoe), landlubber.

17.20
goober (peanut), juba (Negro dance), Luba (African people), Cuba, scuba, Nuba (Sudanese people), tuber, tuba, Tshiluba (African language), Aruba (West Indian island), simarouba (tropical tree).

17.21
Aqaba (port of Jordan), cordoba (Nicaraguan currency), dagoba (Buddhist shrine), jellaba (hooded cloak), Annaba (Algerian port), mastaba (pyramid prototype), Addis Ababa.

17.22
Elba, Melba.

17.23
amber, camber, clamber, mamba, samba, sambar (Asian deer), caramba (Asian tree), liquidambar (yellow balsam), viola da gamba.

17.24
ember, Bemba (African people), member, Pemba (Tanzanian island), remember, nonmember, dismember, December, September, November.

17.25
limber, timber, marimba.

17.26
ombre (card game), sombre, Zomba (Malawi city).

17.27
umber, cumber (to hinder), Humber, lumbar, lumber, clumber (type of spaniel), slumber, number, rumba, cucumber, encumber, Columba, outnumber, disencumber.

17.28
backer, Dakar (capital of Senegal), Dacca (capital of Bangladesh), lacquer, slacker, smacker, knacker, packer, cracker, tracker, stacker, hijacker, Malacca (Malaysian state), malacca (walking stick), alpaca, maraca, firecracker, nutcracker, attacker, greywacke (dark rock), bushwhacker (*Austral* travelling woodlander), portulaca (tropical plant).

17.29
barker, kaka (New Zealand parrot), charkha (Indian spinning wheel), marker, parka, Parker, paca (large rodent), bidarka (Eskimo canoe), sifaka (Madagascan mammal), Osaka (Japanese port), moussaka, Lusaka (capital

of Zambia), nosy-parker, anasarca (medical term), koulibiaca (Russian fish pie), Hamilcar Barca (Carthaginian general).

17.30
acre, baker, faker, laker (lake cargo boat), maker, naker (small kettledrum), nacre (mother-of-pearl), Quaker, breaker, saker (large falcon), shaker, taker, weka (New Zealand bird).

cloaca, haymaker, shoemaker, Jamaica, clockmaker, bookmaker, matchmaker, watchmaker, pacemaker, dressmaker, peacemaker, tiebreaker, jawbreaker, lawbreaker, backbreaker, strikebreaker, icebreaker, housebreaker, heartbreaker, moonraker (square sail), boneshaker, caretaker, wiseacre, stavesacre (Eurasian plant).

moneymaker, merrymaker, boilermaker, troublemaker, undertaker.

17.31
chequer, checker, Mecca, pecker, wrecker, trekker, Rebecca, exchequer, woodpecker, oxpecker (African starling), Voortrekker (Afrikaner settler), Rijeka (Yugoslavian port), doubledecker.

17.32
burka (Muslim garment), Gurkha, circa, shirker, worker, tear-jerker, outworker, mazurka, wonder-worker.

17.33
beaker, speaker, Spica (star), squeaker, streaker, seeker, sika (Japanese deer), theca (biology term), Guernica, loudspeaker, eureka, Dominica, Costa Rica, spermatheca (biology term), Tanganyika, Judaica (Jewish literature), bibliotheca (library), Cyrenaica (region of Libya).

17.34
bicker, kicker, dicker (*US* to barter), liquor, clicker (factory foreman), flicker, slicker (*US* sly person), nicker, snicker, picker, pricker (*US* prickle),

shicker (*Austral* alcoholic drink), ticker, sticker, vicar, wicker, whicker (whinny).

Baedeker (travel guidebook), Boudicca (Latin name of Boadicea), trafficker, silica, replica, bootlicker, arnica (plant genus), Seneca, picnicker, areca (Asian palm), Africa, paprika, brassica (vegetable genus), Jessica, vesica (bladder), Corsica, Utica (ancient African city), swastika, spitsticker (wood-engraving tool).

angelica, basilica (Roman building), nux vomica (tree yielding poisonous seeds), amphitricha (bacteria), peritricha (bacteria), erotica, exotica, Antarctica, materia medica (study of drugs).

17.34.1
Monica, moniker, Salonika (Greek port), harmonica, japonica (Japanese quince), Veronica, santonica (Oriental plant).

17.34.2
Erica, America.

17.34.3
Attica, sciatica, hepatica (woodland plant).

17.35
duiker (African antelope), hiker, plica (anatomical fold), Micah, mica, pica, piker (*Austral* wild bullock), pika (burrowing mammal), spica (spiral bandage), striker, hitchhiker, Formica (*Trademark*), myrica (medicinal root bark), lorica (protective shell), balalaika.

17.36
ocker (*Austral* boorish person), cocker, chocker (*Austral* full up), docker, Fokker, locker, blocker, mocha, knocker, quokka (small wallaby), rocker, soccer, shocker, stocker, Knickerbocker (*US* New Yorker).

17.37
corker, hawker, porker, talker, stalker, walker, yorker (cricket term), Minorca, deerstalker, jaywalker, sleepwalker, shopwalker, streetwalker, Majorca, kwashiorkor (protein deficiency).

17.38
ochre, oka (Turkish weight), oca (South American plant), coca (Andean shrub), choker, joker, smoker, poker, broker, croaker (tropical fish), stoker, nonsmoker, stockbroker, pawnbroker, Cape Roca (westernmost point of Europe), Asoka (Indian emperor), mediocre, tapioca, carioca (Brazilian dance), Fukuoka (Japanese city), Shizuoka (Japanese city).

17.39
UCCA, chukker (polo term), fucker, mucker (*Slang* friend), pukka, pucker, trucker, succour, sucker, tucker, yucca, felucca (Mediterranean boat), seersucker, bloodsucker, sapsucker (US woodpecker), goatsucker (*US* nightjar), motherfucker, honeysucker (nectarfeeding bird).

17.40
cooker, hooker, hookah, looker, onlooker.

17.41
lucre, snooker, euchre (US card game), nucha (nape of neck), palooka (*US* clumsy person), manuka (New Zealand tree), verruca, bazooka, noctiluca (light-emitting organism), melaleuca (Australian shrub), involucre (botany term), Juan de Fuca (US–Canadian strait).

17.42
abaca (Philippine plant), stomacher (decorative piece of material), Hanukkah (Jewish festival), spinnaker, massacre, Whitaker, Ithaca, Karnataka (Indian state).

17.43
anchor, banker, Bangka (Indonesian island), canker, hanker, flanker, spanker, rancour, ranker, chancre, tanker, tanka (Japanese verse), Sri Lanka, barranca (*US* ravine), Casablanca, lingua franca (common language).

17.44
Inca, Dinka (Sudanese people), blinker, clinker, drinker, sinker, tinker, stinker, thinker, winker, Treblinka (Nazi concentration camp), headshrinker, stotinka (Bulgarian coin), freethinker.

17.45
conquer, conker, concha (shell-shaped body part), tonka (tree yielding fragrant seeds), Dzongka (Asian language).

17.46
bunker, punka (palm-leaf fan), Junker (Prussian landowner), mossbunker (US fish), spelunker (cave explorer).

17.47
lascar (East Indian sailor), Alaska, marasca (European cherry tree), Nebraska, Athabaska (Canadian lake), Madagascar.

17.48
risker, frisker, whisker.

17.49
busker, Musca (constellation), tusker.

17.50
catcher, dacha (Russian country house), stature, Thatcher, thatcher, viscacha (South American rodent), backscratcher, oystercatcher, baby-snatcher, body-snatcher, cradle-snatcher, oboe da caccia (former musical instrument).

17.51
archer, marcher, departure.

17.52
nature, denature, legislature.

17.53
lecher, Fletcher, fletcher (maker of arrows), stretcher.

17.54
lurcher, nurture, searcher, researcher, gutta-percha (rubbery substance).

17.55
feature, Nietzsche (German philosopher), creature, preacher, teacher, schoolteacher.

17.56
pitcher, twitcher, dowitcher (arctic bird), forfeiture, garniture (decoration), furniture, miniature, Onitsha (Nigerian port), signature, portraiture, expenditure, discomfiture, literature, temperature, investiture, primogeniture (legal term).

17.57
botcher, boccia (Italian bowls game), watcher, topnotcher.

17.58
scorcher, torture.

17.59
cloture (closure in US Senate), poacher, panocha (coarse sugar).

17.60
sloucher, voucher.

17.61
suture, future, cachucha (Spanish dance).

17.62
cubature (cubic contents), arcature (small arcade), ligature, filature (silk-spinning), tablature (form of musical notation), aperture, quadrature (maths term), curvature, coverture (legal term), judicature, musculature, nomenclature.

17.63
fracture, contracture, manufacture.

17.64
lecture, conjecture, architecture.

17.65
picture, stricture.

17.66
structure, substructure, superstructure, infrastructure.

17.67
cincture (surround), tincture.

17.68
juncture, puncture, conjuncture, venipuncture (puncturing of a vein), acupuncture.

17.69
culture, multure (miller's fee), vulture, sepulture (burial), viniculture, sericulture (silkworm rearing), agriculture, viticulture (grape cultivation), horticulture, monoculture (single-crop cultivation), aquaculture (biology term), counterculture (alternative social culture), arboriculture.

17.70
bencher (a judge), denture, trencher (wooden platter), venture, debenture, backbencher, indenture, adventure, peradventure, misadventure.

17.71
lyncher, clincher, flincher, wincher.

17.72
capture, rapture, recapture, enrapture.

17.73
gesture, vesture (garment).

17.74
posture, imposture.

17.75
texture, contexture (weaving).

17.76
fixture, mixture, affixture, admixture, intermixture.

17.77
adder, ladder, bladder, madder, stepladder.

17.78
ardour, khaddar (Indian cotton cloth), cadre (nucleus of trained personnel), Garda (Italian lake), larder, RADA, cicada, Haggadah (part of Jewish literature), armada, monarda (US plant), retarder, Nevada, enchilada (Mexican food), autostrada (Italian motorway).

17.78.1
panada (thick sauce), Granada (Spanish city), promenader.

17.79
aider, Ada, Ede (Dutch city), raider, grader (earth-levelling machine), trader, Seder (Jewish ceremonial meal), Veda (Hindu scriptures), wader, Grenada, crusader, Bethsaida (Israeli town), Rig-Veda (Hindu poetry), invader, alameda (*US* tree-lined promenade), Ayurveda (Hindu medical treatise).

17.80
Edda (Old Norse poems), bedder (college servant), Kedah (Malaysian state), kheda (elephant enclosure), Cheddar, header, spreader, shredder, shedder (animal that moults), tedder, Vedda (Sri Lankan people), homesteader.

17.81
girder, herder, murder, purdah.

17.82
feeder, leader, Leda (Greek mythological character), bleeder, Blida (Algerian city), pleader, reader, breeder, Breda (Dutch city), cedar, seeder, cheerleader, ringleader, stockbreeder, proofreader, lip-reader, interpleader (legal term), olla podrida (Spanish stew).

17.83
bidder, Jidda (Saudi Arabian port), whydah (African weaverbird), Saida (Lebanese port), Florida, reseda (Mediterranean plant), Cressida, consider, Andromeda, reconsider, spina bifida, asafoetida (foul-smelling resin), primigravida (obstetrics term), multigravida (obstetrics term), camera lucida (microscope attachment).

17.84
eider, Ida, guider, Haida (American Indian people), glider, slider, spider, rider, cider, Oneida (US lake), joyrider, nightrider, outrider, decider, insider, outsider, divider.

17.85
dodder, fodder, plodder.

17.86
order, boarder, border, hoarder, Lauder (Scottish singer), sawder (to flatter), warder, suborder (biology term), recorder, marauder, disorder.

17.87
moider (*Dialect* to bother), embroider.

17.88
odour, Oder (European river), coda, coder, loader, soda, decoder, encoder, Sargodha (Pakistani city), pagoda, Baroda (Indian state), Fashoda (Sudanese town).

17.89
chowder (thick clam soup), Gouda, howdah (seat on elephant), powder, gunpowder.

17.90
udder, chuddar (Indian shawl), judder, rudder, shudder.

17.91
Judah, brooder, Tudor, Barbuda (West Indian island), mouthbrooder (African fish), intruder, Bermuda, draught-excluder, barracuda.

17.92
gelada (African baboon), Canada, Kannada (Indian language), forwarder (bookbinder), ambassador.

17.93
elder, welder.

17.94
fielder, shielder, wielder.

17.95
builder, guilder, Hilda, tilde (phonetic symbol), shipbuilder, Saint Kilda (Hebridean island), Matilda, bewilder.

17.96
alder, Balder (Norse god).

17.97
older, boulder, folder, holder, moulder, smoulder, polder, solder, shoulder, shareholder, freeholder, beholder, stockholder, stadholder (Dutch chief magistrate), smallholder, gasholder, leaseholder, householder.

17.98
candour, dander, gander, panda, pander, sander, vanda (orchid), Luanda (capital of Angola), Rwanda (African republic), Buganda (Ugandan state), Uganda, backhander, right-hander, left-hander, philander, solander (botanical specimen box), outlander (stranger), germander (flowering plant), pomander, Menander (Greek dramatist), expander, Miranda, Lysander, goosander (type of duck), dittander (small plant), bystander, propaganda, gerrymander, calamander (hard wood), salamander, Anaximander (Greek philosopher).

17.98.1
Leander (Greek mythological character), meander, oleander, coriander.

17.98.2
veranda, jacaranda (tropical tree), memoranda.

17.99
Lahnda (Pakistani language), slander, commander, Alexander.

17.100
remainder, attainder (former legal term).

17.101
bender, fender, gender, lender, blender, splendour, slender, mender, spender, render, sender, tender, vendor, Venda (African people), weekender, defender,

offender, agenda, engender, suspender, surrender, descender (printing term), ascender (printing term), bartender, pretender, attender, extender, hacienda, moneylender.

17.102
hinder, Pindar (Greek poet), cinder, tinder, calendar, calender (machine for smoothing cloth), cylinder, provender (feed for livestock).

17.103
binder, finder, hinder (at the rear), minder, grinder, winder, bookbinder, viewfinder, rangefinder, pathfinder, reminder, rewinder, sidewinder.

17.104
Fonda, Honda (*Trademark*), ponder, squander, Rhondda, wander, yonder, Golconda (ruined Indian town), transponder (radio transmitter–receiver), anaconda.

17.105
launder, maunder (behave aimlessly).

17.106
joinder (legal term), rejoinder, nonjoinder (legal term), misjoinder (legal term).

17.107
bounder, founder, flounder, rounder, sounder.

17.108
under, chunder, blunder, plunder, sunder, thunder, wonder, osmunda (fern), thereunder, hereunder, asunder, rotunda (circular domed building), floribunda (cultivated rosebush), barramunda (Australian fish).

17.109
seconder, bilander (small cargo ship), islander, Highlander, colander, Jullundur (Indian city), woodlander, Greenlander, Laplander, lavender, New Zealander.

17.110
chaffer (haggle), gaffer, Jaffa, Staffa, zaffer (impure cobalt oxide).

17.111
chafer (beetle), wafer, cockchafer.

17.112
heifer, zephyr.

17.113
ephah (Hebrew unit of measure), FIFA, reefer, Recife (Brazilian port), synalepha (linguistics term).

17.114
differ, conifer, aquifer (water-containing rock), thurifer (incense carrier), Lucifer, crucifer (family of plants), Potiphar (biblical character), rotifer (minute aquatic animal), Apocrypha.

17.115
Haifa (Israeli port), hypha (part of fungus), lifer, cipher, sypher (woodworking term), decipher, encipher.

17.116
offer, Offa (king of Mercia), coffer, scoffer, proffer.

17.117
Ophir (biblical region), gopher, goffer (to crimp), loafer, sofa, chauffeur.

17.118
buffer, duffer, luffa (tropical climbing plant), bluffer, snuffer, puffer, suffer, chufa (tropical sedge).

17.119
loofah, woofer (loudspeaker), tufa (soft rock).

17.120
agrapha (unrecorded sayings of Christ), metaphor, Christopher, telegrapher, philosopher, Pseudepigrapha (Jewish writings).

17.120.1 [further rhymes may be derived from **16.90.2**]
biographer, stenographer (*US* shorthand typist), photographer, radiographer, Hagiographa (section of Old

Testament), choreographer, historiographer (historian).

17.121
alpha, pedalfer (lime-deficient soil), alfalfa, Wadi Halfa (Sudanese town).

17.122
camphor, chamfer.

17.123
dagger, gagger, Jagger, nagger, quagga (extinct horse), bragger, saggar (fireproof box for pottery), stagger, swagger, zigzagger (sewing-machine attachment), carpetbagger.

17.124
aga (Turkish title), laager (African camp), lager, raga (Indian musical term), saga.

17.125
agar, eagre (tidal bore), jaeger, telega (Russian four-wheeled cart), rutabaga (*US* swede).

17.126
egger (moth), beggar, bootlegger.

17.127
burger, burgher, turgor (biology term), virga (meteorology term), beefburger, hamburger, Limburger (strong white cheese).

17.128
eager, meagre, Riga (Russian port), Vega (bright star), bodega (Spanish wine shop), beleaguer, quadriga (chariot), Antigua.

17.129
chigger (mite larva), digger, figure, jigger, snigger, rigour, rigger, trigger, vigour, prefigure, disfigure, transfigure, alegar (malt vinegar), omega, senega (milkwort plant), vinegar, Honegger (French composer), outrigger.

17.130
Eiger, Geiger, liger (lion–tiger hybrid), saiga (Asian antelope), tiger, taiga (coniferous forests), canaigre (US dock plant), Auriga (constellation).

17.131
Dogger, dogger (Dutch fishing vessel), jogger, logger, wagga (*Austral* blanket), pettifogger, Wagga Wagga (Australian city).

17.132
auger (boring tool), augur (predict), sauger (US fish), massasauga (US venomous snake), Mississauga (Canadian town).

17.133
ogre, toga, yoga, Saratoga, Ticonderoga (US battle site).

17.134
bugger, lugger (small boat), slugger (*US* hard-hitting person), mugger, nuggar (Egyptian sailing boat), rugger, Srinagar (Indian city), huggermugger.

17.135
sugar, Yuga (Hindu age of mankind).

17.136
cougar, Luger, ruga (biology term), Kruger (Boer statesman), beluga (large sturgeon), sastruga (ridge on snowfield), Chattanooga.

17.137
realgar (rare mineral), Trafalgar.

17.138
Olga, brolga (Australian bird), Volga.

17.139
mulga (Australian acacia), vulgar.

17.140 [see also **17.245**]
anger, Bangor, languor, clangour, panga (African knife), Tanga (Tanzanian port), Kananga (city in Zaîre), Zamboanga (Philippine port).

17.141 [see also **17.246**]
finger, linger, forefinger, fishfinger, anhinga (aquatic bird), malinger, syringa (flowering shrub), churinga (Aboriginal sacred amulet), cotinga (tropical bird), alcheringa (Aboriginal mythical golden age).

17.142
conger, conga, Tonga, Tsonga (African people), Alba Longa (city of ancient Latium), Rarotonga (Pacific island).

17.143
hunger, munga (*Austral* food), scaremonger, whoremonger, warmonger, fellmonger (dealer in animal skins), fishmonger, costermonger, scandalmonger, ironmonger.

17.144
agger (Roman earthwork), badger, cadger.

17.145
charger, Djaja (Indonesian mountain), rajah, enlarger, turbocharger, supercharger (compressor), maharajah.

17.146 [see also **17.3.12**]
gauger (customs officer), major, stager (experienced person), wager, teenager.

17.147
ledger, dredger, Saint Leger.

17.148
merger, perjure, verger, verdure.

17.149 [see also **17.3.13**]
Ouija, procedure, supersedure.

17.150 [see also **17.3.14**]
voyager, mortgagor, packager, veliger (larva of mollusc), villager, armiger (heraldic term), manager, cottager, integer, vintager (grape harvester).

17.151
Niger, Elijah.

17.152
bodger, codger, dodger, loggia, lodger, Roger.

17.153
Borgia, forger, gorger, Georgia.

17.154
dowager, tanager (US songbird), onager (Iranian wild ass), sockdologer (*US* decisive blow), astrologer.

17.155
grandeur, phalanger (arboreal marsupial).

17.156
danger, manger, ranger, stranger, endanger, arranger, hydrangea, bushranger (person living in bush), moneychanger, autochanger (record-changing device).

17.157
injure, ginger, Jinja (Ugandan town), harbinger, wharfinger (wharf manager), challenger, Salinger (US writer), derringer (US pistol), porringer (small dish), Massinger (English dramatist), passenger, messenger, Kissinger, scavenger.

17.158
lounger, scrounger.

17.159
conjure, blunger (large vat), plunger, sponger.

17.160
Allah, Bala (Welsh lake), calla (African plant), caller (*Scot* fresh food), pallor, valour, Whyalla (Australian port), Valhalla, cavalla (tropical fish), boobialla (Australian shrub), Caracalla (Roman emperor).

17.161
gala, Galle (Sri Lankan port), challah (Jewish plaited loaf), haler (Czech coin), Mahler, parlour, thaler (silver coin), nyala (African antelope), koala, cabbala (ancient Jewish tradition), Ambala (Indian city), trehala (sugary substance), Kampala, impala, Marsala, Uppsala (Swedish city), cantala (tropical plant).

17.161.1
kamala (East Indian tree), Guatemala.

17.162
ala (winglike structure), alar (relating to wings), bailor, baler, scalar, scaler, chela (Hindu religious disciple), jailer, mailer, malar (relating to the cheek),

kwela (South African beat music), trailer, sailor, tailor, Taylor, whaler, Waler (*Austral* saddle horse), Akela, loud-hailer, inhaler, shillelagh, blackmailer, wholesaler, retailer, zarzuela (Spanish operetta), Venezuela.

17.163
Keller, feller, fellah (Arab peasant), heller (old German coin), Pella (ancient Greek city), speller, seller, cellar, cella (room in temple), teller, stellar, dweller.

paella, Viyella (*Trademark*), mabela (African ground corn), rubella, bierkeller, shigella (bacterium), lamella (thin layer), prunella (strong fabric), canella (West Indian spice), Capella (bright star), propeller, chlorella (microscopic plant), umbrella, micella (chemical term), bonsela (African gift), saltcellar, novella, rosella (Australian parrot).

Rockefeller, columella (biology term), villanella (Neapolitan song), salmonella, citronella (Asian grass), gentianella (flowering plant), fustanella (Greek man's white skirt), Cinderella, mozzarella, varicella (chickenpox), vorticella (small animal), storyteller, fortune-teller, tarantella, fenestella (small opening in wall).

17.163.1
glabella (medical term), clarabella (organ stop), Isabella.

17.163.2
patella, panatella.

17.164
curler, pearler (pearl-fishing boat), purler (headlong fall).

17.165
chela (claw), dealer, feeler, healer, kneeler, peeler, spieler (*US* glib talker), sealer, Sheila, tela (web-like structure), vealer (veal calf), velar (linguistics term), wheeler, tequila, candela (unit of luminous intensity), weigela (Asian shrub), sequela (medical term), side-wheeler (paddle-wheeled riverboat), Philomela (Greek mythological princess).

17.166
killer, filler, miller, pillar, squilla (shrimp), thriller, Scylla (Greek sea nymph), scilla (bell-flowered plant), Schiller, schiller (metallic lustre), tiller, villa.

weedkiller, painkiller, chinchilla, spinechiller, cedilla, megillah (Hebrew scroll), mamilla, similar, Aquila (constellation), Priscilla, pteryla (ornithology term), pralltriller (musical term), basilar (anatomy term), Attila, flotilla, mantilla (Spanish scarf), scintilla (minute amount), distiller, Anguilla (West Indian island), axilla (armpit), maxilla (upper jawbone).

sabadillá (tropical plant), granadilla (passion-flower), sapodilla (tropical evergreen tree), drosophila (fruit fly), gypsophila (Mediterranean plant), dissimilar, verisimilar (likely to be true).

17.166.1
manilla, Manila (Philippine port), vanilla, manzanilla (very dry sherry).

17.166.2
papilla (small protuberance), caterpillar.

17.166.3
barilla (salty plant extract), guerrilla, gorilla, zorilla (African mammal), cascarilla (West Indian shrub), camarilla (Spanish cabal), sarsaparilla.

17.167
filar (relating to thread), hyla (tree frog), miler, tiler, Tyler, strobila (body of tapeworm), Delilah, compiler, astylar (architectural term), Rottweiler (breed of dog), amphistylar (architectural term).

17.168
olla (Spanish cooking pot), collar, choler (anger), scholar, dollar, dolour

(grief), holler, squalor, wallah, rix-dollar (former Dutch silver coin), corolla, Eurodollar, petrodollar (money earned exporting petroleum), ayatollah.

17.169
caller, faller (*Austral* lumberjack), mauler, brawler, crawler, trawler, footballer, mandorla (art term).

17.170
oiler, boiler, boyla (Aboriginal witch doctor), spoiler, broiler.

17.171
bowler, bola (South-American Indian weapon), cola, coaler (coal transporter), Ndola (Zambian city), Lola, molar, mola (a fish), poler (*Austral* idler), polar, roller, stroller, solar, tola (Indian weight), volar (anatomy term), Zola (French novelist).

payola (*US* bribe), viola, tombola, Angola, Gongola (Nigerian state), potholer, premolar, bipolar, transpolar, roadroller, steamroller, controller, scagliola (imitation marble).

hemiola (musical term), Carniola (region of Yugoslavia), Moviola (*Trademark*), Coca-Cola (*Trademark*), Pianola (*Trademark*), Hispaniola (West Indian island), Gorgonzola.

17.172
Fowler (English grammarian), howler, growler, prowler, bobowler (*Dialect* large moth).

17.173
colour, mullah (Muslim religious leader), muller (heavy grinding instrument), cruller (US cake), Sulla (Roman dictator), discolour, medulla, Technicolor (*Trademark*), watercolour, nulla-nulla (Aboriginal wooden club), Gujranwala (Pakistani city).

17.174
bulla (seal on papal bull), fuller.

ampulla (flask), ferula (Mediterranean plant), spirula (tropical mollusc), gastrula (animal embryo), nebula, globular, tubular, vascular, oscular (relating to the mouth), radula (part of mollusc's tongue), modular, nodular, glandular, scrofula, regular, ligula (part of insect's lip), jugular, angular, singular, ungula (maths term), alula (tuft of feathers), cellular, stellular (resembling small stars), primula, formula, nummular (coin-shaped), tumular (mound-like), pinnula, lunula, scapula, scapular (part of monastic habit), morula (biology term), Ursula, consular, spatula, blastula (animal embryo), fistula, Vistula (Polish river), pustular, uvula, valvular.

carbuncular, avuncular, calendula (flowering plant), irregular, Caligula, triangular, rectangular, manipular (relating to manipulation), discipular, bicapsular (botany term), tarantula, equiangular.

17.174.1
tabular, incunabula (book printed before 1500).

17.174.2
fibula, mandibular, vestibular.

17.174.3
facula (bright area on sun), macula, piacular (atonement for sacrilegious act), vernacular, oracular (wise and prophetic), spectacular, tentacular, sustentacular (supporting).

17.174.4
fecula (plant starch extract), specular (having mirror-like properties), secular, nubecula (small galaxy), trabecula (botany term), molecular, vallecula (biology term), Vulpecula (constellation).

17.174.5
furcula (fork-like organ), circular, tubercular, semicircular.

17.174.6
orbicular (circular), corbicula (bee's pollen carrier), pedicular (infested with lice), vehicular, follicular, vermicular

(worm-like), funicular, auricula (cultivated alpine primrose), ventricular (swollen), acicula (needle-shaped structure), articular, cuticula (cuticle), particular, lenticular (lens-shaped), navicular (boat-shaped), appendicular, perpendicular, extravehicular (outside a spacecraft), extracurricular.

17.174.7
ocular, jocular, locular (biology term), binocular, monocular.

17.174.8
muscular, crepuscular, corpuscular, neuromuscular, intramuscular.

17.174.9
annular, cannula (small surgical tube), planula (larval form), granular, campanula.

17.174.10
copula (type of verb), scopula (spider's tuft of hair), popular, unpopular.

17.174.11
insula, insular, peninsula, peninsular.

17.174.12
situla (Iron Age container), titular, capitular (relating to cathedral chapter).

17.175
cooler, kula (Pacific island ceremony), Fula (African people), gular (relating to the throat), hula (Hawaiian dance), ruler, Beulah (biblical name for Israel), Lobengula (Matabele king).

17.176
jeweller, dueller, labeller, falbala (gathered frill), bachelor, modeller, gondola, pergola (framework supporting plants), signaller, cupola, gospeller, quarreller, chancellor, councillor, counsellor, hosteller, traveller, leveller, reveller, shoveler (duck).

rubeola (measles), areola (biology term), alveolar (anatomy term), roseola (red rash), parabola, hyperbola, amygdala (almond-shaped body part), po-

lygala (herbaceous plant), teetotaller, epistoler, Methuselah.

17.176.1
dialler, viola (flowering plant), variola (smallpox).

17.176.2
tricolour, Agricola.

17.176.3
victualler, hospitaller.

17.177
dabbler, gabbler.

17.178
cobbler, gobbler.

17.179
gambler, rambler, scrambler.

17.180
bumbler, fumbler, mumbler, grumbler, tumbler.

17.181
tickler, stickler, chronicler.

17.182
sprinkler, twinkler.

17.183
Adler, paddler, saddler.

17.184
meddler, medlar (fruit), pedlar.

17.185
curdler, hurdler.

17.186
fiddler, tiddler.

17.187
idler, sidler, bridler.

17.188
coddler, toddler, waddler, mollycoddler.

17.189
kindler, swindler.

17.190
riffler (a file), whiffler.

17.191
muffler, ruffler, shuffler.

17.192
haggler, straggler.

17.193
juggler, smuggler, struggler.

17.194
angler, wrangler, strangler.

17.195
Doppler (Austrian physicist), poplar.

17.196
Templar, exemplar (a model).

17.197
nestler, wrestler.

17.198
ostler, jostler.

17.199
bustler, hustler, rustler.

17.200
battler, rattler, prattler, tattler.

17.201
Hitler, whittler.

17.202
butler, cutler, sutler (former army provisions merchant).

17.203
antler, dismantler.

17.204
guzzler, muzzler, puzzler.

17.205
dammar (resin), gammer (*Dialect* old woman), gamma (Greek letter), hammer, clamour, glamour, mamma (breast), crammer, grammar, shammer, stammer, yammer, windjammer, sledgehammer, enamour, programmer, Alabama, yellowhammer.

17.206
armour, amah (Eastern nurse), karma (destiny), Kama (Russian river), charmer, dharma (Hindu custom), farmer, llama, lama (Tibetan priest), Nama (Hottentot people), Parma, Rama (Hindu mythological hero), Brahma (Hindu god), drama, grama (pasture grass), Zama (ancient African city), embalmer, pyjama, Manama (capital of Bahrain), Dalai Lama, diorama (small three-dimensional scene), cyclorama (picture around cylindrical room), panorama, Cinerama (*Trademark*), psychodrama, melodrama, Vasco da Gama.

17.207
squama (scale), framer, tamer, disclaimer, Macias Nguema (Guinean island).

17.208
emmer (variety of wheat), gemma (plant reproductive structure), hemmer, lemma (logic term), tremor, stemma (family tree), dilemma, trilemma (situation presenting three choices), maremma (marshy maritime region), neurolemma (nerve-fibre sheath), analemma (type of sundial).

17.209
Burma, derma (deep inner skin layer), murmur, termor (legal term), Sturmer (eating apple), leucoderma (unpigmented area of skin), scleroderma (skin disease), xeroderma (abnormally dry skin), pyoderma (skin disase), terra firma.

17.210
bema (Athenian speaker's platform), schema, schemer, femur, lemur, Lima, reamer (steel tool), creamer, screamer, dreamer, prima, streamer, Tema (Ghanaian port), steamer.

oedema, redeemer, blasphemer, daydreamer, blastema (biology term).

seriema (South American bird), empyema (accumulation of pus), myxoedema (disease of thyroid gland), Iwo Jima (Pacific island), chromonema (biology term), treponema (bacterium), emphysema, Hiroshima, erotema (rhetorical question), diastema (abnormal fissure), erythema (red patches on skin), exanthema (a rash).

17.211
skimmer, dimmer, glimmer, slimmer, krimmer (Crimean lambswool), trimmer, simmer, shimmer, swimmer.

polymer, ulema (Muslim scholar), anima, enema, minima (*plural of* minimum), cinema, lorimer, dulcimer, Fatima, Mortimer, ultima (final syllable of word), intima (innermost layer of organ), ecthyma (inflammation of skin), nonswimmer, maxima (*plural of* maximum), eczema, Proxima (star).

sclerenchyma (supporting plant tissue), parenchyma (soft plant tissue).

Alma-Tadema (painter), Quinquagesima, Quadragesima, Sexagesima, Septuagesima.

17.212
dimer (chemistry term), lima (US bean), climber, primer, trimer (chemistry term), tryma (hard-shelled fruit), sima (layer of earth's crust), timer, old-timer, full-timer, part-timer, Oppenheimer, Maritimer (inhabitant of Canadian Maritimes), autotimer.

17.213
bomber, comma, homa (sacred plant).

17.214
ormer (edible mollusc), korma (Indian food), dormer, former, Norma, trauma, warmer, reformer, performer, informer, transformer, bedwarmer.

17.215
omer (ancient Hebrew measure), coma, comber, ngoma (East African drum), Homer, homer, noma (inflammation of the mouth), roamer, stroma (biology term), soma, stoma (mouthlike part), vomer (thin flat bone).

glioma (tumour), myoma (muscle tumour), sarcoma, glaucoma, trachoma (eye disease), Tacoma (Washington port), beachcomber, diploma, misnomer, lipoma (fatty tumour), scleroma (patch of hard tissue), aroma, fibroma

(fibrous tumour), scotoma (blind spot), xanthoma (yellowish nodule on skin).

angioma (tumour), osteoma (bone tumour), Oklahoma, condyloma (tumour), papilloma (tumour), myeloma (tumour of bone marrow), adenoma (glandular tumour), carcinoma, atheroma (obstruction in artery), haematoma (tumour of clotted blood), encephaloma (brain tumour).

17.216
bummer, gumma (syphilitic tumour), plumber, mummer, rummer (drinking glass), drummer, summer, newcomer, latecomer, midsummer.

17.217
boomer, bloomer, rumour, Nkrumah, struma (a swelling), Sumer (region of Babylon), humour, pneuma (soul), puma, tumour, stumer (*Slang* forgery), satsuma, perfumer, consumer, mazuma (*US* money), empyreuma (burning smell), Montezuma (Aztec emperor).

17.218
agama (small lizard), isomer (chemistry term), gossamer, Latimer, metamer (chemistry term), tautomer (chemistry term), Gautama (early name of Buddha), customer, elastomer (rubbery material), scyphistoma (zoology term), anathema.

17.218.1
monomer (chemistry term), gastronomer, astronomer.

17.219
chacma (baboon), drachma.

17.220
agma (phonetic symbol), magma, syntagma (linguistics term).

17.221
smegma, bregma (part of skull).

17.222
sigma (Greek letter), stigma, enigma, sterigma (botany term).

17.223
plasma, miasma, chiasma (biology term).

17.224
melisma (musical term), charisma.

17.225
Anna, banner, canner, canna (tropical plant), scanner, Hannah, lanner (large falcon), planner, manner, manor, manna, nanna, spanner, tanner, Diana, Guyana (South American republic), goanna (Australian monitor lizard), bandanna, alannah (Irish term of endearment), Fermanagh, Montana, Havana, Savannah (US port), savanna (open grassland), hosanna, Susanna, Susquehanna (US river), ipecacuanha (purgative drug).

17.225.1
Indiana, Pollyanna, Louisiana.

17.226
ana (anecdotes about a person), kana (Japanese syllabic writing), Ghana, garner, mana (power), Tana (Ethiopian lake), tana (Madagascan lemur), varna (Hindu caste), bwana, Tswana (African people).

Tucana (constellation), gymkhana, Fergana (region of Asia), nagana (animal disease), zenana (women's part of house), banana, piranha, Tirana (capital of Albania), Purana (Sanskrit writings), curtana (coronation sword), sultana, nirvana, Tijuana, Botswana, iguana, Ljubljana (Yugoslavian city).

ikebana (Japanese flower-arranging), katakana (Japanese syllabic writing), hiragana (Japanese syllabic writing), pozzuolana (volcanic ash), vox humana, Weimaraner (breed of dog), Lippizaner (breed of horse), Rosh Hashanah (Jewish New Year), marijuana, Mahayana (school of Buddhism), Hinayana (early form of Buddhism), Tell el Amarna (Egyptian ruins).

17.226.1
liana, Ludhiana (Indian city), Juliana, dulciana (organ stop), poinciana (tropical tree), Australiana, Shakespeareana, Victoriana, nicotiana (fragrant flowering plant).

17.226.2
Afrikaner, Americana.

17.227
Cana (biblical town), Gaynor, gainer, planar, planer, drainer, trainer, strainer, arcana (tarot cards), coplanar (in the same plane), Ndjamena (capital of Chad), campaigner, restrainer, detainer, retainer, lantana (tropical shrub), container, sustainer, abstainer, cantilena (musical term), Magdalena (Colombian river), entertainer.

17.228
Jenner (English physician), henna, penna (large feather), senna, tenner, tenor, sienna, Siena, Vienna, duenna, Gehenna (place of torment), antenna, Ravenna (Italian city), Avicenna (Arab philosopher), countertenor.

17.229
earner, burner, learner, Smyrna, turner, cisterna (space containing body fluid), afterburner.

17.230
Lena, cleaner, Nina, Tina, vina (Indian stringed instrument), vena (vein), wiener (*US* smoked sausage), weaner (newly weaned animal), Zena.

hyena, verbena, coquina (soft limestone), kachina (American Indian spirit), Medina (Saudi Arabian city), saphena (leg vein), lagena (narrow-necked bottle), congener (member of category), tahina (sesame-seed paste), dolina (depression in limestone), galena (heavy mineral), euglena (microscopic freshwater organism), demeanour, subpoena, tsarina, Messina, piscina (basin in Catholic church), dracaena (tropical plant), Katsina (Nigerian city), retsina, catena (connected series), phlyctena (small blister), cantina (Spanish bar), sestina (Italian verse form), Christina, Athena, novena (Catholic devotion), convener, rendzina (dark soil).

anabaena (freshwater plant), karabiner (clip used in mountaineering), amphisbaena (worm lizard), hagedena (ulcer), Pasadena, Saint Helena, semolina, Messalina, misdemeanour, Wilhelmina, Agrippina, signorina, orchestrina (musical instrument), scarlatina, sonatina, concertina, cavatina (musical composition), Argentina, Bukovina (region of central Europe).

Herzegovina (region of Yugoslavia), Quezon y Molina (first Philippine president).

17.230.1
arena, Carina (constellation), farina (flour), marina, ocarina, ballerina, Incaparina (high-protein food).

17.231
inner, skinner, dinner, finner (whale), Minna (Nigerian city), pinner (small dainty apron), pinna (biology term), spinner, sinner, Cinna (Roman aristocrat), thinner, winner.

tachina (bristly fly), Kitchener, beginner, bigener (hybrid organism), Eleanor, milliner, mariner, foreigner, parcener (coheir), Porsena (legendary Etruscan king), platina (platinum alloy), patina (shallow Roman dish), retina, breadwinner.

determiner, phenomena, alumina (aluminium oxide), Proserpina (Roman goddess), submariner, Polyxena (Greek mythological princess).

17.231.1
lamina, stamina, examiner.

17.232
China, china, diner, Dinah, liner, miner, mynah, minor, shiner.

trichina (parasitic roundworm), refiner, Aegina (Greek island), Regina, vagina, angina, airliner, eyeliner, salina (salt lake), recliner, headliner, freightliner, jetliner, Lucina (Roman goddess), consignor, moonshiner (*US* whisky smuggler), diviner, designer.

Indochina, Carolina.

casuarina (Australian tree), globigerina (microscopic animal).

17.233
honour, Donna, goner, gonna, wanna, O'Connor, dishonour.

17.233.1
Madonna, belladonna, prima donna.

17.234
corner, fauna, mourner, sauna, avifauna (birds of particular region).

17.235
joiner, amboyna (Indonesian tree), Amboina (Indonesian island).

17.236
owner, boner, donor, Jonah, loner, moaner, Mona, mona (African monkey), krone, trona (greyish mineral), toner, Iona, cinchona (quinine-producing tree bark), Dodona (Greek town), landowner, Bellona (Roman war goddess), Pamplona (Spanish city), Cremona, Pomona (Roman goddess), shipowner, corona, Verona, persona, Daytona, Altona (German port), canzona (musical term), Barcelona, Arizona.

17.237
scunner (*Scot* aversion), dharna (Indian sit-in), gunner, runner, Sunna (Islamic law), stunner, oner (something outstanding), forerunner, Corunna (Spanish port), roadrunner (crested bird), gunrunner, outrunner, frontrunner.

17.238
schooner, lunar, Luna (Roman moon goddess), Poona, crooner, pruner,

sooner, tuna, tuner, Kaduna (Nigerian state), cislunar (between earth and moon), koruna (Czechoslovak currency), vicuña, lacuna (gap), lacunar (ceiling with sunken panels), Fortuna (Roman goddess), semilunar, circumlunar, honeymooner.

17.239
vahana (Indian mythological vehicle), baconer (type of pig), reckoner, thickener, falconer, questioner, Adana (Turkish city), Londoner, stiffener, softener, wagoner, Helena, almoner, Brahmana (Hindu sacred treatise), commoner, sharpener, opener, coroner, fastener, freshener, pensioner, sweetener, lightener, whitener, Westerner, Easterner, strengthener, Northerner, Southerner, taverner, governor, alienor (legal term), prisoner, poisoner.

reversioner (legal term), confectioner, redemptioner (early emigrant to America), Ecbatana (ancient Iranian city).

executioner, paralipomena (supplementary writings).

17.239.1
stationer, probationer, vacationer.

17.239.2
conditioner, commissioner, parishioner, petitioner, practitioner, exhibitioner (scholarship student).

17.240
Gardiner, gardener, hardener, pardner.

17.241
Pydna (ancient Macedonian town), echidna.

17.242
Jumna (Indian river), alumna (*US* female graduate), columnar.

17.243
Mishnah (Jewish precepts), Krishna, Ramakrishna (Hindu religious reformer).

17.244
Etna, Gretna.

17.245 [see also **17.140**]
banger, ganger (foreman of labour gang), hangar, hanger, clanger, franger (*Austral* condom), cliffhanger, straphanger, Selangor (Malaysian state), Tauranga (New Zealand port), paperhanger, Doppelgänger.

17.246 [see also **17.141**]
clinger, pinger, ringer, wringer, springer, stringer (architectural term), singer, stinger (iced whisky and soda), winger, swinger, humdinger, gunslinger, klipspringer (small African antelope), minnesinger (medieval German minstrel), Meistersinger (German poet or musician).

17.247
kappa (Greek letter), dapper, clapper, flapper, napper, nappa (*Slang* head), snapper, wrapper, rapper, grappa, trapper, strapper (*US* strapping person), sapper, schappe (silk yarn or fabric), kidnapper, Harappa (Pakistani city), handicapper (sports handicap assigner), whippersnapper, Phi Beta Kappa (US academic society).

17.248
scarper, Harper, sharper, tapa (paper mulberry bark), cardsharper.

17.249
caper, neper (unit in physics), paper, scraper, draper, shaper, tapir, taper, vapour, flypaper, sandpaper, endpaper, wallpaper, notepaper, newspaper, skyscraper.

17.250
leper, pepper, stepper.

17.251
chirper, Sherpa, usurper.

17.252
keeper, sleeper, nipa (palm tree), Dnieper (Russian river), peeper, pipa (South American toad), reaper, creeper, weeper, sweeper, beekeeper, door-

keeper, storekeeper, book-keeper, goal-keeper, gamekeeper, timekeeper, innkeeper, shopkeeper, housekeeper, gatekeeper, minesweeper, Arequipa (Peruvian city), wicketkeeper.

17.253
kipper, skipper, chipper, dipper, Lippe (German river), clipper, flipper, slipper, nipper, ripper, tripper, stripper, sipper (*US* drinking straw), shipper, tipper, zipper, mudskipper (tropical coastal fish), calliper, juniper, Agrippa (Roman general), day-tripper, worshipper.

17.254
sniper, piper, viper, wiper, sandpiper (bird).

17.255
copper, chopper, Dopper (Afrikaner Church member), Joppa, hopper, popper, cropper, dropper, proper, shopper, topper, stopper, whopper, treehopper (insect), clodhopper, froghopper (small leaping insect), grasshopper, sharecropper (*US* tenant farmer), eavesdropper, improper, gobstopper, teenybopper.

17.256
scorper (fine chisel), pauper, torpor.

17.257
coper (horse dealer), groper, sopor (abnormally deep sleep), toper, L-dopa (natural body substance), landloper (*Scot* vagrant), Europa (satellite of Jupiter), NATSOPA, methyldopa (a drug), interloper.

17.258
upper, cuppa, scupper, crupper (saddle strap), supper.

17.259
Cooper, cooper (barrel-maker), looper (moth larva), blooper (*US* blunder), snooper, grouper (tropical fish), trouper, trooper, super, whooper (white swan), pupa, stupor, mosstrooper (border country raider), peasouper, super-duper.

17.260
walloper (*Austral* policeman), hanaper (wickerwork basket), developer.

17.261
camper, scamper, damper, hamper, clamper (spiked frame on sole), pamper, tamper, Tampa (Florida resort).

17.262
temper, distemper.

17.263
crimper, shrimper, simper, whimper.

17.264
bumper, dumper, jumper, lumper (*US* stevedore), plumper (actor's mouth pad), show-jumper, buckjumper (*Austral* untamed horse).

17.265
asper (Turkish coin), Caspar (one of the Magi), jasper.

17.266
crisper, whisper.

17.267
ROSPA (accident prevention society), prosper.

17.268
Ara (constellation), Harar (Ethiopian city), Nara (Japanese city), para (Yugoslavian coin), vara (Spanish length), cascara, mascara, Bukhara (Russian city), Sahara, Amhara (Ethiopian province), Damara (African people), samara (winged fruit), Asmara (Ethiopian city), Carrara (Italian town), Ferrara, Guevara, gurdwara (Sikh place of worship), capybara, caracara (bird of prey), Tsukahara (Japanese gymnast), Connemara, tuatara, solfatara (sulphurous volcanic vent).

17.268.1
tiara, Honiara (capital of Solomon Islands).

17.269
error, terror, naira (Nigerian currency), Kagera (African river), busera (Ugandan alcoholic drink).

17.270
stirrer, preferrer, conferrer.

17.271
Eire, eyra (feline mammal), bearer, Sarah, wearer, sierra, torchbearer, trainbearer, cupbearer, macebearer, caldera (volcanic crater), wayfarer, seafarer, declarer, Dun Laoghaire, repairer, pareira (medicinal plant root), Riviera, tapadera (US stirrup covering), pintadera (Neolithic decorative stamp), habanera (Cuban dance), demerara, cordillera.

17.272
era, gerah (ancient Hebrew weight), hearer, Hera, lira, sclera (outer covering of eyeball), sera (*plural of* serum), Madeira, chimera (hybrid monster), lempira (Honduran currency), sheepshearer, hetaera (female prostitute), Cythera (Greek island), Gezira (region of Sudan), Hegira (flight of Mohammed), Mufulira (Zambian town), phylloxera (insect that attacks vines).

17.273
mirror, Pyrrha (Greek mythological character), sirrah, wirra (Irish exclamation of sorrow).

17.274
Beira (Mozambique port), hirer, Lyra (constellation), tayra (arboreal mammal), wirer, Sapphira (biblical character), Stagira (ancient Macedonian city), admirer, palmyra (tropical palm), enquirer, spirogyra (freshwater alga).

17.275
horror, begorra, Camorra (Neapolitan secret society), Gomorrah, Illawarra (Australian coastal district).

17.276
aura, borer, bora (violent north wind), Cora, corer, scorer, Dora, hora (traditional circle dance), Laura, flora, Flora, Morar (Scottish loch), Nora, snorer, schnorrer (*US* professional beggar), pourer, sora (US bird).

woodborer (beetle larva), bombora (submerged reef), rasbora (tropical fish), fedora (brimmed hat), Andorra, Pandora, angora, explorer, menorah (Jewish ceremonial candelabrum), aurora, Masora (Hebrew bible text), restorer, signora.

Bora Bora (Pacific island), Tuscarora (American Indian people).

17.277
juror, Jura, pleura (membrane enveloping lungs), crura (leglike structures), surah (twill fabric), tourer, tamboura (Indian musical instrument), Madura (Indonesian island), nonjuror, insurer, Mathura (Indian city), procurer, datura (narcotic plant), bravura, caesura, Kamakura (Japanese city), Djajapura (Indonesian port), El Mansura (Egyptian city), tessitura (musical term), angostura, acciaccatura (musical term), appoggiatura (musical term), coloratura, Bonaventura (Italian saint), camera obscura (optical device).

17.278
borough, durra (cereal grass), thorough, demurrer (objection), kookaburra.

17.279
Scarborough, labourer, Deborah, Berbera (Somalian port), Loughborough, Marlborough, Flamborough, slumberer, Canberra, Farnborough, Atbara (Sudanese town), Gainsborough, Greensboro (US city), Ankara, conqueror, torturer, lecturer, murderer, borderer, solderer, wanderer, plunderer, sufferer, amphora, agora (ancient Greek marketplace), Megara (Greek town), perjurer, conjurer, cellarer (monastic official), cholera, camera, stammerer, armourer, Marmara (Turkish inland sea), Woomera, woomera (Aboriginal spear thrower), genera (*plural of* genus), corpora (*plural of* corpus), emperor, Klemperer (orchestral conductor), tempera (painting medium), whisperer, tessera

(square mosaic tile), sorcerer, treasurer, usurer, chatterer, flatterer, caterer, slaughterer, stutterer, fruiterer, poulterer, tantara (trumpet fanfare), plasterer, plethora, cithara (stringed instrument).

Peterborough, Attenborough, Edinburgh, adventurer, Vadodara (Indian city), philanderer, anaphora (rhetorical device), mandragora (narcotic plant), malingerer, in camera, nullipara (obstetrics term), primipara (obstetrics term), multipara (obstetrics term), Diaspora (Jews' dispersion from Palestine), adulterer, upholsterer, deliverer, discoverer.

manufacturer, sesquialtera (organ stop).

17.279.1
remora (marine fish), ephemera.

17.279.2
Sisera (biblical character), viscera (large internal body organs), chelicera (spider's claw), lonicera (honeysuckle).

17.280
Aldabra (Indian Ocean islands), abracadabra.

17.281
sabra (Israeli-born Jew), macabre.

17.282
zebra, cause célèbre (famous lawsuit).

17.283
Libra, algebra, vertebra.

17.284
timbre, Alhambra, Anambra (Nigerian state).

17.285
umbra, penumbra.

17.286
Phaedra (wife of Theseus), ex cathedra (with authority).

17.287
Alexandra, double entendre.

17.288
tundra, Ramachandra (Hindu mythological character).

17.289
Niagara, podagra (gout), pellagra (vitamin deficiency disease).

17.290
opera, copra (dried coconut kernel).

17.291
quatre (playing card), Cleopatra.

17.292
Chartres, Sumatra, Sinatra.

17.293
Petra (ancient Jordanian city), tetra (tropical fish), et cetera.

17.294
sutra (Sanskrit sayings), Brahmaputra (Asian river), Kamasutra.

17.295
spectra, Electra.

17.296
mantra, Tantra (Sanskrit sacred books).

17.297
orchestra, aspidistra.

17.298
Assur (Assyrian god), gasser, placer (gold-containing sediment), NASA, Mombasa, Makasar (Indonesian port), Cabora Bassa (African dam), antimacassar.

17.299
chaser, facer, mesa (tableland), macer (macebearer), pacer, spacer, racer, bracer, tracer, Hargeisa (Somalian city), embraceor (legal term), steeplechaser.

17.300
lesser, dresser, pressor (producing increased blood pressure), cesser (legal term), Odessa, professor, confessor, hairdresser, aggressor, depressor, oppressor, compressor, processor, asses-

sor, successor, possessor, predecessor, microprocessor.

17.301
bursar, bursa, cursor, mercer, purser, precursor, vice versa.

17.302
kisser, purchaser, officer, Orissa (Indian state), Larisa (Greek city), vibrissa (whisker), abscissa (maths term), mantissa (maths term), artificer (skilled craftsman).

17.303
slicer, Neisse (German–Polish river), ricer (*US* sieve), de-icer.

17.304
Ossa (Greek mountain), dosser, fossa (anatomical depression), glossa (tongue), Canossa (Italian castle), Saragossa (Spanish city), Barbarossa (Holy Roman Emperor).

17.305
courser, Chaucer, Horsa (leader of Jutes), saucer.

17.306
grocer, mucosa (mucous membrane), mimosa, Formosa, serosa (delicate body membrane), greengrocer, Via Dolorosa (road to Calvary), anorexia nervosa.

17.307
douser, Hausa (African people).

17.308
Susa (ancient Iranian city), Teucer (Greek mythological character), anchusa (Eurasian plant), reducer, seducer, producer, transducer, Appaloosa (US breed of horse), Jebel Musa (Moroccan mountain), babirusa.

17.309
trespasser, canvasser.

17.310
balsa, waltzer.

17.311
ulcer, Tulsa.

17.312
cancer, Cancer, merganser (marine diving duck).

17.313
answer, dancer, lancer, enhancer.

17.314
fencer, Mensa, Spencer, censor, sensor, censer (incense burner), tensor (tensing muscle), condenser, dispenser, extensor (extending muscle).

17.315
mincer, pincer, rinser.

17.316
sponsor, responser (radio receiver).

17.317
bouncer, denouncer, announcer.

17.318
balancer, silencer, sequencer (electronic device), encumbrancer (legal term).

17.319
matza (Jewish biscuit), tazza (wine cup), piazza.

17.320
bitser (*Austral* mongrel dog), Switzer (Swiss), howitzer, Pulitzer, tsaritsa (wife of tsar), Amritsar (Indian city).

17.321
Asher, dasher (plunger in a churn), flasher, splasher (protection against splashes), masher, smasher, pasha (Turkish title), rasher, thrasher (US songbird), tamasha (Indian entertainment), gate-crasher, haberdasher.

17.322
Asia, fascia, geisha, Croatia (Yugoslavian republic), acacia, Ilesha (Nigerian town), Galatia, Dalmatia, Laurasia (hypothetical prehistoric land mass), Eurasia, ex gratia, osteomalacia (bone disease).

17.323
flesher (*Scot* butcher), fresher, pressure, tressure (heraldic term), thresher, refresher.

17.324
Persia, inertia.

17.325
Esher, Rhodesia, godetia, Belisha, Portlaoise (Irish town), Venetia (region of ancient Italy), magnesia, aubrietia (trailing plant), montbretia (African plant), Ossetia (region of Russia), Lutetia (ancient name for Paris), Helvetia (Latin name for Switzerland), alopecia.

17.326 [see also **17.3.49**]
fisher, fissure, wisher, Frobisher, kingfisher, militia, polisher, publisher, varnisher, furnisher, finisher, Britisher, well-wisher, extinguisher.

17.327
cosher, quassia (tropical tree), washer, dishwasher.

17.328
kosher, scotia (architectural moulding), Boeotia (region of ancient Greece), Nova Scotia.

17.329
usher, gusher, blusher, Russia, crusher, Prussia.

17.330
censure, dementia (mental deterioration), amentia (congenital mental deficiency).

17.331
affenpinscher (breed of dog), Doberman pinscher.

17.332 [see also **17.3.59**]
erasure, embrasure.

17.333
leisure, pleasure, measure, treasure, displeasure, commeasure (be the same as), admeasure (share out), countermeasure.

17.334 [see also **17.3.60**]
freesia, seizure, nemesia (cultivated plant), Polynesia, Melanesia, Micronesia, Austronesia.

17.335 [see also **17.3.62**]
closure, foreclosure, enclosure, disclosure, exclosure (fenced forest area), composure, exposure, discomposure, underexposure, overexposure.

17.336
attar (oil used in perfume), batter, scatter, chatter, hatter, latter, clatter, flatter, platter, splatter, matter, smatter, natter, patter, spatter, ratter, satyr, shatter, tatter, wildcatter (*US* oil prospector), regatta, bespatter, Kenyatta, antimatter, pitter-patter.

17.337
barter, Carter, charter, darter (aquatic tropical bird), garter, martyr, Sparta, rata (New Zealand tree), strata, sartor (tailor), tartar, Tartar, starter, riata (a lasso), Djakarta (capital of Indonesia), toccata, Siddhartha (personal name of Buddha), sonata, errata, pro rata, cassata (ice cream), cantata, nonstarter, Magna Carta, alma mater, Stabat Mater (Latin hymn), serenata (18th-century cantata).

17.337.1
chipolata, taramasalata (fish-roe paté).

17.337.2
Maratha (Indian people), desiderata, inamorata.

17.338
eta (Japanese outcast), cater, skater, data, gaiter, hater, later, plater, slater, mater, Meta (Colombian river), pater, crater, freighter, frater (friar), grater, traitor, tater, stater (ancient Greek coin), stator (stationary part of machine), waiter.

debater, abator (legal term), albata (variety of nickel silver), Mercator, dilator, collator, ablator (heat shield), translator, pronator (type of muscle), equator, curator, vibrator, glossator (writer of glosses), peseta, pulsator, rotator, scrutator (examiner), spectator, dictator, testator, dumbwaiter.

incubator, educator, evocator (biology term), liquidator, percolator, escalator, inhalator (device aiding breathing), nomenclator (person who invents names), legislator, collimator (optical device), animator, lacrimator (substance causing tear flow), imprimatur (church licence to publish), pia mater (membrane enclosing brain), dura mater (membrane enclosing brain), exequatur (official authorization), aspirator, procurator, integrator (computer term), perpetrator, illustrator, demonstrator, crux ansata (symbolic cross), commutator, sternutator (substance causing sneezing), commentator, excavator, conservator (custodian).

attenuator, continuator, vasodilator, administrator, totalizator (betting system).

17.338.1
creator, gladiator, radiator, mediator, aviator, caveator (legal term), delineator (tailor's pattern), negotiator, annunciator (location indicator).

17.338.2
judicator (judge), indicator, trafficator (car indicator), applicator, duplicator, lubricator, desiccator (drying apparatus), adjudicator, vinificator (wine-making apparatus), scarificator (surgical instrument), purificator (Communion cloth), divaricator (zoology term).

17.338.3
negator (electronic circuit), alligator, navigator, investigator.

17.338.4
propagator, corrugator (brow-wrinkling muscle), interrogator.

17.338.5
relator (legal term), oscillator, ventilator, scintillator (physics term), invigilator, defibrillator (medical apparatus).

17.338.6
tabulator, speculator, calculator, modulator, regulator, simulator, stimulator,

insulator, postulator (advocate for person's canonization), perambulator, articulator, accumulator.

17.338.7
terminator (dividing line on planet), supinator (muscle of forearm), buccinator (muscle in cheek), coordinator, exterminator, discriminator (electronic circuit), denominator.

17.338.8
detonator, alternator, resonator, impersonator.

17.338.9
narrator, liberator, decorator, moderator, stellarator (physics apparatus), numerator, generator, cinerator (cremation furnace), separator, operator, corporator (member of corporation), respirator, literator (professional writer), collaborator, reverberator (metallurgical furnace), refrigerator, accelerator, enumerator (person taking census), incinerator, recuperator (gun-resetting device).

17.338.10
agitator, imitator, resuscitator.

17.338.11
levator (raising muscle), elevator, activator, cultivator.

17.339
better, betta (fighting fish), debtor, fetter, feta (Greek cheese), getter, letter, Quetta (Pakistani city), setter, tetter (skin eruption), sweater.

Gambetta (French statesman), vendetta, unfetter, go-getter, muleta (matador's small cape), Valletta (capital of Malta), newsletter, biretta (clerical cap), cabretta (soft leather), bonesetter, typesetter, pacesetter, jetsetter, mozzetta (clerical cape), Rosetta.

Damietta (Egyptian town), arietta (short aria), mantelletta (clerical vestment), carburettor, operetta, anchoveta (small anchovy), sinfonietta (short symphony).

17.340

skirter (*Austral* fleece trimmer), hurter (protective object), stertor (laborious noisy breathing), Alberta, frankfurter, Lacerta (constellation), evertor (type of muscle), inverter (electrical circuit), converter, Bizerte (Tunisian port), deserter.

17.341

eater, beater, beta, chaeta (small bristle on worm), cheetah, dita (tropical shrub), fetor (offensive smell), heater, litre, pleater, meter, metre, peter, Peter, pita (fibre-yielding plant), rhetor (teacher of rhetoric), praetor (Roman magistrate), seta (small bristle), teeter, theta, tweeter (loudspeaker).

eggbeater (*US* helicopter), windcheater, beefeater, veleta, Demeter (Greek goddess), Machmeter, ammeter, repeater, saltpetre, ureter, excreta, amrita (Hindu ambrosia), propraetor (Roman ex-magistrate), masseter (cheek muscle), receiptor (issuer of receipts), two-seater, Peshitta (version of Bible), partita (musical composition), anteater.

honey-eater (small songbird), millilitre, centilitre, millimetre, centimetre, taximeter, nanometre, kilometre, señorita, margarita (cocktail), Bhagavad-Gita (sacred Hindu text).

17.342

bitter, skitter (scamper), chitter (*US* twitter), fitter, jitter, hitter, litter, lytta (cartilage beneath dog's tongue), flitter, glitter, knitter, pitta (flat Greek bread), quitter, quittor (horse's foot infection), critter, fritter, sitter, shittah (biblical tree), titter, vitta (biology term), twitter.

rabbiter, arbiter, embitter, presbyter, cricketer, traditor (early Christian betrayer), auditor, taffeta, outfitter, Sagitta (constellation), aglitter, transmitter,

janitor, genitor (biological father), monitor, chapiter (upper part of column), Jupiter, trumpeter, heritor, bedsitter, catheter, servitor, Exeter.

inhibitor, exhibitor, counterfeiter, Hippolyta (Greek mythological queen), diameter, parameter, voltameter, pentameter, hexameter, telemeter (distance measurer), hypermeter (verse line), volumeter, progenitor, per capita, accipiter (hawk), non sequitur, apparitor (ecclesiastical court officer), inheritor, interpreter, capacitor, solicitor, competitor, primogenitor.

17.342.1

editor, creditor, subeditor.

17.342.2

emitter, dimeter (verse line), remitter, trimeter (verse line), scimitar, planimeter (plane-area measurer), dosimeter (radiation measurer), tasimeter (temperature-change measurer), pulsimeter, densimeter, altimeter, acidimeter, alkalimeter.

17.342.2.1

perimeter, saccharimeter (sugar-concentration measurer), calorimeter, polarimeter (light-polarization measurer), solarimeter (solar-radiation measurer), colorimeter, vaporimeter (vapour-pressure measurer).

17.342.3

cryometer (low-temperature thermometer), tachometer, viscometer, pedometer, speedometer, odometer, algometer (sensitivity measurer), mileometer, bolometer (radiant-energy measurer), coulometer, cyclometer, atmometer (evaporation measurer), planometer (plate for testing flatness), clinometer, monometer (verse line), pycnometer (bottle for weighing liquids), swingometer, aerometer, sclerometer (mineral-hardness measurer), pyrometer, spirometer (lung-capacity measurer), micrometer, hydrometer, hygrometer (humidity measurer), nitrometer, gasometer, optometer, Comptometer (*Trademark*), plastometer (plasticity measurer), bathometer.

cephalometer (head measurer), anemometer (wind-speed measurer), salinometer, inclinometer (aircraft instrument), actinometer (sun-radiation measurer), fluorometer (fluorescence measurer), tellurometer (surveying instrument), magnetometer, densitometer, sensitometer, dilatometer (dimension-change measurer), refractometer, piezometer (pressure measurer), alcoholometer.

17.342.3.1
rheometer (blood-flow measurer), geometer (person who studies geometry), tacheometer (surveying instrument), radiometer, audiometer, eudiometer (chemistry apparatus), heliometer (type of telescope), craniometer, goniometer (angle measurer), variometer, tensiometer, potentiometer.

17.342.3.2
thermometer, dynamometer (power measurer).

17.342.3.3
tonometer, phonometer (sound-intensity measurer), manometer (instrument for comparing pressures), chronometer (nautical timepiece), galvanometer (electric-current measurer).

17.342.3.4
barometer, interferometer, decelerometer, accelerometer.

17.342.3.5
spectrometer (spectrum producer and measurer), electrometer (electrical-potential measurer).

17.342.4
visitor, inquisitor.

17.342.5
prepositor (prefect), depositor, compositor, expositor (person who ex-

pounds), ovipositor (insect's egg-laying organ).

17.343
fighter, lighter, blighter, mitre, nitre, writer, sighter (practice shot in competition), titre, bullfighter, gunfighter, prizefighter, Gauleiter (German governor under Hitler), moonlighter, lamplighter, igniter, songwriter, typewriter, scriptwriter, ghostwriter, exciter (oscillator), excitor (a nerve), amanita (genus of fungi), telewriter, copywriter, underwriter.

17.344
otter, cotter, cotta (clerical surplice), gotta, jotter, blotter, plotter, potter, spotter, squatter, rotter, trotter, totter, stotter (*Scot* good-looking woman), swatter, ricotta (soft white cheese), pelota (Spanish ball game), globetrotter, terra cotta.

17.345
daughter, slaughter, mortar, snorter, porter, quarter, sorter, water.

aorta, goddaughter, granddaughter, stepdaughter, manslaughter, ripsnorter, reporter, supporter, colporteur (book pedlar), importer, transporter, exporter, backwater, breakwater, forequarter, hindquarter, shearwater, firewater (whisky), Bridgwater, freshwater, dishwater, saltwater, Ullswater, kicksorter (physics apparatus).

underwater, Derwentwater.

17.346
Oita (Japanese city), goitre, loiter, Reuter, reconnoitre.

17.347
boater, Kota (Indian city), scoter, lota (brass water container), bloater, floater, motor, notour (Scottish legal term), quota, rota, rotor, voter, iota, biota (biology term), Dakota, promoter, sapota (tropical fruit), acroter (architectural term), nonvoter, locomotor (relating to locomotion), dynamotor

(current-converting machine), Minnesota, sensorimotor (physiology term).

17.348
outer, scouter, doubter, pouter (domestic pigeon), router (cutting tool).

17.349
utter, butter, cutter, scutter (scurry), gutter, gutta (architectural ornament), clutter, flutter, splutter, mutter, nutter, putter, sputter, shutter, stutter, rebutter (legal term), abutter (owner of adjoining property), woodcutter, leafcutter (South American ant), Calcutta, stonecutter, daisycutter (cricket term).

17.350
first-footer, six-footer, shot-putter, coadjutor (bishop's assistant), contributor, distributor, executor, prolocutor (Anglican Church official), interlocutor.

17.351
scooter, hooter, looter, fluter, fruiter, suitor, souter (*Scot* cobbler), neuter, pewter, tutor, freebooter, accoutre, valuta (currency exchange rate), peashooter, crapshooter (*US* craps player), sharpshooter, commuter, computer, barracouta (predatory fish), troubleshooter, persecutor, prosecutor, collocutor (person making conversation), Abeokuta (Nigerian town).

17.352
theatre, predator, comforter, balata (tropical tree, Galata (Turkish port), elater (biology term), amateur, stigmata, senator, orator, waratah (Australian shrub), idolater, automata (*plural of* automaton), Antipater (Macedonian general), declarator (Scottish legal term), comparator (comparing device), conspirator, amphitheatre, Mahabharata (Indian poem).

17.352.1
dieter, rioter, proprietor.

17.353
actor, factor, tractor, reactor, varactor (electronic device), refractor, retractor,

protractor, contractor, extractor, contactor (type of switch), malefactor, benefactor, chiropractor, subcontractor, azotobacter (bacterium).

17.354
hector, nectar, spectre, rector, recta (*plural of* rectum), sector, vector, effector (nerve ending), defector, ejector, ejecta (expelled volcanic material), dejecta (solid body waste), projector, injector, elector, collector, selector, reflector, connector, respecter, prospector, inspector, erector, director, bisector, prosector (person who dissects), detector, protector, convector.

17.355
dicta (*plural of* dictum), lictor (Roman official), victor, predictor, character, constrictor, vasoconstrictor (substance constricting blood vessels).

17.356
okta (meteorological unit), doctor, proctor.

17.357
adductor (type of muscle), inductor (electrical component), conductor, destructor (furnace for burning refuse), instructor, nonconductor, semiconductor.

17.358
after, laughter, rafter, grafter, wafter (fan), thereafter, hereafter.

17.359
snifter, drifter, swifter (nautical term), shoplifter, weightlifter, CARIFTA (Caribbean Free Trade Area).

17.360
kofta (Indian meatballs), lofter (golf club), crofter, softa (Muslim student).

17.361
kelter (condition), delta, smelter, spelter (impure zinc), shelter, Shelta (Irish tinkers' secret language), welter, swelter, helter-skelter.

17.362
filter, philtre (love potion), milter (sexually mature male fish), ultrafilter (filter with tiny pores).

17.363
alter, altar, falter, halter, Malta, palter (be insincere), salter, psalter, defaulter, Gibraltar.

17.364
bolter (*Austral* outsider in race), coulter (plough blade), Volta (Italian physicist).

17.365
antre (cavern), anta (architectural term), banter, canter, plantar, manta (large ray fish), Granta (River Cam), Santa, Tanta (Egyptian city), decanter, trochanter (projection on femur), Vedanta (Hindu school of philosophy), infanta, Atlanta, instanter (without delay), levanter (Mediterranean easterly wind), almucantar (astronomy term), tam-o'-shanter.

17.366
chanter, planter.

17.367
fainter, painter.

17.368
enter, renter, centre, tenter (cloth-stretching frame), venter (belly), scienter (wilfully), magenta, polenta (Italian porridge), tormentor, assentor, placenta, Jobcentre, concentre, preventer (nautical term), inventor, accentor (small songbird), succentor (cathedral cleric), presenter, hypocentre (area below nuclear explosion), orthocentre (maths term), impedimenta.

17.368.1
dissenter, precentor (cathedral cleric), epicentre (area above earthquake. origin), barycentre (centre of mass).

17.369
linter (fibre-stripping machine), splinter, Pinter (English dramatist), pinta (skin disease), printer, sprinter, sinter

(deposit from hot springs), winter, carpenter, midwinter, calcsinter (porous rock), teleprinter, overwinter (spend the winter).

17.370
saunter, taunter.

17.371
jointer (pointing tool), pointer, appointor (legal term).

17.372
counter, encounter.

17.373
chunter (mutter), junta, hunter, punter, grunter, shunter, pothunter (prize-seeking competitor), marabunta (West Indian wasp).

17.374
captor, chapter, raptor (bird of prey), adapter.

17.375
sceptre, septa (*plural of* septum), receptor, preceptor (teacher), acceptor (electronics term), amboceptor (immune body in blood), interceptor (fighter aircraft), proprioceptor (nerve ending).

17.376
anaglypta, lex non scripta (unwritten law).

17.377
copter (*short for* helicopter), dioptre, helicopter, ornithopter (aircraft with flapping wings).

17.378
tempter, pre-emptor, attempter.

17.379
aster, Astor, pasta, Rasta, raster (electronics term), piastre (South Vietnamese currency), diaster (biology term), Jocasta (mother of Oedipus), cadaster (property register), pilaster (rectangular column in wall), pinaster (Mediterranean pine), canasta, amphiaster (biology term), oleaster (flowering shrub), Zoroaster (Persian prophet), poetaster (inferior poet), cotoneaster,

Antofagasta (Chilean port), verticillaster (botany term).

17.380
castor, caster, plaster, master, pastor, forecaster, broadcaster, newscaster, paymaster, choirmaster, taskmaster, headmaster, bandmaster, grandmaster, schoolmaster, ringmaster, housemaster, scoutmaster, postmaster, toastmaster, quizmaster, disaster, alabaster, quartermaster, stationmaster.

17.381
slaister (*Scot* confused mess), taster, shirtwaister.

17.382
Esther, ester, Chester, fester, jester, Leicester, mester (*Dialect* master), pester, cuesta (long low ridge), tester, testa (outer layer of seed), Vesta, vesta (wooden match), wester (to move towards west).

podesta (Italian magistrate), egesta (body waste), digester, ingesta (food taken by mouth), celesta (keyboard instrument), molester, semester, trimester, sequester, arrester, ancestor, protester, Avesta (Zoroastrian scriptures), investor, sou'wester, Cirencester.

17.382.1
fiesta, siesta, polyester.

17.383
Easter, keister (*US* buttocks), leister (pronged fishing spear), Dniester (Russian river), quaestor (Roman magistrate), autopista (Spanish motorway).

17.384
bistre (drawing pigment), Lister, lister (a plough), blister, clyster (enema), glister, Mr., mister, crista (biology term), sister, vista, twister, xyster (surgical file).

Chichester, Rochester, Dorchester, Colchester, Manchester, Winchester, sophister (second-year undergraduate), register, fillister (adjustable plane),

ballista (ancient catapult), thermistor (electronic component), banister, canister, ganister (sedimentary rock), barrister, thyristor (electronic component), chorister, forester, arista (a bristle), varistor (electronic component), stepsister, harvester, resistor, transistor. deregister.

17.384.1
minister, sinister, administer, maladminister.

17.385
costa (a rib), foster, goster (*Dialect* laugh uncontrollably), hosta (Oriental plant), Gloucester, roster, zoster (shingles), impostor, defroster, paternoster.

17.386
oyster, cloister, roister.

17.387
coaster, poster, throwster (yarn spinner), toaster, four-poster, billposter.

17.388
buster, Custer, duster, lustre, bluster, cluster, fluster, muster, thruster (rocket engine), Worcester, blockbuster, combustor (part of jet engine), Augusta, lacklustre, lincrusta (embossed wallpaper), filibuster, broncobuster, knuckle-duster, Famagusta (Cypriot port).

17.389
booster, rooster.

17.390
Lancaster, Doncaster, baluster, canaster (dried tobacco leaves).

17.391
lobster, mobster.

17.392
bolster, holster, pollster (person who conducts polls), upholster.

17.393
deemster (Manx magistrate), teamster.

17.394
minster, spinster, Westminster, Axminster, Kidderminster.

17.395
Munster, punster.

17.396
hipster, quipster, tipster.

17.397
Arthur, Martha.

17.398
aphtha (small ulceration), naphtha (chemical compound).

17.399
anther, panther, pyracantha (ornamental shrub).

17.400
gather, blather, forgather (assemble), ingather.

17.401
father, farther, lather, slather (large quantity), rather, forefather, godfather, grandfather, stepfather.

17.402
feather, heather, leather, nether, tether, whether, weather, wether (castrated male sheep), together, aweather (nautical term), bellwether (leader of flock), altogether.

17.403
further, murther (murder).

17.404
breather, bequeather.

17.405
dither, hither, slither, thither, whither, wither, swither (*Scot* hesitate), zither.

17.406
either, neither.

17.407
bother, pother (commotion).

17.408
other, mother, smother, brother, godmother, grandmother, stepmother, another, stepbrother.

17.409
carver, kava (Polynesian shrub), Java, larva, lava, laver (seaweed), Drava (European river), Sava (Yugoslavian river), guava, palaver, Delmarva (US peninsula), Morava (Czechoslovakian river), cassava (tropical plant), ottava (octave), Balaclava, Bratislava (Czechoslovakian port), Costa Brava, piassava (South American palm tree).

17.410
deva (Hindu–Buddhist god), favour, haver (dither), laver (baptismal font), claver (*Scot* to gossip), flavour, slaver, quaver, raver, graver (engraving tool), savour, saver, shaver, waiver, waver, cadaver, disfavour, Ungava (region of Canada), engraver, vena cava (large vein), clishmaclaver (*Scot* gossip), semiquaver.

17.411
ever, clever, never, sever, however, whoever, whichever, endeavour, whomever, whenever, wherever, forever, dissever (break off), whatever, howsoever, whatsoever.

17.412
fervour, Nerva (Roman emperor), server, conferva (freshwater alga), Minerva, timeserver, observer, contrayerva (medicinal plant root).

17.413
beaver, kiva (Pueblo Indian underground room), diva, fever, lever, cleaver, Neva (Russian river), Siva (Hindu god), viva (long live!), weaver, weever (marine fish), believer, Geneva, retriever, deceiver, receiver, transceiver (radio transmitter–receiver), unbeliever, cantilever, underachiever.

17.414
giver, liver, flivver (cheap old car), sliver, quiver, river, shiver, lawgiver, gingiva (gum), deliver, Oliver, miniver (fur on ceremonial robes), Nineveh, vetiver (tall Asian grass).

17.415
skiver, diver, fiver, driver, Saiva (Hindu worshipper), stiver (former Dutch

coin), viva (oral examination), Godiva, helldiver (*US* grebe), saliva, co-driver, screwdriver, survivor, conjunctiva.

17.416
bovver, hover, windhover (*Dialect* kestrel).

17.417
ova, over, Dover, clover, nova, rover, drover, trover (legal term), stover (fodder).

flyover, Markova, walkover, Sadowa (battle site in Czechoslovakia), Andover, changeover, Jehovah, pullover, Pavlova, Hanover, ars nova (14th-century music style), hangover, wingover (aircraft manoeuvre), wrapover, slipover, stopover, moreover, Passover, crossover, flashover (electric discharge), pushover, leftover.

supernova, Casanova, bossa nova.

17.418
cover, lover, glover, plover, recover, uncover, discover, undercover, rediscover.

17.419
Hoover (*Trademark*), louvre, mover, Suva (capital of Fiji), Vancouver, remover, manoeuvre, outmanoeuvre, Lietuva.

17.420
salvor (person salvaging boats), salver, quacksalver (quack doctor).

17.421
elver, selva (dense equatorial forest).

17.422
silver, sylva (trees of particular region), quicksilver.

17.423
volva (botany term), revolver.

17.424
culver, vulva.

17.425
Oshawa (Canadian city), Ottawa, pipsissewa (evergreen plant).

17.426
flexor, plexor (medical hammer), indexer.

17.427
fixer, mixer, nixer (*Dialect* spare-time job), elixir.

17.428
boxer, coxa (hip bone or joint), moxa (Oriental medicinal plant substance), bobbysoxer, chionodoxa (Eurasian plant).

17.429
coaxer, hoaxer.

17.430 [see also **17.5**]
lawyer, sawyer.

17.431
bowyer (maker of archery bows), Nagoya (Japanese city), kabaragoya (large monitor lizard).

17.432
thuja (coniferous tree), alleluia.

17.433 [see also **17.3.18**]
failure, derailleur (bicycle gear-changing device).

17.434 [see also **17.3.29**]
Nyanja (African people), lasagne.

17.435 [see also **17.3.33**]
senior, Tigrinya (Ethiopian language), Monsignor.

17.436 [see also **17.3.53**]
paviour (material for paving), saviour, behaviour, misbehaviour.

17.437
lazar (leper), Belshazzar (biblical character), Salmanazar (large wine bottle).

17.438
Gaza, plaza, Kinshasa (capital of Zaïre).

17.439
laser, blazer, maser (microwave laser), razor, Fraser, stargazer, chalaza, trailblazer, eraser, impresa (emblem).

17.440
beezer (*Slang* fellow), geezer, geyser, Pisa, squeezer, freezer, Caesar, teaser, visa, genizah (synagogue storeroom), Theresa, Mona Lisa, Ebenezer.

17.441
Kaiser, miser, riser, sizar (maintained college undergraduate), visor, incisor, devisor (legal term), divisor, adviser, liquidizer, stabilizer, tranquillizer, sterilizer, fertilizer, dialyser, equalizer, neutralizer, totalizer, Breathalyzer (*Trademark*), atomizer, organizer, womanizer, moisturizer, synthesizer, exerciser, appetizer, advertiser, sympathizer, supervisor.

17.441.1
coryza (head cold), mycorrhiza (botany term), tenderizer, vaporizer, pasteurizer, coleorhiza (grass root sheath).

17.442
dozer (*short for* bulldozer), closer, poser, Rosa, bulldozer, Mendoza (Argentine city), Spinoza, composer, sub rosa (in secret), proposer, mariposa (flowering plant), decomposer (organism causing decay).

17.443
bowser (fuel tanker), dowser (water diviner), Mauser, mouser, browser, wowser (*Austral* puritanical person), carouser.

17.444
boozer, loser, bruiser, cruiser, Sousa, user, accuser, medusa (jellyfish), diffuser, infuser (tea-making device), misuser, Lampedusa (Mediterranean island), arethusa (US orchid).

17.445
panzer, kwanza (Angolan currency), stanza, organza, bonanza, extravaganza.

17.446
cleanser, credenza (small sideboard), cadenza, influenza.

18 -ab
cab, scab, dab, fab, gab, jab, lab, blab, flab, slab, Mab (fairy queen), nab, crab, drab, grab, tab, stab.

Joab (biblical character), Moab (biblical kingdom), kebab, vocab, serdab (chamber in Egyptian tomb), prefab, confab, Ahab (biblical king), Skylab, lablab (African bean plant), Chenab (Himalayan river), mihrab (niche in mosque), Cantab.

baobab (African tree), pedicab (Asian passenger-carrying tricycle), minicab.

19 -arb
barb, garb, Saab (*Trademark*), doab (land between converging rivers), rhubarb, bicarb, Punjab, nawab (Muslim prince), inqilab (revolution in India).

20 -abe
babe, astrolabe (former astronomers' instrument).

21 -eb
ebb, deb, bleb (a blister), pleb, neb (*Dialect* projecting part), reb (*US* Confederate soldier), web, cubeb (Asian climbing plant), ardeb (Egyptian unit of measure), Deneb (star), Zagreb, cobweb.

22 -erb
kerb, curb, herb, blurb, Serb (Serbian), verb, suburb, cowherb (flowering plant), potherb (plant used in cooking), superb, perturb, disturb, proverb, adverb, willowherb.

23 -ebe
Beeb, glebe, grebe, ephebe (ancient Greek youth), sungrebe (aquatic bird).

24 -ib
bib, dib, fib, jib, gib (metal bearing), lib, glib, nib, snib (*Scot* door fastening), squib, rib, crib, sib (kin), sahib, ad-lib, Carib (American Indian peo-

ple), sparerib, corncrib (*US* maize store), midrib (leaf vein), memsahib, Sennacherib (Assyrian king).

25 -ibe
kibe (chilblain), gibe, gybe (nautical term), bribe, scribe, tribe, imbibe, describe, prescribe, proscribe, ascribe, subscribe, transcribe, inscribe, circumscribe, diatribe.

26 -ob
bob, cob, kob (African antelope), fob, gob, job, hob, lob, blob, glob, slob, mob, nob, knob, snob, squab (young pigeon), rob, throb, sob, stob (*Dialect* a stump), swab, yob, nabob (rich person), skibob (vehicle running on skis), corncob, kincob (Indian silk fabric), demob, hobnob, thingumabob.

27 -orb
orb, daub, sorb (tree), warb (*Austral* dirty person), bedaub, desorb (chemistry term), resorb, absorb, adsorb, chemisorb (chemistry term).

28 -obe
daube (meat stew), Job, lobe, globe, robe, probe, strobe, aerobe (organism needing oxygen), microbe, wardrobe, enrobe, saprobe (organism inhabiting foul water), disrobe, bathrobe, Francophobe, Anglophobe, Negrophobe, Russophobe, xenophobe (fearer of strangers), Germanophobe, ailurophobe (fearer of cats).

29 -ub
cub, chub, dub, hub, blub, club, slub, nub, snub, pub, rub, scrub, drub (to beat), grub, shrub, sub, tub, stub, hubbub, nightclub, washtub, bathtub, syllabub, Beelzebub.

30 -ube
boob, jube (church gallery), rube (*US* country bumpkin), cube, tube, jujube, flashcube, Danube, drawtube (telescop-

ic tube), teletube (*short for* television tube).

31 -'b
Jacob, Arab, carob, scarab, cherub, Maghreb (northwest Africa).

32 -ack
back, jack, Jack, hack, lack, lac (resin), black, clack, claque (hired applauders), flak, plaque, slack, mac, smack, knack, snack, pack, quack, rack, wrack (seaweed), crack, track, sac, sack, shack, tack, stack, vac, whack, thwack, yak.

kayak, chiack (*Austral* to tease), Dyak (Malaysian people), playback, greyback (hooded crow), bareback, dieback (tree disease), tieback (*US* curtain fastening), zwieback (toasted rusk), drawback, roorback (*US* false report), throwback, kickback, hatchback, switchback, hunchback, hardback, feedback, halfback, hogback (narrow ridge), tailback, shellback (experienced sailor), fullback, tombac (an alloy), comeback, greenback, thornback (a fish), slingback, humpback, leaseback (property transaction), mossback (*US* conservative person), horseback, flashback, splashback, fatback (pork fat), outback, cutback, fastback (type of car), ack-ack, skyjack, hijack, blackjack, smokejack (spit-turning device), flapjack, slapjack (card game), skipjack, crossjack (type of sail), muntjac (small Asian deer), hardhack (US flowering plant), kulak (Russian peasant), alack, shellac, shoeblack, boneblack (black pigment), lampblack (form of carbon), bootblack, Senlac (Battle of Hastings site), Tarmac (*Trademark*), sumach (shrub), Micmac (American Indian people), knickknack, gopak (Russian dance), mudpack, calpac (brimless hat), woolpack, champac (Indian tree), unpack, hayrack, sérac (ice pinnacle), Dirac (English physicist), tribrach (metrical foot), barn-brack (*Dialect* fruit muffin), rickrack, gimcrack, wisecrack, Shadrach, backtrack, trictrac (board game), sidetrack, soundtrack, racetrack, Barsac (sweet French wine), Cossack, corsac (Asian fox), mailsack, woolsack, ransack, knapsack, hopsack, Meshach, Dvořák, Cuttack (Indian city), ticktack (bookmakers' sign language), hardtack (hard biscuit), thumbtack, haystack, smokestack, Slovak, bushwhack (travel through woods), rucksack, galyak (fur), Cognac, Muzak (*Trademark*), Balzac, Anzac.

Kerouac (US writer), bivouac, piggyback, stickleback, turtleback (part of ship), canvasback (US duck), ipecac (purgative drug), solonchak (type of soil), amberjack (Atlantic fish), lumberjack, crackerjack, natterjack (toad), applejack (apple brandy), steeplejack, supplejack (US vine), Cadillac (*Trademark*), almanac, Sassenach, Pasternak (Russian writer), amphibrach (metrical foot), bric-a-brac, tetrabrach (metrical foot), ovisac (egg sac), Gay-Lussac (French scientist), cul-de-sac, haversack, paddywhack (a smack), Armagnac.

biofeedback (medical term), diamondback (US terrapin), Aniakchak (Alaskan volcanic crater), tacamahac (resinous gum), Apurimac (Peruvian river), Czechoslovak.

32.1
cardiac, Kodiak (large bear), zodiac, coeliac (of the abdomen), umiak (Eskimo boat), maniac, Syriac (former Syrian dialect), Votyak (Finnish people), Pontiac (Indian chief), demoniac (like a demon), simoniac (person who practises simony), ammoniac (gum resin), insomniac, celeriac (vegetable), amnesiac, symposiac (relating to a symposium), nymphomaniac, egomaniac, pyromaniac, dipsomaniac, kleptomaniac, hypochondriac, aphrodisiac,

Dionysiac (relating to Dionysus), megalomaniac.

32.1.1
ileac (relating to the ileum), iliac (relating to the ilium), sacroiliac (joint of pelvis), haemophiliac.

32.2
aback, pickaback, huckaback (coarse fabric), leatherback (turtle), paperback, quarterback, razorback (whale).

32.3
Bacharach, bladderwrack (seaweed), sandarac (tree yielding resin), Skagerrak, tamarack (US larch), anorak, sazerac (US cocktail), azedarach (bark of chinaberry tree).

32.4
attack, nunatak (isolated rock peak), counterattack.

33 -ark
ark, arc, bark, Bach, barque (sailing ship), dark, dhak, hark, haugh (*Dialect* flat valley base), lark, lakh (100 000 Indian rupees), clerk, Clark, Vlach (medieval European people), Mark, mark, marc (remnants of pressed fruit), marque (brand of car), nark, park, spark, quark, Sark, shark, stark.

diarch (botany term), debark (disembark), shagbark (US tree), embark, tanbark (bark producing tannin), soapbark (South American tree), macaque, endarch (botany term), skylark, salesclerk, mudlark, woodlark, seamark, earmark, nomarch (ancient Egyptian administrator), pockmark, bookmark, matchmark (mark on engine components), touchmark (maker's mark on pewter), trademark, tidemark, landmark, hallmark, Denmark, Finnmark (Norwegian county), pressmark (code on library book), sitzmark (skiing term), platemark (hallmark), footmark, ostmark (East German currency), postmark, birthmark, Reichsmark (former German currency), Bismarck, ethnarch (ruler of province), eparch (Orthodox Church bishop), hipparch (ancient Greek cavalry commander), toparch (ruler of small state), ballpark, Arak (Iranian town), xerarch (ecology term), Iraq, Petrarch, tetrarch, Pesach (Passover), mesarch (botany term), Rorschach, landshark (land profiteer), Plutarch, Landtag (German legislative assembly), futhark (phonetic alphabet), aardvark, boschvark (wild pig), exarch (head of Orthodox Church).

paperbark (Australian tree), disembark, ironbark (Australian eucalyptus tree), Offenbach, oligarch, meadowlark, fingermark, monomark (identification mark on goods), watermark, hierarch, perisarc (zoology term), coenosarc (zoology term), ectosarc (ectoplasm of amoeba).

33.1
matriarch, patriarch, gymnasiarch (Greek education magistrate), heresiarch (leader of heretical movement).

33.2
remark, remarque (mark on engraved plate), telemark (skiing term), polemarch (ancient Greek official).

34 -ake
ache, bake, cake, fake, hake, lake, laik (*Dialect* to play), Blake, flake, splake (Canadian hybrid trout), slake, make, snake, spake, quake, rake, brake, break, crake (bird), drake, strake (metal part of wheel), sake, sheik, shake, take, steak, stake, wake.

hardbake (almond toffee), clambake, sunbake (*Austral* sunbathing), backache, teacake, seedcake, beefcake, pancake, queencake, cupcake, shortcake, oatcake, fruitcake, cheesecake, headache, Hoylake, snowflake, remake, unmake, blacksnake (venomous snake), opaque, seaquake (earthquake on seabed), lyke-wake (night vigil over corpse), moonquake (moon tremor),

earthquake, earache, daybreak, firebreak, wordbreak, handbrake, windbreak, jailbreak, canebrake (*US* thicket of canes), heartbreak, outbreak, muckrake, corncrake, firedrake (fire-breathing dragon), sheldrake, mandrake, lapstrake (nautical term), forsake, namesake, keepsake, handshake, heartache, partake, retake, betake, intake, uptake, mistake, beefsteak, sweepstake, toothache, awake.

stomachache, griddlecake, rattlesnake, parabrake (aircraft parachute), undertake, overtake, wapentake (former county subdivision), kittiwake, radiopaque (impervious to radiation).

35 -eck
beck, keck (retch), Czech, check, cheque, deck, heck, Lech (European river), lek (Albanian currency), cleck (*Dialect* gossip), fleck, meck (*Dialect* small coin), neck, nek (mountain pass), sneck (*Dialect* latch), peck, spec, speck, wreck, rec (*short for* recreation), trek, sec.

Purbeck, rebec (former stringed instrument), Seebeck (philately term), xebec (Mediterranean sailing ship), Quebec, Warbeck (pretender to English throne), Brubeck (US jazz musician), pinchbeck (imitation gold), Baalbek (Lebanese town), crombec (African songbird), Steinbeck, Kazbek (Russian volcano), háček (phonetic symbol), raincheck, crosscheck, bedeck, foredeck, cromlech (prehistoric stone structure), fartlek (sports term), fennec, wryneck (woodpecker), crew-neck, breakneck, redneck, roughneck, rollneck, gooseneck (nautical term), OPEC, kopeck (Russian coin), henpeck, flyspeck (small speck), varec (seaweed), tenrec (small mammal), shipwreck, parsec (unit of astronomical distance), cusec (unit of flow), Toltec (American Indian people), Mixtec (American Indian people), Aztec.

bodycheck (sports term), overcheck, quarterdeck, afterdeck, rubberneck (*Slang* sightseer), leatherneck (*Slang* US marine), turtleneck, bottleneck, Chiang Kai-shek, Kohoutek (comet), discotheque, Zapotec (American Indian people), Tehuantepec (region of Mexico).

36 -erk

erk, irk, berk, burke (murder by suffocation), kirk, dirk, jerk, lurk, murk (gloomy darkness), smirk, perk, quirk, cirque (semicircular depression in mountains), shirk, Turk, stirk (heifer), work.

hauberk (long coat of mail), Selkirk, Falkirk, brickwork, clockwork, taskwork (unpleasant work), rework, firework, wirework, cribwork (heavy timber framework), patchwork, coachwork, spadework, roadwork, woodwork, fieldwork, groundwork, legwork, bridgework (small dental plate), framework, teamwork, timework, formwork (wooden mould for concrete), homework, stonework, crownwork (dental crown manufacture), slopwork (manufacture of shoddy goods), glasswork, casework, guesswork, presswork (operation of printing press), piecework, housework, falsework (framework supporting unfinished construction), brushwork, artwork, network, fretwork, brightwork (metal car trimmings), outwork, footwork, breastwork, earthwork, waxwork, berserk.

Atatürk (Turkish general), bodywork, handiwork, fancywork, timberwork, wickerwork, wonderwork (miracle), paperwork, counterwork, overwork, needlework, metalwork, ironwork, openwork, trelliswork, basketwork.

37 -eek

eke, beak, keek (*Scot* peep), cheek, deek (*Dialect* look at), geek (animal-eating sideshow performer), leak, leek, bleak, clique, cleek (golf club), sleek, meek, sneak, pique, peke, peek, peak, speak, squeak, reek, wreak, creek, creak, screak (*Dialect* screech), freak, Greek, shriek, streak, seek, Sikh, chic, teak, week, weak, tweak.

caïque (boat), halfbeak (a fish), grosbeak (bird), Belleek (delicate porcelain), oblique, houseleek (a plant), unique, technique, forepeak (nautical term), bespeak, newspeak, pipsqueak, perique (strong tobacco), tugrik (Mongolian currency), hairstreak (butterfly), cacique (American Indian chief), pratique (permission to use port), critique, boutique, antique, triptyque (permission to import vehicle), mystique, midweek, bezique, physique.

stickybeak (*Austral* inquisitive person), Mozambique, Martinique, ortanique (orange–tangerine hybrid), Chesapeake, fenugreek, hide-and-seek.

38 -ick [further rhymes may be created by removing -al from some adjectives in 228.23]

kick, chick, Dick, hic, hick, lick, click, flick, slick, Mick, nick, snick, pick, quick, rick, brick, crick, prick, trick, strick (unprepared textile fibres), sick, sic, tick, tic, stick, stich (line of poetry), thick, Wick, wick.

spruik (*Austral* speak in public), Bewick (English wood engraver), rhombic, Turkic (language group), psychic, sidekick, dabchick, Dardic (language group), Vedic (relating to Hindu scriptures), medic, medick (a plant), herdic (*US* small carriage), Nordic, dik-dik (small African antelope), Indic (language group), syndic (business agent), asdic (echo sounder), Kufic (early Arabic script), Delphic, georgic (poem about rural life), garlic, Gaelic, cowlick, niblick, public, cyclic, suslik (Eurasian ground squirrel), shashlik (kebab), bootlick, formic (relating to ants), gnomic (relating to aphorisms), bromic (containing bromine), chromic (containing chromium), sphygmic (relating to the pulse), seismic, cosmic, dornick (heavy cloth), runic, Munich, Punic, tunic, picnic, pyknic (having broad squat build), strychnic (relating to strychnine), splanchnic (relating to abdominal organs), Chetnik (Serbian nationalist), beatnik, sputnik, ethnic, epic, unpick, aspic, toothpick, baric (relating to atmospheric pressure), hayrick, xeric (growing in dry conditions), fabric, airbrick, firebrick, rubric, Kubrick (US film director), redbrick, cambric, hydric (containing hydrogen), quadric (maths term), baldric (sash for carrying sword), Ugric (language group), Cymric (Welsh language), cupric (containing copper), pinprick, citric, vitric (relating to glass), nitric, gastric, carsick, basic, airsick, seasick, calcic (containing calcium), homesick, brainsick, heartsick, lovesick, muzhik (Russian peasant), quartic (maths term), deictic (logic term), Celtic, Baltic, haptic (relating to touch), caustic, fustic (tree yielding yellow dye), rustic, crabstick (crab-apple stick), matchstick, swordstick, pigstick (hunt wild boar), maulstick (artist's hand-steadying stick), drumstick, broomstick, greenstick, nonstick, unstick, chapstick (*US* lip salve), slapstick, dipstick, lipstick, ethic, Gothic, Sothic (relating to Sirius), Slavic, Narvik (Norwegian port), pelvic, Lerwick (Scottish town), Brunswick, Keswick, physic, music.

ichthyic (relating to fishes), syllabic, amoebic, acerbic (bitter), Arabic, alembic, anarchic, druidic, bromidic (dull), acidic, fatidic (prophetic), heraldic, malefic, benefic, lethargic, neuralgic, nephralgic, gastralgic, arthralgic, nostalgic, pilgarlic (*Dialect* pitiful person), pashalik (region governed by pasha), catholic, Catholic, republic, acyclic

(chemistry term), bicyclic (forming two circles), ophthalmic, orgasmic, Adonic (type of verse line), arsenic, Dubrovnik, Olympic, epeiric (relating to continental drift), oneiric (relating to dreams), Frederick, bishopric, undertrick (bridge term), gastrotrich (minute aquatic animal), overtrick (bridge term), electric, dioptric, digastric (jaw muscle), silicic (containing silicon), banausic (utilitarian), Tungusic (language group), forensic, intrinsic, extrinsic, cathartic (purgative), elenctic (logic term), acoustic, monostich (single-line poem), tetrastich (four-line poem), pentastich (five-line poem), hexastich (six-line poem), fiddlestick, candlestick, singlestick (wooden sword-substitute), alethic (logic term), helminthic (relating to parasitic worms), Reykjavik, bailiwick, candlewick, dyslexic.

orthorhombic (crystallography term), demagogic, cataclysmic, microcosmic, polytechnic, pyrotechnic (relating to fireworks), archbishopric, dielectric (physics term), pneumogastric (anatomy term), geodesic (maths term), anthelmintic (substance destroying intestinal worms), anacoustic (soundless), ataraxic (calming), analgesic, metaphysic.

polysyllabic, monosyllabic, turbo-electric, thermoelectric (physics term), hydroelectric, isoelectric (having same electric potential), photoelectric, onomatopoeic.

38.1
laic, archaic, trochaic (verse form), Alcaic (verse form), Judaic, Altaic (language group), voltaic, prosaic, mosaic, formulaic, Ptolemaic, Aramaic, Pharisaic, apotropaic (preventing evil), deoxyribonucleic.

38.1.1
Hebraic, algebraic.

38.2

stoic, echoic, heroic, anechoic, amphichroic (producing two colours), polyzoic (zoology term), epizoic (zoology term), Eozoic, Neozoic, holozoic (biology term), Cenozoic, saprozoic (biology term), Mesozoic, entozoic (living inside an animal), cryptozoic (living in dark places), Palaeozoic.

38.3

phobic, strobic (spinning), aerobic (requiring oxygen), xenophobic (afraid of foreigners), aerophobic (afraid of draughts), acrophobic (afraid of heights), necrophobic (afraid of death), hydrophobic, claustrophobic, anaerobic (not requiring oxygen), agoraphobic.

38.4

cubic, pubic, cherubic.

38.5

iambic (metrical foot), galliambic (verse metre), dithyrambic (passionately eloquent).

38.6

Bacchic, Noachic (relating to Noah), stomachic.

38.7

Chadic (language group), dyadic (twofold), dryadic, nomadic, tornadic, faradic (physics term), sporadic.

38.8

comedic (relating to comedy), logaoedic (verse form), orthopaedic, encyclopedic.

38.9

iodic (containing iodine), melodic, psalmodic, spasmodic, synodic, parodic, rhapsodic, periodic, episodic, aperiodic (at irregular intervals), antispasmodic.

38.10

scandic (containing the element scandium), Icelandic.

38.11

[further rhymes may be derived from 16.90.2 and 158.1]

graphic, traffic, Sapphic (verse form), edaphic (relating to soil), seraphic, telegraphic, epigraphic, pornographic, photographic, epitaphic.

38.12

deific (godlike), morbific (causing disease), prolific, omnific, horrific, febrific (causing fever), specific, Pacific, pacific, calcific (forming lime), conspecific (within the same species), transpacific, beatific, scientific, hieroglyphic, unscientific, stereospecific (chemistry term).

38.12.1

terrific, sudorific (causing sweating), calorific (relating to heat), colorific (relating to colour), honorific, vaporific (producing vapour), soporific.

38.13

trophic (relating to nutrition), strophic (poetry term), eutrophic (ecology term), atrophic, polytrophic (biology term), autotrophic (biology term), prototrophic (biology term), geostrophic (meteorology term), apostrophic, catastrophic, philosophic, oligotrophic (ecology term), heterotrophic (biology term).

38.14

Orphic (mysterious), geomorphic (concerning the earth's surface), endomorphic (having heavy build), monomorphic (having only one form), mesomorphic (having muscular build), metamorphic, protomorphic (primitive), ectomorphic (having thin build), theriomorphic (depicted in animal form), anthropomorphic (depicted in human form), heteromorphic (having different forms).

38.15

magic, tragic, pelagic (relating to open sea), haemorrhagic, anthropophagic (cannibalistic), archipelagic.

38.16

allergic, anergic (lacking energy), lysergic (type of acid), endoergic (energy-absorbing), exoergic (energy-emitting), metallurgic, cholinergic (biology term), adrenergic (biology term).

38.17
strategic, hemiplegic, quadriplegic, paraplegic.

38.18
logic, choplogic, pedagogic, hypnagogic (psychology term).

38.19
Alec, phallic, Gallic, salic (having high silica content), vocalic (relating to a vowel), alkalic (having high alkali content), medallic, cephalic (relating to the head), Uralic (language group), smart aleck, prevocalic (coming before a vowel), encephalic (relating to the brain), intervocalic (between vowels).

38.19.1
italic, metallic, bimetallic, nonmetallic, genitalic.

38.20
melic (meant to be sung), relic, telic (purposeful), nickelic, Goidelic (language group), angelic, Gadhelic (Gaelic language), scalpellic, psychedelic, philatelic.

38.21
killick (small stone anchor), idyllic, Menelik (Abyssinian emperor), vanillic (relating to vanilla), Cyrillic, acrylic, cresylic (relating to creosote), dactylic (metrical foot), ethylic, methylic, basilic (vein in arm), lyophilic (chemistry term), cryophilic (thriving at low temperatures), zoophilic (fond of animals), haemophilic, thermophilic (thriving in warm conditions), lipophilic (chemistry term), hydrophilic (chemistry term).

38.22
colic, rollick, frolic, Aeolic (ancient Greek dialect), carbolic, ecbolic (inducing labour or abortion), embolic, symbolic, bucolic, Mongolic, petrolic (relating to petroleum), systolic, vitriolic, diabolic, anabolic, hyperbolic, parabolic, catabolic, metabolic, melancholic, hypergolic (spontaneously flammable), alcoholic, diastolic, apostolic.

38.23
aulic (relating to royal court), hydraulic.

38.24
gamic (biology term), agamic (biology term), Islamic, dynamic, ceramic, balsamic, potamic (relating to rivers), panoramic, thermodynamic, aerodynamic, hydrodynamic (physics term), isodynamic (having equal force).

38.25
alchemic, pandemic (widespread epidemic), endemic, polemic, Moslemic, totemic, systemic, polydemic (ecology term), epidemic, academic.

38.26
spermic, endermic (absorbed through skin), taxidermic, hypodermic, diathermic (medical term), endothermic (chemistry term), photothermic (of light and heat), exothermic (chemistry term).

38.27
haemic (relating to blood), anaemic, phonemic (relating to speech sounds), racemic (chemistry term), epistemic (relating to knowledge).

38.28
gimmick, mimic, acronymic, metronymic (relating to maternal name), patronymic.

38.29
comic, syndromic, atomic, entomic (relating to insects), pentomic (dividing into five groups), tragicomic, diatomic (containing two atoms), triatomic (containing three atoms), subatomic, monatomic (containing one atom), physiognomic, intra-atomic, interatomic.

38.29.1
economic, metronomic, astronomic, gastronomic, autonomic (occurring involuntarily), taxonomic, uneconomic, socioeconomic.

38.30
rhythmic, eurhythmic (having pleasing rhythm), logarithmic, isorhythmic (musical term).

38.31
manic, panic, tannic, stannic (containing tin), mechanic, volcanic, Sudanic (language group), organic, Brahmanic, Germanic, tympanic, Hispanic, uranic (containing uranium), Britannic, titanic, satanic, tetanic, sultanic, galvanic, homorganic (linguistics term), inorganic, aldermanic, Alemannic (language group), talismanic, aeromechanic.

38.31.1
messianic (relating to the Messiah), oceanic, suboceanic, transoceanic.

38.32
genic (relating to a gene), splenic (relating to the spleen), phrenic (relating to the diaphragm), sthenic (energetic and strong), sphenic (wedge-shaped), eugenic, Hellenic, asthenic (weak), telegenic (looking good on television), oxygenic, schizophrenic, Saracenic, callisthenic.

38.32.1
myogenic (muscle-forming), psychogenic, oncogenic (tumour-forming), typhogenic (causing typhoid), allergenic, chromogenic (colour-producing), pyrogenic (heat-producing), neurogenic (of nervous origin), androgenic, oestrogenic, allergenic, phytogenic (obtained from plants), photogenic, lactogenic, cryptogenic (of unknown origin), pathogenic, orthogenic (medical term), toxicogenic, immunogenic, hysterogenic, radiogenic (caused by radioactive decay), audiogenic (caused by sound), cariogenic (producing tooth decay),

erotogenic (erogenous), teratogenic (causing fetal deformity).

38.32.1.1
carcinogenic, hallucinogenic.

38.33
scenic, hygienic, irenic (conciliatory), axenic (uncontaminated).

38.34
Finnic (language group), clinic, cynic, rabbinic, albinic, triclinic (crystallography term), Brahminic, Dominic, actinic (denoting type of radiation), succinic (relating to amber), kinnikinnick (mixture for smoking), polyclinic (general hospital), monoclinic (crystallography term), histaminic, nicotinic, haematinic (substance stimulating haemoglobin production), diactinic (physics term).

38.35
conic, phonic, clonic (medical term), chronic, sonic, tonic.

ionic, Ionic, bionic, thionic (relating to sulphur), carbonic, bubonic, iconic, laconic, draconic, obconic (cone-shaped), sardonic, typhonic, euphonic, symphonic, colonic, cyclonic, harmonic, sermonic, demonic, mnemonic, pneumonic, pulmonic, Pharaonic, ironic, Byronic, moronic, vibronic (physics term), synchronic (linguistics term), subsonic, transonic (around the sound barrier), atonic (unstressed), plutonic (geology term), Teutonic, subtonic (musical note), tectonic, planktonic, Miltonic, syntonic (psychology term), gnathonic (deceitfully flattering), Brythonic (language group), pythonic, Slavonic, ozonic.

polyconic (maths term), aniconic (forbidding idol worship), telephonic, polyphonic (musical term), isogonic (maths term), philharmonic, enharmonic (musical term), nonharmonic, geoponic (relating to agricultural science), macaronic (type of verse), diachronic (linguistics term), anachronic (out of date), electronic.

anticyclonic, architectonic (relating to architectural qualities), geotectonic (relating to earth's crust), microelectronic.

38.35.1
thermionic (physics term), embryonic, histrionic, avionic, chameleonic, Napoleonic.

38.35.2
aphonic (voiceless), diaphonic (musical term), megaphonic, xylophonic, homophonic (having identical pronunciation), monophonic, microphonic, quadraphonic, saxophonic, radiophonic, stereophonic, dodecaphonic (musical term).

38.35.3
ammonic, Solomonic, pathognomonic (indicating a particular disease).

38.35.4
masonic, freemasonic, supersonic, infrasonic (below frequency of sound), ultrasonic.

38.35.5
Platonic, diatonic (musical term), hypotonic (lacking tension), hypertonic (having high tension), supertonic (musical note), isotonic (having equal tension), phototonic (responding to light), pentatonic (musical term).

38.36
philippic (speech of bitter denunciation), polytypic (having several different types), monotypic (having only one type), heterotypic (biology term), homeotypic (biology term), stereotypic.

38.37
tropic, topic, myopic, metopic (relating to the forehead), ectopic, entopic (in normal position), Ethiopic, telescopic, periscopic, eurytropic (ecology term), isentropic (physics term), isotopic, radioisotopic.

38.37.1 [further rhymes may be derived from 16.254.2 and 278.1]
stroboscopic, macroscopic, microscopic, hygroscopic (absorbing moisture from air), orthoscopic (relating to normal vision), stereoscopic, kaleidoscopic.

38.37.2
vagotropic (affecting the vagus nerve), allotropic (existing in several forms), stenotropic (ecology term), inotropic (affecting muscle contraction), hydrotropic (growing towards water), phototropic (growing towards light), thixotropic (becoming thinner when stirred), heliotropic (growing towards sunlight).

38.37.3
philanthropic, misanthropic, palaeanthropic (relating to early man), neoanthropic (resembling modern man), therianthropic (part animal, part human).

38.38
baric (relating to atmospheric pressure), daric (ancient Persian coin), Garrick, skerrick (US small fragment), stearic (relating to suet), barbaric, Pindaric (type of ode), margaric (resembling pearl), Amharic (Ethiopian official language), tartaric, Balearic, centrobaric (of centre of gravity), isobaric, hyperbaric (relating to high pressures).

38.39
Eric, Berwick, skerrick (US small fragment), derrick, Derek, ferric, cleric, steric (chemistry term), valeric (relating to valerian), Homeric, numeric, mesmeric, dineric (chemistry term), generic, glyceric (containing glycerol), enteric, hysteric, hemispheric, atmospheric, stratospheric, polymeric, poromeric (permeable to water vapour), esoteric, exoteric (comprehensible), amphoteric (chemistry term), isosteric (chemistry term), alphanumeric, gastroenteric.

38.40
lyric, pyrrhic, vampiric, empiric, satiric, satyric, panegyric (speech of praise).

38.41
choric (relating to a chorus), Doric (architectural term), Warwick, euphoric, camphoric, phosphoric, caloric, folkloric, historic, meteoric, pyrophoric (igniting spontaneously), semaphoric, metaphoric, allegoric, categoric, prehistoric, phantasmagoric.

38.42
auric (containing gold), boric, chloric, fluoric (relating to fluorine), hydrochloric.

38.43
Rurik (Scandinavian Viking leader), uric, Zürich, mercuric, sulphuric, telluric (terrestrial).

38.44
agaric, Alaric (king of the Visigoths), choleric, turmeric, limerick, Limerick, rhetoric, maverick, Theodoric (king of the Ostrogoths), Ermanaric (king of the Ostrogoths), climacteric.

38.45
Patrick, iatric (relating to medicine), Kirkpatrick, sympatric (biology term), Downpatrick (Irish town), psychiatric, paediatric, geriatric, allopatric (biology term).

38.46 [further rhymes may be derived from **16.285.2** and **17.342.3**]
metric, dimetric (crystallography term), trimetric (relating to verse line), obstetric, asymmetric, bisymmetric, geometric, diametric, kilometric, barometric, isometric.

38.47
centric, acentric, concentric, eccentric, theocentric (theology term), geocentric (having earth at centre), endocentric (linguistics term), egocentric, homocentric (having the same centre), exocentric (linguistics term).

38.48
classic, Liassic, Triassic, thalassic (relating to the sea), thoracic, Jurassic, boracic.

38.49
Attic, attic, batik, phatic (relating to social conversation), static, vatic (relating to a prophet).

sciatic, emphatic, lymphatic, villatic (rustic), spermatic, haematic, climatic, traumatic, komatik (Eskimo sledge), somatic (relating to the body), stomatic (relating to the mouth), pneumatic, rheumatic, magmatic, pragmatic, phlegmatic, dogmatic, dalmatic (tunic-like vestment), asthmatic, Carnatic (region of India), venatic, hepatic, aquatic, erratic, piratic, Socratic, quadratic, astatic (unstable), eustatic (geology term), ecstatic, sylvatic (growing in a wood).

Eleatic (school of philosophy), pancreatic, Adriatic, mydriatic (causing pupil dilation), Hanseatic, Asiatic, acrobatic, aliphatic (chemistry term), subaquatic, hieratic (relating to priests), operatic, biquadratic (maths term), antistatic.

proceleusmatic (metrical foot), semi-aquatic, idiosyncratic.

38.49.1
schematic, nematic (chemistry term), sematic (zoology term), thematic, dilemmatic, cinematic, systematic, episematic (zoology term), aposematic (zoology term), athematic (musical term), unsystematic.

38.49.2
chromatic, dramatic, problematic, emblematic, diplomatic, aromatic, achromatic (without colour), dichromatic (having only two colours), trichromatic (relating to three colours), programmatic, automatic, symptomatic, idiomatic, axiomatic (self-evident), iconomatic (representing sounds with pictures), polychromatic, monochro-

matic, apochromatic (physics term), melodramatic, epigrammatic, diagrammatic, anagrammatic, monogrammatic, psychosomatic, asymptomatic, semiautomatic.

38.49.3
stigmatic, enigmatic, astigmatic, paradigmatic (linguistics term), anastigmatic.

38.49.4
prismatic, schismatic, melismatic (musical term), numismatic, charismatic.

38.49.5
fanatic, morganatic, aplanatic (physics term).

38.49.6 [further rhymes may be derived from 16.307.5]
leucocratic (geology term), democratic, Hippocratic, bureaucratic, mesocratic (geology term), autocratic, plutocratic, aristocratic.

38.49.7
geostatic (geology term), haemostatic (stopping blood flow), thermostatic, hypostatic, gyrostatic (concerned with rotating bodies), hydrostatic (physics term), electrostatic.

38.50
metic (ancient Greek alien), thetic (relating to metrical stress).

hebetic (relating to puberty), eidetic (psychology term), syndetic (linguistics term), prophetic, balletic, phyletic (biology term), athletic, hermetic, emetic, mimetic (imitative), cosmetic, tonetic (linguistics term), magnetic, limnetic (ecology term), pyretic (relating to fever), uretic (relating to urine), ascetic, enthetic (medical term), synthetic, aesthetic, prosthetic, Helvetic (Swiss).

geodetic (geography term), asyndetic (without cross references), exegetic (explanatory), homiletic (relating to a sermon), arithmetic, apyretic (without fe-

ver), diuretic, dietetic, parenthetic, anaesthetic.

antimagnetic, thermomagnetic (physics term), gyromagnetic (physics term), isomagnetic (having equal magnetic force), antipyretic (preventing fever), diaphoretic (causing perspiration), peripatetic, polysynthetic (linguistics term), photosynthetic.

galactopoietic (inducing milk production), electromagnetic.

38.50.1
noetic (relating to the mind), poetic, dianoetic (relating to thought).

38.50.2
diabetic, alphabetic, analphabetic.

38.50.3
energetic, synergetic (acting together), apologetic.

38.50.4
kinetic, phenetic (biology term), genetic, splenetic, frenetic, Venetic (ancient Italian language), telekinetic, hydrokinetic (relating to moving fluids), autokinetic (self-moving), pathogenetic (relating to disease).

38.50.5
phonetic, cybernetic.

38.50.6
bathetic, pathetic, nomothetic (giving laws), apathetic, empathetic, sympathetic, antipathetic, parasympathetic.

38.51
Rhaetic (geology term), cretic (metrical foot), acetic.

38.52
lytic (biology term), clitic (unstressed), critic.

phlebitic, rachitic (having rickets), trachytic (geology term), bronchitic, mephitic (poisonous), graphitic, politic, proclitic (linguistics term), enclitic (linguistics term), Hamitic (language group), Semitic, Sinitic (language group), granitic, ncritic (ecology term), Sanskritic, nephritic (relating to the kidneys), Negritic (relating to Negroes), arthritic, Cushitic (language group).

Jesuitic, troglodytic, holophytic (biology term), meningitic, laryngitic, syphilitic, tonsillitic, impolitic, anaclitic (psychology term), stalagmitic, porphyritic (geology term), diacritic, stalactitic.

hermaphroditic, anti-Semitic, Protosemitic (language group), osteoarthritic.

38.52.1
oolitic, thermolytic (relating to heat loss), analytic, paralytic, hydrolytic (chemistry term), catalytic, electrolytic, sympatholytic (inhibiting nerve impulses), bacteriolytic (destroying bacteria), psychoanalytic.

38.52.2
sybaritic, Ugaritic (extinct Semitic language), Himyaritic (language group), meteoritic.

38.52.3
lymphocytic, parasitic, anthracitic, erythrocytic, semiparasitic.

38.53
glottic (relating to the tongue), chaotic, thrombotic, narcotic, mycotic (relating to fungal infections), psychotic, aphotic (growing without light), Nilotic (relating to the Nile), demotic (of the common people), zymotic (relating to fermentation), osmotic, nepotic, despotic, sclerotic, erotic, cirrhotic, neurotic, parotic (situated near the ear), necrotic (relating to dead tissue), dicrotic (having a double pulse), tricrotic (having a triple pulse), quixotic, azotic (relating to nitrogen), exotic.

idiotic, symbiotic (mutually dependent), semiotic (relating to symbols), amniotic, patriotic, enzootic (veterinary term), creosotic, asymptotic.

epizootic (veterinary term), psychoneurotic.

38.53.1
biotic (relating to living organisms), meiotic, amphibiotic (zoology term), antibiotic, macrobiotic (relating to vegetarian diet).

38.53.2
hypnotic, posthypnotic, agrypnotic (relating to insomnia), autohypnotic.

38.54
aortic, astronautic.

38.55
otic (relating to the ear), photic (relating to light), lotic (inhabiting flowing water), rhotic (linguistics term), euphotic (ecology term), periotic (around the ear).

38.56
maieutic (philosophy term), scorbutic, propaedeutic (preparation before further study), hermeneutic (relating to biblical interpretation), therapeutic, antiscorbutic, radiotherapeutic.

38.57
lunatic, heretic, arithmetic.

38.58
lactic, tactic, didactic, galactic, climactic, atactic (chemistry term), syntactic, prophylactic, parallactic (relating to parallax), ataractic (tranquillizing), chiropractic, anaphylactic, extragalactic, anticlimactic, heliotactic (moving towards sunlight).

38.59
arctic, Nearctic (zoogeographical term), subarctic, Holarctic (zoogeographical term), Antarctic, subantarctic.

38.60
hectic, smectic (chemistry term), eclectic, dyslectic, orectic (relating to desire), eutectic (physics term), cathectic (psychology term), dialectic, catalectic (relating to verse line), apoplectic.

38.61
systaltic (relating to heartbeat), peristaltic.

38.62
antic, mantic (relating to prophecy), frantic, pedantic, gigantic, Atlantic, semantic, romantic, sycophantic, transatlantic.

38.63
lentic (inhabiting still water), argentic (containing silver), crescentic, authentic.

38.64
Pontic (of the Black Sea), quantic (maths term), deontic (logic term), orthodontic.

38.65
sceptic, peptic, septic, dyspeptic, aseptic, epileptic, analeptic (restorative drug), antiseptic.

38.66
diptych, glyptic (relating to engraving), cryptic, triptych, styptic, elliptic, polyptych (altarpiece), ecliptic, procryptic (protectively coloured), apocalyptic.

38.67
optic, Coptic (language group), bioptic, panoptic (taking in all viewpoints), synoptic, orthoptic (relating to binocular vision).

38.68
clastic (geology term), plastic, mastic (aromatic resin), spastic, drastic.

bombastic, sarcastic, stochastic (statistics term), elastic, scholastic, synclastic (maths term), aplastic, euplastic (healing quickly), dynastic, monastic, gymnastic, fantastic, doxastic (logic term).

inelastic, anticlastic (maths term), thromboplastic (forming a blood clot), thermoplastic (becoming soft when heated), anaplastic (relating to plastic surgery), ceroplastic (relating to wax-modelling), esemplastic (unifying), onomastic (relating to proper names),

epispastic (producing a blister), hudibrastic (mock-heroic), periphrastic (circumlocutory).

interscholastic, iconoclastic.

38.68.1
orgiastic, ecclesiastic, enthusiastic.

38.69
majestic, telestich (short poem), domestic, agrestic (rural), isopiestic (having equal atmospheric pressure).

38.70 [further rhymes may be derived from 242.35]
distich (two-line poem), fistic (relating to boxing), mystic, tristich (three-line poem), cystic.

sadistic, sophistic, stylistic, simplistic, hemistich (half line of verse), eristic (logic term), floristic, touristic, heuristic (helping to learn), juristic, patristic (relating to Church Fathers), artistic, autistic, linguistic.

atheistic, egoistic, jingoistic, altruistic, casuistic, masochistic, Hellenistic (relating to Greek civilization), chauvinistic, communistic, narcissistic, inartistic.

evangelistic, relativistic, sadomasochistic.

38.70.1
logistic, phlogistic (relating to inflammation), syllogistic, eulogistic, synergistic (acting together), antiphlogistic (alleviating inflammation).

38.70.2
ballistic, symbolistic, journalistic, socialistic, fatalistic, novelistic, cannibalistic, nationalistic, rationalistic, naturalistic, commercialistic, capitalistic, sensationalistic, individualistic.

38.70.2.1
realistic, idealistic, surrealistic, materialistic.

38.70.3
euphemistic, pessimistic, optimistic.

38.70.4

mechanistic, modernistic, agonistic (combative), antagonistic, anachronistic, impressionistic.

38.70.5

meristic (biology term), futuristic, aphoristic, humoristic, terroristic, voyeuristic, characteristic, behaviouristic.

38.70.6

statistic, egotistic, chrematistic (relating to money-making).

38.71

gnostic, agnostic, prognostic, acrostic, diagnostic.

38.72

gnathic (relating to the jaw), spathic (resembling the mineral spar), empathic, photobathic (biology term), telepathic, psychopathic, allopathic, idiopathic (medical term), homeopathic, osteopathic, naturopathic.

38.73

lithic (made of stone), ornithic (relating to birds), Eolithic, Neolithic, chalcolithic (archaeology term), megalithic, monolithic, Mesolithic, protolithic (of the Stone Age), Palaeolithic, heliolithic (of sun-worshipping civilization).

38.74

civic, Bolshevik, Menshevik.

38.75

toxic, hypoxic (relating to oxygen deficiency), radiotoxic.

39 -ike

bike, dyke, fyke (*US* fishing net), hike, haik (Arabian outer garment), like, mike, pike, spike, Reich, shrike, trike, strike, psych, sike (*Dialect* small stream), tyke.

Vandyke, Klondike, Thorndike, hitchhike, hairlike, warlike, alike, snakelike, suchlike, godlike, swordlike, childlike, lifelike, shell-like, dreamlike, manlike, swanlike, unlike, apelike, glasslike, cat-like, antlike, Christlike, ghostlike, van Eyck, garpike (freshwater fish), turnpike, handspike (metal lever), alsike (Eurasian clover).

motorbike, ladylike, workmanlike, sportsmanlike.

39.1

dislike, businesslike.

40 -ock

och, bock (beer), cock, chock (wooden wedge), dock, doc, Jock, hock, lock, lough, loch, bloc, block, clock, flock, schlock (*US* inferior goods), mock, smock, knock, nock (notch on arrow), pock, Spock, rock, roc, brock (badger), broch (Scottish circular tower), crock, frock, sock, shock, stock, wok.

blaubok (large antelope), sjambok (heavy whip), Lombok (Indonesian island), steinbok (small antelope), springbok, grysbok (small antelope), gemsbok (large antelope), haycock (small pile of hay), Leacock (Canadian humorist), peacock, seacock, gorcock (male red grouse), moorcock, bibcock (tap with bent nozzle), blackcock (male black grouse), spatchcock, Hitchcock, spitchcock, pinchcock (clamp compressing rubber tube), woodcock, Alcock (British aviator), ball cock, gamecock (fighting cock), Hancock, turncock (Water Authority official), Bangkok, stopcock, petcock (valve on steam boiler), Médoc, burdock, Murdoch, Kodok (Sudanese town), Van Gogh, forehock, Mohock (18th-century aristocratic ruffian), ad hoc, charlock, Belloc, airlock, Shylock, oarlock, forelock, warlock, Moloch, breechblock (metal block in firearm), roadblock, picklock (person who picks locks), o'clock, padlock, deadlock, headlock (wrestling hold), wedlock, elflock (tangled lock of hair), daglock (dung-encrusted sheep's wool), hemlock, unlock, gunlock, Matlock, fetlock, wristlock (wrestling hold), have-lock (protective cap cover), lovelock (lock of hair), Enoch, kapok, epoch, Duroc (US breed of pig), baroque, pibroch, bedrock, defrock, unfrock, shamrock, rimrock (geology term), traprock (fine-grained rock), windsock, foreshock (*US* minor earthquake), Bartók, ticktock, Gangtok (Indian city), diestock (screw-cutting tool), nostoc (blue-green alga), Rostock (East German port), Vostok (Russian spacecraft), headstock (part of machine tool), bloodstock, tailstock (part of machine tool), drillstock (part of machine tool), penstock (water channel), linstock, gunstock, whipstock (whip handle), bitstock (handle of drilling tool), rootstock, livestock.

· manioc (tropical plant), Antioch, poppycock, weathercock, monocoque (car or aircraft body), shuttlecock, kazachok (Russian folk dance), hollyhock, interlock, antiknock (petrol additive), monadnock (hill of hard rock), aftershock, alpenstock, Eniwetok (Pacific atoll).

41 -ork
auk, orc (whale), balk, baulk (billiards term), cork, Cork, calk (metal spike on shoe), caulk (fill cracks), chalk, fork, gawk (clumsy person), hawk, nork (*Austral* female breast), pork, squawk, talk, torque, stalk, stork, walk, York.

uncork, Dundalk (Irish town), hayfork, pitchfork, Mohawk, goshawk, nighthawk, newshawk (*US* newspaper reporter), cakewalk, shoptalk, crosstalk, leafstalk, beanstalk, cornstalk (*Austral* native Australian), jaywalk, sidewalk, boardwalk (*US* wooden promenade), sleepwalk, sheepwalk (land for sheep-grazing), ropewalk (narrow rope-making passage), spacewalk, crosswalk (*US* pedestrian crossing), catwalk.

sparrowhawk, tomahawk.

42 -oke
oak, coke, choke, folk, joke, hoke (overact), bloke, cloak, moke, smoke, poke, spoke, roque (US game resembling croquet), broke, croak, stroke, soak, soke (former legal term), toque, stoke, woke, yoke, yolk.

decoke, workfolk, menfolk, tradesfolk, kinsfolk, slowpoke (*US* slowcoach), mopoke (Australian owl), bespoke, keystroke, sidestroke, handstroke (bell-ringing term), sunstroke, upstroke, heatstroke, breaststroke, backstroke, evoke, revoke, provoke, invoke, convoke, awoke, unyoke.

artichoke, okey-doke, gentlefolk, womenfolk, Roanoke (US island), masterstroke, Basingstoke.

43 -uck
buck, chuck, duck, fuck, guck (slimy substance), luck, cluck, pluck, muck, puck, ruck, cruck (roof timber), truck, struck, suck, shuck, tuck, stuck, yuk.

roebuck, blackbuck (Indian antelope), reedbuck (African antelope), jumbuck, bushbuck (small African antelope), woodchuck, shelduck, mukluk (Eskimo's sealskin boot), potluck, amok, Kalmuck (Mongoloid people), dumbstruck, moonstruck, untuck, unstuck.

waterbuck (African antelope), chempaduk (Malaysian fruit tree), mallemuck (sea bird), thunderstruck.

44 -ook
book, cook, doek (African headscarf), hook, look, nook, schnook (*US* stupid person), rook, brook, crook, sook (coward), shook, took.

daybook, flybook (angler's case for flies), boobook (Australian owl), bluebook (British government publication), chequebook, workbook, cookbook, bankbook, sketchbook, studbook, handbook, logbook, chapbook (book of popular ballads), scrapbook, passbook, notebook, textbook, Kirkuk (Iraqi city), billhook, unhook, grasshook (sickle), pothook, boathook, Windhoek (African city), taluk (Indian district), outlook, Sherbrooke (Canadian city), Pembroke, Innsbruck, forsook, nainsook (soft cotton fabric), partook, betook, mistook.

copybook, storybook, pocketbook, overcook, tenterhook, buttonhook (thin hooked instrument), overlook, gerenuk (African antelope), inglenook, Volapuk (artificial language), donnybrook (rowdy brawl), Alanbrooke (British field marshall), Bolingbroke, undertook, overtook.

44.1
Tobruk (Libyan port), Beaverbrook.

45 -uke
kook (*US* eccentric person), douc (Asian monkey), Luke, fluke, snook, spook, tuque (Canadian knitted cap), stook, duke, nuke, puke, chibouk (Turkish tobacco pipe), caoutchouc (rubber material), Seljuk (member of Turkish dynasty), Nanook, Chinook, Farouk, peruke (men's wig), rebuke, archduke, Mameluke (military Egyptian ruler), Pentateuch, Heptateuch, Hexateuch, gobbledegook, bashibazouk (19th-century Turkish soldier).

46 -'ck
Newark, Lubbock (Texan city), Southwark, haddock, paddock, shaddock (tropical fruit tree), piddock (mollusc), ruddock (*Dialect* robin), Norfolk, Suffolk, hillock, lilac, pollack (Atlantic fish), rowlock, mullock (*Dialect* mess), bullock, hammock, mammock (*Dialect* shred), hummock, stomach, bannock (Scottish cake), Cannock, Lanark, Greenock, jonnock (*Dialect* genuine), monarch, dunnock (hedge sparrow), eunuch, arrack (alcoholic spirit), barrack, carrack, borak (*Austral* non-

sense), cassock, hassock, tussock, mattock (agricultural tool), buttock, futtock (part of boat), havoc, bulwark, Isaac.

Habakkuk (Old Testament prophet), agalloch (tree yielding fragrant wood), Potomac, Kilmarnock, coronach (*Scot* dirge), laverock (*Dialect* skylark), Sarawak (Malaysian state).

elegiac, paranoiac.

47 -alk
calque (linguistics term), talc, catafalque (platform for coffin).

48 -elk
elk, spelk (*Dialect* wood splinter), whelk.

49 -ilk
ilk, bilk (thwart), milk, silk, Liebfraumilch, buttermilk.

50 -ulk
bulk, skulk, hulk, sulk.

51 -ank
ankh (symbolic cross), bank, banc (legal term), dank, hank, lank, blank, clank, flank, plank, spank, rank, crank, drank, franc, frank, Frank, prank, shrank, sank, shank, tank, stank, thank, wank, swank, yank, Yank.

claybank (*US* dull brownish colour), Clydebank, sandbank, embank, outflank, gangplank, outrank, Cruickshank, redshank (red-stemmed plant), scrimshank (*Slang* shirk work), greenshank (European shore bird), sheepshank.

mountebank, antitank.

52 -ink
ink, kink, skink (tropical lizard), chink, dink (*Scot* neat), fink, gink, jink, link, blink, clink, slink, mink, pink, rink, brink, drink, prink, shrink, sink, sync,

stink, think, wink, swink (*Dialect* to toil), twink, zinc.

ratfink, snowblink (luminosity reflected from snow), iceblink (luminosity reflected from ice), Haitink (Dutch conductor), Bentinck (governor-general of India), rethink, unthink, outthink, hoodwink.

bobolink (US songbird), Maeterlinck (Belgian poet), interlink, countersink, doublethink.

53 -onk
conk, conch, gonk, honk, clonk, plonk, cronk (*Austral* unsound), tonk (*Austral* effeminate man), stonk (bombard with artillery), honky-tonk.

54 -unk
bunk, skunk, chunk, dunk, funk, gunk (*Slang* slimy substance), junk, hunk, clunk, flunk, plunk (to pluck), slunk, monk, punk, spunk, drunk, shrunk, trunk, sunk, stunk, debunk, chipmunk, quidnunc (gossipmonger), preshrunk.

55 -ask
Basque, casque (helmet-like structure), hask (*Dialect* dry cough), Monegasque (citizen of Monaco).

56 -arsk
ask, bask, cask, flask, mask, masque, task, unmask, antimasque (grotesque dance), overtask.

57 -esk
desk, burlesque, Moresque (Moorish decoration), grotesque, Junoesque, statuesque, arabesque, Romanesque (architectural style), picaresque, picturesque, sculpturesque, humoresque.

58 -isk
bisque, disc, disk, risk, brisk, frisk, whisk, obelisk, basilisk (tropical lizard), odalisque (female slave), tamarisk (ornamental tree), asterisk.

59 -osk
bosk (small wood), mosque, kiosk, abelmosk (tropical plant).

60 -usk
Usk (British river), busk, dusk, husk, musk, rusk, brusque, tusk, subfusc (drab), cornhusk.

61 -'sk
mollusc, damask.

62 -atch
batch, catch, hatch, latch, match, natch, snatch, patch, cratch (rack for cattle fodder), scratch, thatch, crosshatch, nuthatch, unlatch, potlatch (American Indian ceremonial activity), rematch, mismatch, dispatch, crosspatch, detach, attach, Saguache (US mountain range).

63 -arch
arch, larch, march, March, parch, starch, frogmarch, routemarch, cornstarch, countermarch, overarch, Dedéagach (Greek port).

64 -etch
etch, ketch, sketch, fetch, lech, fletch (fit with a feather), wretch, retch, stretch, vetch, Dolmetsch (British musician), outstretch.

65 -erch
birch, church, lurch, smirch (to soil), perch, search, unchurch (excommunicate), Christchurch, besmirch, pikeperch (freshwater fish), surfperch (marine fish), research.

66 -eech
each, beach, beech, leech, leach, bleach, pleach (interlace shoots in hedge), peach, speech, reach, breach, breech, screech, preach, teach, horseleech (freshwater leech), impeach, forereach (nautical term), headreach (nau-

tical term), outreach, beseech, unteach, overreach.

67 -itch

itch, bitch, kitsch, ditch, fitch (polecat), hitch, flitch, mitch (*Dialect* play truant), niche, snitch, pitch, quitch (type of grass), rich, stitch, which, witch, switch, twitch.

cowitch (tropical climbing plant), Redditch, orache (herbaceous plant), eldritch (unearthly), enrich, ostrich, hemstitch, backstitch, bewitch, Ipswich, Prestwich, Northwich.

overpitch (cricket term), featherstitch, tsarevitch.

Shostakovich, Rostropovich, Mohorovičić (Yugoslav geologist).

68 -otch

botch, scotch, Scotch, blotch, splotch, notch, potch (*Austral* inferior opal), crotch, watch, swatch, hopscotch, topnotch, hotchpotch, dogwatch, stopwatch, wristwatch, deathwatch, butterscotch, overwatch.

69 -orch

scorch, nautch (traditional Indian dance), porch, torch, debauch, blowtorch.

70 -oach

coach, loach, poach, roach, broach, brooch, slowcoach, stagecoach, mailcoach, cockroach, encroach, reproach, approach, motorcoach.

71 -ouch

ouch, couch, slouch, pouch, crouch, grouch, vouch, debouch (move into larger space).

72 -utch

Kutch (former Indian state), cutch (resinous substance), Dutch, hutch, clutch, much, mutch (close-fitting linen

cap), smutch (to smudge), crutch, such, touch, declutch, nonesuch (flowering plant), retouch, insomuch, overmuch, inasmuch, forasmuch.

73 -ootch

butch, cootch (hiding place).

74 -ooch

hooch, mooch, smooch, pooch.

75 -elch

belch, squelch.

76 -ilch

filch, milch (milk-yielding), pilch (infant's outer garment), zilch.

77 -ulch

culch (base of oyster bed), gulch, mulch.

78 -anch

blanch, ranch, branch, stanch, carte blanche, disbranch, avalanche, anabranch (stream branching from river).

79 -ench

bench, blench (shy away), clench, quench, wrench, drench, French, trench, tench, stench, wench, workbench, retrench, entrench.

80 -inch

inch, chinch (*US* bedbug), finch, lynch, clinch, flinch, Minch (Atlantic channel off Scotland), pinch, squinch (supporting arch in tower), cinch, winch, chaffinch, hawfinch, goldfinch, bullfinch, greenfinch, grassfinch.

81 -ornch

haunch, launch, flaunch (slope around chimney top), paunch, craunch (*Dialect* crunch), staunch.

82 -unch

bunch, hunch, lunch, munch, punch, runch (flowering plant), brunch, crunch, scrunch, sarpanch (Indian village council leader), honeybunch.

83 -ad

ad, add, bad, bade, cad, scad (marine fish), Chad, dad, fad, gad, had, lad, clad, glad, plaid, mad, pad, rad (unit of absorbed radiation), brad (small nail), grad (*short for* graduate), trad, sad, shad, tad (*US* small boy).

forbade, Akkad (ancient Babylonian city), ecad (ecology term), cycad (tropical plant), caudad (towards the tail), Baghdad, granddad, egad, jihad (Islamic holy war), Mashhad (Iranian city), unclad, nomad, maenad (priestess of Bacchus), kneepad, footpad, Arad (Rumanian city), Conrad, tetrad (group of four), dorsad (towards the back), octad, pentad, heptad, hexad.

alidad (surveying instrument), Trinidad, aoudad (wild mountain sheep), Galahad, cephalad (towards the head), ironclad, superadd (add as extra), Petrograd, Stalingrad, Leningrad, Upanishad (ancient Hindu sacred book).

83.1

Iliad, chiliad (group of one thousand), Gilead, ennead (group of nine), gwyniad (freshwater fish), oread (Greek mountain nymph), bromeliad (fleshyleaved plant), Olympiad.

83.2

dyad (maths term), pleiad (talented group of seven), naiad, dryad, triad, Omayyad (caliph), jeremiad (long mournful lamentation), hamadryad (tree nymph).

83.3

gonad (sex organ), monad (philosophy term), trichomonad (microscopic parasitic animal).

84 -ard [also 1 + -ed]

bard, card, chard, guard, hard, lard, nard (aromatic plant), pard, Sade, sard (gemstone), shard, yard.

Liard (Canadian river), liard (former European coin), Fuad (Egyptian king), bombard, Jacquard (fabric with patterned weave), placard, scorecard, filecard, timecard, racecard, discard, falsecard (bridge term), postcard, Goddard, blackguard, rearguard, fireguard, Bogarde, Midgard (Norse mythological place), mudguard, safeguard, lifeguard, vanguard, Asgard (home of Norse gods), Utgard (Norse mythological place), coastguard, die-hard, blowhard (boastful person), ballade (verse form), mallard, foulard (soft light fabric), poulard (spayed hen), roulade, pomade (perfumed hair oil), chamade (former military signal), canard (rumour or hoax), Barnard, spikenard (aromatic Indian plant), Arpád (9th-century Magyar chieftain), Stoppard, charade, estrade (dais), brassard (identifying armband), pesade (dressage term), glissade (ballet step), façade, Hansard, mansard, petard, retard, ill-starred, noyade (execution by drowning), oeillade (suggestive glance), Riyadh (capital of Saudi Arabia), dooryard (*US* yard outside door), foreyard (nautical term), brickyard, dockyard, stockyard, junkyard, churchyard, kaleyard (*Scot* vegetable garden), steelyard, farmyard, barnyard, vineyard, boneyard, shipyard, courtyard, tiltyard (enclosed area for jousting), graveyard.

milliard (thousand million), Savoyard (native of Savoy), Kierkegaard, avant-garde, Abelard, interlard, communard (member of a commune), promenade, leotard, Kristianstad (Swedish town), timberyard, lumberyard, Montagnard (member of mountain people), camelopard (giraffe).

84.1
regard, bodyguard, disregard.

85 -ade [also 2 + -ed]
aide, aid, cade (juniper tree), fade, jade, hade (geology term), laid, lade (load cargo), blade, glade, maid, made, paid, spade, raid, braid, grade, trade, shade, staid, they'd, wade, suede.

arcade, decade, cockade, blockade, stockade, brocade, alcaide (Spanish castle commander), cascade, twayblade (orchid), creamlaid, inlaid, unlade (unload), barmaid, mermaid, remade, limeade, milkmaid, handmade, bondmaid (unmarried female slave), self-made, unmade, nursemaid, housemaid, bridesmaid, prepaid, well-paid, unpaid, postpaid, tirade, corrade (geology term), abrade, upbraid, afraid, Belgrade, downgrade, upgrade, comrade, torsade (ornamental twist on hat), crusade, cliché'd, eyeshade, sunshade, nightshade, pervade, evade, invade, unweighed, dissuade, persuade.

El Obeid (Sudanese city), Medicaid (*US* health assistance programme), barricade, autocade (*US* motorcade), motorcade, cavalcade, ambuscade (an ambush), alidade (surveyor's instrument), orangeade, Almohade (former Muslim ruler), Adelaide, defilade (military term), enfilade (military term), fusillade (rapid gunfire), accolade, escalade (scaling walls with ladders), underlaid, marmalade, phylloclade (leaflike plant stem), chambermaid, escapade, underpaid, overpaid, unafraid, overtrade, balustrade, rodomontade (boastful talk).

85.1
brigade, renegade.

85.2
grenade, pasquinade (satire), marinade, serenade, harlequinade.

85.3
carbonade, gasconade (boastful talk), dragonnade (persecution by dragoons), colonnade, esplanade, lemonade, cannonade, carronade (obsolete light cannon), cottonade (coarse fabric), gabionade (construction controlling water flow).

85.4
parade, masquerade.

85.5
degrade, tardigrade (minute segmented animal), taligrade (zoology term), saltigrade (moving by jumps), plantigrade (zoology term), centigrade, unguligrade (walking on hooves), digitigrade (walking on toes).

85.6
aggrade (geology term), retrograde, intergrade (biology term).

86 -ed
bed, dead, fed, head, lead, led, fled, sled, Med, sned (*Dialect* to prune), sped, red, read, redd (*Dialect* to tidy), bread, bred, dread, spread, shred, tread, thread, said, shed, ted, stead, wed, zed.

co-ed, seedbed, roadbed, childbed, embed, hotbed, deathbed, sheep-ked (parasitic fly), airhead (military term), stairhead, spearhead, sorehead (*US* peevish person), warhead, blackhead, blockhead, bulkhead, deadhead, redhead, Godhead, Roundhead, egghead, bighead, nailhead (decorative device), railhead (end of railway), wellhead, steelhead (Pacific trout), bullhead (a fish), drumhead, greenhead (male mallard), bonehead, springhead (source of stream), crosshead, sheepshead (Atlantic fish), Gateshead, cathead (nautical term), fathead, flathead (Pacific fish), pithead, Spithead, hothead, pothead (*Slang* cannabis user), gilthead (Atlantic fish), masthead, hogshead, unlead (printing term), misled, Ahmed, premed, biped, moped, beebread (food for bee larvae), purebred, lowbred, shewbread (Old Testament bread), sowbread (European plant), homebred, inbred, unbred, crispbread, crossbred, sweetbread, shortbread, well-read, unread, bespread, bedspread, widespread, outspread, re-tread, packthread, goldthread (US woodland plant), unthread, unsaid, snowshed (shelter over railway track), bloodshed, woodshed, oersted (unit in physics), bedstead, roadstead, farmstead, homestead, instead, Dyfed, Enzed (New Zealand).

underfed, overfed, knucklehead (foolish person), fiddlehead (nautical term), bufflehead (diving duck), shovelhead (common shark), Birkenhead, maidenhead, Maidenhead, woodenhead (stupid person), dragonhead (flowering plant), quadruped, infrared, underbred (of impure stock), gingerbread, thoroughbred, Ethelred, aforesaid, watershed, Holinshed, newlywed, Samoyed.

86.1
abed, flowerbed, slugabed, riverbed.

86.2
behead, Holyhead, sleepyhead, poppyhead.

86.3
bowhead (arctic whale), towhead (blond-haired person), arrowhead.

86.4
skinhead, pinhead, fountainhead.

86.5
ahead, go-ahead, timberhead (nautical term), Leatherhead, leatherhead (Australian songbird), rudderhead (nautical term), dunderhead, thunderhead (anvil-shaped cloud top), figurehead, loggerhead, hammerhead (shark), copperhead (venomous snake), letterhead, overhead.

86.6
aliped (having wing-like limbs), taliped (having a club foot), pinniped (having flipper-like limbs), fissiped (having separate toes), maxilliped (zoology term), pinnatiped (ornithology term).

87 -erd [also 3 + -ed]
urd (bean plant), bird, Byrd, curd, Kurd (nomadic Turkic people), furred, gird, heard, herd, surd, turd, third, word.

firebird, lyrebird, snowbird, bluebird, blackbird, puffbird, jailbird, rainbird, sunbird, songbird, lovebird, potsherd, begird (to surround), cowherd, swineherd, swanherd, unheard, goatherd, absurd, swearword, reword, byword, foreword, catchword, watchword, headword, password, crossword.

ladybird, whirlybird, friarbird, bowerbird, butcherbird, thunderbird, tailorbird, dollarbird, weaverbird, riflebird, wattlebird, mockingbird, hummingbird, undergird, overheard, undeterred, Mesa Verde (high plateau in Colorado), afterword (postscript), overword (repeated phrase or word).

88 -aird [also 4 + -ed]
Baird, laird, tow-haired, long-haired, short-haired, unaired, unrepaired, unprepared, unimpaired.

89 -eed [also 5 + -ed]
Bede, bead, deed, feed, heed, he'd, lead, lied (type of song), bleed, plead, mead, Mede, knead, need, speed, reed, read, Reid, breed, creed, screed, greed, cede, seed, she'd, steed, weed, we'd, swede, Swede, tweed, Tweed.

indeed, misdeed, handfeed, spoon-feed, fairlead (nautical term), nosebleed, misplead (plead incorrectly), mislead, knock-kneed, stampede, impede, airspeed, Godspeed, groundspeed, jerid (wooden javelin), inbreed, crossbreed, outbreed, proofread, Siegfried, agreed, lip-read, misread, sight-read, birdseed, allseed (plant producing many seeds), wormseed (plant producing medicinal seeds), moonseed (climbing plant), rapeseed, axseed (flowering plant), flaxseed, Jamshid (Persian mythological king), Flamsteed (English astronomer), mayweed, seaweed, fireweed, rockweed (seaweed growing on rocks), pokeweed, duckweed, milkweed, stinkweed, bindweed, pondweed, gulfweed (brown seaweed), ragweed, pigweed, hogweed, knapweed, knotweed, goutweed, accede, exceed, stickseed (plant producing prickly fruits), succeed.

underfeed, winterfeed, overfeed, invalid, interplead (legal term), Ganymede, Runnymede, copyread (*US* subedit), interbreed, beggarweed, waterweed, silverweed, cottonweed.

Harun al-Rashid (8th-century caliph), Berwick-upon-Tweed.

89.1
millipede, cirripede (marine animal), centipede, velocipede (early type of bicycle).

89.2
recede, precede, secede, aniseed, antecede.

89.3
proceed, supersede, retrocede (give back), intercede.

89.4
linseed, pumpkinseed (US fish).

89.5
concede, cottonseed.

89.6
chickweed, stickweed, colicweed.

89.7
thimbleweed, tumbleweed, bugleweed, pickerelweed.

90 -eerd [also 6 + -*ed*]
eared, beard, fyrd (Anglo-Saxon local militia), weird, greybeard (old man), Bluebeard, Blackbeard (English pirate), goatsbeard (plant with woolly stem), lop-eared.

91 -id [Also 16 + -*ed*. Further rhymes may be created by adding -*ed* to appropriate verbs and nouns.]
id, bid, kid, Kidd (Scottish pirate), skid, did, fid (nautical term), gid (disease of sheep), hid, lid, slid, mid, quid, squid, rid, grid, Sid.

sayyid (Muslim title), rabid, crabbed, turbid, verbid (linguistics term), morbid, Irbid (Jordanian town), outbid, naked, wicked, orchid, crooked, tailskid, wretched, bearded, voided (heraldic term), crowded, hooded, wooded, winded, minded, bonded, fronded, undid, wounded, outdid, aphid, syrphid (type of fly), bifid, trifid, jagged, ragged, cragged (*US* craggy), dogged, rugged, pongid (type of ape), aged, turgid, algid (chilly), masjid (Arab mosque), eyelid, cichlid (tropical fish), Euclid, skidlid, timid, humid, tumid, desmid (freshwater alga), phasmid (plant-eating insect), learned, honeyed, moneyed, rapid, sapid (having a pleasant taste), vapid, torpid, Cupid, stupid, limpid, vespid (wasplike), hispid (covered with bristles), cuspid (tooth having one point), liquid, varied, serried, storied, lurid, hurried, hybrid, acrid, sacred, Madrid, kindred, Alfred, hatred, putrid, blessed, cursed, cussed, muscid (type of fly), chalcid (tiny insect), El Cid, fancied, rancid, gifted, tufted, kilted, stilted, tinted, wonted, hunted, stunted, plastid (microscopic cell structure), waisted, frosted, worsted, Hampstead, avid, gravid, David, livid, vivid, ivied, Ovid, bovid, languid, pinguid (fatty or greasy), palsied, frenzied.

noctuid (nocturnal moth), half-naked, unheeded, unseeded, katydid, secluded, included, overdid, long-winded, high-minded, like-minded, broad-minded, quadrifid, multifid, three-legged, bow-legged, cross-legged, carangid (marine fish), nymphalid (brightly-coloured butterfly), annelid (segmented worm), pyralid (tropical moth), Ozalid (*Trademark*), Mohammed, serranid (marine fish), unlearned, hominid, cyprinid (freshwater fish), elapid (venomous snake), bicuspid, tricuspid, illiquid, satyrid (type of butterfly), unwearied, unhurried, dihybrid (genetics term), colubrid (type of snake), eupatrid (ancient Greek landowner), accursed, Abbasid (caliph of Muslim dynasty), assorted, undoubted, sure-footed, club-footed, flat-footed, hydatid (cyst containing tapeworm larva), bigoted, spermatid (immature sperm), chromatid (part of chromosome), propertied, impacted, unbolted, enchanted, unwanted, unwonted, unscripted, adopted, beloved.

disembodied, bloody-minded, narrow-minded, feeble-minded, single-minded, open-minded, prehominid (extinct man-like primate), tertium quid, scolopendrid (type of centipede), geometrid (type of moth), ill-assorted, self-inflicted, unrestricted, anabantid (spiny-finned fish), malimprinted, unadopted, Hemel Hempstead.

antherozoid (botany term), unreconstructed, isoniazid (crystalline compound).

91.1
Aeneid, scarabaeid.

91.2
tracheid (plant cell), tineid (type of moth), clupeid (type of fish), Nereid (Greek nymph), araneid (spider), saturniid (tropical moth), reduviid (type of bug), euphausiid (small shrimp-like animal).

91.3
Clwyd, fluid, druid, semifluid, superfluid (physics term).

91.4
forbid, underbid, carabid (dark-coloured beetle), overbid.

91.5
guarded, unguarded, retarded.

91.6
faded, gadid (marine fish), jaded, braided, unaided, unshaded, colonnaded.

91.7
leaded, wedded, bareheaded, baldheaded, bigheaded, light-headed, unleaded (printing term), interbedded (geology term), muddleheaded, level-headed.

91.8
misguided, decided, one-sided, lopsided, undecided, undivided.

91.9
corded, sordid, prerecorded, unrewarded.

91.10
loaded, woaded, outmoded, unexploded.

91.11
blooded (of good breeding), studied, blue-blooded, cold-blooded, full-blooded, warm-blooded, hot-blooded, unstudied.

91.12
candid, candied, landed, stranded, barehanded, high-handed, forehanded, backhanded, cack-handed, red-handed, right-handed, left-handed, empty-handed, heavy-handed, underhanded, single-handed.

91.13
splendid, commended, intended, undefended, undescended, unattended.

91.14
rounded, unbounded, unfounded, confounded, astounded.

91.15
rigid, Brigid, frigid, nonrigid, semirigid.

91.16
pallid, valid, invalid.

91.17
jellied, gelid, potbellied.

91.18
olid (foul-smelling), squalid, solid, stolid, semisolid.

91.19
amid, pyramid.

91.20
Enid, sciaenid (type of fish), scorpaenid (spiny-finned fish).

91.21
tabanid (blood-sucking fly), balconied, Sassanid (member of Persian dynasty), oceanid (Greek nymph), Achaemenid (member of Persian dynasty), unaccompanied.

91.22
hackneyed, arachnid.

91.23
tepid, intrepid.

91.24
lipid, insipid, phospholipid.

91.25
arid, married, sparid (tropical fish), subarid, unmarried, semiarid.

91.26
forehead, horrid, florid, torrid, subtorrid (subtropical).

91.27
acarid (tick or mite), ascarid (parasitic worm), salaried, leporid (mammal of hare family), liveried, ephemerid (mayfly), elaterid (click beetle), eurypterid (extinct scorpion-like animal).

91.28
acid, flaccid, placid, triacid (chemistry term), subacid (moderately acid), peracid (type of acid), tetracid (chemistry term), antacid, oxyacid (acid containing oxygen), monoacid (chemistry term).

91.29
viscid, bombycid (type of moth), culicid (mosquito), tortricid (small moth), dytiscid (carnivorous aquatic beetle).

91.30
lucid, deuced, mucid (mouldy), pellucid (translucent), Seleucid (member of ancient dynasty).

91.31
capsid (plant-eating bug), therapsid (extinct reptile).

91.32
fatted, matted, dratted, caryatid.

91.33
uncharted, hardhearted, cold-hearted, kind-hearted, half-hearted, wholehearted, downhearted, light-hearted, stouthearted, softhearted, departed, tenderhearted, chicken-hearted, lionhearted, brokenhearted.

91.34
dated, fated, plated, truncated, outdated, cerated (ornithology term), hydrated (containing water), unabated, educated, calculated, simulated, medullated (anatomy term), mentholated, dissipated, constipated, antiquated, celebrated, fenestrated (having windows), elevated, cultivated, dilapidated, self-opinionated, unpremeditated.

91.34.1
trabeated (architectural term), foliated, floriated (architectural term), asteriated (crystallography term), unappropriated, unsubstantiated.

91.34.2
infatuated, superannuated.

91.34.3
dedicated, complicated, desiccated, alembicated (excessively refined), sophisticated, unsophisticated.

91.34.4
variegated, unmitigated.

91.34.5
belated, related, rutilated (mineralogy term), castellated, pixilated (*US* eccentric).

91.34.6
hyphenated, uncoordinated.

91.34.7
serrated, saturated, perforated, unsaturated, unperforated, exaggerated, incorporated, supersaturated (physics term), unadulterated, polyunsaturated.

91.35
fetid, fretted, sweated, indebted, coroneted.

91.36
concerted, perverted, deserted, miniskirted, disconcerted.

91.37
heated, seated, repeated, conceited.

91.38
fitted, knitted, nitid (bright), limited, helmeted, spirited, turreted, lanceted (architectural term), quick-witted, half-witted, dim-witted, sharp-witted, unedited, unlimited, inherited, unmerited, dispirited, high-spirited, multifaceted.

91.39
sighted, whited, delighted, benighted (ignorant), united, far-sighted, clear-sighted, near-sighted, unsighted, long-sighted, sharp-sighted, short-sighted, excited, unrequited, uninvited, overexcited.

91.40
dotted, knotted, potted, spotted, unspotted, carotid, parotid, besotted.

91.41
coated, bloated, noted, devoted.

91.42
booted, fluted, reputed, unsuited, undiluted, unpolluted, convoluted, undisputed.

91.43
affected, dejected, collected, unaffected, unreflected, unconnected, unsuspected, unexpected, undirected, undetected.

91.44
malted, salted, vaulted, exalted.

91.45
sainted, unpainted, acquainted, unacquainted.

91.46
rented, scented, demented, lamented, contented, discontented, unprecedented.

91.47
haunted, undaunted.

91.48
jointed, pointed, disjointed, double-jointed, disappointed.

91.49
mounted, uncounted, unmounted.

91.50
talented, unwarranted, uncovenanted (legal term).

91.51
blasted, flabbergasted.

91.52
crested, vested, buprestid (tropical beetle), undigested, unmolested, double-breasted, unattested.

91.53
listed, tightfisted, unlisted, forested, interested, uninterested, disinterested, unassisted.

91.54
crusted, disgusted, maladjusted.

91.55
fervid, cervid (mammal of deer family), perfervid (extremely ardent).

92 -ide [also 7 + -ed]

eyed, I'd, ide (small fish), bide, chide, dyed, guide, hide, Hyde, Clyde, glide, slide, nide (flock of pheasants), snide, pied, ride, bride, gride (to grate), pride, stride, side, tied, tide, wide.

carbide (chemical compound), abide, cockeyed, raphide (needle-shaped crystal), sulphide, confide, phosphide (chemical compound), misguide, waveguide (electronics term), rawhide, cowhide, horsehide, oxhide, halide (chemical compound), walleyed, bolide (large bright meteor), allied, collide, nuclide (type of atomic nucleus), Strathclyde, applied, landslide, backslide, amide (chemical compound), bromide, popeyed, deride, fluoride, hydride (chemical compound), nitride (chemical compound), outride, well-tried, untried, bestride, astride, Tayside, wayside, quayside, seaside, nearside, fireside, cross-eyed, subside, bedside, broadside, landside (part of plough), offside, hillside, Tyneside, onside (sports term), ringside, depside (chemical compound), upside (upper surface), stateside, Port Said, outside, Teesside, betide, Hocktide (former British festival), yuletide, peptide, riptide (turbulent water in sea), Twelfthtide (Epiphany), Shrovetide, divide, worldwide, backside, azide (chemical compound), reside, preside.

ureide (chemical compound), oroide (metal alloy), iodide (chemical compound), athodyd (type of jet engine), disulphide, trisulphide, aldehyde (chemical compound), ophicleide (obsolete wind instrument), actinide (radioactive element), telluride (chemical compound), East Kilbride, anhydride (chemical compound), Ironside, slickenside (polished rock surface), alongside, mercaptide (chemical compound), dipeptide (biochemical compound), Christmastide, subdivide, nationwide.

hydrosulphide, dissatisfied, formaldehyde, benzaldehyde (fragrant oil), polyamide (polymer), preoccupied, unoccupied, Allhallowtide, polypeptide (biochemical compound).

acetaldehyde (colourless volatile liquid), chlorothiazide (drug).

92.1

qualified, dignified, rarefied, countrified, classified, certified, citified, unqualified, undignified, unclassified, unstratified.

92.2

elide, acetylide (chemical compound), acetanilide (crystalline substance).

92.3

sodamide (crystalline substance), thalidomide, cyanamide (crystalline substance), sulphonamide, chlorpropamide (a drug), tolbutamide (medicinal compound), sulphanilamide (crystalline substance), nicotinamide (component of vitamin B).

92.4

cyanide, uranide (type of element), arsenide (chemical compound), lanthanide (type of element), ferrocyanide (chemical compound), isocyanide (chemical compound), platinocyanide (chemical compound).

92.5

boride (chemical compound), chloride, dichloride, trichloride, hydrochloride, tetrachloride.

92.6

saccharide (a sugar), glyceride (chemical compound), deuteride (chemical compound), override, disaccharide, trisaccharide, polysaccharide, monosaccharide.

92.7

beside, decide.

deicide, suicide, herbicide, regicide, algicide, fungicide, filicide, silicide (chemical compound), stillicide (legal term), Barmecide (illusory), germicide, spermicide, vermicide, homicide, parricide (killing of parent), matricide, patricide, fratricide, countryside, feticide, multicide (mass murder), pesticide, larvicide, Heaviside, Merseyside.

tyrannicide, bactericide, sororicide, uxoricide, liberticide (destruction of freedom), aborticide (destruction of fetus), insecticide, infanticide, rodenticide.

92.7.1
miticide (mite-killing substance), parasiticide.

92.8
aside, biocide (chemical for killing organisms), Humberside, ecocide (destruction of natural environment), glycoside (biochemical compound), underside, genocide, waterside, riverside, overside, silverside, nucleoside (biochemical compound), taeniacide (tapeworm-killing substance).

92.9
inside, coincide, Qaboos bin Said (sultan of Oman).

92.10
topside, diopside (type of mineral).

92.11
phosphatide (biochemical compound), Eastertide, nucleotide (biochemical compound), polynucleotide (biochemical compound).

92.12
Whitsuntide, Passiontide, eventide, Ascensiontide.

92.13
provide, Almoravide (member of Islamic people).

92.14
oxide, dioxide, trioxide, monoxide, epoxide (chemical compound), peroxide, hydroxide, methoxide (chemical compound), ethoxide (chemical com-

pound), superoxide, dimethylsulphoxide (medicinal compound).

93 -ired [also **8** + *-ed*]
oilfired, uninspired, unexpired, overtired.

94 -od
odd, bod, cod, god, hod, Lod (Israeli town), clod, plod, mod, nod, pod, quad, quod (*Slang* jail), squad, rod, scrod (*US* young cod), prod, trod, sod, shod, tod, Todd, wad.

lingcod (Pacific fish), ephod (Old Testament priest's vestment), nid-nod (nod repeatedly), bipod, tripod, ramrod, Nimrod, pushrod, roughshod, slipshod, tightwad.

Hesiod (ancient Greek poet), ostracod (tiny freshwater animal), demigod, amphipod (aquatic organism), polypod, unipod, copepod (plankton constituent), goldenrod (yellow-flowered plant).

94.1
decapod, scaphopod (marine mollusc), chilopod (crawling invertebrate), tylopod (type of mammal), diplopod (crawling invertebrate), chenopod (marine mollusc), pteropod (marine mollusc), theropod (dinosaur), sauropod (dinosaur), tetrapod, gastropod, arthropod, chaetopod (type of worm), octopod, hexapod, rhizopod (minute organism), brachiopod (marine invertebrate), branchiopod (freshwater organism), myriapod (crawling invertebrate), cephalopod (marine mollusc), ornithopod (dinosaur).

95 -ord [also **9** + *-ed*]
oared, board, bawd, baud (unit in computer technology), cord, chord, ford, gaud (cheap trinket), hoard, horde, lord, laud, Maud, maud (Scottish plaid shawl), broad, fraud, sword, ward, sward, fjord, Njord (Norse god).

keyboard, leeboard (board in ship), freeboard (nautical term), seaboard (*US* seashore), scoreboard, floorboard, strawboard (board of compressed straw), backboard, blackboard, blockboard, corkboard, chalkboard (*US* blackboard), buckboard (horse-drawn carriage), duckboard (board covering muddy ground), matchboard, switchboard, cardboard, hardboard, headboard, breadboard, sideboard, surfboard, pegboard, scaleboard (veneer), tailboard, billboard, millboard (strong pasteboard), inboard, signboard, springboard, stringboard (part of staircase), chipboard, clipboard, shipboard, chessboard, dashboard, flashboard (board on dam), splashboard, washboard, dartboard, skateboard, outboard, footboard (foot-operated lever), draughtboard, pasteboard, cheeseboard, record, concord, Concorde, ripcord, whipcord (strong fabric), discord, afford, milord, warlord, landlord, applaud, maraud, abroad, defraud, broadsword, reward, greensward.

shuffleboard, smorgasbord, needlecord, overlord.

95.1
aboard, fibreboard (building material), chequerboard, weatherboard, fingerboard, clapperboard, paperboard (thick cardboard), scraperboard, mortarboard, centreboard (supplementary keel), plasterboard, overboard.

95.2
record, harpsichord, clavichord, misericord.

95.3
accord, monochord (instrument for acoustic analysis), urochord (zoology term), tetrachord (musical term), disaccord, notochord (zoology term), octachord (eight-stringed musical instrument), hexachord (musical term).

95.4
award, toward, untoward.

96 -oord [also **10** + *-ed*]
gourd, Sigurd (Norse mythological hero), assured, insured, self-assured, uninsured, unsecured.

97 -oid [also **11** + *-ed*]
Boyd, Lloyd, Freud, void.

hyoid (bone at tongue base), pyoid (pus-like), zooid (independent animal body), globoid, cuboid, rhomboid, placoid (plate-like), sarcoid (flesh-like), cricoid (cartilage in larynx), trochoid (geometric curve), fucoid (brown seaweed), mucoid, conchoid (geometric curve), discoid, viscoid, gadoid (type of fish), xiphoid (sword-shaped), typhoid, lymphoid, algoid (resembling algae), fungoid, keloid (scar tissue on injury), styloid (stylus-like), xyloid (woody), colloid, tabloid, cycloid (circular), haploid (biology term), diploid (biology term), triploid (biology term), euploid (biology term), dermoid, cymoid (botany term), sphygmoid (pulselike), sigmoid (S-shaped), desmoid (firm tumour), ethmoid (bone of the face), conoid (geometry term), hypnoid, lipoid (fatty), choroid (membrane of eyeball), toroid (geometry term), labroid (marine fish), fibroid, scombroid (marine fish), cancroid (cancerlike), chancroid (soft venereal ulcer), android, dendroid (tree-like), Negroid, centroid (centre of gravity), astroid (maths term), cissoid (geometric curve), schizoid, deltoid, dentoid (tooth-like), mastoid, cestoid (ribbonshaped), histoid (resembling normal tissue), cystoid, lithoid (stone-like), devoid, ovoid, avoid, toxoid (toxin used in immunization), rhizoid (root-like plant structure).

gobioid (spiny-finned fish), blennioid (marine fish), scorpioid (scorpion-like), osteoid, ichthyoid, amoeboid, coracoid (zoology term), anthracoid, autacoid (natural internal body secretion), Celluloid (*Trademark*), unemployed, echinoid (marine animal), arachnoid (membrane covering brain), polypoid, anthropoid, porphyroid (geology term), sciuroid (squirrel-like), lemuroid, cylindroid, sinusoid (maths term), emulsoid, suspensoid (chemistry term), ellipsoid, parotoid (poison gland on toad), haematoid, rheumatoid, prismatoid (geometric solid), keratoid (horny), teratoid (monster-like), allantoid (sausage-shaped), acanthoid (spiny), obovoid (egg-shaped), trapezoid, Caucasoid.

paratyphoid, epicycloid (geometric curve), hypocycloid (geometric curve), underemployed, epileptoid.

97.1
geoid (shape of earth), scarabaeoid.

97.2
percoid (type of fish), cysticercoid (tapeworm larva).

97.3
trichoid (hair-like), helicoid (spiral-shaped), gynaecoid (woman-like), lumbricoid (worm-like), cercopithecoid (monkey), mineralocorticoid (steroid hormone).

97.4
meloid (long-legged beetle), varicelloid (resembling chickenpox).

97.5
phylloid (leaf-like), myeloid (anatomy term), condyloid (anatomy term), amyloid (starch-like protein), cotyloid (cup-shaped), nautiloid (mollusc), erysipeloid (type of dermatitis).

97.6
hyaloid (transparent), sialoid (saliva-like), alkaloid, mongoloid, unalloyed, coralloid, metalloid (type of element), petaloid, crystalloid, varioloid (resembling smallpox), paraboloid (geometric surface), hyperboloid (geometric surface), amygdaloid (volcanic rock).

97.7
sphenoid (wedge-shaped), glenoid (having a shallow cavity), ctenoid (comb-like), scorpaenoid (spiny-finned fish).

97.8
crinoid (marine animal), adenoid, solenoid, hominoid, cyprinoid (carp-like), actinoid (having a radiate form), resinoid, albuminoid, carotenoid (red or yellow pigment).

97.8.1
platinoid (platinum-like), gelatinoid.

97.9
annoyed, melanoid (dark-coloured), humanoid, salmonoid, paranoid, bioflavonoid (vitamin).

97.10
spheroid, scleroid (hardened), steroid, theroid (beast-like), hemispheroid, corticosteroid.

97.11
spiroid (spiral), thyroid, parathyroid.

97.12
amberoid (synthetic amber), acaroid (mite- or tick-like), saccharoid, Polaroid (*Trademark*), haemorrhoid, bacteroid, asteroid, hysteroid (resembling hysteria), meteoroid.

98 -ode [also 12 + -*ed*]
ode, bode, code, goad, lode, load, mode, node, Spode, road, rode, strode, toad, woad.

geode (crystal-lined rock cavity), diode, triode (electronic valve), forebode, abode, decode, encode, postcode, cladode (leaflike stem), hallowed, payload, reload, freeload (*US* be a sponger), workload, truckload, unload, shipload, implode (collapse inwards violently), explode, cartload, boatload, anode, dynode (type of electrode), crunode (maths term), acnode (maths term), epode (part of Greek ode), erode, byroad, highroad, corrode, railroad, inroad, tetrode (electronic valve), pentode (electronic valve), cestode, cathode.

Kozhikode (Indian port), unhallowed, overload, wagonload, à la mode, staminode (nonfunctioning stamen), antinode (physics term), internode (part of plant stem), hemipode (quail-like bird), antipode (the exact opposite), megapode (ground-living bird), nesselrode (rich frozen pudding), electrode, episode, nematode, trematode (parasitic flatworm), hydathode (water-secreting plant pore).

98.1
commode, incommode, discommode, alamode (light silk).

99 -oud [also **13** + *-ed*]
Oudh (region of India), loud, cloud, crowd, proud, shroud, stroud (coarse woollen fabric), Saud, showd (*Scot* to rock), unbowed, aloud, becloud (to muddle), enshroud, avowed, well-endowed, overcrowd, ibn-Saud.

99.1
Macleod, thundercloud, overcloud.

100 -ud
bud, cud, scud, dud, blood, flood, mud, spud, rudd (freshwater fish), crud, sudd (floating weed in Nile), stud, thud, redbud (US tree), disbud, rosebud, lifeblood, oxblood (dark reddish-brown colour), m'lud, photoflood (very bright tungsten lamp).

101 -ood
could, good, hood, should, stood, would, wood.

Gielgud, boyhood, monkhood, godhood, childhood, selfhood, girlhood, manhood, nunhood, falsehood, knighthood, sainthood, priesthood, monkshood (poisonous plant), Talmud, Blackwood (bridge term), blackwood (Australian acacia tree), withstood, Larwood (English cricketer), baywood

(light soft wood), Heywood, Sherwood, dyewood (wood yielding dye), plywood, firewood, matchwood, touchwood, hardwood, deadwood, redwood, bogwood (wood preserved in bogs), dogwood (European shrub), logwood (tree yielding red dye), Wedgwood, wormwood, greenwood, kingwood (violet-tinted wood), springwood (wood produced in spring), sapwood (wood directly beneath bark), pulpwood (wood used in papermaking), brushwood, heartwood (central core of tree), Fleetwood, whitewood, driftwood, softwood, bentwood, Brentwood, boxwood (close-grained yellow wood), rosewood.

babyhood, hardihood, likelihood, livelihood, widowhood, neighbourhood, sisterhood, fatherhood, motherhood, brotherhood, maidenhood, womanhood, adulthood, parenthood, understood, Hollywood, leatherwood (US flowering shrub), Isherwood, summerwood (late season's wood growth), zebrawood (tree yielding striped wood), bitterwood (tree yielding medicinal bark), orangewood, candlewood (resinous wood), sandalwood, eaglewood (tree yielding aromatic resin), satinwood, ironwood (very hard wood), ribbonwood (New Zealand evergreen tree), southernwood (European wormwood tree), sappanwood (tree yielding red dye), cottonwood (US poplar), buttonwood (US plane tree), misunderstood.

102 -ude [also **15** + *-ed*]
food, Jude, who'd, lewd, mood, snood, pood (Russian unit of weight), rood, rude, brood, crude, prude, shrewd, you'd, dude, feud, hued, nude, pseud.

seafood, wholefood, elude, illude, delude, preclude, seclude, occlude, include, conclude, exclude, postlude (concluding piece of music), detrude (thrust out), protrude, obtrude, intrude, extrude, subdued, prelude, denude, transude, étude, exude.

Safid Rud (Iranian river), unvalued.

102.1
allude, collude, interlude.

102.2
quietude, longitude, solitude, amplitude, plenitude (abundance), magnitude, turpitude (baseness), pulchritude, lassitude, certitude, fortitude, rectitude, sanctitude, altitude, multitude, aptitude, promptitude, servitude, mansuetude (gentleness), consuetude (established custom).

inquietude (restlessness), disquietude (unease), desuetude (state of disuse), similitude, decrepitude, solicitude, vicissitude, incertitude, exactitude, correctitude, ineptitude.

dissimilitude, inexactitude, verisimilitude (appearance of truth).

102.2.1
attitude, latitude, platitude, gratitude, beatitude, colatitude (astronomy coordinate), ingratitude.

103 -'d [also **17** + -ed]
froward (obstinate), coward, Howard, steward, scabbard, tabard, larboard, starboard, cupboard, Hubbard, halberd (spear with axe head), Lombard, acred (having acres of land), chequered, tankard, drunkard, whiskered, Richard, orchard, pochard (diving duck), pilchard, cultured, standard, Stafford, Rockford (US city), Crockford (directory of Anglican clergy), Bradford, Telford, Guildford, Salford, Longford (Irish county), Stratford, Dartford, Hertford, Hartford, Watford, Wexford (Irish county), Oxford, Chelmsford, haggard, laggard, staggard (male red deer), jiggered, niggard, sluggard, ballad, salad, armoured, mannered, Reynard, gurnard (European marine fish), synod, leopard, shepherd, backward,

awkward, farad, Herod, hundred, dotard, sceptred, dastard, bastard, plastered, cloistered, bustard, custard, mustard, method, Harvard, fevered, louvred, wayward, leeward, seaward, Edward, headward (eroding upstream of source), sideward, landward, windward, homeward, inward, onward, downward, upward, outward, westward, eastward, northward, southward, galliard (17th-century dance), halyard, billiard, goliard (medieval European wandering scholar), lanyard, Spaniard, poniard (small dagger), hazard, izard (chamois), gizzard, lizard, blizzard, vizard (a mask), wizard, trousered, buzzard.

unnumbered, good-natured, unstructured, substandard, nonstandard, Hereford, Waterford, Rutherford, Muhammad, enamoured, unanswered, untutored, self-centred, Hereward, northwestward, southwestward, northeastward, southeastward, haphazard, butterfingered.

103.1
period, myriad, photoperiod (period of daylight).

103.2
Bedford, Redford, cisteddfod.

103.3
bollard, collard (variety of cabbage), Lollard, pollard, Bacolod (Philippine town).

103.4
coloured, dullard, varicoloured, particoloured, multicoloured.

103.5
rumoured, good-humoured.

103.6
leisured, measured, treasured, unmeasured.

103.7
uncovered, undiscovered.

103.8
forward, shoreward, henceforward, straightforward.

104 -ebbed
ebbed, webbed, cobwebbed.

105 -erbed [also **22** + *-ed*]
uncurbed, unperturbed, undisturbed.

106 -ogged [also **185** + *-ed*]
fogged (photography term), hogged (nautical term), waterlogged.

107 -inged
stringed, winged, stockinged.

108 -aged [also **193** + *-ed*]
uncaged, engaged, unpaged (having no page numbers), unengaged.

109 -edged [also **194** + *-ed*]
alleged, unfledged, fully-fledged.

110 -idged [also **197** + *-ed*]
privileged, unabridged, disadvantaged, underprivileged.

111 -anged [also **207** + *-ed*]
estranged, prearranged.

112 -aled [also **214** + *-ed*]
veiled, hobnailed, detailed, pigtailed, fan-tailed.

113 -eld [also **215** + *-ed*]
geld, held, meld, weld, fjeld (rocky Scandinavian plateau), Krefeld (West German city), Ziegfeld, Danegeld, beheld, upheld, withheld, self-propelled, unparalleled.

114 -erld [also **216** + *-ed*]
world, unfurled, antiworld (world composed of antimatter), underworld, afterworld.

115 -eeld [also **217** + *-ed*]
bield (*Dialect* refuge), field, heeled, shield, Weald, wield, yield.

Sheffield, airfield, Scofield, snowfield, Nuffield, Wakefield, Lichfield, midfield, oilfield, coalfield, canfield (gambling card game), Enfield, urnfield (cemetery of cremation urns), infield, minefield, cornfield, Springfield (US city), Masefield, Mansfield, Hatfield, outfield, well-heeled, windshield, gumshield.

battlefield, Huddersfield, Macclesfield, Beaconsfield, Sutton Coldfield.

115.1
afield, chesterfield, Chesterfield.

116 -ild [also **218** + *-ed*]
build, skilled, gild, guild, sild, rebuild, upbuild, unskilled, wergild (price on man's life), Brunhild (legendary German queen), self-willed, unwilled, overbuild, semiskilled.

117 -iled [also **219** + *-ed*]
child, Fylde, mild, wild, Wilde, godchild, grandchild, brainchild, stepchild, Rothschild, undefiled.

118 -orld [also **221** + *-ed*]
auld, bald, scald, skald (ancient Scandinavian bard), walled, piebald, skewbald, close-hauled (with the sails flat), Cumbernauld.

119 -oiled [also **222** + *-ed*]
well-oiled, unspoiled, shopsoiled.

120 -oled [also **223** + *-ed*]
old, bold, cold, scold, fold, gold, hold, mould, sold, told, wold.

kobold (German mythological mischievous spirit), threefold, fourfold, twofold, blindfold, billfold, tenfold, enfold, pinfold (cattle pen), ninefold, unfold, sheepfold, eightfold, gatefold (folded oversize page), fivefold, sixfold, freehold, toehold, stokehold (coal bunker in ship), handhold, stronghold, uphold, leasehold, household, foothold, withhold, remould, Detmold (German city), unpolled, unsold, threshold, foretold, untold, Cotswold.

semibold (printing term), manifold, centrefold, overfold (geology term), sevenfold, marigold, stranglehold, buttonmould (core of covered button), Leopold, Hammarskjöld.

120.1
behold, copyhold (legal term).

121 -uled [also **227** + *-ed*]
Gould, unruled, unschooled, unscheduled.

122 -'ld [also **228** + *-ed*]
marbled, fabled, gabled, ribald, freckled, pickled, cuckold, raddled, handled, brindled, scaffold, Arnold, pimpled, Harold, titled, gruntled (contented), Tynwald, measled (infested with tapeworm larvae), chiselled, grizzled, sozzled.

spectacled, unbridled, unruffled, bedraggled, newfangled, oldfangled, Macdonald, principled, unequalled, emerald, untitled, disgruntled, untravelled, dishevelled, unrivalled, bespectacled, unprincipled.

122.1
Gerald, herald, Fitzgerald.

122.2
mettled (brave), unsettled.

123 -armed [also **230** + *-ed*]
armed, becalmed, unharmed, alarmed, unarmed.

124 -amed [also **231** + *-ed*]
forenamed, unaimed, unnamed, unframed, ashamed, untamed, unacclaimed, unashamed.

125 -ormed [also **238** + *-ed*]
deformed, reformed, malformed, unformed, uninformed.

126 -imed [also **236** + *-ed*]
unrhymed, well-timed.

127 -'md [also **242** + *-ed*]
envenomed, accustomed, unfathomed, unaccustomed.

128 -and [Some *-land* words in **143** may be pronounced to rhyme with this group. Also **245** + *-ed*.]
and, band, canned, hand, land, bland, gland, manned, rand, brand, grand, strand, Strand, sand, stand.

proband (person in genealogical study), browband (part of bridle), neckband, headband, sideband (electronics term), fahlband (thin bed of rock), armband, rainband (band in solar spectrum), trainband (16th-century English militia), spaceband (printing term), disband, hatband, sweatband, waistband, waveband, noseband (part of bridle), forehand, backhand, offhand, stagehand, unhand, longhand, shorthand, summand (part of a sum), unmanned, repand (having a wavy margin), expand, firebrand, Streisand, quicksand, greensand (olive-green sandstone), suntanned, headstand, bandstand, handstand, grandstand, washstand, withstand, newsstand, kickstand (stand for bicycle), inkstand.

graduand, bellyband (part of harness), saraband, contraband, Samarkand, deodand (former legal term), beforehand, underhand, overhand, behindhand, second-hand, confirmand, Ferdinand, ordinand, operand (maths term), integrand (mathematical function), ampersand, Kristiansand (Norwegian port), understand.

Witwatersrand (South African region), analysand (person undergoing psychoanalysis), misunderstand.

128.1
radicand (maths term), multiplicand (number multiplied).

129 -arned
darned, demand, remand, command, allemande (musical term), reprimand, countermand.

130 -aned [also **247** + *-ed*]
pained, strained, harebrained, crackbrained, ingrained, close-grained, unstrained, bloodstained, scatterbrained, featherbrained, unrestrained, self-contained.

131 -end
end, bend, fend, lend, blend, mend, pend, penned, spend, rend, friend, trend, send, scend (nautical term), tend, vend, wend.

backbend (gymnastic exercise), unbend, unkenned (*Dialect* unknown), addend (number added to), defend, forfend (*US* protect), offend, augend (number added), pitchblende, hornblende, emend, stipend, upend, append, perpend, impend, misspend, expend, befriend, boyfriend, girlfriend, descend, ascend, godsend, transcend, portend, attend, subtend, intend, contend, distend, Ostend, extend, Southend, Wallsend, Gravesend.

minuend (number subtracted from), dividend, subtrahend (number subtracted), condescend, coextend, Demavend (Iranian volcanic peak), superintend.

131.1
apprehend, reprehend, comprehend, misapprehend.

131.2
amend, commend, recommend, discommend.

131.3
depend, vilipend (treat with contempt).

131.4
suspend, overspend.

131.5
pretend, repetend (repeated digit).

132 -erned [also **249** + *-ed*]
unearned, concerned, unturned, unconcerned.

133 -eened [also **251** + *-ed*]
fiend, archfiend, uncleaned, unscreened.

134 -ind [also **252** + *-ed*]
Ind (poetic name for India), finned, Sind (region of Pakistan), tinned, wind, thick-skinned, thin-skinned, sequined, rescind, destined, spavined (veterinary term), forewind (favourable wind), headwind, woodwind, tailwind, whirlwind, downwind, upwind, crosswind, exscind (cut off), wunderkind (child prodigy), determined, tamarind, undetermined.

135 -ined [also **253** + *-ed*]
bind, kind, find, hind, blind, mind, rind, grind, wind, wynd (*Scot* narrow lane).

cowbind (climbing plant), spellbind, unbind, mankind, unkind, refined, affined (closely related), behind, purblind (partly blind), inclined, streamlined, unlined, remind, unsigned, rewind, enwind, unwind.

gavelkind (former land tenure system), womankind, humankind, unrefined, nonaligned, mastermind, undersigned, overwind.

136 -ond

bond, donned, fond, Gond (former tribal Indian), blonde, blond, pond, frond, Fronde, sonde (device for observing atmosphere), wand, Zond (unmanned Russian spacecraft), second, seconde (fencing position), abscond, keeshond, beau monde, millpond, respond, dropsonde (meteorological device), beyond, vagabond, demimonde, Garamond (typeface), correspond, rawinsonde (meteorological balloon), Trebizond (Turkish port), radiosonde (meteorological device).

137 -orned [also **255** + *-ed*]

corned, horned, maund (Asian unit of weight), unmourned, unadorned.

138 -oaned [also **257** + *-ed*]

stoned, rawboned (having bony physique), unboned, unowned, unatoned, unchaperoned.

139 -ound [also **258** + *-ed*]

bound, found, hound, mound, pound, round, ground, sound, stound (*Dialect* short period), wound, swound (*Dialect* swoon).

rebound, snowbound, abound, strikebound, hidebound, windbound (nautical term), hoofbound (veterinary term), fogbound, spellbound, stormbound, inbound, unbound, brassbound, casebound, icebound, housebound, outbound, westbound, eastbound, earthbound, clothbound, northbound, southbound, redound (have an effect on), profound, dumbfound, confound, greyhound, deerhound, boarhound, horehound (flowering plant), elkhound, bloodhound, wolfhound, draghound, staghound, hellhound (fiend), sleuthhound, foxhound, renowned, geepound (unit of mass), propound, impound, compound, expound, uncrowned, playground, fairground, foreground, background, stoneground, unsound,

astound, unwound, shunt-wound (electrical term), resound.

ironbound (unyielding), decompound (describing type of leaf), ultrasound, series-wound (electrical term).

superabound, merry-go-round.

139.1

around, surround, turnaround.

139.2

aground, underground, overground.

140 -und [also **259** + *-ed*]

bundh (general strike in India), bund (embankment), fund, secund (botany term), refund, re-fund, rotund, obtund (deaden), moribund, cummerbund, iracund (easily angered), Bundelkhand (region of India), orotund.

141 -oond

Bund (federation), Lund (Swedish city), dachshund.

142 -ooned [also **260** + *-ed*]

wound, marooned.

143 -'nd [also **261** + *-ed*]

viand (type of food), prebend (church stipend), riband (ribbon awarded for achievement), roband (nautical term), husband, second, fecund, jocund, hardened, ligand (chemistry term), brigand, legend, taloned, garland, Wayland (character in European folklore), island, highland, Thailand, Ireland, Holland, holland (coarse linen cloth), foreland (headland), Courland (region of Russia), moorland, lowland, Poland, Roland, Dowland (English musician), clubland, scrubland, parkland, Lakeland, dockland, Auckland, Falkland, midland, woodland, England, farmland, homeland, mainland, Greenland, inland, Finland, Vinland (stretch of US coast), Rhineland, gangland, Langland (English poet), Lapland, upland, grassland, Iceland, marshland, heartland, Shetland, Scotland, Gotland (Swedish island), Portland, Jutland, Rutland, wasteland, Cleveland, Friesland (Dutch province), Queensland, Hammond, almond, dromond (medieval sailing vessel), gourmand, Lomond, Richmond, Edmund, Redmond, Sigmund, Dortmund, perpend (large stone in wall), errand, gerund, wizened, thousand.

infecund, rubicund, unquestioned, abandoned, Zululand, Newfoundland, tableland, diamond, Sigismund (Holy Roman Emperor), unopened, reverend, old-fashioned, impassioned, unleavened.

millisecond, nanosecond, microsecond, Sudetenland (region of Czechoslovakia), aforementioned, undermentioned, well-intentioned.

143.1
eland, hieland (*Scot* easily tricked), Zealand, New Zealand.

143.2
Disneyland, fairyland, Maryland, Dixieland, Swaziland, Somaliland, Matabeleland.

143.3
Pondoland (region of South Africa), Togoland, Heligoland (North Sea island).

143.4
Oberland, timberland, borderland, Gelderland (Dutch province), Sunderland, wonderland, Nagaland (Indian state), Westmorland, Switzerland, hinterland, fatherland, motherland, Sutherland, overland, Bechuanaland, Gondwanaland, Nyasaland.

143.4.1
Cumberland, Northumberland.

143.5
conditioned, unconditioned, noncommissioned.

143.6
reasoned, weasand (windpipe), unseasoned.

144 -athed [also **473** + *-ed*]
unscathed, enswathed.

145 -othed [also **478** + *-ed*]
unclothed, betrothed.

146 -aved [also **482** + *-ed*]
unpaved, depraved, unsaved, well-behaved.

147 -erved [also **483** + *-ed*]
decurved (bent downwards), reserved, undeserved, unreserved, well-preserved, unobserved.

148 -eeved [also **484** + *-ed*]
leaved, relieved, well-received, unperceived.

149 -ived [also **486** + *-ed*]
deprived, contrived.

150 -ooved [also **490** + *-ed*]
moved, removed, unmoved, approved, unproved, unimproved.

151 -olved [also **493** + *-ed*]
unsolved, involved, resolved, unresolved, undissolved.

152 -azed [also **509** + *-ed*]
crazed, unglazed.

153 -eezed [also **513** + *-ed*]
pleased, well-pleased, diseased.

154 -ized [also **516** + *-ed*]
sized, pearlized, advised, undisguised, civilized, creolized (linguistics term), undersized, oversized, ill-advised, unadvised, uncivilized, well-organized, disorganized, unauthorized, uncircumcised.

155 -ozed [also **520** + *-ed*]

closed, composed, unposed, disposed, exposed, undisclosed, indisposed, unexposed, undiagnosed.

155.1

supposed, unopposed.

156 -oozed [also **523** + *-ed*]

used, bruised, accused, bemused, amused, disused.

157 -aff

caff, daff, faff, gaff, gaffe, sclaff (golf stroke), raff (*Dialect* rubbish), draff (husks remaining after fermentation), waff (*Dialect* gust), WAAF, piaffe (dressage term), chiffchaff (European warbler), Llandaff, kenaf (jute-like fibre), carafe, riffraff, agraffe (a fastening), bathyscaph, shandygaff.

158 -arf

calf, scarf, chaff, half, haaf (deep-sea fishing ground), laugh, graph, staff, zarf (coffee-cup holder), mooncalf (fool), headscarf, behalf, giraffe, digraph (two-letter sound), trigraph (three-letter sound), distaff, ploughstaff, flagstaff, tipstaff, pikestaff, telegraph, polygraph (lie detector), epigraph (opening quotation in book), serigraph (silk-screen print), shadowgraph, Stevengraph (picture woven in silk), epitaph, cenotaph, quarterstaff (former English weapon).

158.1

myograph (muscular-contraction recorder), tachograph, arcograph (geometric instrument), zincograph (zinc printing-plate), Van de Graaff (US physicist), ondograph (alternating-current recorder), nephograph (cloud-photographing instrument), allograph (signature written for another), stylograph (type of pen), xylograph (wood engraving), holograph (original manu-

script), thermograph, kymograph (medical instrument), homograph, pneumograph, sphygmograph (blood-pressure recorder), seismograph, stenograph, Chinagraph (*Trademark*), monograph, chronograph, barograph, paragraph, spirograph (breathing-movement recorder), macrograph (drawing showing enlarged image), micrograph (picture of microscope image), hygrograph (humidity recorder), autograph, photograph, hectograph (copying process), pictograph, pantograph (instrument for scale drawing), cryptograph (code), lithograph.

oscillograph, Addressograph (*Trademark*), hyetograph (rainfall chart), odontograph (gear-tooth marking aid).

meteorograph, photomicrograph (photograph of microscope image), cinematograph (type of cine-projector), microphotograph (photograph showing reduced image), electroencephalograph.

158.1.1

cardiograph, radiograph, heliograph, oleograph (lithograph imitating oil-painting), Mimeograph (*Trademark*), stereograph (three-dimensional picture), choreograph, phraseograph (phrase representable by symbol), myocardiograph, autoradiograph (photograph of radioactive object), spectroheliograph (instrument for photographing sun), electrocardiograph.

158.1.2

phonograph, coronagraph (optical instrument).

158.1.3

spectrograph (instrument for photographing spectrum), electrograph.

159 -afe

chafe, strafe, safe, waif, vouchsafe, unsafe.

160 -eff

eff, deaf, lev (Bulgarian currency), clef, ref, chef, tef (African grass), ASLEF, Brezhnev, UNICEF.

160.1
Kiev, Prokofiev.

161 -erf
kerf (cut made by saw), scurf, serf, surf, turf.

162 -eef
beef, chief, fief (property granted to vassal), leaf, lief, reef, brief, grief, sheaf, thief, naïf, enfeoff (legal term), flyleaf, thickleaf (succulent plant), broadleaf (tobacco plant), sherif (descendant of Mohammed), debrief, massif, motif, interleaf, overleaf, cloverleaf, leitmotiv, apéritif.

162.1
belief, relief, unbelief, disbelief, misbelief (unorthodox belief), bas-relief, demirelief.

162.2
kharif (autumn-harvested crop), Tenerife.

163 -iff
if, biff, kif (marijuana), skiff, cliff, glyph (groove on frieze), miff, niff, sniff, quiff, Rif (Moroccan people), riff (jazz term), griffe (claw-shaped carved ornament), tiff, stiff, whiff, ziff (*Austral* beard).

kerchief, mischief, Cardiff, Aycliffe (English town), Wycliffe (English religious reformer), Radcliffe, Sutcliffe, triglyph (architectural term), tariff, Er Rif (mountainous region of Morocco), hairif (Eurasian plant), midriff, caitiff (cowardly person), plaintiff, pontiff, mastiff, skewwhiff, Joseph.

neckerchief, handkerchief, anaglyph (stereoscopic picture), hieroglyph, petroglyph (prehistoric rock carving),

logogriph (word puzzle), hippogriff (Greek mythological monster), positif (organ keyboard).

163.1
bailiff, caliph, bumbailiff (debt collector).

163.2
serif, sheriff, sanserif, undersheriff.

164 -ife
fife, Fife, life, knife, rife, strife, wife, highlife, wildlife, half-life, nightlife, drawknife (woodcutting tool), jackknife, penknife, wakerife (*Dialect* wakeful), loosestrife, midwife, goodwife, oldwife (long-tailed sea duck), alewife (herring-like fish), housewife, fishwife, afterlife, paperknife, pocketknife, sweetiewife (*Scot* talkative woman).

165 -off
off, cough, coff (*Scot* buy), scoff, doff, quaff, prof, shroff (detector of counterfeit money), trough, toff, takeoff, Chekhov, Khrushchev, sendoff, Wolof (African people), brushoff, liftoff, blastoff, waveoff (signal to aircraft), Nabokov, whooping cough, Godunov (Russian tsar), stroganoff, Romanov (Russian imperial dynasty), Molotov, Rimsky-Korsakov.

165.1
Ustinov, Rachmaninoff.

166 -orf
orfe, Orff (German composer), corf (wagon used in mines), morph (linguistics term), wharf, dwarf, swarf, Waldorf, bimorph (electronics term), dimorph (one of two forms), trimorph (one of three forms), Düsseldorf, polymorph, perimorph (mineral enclosing another).

166.1
pseudomorph (mineral of uncharacteristic form), endomorph, lagomorph

(type of mammal), allomorph, paramorph (mineralogy term), mesomorph, isomorph (organism with similar form), ectomorph, rhizomorph (rootlike fungal structure), hystricomorph (type of rodent), gynandromorph (biology term), enantiomorph (form of crystal).

167 -oaf
oaf, loaf, limitrophe (near a frontier).

168 -uff
buff, cuff, scuff, chuff, chough, duff, guff (*Slang* ridiculous talk), huff, luff (leading edge of sail), bluff, clough (*Dialect* a gorge), fluff, slough, muff, snuff, puff, ruff, rough, scruff, gruff, sough (*Dialect* a drain), tough, tuff (volcanic rock), stuff.

rebuff, handcuff, earmuff, enough, woodruff (flowering plant), crossruff (bridge term), dyestuff, foodstuff, greenstuff, overstuff.

169 -oof
poof, woof.

170 -ufe
oof (*Slang* money), goof, hoof, kloof (South African mountain pass), pouffe, spoof, roof, proof, woof.

shadoof, aloof, sunroof, reproof, wearproof, fireproof, shockproof, skidproof, soundproof, shellproof, foolproof, flameproof, stormproof, rainproof, disproof, rustproof, mothproof.

Al Hufuf (Saudi Arabian town), showerproof, weatherproof, shatterproof, waterproof, counterproof (printing term), bulletproof.

171 -'f
ganef (*US* unscrupulous opportunist), daraf (unit in physics), paraph (flourish following a signature), seraph, ter-

aph (Old Testament household god), dandruff.

172 -elf
elf, skelf (*Dialect* wood splinter), pelf (money), self, shelf, Guelph (Italian political faction member), thyself, myself, yourself, herself, himself, oneself, itself.

173 -olf
golf, Rolf, Rudolf, Randolph.

174 -ulf
gulf, engulf.

175 -oolf
wolf, Woolf, Wolfe, werewolf, aardwolf (nocturnal mammal), Cynewulf (Anglo-Saxon poet), Beowulf (Old English epic poem), Fenriswolf (Norse mythological wolf).

176 -imph
lymph, nymph, perilymph (fluid in ear), endolymph (fluid in ear), karyolymph (part of cell nucleus).

177 -umph
bumph, humph, triumph, galumph.

178 -ag
bag, scag (*Dialect* to tear), fag, gag, jag, hag, lag, flag, slag, mag, nag, knag (knot in wood), snag, spag (*Welsh* scratch with claws), rag, brag, crag, scrag, drag, frag (US military slang term), sprag (prop used in mining), sag, shag, tag, stag, vag (*Austral* a vagrant), wag, swag.

debag, fleabag, workbag, feedbag, handbag, sandbag, windbag, ragbag, mailbag, beanbag, gasbag, ratbag, postbag, nosebag, stalag, greylag, Gulag, cagmag (*Dialect* chat idly), washrag (*US* face cloth), ragtag (the rabble), wigwag (wave flags in signalling), chinwag, zigzag.

saddlebag, lallygag (*US* loiter aimlessly), bullyrag (bully with practical jokes), scallywag.

178.1
kitbag, carpetbag.

179 -arg
bagh (Indian garden), darg (*Dialect* day's work), Prague, Reichstag, Laoag (Philippine city), Bundestag (West German legislative assembly).

180 -aig
Haig, Hague, plague, Craig, vague, stravaig (*Dialect* wander aimlessly).

181 -eg
egg, beg, keg, skeg (nautical term), leg, cleg (horsefly), peg, dreg, teg, muskeg (boggy hollow), foreleg, proleg (larva's abdominal limb), blackleg, dogleg, bootleg, nutmeg, unpeg, Tuareg (member of Berber people), thalweg (geography term), filibeg (Scottish Highlander's kilt), Scanderbeg (Albanian patriot), Winnipeg.

182 -erg
erg, burg (town), berg (*short for* iceberg).

Marburg, Coburg, coburg (type of loaf), Newburg (cookery term), Lindbergh, Strindberg, Bamberg (German town), Hamburg, Limburg, Gomberg (US chemist), homburg, Romberg (US composer), Schoenberg, iceberg, Hapsburg, Vicksburg (American Civil War site), Strasbourg, exergue (inscription on coin).

Magdeburg, Bundaberg (Australian city), osnaburg (coarse cotton fabric), Middelburg (Dutch city), Heidelberg, inselberg (isolated rocky hill), Nuremberg, Württemberg, Luxembourg, Oldenburg (German city), Brandenburg, Hindenburg, Mecklenburg (region of Germany), Orenburg (Russian city),

Battenburg, Gutenberg, Gothenburg (Swedish port), Gettysburg, Petersburg (American Civil War site), Williamsburg (former capital of Virginia), Drakensberg (African mountain range), Saint Petersburg.

182.1
Louisburg (Canadian fortress), Harrisburg (capital of Pennsylvania), Johannesburg.

182.2
Pittsburgh, Pietermaritzburg (capital of Natal).

183 -eeg
league, Grieg, gigue, colleague, renege, blitzkrieg, sitzkrieg, intrigue, squeteague (Atlantic fish), fatigue.

184 -ig
big, dig, fig, gig, jig, pig, rig, brig, frig, grig (*Dialect* lively person), prig, sprig, trig, cig, Whig, wig, swig, twig.

shindig, fishgig (pole for impaling fish), rejig (re-equip), pfennig, bushpig (African wild pig), unrig, Danzig (fancy pigeon), Leipzig, earwig, bagwig (18th-century wig), bigwig.

infra dig, caprifig (wild fig), whirligig, guinea pig, thimblerig (game of chance), periwig, Zagazig (Egyptian city), thingumajig.

185 -og
bog, cog, dog, fog, Gog, jog, Hogg, hog, log, clog, flog, glogg (hot alcoholic drink), slog, mog, smog, nog, snog, pogge (European fish), frog, grog, prog, trog (to stroll), tog.

seadog, firedog, watchdog, fogdog (whitish spot in fog), bulldog, sundog (small rainbow near horizon), hangdog, sheepdog, hot dog, Magog, goosegog, quahog, sandhog (*US* underground worker), hedgehog, prologue, backlog, eclogue, unclog, loglog (logarithm of logarithm), footslog, putlog (beam supporting scaffold floor), eggnog, bullfrog, leapfrog, Hertzog, tautog (Atlantic fish).

underdog, Tagalog, epilogue, antilog, dialogue, duologue, Decalogue, homologue, analogue, monologue, apologue (moral fable), catalogue, travelogue, golliwog, polliwog, Memphremagog (US–Canadian lake).

185.1
befog, pettifog.

185.2
agog, pedagogue, demagogue, haemagogue (promoting blood flow), synagogue, mystagogue (teacher of mystical doctrines), sialagogue (substance stimulating saliva flow), emmenagogue (substance increasing menstrual flow), galactagogue (inducing milk secretion).

186 -org
Borg, morgue, Swedenborg (Swedish scientist and theologian).

187 -oorg
bourg (French market town), Coorg (former province of India), Cherbourg, faubourg.

188 -oag
rogue, brogue, drogue (funnel-shaped device), vogue, collogue (conspire), pirog (large pie), pirogue (canoe), prorogue, pishogue (*Irish* sorcery), disembogue (discharge or flow out).

189 -ug
bug, chug, dug, fug, jug, hug, lug, plug, slug, mug, smug, snug, pug, rug, drug, shrug, trug, tug, thug, vug (mining term).

debug, firebug (arsonist), bedbug, redbug (parasitic larva), humbug, earplug, unplug.

jitterbug, litterbug, doodlebug, spittlebug (leaping insect).

190 -oog
Moog (*Trademark*), fugue.

191 -adge
badge, cadge, fadge (*Dialect* agree), hajj (Muslim pilgrimage to Mecca).

192 -arge
barge, charge, large, marg, marge, sparge (sprinkle), raj, sarge, taj (Muslim's tall cap), surcharge, recharge, discharge, enlarge, Al Marj (ancient Libyan town), swaraj (self-government in India), litharge (lead monoxide), undercharge, supercharge, countercharge, overcharge, lithomarge (type of kaolin).

193 -age
age, cage, phage (virus that destroys bacteria), gauge, gage (a pledge), page, rage, sage, stage, wage, swage (shaped tool).

birdcage, encage, prophage (parasitic virus in bacterium), greengage, engage, teenage, rampage, enrage, outrage, Osage (American Indian people), substage (part of microscope), offstage, downstage, upstage, backstage, assuage.

disengage, archimage (great magician), interpage, underage, overage, saxifrage, multistage.

193.1
macrophage (cell in animal tissue), bacteriophage (virus that destroys bacteria).

194 -edge
edge, kedge (nautical term), hedge, ledge, fledge, pledge, sledge, dredge, sedge, veg, wedge, allege, frankpledge (medieval tithing system), straightedge

(strip used as ruler), featheredge (plank with thin edge).

195 -erge

urge, scourge, dirge, splurge, merge, purge, spurge, serge, surge, verge, emerge, submerge, resurge (rise again), deterge (cleanse), diverge, converge, demiurge (philosophy term), dramaturge, thaumaturge (performer of miracles).

196 -eege

liege, siege, besiege.

197 -idge

midge, ridge, bridge, fridge.

triage (sorting according to priority), buoyage, voyage, flowage, towage, stowage, cowage (tropical climbing plant), brewage, sewage, Babbage (English mathematician), cabbage, garbage, Burbage (English actor), herbage (vegetation for grazing), cribbage, cubage (cubic contents), package, breakage, leakage, dockage (charge for docking ships), lockage (canal lock system), blockage, socage (former legal term), corkage, linkage, shrinkage, boscage (thicket), adage, wordage, cordage (ship's rigging), bandage, blindage (military protective screen), bondage, poundage, groundage (fee for anchorage), roughage, baggage, mortgage, luggage, scalage (*US* percentage price reduction), treillage (trellis), pelage (coat of mammal), mileage, silage, haulage, spoilage, soilage (green fodder), ullage (unfilled part of container), sullage (sewage), Coolidge, Sutlej (Asian river), kentledge (ship's ballast), damage, rummage, scrummage, plumage, carnage, cranage (use of crane), drainage, nonage (being under legal age), dunnage (material for packing cargo), tonnage, seepage, pipage (system of pipes), stoppage, peerage, steer-

age, borage (flowering plant), forage, Norwich, porridge, floorage, storage, moorage, weighbridge, drawbridge, Trowbridge, Stourbridge, abridge, Cambridge, umbrage, Tonbridge, footbridge, Lethbridge (Canadian city), Oxbridge, Uxbridge, suffrage, cartridge, partridge, passage, sausage, dosage, usage, cartage, eatage (*Dialect* grazing rights), metage (official measuring of goods), cottage, pottage, wattage, portage (transport), shortage, outage (missing goods), footage, voltage, vantage, mintage, vintage, frontage, wastage, vestige, hostage, postage, Carthage, lavage (medical procedure), ravage, savage, pavage (tax towards paving streets), cleavage, lovage, salvage, selvage, language, sandwich, messuage (legal term), visage, prisage (customs duty on wine).

verbiage, foliage, lineage, ferriage (transportation by ferry), appendage, diallage (mineral), vassalage, assemblage, endamage, peonage (working to pay debts), orphanage, gallonage, commonage (legal term), baronage, patronage, matronage, parsonage, personage, Stevenage, sewerage, harbourage, acreage, vicarage, brokerage, anchorage, pasturage, plunderage (embezzlement of ship's goods), telpherage (overhead transport system), pilferage, cellarage, Coleridge, haemorrhage, porterage (charge for porter's work), quarterage (quarterly payment), waterage (transportation by ship), fosterage, average, beverage, leverage, coverage, agiotage (business of currency exchange), pilotage, advantage, parentage (ancestry), envisage.

vagabondage, overdosage, disadvantage, protolanguage (reconstructed extinct language), paralanguage (linguistics term), metalanguage (linguistics term).

197.1
pillage, spillage, grillage (arrangement of beams), tillage, stillage (low supporting platform), village, pupillage, sacrilege, mucilage, ensilage (process of storing fodder), cartilage, curtilage (enclosed area of land), sortilege (divination by drawing lots), tutelage, privilege.

197.2
college, knowledge, foreknowledge, acknowledge.

197.3
image, scrimmage, pilgrimage, afterimage.

197.4
homage, West Bromwich.

197.5
manage, pannage (pasturage for pigs), tannage (process of tanning), mismanage.

197.6
ennage (printing term), empennage (rear part of aircraft).

197.7
spinach, Greenwich, concubinage.

197.8
slippage, equipage (horse-drawn carriage).

197.9
carriage, Harwich, marriage, miscarriage, remarriage, disparage, undercarriage, intermarriage.

197.10
courage, encourage, discourage, demurrage (delay of carrier's departure).

197.11
message, presage, expressage (conveyance by express).

197.12
hermitage, maritage (feudal right), heritage, baronetage.

197.13
dotage, flotage, anecdotage.

197.14
tentage (tents), ventage (small hole), percentage.

198 -ige
oblige, disoblige.

199 -odge
bodge, dodge, lodge, plodge (*Dialect* wade), splodge, modge (*Dialect* to botch), stodge, wodge, dislodge, hodgepodge, horologe (timepiece).

200 -orge
forge, gorge, George, regorge (to vomit), engorge, disgorge.

201 -oge
doge, gamboge (gum resin).

202 -ouge
gouge, scrouge (*Dialect* to crowd).

203 -udge
budge, fudge, judge, bludge (*Austral* to scrounge), sludge, smudge, nudge, drudge, grudge, trudge, prejudge, forejudge, forjudge (legal term), adjudge (pronounce formally), misjudge, begrudge.

204 -uge
smoodge (*Austral* smooch), Scrooge, stooge, huge, refuge, deluge, vermifuge (worm-expelling drug), febrifuge (fever-reducing drug), centrifuge, calcifuge (botany term), subterfuge.

205 -ulge
bulge, indulge, divulge.

206 -ange
flange, phalange (finger- or toe-bone), Falange (Spanish Fascist movement).

207 -ainge
change, mange, range, grange, strange, exchange, arrange, estrange, inter-

change, counterchange, rearrange, disarrange.

207.1
derange, omnirange (radio navigational system).

208 -enge
henge (area with stone circle), Stonehenge, revenge, avenge.

209 -inge
binge, dinge, hinge, cringe, fringe, springe (small snare), singe, tinge, whinge, swinge, twinge, unhinge, challenge, impinge, syringe, orange, infringe, scavenge, lozenge.

210 -ounge
lounge, scrounge.

211 -unge
scunge (*Austral* borrow), gunge, lunge, blunge (ceramics term), plunge, sponge, expunge, muskellunge (US game fish), Narayanganj (Bangladeshi city).

212 -al
gal, pal, sal (salt), shall, cabal, decal (transferred design), coucal (ground-living bird), fallal (showy ornament), formal (chemical compound), grand mal, canal, neral (chemistry term), La Salle (Canadian city), Laval (Canadian city), pedocal (lime-rich soil), caracal (desert lynx), warrigal (*Austral* dingo), methylal (chemical compound), petit mal, rhodinal (fragrant natural oil), falderal (worthless trifle), chaparral (dense growth of trees), acetal (chemical compound), citronellal (fragrant natural oil), Guadalcanal (Pacific island), piperonal (chemical compound), Ashurbanipal (Assyrian king).

213 -arl
Basle, Baal, Carl, dhal (tropical shrub), dal (Indian food), farl (oatmeal cake), marl, gnarl, snarl, rale (medical term), kraal (South African hut village), Vaal (South African river), joual (Canadian French dialect), toile, jarl (medieval Scandinavian chieftain).

Taal (Philippine volcano), real (former Spanish coin), timbale (dish cooked in mould), Baikal (Russian lake), locale, housecarl (medieval Danish household servant), Heimdall (Norse god), Ruisdael (Dutch painter), Imphal (Indian city), halal (Muslim custom), hamal (Oriental servant), unsnarl, Bhopal (Indian city), corral, chorale, morale, Transvaal, riyal (Saudi Arabian currency), khayal (Indian classical vocal music), Chogyal (title of Indian ruler).

Taj Mahal, Ar Rimal (Arabian desert), caporal (strong tobacco), pastorale, Provençal, Nembutal (*Trademark*), Emmenthal, Van der Waal (Dutch chemist).

Escorial (Spanish architectural site), Neanderthal.

213.1
banal, rationale.

214 -ale
ail, ale, bale, bail, kale, scale, dale, fail, faille (soft light fabric), gale, Gael (Gaelic-speaking person), gaol, jail, hail, hale, flail, male, mail, nail, snail, pail, pale, quail, rail, Braille, brail (nautical term), drail (angler's weighted hook), frail, Grail, trail, sail, sale, shale, tale, tail, stale, they'll, veil, vale, wail, whale, wale (weal on skin), dwale (deadly nightshade).

percale (closely-woven cotton fabric), Airedale, Rochdale, Drysdale, Clydesdale, regale, Longueuil (Canadian city), inhale, exhale, Hallel (Jewish chant of praise), camail (part of armour), vermeil (gilded metal), female, blackmail, tenaille (part of fortification), treenail (dowel joining planks), doornail, toenail, hobnail, thumbnail, hangnail, impale, derail, guardrail, handrail, taffrail (rail at ship's stern), engrail (indent edge of), Sangraal (Holy Grail), contrail (vapour trail from aircraft), staysail, resale, skysail, trysail, wassail, foresail, assail, abseil, wholesale, mainsail, topsail, curtail, hairtail (marine fish), detail, retail, hightail, bobtail, cocktail, broadtail (fur from Persian lambs), swordtail (tropical fish), wagtail, pigtail, telltale, fantail, ventail (part of armour), entail, pintail (greyish-brown duck), fishtail (ballroom-dancing step), dovetail, oxtail, foxtail, travail, prevail, avail, unveil, bewail, grisaille (painting technique).

Wensleydale, Corriedale (breed of sheep), amygdale (geology term), Chippendale, Skelmersdale, Abigail, Fine Gael (Irish political party), martingale (strap in horse's harness), galingale (European plant), nightingale, farthingale (framework worn under skirts), fingernail, monorail, ponytail, swallowtail (type of butterfly), tattletale, cottontail, Ebbw Vale, countervail (act with equal force).

215 -ell

ell, bell, belle, bel, dell, fell, jell, gel, hell, Hel (Norse mythological goddess), mel (pure form of honey), smell, knell, spell, quell, cell, sell, shell, tell, well, dwell, swell, yell.

Nowell, gabelle (former French salt tax), barbell, harebell, rebel, doorbell, Nobel, cowbell, bluebell, handbell, dumbbell, chandelle (aeronautics term), Bendel (Nigerian state), Scafell, befell, pell-mell, Parnell, fresnel (unit of frequency), spinel (mineral), Brunel, prunelle (French liqueur), quenelle (meat or fish dumpling), rappel (mountaineer's method of descent), repel, appel (fencing term), lapel, propel, impel, compel, dispel, misspell, expel,

Bakewell, inkwell, morel (edible fungus), jurel (Atlantic fish), marcel (hair style), Purcell, outsell, seashell, eggshell, bombshell, nutshell, artel (Russian cooperative union), cartel, Ravel, Tavel (French rosé wine), farewell, stairwell, speedwell, bridewell (jail), Caldwell, indwell, Cromwell, unwell, excel, Moselle, gazelle.

decibel, Jezebel, Isabel, aludel (vessel used in chemistry), Zinfandel (Californian wine grape), plasmagel (jelly-like protoplasm), aerogel (solid foam), parallel, calomel (purgative powder), philomel (nightingale), oenomel (wine and honey drink), béchamel, organelle (tiny structure inside cell), mangonel (stone-throwing war engine), villanelle (verse form), pimpernel, petronel (17th-century firearm), personnel, fontanelle, amarelle (variety of sour cherry), aquarelle, chanterelle (edible fungus), pipistrelle, radicel (tiny root), pedicel (flower stalk), filoselle (embroidery thread), photocell, cockleshell, tortoiseshell, brocatelle (heavy brocade), moschatel (small flowering plant), muscatel (rich sweet wine), bagatelle, clientele, caravel (sailing ship), Camberwell, demoiselle (small Eurasian crane).

spirituel (having refined wit), materiel (materials and equipment), involucel (botany term), eau de Javelle (bleaching solution), mademoiselle.

215.1
cadelle (small beetle), asphodel.

215.2
nacelle (part of aircraft), undersell, carousel, oversell.

215.3
Courtelle (*Trademark*), foretell, immortelle (everlasting flower).

215.4
boatel, hotel, motel, maître d'hôtel.

216 -erl

earl, burl (small lump in wool), curl, skirl (*Dialect* play bagpipes), churl, furl, girl, hurl, herl (angling term), merle (*Scot* blackbird), knurl (small ridge), purl, pearl, thirl (*Dialect* to drill), whirl, swirl, twirl, uncurl, unfurl, showgirl, cowgirl, switchgirl (*Austral* female switchboard operator), impearl (adorn with pearls), papergirl, mother-of-pearl.

217 -eel

eel, Biel (Swiss town), keel, Kiel (West German port), deal, deil (*Scot* devil), feel, heel, heal, he'll, leal (*Scot* loyal), meal, kneel, Neil, peel, peal, speel (*Dialect* wood splinter), spiel, squeal, reel, creel, seal, seel (falconry term), she'll, teal, steel, steal, veal, we'll, wheel, weal (raised mark on skin), zeal.

abele (white poplar tree), ordeal, misdeal, congeal, selfheal, allheal, allele (genetics term), schlemiel (*US* clumsy), inchmeal (inch by inch), wholemeal, piecemeal, sweetmeal, oatmeal, fistmele (archery term), repeal, appeal, kriegspiel (war game), bonspiel (curling match), newsreel, unseal, conceal, genteel, Bastille, Castile, reveal, Deauville, freewheel, gearwheel, flywheel, sidewheel (riverboat's paddle-wheel), aiguille (needle-shaped mountain peak), cogwheel, millwheel, pinwheel, cartwheel.

dishabille, traymobile (*Austral* trolley), Dormobile (*Trademark*), snowmobile, urodele (type of amphibian), Israfil (archangel in the Koran), cochineal, manchineel (tropical tree), glockenspiel, imbecile, cockatiel, commonweal, automobile.

217.1

anneal, chenille, eau de nil (pale yellowish-green colour).

217.2

underseal, hydrocele, rectocele, blastocoel (embryology term), haemocoel (invertebrate's body cavity), cystocele, haematocele (blood cyst), bubonocele (partial hernia in groin).

218 -ill

ill, bill, kill, skill, chill, dill, fill, gill, hill, mill, mil (unit of length), nil, pill, spill, quill, squill (Mediterranean plant), rill, brill, krill, drill, frill, grill, grille, shrill, trill, thrill, sill, till, still, will, swill, twill.

playbill (poster advertising a play), waybill, Erbil (Iraqi city), gerbil, sibyl (ancient Greek prophetess), wrybill, twibill (agricultural implement), bluebill, shoebill, handbill, bulbil (small bulb-like plant organ), hornbill, thornbill, spoonbill, waxbill, hawksbill (small tropical turtle), storksbill (flowering plant), cranesbill (flowering plant), alkyl (chemical group), Gaitskell, Churchill, idyll, condyle (rounded projection on bone), refill, fulfil, argil (potter's clay), Virgil, strigil (ancient Roman's body-scraper), vigil, Edgehill, molehill, downhill, dunghill, uphill, foothill, allyl (chemical group), amyl (chemical group), Tamil (member of Asian people), sawmill, De Mille, treadmill, windmill, gristmill, anil (West Indian shrub), manille (trump in card game), phenyl (chemical group), vinyl, tranquil, jonquil, fibril (small fibre), nombril (heraldic term), quadrille, mandrill, tendril, nostril, Bovril (*Trademark*), acyl (chemical group), doorsill, groundsill (joist in timber frame), butyl (chemical group), dactyl, dentil (architectural term), lentil, until, pastille, distil, pistil, standstill, instil, ethyl, methyl, chervil, Melville, anvil, Nashville, dullsville, goodwill, pigswill, axil, Brazil, benzyl (chemical group).

razorbill, winterkill (kill by frost exposure), overkill, cacodyl (oily poisonous liquid), daffodil, thionyl (chemical group), uranyl (chemical group), minipill, overspill, escadrille (French aircraft squadron), espadrille, codicil, verticil (biology term), windowsill, uracil (biochemical compound), nitrosyl (chemical group), acetyl, tormentil (Eurasian plant), Bougainville (Pacific island), Jacksonville (US port), whippoorwill, carboxyl (chemical group).

Invercargill, pterodactyl, Merthyr Tydfil.

218.1
sclerophyll (woody evergreen plant), sporophyll (botany term), mesophyll (middle layer of leaf), xanthophyll (plant pigment), cladophyll (botany term), chlorophyll, neutrophil (white blood cell), eosinophil (white blood cell).

218.2
beryl, Beryl, peril, imperil.

218.3
Seville, Baskerville, vaudeville, Stoke Mandeville.

219 -ile
isle, aisle, I'll, bile, chyle (milky fluid in intestine), kyle (*Scot* narrow strait), file, guile, lisle, mile, smile, Nile, pile, spile (heavy timber stake), rile, sile (*Dialect* rain heavily), tile, style, stile, vile, Weill (German composer), wile, while.

labile (unstable), stabile (stationary abstract construction), mobile, nubile, Kabyle (member of Berber people), aedile, defile, profile, nailfile, symphile (entomology term), misfile, Argyll, beguile, agile, fragile, Carlisle, Carlyle, anile (like an old woman), penile, senile, stockpile, woodpile, compile, sterile, virile, febrile, facile, gracile (gracefully slender), sessile (botany term), docile, fertile, quartile (statistics term), motile, protyle (hypothetical sub-

stance), rutile (mineral), futile, fictile (moulded from clay), ductile, pantile, quintile (astrology term), reptile, hairstyle, freestyle, hostile, prostyle (architectural term), turnstile, servile, revile, awhile, meanwhile, erstwhile, worthwhile, resile (spring back), fusile (easily melted), exile.

immobile, crocodile, camomile, Chari-Nile (language group), juvenile, thermopile (radiant energy detector), micropyle (biology term), puerile, afebrile (without fever), indocile, expansile (able to expand), reconcile, infertile, volatile, versatile, pulsatile (beating rhythmically), inductile (not pliant), mercantile, infantile, epistyle (architectural term), peristyle (colonnade surrounding building).

aeolipile (model steam turbine), antifebrile, coleoptile (botany term), acrylonitrile (colourless liquid).

219.1
zoophile (animal lover), Francophile, discophile (collector of gramophone records), paedophile, Anglophile, thermophile (organism thriving in warmth), spermophile (US ground squirrel), xenophile (admirer of foreigners), Negrophile, Russophile, audiophile (hi-fi enthusiast), bibliophile, myrmecophile (animal living with ants), Germanophile, ailurophile (cat lover).

219.2
fissile, missile, scissile (capable of being cut), domicile, antimissile, circumscissile (botany term).

219.3
ensile (store in silo), pensile (ornithology term), tensile, prehensile, thermotensile (physics term).

219.4
tractile (ductile), tactile, retractile (able to be withdrawn), protractile (able to be extended), contractile.

219.5
sectile (easily sliced), projectile, erectile.

219.6
Gentile, percentile (statistics term).

219.7
hypostyle (architectural term), urostyle (zoology term), cyclostyle, amphiprostyle (architectural term).

219.8
sextile, textile, bissextile (relating to leap year).

220 -oll
col, doll, dol (unit of pain intensity), loll, moll.

obol, COBOL, glycol (liquid used as antifreeze), aldol (chemical compound), argol (deposit in wine vats), Gogol, googol (large number), ALGOL, Algol (bright star), Mongol, Jehol (region of China), salol (crystalline substance), xylol (chemical compound), thymol (crystalline compound), enol (chemical compound), phenol (carbolic acid), redpoll (finch), sterol (biochemical compound), cresol (chemical compound), atoll, metol (chemical compound), naphthol (crystalline substance), menthol, AWOL, podzol, benzol (chemical compound).

guaiacol (yellowish oily liquid), protocol, alcohol, mestranol (synthetic hormone), ethanol, methanol (chemical compound), Interpol, cortisol (hormone), creosol (yellow oily liquid), regosol (type of soil), Limassol (Cypriot port), plasmasol (fluid form of protoplasm), planosol (type of soil), parasol, aerosol, girasol (type of opal), entresol (mezzanine floor), lithosol (type of soil), amatol (explosive substance).

dimercaprol (colourless oily liquid), eucalyptol (colourless oily liquid), chloramphenicol (antibiotic).

220.1
borneol (chemical compound), vitriol, oestriol (hormone), geraniol (chemical compound), terpineol (chemical compound), urushiol (poisonous liquid).

220.2
Komsomol (Russian youth association), paracetamol.

220.3
quinol (crystalline substance), eugenol (oily liquid), orcinol (crystalline substance), retinol (biochemical compound), allopurinol (synthetic drug).

220.4
glycerol (syrupy liquid), calciferol (vitamin), tocopherol (vitamin), stigmasterol (biochemical compound), cholesterol, zoosterol (biochemical compound), ergosterol (biochemical compound), sitosterol (extract from soya beans).

221 -orl
awl, all, orle (border around a shield), ball, bawl, caul, call, scall (disease of the scalp), fall, Gaul, gall, hall, haul, maul, mall, small, pall, Paul, pawl (part of ratchet mechanism), spall (rock splinter), squall, brawl, crawl, scrawl, drawl, sprawl, trawl, thrall, Saul, shawl, schorl (black tourmaline), tall, stall, wall, waul (wail like a cat), yawl.

hairball, eyeball, highball, fireball, snowball, screwball, blackball, punchball, oddball, handball, pinball, baseball, netball, meatball, football, mothball, jackal, catcall, withal, bradawl, holdall, befall, snowfall, landfall, windfall, rainfall, downfall, catfall (nautical term), pratfall, pitfall, nightfall, shortfall, footfall, windgall (swelling on horse's fetlock), Bengal, Bohol (Philippine island), guildhall, keelhaul, downhaul (nautical term), townhall, Whitehall, monal (Asian pheasant), Nepal, appal, Blackwall, enthral, Walsall, forestall, thumbstall, install, footstall (base of column), bookstall, sidewall, Cornwall, stonewall.

carryall, Montreal, volleyball, cannonball, basketball, wherewithal, waterfall, Senegal, Donegal, overhaul, overall, disenthral, tattersall (patterned fabric), fingerstall, caterwaul.

221.1
recall, nudicaul (having leafless stems), amplexicaul (botany term).

222 -oil
oil, boil, Boyle, coil, Doyle, foil, noil (short textile fibres), spoil, roil, broil, soil, toil, voile, parboil, gumboil, recoil, uncoil, trefoil, airfoil, cinquefoil (type of plant), milfoil (yarrow), tinfoil, gargoyle, turmoil, despoil, embroil, subsoil, topsoil, multifoil (looped design), disembroil, undersoil.

222.1
aerofoil, hydrofoil, quatrefoil (architectural ornament), counterfoil, Fianna fail (Irish political party).

223 -ole
bowl, boll, bole, coal, kohl, cole (plant of cabbage family), skoal (drinking toast), dole, dhole (fierce canine mammal), foal, goal, whole, hole, mole, knoll, Pole, pole, poll, role, roll, scroll, droll, prole, troll, stroll, soul, sole, Seoul (capital of South Korea), sol (former French coin), shoal, toll, tole (enamelled metal ware), stole, thole (wooden peg in boat), vole.

creole, Sheol (abode of the dead), punchbowl, fishbowl, charcoal, clearcole (size for painting walls), bricole (billiards term), indole (crystalline substance), de Gaulle, cajole, keyhole, kneehole, frijol (variety of French bean), eyehole, blowhole, hellhole, armhole, manhole, pinhole, peephole, loophole, knothole, pothole, porthole, foxhole, anole (small tropical lizard),

maypole, dipole (pair of electric charges), blackpoll (US warbler), catchpole (medieval sheriff's officer), tadpole, flagpole, bargepole, ridgepole, Walpole, beanpole, payroll, pyrrole (colourless toxic liquid), Tyrol, bankroll, bedroll, safrole (plant oil), enrol, unroll, patrol, control, turnsole (plant turning towards sun), insole, console, skatole (crystalline substance), pistole (former European gold coin), extol, azole (chemical compound).

vacuole, amphibole (type of mineral), rocambole (garlic-like plant), caracole (half turn in dressage), pratincole (swallow-like bird), cubbyhole, pigeonhole, buttonhole, Seminole (American Indian), multirole, rock-and-roll, decontrol, self-control, oversoul (spiritual essence of everything), carmagnole (French Revolutionary costume), thiazole (chemical compound), carbazole (chemical compound), bibliopole (dealer in rare books).

223.1
bronchiole, cariole (horse-drawn cart), dariole (mould used in cookery), oriole, aureole (halo), cabriole, capriole (leap), centriole (biology term), petiole (leaf stalk), ostiole (small pore), arteriole (subdivision of artery).

223.2
condole, farandole (lively Provençal dance), girandole (ornamental candleholder).

223.3
parole, barcarole, banderole (long narrow ship's flag), fumarole (vent in volcano), rigmarole, casserole, profiterole.

223.4
rissole, camisole, anisole (colourless fragrant liquid).

224 -owl
owl, cowl, scowl, foul, fowl, jowl, howl, growl, prowl, yowl, peafowl, be-

foul, moorfowl, afoul, wildfowl, water-fowl.

225 -ull

cull, scull, skull, dull, gull, Hull, hull, lull, mull, Mull, null, Tull (English agriculturalist), stull (timber prop in mining), numbskull, annul, caracul (Persian lamb), Solihull, multihull, disannul.

226 -ul [further rhymes may be created by adding -ful to appropriate nouns]

bull, full, pull, wool.

Kabul (capital of Afghanistan), bulbul (tropical songbird), playful, careful, prayerful, gleeful, earful, cheerful, fearful, tearful, eyeful, joyful, rueful, wakeful, tankful, thankful, watchful, dreadful, heedful, needful, handful, mindful, changeful, vengeful, baleful, guileful, bowlful, doleful, soulful, armful, harmful, blameful, shameful, brimful, roomful, manful, skinful, sinful, scornful, mournful, spoonful, tuneful, wrongful, songful, hopeful, helpful, graceful, peaceful, blissful, useful, bashful, wishful, artful, cartful, hurtful, fitful, potful, thoughtful, doubtful, fruitful, tactful, restful, wistful, boastful, faithful, mirthful, wrathful, slothful, mouthful, healthful, stealthful, easeful.

Istanbul, bellyful, merciful, fanciful, pitiful, beautiful, dutiful, plentiful, bountiful, powerful, wonderful, colourful, masterful, flavourful, quiverful, reproachful, regardful, remindful, unmindful, revengeful, thimbleful, needleful, meaningful, worshipful, disgraceful, purposeful, deceitful, pocketful, unfaithful.

226.1
awful, lawful, unlawful.

226.2
woeful, sorrowful.

226.3
skilful, wilful, unskilful.

226.4
baneful, gainful, painful, disdainful.

226.5
stressful, successful.

226.6
forceful, remorseful, resourceful.

226.7
fateful, hateful, plateful, grateful, ungrateful.

226.8
fretful, forgetful, regretful.

226.9
spiteful, rightful, frightful, delightful.

226.10
neglectful, respectful, disrespectful.

226.11
eventful, resentful, uneventful.

226.12
tasteful, wasteful, distasteful.

226.13
lustful, trustful, distrustful.

226.14
ruthful, truthful, toothful (small draught of liquor), youthful, untruthful.

227 -ool

boulle (denoting type of marquetry), boule (pear-shaped imitation gemstone), Boole (British mathematician), cool, school, fool, ghoul, Goole (English inland port), joule, who'll, pool, Poole, pul (Afghan coin), spool, rule, drool, shul (synagogue), tool, stool, yule, you'll, mule, mewl, pule (to whimper), tulle.

babul (type of acacia), Stambul (old part of Istanbul), playschool, deschool, preschool, befool (make a fool of), tomfool, cagoule, Banjul (capital of Gambia), Blackpool, whirlpool, ampoule, cesspool, ferrule (metal cap), ferule (flat cane for punishment), spherule (tiny sphere), chondrule (meteorology term), misrule, toadstool, faldstool (bishop's backless seat), close-stool, footstool, lobule, globule, tubule, macule, saccule, locule (biology term), floccule (small mass of particles), bascule (type of bridge), schedule, module, nodule, virgule (printing term), cellule, pilule, granule, venule (small vein), papule (small pimple), cupule (cup-shaped structure), capsule, noctule (insectivorous bat), pustule, frustule (botany term), ovule, valvule.

supercool (cool without freezing), Hartlepool, Pontypool, Liverpool, overrule, vestibule, majuscule, minuscule, gallinule (aquatic bird).

animalcule, hierodule (ancient Greek temple slave).

227.1
spicule (slender pointed structure), ridicule, lodicule (botany term), molecule, fascicule (published instalment of book), graticule (grid), reticule (woman's bag), monticule (small hill).

228 -'l
babble, scabble (shape roughly), dabble, gabble, rabble, scrabble, drabble (make wet or dirty), grabble (grope about), barbel (European fish), garble, marble, Schnabel (US musician), jebel (hill in Arab country), pebble, rebel, treble, burble, herbal, verbal, feeble, Bible, libel, tribal, bobble, cobble, gobble, hobble, nobble, squabble, wobble, bauble, corbel, warble, foible, Jubal (biblical character), rouble, bubal (African antelope), tubal, fimble (male hemp plant), nimble, cymbal, symbol, timbal (type of kettledrum), thimble, wimble (hand tool), umbel (type of inflorescence), bumble, scumble (art term), fumble, jumble, humble, mumble, rumble, crumble, grumble, tumble, stumble, faecal, treacle, faucal (anato-

my term), snorkel, paucal (linguistics term), ducal, ankle, fankle (*Scot* entangle), rankle, Wankel (German engineer), Gaskell (English writer), pascal (unit of pressure), mascle (heraldic term), rascal, fiscal, hatchel (to comb flax), satchel, Rachel, Mitchell, fardel, hadal (relating to ocean depths), ladle, cradle, heddle (part of loom), medal, meddle, pedal, peddle, treadle, curdle, girdle, hurdle, beadle, needle, pedal (relating to the foot), wheedle, caudal, dawdle, modal, nodal, yodel, Kendal, Mendel (Austrian botanist), Grendel (legendary man-eating monster), sendel (fine silk fabric), dirndl, fondle, rondel (type of poem), poundal (unit of force), roundel (circular mark or object), bundle, rundle (ladder rung), trundle, baffle, snaffle, raffle, Eiffel, rifle, trifle, stifle, offal, coffle (line of chained slaves), waffle, gargle, burgle, gurgle, ogle, bogle (*Dialect* bogey), mogul, Vogul (member of Siberian people), juggle, smuggle, snuggle, struggle, mongol, bungle, fungal, jungle, cudgel, angel, dermal, thermal, primal, hummel (*Scot* hornless), pommel (part of saddle), pummel, Brummell, carnal, charnel (sepulchral), darnel (type of grass), tarnal (*US* damned), Chunnel, funnel, gunnel (eel-like fish), gunwale (nautical term), runnel (small stream), tunnel, Bracknell, cracknel, spignel (European plant), signal, hymnal, simnel, grapnel, shrapnel, carpal (wrist bone), carpel (female part of flower), maple, papal, staple, sepal, purple, couple, supple, scruple, cupel (gold-refining vessel), duple, pupil, scalpel, ample, trample, temple, dimple, pimple, crimple (crumple), simple, wimple, rumple, crumple, gospel, rorqual, mayoral, feral (wild), spheral (spherical), squirrel, Cyril, Wirral, gyral (rotating), viral, spiral, timbrel (tambourine), whimbrel (European curlew), sacral, mandrel (spindle in machine tool), spandrel (architectural term), scoundrel, mongrel, April, petrol, petrel, neutral, spectral, astral, wastrel, cloistral, minstrel, hassle, tassel, vassal, basal, chessel (cheese-making mould), nestle, pestle, wrestle, trestle, Cecil, vessel, Faisal, sisal, dorsal, morsel, plimsoll, cancel, handsel (*Dialect* new year gift), spancel (rope for fettering horse), chancel, tinsel, council, counsel, groundsel, Etzel (legendary German king), quetzal (crested bird), pretzel, schnitzel, special, bushel, crucial, nuptial, hurtle, myrtle, turtle, rectal, lintel, pintle (hinge pin), quintal (unit of weight), pastel, coastal, postal, Bethel, lethal, brothel, larval, marvel, navel, naval, serval, hovel, novel, grovel, oval, Lovell, shovel, narwhal (arctic whale), Orwell, lingual, Cromwell, gromwell (flowering plant), Sitwell, Maxwell, Boswell, axle, axel (ice-skating jump), bezel (surface on cutting tool), easel, diesel, teasel, weasel, chisel, fizzle, mizzle (*Dialect* drizzle), drizzle, frizzle, grizzle, sizzle, swizzle, nozzle, schnozzle (*US* nose), causal, guzzle, muzzle, nuzzle, puzzle, damsel.

enfeeble, ensemble, archducal, Arundel, triumphal, conjugal, Portugal, Tintagel, archangel, caramel, communal, tribunal, autumnal, uncouple, quadruple, octuple, quintuple, septuple, sextuple, catarrhal, deferral, referral, palpebral (relating to the eyelid), cerebral, vertebral, sepulchral, integral, urethral, especial, provincial, palatal, pivotal, betrothal, interval, bilingual, trilingual, sublingual, embezzle, reprisal, devisal (act of devising).

chromosomal, metacarpal, thermocouple, episcopal, Sebastopol (Russian port), equinoctial, multilingual, monolingual.

228.1
bael (Indian tree), Jael (biblical character), Raphael, Ishmael (biblical character), betrayal, portrayal, Israel.

228.2
real, ideal, genial (relating to the chin), corneal, surreal, unreal, epigeal (living on soil surface), hypogeal (living below soil surface), pharyngeal, laryngeal, perineal, peroneal (relating to outer leg), oesophageal, peritoneal.

228.3
labial (relating to a lip), brachial (relating to the arm), bronchial, radial, prandial, mondial (of the whole world), Belial (demon), cuneal (wedge-shaped), burial, Gabriel, Umbriel (satellite of Uranus), atrial, patrial, uncial (type of capital letter), lacteal (relating to milk), osteal (relating to bone), bathyal (relating to ocean depths), gavial (Asian crocodile), mesial (in the middle).

proverbial, adverbial, connubial (relating to marriage), Ezekiel, parochial, allodial (former property law term), custodial, postprandial, lymphangial (relating to lymphatic vessel), phalangeal (anatomy term), binomial, trinomial, monomial, biennial, triennial, millennial, perennial, centennial, colloquial, mercurial, industrial, carnassial (type of tooth), popliteal (behind the knee).

myocardial, endocardial, polynomial, entrepreneurial.

228.3.1
medial, predial (relating to land), remedial.

228.3.2
cordial, primordial.

228.3.3
effigial, vestigial, apterygial (zoology term).

228.3.4
filial, familial.

228.3.5
cranial, geranial (chemistry term), intracranial.

228.3.6
genial, menial, venial, congenial.

228.3.7
lineal, pineal, matrilineal, patrilineal.

228.3.8
colonial, baronial, ceremonial, matrimonial, patrimonial, antimonial (containing antimony), testimonial.

228.3.9
troupial (South American songbird), marsupial.

228.3.10
aerial, ariel (Arabian gazelle), Ariel (satellite of Uranus), narial (relating to the nostrils), vicarial, malarial, bursarial, actuarial, estuarial, secretarial, antimalarial.

228.3.11
ferial (relating to weekday), cereal, serial, sidereal, venereal, funereal, imperial, arterial, material, bacterial, ethereal, diphtherial, managerial, presbyterial, immaterial, magisterial, ministerial, monasterial.

228.3.12
oriel, boreal (relating to the north).

arboreal, enchorial (of a particular country), armorial, marmoreal (relating to marble), memorial, manorial, corporeal, gressorial (adapted for walking), cursorial (adapted for running), fossorial (used for burrowing), scansorial (adapted for climbing), sensorial (relating to the senses), tonsorial, sartorial, tutorial, factorial, pictorial, auctorial (relating to an author), tinctorial (relating to dyeing), raptorial (predatory), uxorial.

immemorial, incorporeal, insessorial (adapted for perching), professorial, prefectorial, directorial.

ambassadorial, gladiatorial, multifactorial (genetics term).

228.3.12.1
editorial, territorial, inquisitorial, extraterritorial.

228.3.12.2
piscatorial (relating to fish), purgatorial, grallatorial (ornithology term), clamatorial (ornithology term), senatorial, equatorial, dictatorial, saltatorial (adapted for jumping), legislatorial, gubernatorial (relating to a governor), subequatorial, conspiratorial, visitatorial (relating to official visitation), accusatorial.

228.3.13
bimestrial (lasting for two months), terrestrial, extraterrestrial.

228.3.14
bestial, celestial.

228.3.15
trivial, quadrivial (having four roads meeting), convivial.

228.3.16
jovial, synovial.

228.3.17
fluvial (relating to a river), pluvial (relating to rain), diluvial (produced by a flood), alluvial.

228.3.18
axial, preaxial (anatomy term), biaxial, triaxial, coaxial, abaxial (away from the axis), adaxial (facing towards the axis), uniaxial, epitaxial (electronics term).

228.4
dial, phial, myall (Australian acacia), rial (Iranian currency), trial, sial (part of earth's crust), viol, sundial, denial, espial, retrial, mistrial, self-denial.

228.5
knawel (Eurasian plant), withdrawal.

228.6
loyal, royal, disloyal, pennyroyal (Eurasian plant).

228.7
Noel, bestowal.

228.8
bowel, dowel, Powell, rowel (spiked wheel on spur), trowel, towel, vowel, embowel, avowal, disembowel, semivowel (phonetics term), disavowal.

228.9
menstrual, gradual, Samuel, sensual, casual, visual, usual, virtual, mutual, punctual, textual, sexual.

premenstrual, continual, consensual (legal term), unusual, perpetual, accentual (rhythmical), eventual, conventual (relating to a convent), perceptual, conceptual, contextual, asexual, bisexual, transsexual.

pari-mutuel (betting system), unisexual, homosexual.

audiovisual, heterosexual.

228.9.1
residual, individual.

228.9.2
annual, manual, biannual, Emmanuel.

228.9.3
ritual, habitual, spiritual.

228.9.4
actual, factual, tactual (caused by touch), contractual.

228.9.5
effectual, aspectual (linguistics term), ineffectual, intellectual.

228.10
jewel, cruel, crewel, gruel, dual, duel, fuel, newel, bejewel, refuel, renewal.

228.11
Abel, able, Babel, cable, fable, gable, label, sable, table, stable, enable, unable, disable, retable (screen behind altar), worktable, timetable, turntable, unstable, disenable.

228.12
kibble (bucket for hoisting material), dibble (small garden tool), nibble, quibble, Ribble, scribble, dribble, fribble (fritter away), gribble (small marine animal), Sybil, mandible, cannibal, Hannibal, thurible (container for burning incense), crucible.

228.13
coble (*Scot* fishing boat), global, noble, ennoble, Grenoble, ignoble.

228.14
bubble, double, nubble (small lump), rubble, trouble, stubble, redouble.

228.15
Hasdrubal (Carthaginian general), soluble, voluble, chasuble, insoluble, resoluble, indissoluble, irresoluble.

228.16 [further rhymes may be created by adding -*able* or -*ible* to appropriate verbs]
playable, payable, probable, placable, peccable (liable to sin), workable, likable, lockable, vocable (vocal sound), bankable, stretchable, touchable, quenchable, readable, affable, laughable, effable, chargeable, legible, changeable, fallible, gullible, tenable, tunable, pregnable, damnable, stoppable, palpable, culpable, equable, arable, parable, sparable (small nail), terrible, horrible, passable, peaceable, possible, forcible, satiable, washable, notable, potable (drinkable), quotable, tractable, liftable, printable, constable, Dunstable, tithable, lovable, taxable, flexible, feasible, plausible.

unknowable, improbable, implacable, remarkable, impeccable, unspeakable, dislikable, educable, revocable, detachable, untouchable, degradable, unreadable, avoidable, refundable, ineffable, illegible, infallible, indelible, redeemable, estimable, conformable, consumable, presumable, fathomable, untenable, amenable, impregnable, unflappable, unstoppable, impalpable, inculpable (guiltless), transferable, desirable, adorable, deplorable, execrable, demonstrable, manoeuvrable, irascible, impassable, impossible, reducible, purchasable, expansible, responsible, pronounceable, collapsible, insatiable, compatible, redoubtable, comfortable, vegetable, palatable, retractable, intractable, perfectible, delectable, respectable, expectable, detectable, predictable, unprintable, adaptable, corruptible, attemptable, contemptible, resistible, exhaustible, observable, forgivable, inflexible, erasable, implausible, opposable, disposable.

imperturbable, ineducable, irrevocable, unavoidable, interchangeable, reconcilable, inviolable, irredeemable, inestimable, unfathomable, undesirable, impenetrable, indemonstrable, irreducible, irresponsible, unpronounceable, incompatible, uncomfortable, unpredictable, incorruptible, irresistible, inexhaustible, unforgivable, irresolvable.

biodegradable, irreconcilable.

228.16.1
agreeable, foreseeable, disagreeable, unforeseeable.

228.16.2
malleable, amiable, permeable, expiable, variable, pitiable, dutiable, leviable, enviable, impermeable, invariable, justiciable (subject to jurisdiction), unenviable, irremediable, semipermeable, differentiable.

228.16.3
liable, pliable, friable, triable, viable, reliable, deniable, inviable, unreliable, undeniable.

228.16.3.1
modifiable, magnifiable, verifiable, classifiable, specifiable, certifiable, notifiable, rectifiable, quantifiable, justifiable, identifiable.

228.16.4
enjoyable, employable, unemployable.

228.16.5
dowable (legal term), allowable.

228.16.6
arguable, valuable, issuable, invaluable.

228.16.7
doable, suable, viewable, renewable.

228.16.8
bribable, describable, indescribable.

228.16.9
breakable, unbreakable, unshakable, mistakable, unmistakable.

228.16.10
medicable, predicable (able to be affirmed), applicable, explicable, amicable, despicable, extricable, practicable, eradicable, inapplicable, inexplicable, communicable, inextricable, impracticable, ineradicable, incommunicable.

228.16.11
drinkable, sinkable, thinkable, undrinkable, unsinkable, unthinkable.

228.16.12
reachable, teachable, impeachable, unteachable, unimpeachable.

228.16.13
approachable, reproachable, irreproachable, unapproachable.

228.16.14
edible, credible, beddable, inedible, incredible.

228.16.15
biddable, formidable.

228.16.16
audible, fordable, laudable, recordable, inaudible, rewardable.

228.16.17
expandable, understandable.

228.16.18
mendable, vendible, unbendable, commendable, dependable, expendable, extendible, recommendable.

228.16.19
litigable, mitigable, navigable, indefatigable, circumnavigable.

228.16.20
knowledgeable, negligible, manageable, marriageable, dirigible, corrigible, salvageable, exigible (liable to be demanded), incorrigible.

228.16.20.1
eligible, ineligible, intelligible, unintelligible.

228.16.21
frangible (breakable), tangible, refrangible (able to be refracted), infrangible, intangible, irrefrangible (inviolable).

228.16.22
bailable, scalable, saleable, sailable, resaleable, available, unassailable, unavailable.

228.16.23
syllable, willable, refillable, monosyllable.

228.16.24
controllable, uncontrollable, inconsolable.

228.16.25
calculable, regulable, inoculable, incalculable.

228.16.26
flammable, inflammable, nonflammable, programmable.

228.16.27
explainable, attainable, obtainable, unexplainable, unattainable, unobtainable.

228.16.28
discernible, returnable, indiscernible, nonreturnable.

228.16.29
terminable, imaginable, determinable, interminable, abominable, unimaginable, indeterminable.

228.16.30
finable (liable to a fine), definable, reclinable, inclinable, indefinable, indeclinable.

228.16.31
questionable, pardonable, personable, fashionable, actionable, conscionable, governable, alienable, unquestionable, impressionable, objectionable, unconscionable, ungovernable, inalienable, companionable.

228.16.31.1
pensionable, unmentionable.

228.16.31.2
reasonable, seasonable, unreasonable, unseasonable.

228.16.32
capable, incapable, inescapable.

228.16.33
bearable, tearable, wearable, unbearable, repairable, untearable, unwearable.

228.16.34
curable, durable, insurable, incurable, endurable.

228.16.35
saturable, preferable, tolerable, colourable, memorable, admirable, generable (able to be generated), venerable, honourable, vulnerable, operable, superable, comparable, answerable, mensurable, alterable, favourable, miserable.

considerable, imponderable, insufferable, intolerable, innumerable, dishonourable, invulnerable, inoperable, insuperable, incomparable, unanswerable, commensurable, immensurable, unutterable, inalterable, unfavourable, inexorable.

inconsiderable, indecipherable, irrecoverable.

228.16.35.1
reparable, separable, irreparable, inseparable.

228.16.35.2
pleasurable, measurable, immeasurable.

228.16.36
traceable, effaceable, replaceable, ineffaceable, irreplaceable.

228.16.37
expressible, accessible, irrepressible, inexpressible, inaccessible.

228.16.38
coercible, submersible, reversible, conversable, incoercible, irreversible.

228.16.39
kissable, miscible, immiscible, omissible, permissible, admissible, rescissible (able to be rescinded), noticeable, serviceable, impermissible, inadmissible.

228.16.40
sensible, tensible (able to be stretched), defensible, dispensable, insensible, ostensible, extensible, indefensible, apprehensible, reprehensible, comprehensible, indispensable, incomprehensible.

228.16.41
vincible, invincible, convincible, inconvincible.

228.16.42
depreciable, appreciable, inappreciable.

228.16.43
punishable, perishable, imperishable, distinguishable, extinguishable, indistinguishable, inextinguishable.

228.16.44
sociable, negotiable, dissociable, unsociable.

228.16.45
rateable, debatable, inflatable, untranslatable.

228.16.46
forgettable, regrettable, unforgettable.

228.16.47
convertible, inconvertible, incontrovertible.

228.16.48
eatable, beatable, unbeatable, repeatable.

228.16.49
habitable, dubitable, marketable, creditable, profitable, hospitable, equitable, charitable, heritable, veritable, irritable, indubitable, discreditable, unprofitable, illimitable, inimitable, indomitable, inhospitable, inequitable, inevitable.

228.16.50
indictable, excitable, extraditable.

228.16.51
portable, supportable, insupportable.

228.16.52
reputable, attributable, irrefutable, disreputable.

228.16.53
suitable, mutable, inscrutable, unsuitable, immutable, commutable, imputable, disputable, incommutable, incomputable, indisputable.

228.16.54
deductible, destructible, ineluctable (inescapable), indestructible.

228.16.55
preventable, presentable, unpreventable, unpresentable.

228.16.56
accountable, surmountable, unaccountable, insurmountable.

228.16.57
merchantable, lamentable, warrantable, unwarrantable.

228.16.58
perceptible, susceptible, acceptable, imperceptible, unacceptable.

228.16.59
suggestible, comestible, digestible, arrestable, detestable, contestable, indigestible, incontestable.

228.16.60
combustible, adjustable, incombustible.

228.16.61

achievable, believable, retrievable, conceivable, unbelievable, irretrievable, inconceivable.

228.16.62

movable, provable, immovable, removable, improvable, irremovable.

228.16.63

risible, visible, cognizable (perceptible), divisible, invisible, indivisible.

228.16.64

sizable, devisable, advisable, realizable, recognizable, inadvisable, unrecognizable.

228.16.65

usable, fusible (able to be melted), excusable, infusible, irrecusable (unable to be rejected), inexcusable.

228.17

amble, Campbell, gamble, gambol, ramble, bramble, scramble, shamble, preamble, unscramble.

228.18

Kemble (English acting family), tremble, dissemble, assemble, resemble, disassemble.

228.19

Acol (bridge term), cackle, hackle, mackle (printing term), crackle, grackle (US songbird), shackle, tackle, hamshackle (fetter a horse), ramshackle, tabernacle.

228.20

darkle (grow dark), sparkle, debacle, monarchal.

228.21

deckle, Jekyll, heckle, speckle, freckle, shekel, kenspeckle (*Scot* easily recognized).

228.22

circle, encircle, semicircle, homocercal (zoology term), heterocercal (zoology term).

228.23 [also **38** + *-al*]

chicle (ingredient of chewing-gum), fickle, mickle (*Dialect* much), nickel, pickle, picul (Oriental unit of weight), brickle (*Dialect* brittle), prickle, trickle, strickle, sickle, tickle, stickle (argue about trifles).

vehicle, stoical, cubicle, cubical (relating to volume), radicle (embryonic plant root), radical, nodical (astronomy term), magical, calycle (biology term), caulicle (small plant stalk), biblical, chemical, rhythmical, funicle (botany term), tunicle (Catholic bishop's vestment), technical, apical (at the apex), typical, auricle (heart's upper chamber), curricle (two-wheeled open carriage), metrical, utricle (part of ear), ventricle, fascicle (bundle of branches), classical, farcical, vesical (relating to bladder), vesicle (small cavity), versicle, icicle, bicycle, tricycle, ossicle (small bone in ear), Popsicle (*Trademark*), dropsical, article, particle, vertical, nautical, canticle, sceptical, optical, testicle, ethical, mythical, clavicle, cervical, lexical (relating to vocabulary), musical, whimsical.

veridical (truthful), juridical (relating to law), pontifical, encyclical, inimical, cupronickel, pumpernickel, atypical, cylindrical, theatrical, symmetrical, electrical, nonsensical, elliptical, unmusical.

hierarchical, philosophical, biochemical, aeronautical, dialectical, paradoxical, lackadaisical, ecclesiastical.

228.23.1

medical, pedicle (small plant stalk), premedical, paramedical.

228.23.2

methodical, periodical, immethodical.

228.23.3

graphical, geographical, biographical, typographical, autobiographical.

228.23.4
surgical, liturgical, metallurgical, neurosurgical.

228.23.5 [further rhymes may be derived from **16.108.4**]
logical, illogical, geological, biological, zoological, ecological, psychological, chronological, technological, pathological, mythological.

228.23.6
helical, pellicle (thin surface layer), angelical, evangelical.

228.23.7
silicle (type of fruit), umbilical.

228.23.8
follicle, symbolical, diabolical.

228.23.9
comical, economical, astronomical, gastronomical, anatomical.

228.23.10
panicle (type of inflorescence), sanicle (flowering plant), mechanical, tyrannical, botanical, puritanical.

228.23.11
galenical (pharmacology term), arsenical, ecumenical.

228.23.12
clinical, cynical, rabbinical, dominical (relating to the Lord), adminicle (legal term).

228.23.13
conical, chronicle, canonical, ironical, acronychal (occurring at sunset).

228.23.14
tropical, topical, subtropical.

228.23.15
spherical, clerical, chimerical (fanciful), numerical, hysterical, anticlerical.

228.23.16
lyrical, empirical, satirical.

228.23.17
rhetorical, historical, metaphorical, allegorical, categorical, oratorical.

228.23.18
sabbatical, grammatical, fanatical, mathematical, ungrammatical.

228.23.19
reticle (grid in optical instrument), heretical, alphabetical, catechetical (by question and answer), theoretical, antithetical, hypothetical.

228.23.20
critical, political, analytical, apolitical, diacritical, hypocritical, hypercritical.

228.23.21
cuticle, pharmaceutical.

228.23.22
practical, tactical, impractical.

228.23.23
denticle (small tooth), identical, conventicle (secret group of worshippers).

228.23.24
mystical, statistical, egotistical.

228.23.25
physical, quizzical, metaphysical.

228.24
Michael, cycle, recycle, unicycle, motorcycle.

228.25
cockle, grockle, socle (plinth), corncockle (European wayside plant), streptococcal.

228.26
focal, local, trochal (wheel-shaped), vocal, yokel, bifocal, matrilocal (living with wife's family), patrilocal (living with husband's family).

228.27
buckle, buccal (relating to the cheek), chuckle, muckle (*Scot* much), knuckle, truckle, suckle, parbuckle (rope sling), turnbuckle (device for tightening wire), unbuckle, pinochle (card game), honeysuckle.

228.28
tubercle, manacle, barnacle, cenacle (supper room), binnacle (housing for

ship's compass), pinnacle, monocle, monachal (monastic), miracle, spiracle (respiratory aperture), oracle, coracle, spectacle, pentacle (star-shaped figure), tentacle, obstacle, reciprocal, receptacle, conceptacle (botany term), equivocal, unequivocal.

228.28.1
zodiacal, maniacal, ammoniacal, paradisiacal.

228.29
inkle (linen tape), wrinkle, crinkle, sprinkle, tinkle, winkle, twinkle, besprinkle, periwinkle, Rip Van Winkle.

228.30
uncle, nuncle (*Dialect* uncle), carbuncle, peduncle (flower stalk), furuncle (a boil), caruncle (fleshy outgrowth).

228.31
addle, paddle, raddle, straddle, saddle, staddle, skedaddle, unsaddle, packsaddle, fiddle-faddle.

228.32
kiddle (device for catching fish), diddle, fiddle, middle, piddle, riddle, griddle, twiddle, infidel, unriddle (puzzle out), tarradiddle (nonsense), pyramidal.

228.33 [also 92.7 + -*al*]
idol, idle, Rydal (English village), bridal, bridle, sidle, tidal, unbridle, suicidal, spermicidal, homicidal.

228.34
coddle, doddle, model, noddle, broddle (*Dialect* to poke), toddle, waddle, swaddle, twaddle, remodel, mollycoddle, niddle-noddle (nod rapidly).

228.35
Goidel (Gaelic-speaking Celt), conchoidal (geology term), spheroidal (approximately spherical), adenoidal, sinusoidal (maths term), amygdaloidal (geology term).

228.36
buddle (trough for washing ore), cuddle, fuddle, huddle, muddle, puddle, ruddle (red dye for sheep), befuddle, Tolpuddle.

228.37
boodle, doodle, noodle, poodle, strudel, udal (legal term), feudal, caboodle, flapdoodle (*Slang* foolish talk), canoodle.

228.38
apodal (without feet), citadel, hebdomadal, antipodal.

228.39
candle, scandal, dandle (bounce child on knee), Handel, handle, sandal, vandal, manhandle, panhandle, mishandle.

228.40
kindle, Mindel (European glaciation period), spindle, brindle, Tyndale (English Protestant), dwindle, swindle, rekindle, enkindle.

228.41
skiffle, sniffle, piffle, riffle, whiffle (behave unpredictably), apocryphal.

228.42
scuffle, duffel, muffle, snuffle, ruffle, truffle, shuffle, kerfuffle, reshuffle.

228.43
gaggle, haggle, draggle (hang trailing), straggle, waggle, bedraggle, raggle-taggle (unkempt).

228.44
bagel (Jewish ring-shaped roll), Hegel (German philosopher), plagal (musical term), paigle (cowslip or oxlip), vagal (anatomy term), finagle.

228.45
eagle, beagle, legal, regal, porbeagle, illegal, viceregal, inveigle.

228.46
giggle, jiggle, niggle, sniggle (fish for eels), squiggle, wriggle, wiggle, prodigal, madrigal.

228.47

boggle, goggle, joggle, toggle, woggle, boondoggle (*US* do futile work), hornswoggle (*Slang* to cheat).

228.48

jugal (relating to the cheekbone), frugal, bugle, fugal, centrifugal.

228.49

angle, bangle, dangle, jangle, mangle, spangle, wrangle, strangle, tangle, wangle, triangle, fandangle (elaborate ornament), galangal (Oriental plant), bespangle, quadrangle, rectangle, entangle, untangle, disentangle.

228.50

ingle, bingle (*Austral* minor car crash), dingle (small wooded dell), jingle, mingle, cringle (nautical term), single, shingle, tingle, swingle (flax-beating instrument), commingle (to mix), Kriss Kringle (*US* Santa Claus), surcingle (horse's girth), intermingle.

228.51

camel, mammal, trammel (hindrance), stammel (coarse red woollen cloth), enamel, entrammel.

228.52

gimmal (part of rotating joint), animal, minimal, lacrimal, optimal, maximal, proximal, approximal (situated side by side).

228.52.1

decimal, vigesimal (relating to number twenty), millesimal, centesimal, duodecimal (relating to number twelve), hexadecimal (number system), Quadragesimal (relating to Lent), infinitesimal.

228.53

cormel (tiny new corm), formal, normal, informal, conformal (maths term), abnormal, subnormal, paranormal.

228.54

dismal, abysmal, baptismal, paroxysmal.

228.55

annal, cannel (type of coal), channel, flannel, panel, branle (French country dance), empanel.

228.56

anal, decanal (relating to a dean).

228.57

kennel, fennel, crenel (indentation in battlement), unkennel.

228.58

colonel, kernel, journal, vernal, diurnal, hibernal, infernal, supernal (celestial), eternal, maternal, paternal, fraternal, nocturnal, internal, asternal (unconnected to the sternum), external, sempiternal (everlasting).

228.59

penal, renal, venal, adrenal, duodenal.

228.60

ginnel (*Dialect* passageway between buildings), cardinal, ordinal, marginal, virginal, germinal (embryonic), terminal, Quirinal (hill of ancient Rome), actinal (zoology term), sentinel, Juvenal (Roman satirist), inguinal, vaccinal, original, cacuminal (phonetics term), intestinal, aboriginal.

228.60.1

testudinal (relating to tortoises), longitudinal, latitudinal.

228.60.2

paginal (page-for-page), imaginal (relating to an image).

228.60.3

seminal, trigeminal (anatomy term).

228.60.4

liminal (psychology term), criminal, Viminal (hill of ancient Rome), subliminal.

228.60.5

nominal, abdominal, prenominal (placed before a noun), phenomenal, binominal (biology term), pronominal (relating to a pronoun), adnominal (word modifying a noun).

228.60.6
vicinal (neighbouring), medicinal.

228.61
binal (twofold), final, spinal, rhinal (relating to the nose), vaginal, urinal, doctrinal, semifinal, quarterfinal, periclinal (botany term), anticlinal (botany term), isoclinal (sloping in same direction), anaclinal (geology term), cataclinal (geology term), matutinal (occurring in the morning), cerebrospinal.

228.62
tonal, zonal, hormonal, coronal (anatomy term), atonal.

228.63
regional, ammonal (an explosive), coronal (garland for head), arsenal, personal, factional, fractional, fictional, frictional, functional, optional, seasonal, antiphonal, diagonal, tetragonal (crystallography term), octagonal, hexagonal, orthogonal (relating to right angles), isochronal (having the same duration), impersonal, proportional, instructional, constructional, exceptional, occasional, divisional, provisional, meridional, unexceptional.

228.63.1
bacchanal (drunken celebration), diaconal (relating to a deacon).

228.63.2
national, passional, rational, irrational, multinational, international.

228.63.3
vocational, sensational, recreational, educational, irrigational, congregational, navigational, occupational, inspirational, operational, conversational, gravitational, progestational (before pregnancy), coeducational, denominational, representational.

228.63.4
professional, confessional, congressional, recessional, processional, unprofessional, semiprofessional.

228.63.5
additional, traditional, conditional, salicional (organ stop), nutritional, transitional, unconditional.

228.63.6
notional, emotional, promotional, devotional.

228.63.7
institutional, constitutional, unconstitutional.

228.63.8
sectional, directional.

228.63.9
intentional, conventional, three-dimensional, two-dimensional, unintentional, unconventional.

228.64
apple, chapel, dapple, grapple, crabapple, Whitechapel, pineapple.

228.65
peepul (Indian tree), people, tepal (botany term), steeple, unpeople, townspeople.

228.66
fipple (mouthpiece of wind instrument), nipple, ripple, cripple, triple, tipple, stipple, swipple (part of flail), maniple (unit of Roman soldiers), manciple (steward who buys provisions), principle, principal, multiple, municipal, participle.

228.67
Siple (mountain in Antarctica), stipel (small leaflike structure), disciple, archetypal.

228.68
hopple (hobble), popple, topple, estoppel (legal term).

228.69
opal, copal (hard aromatic resin), nopal (red-flowered cactus), Constantinople.

228.70
sample, example.

228.71
equal, sequel, unequal.

228.72
barrel, Carol, carol, carrel (study cubicle in library), parrel (nautical term), apparel.

228.73
coral, laurel, moral, quarrel, sorrel, amoral, immoral, Balmoral.

228.74
aural, oral, choral, goral (small goat antelope), chloral (oily liquid), floral, aboral (away from the mouth), binaural, monaural.

228.75
jural (relating to law), plural, pleural, rural, crural, Ural, mural, neural, sural (anatomy term), epidural, intramural, extramural.

228.76
liberal, pickerel (US freshwater fish), cockerel, mackerel, natural, structural, cultural, scriptural, sculptural, federal, ruderal (plant growing on wasteland), doggerel, cameral (relating to judicial chamber), humeral, numeral, admiral, general, mineral, funeral, corporal, temporal, nonpareil, vesperal (prayer book), visceral, mensural, lateral, literal, littoral, guttural, doctoral, enteral, apteral (architectural term), dipteral (architectural term), pastoral, several.

illiberal, unnatural, peripheral, bicameral, puerperal, bilateral, trilateral, collateral, postdoctoral, parenteral (medical term), Canaveral, inaugural, behavioural.

supernatural, preternatural, horticultural, unicameral, unilateral, equilateral, quadrilateral, multilateral.

228.76.1
conjectural, architectural.

228.76.2
femoral, ephemeral.

228.76.3
pectoral, electoral.

228.77
tumbrel, adumbral (shadowy).

228.78
dihedral (two-sided), anhedral (aircraft wing's downward inclination), cathedral, polyhedral, hemihedral (crystallography term), rhombohedral, procathedral (church serving as cathedral).

228.79
citral (fragrant plant oil), arbitral (relating to arbitration), diametral (relating to diameter).

228.80
central, ventral, dorsoventral.

228.81
kestrel, orchestral, campestral (relating to fields), ancestral.

228.82
mistral, magistral (pharmacology term), sinistral (relating to left side).

228.83
castle, parcel, tarsal, warsle (*Dialect* wrestle), Newcastle, metatarsal.

228.84
tercel (male falcon or hawk), succursal (subsidiary), rehearsal, demersal (living in deep water), dispersal, reversal, transversal, universal, quaquaversal (geology term).

228.85
kissel (Russian fruit dessert), scissel (waste metal), missal, bristle, gristle, thistle, whistle, abyssal, dismissal, epistle, cacomistle (cat-like mammal).

228.86
dossal (ornamental church hanging), fossil, jostle, throstle, colossal, apostle, hypoglossal (beneath the tongue).

228.87
bustle, justle (jostle), hustle, mussel, muscle, Russell, rustle, tussle, corpuscle.

228.88
pencel (small flag), pencil, stencil, commensal (biology term), utensil.

228.89
consul, tonsil, proconsul.

228.90
martial, marshal, partial, impartial.

228.91
facial, glacial, spatial, racial, abbatial, palatial, preglacial, subglacial, postglacial, multiracial.

228.92
Herschel (English astronomer), tertial (ornithology term), commercial, uncommercial, controversial.

228.93
judicial, official, seneschal (medieval household steward), initial, altricial (ornithology term), prejudicial, beneficial, sacrificial, artificial, unofficial, superficial, interstitial.

228.94
social, precocial (ornithology term), asocial, unsocial, antisocial.

228.95
financial, substantial, insubstantial, circumstantial.

228.96
sciential (knowledgeable), prudential, tangential, sequential, essential, potential, influential, pestilential, exponential, consequential, inessential, nonessential, quintessential, penitential, existential, expediential, experiential, inconsequential.

228.96.1
credential, confidential, precedential, evidential, providential, residential, presidential.

228.96.2
torrential, deferential, preferential, differential, inferential, reverential.

228.97
battle, cattle, chattel, rattle, prattle, tattle, Seattle, embattle, tittle-tattle, Quetzalcoatl (Aztec god).

228.98
startle, Nahuatl (American Indian).

228.99
fatal, natal, ratel (burrowing mammal), ratal (rateable value), prenatal, postnatal, perinatal, antenatal.

228.100
kettle, fettle, metal, mettle, nettle, petal, settle, nonmetal, gunmetal, resettle, unsettle, Citlaltépetl (Mexican volcano), Popocatépetl (Mexican volcano).

228.101
betel, beetle, chital (Asian deer), fetal, decretal (papal edict), centripetal.

228.102
it'll, kittle (*Scot* capricious), skittle, little, spittle, brittle, tittle, victual, whittle.

orbital, cubital (relating to the forearm), sagittal (resembling an arrow), vegetal (relating to plant life), digital, skeletal, belittle, Doolittle, remittal, committal, genital, Capitol, capital, hospital, lickspittle (servile person), acquittal, marital.

parietal (anatomy term), varietal (relating to biological variety), noncommittal, congenital, basipetal (botany term), bicipital (relating to the biceps), occipital (anatomy term), premarital, extramarital.

228.103
title, vital, requital, recital, subtitle, entitle, disentitle.

228.104
bottle, dottle (tobacco remnant in pipe), glottal, mottle, rotl (unit of weight), throttle, wattle, bluebottle, greenbottle (type of fly), axolotl, Aristotle.

228.105
chortle, mortal, portal, immortal.

228.106
total, teetotal, subtotal, sacerdotal (relating to priests), anecdotal.

228.107
cuttle, scuttle, subtle, shuttle, rebuttal.

228.108
Bootle, footle, rootle, brutal, tootle, Kwakiutl (American Indian).

228.109
cantle (part of saddle), mantle, mantel, Fremantle, dismantle, overmantel (shelf over mantlepiece), consonantal.

228.110
dental, gentle, mental, rental, cental (unit of weight), submental (beneath the chin), fragmental, segmental, parental, placental, oriental, transcendental, monumental, departmental, compartmental, continental, developmental, transcontinental, intercontinental.

228.110.1
incidental, accidental, Occidental, coincidental.

228.110.2
sedimental, regimental, elemental, incremental, detrimental, sentimental, experimental.

228.110.3
fundamental, ornamental, sacramental, instrumental, temperamental.

228.110.4
governmental, environmental.

228.111
quantal (physics term), horizontal, periodontal (around a tooth).

228.112
buntal (straw from palm leaves), frontal, prefrontal (zoology term), full-frontal, disgruntle, balibuntal (Philippine straw hat), contrapuntal.

228.113
festal (festive), vestal, agrestal (growing as a weed).

228.114
distal (anatomy term), listel (architectural term), mistal (*Scot* cowshed), pistol, Bristol, crystal, pedestal.

228.115
costal, hostel, Pentecostal, intercostal.

228.116
borstal, Saint Austell.

228.117
cavil, gavel, ravel, gravel, travel, unravel.

228.118
bevel, kevel (nautical term), devil, level, revel, daredevil, bedevil, dishevel.

228.119
evil, shrieval (relating to a sheriff), weevil, coeval (belonging to same age), medieval, upheaval, primeval, retrieval.

228.120
snivel, drivel, frivol (behave frivolously), shrivel, civil, swivel, carnival, Percival, uncivil, festival.

228.121
nival (growing in snow), rival, arrival, aestival (occurring in the summer), revival, survival, adjectival.

228.122
removal, approval, disapproval.

228.123
Daniel, spaniel, Nathaniel.

228.124
basil, Basil, dazzle, frazzle, bedazzle, razzle-dazzle.

228.125
hazel, nasal, phrasal, appraisal.

228.126
kursaal (building at health resort), mangelwurzel (Eurasian beet plant).

228.127
losel (*Dialect* worthless person), deposal, proposal, disposal, counterproposal.

228.128
ouzel, foozle (bungle golf shot), fusel (poisonous oily liquid), bamboozle, perusal, accusal, refusal.

228.129
housel (medieval name for Eucharist), spousal (marriage ceremony), tousle, espousal, arousal, carousal.

229 -am
am, Cam, cam, damn, dam, gam (school of whales), jam, jamb, ham, lam, lamb, clam, flam (*Dialect* falsehood), slam, mam, Spam (*Trademark*), ram, cram, scramb (*Dialect* scratch with fingernails), scram, dram, gram, pram, tram, sham, wham, swam, yam.

iamb, Siam, pro-am, ferbam (black powder), Edam, goddamn, milldam, quondam (former), Potsdam (East German city), Corfam (*Trademark*), doorjamb, mallam (West African Islamic scholar), Balaam (Old Testament character), flimflam (nonsense), Annam (part of Vietnam), Menam (Thai river), Hungnam (North Korean port), dirham (Moroccan currency), Ceram (Indonesian island), Bairam (Muslim festival), programme, engram (psychology term), tangram, Assam, cheongsam (Chinese dress), lactam (chemical group), wigwam, nizam (former Turkish soldier), exam.

cofferdam (watertight underwater chamber), Rotterdam, Amsterdam, commendam (temporary Church office), cryptogam (non-flowering plant), Abraham, oriflamme (scarlet medieval French flag), Surinam, Vietnam, dithyramb, epiphragm (part of snail's shell), diaphragm, telegram, milligram, epigram, centigram, cablegram, cocoyam (African food plant), ad nauseam.

229.1
diagram, nephogram (photograph of a cloud), logogram, hologram, nomogram (type of graph), anagram, monogram, chronogram (phrase concealing Roman numerals), phonogram (symbol representing sound), barogram, aerogram, tetragram (four-letter word), cartogram (map showing statistical information), photogram (type of photograph), hectogram, cryptogram (secret symbol), histogram, hexagram (star-shaped figure), roentgenogram (*US* x-ray), hierogram (sacred symbol), parallelogram, encephalogram, pneumoencephalogram, electroencephalogram.

229.1.1
cardiogram, radiogram, ideogram (symbol representing concept), stereogram, phraseogram (symbol representing phrase), electrocardiogram.

229.1.2
kilogram, oscillogram (oscilloscope record), dactylogram (*US* fingerprint).

230 -arm
arm, balm, barm (*Dialect* yeast), calm, charm, farm, harm, malm (greyish limestone), ma'am, smarm, palm, qualm, gram (Indian village), pram (light boat), psalm, Guam (Pacific island).

rearm, embalm, gendarme, Ratlam (Indian city), Islam, imam (Islamic prayer leader), schoolmarm, unarm, napalm, copalm (brown resin), ihram (Muslim pilgrim's white robes), firearm, forearm, disarm, gisarme (battle-axe), Nizam (title of Indian ruler).

Notre Dame, underarm, overarm, Omar Khayyam.

230.1
alarm, salaam, Dar es Salaam (capital of Tanzania).

231 -ame

aim, came, kame (mound formed by glacier), dame, fame, game, hame, lame, blame, claim, flame, maim, name, frame, same, Sejm (Polish legislature), shame, tame, wame (*Dialect* belly or womb).

became, defame, endgame, declaim, reclaim, acclaim, proclaim, disclaim, quitclaim (legal term), exclaim, aflame, inflame, surname, rename, forename, nickname, airframe (part of aircraft), doorframe, selfsame, overcame, counterclaim.

232 -em

em (printer's measure), feme (legal term for woman), gem, hem, clem (*Dialect* be hungry), phlegm, crème, Shem (Noah's eldest son), stem, them.

phloem, proem (preface), Yquem (French vineyard), modem, condemn, mayhem, ahem, xylem, golem (resurrection in Jewish legend), in rem (legal term), item (likewise), contemn (to scorn), millieme (Tunisian coin).

requiem, per diem, diadem, anadem (garland), Bethlehem, periblem (plant tissue), meristem (plant tissue), apothem (geometry term), apophthegm, chernozem (black soil).

233 -erm

berm (narrow ledge), chirm (chirp), firm, germ, perm, sperm, squirm, term, therm, worm.

affirm, infirm, confirm, bookworm, hookworm, silkworm, midterm, inchworm, threadworm, woodworm, blindworm, roundworm, pinworm, ringworm, tapeworm, flatworm, earthworm.

pachyderm, periderm (protective plant layer), endoderm (part of embryo), phelloderm (botany term), mesoderm (part of embryo), ectoderm (part of embryo), blastoderm (embryology term), reaffirm, disaffirm, endosperm (seed's nutritive tissue), gymnosperm (cone-bearing plant), zoosperm (spermatozoon), isotherm.

234 -eem

beam, scheme, deem, deme (biology term), haem, fleam (blood-letting lancet), gleam, ream, bream, cream, scream, dream, stream, seam, seem, team, teem, steam, theme.

abeam, hornbeam (Eurasian tree), sunbeam, moonbeam, crossbeam, whitebeam (European tree), hakim (Muslim judge), redeem, grapheme (letter), morpheme (grammatical unit), blaspheme, agleam, sememe (unit of meaning), phoneme (distinguishable speech sound), toneme (linguistics term), harem, Tarim (Chinese river), bireme, spireme (tangled mass of chromosomes), trireme, ice cream, daydream, supreme, airstream, headstream, thirdstream (type of jazz), millstream, mainstream, downstream, slipstream, upstream, extreme, berseem (Mediterranean clover), glosseme (linguistics term), raceme, regime, centime, septime (fencing position), esteem, lexeme (minimal unit in vocabulary), oxime (chemical compound).

Hasidim (Jewish sect), academe (place of learning), quinquereme, monotreme, self-esteem, disesteem.

235 -im

Bim (native of Barbados), skim, dim, gym, him, hymn, limb, limn (represent in drawing), glim (*Slang* lamp), slim, mim (*Dialect* prim), nim (a game), quim, rim, brim, crim (*Austral* criminal), scrim (strong fabric), Grimm, grim, prim, trim, shim (thin washer), vim, whim, swim.

poem, Sikkim (Indian state), bedim, forelimb, dislimn (efface), Muslim, paynim, denim, Blenheim, minim, Purim (Jewish holiday), minim, Purim (Jewish holiday), broadbrim (type of hat), megrim, pilgrim, Leitrim, Antrim, Shittim (Old Testament place), victim, maxim.

Ephraim (Old Testament character), cherubim, seraphim, pseudonym, allonym (assumed name), homonym, anonym (pseudonym), synonym, eponym, toponym, acronym, metonym (linguistics term), antonym, exonym (foreigner's version of placename), Kuskokwim (Alaskan river), interim, Abd-el-Krim (Moroccan chief), verbatim.

seriatim (in a series), literatim (letter for letter).

236 -ime
I'm, chyme (digested food in stomach), chime, dime, lime, climb, clime, slime, mime, rime, rhyme, crime, grime, prime, cyme (type of inflorescence), time, thyme.

Trondheim (Norwegian port), Sondheim (US songwriter), Mannheim (West German city), sublime, quicklime, brooklime (trailing plant), birdlime, begrime, daytime, playtime, foretime (the past), wartime, bedtime, halftime, lifetime, ragtime, full-time, sometime, meantime, noontime, springtime, longtime, pastime, peacetime, mistime, part-time, enzyme.

isocheim (line on map), mesenchyme (embryology term), paradigm, Anaheim (Californian city), pantomime, maritime, flexitime, summertime, wintertime, overtime, lysozyme (enzyme), coenzyme (biochemical compound).

237 -om
bomb, dom (title of Catholic monks), hom (ancient Persian sacred plant), mom, pom, from, prom, Tom, tom, firebomb, Syncom (communications

satellite), non-com (*short for* noncommissioned officer), sitcom, coulomb, aplomb, pom-pom, therefrom, wherefrom, maelstrom, intercom, abcoulomb.

238 -orm
corm, dorm, form, forme (printing equipment), haulm (thatching material), Maugham, norm, shawm (medieval type of oboe), storm, warm, swarm.

re-form, biform, landform, planform (silhouette viewed from above), inform, conform, transform, platform, waveform, Cairngorm, cairngorm (variety of quartz), lukewarm, snowstorm, sandstorm, windstorm, hailstorm, barnstorm, rainstorm, brainstorm, aswarm.

Cominform (Communist Information Bureau), misinform, thunderstorm.

238.1
deform, reform.

deiform (godlike in form), cubiform, pediform, cordiform (heart-shaped), scyphiform (cup-shaped), fungiform, aliform (wing-shaped), stelliform, cheliform (pincer-like), filiform (threadlike), piliform (hairlike), ramiform (branchlike), vermiform, reniform (kidney-shaped), uniform, cuneiform, ligniform (wood-like), napiform (turnip-shaped), aeriform (gaseous), variform, pyriform (pear-shaped), cribriform (sievelike), fibriform, dendriform (branching), vitriform (resembling glass), gasiform, pisiform (resembling a pea), cruciform, falciform (sickle-shaped), unciform (hook-shaped), scutiform (shield-shaped), multiform, dentiform (tooth-shaped), lentiform (lens-shaped), oviform, linguiform, plexiform (intricate), fusiform (spindle-shaped).

cumuliform, cuculiform (ornithology term), baculiform (rod-shaped), dolabriform (hatchet-shaped), diversiform, digitiform.

238.2

perform, bromoform (chemical compound), chloroform, salverform (botany term), iodoform (crystalline substance), electroform (form by electrolysis), nitrochloroform.

239 -ome

ohm, Om (Hindu sacred syllable), comb, dome, foam, home, heaume (medieval helmet), holm (*Dialect* river island), loam, gnome, nome (modern Greek province), pome (fruit of apple), Rome, roam, brome (type of grass), chrome, tome.

abohm, Beerbohm, trichome (hairlike plant structure), backcomb, cockscomb, radome (radar antenna's protective housing), megohm (one million ohms), Stockholm, phyllome (leaf-like organ), genome (group of chromosomes), Jerome, prodrome (symptom indicating disease), syndrome, rhizome.

honeycomb, currycomb, semidome, astrodome (transparent dome on aircraft), tumblehome (nautical term), metronome, gastronome, polychrome (multicoloured), urochrome (pigment in urine), haemochrome (blood pigment), monochrome, velodrome (cycle-racing arena), cosmodrome (spacecraft launching-site), hippodrome, aerodrome, acrodrome (botany term), palindrome, biostrome (fossil-rich rocky layer), endosome (part of cell nucleus), ribosome (part of living cell), chromosome, monosome (type of chromosome), centrosome (part of living cell), autosome (type of chromosome), leptosome (slender person), schistosome (blood parasite), microtome (biologist's cutting instrument), dermatome (surgical instrument), cyclostome (primitive aquatic vertebrate), monostome (having one mouth).

240 -um

bum, come, scum, chum, dumb, gum, hum, glum, plumb, plum, slum, mum, numb, rum, crumb, scrum, drum, strum, thrum, sum, some, tum, stum (partly fermented wine), thumb, swum.

become, succumb, income, outcome, dumdum, benumb, eardrum, humdrum.

misbecome (be unsuitable for), overcome, Tweedledum, sugarplum, kettledrum.

241 -oom

boom, cwm (valley or hollow), coomb (short valley), doom, whom, loom, bloom, flume (narrow ravine), gloom, glume (botany term), plume, rheum, room, broom, groom, vroom, tomb, womb, fume, Hume, neume (early musical symbol), spume, zoom.

foredoom, heirloom, illume (illuminate), abloom (in flower), broadloom, deplume (deprive of feathers), simoom (desert wind), barroom, playroom, tearoom, storeroom, showroom, darkroom, workroom, stockroom, cloakroom, guardroom, bedroom, headroom, boardroom, wardroom, legroom, bridegroom, saleroom, grillroom, ballroom, greenroom, strongroom, taproom, classroom, houseroom, washroom, mushroom, stateroom, courtroom, bathroom, boxroom, Batum (Russian city), Khartoum, pantoum (verse form), entomb, enwomb, perfume, legume, inhume (to inter), exhume, volume, assume, subsume, consume, costume, resume, presume.

catacomb, checkerbloom (Californian plant), nom de plume, filoplume (hairlike feather), anteroom, elbowroom, hecatomb, disentomb, El Faiyum (Egyptian city).

242 -'m

'em, Graham, Priam, brougham, Newham, sebum, album, plumbum, Rackham, Shechem (ancient Jordanian town), caecum, Ockham (English philosopher), Morecambe, oakum (fibre from unravelled rope), hokum, Malcolm, welcome, dinkum, bunkum, Beecham, stardom, heirdom, Edom, freedom, sedum (fleshy-leaved plant), Sodom, boredom, whoredom, serfdom, sheikdom, dukedom, seldom, earldom, Oldham, condom, kingdom, popedom, princedom, wisdom, begum, Egham, sorghum, Dodgem (*Trademark*), Belgium, Nahum (Old Testament prophet), alum, Harlem, slalom, Salem, Elam (ancient Asian kingdom), Caelum (constellation), coelom (body cavity), velum (biology term), column, solemn, solum (upper layer of soil), problem, emblem, bedlam, hoodlum, peplum (flared ruffle on garment), Moslem, Barnum, Arnhem, Farnham, venom, sphagnum (bog moss), magnum, Clapham, wampum (American Indian shell money), carom (billiards term), marram, durum, Durham, labrum (lip), sacrum, buckram, fulcrum, wolfram, pogrom, grogram (coarse fabric), ashram (Hindu religious retreat), antrum (anatomy term), tantrum, threesome, fearsome, tiresome, awesome, dorsum (the back), foursome, noisome, gruesome, twosome, gladsome, handsome, balsam, toilsome, wholesome, fulsome, gamesome (merry), hansom, ransom, transom, winsome, lonesome, Epsom, gypsum, eightsome, jetsam, lightsome, flotsam, toothsome, lithesome, blithesome, loathsome, Heysham, Qeshm (island in Persian Gulf), Gresham, Evesham, atom, Chatham, bottom, scutum, sputum, rectum, dictum, sanctum, bantam, phantom, quantum, septum (biology term), symptom, system, anthem, fathom, ovum, darksome, Wrexham, irksome, buxom, trillium (three-leaved plant), William, besom, seism (earthquake), bosom.

unwelcome, poppadom, martyrdom, corundum (very hard mineral), Christendom, heathendom, amalgam, stratagem, Brummagem, amylum (starch), spirillum (type of bacterium), sensillum (insect's sense organ), exemplum, minimum, optimum, maximum, cardamom, Pergamum (ancient Asian city), per annum, arcanum (profound secret), solanum (plant genus), envenom, jejunum, cerebrum, panjandrum, Trivandrum (Indian city), conundrum, pyrethrum, sargassum (floating brown seaweed), omasum (compartment of cow's stomach), cumbersome, venturesome, humoursome (capricious), bothersome, Hilversum, unwholesome, troublesome, meddlesome, cuddlesome, quarrelsome, nettlesome (causing irritation), burdensome, nasturtium, Lewisham, petersham, cementum (part of a tooth), omentum (anatomy term), lomentum (plant pod), momentum, tomentum (biology term), Chrysostom (Greek patriarch), frolicsome, unbosom.

rehoboam, jeroboam, Eboracum (Roman name for York), taraxacum (plant genus), crinkum-crankum (twisted object), officialdom, duodenum, jus divinum (divine law), interregnum, hydrargyrum, candelabrum, hippeastrum (South American plant), ecosystem, microcosm, macrocosm.

242.1

geum, Te Deum, lyceum, museum, stomodaeum (embryonic mouth cavity), hypogeum (underground burial vault), propylaeum (portico forming temple entrance), mausoleum, perineum, athenaeum (institution promoting learning), gynaeceum (ancient Roman women's apartments), colosseum, peritoneum.

242.2

labium, erbium (element), terbium (element), cambium, brachium (arm or armlike part), ischium, scandium, indium (element), allium (plant genus), gallium (element), pallium (vestment or mantle), thallium (element), Valium (*Trademark*), pileum (top of bird's head), thulium (element), fermium (element), cadmium, holmium (element), osmium, hafnium (element), Samnium (ancient Italian city), atrium, yttrium (element), calcium, francium (element), Latium (region of Italy), protium (isotope of hydrogen), Actium, strontium, ostium (biology term), lithium, axiom.

ytterbium (element), aerobium (organism requiring oxygen), rhizobium (rod-shaped bacterium), niobium (element), exordium (beginning of a speech), compendium, patagium (zoology term), contagium (transmission of disease), sporangium (spore-producing plant organ), dentalium (marine mollusc), nobelium (element), triennium, millennium, quinquennium, quadrennium, decennium, septennium, Capernaum, selenium (element), hymenium (fungal tissue), proscenium, ruthenium (element), principium (fundamental principle), marsupium, colloquium, tellurium, masurium (element), anthurium (tropical plant), opprobrium, manubrium (zoology term), potassium, gynoecium (female part of flower), androecium (stamens of flower), technetium (element), lutetium (element), spermatium (reproductive cell in algae), cymatium (architectural moulding), sestertium (ancient Roman currency), consortium, Byzantium, endosteum (membrane within bone), promethium (element), Erechtheum (temple on the Acropolis), quadrivium (medieval branch of learning), lixivium (alkaline solution), eluvium (mass of rock particles), diluvium (geology term), alluvium, colluvium (mixture of rock fragments), effluvium, Elysium, symposium, indusium (enveloping membrane).

epicardium, pericardium, endocardium, myocardium, horologium (clock tower), Verulamium, neodymium (element), californium (element), equilibrium, perichondrium (membrane covering cartilage), hypochondrium (part of abdomen), perinephrium (tissue surrounding kidney), endometrium, epigastrium (part of abdomen), hypogastrium (part of abdomen), corpus luteum (tissue in ovary), periosteum (membrane covering bone), mendelevium (element).

perionychium (skin surrounding fingernail), praseodymium (element), disequilibrium.

242.2.1

radium, stadium, caladium (cultivated tropical plant), palladium, vanadium (element).

242.2.2

medium, tedium, soredium (reproductive organ of lichens), uredium (spore-producing fungal structure), cypripedium (large-flowered orchid).

242.2.3

idiom, oidium (chain of fungal spores), rubidium, glochidium (biology term), ctenidium (mollusc's gill), conidium (fungal spore), gonidium (botany term), iridium, peridium (botany term), nephridium (tubelike excretory organ), clostridium (rod-shaped bacterium), basidium (fungal structure), aecidium (fungal structure), presidium, ascidium (pitcher-shaped plant part), osmiridium (alloy), post meridiem, hesperidium (citrus fruit), antheridium (plant's male sex organ), miracidium (larva of parasitic fluke), ante meridiem.

242.2.4

odium, odeum (building for musical performances), podium, rhodium, sodium, allodium (former property law term), plasmodium (biology term), sympodium (botany term), pseudopodium, lycopodium (non-flowering plant), monopodium (botany term), parapodium (zoology term).

242.2.5

helium, Sealyham, telium (spore-producing fungal structure), berkelium (element), mycelium (fungal body), epithelium, endothelium, mesothelium.

242.2.6

Ilium (ancient Troy), ileum (part of small intestine), ilium (part of hipbone), milium (nodule on skin), cilium, beryllium, penicillium.

242.2.7

scholium (marginal note), folium (geometrical curve), trifolium (clover-like plant), linoleum, petroleum.

242.2.8

premium, gelsemium (climbing shrub).

242.2.9

chromium, encomium, prostomium (zoology term), ferrochromium (iron—chromium alloy).

242.2.10

cranium, germanium, geranium, uranium, titanium, succedaneum (drug substituted for another), Herculaneum (ancient Italian city), pericranium, endocranium, actinouranium (isotope of uranium).

242.2.11

minium (red lead), delphinium, virginium (element), illinium (element), triclinium (ancient Roman dining room), dominium (property law term), actinium, gadolinium, androclinium (cavity in orchid flower), aluminium, condominium, protactinium (element).

242.2.12

conium (hemlock), zirconium (element), meconium, syconium (fig fruit), euphonium, polonium (element), har-

monium, ammonium, stramonium (drug), plutonium, archegonium (plant's female sex organ), sporogonium (spore-bearing plant part), oogonium (biology term), ascogonium (fungal reproductive body), pelargonium, spermogonium (plant reproductive body), carpogonium (plant reproductive body), pandemonium, positronium (physics term).

242.2.13

opium, europium (element).

242.2.14

barium, herbarium (collection of dried plants), sudarium (cloth for wiping face), caldarium (Roman hot-bath room), velarium (awning in Roman theatre), solarium, samarium (element), puparium (entomology term), aquarium, terrarium (container for small organisms), sacrarium (church sanctuary), vivarium, rosarium, columbarium (dovecote), oceanarium, cinerarium (place for cremation ashes), honorarium, leprosarium (hospital for lepers), termitarium (termite nest), planetarium, sanitarium, insectarium, polyzoarium (animal colony), armamentarium (doctor's equipment).

242.2.15

cerium (element), imperium (ancient Roman supreme power), deuterium, bacterium, psalterium (part of cow's stomach), mezereum (fragrant Eurasian shrub), puerperium, elaterium (greenish sediment), ministerium (body of Lutheran ministers), nototherium (extinct marsupial).

242.2.16

Miriam, delirium, collyrium (eye lotion).

242.2.17

corium (deep layer beneath skin), thorium, ciborium (Christian communion vessel), triforium (part of a church), emporium, sensorium (area of the brain), scriptorium (writing room in monastery), haustorium (organ of parasitic plant), in memoriam, synclinorium (geology term), aspersorium (basin containing holy water), auditorium, sudatorium (Roman steam-bath room), crematorium, fumatorium (airtight fumigation chamber), sanatorium, eupatorium (cultivated tropical plant), moratorium, anticlinorium (geology term).

242.2.18
tritium (isotope of hydrogen), syncytium (zoology term), satellitium (astrology term).

242.2.19
dichasium (type of inflorescence), gymnasium, polychasium (type of inflorescence), monochasium (type of inflorescence).

242.2.20
caesium, magnesium, trapezium.

242.3
menstruum (a solvent), vacuum, residuum, continuum.

242.4
colchicum (Eurasian plant), modicum, Noricum (Celtic Alpine kingdom), capsicum, triticum (cereal grass), High Wycombe, doronicum (Eurasian plant), hypericum (flowering plant), Illyricum (ancient Roman province), viaticum.

242.5
Adam, madam, macadam.

242.6
random, tandem, memorandum, avizandum (Scottish legal term), nil desperandum.

242.7
credendum (Christian article of faith), pudendum, addendum, corrigendum, referendum, definiendum (something to be defined).

242.8
phellem (cork), pelham (horse's bit), vellum, cribellum (spider's spinning organ), labellum (part of orchid flower), flabellum (fan-shaped insect organ), post-bellum, flagellum, clitellum (part of earthworm's body), scutellum (shield-shaped structure), rostellum (beak-like projection), haustellum (entomology term), cerebellum, antebellum.

242.9
phylum, filum (thread-like anatomical part), hilum (botany term), subphylum, asylum.

242.10
Fulham, speculum, vinculum (maths symbol), vasculum (botanist's specimen container), osculum (mouth-like aperture), Tusculum (ancient city near Rome), pendulum, cingulum (girdle-like anatomical part), frenulum (bristle on insect's wing), tenaculum (surgical instrument), vibraculum (type of polyp), operculum (biology term), inoculum (material used for inoculation), coagulum (coagulated mass), Triangulum (constellation), capitulum (biology term), tintinnabulum (small high-pitched bell), acetabulum (cavity in hipbone), infundibulum (funnel-shaped anatomical part).

242.10.1
cubiculum (Roman underground burial chamber), Janiculum (ancient Roman hill), curriculum, aciculum (zoology term), reticulum, diverticulum.

242.11
cimbalom (type of dulcimer), Absalom, tantalum (element), tropaeolum (flowering plant), Jerusalem.

242.12
chrysanthemum, mesembryanthemum.

242.13
Burnham, sternum, viburnum, laburnum, xiphisternum (part of breastbone), episternum (part of breastbone).

242.14
platinum, molybdenum.

242.15

crinum (tropical plant), glucinum (element), antirrhinum, mediastinum (anatomy term).

242.16

galbanum (bitter gum resin), Twickenham, laudanum, labdanum (resinous plant juice), Dagenham, tympanum, Cheltenham, lanthanum (element), olibanum (frankincense), polygonum (plant with jointed stems).

242.17

gingham, Buckingham, Gillingham, Immingham, Sandringham, Altrincham, Walsingham, Nottingham.

242.18

arum, Fareham, Sarum, harum-scarum.

242.19

serum, theorem, disulfiram (a drug), antiserum.

242.20

aurum (gold), forum, jorum (large drinking bowl), quorum, decorum, Mizoram (Indian union territory), variorum (containing scholarly annotations), indecorum, Karakoram (mountain system in Kashmir), cockalorum (self-important person), ad valorem (according to value), pons asinorum (geometry theorem), sanctum sanctorum, schola cantorum.

242.21

labarum (Christian banner), marjoram, asarum (dried wild ginger root), Rotherham, Kanchipuram (Indian city), omnium-gatherum (miscellaneous collection).

242.22

plectrum, spectrum, electrum (gold−silver alloy).

242.23

nostrum, rostrum, colostrum.

242.24

jissom, lissom, crissum (ornithology term), alyssum, wearisome, worrisome, fideicommissum (civil law term).

242.25

blossom, possum, opossum, odontoglossum (tropical orchid).

242.26

stratum, satem (linguistics term), postpartum, erratum, substratum, superstratum, desideratum.

242.27

datum, relatum (logic term), ideatum (philosophy term), petrolatum (petroleum jelly), ultimatum, ageratum (tropical plant), corpus striatum (part of brain).

242.28

pinetum (conifer plantation), tapetum (biology term), acetum (vinegar), Antietam (US battle site), arboretum, equisetum (a plant).

242.29

item, ad infinitum.

242.30

autumn, postmortem.

242.31

notum (entomology term), scrotum, totem, teetotum (spinning top), factotum.

242.32

custom, frustum, accustom, disaccustom.

242.33

rhythm, polyrhythm (style of musical composition), logarithm, algorithm.

242.34

chasm, plasm (type of protoplasm), spasm, sarcasm, orgasm, phantasm, chiliasm (Christian belief), endoplasm, cytoplasm, protoplasm, ectoplasm, pleonasm (use of superfluous words), enthusiasm, iconoclasm (attack on traditional concepts).

242.35
ism, chrism (oil used for anointing), chrisom (baptismal robe), prism, schism.

Maoism, cubism, plumbism (lead poisoning), tychism (philosophy term), sadism, Buddhism, nudism, sophism, Sufism (mystical doctrine), Gaullism, holism (philosophy term), momism (excessive dependence on mother), nomism (theology term), bromism (bromine poisoning), Thomism (doctrine of Thomas Aquinas), Jainism (Hindu sect), monism (philosophy term), bonism (semi-optimistic doctrine), tropism, tsarism, verism (extreme realism), porism (mathematical proposition), tourism, purism, Tantrism (Hindu or Buddhist movement), Graecism, Nazism, fascism, statism (state control), rightism, autism, leftism, baptism, Marxism, sexism.

Dadaism, Bahaism (religious system), fideism (trust placed in faith), Judaism, Hebraism, Mithraism (ancient Persian religion), prosaism (prosaic style), Mazdaism (ancient Persian religion), Lamaism (form of Buddhism), ultraism (extreme philosophy), Sivaism (Hindu cult), Lamarckism, catechism, iodism (iodine poisoning), monadism (philosophical doctrine), faradism (medical use of electricity), Methodism, pacifism, imagism (poetic movement), cataclysm, alarmism, extremism, euphemism, dysphemism (substitution of offensive word), Muslimism, animism (primitive belief), pessimism, optimism, dynamism (philosophical theory), atomism (philosophical theory), totemism, cocainism, communism, escapism, priapism, sinapism, vampirism, tenebrism (style of painting), helichrysum (flowering plant), pentaprism (five-sided prism), erythrism (abnormal red coloration), ostracism, exorcism, solipsism (philosophy term), Englishism, Irishism, fetishism, Britishism, de-

featism, elitism, occultism, gigantism, erethism (high degree of sensitivity), atavism (recurrence of primitive characteristics), paroxysm, Spinozism.

invalidism (being an invalid), diastrophism (movement of earth's crust), catastrophism (geological theory), parallelism, alcoholism, nicotinism, opportunism, malapropism, ventriloquism, polycentrism (political theory), egocentrism, ethnocentrism (belief in race's superiority).

hypothyroidism, hyperthyroidism, Eurocommunism.

242.35.1
deism, Shiism (Islamic belief), theism, misoneism (hatred of anything new), absenteeism.

242.35.2
archaism, Trotskyism, Gandhiism, cockneyism, atheism, ditheism (belief in two gods), tritheism (belief in the Trinity), pantheism, McCarthyism, polytheism, monotheism.

242.35.3
Foism (Chinese Buddhism), Taoism (Chinese philosophy), echoism (linguistics term), locoism (disease of cattle), egoism, jingoism, heroism, dichroism (crystallography term), trichroism (crystallography term), Titoism, xanthochroism (skin condition in goldfish), hylozoism (philosophical doctrine).

242.35.4
truism, Hinduism, altruism, euphuism (Elizabethan prose style).

242.35.5
abysm, syllabism (system of writing).

242.35.6
anarchism, monarchism, masochism, sadomasochism.

242.35.7
Orphism (ancient Greek religion), dwarfism, polymorphism (existence of

different forms), endomorphism (geology term), isomorphism (similarity of form), allomorphism (variation in crystalline form), metamorphism, anthropomorphism.

242.35.8

syllogism, synergism (medical term), geophagism (practice of eating earth), dialogism (philosophy term), paralogism (invalid argument), antilogism (philosophy term), neologism, psychologism (belief in psychology).

242.35.9

nihilism, pugilism, virilism (medical term), pointillism, immobilism (reactionary political policy), probabilism (philosophical doctrine), zoophilism (emotional attachment to animals), necrophilism (desire to be dead), evangelism, puerilism (immature behaviour by adult), infantilism, mercantilism (economic theory).

242.35.10

formulism (adherence to formulas), botulism, somnambulism.

242.35.11

myalism (type of witchcraft), ptyalism (excessive excretion of saliva), loyalism, royalism, dualism, verbalism, tribalism, embolism, symbolism, localism, vocalism (exercise of the voice), feudalism, vandalism, Mendelism (science of heredity), legalism (strict adherence to law), mongolism, formalism, finalism (philosophical doctrine), moralism, pluralism, neutralism, centralism, racialism, specialism, socialism, fatalism, vitalism (philosophical doctrine).

diabolism (devil worship), anabolism (metabolic process), metabolism, catabolism (metabolic process), cannibalism, radicalism, syndicalism (workers' revolutionary movement), clericalism (power of the clergy), classicalism (architectural style), physicalism (philosophical doctrine), animalism (preoccupation with physical matters),

liberalism, structuralism, literalism, naturalism, commercialism, provincialism, symmetallism (economic doctrine), bimetallism (economic doctrine), digitalism (digitalis poisoning), capitalism, medievalism, revivalism.

thromboembolism, phenomenalism (philosophy term), universalism (universal characteristic), existentialism, monometallism (economic doctrine), sacerdotalism (principles of the priesthood).

242.35.11.1

realism, idealism, surrealism.

242.35.11.2

colonialism, colloquialism, mercurialism (mercury poisoning), industrialism, territorialism.

242.35.11.2.1

serialism, imperialism, materialism, immaterialism (philosophy term).

242.35.11.3

gradualism (seeking change gradually), sensualism, ritualism, textualism (adherence to text), spiritualism, conceptualism (philosophy term), transsexualism, intellectualism, individualism.

242.35.11.4

journalism, paternalism, externalism (philosophical doctrine).

242.35.11.5

regionalism, personalism (idiosyncrasy), functionalism, professionalism, traditionalism, emotionalism, conventionalism, occasionalism (philosophical theory), institutionalism, constitutionalism.

242.35.11.5.1

nationalism, rationalism, internationalism.

242.35.11.5.2

sensationalism, Congregationalism, operationalism (philosophy of science term), denominationalism, representationalism (philosophy term).

242.35.11.6
mentalism (philosophy term), Orientalism, transcendentalism, sentimentalism, fundamentalism, sacramentalism (theology term), instrumentalism (philosophy term), departmentalism (division into departments), experimentalism, environmentalism (psychology term).

242.35.12
reformism, transformism (theory of evolution), nonconformism.

242.35.13
rabbinism (teachings of rabbis), albinism, morphinism, Stalinism, Galenism (former theory of medicine), Hellenism, feminism, Leninism, strychninism, alpinism, foreignism, Latinism, cretinism, chauvinism, Calvinism, Darwinism, determinism, illuminism (belief in special enlightenment), indeterminism (philosophy term), ultramontanism (Roman Catholic doctrine), hyperinsulinism.

242.35.14
eonism (psychiatry term), pianism (piano-playing skill), Zionism, mechanism, tokenism (doing the minimum necessary), volcanism (formation of volcanoes), hedonism, modernism, paganism, organism, melanism, shamanism (Asian religion), Brahmanism, Germanism, demonism (worship of demons), Mormonism, Romanism (Roman Catholicism), humanism, pelmanism (card game), onanism, prochronism (error in dating), synchronism (simultaneous occurrence), Jansenism, saturnism (lead poisoning), Platonism, Satanism, Titanism (spirit of rebellion), Teutonism, daltonism, westernism, galvanism, unionism.

antagonism, hooliganism, eudemonism (philosophical doctrine), anachronism, parachronism (error in dating), asynchronism (occurrence at different times), immersionism (Christian doctrine), traducianism (theology term),

Confucianism, abstractionism (theory of abstract art), perfectionism, protectionism, expansionism, divisionism (art term), revisionism (deviation from true Marxism), illusionism, infusionism (theology term), charlatanism, Italianism, nonunionism.

servomechanism, Mohammedanism, microorganism, exhibitionism.

242.35.14.1
Fabianism, lesbianism, Canadianism, Pelagianism (heretical Christian doctrine), Australianism, Nestorianism (theological doctrine), Erastianism (state supremacy over church), Swedenborgianism (religious movement), Saint-Simonianism (form of socialism), presbyterianism, Zoroastrianism.

242.35.14.1.1
Arianism (heretical doctrine), Tractarianism, millenarianism (Christian belief), vegetarianism, unitarianism, hereditarianism (psychology term), utilitarianism, humanitarianism, necessitarianism (philosophy term), parliamentarianism, uniformitarianism (geological theory).

242.35.14.2
Gallicanism (French Catholic movement), Anglicanism, Africanism, Vaticanism, republicanism, Americanism.

242.35.14.3
creationism (theological belief), inflationism, deviationism (ideological deviation), isolationism, restorationism (theological belief), presentationism (philosophy term), associationism (psychology term).

242.35.14.4
impressionism, expressionism, postimpressionism, neoimpressionism.

242.35.15
barbarism, labourism, Quakerism, naturism, futurism, aphorism, rigorism (strictness in judgment), algorism (decimal system of counting), vulgarism,

Gongorism (affected literary style), plagiarism, bowdlerism, Hitlerism, mesmerism, mannerism, spoonerism, terrorism, asterism (printing symbol), pasteurism (treatment of rabies), Lutherism, aneurysm, Caesarism (autocratic system of government).

anachorism (geographical misplacement), hypocorism (pet name), adventurism, metamerism (animal's division into segments), euhemerism (historical interpretation of myths), allomerism (chemistry term), isomerism (chemistry term), tautomerism (chemistry term), consumerism, militarism, voluntarism (philosophy term), behaviourism.

adiaphorism (Protestant theological theory), vernacularism, particularism (attention to minority interest).

242.35.16
stoicism, logicism (theory of mathematics), Anglicism, cynicism, classicism, narcissism, Briticism, criticism, witticism, vorticism (English art movement), scepticism, mysticism, Gnosticism, Gothicism, organicism (biological theory), Hispanicism (word borrowed from Spanish), Hibernicism (Irishism), historicism (theory of history), athleticism, asceticism, aestheticism, romanticism, agnosticism, academicism (conventionalism), neoclassicism.

242.35.16.1
phallicism (worship of phallus), Gallicism (word borrowed from French), Italicism.

242.35.16.2
solecism, Catholicism.

242.35.16.3
lyricism, empiricism.

242.35.16.4
Atticism (simple clear expression), fanaticism, dichromaticism (crystallography term).

242.35.16.5
Scotticism, eroticism, neuroticism.

242.35.16.6
scholasticism, monasticism, neoplasticism (style of abstract painting), ecclesiasticism.

242.35.17
Chartism (English reform movement), Bonapartism.

242.35.18
magnetism, syncretism (tendency to combine beliefs), Docetism (early Christian heresy), synthetism (art term), sovietism, Jesuitism, fortuitism (philosophy term), favouritism, anti-Semitism, diamagnetism, geomagnetism, ferromagnetism, paramagnetism, electromagnetism.

242.35.19
mutism, absolutism.

242.35.20
quietism (form of mysticism), narcotism, ergotism, egotism, helotism (sociopolitical system), prelatism (Church government by prelates), schematism (general arrangement), traumatism, rheumatism, pragmatism, stigmatism, dogmatism, hypnotism, nepotism, despotism, teratism (malformed fetus), patriotism, suprematism, animatism, systematism (practice of classifying), automatism, astigmatism, separatism, conservatism, monochromatism (visual defect).

242.35.21
scientism, tarantism (nervous disorder), immanentism (belief in God's omnipresence), Protestantism, indifferentism (indifference to religion).

242.35.22
passivism, nativism (protection of native cultures), activism, recidivism (habitual relapse into crime), primitivism, positivism, negativism, relativism, objectivism, subjectivism, collectivism, Perspectivism (philosophical doctrine),

constructivism (abstract art movement).

243 -elm
elm, helm, realm, wych-elm (Eurasian elm tree), Wilhelm, unhelm (remove the helmet of), Anselm, overwhelm.

244 -ilm
film, microfilm.

245 -an [some *-man* words in **261** may be pronounced to rhyme with this group]
Anne, an, ban, can, Cannes, scan, dan, Dan, fan, gan (*Dialect* to go), Han (Chinese dynasty), clan, flan, plan, man, nan, pan, Pan, panne (velvet fabric), span, ran, bran, cran (measure of fresh herring), scran (*Slang* food), tan, than, van.

cyan (greenish-blue colour), Cheyenne, koan (Buddhist riddle), yuan (Chinese currency), pecan, oilcan, cancan, cooncan (card game), Houdan (breed of domestic fowl), randan (rowing boat), began, Afghan, tolan (crystalline substance), yulan (Chinese magnolia), Gosplan (Russian state planning commission), unman, outman, Hainan (Chinese island), Tainan (Chinese city), honan (silk fabric), Hunan (Chinese province), tarpan (extinct wild horse), claypan (subsurface clay layer), kneepan (kneecap), Saipan (Pacific island), taipan (venomous snake), Chopin, bedpan, deadpan, skidpan, jampan (sedan chair), sampan, brainpan (skull), wingspan, dustpan, pyran (chemical compound), shoran (short-range radar system), furan (flammable toxic liquid), FORTRAN, outran, Pusan (South Korean port), Wonsan (North Korean port), Bashan (biblical region), Anshan (Chinese city), Nan Shan (Chinese mountain range), rattan, kaftan, suntan, divan, Qairwan (Tunisian city), Lausanne, Kazan (Russian city).

Caliban, billycan, astrakhan, turbofan (fan driven by turbine), Kordofan (Sudanese province), tryptophan (amino acid), Callaghan, Catalan, Ku Klux Klan, overman, cocopan (South African mining wagon), spick-and-span, also-ran, pentosan (biochemical compound), hexosan (biochemical compound), constantan (copper–nickel alloy), mercaptan (chemical compound), caravan.

245.1
redan (type of fortification), sedan, shandrydan (two-wheeled cart).

245.2
Milan, gamelan (East Indian percussion orchestra), Acrilan (*Trademark*).

245.3
trepan (surgical instrument), marzipan.

245.4
Japan, tragopan (Asian pheasant), Belmopan (capital of Belize), Matapan (promontory in southern Greece).

245.5
Oran, saran (resin), Teleran (*Trademark* navigational aid), trimaran, overran, catamaran.

245.6
soutane (Catholic priest's cassock), orang-utan.

245.7
tisane, ptisan (grape juice), Parmesan, artisan, partisan, courtesan, bipartisan, nonpartisan.

246 -arn
Arne (English composer), barn, khan, darn, Han (Chinese imperial dynasty), Marne (French river), San (language group), Shan (Mongoloid people), tarn, Van (Turkish city), guan (South American bird), yarn.

barchan (sand dune), lucarne (dormer window), machan (tiger-hunting platform), maidan (Indian open meeting place), Sudan, goldarn, Tzigane, uhlan (Polish lancer), Kirman (Persian carpet), Oman, Amman, toman (gold coin), Teheran, Iran, Koran, buran (Asian blizzard), Tourane (Vietnamese port), Cwmbran, Khotan (Chinese oasis), Wotan (Germanic god), Bhutan (central Asian kingdom), Multan (Pakistani city), Sevan (Russian lake), pavane, dewan (Indian minister of state), Taiwan, Jawan (Indian soldier), Szechwan (Chinese province), San Juan, Aswan, Dayan, kalian (Oriental pipe), azan (Islamic call to prayer), Fezzan (region of Libya).

skokiaan (South African alcoholic beverage), Vientiane, autobahn, Kublai Khan, Aga Khan, balmacaan (man's knee-length overcoat), Genghis Khan, Abadan (Iranian port), Ramadan (period in Muslim year), Lindisfarne, Abidjan (capital of Ivory Coast), Omdurman (Sudanese city), Suleiman (sultan of Ottoman empire), Hanuman (monkey), Alcoran (Koran), Yucatán (Mexican state), Hindustan, Bantustan, Kwangchowan (region of China), macedoine, Azerbaijan (region of Iran).

246.1
Pakistan, Turkestan (region of Asia), Kurdistan (Asian plateau), Nuristan (region of Afghanistan), Baluchistan (region of Asia), Afghanistan, Waziristan (region of Asia), Kafiristan (region of Afghanistan).

247 -ane
ain (*Scot* own), ane (*Scot* one), bane, Cain, cane, skein, chain, Dane, deign, feign, fain, gain, Jane, lain, lane, blain (blister or sore), plain, plane, slain, Maine, mane, main, pane, pain, Spain, rein, reign, rain, brain, crane, drain, grain, sprain, train, strain, sane, Seine, tain (tinfoil mirror-backing), stain, Steen (Dutch painter), thane, vein, vain, vane, Wayne, wane, wain, swain, twain, Twain.

cowbane (marsh plant), urbane, fleabane (daisy-like plant), cubane (chemical compound), wolfbane (poisonous plant), bugbane (insect-repelling plant), henbane (poisonous plant), ratsbane (rat poison), arcane, decane (chemical compound), Cockaigne (medieval imaginary land), procaine, alkane (chemical compound), cinquain (five-line poem), enchain, unchain, ordain, lindane (crystalline substance), mundane, disdain, Sinn Fein, regain, Ujjain (Indian city), Elaine, poleyn (armour protecting knee), chilblain, Maclean, airplane, terreplein (top of rampart), skiplane, deplane (disembark from aircraft), seaplane, biplane, triplane, warplane, sailplane (high-performance glider), tailplane (aerofoil at aircraft's tail), volplane (glide without power), emplane (board an aircraft), complain, explain, germane, pearmain, demesne, remain, romaine (*US* cos lettuce), ptomaine (chemical compound), chow mein, humane, mortmain (legal term), propane, Bahrain, terrane, terrain, Lorraine, moraine, borane (chemical compound), forebrain, crackbrain (insane person), midbrain, endbrain, hindbrain, membrane, Ukraine, refrain, migraine, Igraine (King Arthur's mother), grosgrain (heavy ribbed fabric), ingrain, vicereine (viceroy's wife), detrain (disembark from train), vitrain (type of coal), quatrain, entrain (board a train), distrain, restrain, eyestrain, constrain, Bassein (Burmese city), Hussein, insane, butane, obtain, octane, Beltane (ancient Celtic festival), maintain, contain, sustain, abstain, bloodstain, ethane, methane, vervain (flowering plant), dogvane (nautical wind vane), sixain (six-line poem), fusain (fine charcoal pencil).

Tubal-cain (biblical character), preordain, foreordain, transmundane (beyond this world), peneplain (flattish land surface), multiplane (multi-winged aircraft), taxiplane (*US* aircraft for hire), hydroplane (motorboat), aquaplane, aeroplane, gyroplane (self-propelled aircraft), inhumane, frangipane (almond-flavoured pastry), windowpane, counterpane, scatterbrain, featherbrain, Pontchartrain (US lake), hovertrain (hovercraft train), halothane (chemical compound), paravane (device on minesweeper).

cycloalkane (chemical compound), demimondaine, cyclohexane (flammable liquid), polyurethane.

247.1
chicane, hurricane.

247.2
cocaine, lignocaine (local anaesthetic), marocain (ribbed crepe fabric), Novocaine (*Trademark*).

247.3
profane, hydrophane (variety of opal), allophane (mineral), cellophane, cymophane (mineral).

247.4
delaine (wool fabric), Kwajalein (Pacific atoll), Tamerlane (Mongol conqueror), chatelaine (mistress of castle).

247.5
domain, leucomaine (biochemical compound), Charlemagne, legerdemain, El Alamein.

247.6
inane, Dunsinane (Scottish hill), catenane (chemistry term).

247.7
campaign, champagne, elecampane (flowering plant).

247.8
arraign, serein (fine tropical rain), souterrain (underground chamber), suzerain (feudal overlord).

247.9
detain, retain, Aquitaine.

247.10
attain, pertain, appertain, chevrotain (Asian mammal), ascertain, entertain.

247.11
Fonteyn, montane, Bloemfontein (South African city), tramontane (across the mountains), submontane (on lower mountain slopes), ultramontane (beyond the mountains).

248 -en
en (printer's measure), Ben, ben, Ken, ken, sken (*Dialect* to squint), den, fen, gen, hen, Len, glen, men, Penn, pen, wren, Bren, sen (Oriental monetary unit), ten, Sten, then, when, wen (cyst on scalp), yen, Zen.

cayenne, doyenne, Chechen (Russian people), Ardennes, again, greyhen (female black grouse), moorhen, amen, semen, hymen, limen (psychology term), vimen (flexible plant shoot), nomen (ancient Roman's clan name), dolmen, playpen, bullpen (*US* large prison cell), Guienne (former French province), Fukien (Chinese province).

Ogaden (region of Ethiopia), thiophen (chemical compound), tappit-hen, madrilène (tomato-flavoured consommé), regimen, praenomen (ancient Roman's first name), agnomen (ancient Roman's fourth name), cognomen (ancient Roman's family name), acumen, samisen (Japanese stringed instrument), Sun Yat-sen (Chinese statesman), Debrecen (Hungarian city), Longyearbyen (Norwegian island village), Sinhailien (Chinese city).

248.1
julienne (cookery term), tragedienne, comedienne, Tyrolienne (Tyrolean peasant dance), equestrienne, Valenciennes (fine lace).

248.2

flamen (Roman priest), stamen, velamen (enveloping membrane of root), foramen (hole in a bone), duramen (woody tissue), putamen (fruit stone), gravamen (legal term), examen (Catholic examination of conscience).

248.3

rumen, numen (ancient Roman deity), cerumen (earwax), hegumen (Eastern Church monastic leader), catechumen (convert receiving pre-baptismal instruction), energumen (possessed person).

249 -ern

urn, earn, erne (eagle), Bern, burn, kern (printing term), churn, fern, föhn (warm Alpine wind), hern (*Dialect* heron), learn, pirn (fishing rod), spurn, quern (stone hand mill), tern, turn, terne (metal alloy), stern, Verne, yearn.

lierne (architectural term), Tyburn, Blackburn, windburn, Swinburne, sunburn, Hepburn, heartburn, sojourn, adjourn, unlearn, inurn, epergne (dinner-table ornament), discern, decern (Scottish legal term), lucerne, Lucerne, concern, Saturn, Sauternes, nocturn (part of Catholic matins), nocturne, intern, upturn, astern, extern, casern (soldier's billet).

Bannockburn, unconcern, overturn, Comintern (international Communist organization).

249.1

gittern (guitar-like instrument), return, cittern (medieval stringed instrument), taciturn.

250 -airn

bairn, cairn, Nairn (Scottish Highland region), Pitcairn (Pacific island), moderne (architectural style), Auvergne (region of France).

251 -een

been, bean, keen, skean (double-edged dagger), dene (narrow wooded valley), dean, sphene (type of mineral), gean (sweet cherry), Jean, gene, lean, clean, glean, spleen, mean, mien, mesne (legal term), pean (heraldic term), peen (part of hammer), queen, reen (*Dialect* ditch), screen, green, preen, treen (wooden), seen, scene, sheen, teen, wean, wheen (*Dialect* few).

shebeen (illegal drinking place), buckbean (marsh plant), Azbine (region of Sahara desert), has-been, takin (large goatlike mammal), achene (one-seeded fruit), Tolkien, nankeen, sardine, sourdine (organ stop), codeine, dudeen (clay pipe), undine (female water spirit), caffeine, trephine (surgical instrument), dauphine (French princess), morphine, phosphene (physiology term), beguine (South American dance), hygiene, phosgene (colourless poisonous gas), praline, phthalein (chemical compound), scalene, squalene (biochemical compound), valine (amino acid), Hellene (a Greek), colleen, choline (biochemical compound), proline (amino acid), unclean, Crimplene (*Trademark*), Kathleen, Amin, ammine (chemical compound), gamine (slim boyish girl), imine (chemical compound), demean, bromine (dark red liquid), Benin (African republic), quinine, strychnine, terpene (chemical compound), chopine (18th-century shoe), spalpeen (*Irish* rascal), McQueen, terrene (relating to the earth), terrine, serene, moreen (heavy furnishing fabric), dourine (infectious disease of horses), fluorine, purine (crystalline compound), windscreen, shagreen (sharkskin), gangrene, vitrine (glass display-case), latrine, fascine (bundle of long sticks), glassine (translucent book-covering), arsine (colourless poisonous gas), narceine (chemical compound), Essene (member of Jewish

sect), foreseen, obscene, unseen, dasheen (Asian plant), archine (Russian
unit of length), ratine (loosely-woven
cloth), sateen (glossy fabric resembling
satin), eighteen, thirteen, poteen (*Irish*
illicit whiskey), fourteen, protein, routine, fifteen, canteen, dentine, pentene
(colourless liquid), nineteen, tontine
(annuity scheme), umpteen, Christine,
pristine, cystine (amino acid), Sistine,
sixteen, nervine (soothing the nerves),
Slovene, subvene, convene, Salween
(Asian river), between, vaccine, cuisine,
benzene.

Hallowe'en, toluene (colourless liquid),
jellybean, terebene (chemical compound), palanquin (Oriental covered
litter), Balanchine (US choreographer),
pethidine, brigandine (medieval coat of
mail), toxaphene (chemical compound),
Josephine, carrageen (edible red seaweed), indigene (native person or organism), epigene (formed at earth's
surface), hypogene (formed beneath
earth's surface), philhellene (lover of
Greece), bellarmine (large earthenware
jar), spodumene (greyish-white mineral), mavourneen (Irish term of endearment), cyanine (blue dye), mezzanine,
reserpine (medicinal plant extract),
Philippine, atropine, Hippocrene (poetic inspiration), multiscreen (type of
film presentation), wintergreen (evergreen shrub), evergreen, unforeseen,
aubergine, subroutine, velveteen, barquentine (sailing ship), brigantine (sailing ship), Argentine, galantine, clementine, quarantine, seventeen, brilliantine,
mangosteen (East Indian tree), poly-
thene, ornithine (amino acid), olivine
(mineral), go-between, bombazine,
magazine, limousine, organzine (strong
silk thread).

piperidine (colourless liquid), tetracycline (antibiotic), physostigmine (medicinal alkaloid), chlorobenzene (colourless liquid), nitrobenzene (chemical
compound).

251.1
gradine (step or ledge), iodine, Aber-
deen, gaberdine, Engadine (Swiss tourist centre), grenadine.

251.2
Terylene (*Trademark*), Vaseline (*Trademark*), ethylene, methylene, acetylene,
polypropylene (plastic), oxyacetylene,
polytetrafluoroethylene.

251.3
baleen (whalebone), malines (silk net
fabric), Abilene (Texan city), percaline
(light cotton fabric), silkaline (fine cotton fabric), mescaline (hallucinogenic
drug), Magdalene, bandoline (hairdressing substance), tourmaline (mineral), trampoline, citrulline (amino acid),
gasoline, messaline (light silk fabric),
naphthalene.

251.4
rhodamine (red dye), melamine, prolamine (plant protein), Dramamine
(*Trademark*), protamine (protein), glutamine (amino acid), catecholamine
(biochemical compound), pyridoxamine
(biochemical compound).

251.5
pyrene (chemical compound), styrene
(colourless liquid), polystyrene.

251.6
chlorine, Maureen, taurine (chemical
compound), euchlorine (explosive gas
mixture), helleborine (type of orchid).

251.7
careen (sway), marine, tureen, tambourine, saccharine, sapphirine (rare blue
mineral), gregarine (microscopic parasitic animal), figurine, margarine, algerine (striped woollen cloth), tangerine, pelerine (woman's narrow cape),
submarine, curarine (muscle relaxant),
butterine (artificial butter), pistareen
(18th-century Spanish coin), wolverine
(large mammal), Nazarene, aquamarine, ultramarine, nitroglycerine.

251.8
colchicine (medicinal alkaloid), epicene (having bisexual characteristics), Plasticine (*Trademark*), australopithecine.

251.9
Pliocene, Miocene, Eocene, Neocene, Holocene, damascene, ferrocene (crystalline compound), kerosene, tyrosine (amino acid), nigrosine (black pigment), Pleistocene, Oligocene, Palaeocene, adenosine (biochemical compound).

251.10
machine, crepe de Chine.

251.11
lateen (having a triangular sail), creatine (compound found in muscles), libertine, nicotine, tricotine (woollen fabric), gelatine, guillotine, carotene, astatine (chemical element), duvetyn (soft fabric), dessiatine (Russian unit of area).

251.12
ravine, supervene, margravine, landgravine, contravene, intervene.

252 -in
in, inn, bin, kin, skin, chin, din, fin, Finn, gin, hin (Hebrew unit of capacity), Lynn, linn (*Scot* waterfall), Min (Chinese dialect), pin, spin, quin, grin, sin, shin, tin, thin, win, whin (gorse), Gwyn, twin.

zein (protein), ruin, bruin, cabin, sabin (physics unit), Harbin (Chinese city), bobbin, dobbin, robin, dubbin, nubbin (*US* undeveloped fruit), Reuben, dustbin, firkin, gherkin, jerkin, merkin (pubic wig), Pekin, Wrekin, bodkin, lambkin, napkin, pipkin (small cooking pot), limpkin (wading bird), bumpkin, pumpkin, gaskin (part of horse's thigh), bearskin, deerskin, griskin (cut of pork), siskin (Eurasian finch), foreskin, doeskin, buskin (type of boot), Ruskin, redskin, kidskin, calfskin, scarfskin (outermost skin layer), pig-

skin, sealskin, oilskin, moleskin, wineskin, sheepskin, goatskin, Pushkin, catkin, sharkskin, snakeskin, buckskin, urchin, kitchen, Odin (Norse god), biffin (red cooking apple), griffin, tiffin, boffin, coffin, dauphin, bowfin (US fish), redfin (small fish), threadfin (tropical fish), dolphin, bargain, begin, biggin (close-fitting cap), piggin (small wooden bucket), noggin, Elgin, margin, virgin, engine, carline (Eurasian plant), marlin (tropical fish), marline (nautical rope), Stalin, Berlin, merlin (small falcon), Merlin, purlin (horizontal roof beam), mullein (Mediterranean plant), Boleyn, moulin (vertical shaft in glacier), goblin, Dublin, Brooklyn, franklin, maudlin, Kremlin, gremlin, drumlin, dunlin, Chaplin, chaplain, Joplin, poplin, purslane (trailing weed), porcelain, ratline (nautical term), javelin, ravelin (type of fortification), Evelyn, muslin, King's Lynn, Brahmin, cumin, lumen, admin, Bodmin, jasmine, plasmin (enzyme), tannin, renin (enzyme), lignin (complex plant substance), Turpin, hairpin, pippin, tiepin, lupin, crankpin, linchpin, tenpin, unpin, kingpin, Crispin, tailspin, topspin, hatpin, breastpin (brooch), backspin, Tarquin, sequin, therein, wherein, Erin, herein, stearin, Turin, urine, burin (a chisel), murrain, chagrin, citrin (vitamin), citrine (gemstone), doctrine, oestrin, brethren, sovereign, pepsin, Latin, matin, satin, martin, Martin, marten, cretin, chitin, actin (protein), pectin, plantain, fountain, mountain, Austin, within, Swithin, spavin (growth on horse's hock), savin (juniper bush), flavine (pigment), Irvine, Calvin, Kelvin (British physicist), Darwin, Edwin, Godwin, Goodwin, Baldwin, anguine (resembling a snake), sanguine, penguin, Colwyn, Gershwin, auxin (hormone), fuchsin (red dye), seisin (legal term), rosin.

casein (protein), crocein (red or orange dye), xanthein (plant pigment), Bedouin, genuine, Menuhin, Scriabin (Russian composer), Jacobin, cannabin (cannabis resin), grimalkin (old female cat), Potemkin (Russian statesman), Algonquin (American Indian people), onionskin, capuchin, Aladdin, Dunedin, gliadin (protein), muscadine (US grape plant), paladin (peer of Charlemagne's court), Saladin, Bernardine (Cistercian monk), Borodin, paraffin, Godolphin (English statesman), imagine, tarpaulin, hobgoblin, Dunfermline, discipline, Ho Chi Minh, albumen, bitumen, illumine, legumen (protein), Vietminh, lichenin (chemical compound), melanin, chinquapin (dwarf chestnut tree), underpin, terrapin, thoroughpin (inflammation on horse's hock), harlequin, porphyrin (pigment), aspirin, ephedrine (medicinal alkaloid), Sanhedrin, Benzedrine (*Trademark*), peregrine, Lohengrin, alpestrine, assassin, myosin (protein), niacin, eosin (red dye), moccasin, characin (freshwater fish), Wisconsin, hoatzin (South American bird), freemartin (female twin calf), biotin (vitamin), gelatin, haematin (dark pigment), chromatin (part of cell nucleus), keratin (protein), nystatin (antibiotic), travertine (porous rock), lecithin (biochemical compound), sympathin (hormone), thick-and-thin, Angevin (inhabitant of Anjou), alevin (young salmon or trout).

haemoglobin, myoglobin (protein), bilirubin (bile pigment), Rumpelstiltskin, biliverdin (bile pigment), prostaglandin (hormone-like compound), calamondin (Philippine citrus tree), digitalin (poisonous chemical compound), tatty-peelin (*Scot* pretentious), indiscipline, bacitracin (antibiotic), Taliesin (Welsh bard), vasopressin (hormone), oxytocin (hormone), acriflavine (brownish antiseptic powder), riboflavin (vitamin).

252.1
Owen, heroin, heroine, fibroin (protein), Halesowen (English town), benzoin (gum resin), hydantoin (crystalline substance).

252.2
Larkin, parkin, Suakin (Sudanese port).

252.3
chicken, spillikin, ramekin, cannikin (small can), mannequin (fashion model), manikin (dwarf), pannikin (*Dialect* small cup), henequen (plant yielding rope fibre), larrikin (*Austral* hooligan), lambrequin (ornamental hanging).

252.4
akin, baldachin (silk and gold brocade), manakin (South American bird), dunnakin (*Dialect* lavatory), catechin (chemical compound).

252.5
muffin, puffin, ragamuffin.

252.6
pidgin, origin.

252.7
Helen, Welwyn, Llewellyn, vitellin (protein), Helvellyn, gibberellin (plant hormone).

252.8
myelin, Kerguelen (archipelago in Indian Ocean), aniline (oily liquid), vanillin (crystalline substance), glutelin (protein), Enniskillen (Northern Irish town), podophyllin (bitter yellow resin), penicillin.

252.9
bowline, francolin (partridge), pangolin (scaly anteater).

252.10
globulin, masculine, inulin (chemical compound), lupulin (hop plant extract), insulin, botulin, tuberculin, folliculin (hormone), immunoglobulin.

252.11
kaolin, hyaline (clear and translucent), ptyalin (enzyme), violin, Gobelin, chamberlain, madeleine, magdalen (reformed prostitute), mandolin, cephalin (biochemical compound), formalin (preservative for biological specimens), lanolin (fatty extract from wool), crinoline, capelin (marine fish), zeppelin, cipolin (Italian marble), amygdalin (extract from bitter almonds), encephalin (chemical in the brain), adrenaline, noradrenaline (hormone).

252.12
famine, gamin (street urchin), examine, re-examine.

252.13
ermine, vermin, determine, predetermine.

252.14
women, specimen, maximin (maths term).

252.15
thiamine, Benjamin, jessamine (jasmine), etamin, vitamin, histamine, arsphenamine (drug containing arsenic), amphetamine, provitamin (precursor of vitamin), antihistamine, cyanocobalamin (crystalline substance).

252.16
Lenin, rennin, venin (poisonous part of venom), antivenin.

252.17
linen, feminine, agglutinin (antibody).

252.18
foreign, florin, Ilorin (Nigerian city).

252.19
tambourin (Provençal folk dance), purpurin (crystalline substance), aventurine (dark metal-flecked glass).

252.20
fiorin (perennial grass), suberin (waxy plant substance), saccharin, muscarine (poisonous chemical compound), mandarin, warfarin, gorgerin (architectural term), tamarin (small monkey), coumarin (chemical compound), heparin (biochemical substance), glycerine, bacterin (vaccine prepared from bacteria), nectarine, Catherine, culverin (heavy cannon), luciferin (light-emitting compound), alizarin (crystalline substance), nitroglycerin.

252.21
medicine, salicin (crystalline substance), sericin (protein), ceresin (white wax), capsaicin (crystalline substance), haemolysin (biochemical compound), fibrinolysin (enzyme).

252.22
lysin (substance that destroys cells), ricin (protein), neomycin (antibiotic), streptomycin, tyrothricin (antibiotic), actinomycin (antibiotic).

252.23
bulletin, palmitin (chemical compound), ferritin (protein), quercetin (yellow plant pigment), precipitin (antibody), phenacetin (crystalline substance).

252.24
cutin (waxy plant substance), Rasputin, highfalutin.

252.25
captain, Sahaptin (American Indian).

252.26
destine, predestine, clandestine, progestin (hormone), intestine.

252.27
Justin, Augustine.

252.28
Bevin (British statesman), Previn, replevin (legal term).

252.29
tocsin, toxin, thyroxine (hormone), digitoxin (poisonous chemical compound), antitoxin, zootoxin (toxin produced by animal), phytotoxin (plant poison), autotoxin (medical term).

252.30

resin, muezzin (Islamic mosque official).

253 -ine

bine (climbing stem), kine (cattle), chine, dyne, dine, fine, Jain (member of Hindu sect), line, cline (ecology term), spline, mine, nine, pine, spine, Rhine, brine, shrine, trine (astrology term), sine, sign, syne (*Scot* since), shine, Tyne, tine, stein, thine, vine, whine, wine, swine, twine.

Sabine, carbine, turbine, stibine (poisonous gas), woodbine, combine, alkyne (chemical compound), turdine (relating to thrushes), indign (undeserving), condign (well-deserved), affine (maths term), define, refine, confine, ralline (ornithology term), saline, airline, hairline, beeline, feline, skyline, dyeline (type of blueprint), Pauline (relating to Saint Paul), shoreline, towline, neckline, touchline, deadline, headline, breadline, guideline, sideline, lifeline, tramline, hemline, streamline, pipeline, baseline, dateline, outline, waistline, coastline, clothesline, carmine, canine, Pennine, rapine (forcible seizure of property), repine (be fretful), orpine (succulent plant), opine (hold an opinion), lupine, supine, alpine, vulpine (relating to foxes), vespine (relating to wasps), equine, larine (relating to gulls), taurine, murine (zoology term), murrhine (Roman vase material), eccrine, caprine (relating to goats), enshrine, Petrine (relating to Saint Peter), ursine, hircine (lascivious), quercine (relating to the oak), piscine, porcine, cosine, phocine (relating to seals), calcine (chemistry term), ensign, consign, shoeshine, sunshine, moonshine, outshine, pontine (relating to bridges), Holstein, Bernstein, Einstein, Epstein, cervine (relating to deer), divine, corvine (relating to crows), ovine,

bovine, grapevine, entwine, design, resign.

concubine, alcidine (ornithology term), hirundine (relating to swallows), celandine, almandine (violet-red garnet), superfine, trichogyne (botany term), androgyne (bisexual), fringilline (ornithology term), aquiline, musteline (zoology term), induline (blue dye), Ursuline (Catholic teaching nun), vituline (relating to calves), monocline (geology term), microcline (feldspar mineral), isocline (geology term), calcimine (pale wash for walls), sycamine (mulberry tree), undermine, calamine, leonine, falconine (relating to falcons), saturnine, pavonine (relating to peacocks), porcupine, subalpine, cisalpine, transalpine, viverrine (zoology term), platyrrhine (zoology term), sciurine (relating to squirrels), colubrine (relating to snakes), endocrine, holocrine (physiology term), apocrine (physiology term), merocrine (physiology term), exocrine (physiology term), auld lang syne, gegenschein (faint glow in sky), vespertine (occurring in the evening), serotine (biology term), Tridentine (orthodox Roman Catholic), Aventine (ancient Roman hill), transpontine (across a bridge), argentine (relating to silver), valentine, eglantine, serpentine, turpentine, Florentine, Constantine, levantine (silk cloth), Hammerstein, Rubinstein, Frankenstein, Liechtenstein, Eisenstein (Russian film director), Wittgenstein, intertwine, disentwine.

Alexandrine, accipitrine (relating to hawks), internecine, terebinthine, labyrinthine, hyacinthine.

253.1

combine, columbine.

253.2

aerodyne (heavier-than-air machine), anodyne, heterodyne (electronics term).

253.3

align, malign, moline (heraldic term), zibeline (sable fur), alkaline, borderline, underline, opaline, Caroline, coralline, metalline, interline, crystalline, limicoline (ornithology term), Capitoline (ancient Roman hill).

253.4

decline, recline, helicline (spiral-shaped ramp), pericline (white mineral), anticline (rock formation), geanticline (rock formation).

253.5

incline, syncline (rock formation), disincline, geosyncline (depression in earth's crust).

253.6

benign, asinine.

253.7

saccharine, vulturine, leporine (relating to hares), piperine (crystalline substance), passerine, anserine (relating to geese), uterine, riverine, estuarine, adulterine (fake), intrauterine, extrauterine.

253.8

assign, thylacine (Tasmanian wolf), limacine (relating to slugs), psittacine (relating to parrots), countersign, haversine (maths term).

253.9

Byzantine, elephantine, diamantine, adamantine (having diamond-like lustre).

253.10

pristine, Philistine, amethystine.

254 -on

on, Bonn, con, scone, don, Don, phon (unit of loudness), gone, John, shone, wan, won (Korean currency), swan, yon.

kaon (physics particle), rayon, neon, Creon (king of Thebes), gluon (hypothetical particle in physics), Huon (Tasmanian river), muon (elementary particle in physics), Gabon, bonbon, zircon, icon, Yukon, chaconne (musical term), mascon (lunar region), radon (radioactive element), chiffon, argon, Sargon (Assyrian king), bygone, trigon (triangular harp), Saigon, doggone, foregone, trogon (tropical bird), salon, nylon, Orlon (*Trademark*), Teflon (*Trademark*), mouflon (wild mountain sheep), gnomon (part of sundial), xenon, chronon (unit of time), Nippon, coupon, jupon (short sleeveless garment), upon, tampon, pompon, thereon, whereon, Chiron (Greek centaur), giron (heraldic term), fleuron (flower-shaped ornament), pleuron (zoology term), neuron (nerve cell), Hebron (Jordanian city), macron (phonetic symbol), Dacron (*Trademark*), micron, nephron (kidney tubule), neutron, Tucson, baton, cretonne, piton, photon, proton, pluton (geology term), mouton (processed sheepskin), crouton, canton, Canton, won ton (Chinese filled dumpling), lepton (Greek coin), krypton, axon, taxon (biology term), bouillon, meson (elementary particle in physics), boson (elementary particle in physics), Luzon (largest Philippine island), blouson.

Ratisbon (German city), vidicon (small television camera tube), Comecon, orthicon (electronic device), Myrmidon (Greek mythological race), Macedon, stegodon (extinct mammal), celadon (Oriental porcelain), sphenodon (tuatara lizard), mastodon, parergon (additional employment), demijohn, eidolon (apparition), etymon (original form of word), kikumon (Japanese royal emblem), thereupon, whereupon, hereupon, elytron (insect's hard outer wing), positron (physics term), phytotron (experimental plant-growing unit), cyclotron (physics apparatus), electron, limaçon (maths term), cabochon (unfaceted polished gem), feuilleton (part of newspaper), magneton (unit in physics), phlogiston (hypothetical substance causing combustion), trilithon (structure comprising three stones), telethon, elevon (aircraft control surface), sabayon (light foamy dessert), Cro-Magnon, liaison, cabezon (Pacific fish), borazon (chemical compound).

Esdraelon (Israeli plain), sine qua non, Agamemnon, antineutron (physics term), hyperbaton (reversed order of words), automaton, demicanton (part of Swiss canton), anacoluthon (rhetoric term).

254.1
logion (authentic saying of Christ), nucleon, baryon (particle in physics), Sicyon (ancient Greek city), gnathion (point on lower jaw), triskelion (three-legged symbol), Anacreon (Greek poet), himation (ancient Greek cloak), antinucleon (particle in physics).

254.2
Laocoon (Greek mythological priest), entozoon (animal living inside another), protozoon, spermatozoon, haematozoon (microscopic blood parasite).

254.3
colophon (publisher's emblem on book), Bellerophon (Greek mythological hero).

254.4
begone, woebegone, polygon.

254.5
isogon (maths term), decagon, glucagon (hormone), undergone, nonagon, Nipigon (Canadian lake), estragon (tarragon), octagon, pentagon, heptagon, hexagon, dodecagon, undecagon, trimetrogon (method of aerial photography).

254.6
Ceylon, Chillon (Swiss castle), papillon (breed of spaniel), epsilon, upsilon, haematoxylon (thorny tree).

254.7
colon (French colonial farmer), Miquelon (French territorial island group), echelon, etalon (physics device), Avalon, encephalon (the brain).

254.8
anon, guenon (African monkey), argonon (a gas), organon (philosophy term), Parthenon, olecranon (projection behind elbow joint), perispomenon (type of Greek word).

254.9
hereon, interferon.

254.10
boron, moron, thoron (radioisotope of radon), oxymoron (rhetoric term).

254.11
Oberon, Acheron (Greek mythological river), megaron (tripartite rectangular room), aileron, hyperon (elementary particle in physics), operon (genetics term), Percheron (breed of carthorse), enteron (animal's digestive tract), hapteron (botany term), ephemeron (short-lived organism), mesenteron (animal's midgut), hexaemeron (the Creation), diatessaron (musical term).

254.12
chignon, filet mignon, boeuf Bourguignon.

255 -orn
awn, born, borne, bourn, corn, scorn, dawn, fawn, faun, horn, lawn, lorn (forsaken), mourn, morn, Norn (Norse goddess), pawn, spawn, brawn, drawn, prawn, thrawn (*Dialect* crooked), sawn, sorn (*Scot* scrounge hospitality), shorn, Sean, torn, thorn, Vaughan, warn, worn, sworn, yawn.

airborne, chairborne, reborn, freeborn, seaborne, highborn, lowborn, newborn, stillborn, inborn, unborn, baseborn, first-born, Eastbourne, Osborne, earth-born, acorn, bicorn (having two horns), tricorn (cocked hat), einkorn (variety of wheat), Runcorn, popcorn, adorn, dehorn, Gijón (Spanish port), shoehorn, inkhorn (ink container), stinkhorn (foul-smelling fungus), leghorn, foghorn, crumhorn (medieval woodwind instrument), greenhorn (inexperienced person), longhorn (breed of cattle), pronghorn (small US deer), alphorn, shorthorn, althorn (brass instrument), saxhorn (brass instrument), forlorn, lovelorn, frogspawn, withdrawn, indrawn, hawthorn, blackthorn, buckthorn, careworn, forewarn, timeworn, forsworn, Mayon (Philippine volcano), Trabzon (Turkish port).

peppercorn, leprechaun, Apeldoorn (Dutch town), Matterhorn, flugelhorn, alpenhorn, overdrawn, weatherworn, waterworn, Finsteraarhorn (Swiss mountain).

255.1
suborn, waterborne, winterbourne (stream caused by rainfall).

255.2
longicorn (beetle), barleycorn, unicorn, Capricorn, cavicorn (having hollow horns), clavicorn (beetle), lamellicorn (beetle).

256 -oin
Boyne, coin, quoin (external corner of wall), join, loin, groyne, groin, sainfoin (Eurasian plant), rejoin, adjoin, subjoin, enjoin, conjoin, disjoin, purloin, sirloin, Boulogne, tenderloin, frankalmoign (English legal history term), talapoin (small monkey), Assiniboine (Canadian river).

257 -oan
own, bone, Beaune, cone, scone, chon (Korean coin), phone, Joan, hone, loan, lone, blown, clone, flown, Sloane, moan, mown, known, pone (maize bread), rone (*Scot* drainpipe), Rhône, roan, crone, drone, grown, groan, prone, throne, thrown, sewn, sown,

sone (unit of loudness), shown, tone, stone, zone.

thighbone, jawbone, backbone, cheekbone, aitchbone (cut of beef), whalebone, trombone, shinbone, hipbone, wishbone, breastbone, dracone (container towed by ship), condone, earphone, sulphone (chemical compound), agon (ancient Greek festival), cogon (tropical grass), chalone (internal secretion), colon (Costa Rican currency), alone, Cologne, cologne, flyblown (contaminated), windblown, full-blown, cyclone, high-flown, bemoan, hormone, unknown, depone (Scottish legal term), repone (Scottish legal term), Capone, postpone, Tyrone, pyrone (chemical compound), neurone, ingrown, oestrone (hormone), dethrone, enthrone, disown, bolson (US desert valley), ketone, tritone (musical term), lactone (chemical compound), halftone, intone, peptone, keystone, freestone (fine-grained stone), kerbstone, touchstone, headstone, lodestone, toadstone (igneous rock), sandstone, grindstone, flagstone, hailstone, millstone, bilestone, milestone, gallstone, gemstone, brimstone, limestone, tombstone, rhinestone, moonstone, copestone, soapstone, whetstone, birthstone, gravestone, flavone (crystalline substance), hexone (chemical compound), ozone, evzone (Greek soldier).

marrowbone, collarbone, knucklebone, anklebone, cuttlebone, herringbone, silicone, methadone (narcotic drug), audiphone (hearing aid), telephone, polyphone (linguistics term), Francophone, chordophone (stringed instrument), megaphone, mellophone (brassband instrument), xylophone, Anglophone, gramophone, homophone (word pronounced like another), vibraphone (percussion instrument), microphone, hydrophone (underwater microphone), Dictaphone (*Trademark*), interphone (telephone system linking rooms), saxophone, sousaphone, heckelphone (bass oboe), overblown, pheromone (chemical substance in animals), unbeknown, rotenone (crystalline substance), ionone (perfumed plant extract), butanone (chemical compound), ethonone (toxic gas), undergrown, overgrown, overthrown, ecdysone (hormone), holystone (sandstone for scrubbing decks), thunderstone (long tapering object), cornerstone, cobblestone, staddlestone, prednisone (steroid drug), cortisone.

radiophone, anticyclone.

enterogastrone (hormone), spironolactone (hormone).

257.1
coumarone (aromatic liquid), chaperon, progesterone, aldosterone, androsterone, testosterone.

257.2
barbitone, semitone, baritone, baryton (bass viol), acetone, phenobarbitone.

257.3
atone, duotone (printing process), sacaton (coarse grass), ecotone (ecology term), undertone, monotone, isotone (chemistry term), overtone.

258 -oun
down, gown, clown, noun, brown, crown, drown, frown, town.

godown (Asian warehouse), hoedown, lowdown, slowdown, showdown, markdown, breakdown, shakedown, touchdown, comedown, sundown, splashdown, shutdown, Piltdown, countdown, nightgown, renown, pronoun, adnoun (adjective used as noun), nutbrown, Motown, midtown, downtown, uptown.

hand-me-down, eiderdown, omadhaun (*Irish* a fool), Portadown, upside-down, tumble-down, thistledown, shantytown, Chinatown, cabbagetown (city slum).

259 -un
bun, dun, done, fun, gun, Hun, none, nun, pun, spun, run, son, sun, sunn (East Indian plant), shun, ton, tonne, tun, stun, one, won.

undone, outdone, begun, handgun, popgun, shotgun, outgun, Falun (Swedish city), Cholon (South Vietnamese city), homespun, finespun, rerun, forerun, millrun, outrun, godson, grandson, stepson, Fushun (Chinese city), someone.

underdone, overdone, overrun, kiloton, megaton, anyone, everyone.

260 -oon
boon, coon, Scone (Scottish parish), goon, June, lune (maths term), loon, moon, noon, poon (Asian tree), spoon, rune, croon, prune, soon, shoon, toon (large tree), swoon, dune, tune.

baboon, tycoon, rockoon (scientifically-equipped rocket), cocoon, puccoon (US plant), raccoon, tuchun (Chinese military governor), cardoon (European plant), bridoon (horse's bit), typhoon, buffoon, lagoon, dragoon, Rangoon, jejune, cohune (US tropical palm), shalloon (light woollen fabric), Walloon, Kowloon, doubloon, forenoon, harpoon, lampoon, teaspoon, gombroon (Oriental pottery), quadroon, Gudrun, gadroon (decorative patterned moulding), poltroon (contemptible coward), Sassoon, gossoon (*Irish* servant boy), bassoon, monsoon, matzoon (fermented milk product), ratoon (crop plant's new growth), cartoon, spittoon, pontoon, spontoon (short pike), festoon, triune (three in one), tribune, immune, commune, repugn, oppugn (to dispute), impugn, Neptune.

rigadoon (old Provençal dance), Dehra Dun (Indian city), demilune (crescent-shaped formation), perilune (point in lunar orbit), honeymoon, tablespoon, dessertspoon, Behistun (Iranian village), picayune (*US* of little value).

Tutankhamun, autoimmune.

260.1
balloon, galloon (decorative cord), saloon, apolune (point in lunar orbit), pantaloon (pantomime character).

260.2
Dunoon, afternoon.

260.3
maroon, macaroon, picaroon (adventurer), Scandaroon (fancy pigeon), Cameroon, octoroon, Iskenderun (Turkish port), vinegarroon (large scorpion-like arachnid).

260.4
platoon, saskatoon (Canadian fruit shrub), Saskatoon (Canadian city).

260.5
fortune, misfortune, importune.

260.6
attune, opportune, inopportune.

261 -'n

ebon, leben (African curdled milk), gibbon, ribbon, auburn, corban (biblical gift), Bourbon, Oban, stubborn, Cuban, Melbourne, Gisborne (New Zealand port), Lisbon, Brisbane, blacken, slacken, bracken, beckon, Deccan, schnecken (*US* bread roll), pekan (US mammal), reckon, Brecon, liken, lichen, silken, Vulcan, Lincoln, Duncan, drunken, shrunken, sunken, scutcheon, scuncheon (part of door jamb), luncheon, puncheon (large cask), truncheon, Christian, Arden, Baden, Dardan (Trojan), garden, harden, lardon (strip of fat), pardon, bourdon (organ stop), hoyden (tomboy), Croydon, loden (thick wool), Snowdon, Woden (Anglo-Saxon god), louden, sudden, wooden, Camden, tendon, linden, Swindon, bounden, London, Hampden, Dresden, deafen, hyphen, siphon, often, soften, orphan, roughen,

druffen (*Dialect* drunk), toughen, lagan (wreckage on sea bed), Skagen (cape in Denmark), Dagan (Babylonian god), jargon, Hagen (German legendary character), Keegan, vegan, tigon (tiger –lion hybrid), bogan (*Canadian* side stream), hogan (American Indian dwelling), Logan, slogan, brogan (heavy boot), roentgen, largen, Georgian, Trojan, Belgian, Injun, St. John, dungeon, Allen, Alan, gallon, talon, Galen (Greek physician), merlon (part of battlement), pylon, fallen, courlan (US wading bird), sullen, woollen, raglan, barman, carman, Raman (Indian physicist), Brahman, Emmen (Dutch city), lemon, German, Herman, merman, sermon, Sherman, pieman, Simon, Cimon (Athenian military commander), fireman, wireman (*US* electrician), common, doorman, foreman, lawman, Mormon, Norman, bowman (oarsman), cowman, ploughman, summon, cabman, kirkman (*Scot* church member), workman, socman (tenant farmer), stockman, milkman, linkman, churchman, Scotchman, watchman, coachman, Dutchman, henchman, Frenchman, adman, badman, madman, Bradman (Australian cricketer), headman, birdman, freedman, goodman, woodman, sandman, bagman (travelling salesman), flagman, ragman, swagman, legman (US newspaper reporter), tegmen (insect's leathery forewing), Bergman, dogman (*Austral* crane-driver's assistant), frogman, dolman (long Turkish robe), coalman, oilman, Pullman, penman, gunman, hangman, strongman, apeman, Helpmann (Australian ballet dancer), gasman, baseman (fielder in baseball), spaceman, horseman, Norseman, houseman, batsman, statesman, Scotsman, yachtsman, sportsman, craftsman, draughtsman, huntsman, freshman, bushman, Welshman, batman, atman (Hindu self), hetman (Cossack leader), Pitman, pitman, titman (smallest piglet in litter), Whitman (US poet), boatman, footman, postman, dustman, caveman, marksman, spokesman, Manxman, Tasman, Osman (Turkish sultan), oarsman, tribesman, guardsman, tradesman, herdsman, sidesman (church warden's assistant), swordsman, bandsman, landsman, roundsman, groundsman, bailsman (person who stands bail), dalesman, salesman, clansman, Klansman (Ku Klux Klan member), kinsman, linesman, townsman, Canaan, Lennon, pennon, tenon, happen, sharpen, tarpon (Atlantic fish), weapon, cheapen, deepen, steepen, Ripon, Crippen, ripen, open, dampen, lampern (European lamprey), crampon, hempen, tympan (resonating membrane), lumpen (stupid), aspen, saucepan, Aran, Arran, barren, baron, Karen, marron (chestnut), Sharon, heron, perron (flight of steps), Aaron, Charon (Greek mythological character), sporran, warren, squadron, children, cauldron, chaldron (unit of capacity), pauldron (armour plate protecting shoulder), saffron, apron, matron, natron (a mineral), patron, citron, plectron, chevron, sovran, bison, hyson (Chinese green tea), grison (predatory mammal), coarsen, Dawson, whoreson, hoarsen, Porson (English classical scholar), moisten, Preussen (German name for Prussia), boatswain, bosun, loosen, Ibsen, Gibson, Hudson, Belsen, kelson (strengthening beam on keel), Nelson, telson (zoology term), Wilson, Samson, Jansen, Nansen, Johnson, sponson (ship's outboard gun platform), Bunsen, Simpson, Thompson, stetson, Whitsun, Watson, tutsan (Eurasian woodland shrub), Martian, cushion, auction, sanction, sponsion (sponsorship), Dayton (US city), phaeton (horse-drawn carriage), straighten, straiten (embarrass financially), Satan, oaten (made of oats), croton (tropical shrub), Acton, Clacton, lectern, Stockton, plankton, chieftain, Carlton,

Charlton, Chiltern, Milton, Stilton, Wilton, Dalton (English scientist), saltern (saltworks), Walton, Bolton, molten, sultan, Danton (French revolutionary leader), lantern, Scranton (Pennsylvanian city), Paignton, Denton (English town), lenten, Trenton (US city), wanton, Taunton, hapten (medical term), Clapton (English rock guitarist), Skipton, Hampton, Aston, pastern, eastern, Boston, postern, pleuston (mass of floating microorganisms), Houston, Gladstone, Maidstone, charleston, Princeton, Dunstan (English saint), tungsten, capstan, Ashton, Caxton, Paxton (English architect), sexton (church caretaker), Folkestone, Buxton, Nathan, earthen, python, luthern (dormer window), lengthen, strengthen, heathen, northern, southern, smoothen, cavern, raven (seize prey), tavern, proven, sylvan (relating to woods), Malvern, seawan (shell beads), Jackson, klaxon, flaxen, Saxon, waxen, Texan, Nixon, vixen, oxen, Oxon., coxswain, bullion, Julian, onion, bunion, Bunyan, Runyon (US writer), grunion (Californian fish), trunnion (pivot), Tarzan, cousin, cozen (to trick), dozen, damson, crimson.

Labuan (Malaysian island), Don Juan, Moroccan, Monacan, Faliscan (ancient Italian language), Franciscan, escutcheon, unchristian, exhaustion, combustion, Basildon, Wimbledon, abandon, Ugandan, Clarendon, Abingdon, Hillingdon, Huntingdon, toboggan, Aragon, paragon, tarragon, suffragan (assistant bishop), martagon (Eurasian lily), Monaghan (Irish county), downfallen (dilapidated), chapfallen (dejected), crestfallen, gonfalon (banner), mamelon (small rounded hillock), ortolan (small bird), biathlon, decathlon, pentathlon, uncommon, discommon (legal term), Roscommon (Irish county), husbandman, Orangeman, patrolman, stableman, nobleman, middleman, rifleman, signalman, muscleman, cattleman, gentleman, midshipman, policeman, businessman, serviceman, warehouseman, Englishman, Irishman, aircraftman, merchantman (merchant ship), harvestman (arachnid), talisman, exciseman, ombudsman, backwoodsman, Lebanon, reopen, half-open, Saharan, Anderson, Jefferson, Emerson, Saracen, Paterson, Peterson, Richardson, Nicholson, Mendelssohn, Williamson, Robinson, Dickinson, Atkinson, Stephenson, pincushion, infarction, decoction (medicinal preparation), concoction, intinction (part of Communion), distinction, extinction, emulsion, repulsion, propulsion, impulsion, compulsion, expulsion, revulsion, divulsion (tearing apart), avulsion (forcible separation), convulsion, pre-emption, redemption, exemption, occasion, equation, abrasion, pervasion, evasion, invasion, persuasion, dissuasion, quieten, Pinkerton, charlatan, tarlatan (cotton fabric), Sheraton, Chatterton, Chesterton, doubleton (bridge term), subaltern, Shackleton, Middleton, singleton, Hamilton, simpleton, Edmonton, Bebington, Tarkington (US novelist), Arlington (Virginian county), Darlington, Ellington (US jazz musician), Wellington, Burlington, Islington, Leamington, Lymington, Warrington, Accrington, Washington, Whittington, Lexington (US city), Kensington, Northampton, Southampton, Augustan, Palmerston, autochthon (country's earliest-known inhabitant), Carmarthen, cordovan (fine leather), Donovan, Amazon.

inescutcheon (heraldic term), Muhammadan, solenodon (shrew-like mammal), Tutankhamen, Landeshauptmann (Austrian state governor), polyhedron, rhombohedron, decahedron, tetrahedron, octahedron, hexahedron, rhododendron, philodendron (climbing plant), hobson-jobson (folk etymolo-

gy), Wolverhampton, Aldermaston, Saskatchewan, Elizabethan.

261.1

crayon, Malayan, Ghanaian, Pompeian.

261.2

Ian, aeon, Behan (Irish writer), peon (Spanish-American farm labourer), paeon (metrical foot), paean (song of praise), Archaean (geology term), Judaean, Andean, Pandean (relating to Pan), Aegean, Fijian, Augean (very dirty), Crimean, Tarpeian, lyncean (resembling a lynx), protean (variable in form).

amoebaean, Caribbean, Hebridean, Sisyphean (endless and futile), herculean, Coeur de Lion, Ponce de León (Spanish explorer), Pyrenean, Cyclopean (architectural term), European, empyrean (relating to the heavens).

antipodean, epicurean.

261.2.1

plebeian, Jacobean, Maccabean, scarabaean (type of beetle).

261.2.2

spelaean (relating to caves), Achillean, Galilean.

261.2.3

Korean, Terpsichorean, Pythagorean.

261.2.4

Odyssean, Laodicean.

261.3

Ian, lien (legal term).

Serbian (language group), Nubian, Albion, lesbian, guardian, Freudian, Scandian (Scandinavian), Mandaean (member of Iraqi sect), Indian, saffian (tanned leather), Orphean, ruffian, galleon, talion (making punishment fit crime), Caerleon (Welsh town), Bodleian, Anglian, ganglion, Wesleyan, camion (lorry), Samian (relating to Samos), Permian, thermion (high-temperature electron), amnion, Jungian, apian (relating to bees), scorpion, campion, champion, lampion (oil-burning lamp), pampean (relating to pampas), rampion (Eurasian plant), Grampian, tampion (plug for gun's muzzle), Caspian, Thespian, Syrian, Tyrian (relating to ancient Tyre), Zyrian (language group), quarrian (Australian bird), Cambrian, Adrian, Hadrian, Cyprian, Bactrian, Austrian, basion (anatomy term), hessian, Ossian (legendary Irish bard), Lucian (ancient Greek writer), halcyon, Haitian, Gratian (Roman emperor), bastion, Parthian, pantheon, Scythian, Pythian (relating to Delphi), Lothian, Latvian, Marxian.

Columbian, Lamarckian, Noachian (relating to Noah), selachian (zoology term), batrachian (amphibian), Pickwickian, Gulbenkian (British industrialist), Algonquian (language group), Comanchean, accordion, Edwardian, cerulean (deep blue), Bohemian, anthemion (ancient Greek floral design), acromion (part of shoulder blade), Hibernian, quaternion (maths term), Mancunian, Neptunian, Olympian, Tocharian (member of Asian culture), Amphitryon (Greek mythological character), pedestrian, equestrian, Circassian, etesian (relating to Mediterranean winds), Gilbertian, nemertean (ribbonlike marine worm), amphictyon (ancient Greek religious councillor), Atlantean, Carpathian, Promethean (creative or original), Erechtheion (temple on Acropolis), Midlothian, Venusian, Carthusian (Roman Catholic monk), Malthusian (relating to population theory), Dickensian.

ornithischian (zoology term), Appalachian, Amerindian, Christadelphian, theologian, Carolingian (Frankish dynasty), Merovingian (Frankish dynasty), Liverpudlian, epilimnion (upper layer in lake), hypolimnion (bottom layer in lake), Mississippian, Alexandrian, mitochondrion (microscopic structure in cell), salientian (type of amphibian), demibastion (type of fortification), Yugoslavian, Czechoslovakian.

261.3.1
Fabian, gabion (stone-filled cylinder), Arabian.

261.3.2
Gibeon (ancient Palestinian town), Libyan, amphibian.

261.3.3
radian, Arcadian, circadian (relating to biological rhythm), Orcadian (relating to the Orkneys), Acadian (French settler in Canada), gammadion (swastika), Canadian, steradian (unit in geometry).

261.3.4
median, tragedian, comedian, Archimedean.

261.3.5
Gideon, Midian (biblical nation), ophidian (snake-like), viridian (green pigment), meridian, ascidian (tiny marine animal), obsidian (volcanic rock), quotidian, Dravidian (language group), solifidian (relating to religious doctrine), nullifidian (sceptic), postmeridian, proboscidean (zoology term), antemeridian.

261.3.6
Rhodian (relating to Rhodes), melodeon (small accordion), collodion (syrupy liquid), custodian, nickelodeon.

261.3.7 [see also 261.37]
Phrygian, Stygian (relating to river Styx), Ogygian (extremely ancient), callipygian (having shapely buttocks), Cantabrigian, crossopterygian (bony fish), malacopterygian (soft-finned fish), acanthopterygian (spiny-finned fish).

261.3.8
alien, Salian (relating to Frankish group), Deucalion (Greek mythological character), mammalian, Pygmalion, Australian, bacchanalian, sesquipedalian (using very long words), episcopalian.

261.3.9 [see also 261.119]
Sabellian (extinct language group), Orwellian, Cromwellian, Machiavellian.

261.3.10
Pelion (Greek mountain), Caelian (ancient Roman hill), parhelion (meteorology term), aphelion (point in planet's orbit), anthelion (meteorology term), chameleon, carnelian (gemstone), Aurelian (Roman emperor), Mingrelian (language group), perihelion (point in planet's orbit), Aristotelian.

261.3.11 [see also 261.120]
Ilion (Greek name for Troy), skillion (*Austral* lean-to), Gillian, penillion (Welsh sung poetry), epyllion (miniature epic poem), caecilian (limbless amphibian), Sicilian, Quintilian (Roman teacher), reptilian, Castilian (relating to Castile), Abbevillian (archaeological period), Basilian (Eastern Christian monk), Brazilian, crocodilian, Maximilian, lacertilian (lizard), vaudevillian.

261.3.12
Aeolian, Mongolian, Napoleon, Anatolian (language group).

261.3.13
scullion, mullion, Tertullian (Carthaginian Christian theologian), slubberdegullion (slovenly person).

261.3.14
Simeon, simian (resembling a monkey), Endymion, prosimian (zoology term).

261.3.15
Albanian, vulcanian (volcanic), Jordanian, Rumanian, Tasmanian, Iranian, Uranian, Ukrainian, Lithuanian, Panamanian, Transylvanian, Pennsylvanian.

261.3.15.1
Pomeranian, subterranean, Mediterranean.

261.3.16
Fenian (19th-century Irish revolutionary), Armenian, Tyrrhenian (part of Mediterranean), sirenian (zoology term), Ruthenian (language group), Athenian.

261.3.17 [see also 261.122]
inion (point on skull), Sardinian, Arminian, Socinian (relating to religious doctrine), Justinian (Byzantine emperor), Darwinian, Carthaginian, Valentinian (Roman emperor), Augustinian.

261.3.18
gonion (anatomy term), chthonian (relating to the underworld), aeonian (everlasting), Ionian, Draconian, Franconian (language group), gorgonian (type of coral), chelonian (tortoise or turtle), Johnsonian, Smithsonian, Shoshonean (language group), Etonian, Plutonian (infernal), Newtonian, Miltonian, Estonian (language group), Devonian, favonian (relating to west wind), Oxonian, Caledonian, Macedonian, Aberdonian, Babylonian, Apollonian, Thessalonian, Ciceronian (eloquent), Hambletonian (breed of horse), Amazonian, Lacedaemonian (Spartan).

261.3.19
Fallopian, Utopian, Ethiopian.

261.3.20
carrion, clarion, Marian, orpharion (large lute).

261.3.21
Arian, Darien (part of Panama), Parian (relating to fine marble).

barbarian, Icarian (relating to Icarus), cnidarian (zoology term), Bulgarian, vulgarian (vulgar person), Hungarian, valerian (Eurasian plant), grammarian, planarian (non-parasitic flatworm), riparian, librarian, agrarian, fruitarian (person eating only fruit), Rotarian, sectarian, ovarian, Bavarian, Caesarean, rosarian (person who cultivates roses).

apiarian (relating to beekeeping), Rastafarian, sertularian (zoology term), antiquarian, Sabbatarian (strict observer of Sabbath), libertarian (believer in free thought).

abecedarian (person learning the alphabet), infralapsarian (theology term), supralapsarian (theology term), parliamentarian.

261.3.21.1
millenarian (relating to a thousand), seminarian (student at seminary), centenarian, octogenarian, nonagenarian, quinquagenarian, quadragenarian, sexagenarian, disciplinarian, veterinarian, predestinarian (believer in predestination), valetudinarian (chronically-sick person), latitudinarian (permitting religious freedom), septuagenarian.

261.3.21.2
vegetarian, proletarian, limitarian, sanitarian (relating to sanitation), Trinitarian (believer in the Trinity), unitarian, egalitarian, totalitarian, utilitarian, futilitarian, humanitarian, communitarian (member of communist community), ubiquitarian (believer in Christ's omnipresence), authoritarian.

261.3.22
Pierian (relating to the Muses), Iberian, Siberian, Nigerian, Algerian, Cimmerian (very dark), Sumerian (ancient Babylonian), Wagnerian, Hyperion, Shakespearean, Chaucerian, criterion, eutherian (zoology term), mezereon (Eurasian shrub), presbyterian, prototherian (zoology term), metatherian (marsupial), Hanoverian.

261.3.23
chorion (embryonic membrane), Dorian (ancient Greek), morion (16th-century helmet), saurian (resembling a lizard), Gregorian, Victorian, stento-rian (extremely loud-voiced), historian, Hyperborean (inhabitant of extreme north), Hypodorian (musical term), prehistorian.

261.3.24
turion (plant bud), durian (Asian tree), Ben-Gurion, tellurian (relating to the earth), tellurion (model showing earth's movement), Silurian, decurion (Roman councillor), pagurian (hermit crab), centurion, Arthurian, Khachaturian (Russian composer), holothurian (sea cucumber).

261.3.25
Umbrian (extinct language group), Cumbrian, Northumbrian.

261.3.26
Lancastrian, Zoroastrian.

261.3.27
fustian, Procrustean (producing conformity ruthlessly).

261.3.28
Corinthian, labyrinthian, pericynthion (point in lunar orbit), apocynthion (point in lunar orbit).

261.3.29
avian, Shavian, subclavian, Moravian, Octavian, Scandinavian.

261.3.30
Vivian, Bolivian, oblivion.

261.3.31
Jovian, Harrovian.

261.3.32
alluvion (overflow), Peruvian, vesuvian (match for lighting cigars), postdiluvian (existing after biblical Flood), antediluvian.

261.3.33
nasion (point on skull), Caucasian, Malaysian, Vespasian, Rabelaisian.

261.3.34 [see also **261.90**]
artesian, Cartesian (relating to Descartes), Polynesian, Indonesian, Melanesian.

261.3.35 [see also **261.91**]
Elysian, Parisian, Dionysian.

261.4
ion, iron, lion, Mayan, Ryan, Brian, scion, Zion, sadiron (heavy iron), midiron (golf club), gridiron, andiron (logstand in fireplace), antlion (tropical insect), anion, cation, flatiron, Hawaiian, dandelion.

261.4.1
Orion, zwitterion (charged particle).

261.5
doyen, Illinoisan, Iroquoian (American Indian language).

261.6
Iowan (Australian bird), rowan, Caddoan (language group), Minoan, dipnoan (lungfish), bryozoan (colonial aquatic animal), hydrozoan (small aquatic animal), sporozoan (microscopic parasitic animal), protozoan (microscopic animal).

261.7
Papuan, gargantuan.

261.8
Schwaben (region of West Germany), carbon, graben (trough of land), hydrocarbon, radiocarbon.

261.9
urban, bourbon, Durban, turban, suburban.

261.10
Aachen, darken, hearken, kraken (legendary sea monster), Interlaken.

261.11
bacon, shaken, taken, waken, Jamaican, forsaken, unshaken, mistaken, awaken, godforsaken, undertaken, overtaken.

261.12
beacon, deacon, weaken, subdeacon, archdeacon, Mohican.

261.13
quicken, stricken, sicken, thicken, Barbican, Rubicon, indican (chemical compound), Helicon (Greek mountain), helicon (bass tuba), pelican, Millikan (US physicist), silicon, publican, Anglican, pemmican (American Indian food), salpicon (chopped food in sauce), hurricane, African, Corsican, Vatican, lexicon, Mexican, catholicon (remedy for all diseases), republican, Dominican, pantechnicon (large van), American, ferrosilicon (iron–silicon alloy), stereopticon (type of projector).

261.14
oaken, spoken, broken, token, woken, Hoboken (Belgian city), unspoken, outspoken, unbroken, heartbroken, betoken, ryokan (traditional Japanese inn).

261.15
Lucan, toucan, lebkuchen (German biscuit), Chinookan (American Indian language).

261.16
Balkan, falcon, gyrfalcon (large rare falcon).

261.17
Tuscan, Etruscan.

261.18
question, digestion, suggestion, ingestion, congestion, indigestion, autosuggestion.

261.19
gladden, madden, sadden, Ibadan (Nigerian city), Abaddon (the devil).

261.20
Aden, Aidan, laden, Blaydon (English town), maiden, menhaden (US fish), unladen, handmaiden.

261.21
deaden, leaden, redden, Armageddon.

261.22
burden, guerdon (reward), lurdan (stupid), unburden, disburden.

261.23
Eden, Sweden, boustrophedon (relating to writing method), cotyledon, dicotyledon, acotyledon, monocotyledon.

261.24
bidden, hidden, midden (*Dialect* rubbish heap), ridden, forbidden, unbidden, oppidan (urban), harridan, Sheridan, bedridden, Mohammedan, parallelepipedon (geometric solid).

261.25
guidon (small military flag), Haydn, Leiden (Dutch city), Dryden, Sidon (Phoenician city), widen, Poseidon.

261.26
hodden (coarse cloth), Flodden (Northumbrian battlefield), modern, trodden, sodden, Culloden (Scottish battlefield), downtrodden, untrodden, ultramodern.

261.27
Auden, cordon, Gordon, Jordan, broaden, warden, firewarden (*US* fire-prevention officer), churchwarden.

261.28
olden, golden, soldan (archaic word for sultan), embolden, beholden.

261.29
griffon, stiffen, antiphon (response).

261.30
flagon, dragon, wagon, pendragon (leader of ancient Britons), snapdragon, bandwagon.

261.31
pagan, Reagan, Nijmegen (Dutch town), Copenhagen.

261.32
Wigan, cardigan, Milligan, mulligan (*US* a stew), hooligan, ptarmigan, larrigan (leather moccasin boot), perigon (angle of 360°), origan (marjoram), Oregon, balbriggan (unbleached cotton fabric), Michigan, Rattigan (English dramatist), shenanigan.

261.33
organ, Gorgon, Morgan, Glamorgan, Demogorgon (mythological god).

261.34
Trajan (Roman emperor), contagion.

261.35
burgeon, gurjun (Asian tree), surgeon, sturgeon, neurosurgeon.

261.36
legion, region, collegian, subregion, Norwegian, Glaswegian.

261.37 [see also **261.3.7**]
smidgen, pigeon, wigeon (Eurasian duck), religion, florigen (hypothetical plant hormone), Harijan (Indian untouchable), cultigen (cultivated plant), antigen, oxygen, irreligion.

261.38
dudgeon, gudgeon, bludgeon, trudgen (swimming stroke), curmudgeon (surly person).

261.39
biogen (hypothetical protein), cryogen (freezing mixture), habergeon (coat of mail), thrombogen (protein), allergen, halogen, glycogen (biochemical compound), phellogen (cork-producing cells), collagen, zymogen (enzyme precursor), chromogen (chemical compound), pyrogen (substance causing fever), acrogen (type of flowerless plant), hydrogen, androgen, nitrogen, oestrogen, mutagen (substance causing mutation), histogen (plant tissue), pathogen, fibrinogen (blood protein), carcinogen, pepsinogen (enzyme), trypsinogen (enzyme), hallucinogen.

261.40
felon, melon, Magellan, muskmelon (type of melon), pademelon (small wallaby), watermelon.

261.41
billon (alloy used for coins), Dylan, villain, villein, Babylon, Macmillan, castellan (keeper of castle), abutilon (flowering shrub).

261.42
pollen, pollan (whitefish), Hohenzollern (German noble family).

261.43
colon, Nolan, Solon (Athenian statesman), stolen, stollen (rich sweet bread), stolon (horizontal plant stem), swollen, semicolon.

261.44
Ammon (biblical character), gammon, mammon, salmon, shaman (Asian priest), backgammon.

261.45
cayman (US crocodile), layman, Bremen, highwayman, railwayman.

261.46
airman, chairman, repairman.

261.47
demon, he-man, freeman, seaman, eudemon (benevolent spirit), pentstemon (US plant), Lacedaemon (Sparta), cacodemon (evil spirit).

261.48
handyman, bogeyman, clergyman, tallyman, journeyman, dairyman, quarryman, juryman, laundryman, nurseryman, poultryman, countryman, Everyman, persimmon (tropical tree), cavalryman, infantryman, committeeman, artilleryman.

261.49
omen, bowman (archer), foeman, snowman, Roman, showman, yeoman, locoman (engine-driver), dragoman (professional interpreter).

261.50
woman, charwoman, churchwoman, horsewoman, sportswoman, batwoman, townswoman, washerwoman, needlewoman, gentlewoman.

261.51
Truman, Schumann, Yuman (language group), human, Newman, subhuman, inhuman, ichneumon (mongoose), superhuman.

261.52
Turkoman (Asian people), Inkerman (Crimean battle site), Betjeman, trencherman (hearty eater), spiderman, abdomen, ealdorman (Anglo-Saxon judicial official), alderman, landammann (Swiss council chairman), telamon (supporting pillar), Solomon, colourman (person dealing in paints), cyclamen, cinnamon, Chinaman, superman, cameraman, ataman (leader of the Cossacks), peterman (*Slang* safe-breaker), ottoman, slaughterman (slaughterhouse employee), waterman (skilled boatman), motorman (electric-train driver), Ulsterman, weatherman, remainderman (legal term), newspaperman.

261.52.1
fisherman, militiaman.

261.53
chessman, desman (small amphibious mammal), pressman, yes-man, Congressman.

261.54
steersman, frontiersman.

261.55
cannon, canon, fanon (papal vestment), Shannon, Buchanan, colcannon (boiled cabbage and potatoes), Clackmannan.

261.56
finnan, noumenon (philosophy term), phenomenon, prolegomenon (critical introduction).

261.57
capon, unshapen, misshapen.

261.58
Byron, Myron (Greek sculptor), siren, environ, lepidosiren (South American fish).

261.59
Huron, aleurone (protein), macruran (type of crustacean), Van Buren (US president), anuran (tailless amphibian),

brachyuran (type of crustacean), thysanuran (primitive wingless insect).

261.60
longeron (part of aircraft), cateran (former Scottish brigand), Lateran (Roman palace), veteran, Lutheran, Aldebaran (star), poriferan (a sponge), erigeron (flowering plant), cladoceran (tiny freshwater animal), hemipteran (type of insect), chiropteran (relating to bats), orthopteran (type of insect).

261.61
arson, Carson, fasten, parson, sarsen (sandstone boulder), unfasten.

261.62
basin, caisson (watertight structure), chasten, Jason, hasten, mason, washbasin, freemason, stonemason.

261.63
lesson, lessen, delicatessen.

261.64
person, worsen, Macpherson, unperson.

261.65
listen, glisten, Nissen, christen, gambeson (medieval padded garment), Addison, Madison, Edison, Tennyson, venison, unison, Morrison, jettison, cavesson (horse's noseband), diocesan, archdiocesan.

261.65.1
garrison, Harrison, parison (unshaped glass before moulding), warison (bugle note ordering attack), caparison (horse's decorated covering), comparison.

261.66
ashen, fashion, passion, ration, impassion, compassion, dispassion, deration.

261.67
Asian, nation, station.

striation, Croatian (language group), libation, vacation, plication (folding), truncation, laudation (praise), foundation, purgation, lallation (speech defect), dilation, collation, ablation, oblation (religious offering), deflation, reflation, stagflation (economics term), inflation, translation, squamation (formation of scales), formation, summation, Dalmatian, planation (erosion of land surface), vernation (leaf arrangement in bud), venation (arrangement of veins), zonation, lunation (lunar month), damnation, crispation (curling), serration, gyration, oration, libration (oscillating), vibration, migration, titration, filtration, castration, prostration, frustration, cassation (legal term), cessation, Alsatian, pulsation, flirtation, fetation (state of pregnancy), citation, dictation, lactation, saltation (biology term), temptation, gustation (tasting), crustacean, substation, outstation, lavation (washing), starvation, nivation (geology term), privation, ovation, novation (legal term), salvation, solvation (chemistry term), fixation, causation.

conurbation, incubation, titubation, education, inculcation, coruscation (gleam of light), retardation, denudation, exudation, inundation, subjugation, conjugation, promulgation, elongation, prolongation, insolation (exposure to solar radiation), contemplation, legislation, deformation, preformation, malformation, conformation, exhumation, subornation, indignation, assignation, designation, resignation, condemnation, usurpation, occupation, syncopation, aspiration, inspiration, expiration, lucubration (laborious study), desecration, consecration, dehydration, conflagration, arbitration, penetration, infiltration, concentration, orchestration, sequestration, illustration, demonstration, conversation, deportation, importation, transportation, exportation, exhortation, exploitation, affectation, delectation, expectation, eructation (belching), exaltation, exultation, auscultation, consultation, supplantation, implantation, transplantation, confrontation, presentation, coaptation (reuniting two surfaces), acceptation, adaptation, forestation, devastation, salivation, elevation, derivation, deprivation, titivation, motivation, activation, cultivation, captivation, aestivation (biology term), excavation, renovation, innovation, aggravation, depravation, conservation, reservation, preservation, observation, accusation.

coeducation, interlunation (period of moon's invisibility), preoccupation, intermigration, superfetation (medical term), preadaptation (biology term).

261.67.1
creation, radiation, mediation, lineation (outline), expiation, variation, recreation, re-creation, procreation, fasciation (abnormal flattening of stems), aviation.

irradiation, repudiation, retaliation, delineation, columniation (arrangement of architectural columns), inebriation, appropriation, repatriation, expatriation, dissociation, association, expatiation, ingratiation, depreciation, appreciation, negotiation, substantiation, asphyxiation.

transubstantiation, consubstantiation, differentiation.

261.67.1.1
filiation (lineage), affiliation, humiliation, conciliation, disaffiliation, reconciliation.

261.67.1.2
foliation, spoliation, defoliation, despoliation.

261.67.1.3
caseation (formation of cheese), glaciation, emaciation.

261.67.1.4
enunciation, denunciation, renunciation, annunciation, pronunciation, mispronunciation.

261.67.1.5
vitiation, officiation, initiation.

261.67.1.6
deviation, abbreviation, alleviation.

261.67.2
menstruation, arcuation (arrangement of arches), graduation, valuation, situation, fluctuation, punctuation, invultuation (making images for witchcraft), evacuation, evaluation, devaluation, revaluation, attenuation, insinuation, continuation, infatuation, perpetuation, accentuation, superannuation.

261.67.3
probation, approbation, reprobation, perturbation, masturbation, disapprobation, exacerbation.

261.67.4
embarkation, demarcation, disembarkation.

261.67.5
dedication, medication, claudication (lameness), abdication, indication, vindication, defecation, publication, application, replication, supplication, duplication, implication, complication, explication, formication (skin sensation), fornication, fabrication, lubrication, imprecation, metrication, mastication.

eradication, adjudication, multiplication, reduplication, communication, prevarication, domestication, sophistication, prognostication, intoxication.

excommunication, intercommunication, telecommunication.

261.67.5.1 [further rhymes may be derived from 7.3]
modification, qualification, ramification, classification, specification, fortifi-

cation, notification, justification, electrification, identification.

261.67.6
location, vocation, bifurcation, suffocation, allocation, collocation, dislocation, embrocation, altercation, evocation, revocation, provocation, advocation, invocation, convocation, equivocation.

261.67.7
predation, sedation, validation, trepidation, cuspidation (architectural term), liquidation, fluoridation, depredation, oxidation, consolidation, intimidation, dilapidation, elucidation.

261.67.8
gradation, backwardation (stock exchange term), degradation, accommodation, biodegradation.

261.67.9
emendation, commendation, recommendation.

261.67.10
legation (diplomatic mission), negation, allegation, delegation, relegation, obligation, fumigation, denegation (denial), abnegation, irrigation, segregation, congregation, litigation, mitigation, castigation, instigation, navigation, desegregation, investigation, circumnavigation.

261.67.11
rogation, propagation, expurgation, abrogation (official cancellation), subrogation (legal term), interrogation.

261.67.12
elation, gelation (freezing), relation.

strobilation (type of asexual reproduction), jubilation, alkylation (chemistry term), flagellation, congelation, appellation, cupellation (metallurgical process), compilation, correlation, fibrillation, vacillation, tessellation, oscillation, cancellation, titillation, scutellation (arrangement of animal's

scales), mutilation, ventilation, scintillation, distillation, constellation.

invigilation, dissimilation, assimilation, horripilation (gooseflesh), interrelation.

malassimilation, hyperventilation.

261.67.13
serrulation (notch), gastrulation (embryology term), tribulation, maculation (spotted pattern), speculation, circulation, calculation, adulation, osculation (maths term), modulation, undulation, regulation, emulation, gemmulation (type of asexual reproduction), formulation, cumulation, annulation (formation of rings), granulation, copulation, population, insulation, postulation, ovulation.

perambulation, ejaculation, vermiculation, matriculation, articulation, denticulation (finely-toothed structure), gesticulation, inoculation, miscalculation, emasculation, demodulation (electronics term), coagulation, accumulation, capitulation, expostulation, recapitulation.

261.67.13.1
tabulation, confabulation, tintinnabulation.

261.67.13.2
angulation, strangulation, triangulation.

261.67.13.3
simulation, stimulation, dissimulation.

261.67.13.4
stipulation, manipulation.

261.67.14
halation (photography term), spallation (nuclear physics reaction), vallation (construction of fortifications), escalation, inhalation, exhalation, immolation, desolation, isolation, consolation, installation, revelation, de-escalation, extrapolation, interpolation, contravallation (fortifications built by besiegers).

261.67.14.1
violation, annihilation.

261.67.15
cremation, sublimation, animation, lacrimation (secretion of tears), decimation, intimation, estimation, approximation, underestimation, overestimation.

261.67.16
affirmation, defamation, reformation, information, confirmation, transformation, acclamation, declamation, reclamation, proclamation, exclamation, inflammation, consummation, automation, misinformation, amalgamation.

261.67.17
carnation, tarnation, incarnation, reincarnation.

261.67.18
crenation (biology term), ruination, combination, machination, pollination, declination, inclination, culmination, fulmination, chlorination, urination, destination, divination, vaccination, recombination, miscegenation (interbreeding of races), desalination, disinclination, insemination, peregrination, indoctrination, hallucination, concatenation (series of interconnected events), agglutination, procrastination, predestination, rejuvenation.

261.67.18.1
ordination, preordination, coordination, subordination, incoordination, insubordination.

261.67.18.2
pagination, imagination, invagination (infolding of tubular structure).

261.67.18.3
lamination, contamination, examination, decontamination, cross-examination.

261.67.18.4
germination, termination, vermination (infestation with vermin), determination, extermination.

261.67.18.5
elimination, recrimination, incrimination, discrimination.

261.67.18.6
commination (threatening vengeance), domination, nomination, abomination, predomination, denomination.

261.67.18.7
rumination, illumination.

261.67.18.8
fascination, assassination.

261.67.19
conation (psychology term), donation, carbonation, eburnation (degenerative condition of bone), hibernation, condonation, profanation, hyphenation, explanation, emanation, coronation, detonation, alternation, intonation, consternation, alienation, impersonation.

261.67.20
obstipation, constipation, emancipation.

261.67.20.1
dissipation, participation, anticipation.

261.67.21
Eurasian, duration, conjuration, carburation, procuration, fulguration (surgical procedure), suppuration, mensuration (measuring), maturation, trituration (grinding into fine powder), transculturation (changing an established culture), prefiguration, configuration, transfiguration, inauguration.

261.67.22
Horatian, narration.

liberation, decoration, saturation, adoration, federation, moderation, perforation, figuration, pejoration (deterioration of word's meaning), toleration, coloration, declaration, exploration, glomeration (cluster), numeration, admiration, reparation, preparation, separation, corporation, desperation, respiration, perspiration, peroration, laceration, ulceration, alteration, restoration, botheration.

melioration (improving), reverberation, deliberation, confederation, consideration, proliferation, exaggeration, refrigeration, deceleration, acceleration, exhilaration, discoloration, commemoration, agglomeration, conglomeration, enumeration, incineration, remuneration, evaporation, recuperation, vituperation, exasperation, trilateration (surveying method), expectoration, perseveration (psychology term), commiseration.

amelioration, deterioration.

261.67.22.1
aberration, collaboration.

261.67.22.2
generation, veneration, degeneration, regeneration.

261.67.22.3
operation, cooperation, disoperation (harmful association between organisms), noncooperation.

261.67.22.4
iteration, literation (representing sounds by letters), reiteration, alliteration, obliteration, transliteration.

261.67.23
calibration, celebration, cerebration (thinking), vertebration, equilibration.

261.67.24
emigration, immigration, integration, redintegration (act of renewal), disintegration.

261.67.25
registration, fenestration (arrangement of windows), ministration, defenestration (throwing person from window), administration, maladministration.

261.67.26
sensation, condensation, compensation, dispensation, aftersensation, overcompensation.

261.67.27
cetacean (whale), habitation, dubitation (doubt), meditation, agitation, vegetation, gurgitation (surging movement), imitation, limitation, sanitation, capitation, palpitation, equitation, irritation, recitation, jactitation (boasting), cavitation (physics term), gravitation, levitation, invitation, excitation, visitation.

cohabitation, premeditation, regurgitation, decapitation, precipitation, interpretation, felicitation, sollicitation, resuscitation.

prestidigitation, rehabilitation, misinterpretation.

261.67.28
dotation (endowment), flotation, notation, potation (drinking), quotation, rotation, annotation, denotation, connotation, misquotation, dextrorotation (rotation to right), laevorotation (rotation to left).

261.67.29
mutation, nutation (nodding), refutation, salutation, permutation, commutation, sternutation (sneezing), deputation, reputation, amputation, imputation, computation, disputation, transmutation.

261.67.30
natation, dilatation, dissertation, constatation (process of establishing truth).

261.67.31
plantation, recantation, incantation.

261.67.32
dentation (tooth-like projections), tentation (method of adjusting machine), indentation, lamentation, fermentation, cementation, fomentation, fragmenta-

tion, segmentation, pigmentation, augmentation, frequentation, assentation (servile agreement), placentation (biology term), ostentation, sustentation (nourishment), orientation, documentation, argumentation, ornamentation, instrumentation, representation, misrepresentation.

261.67.32.1
sedimentation, regimentation, alimentation, implementation, experimentation.

261.67.33
gestation, infestation, molestation, attestation, detestation, protestation, manifestation.

261.67.34
laxation (defecation), taxation, relaxation.

261.67.35
vexation, annexation.

261.67.36 [also **516** + *-ation*]
sterilization, fertilization, civilization, realization, centralization, organization, dramatization, improvisation, nationalization, generalization.

261.68
freshen, session, cession.

profession, confession, discretion, degression (gradual decrease), regression, digression, aggression, progression, transgression, depression, repression, oppression, suppression, impression, compression, expression, recession, precession, secession, obsession, concession, accession, succession, possession.

indiscretion, reimpression, decompression, repossession, prepossession, selfpossession, dispossession.

261.68.1
procession, supersession, intercession.

261.69
Persian, tertian (recurring every other day), version, coercion, recursion (returning), incursion, excursion, emersion

(astronomy term), immersion, dispersion, aspersion, assertion, insertion, Cistercian (member of religious order), reversion, diversion, subversion, inversion, conversion, exertion, desertion, animadversion (criticism).

261.69.1
aversion, perversion, introversion, extroversion.

261.70
Rhaetian (language group), Grecian, deletion, depletion, repletion, suppletion (linguistics term), completion, Venetian, Capetian (relating to French dynasty), secretion, accretion, incretion (secretion into bloodstream), concretion, excretion, Helvetian, Diocletian (Roman emperor).

261.71
fission, mission, Titian.

coition, fruition, tuition, ambition, audition, rendition, condition, logician, magician, emission, demission, remission, submission, admission, transmission, monition (warning), munition, technician, ignition, cognition, suspicion, detrition (wearing away by friction), nutrition, contrition, partition, mortician, sortition (casting lots), beautician, tactician, dentition, optician, musician, transition.

intuition, prohibition, imbibition (absorption), inhibition, exhibition, erudition, recondition, precondition, ammunition, premunition (state of immunity), mechanician, premonition, admonition, inanition, precognition (foreknowledge), recognition, parturition, micturition, apparition, rhetorician, preterition (act of omitting), obstetrician, malnutrition, electrician, repartition, tripartition, deglutition, logistician, statistician, acoustician, superstition, Ordovician (geological period).

equipartition, mathematician, diagnostician.

261.71.1
edition, sedition, expedition.

261.71.2
addition, perdition, tradition, extradition.

261.71.3
volition, coalition, abolition, ebullition, demolition.

261.71.4
omission, commission, Domitian (Roman emperor), permission, intromission (insertion or introduction), intermission, academician.

261.71.5
Phoenician, clinician, definition.

261.71.6
attrition, patrician, paediatrician, geriatrician.

261.71.7
petition, dietitian, politician, cosmetician, phonetician, repetition, competition, aesthetician, theoretician.

261.71.8
physician, acquisition, requisition, inquisition, disquisition (formal discourse), metaphysician.

261.71.9
position, apposition, deposition, preposition, reposition, opposition, proposition, supposition, malposition, imposition, composition, disposition, transposition, exposition, presupposition, juxtaposition, decomposition, predisposition, indisposition.

261.72
caution, portion, torsion, abortion, precaution, retortion (retorting), retorsion (reprisal), intorsion (spiral twisting), contortion, distortion, extortion.

261.72.1
apportion, proportion, disproportion.

261.73
ocean, Goshen (region of ancient Egypt), lotion, motion, notion, potion, groschen (Austrian coin), emotion, demotion, devotion.

261.73.1
promotion, commotion, locomotion.

261.74
Russian, Prussian, percussion, concussion, discussion, repercussion, Byelorussian.

261.75
crucian (European fish), dilution, ablution, Confucian, Rosicrucian, attribution, retribution, contribution, distribution, persecution, prosecution, consecution (sequence of events), execution, diminution, Lilliputian, destitution, restitution, prostitution, substitution, institution, constitution.

261.75.1
pollution, solution, volution (spiral motion), dissolution, absolution, revolution, evolution, devolution, involution (complication), convolution, resolution, circumvolution (turning around central axis), irresolution, counterrevolution.

261.75.2
locution, perlocution (philosophy term), allocution (formal speech), elocution, illocution (philosophy term), interlocution (conversation), circumlocution, electrocution.

261.76
action, faction, fraction, traction.

reaction, inaction, diffraction, refraction, detraction, retraction, attraction, protraction, subtraction, contraction, distraction, abstraction, extraction, exaction, transaction.

abreaction (psychiatry term), retroaction, tumefaction (swelling), benefaction, stupefaction, liquefaction, rarefaction, petrifaction, putrefaction, satisfaction, interaction, dissatisfaction.

261.77
lection (variation in text), flexion, section.

defection, refection, affection, perfection, infection, confection, ejection, dejection, rejection, objection, subjection, injection, bolection (architectural term), collection, deflection, reflection, inflection, complexion, connection, inspection, bisection, subsection, midsection, detection, protection, evection (irregularity in moon's motion), advection (heat transfer in air), convection.

imperfection, disinfection, recollection, retroflexion, genuflection, retrospection, introspection, intersection, overprotection.

261.77.1
projection, introjection (psychology term), interjection.

261.77.2
election, selection, re-election, predilection, intellection (thought).

261.77.3
erection, direction, indirection, misdirection.

261.77.4
correction, insurrection, resurrection.

261.77.5
dissection, resection (surgical removal of part), venesection (incision into vein), vivisection.

261.78
diction, fiction, friction, nonfiction, affliction, depiction, restriction, constriction, eviction, conviction, jurisdiction, crucifixion, dereliction, derestriction.

261.78.1
prediction, malediction, valediction, benediction.

261.78.2
addiction, contradiction, interdiction (prohibition).

261.79
fluxion, ruction, suction, eduction (exhaust stroke of engine), deduction, reduction, seduction, abduction, induction, conduction, transduction (genetics term), destruction, obstruction, instruction, construction, solifluction (downhill soil movement), reconstruction, misconstruction (false interpretation).

261.79.1
adduction, production, reproduction, introduction, underproduction.

261.80
unction, function, junction, malfunction, dysfunction, injunction, conjunction, disjunction, inunction (rubbing ointment into skin), compunction.

261.81
scansion, mansion, stanchion (support), expansion.

261.82
gentian, mention, pension, tension.

indention (indentation), declension, dimension, suspension, Lawrentian, ascension, detention, retention, pretension, intention, contention, abstention, extension, prevention, subvention, invention, convention.

hypotension, contravention, intervention, circumvention.

261.82.1
prehension (act of grasping), apprehension, reprehension, comprehension, misapprehension, incomprehension.

261.82.2
dissension, recension (critical literary revision), condescension.

261.82.3
attention, inattention, hypertension.

261.83

caption, recaption (legal term), contraption.

261.84

obreption (obtaining by deceit), subreption (concealment of facts), deception, reception, subception (subliminal perception), inception, conception, exception, self-deception, preconception, misconception.

261.84.1

perception, apperception (psychology term), contraception, intussusception (medical term).

261.85

Egyptian, conniption (*US* fit of rage), description, prescription, proscription, ascription, subscription, transcription, inscription, conscription, circumscription, teletranscription (video recording).

261.86

option, adoption.

261.87

sorption (adsorption or absorption), absorption, adsorption, desorption (chemistry term), chemisorption (chemistry term).

261.88

eruption, corruption, abruption (breaking off), disruption, interruption.

261.89

gumption, assumption, subsumption (inclusion under general heading), consumption, resumption, presumption.

261.90 [see also **261.3.34**]

lesion, Friesian, Ephesian, cohesion, adhesion, inhesion (inherence).

261.91 [see also **261.3.35**]

Frisian (language of Netherlands), scission, vision, elision, collision, derision, misprision (concealment of treasonable act), abscission (shedding of plant parts), incision, concision, envision, excision, circumcision.

261.91.1

decision, recision (cancellation), precision, precisian (strict observer of rules), indecision, imprecision.

261.91.2

division, revision, prevision, subdivision, television.

261.91.3

provision, Eurovision, supervision, stereovision.

261.92

plosion (phonetics term), eclosion (emergence of insect), implosion (collapsing inwards), explosion, erosion, corrosion.

261.93

fusion, allusion, collusion, prolusion (preliminary written exercise), seclusion, occlusion, inclusion, conclusion, exclusion, protrusion, obtrusion, intrusion, extrusion, effusion, diffusion, affusion (method of baptism), profusion, infusion, confusion, transfusion, contusion, malocclusion (dentistry term).

261.93.1

illusion, delusion, disillusion.

261.94

batten, fatten, latten (thin sheet metal), flatten, platan (plane tree), platen (plate in printing press), slattern, pattern, patten (wooden clog), Patton (US general), paten (silver or gold plate), Grattan, Mountbatten, Manhattan, harmattan.

261.95

Barton, carton, hearten, smarten, partan (*Scot* crab), Spartan, tartan, Dumbarton, dishearten, kindergarten, Akhenaten (Egyptian king), sauerbraten (German beef dish).

261.96

jetton (gambling token), Breton, threaten, Tibetan.

261.97
Burton, burton, curtain, Merton, certain, uncertain.

261.98
Eton, eaten, beaten, Keaton, neaten, Cretan, Seaton, wheaten, sweeten, unbeaten, Nuneaton, weather-beaten.

261.99
bittern, bitten, kitten, mitten, smitten, written, Britain, Briton, Britten, witan (Anglo-Saxon advisory council), frostbitten, skeleton, Honiton, puritan, handwritten, unwritten, Mahometan, Samaritan, endoskeleton, exoskeleton, Neapolitan, cosmopolitan, metropolitan.

261.100
chiton (ancient Greek tunic), heighten, lighten, righten (return to normal position), Brighton, brighten, Crichton, frighten, Triton (Greek sea god), triton (marine mollusc), tighten, Titan, whiten, enlighten.

261.101
cotton, gotten, rotten, guncotton, begotten, forgotten, ill-gotten, misbegotten, unforgotten.

261.102
boughten (*Dialect* bought), Laughton, Morton, quartern (measure of weight), quartan (recurring every third day), shorten, tauten, foreshorten.

261.103
button, glutton, mutton, Sutton, unbutton, bellybutton.

261.104
Luton, gluten, Newton, Teuton (member of Germanic people), rambutan (Asian tree).

261.105
Minton, quintan (recurring every fourth day), badminton.

261.106
Preston, teston (former French silver coin), western, Avestan (ancient language).

261.107
piston, Tristan, cistern, Ilkeston (English town), Eddystone, Germiston (South African city), Coniston, sacristan.

261.108
Kingston, Livingstone.

261.109
Phaëthon (Greek mythological character), Jonathan, marathon, leviathan (biblical sea monster).

261.110
carven, Cuxhaven (West German port), Caernarvon.

261.111
Avon, haven, raven, craven, graven, shaven, Newhaven, clean-shaven, unshaven.

261.112
Bevan (British statesman), Devon, heaven, leaven, Severn, seven, Midheaven (astrology term), eleven.

261.113
even, Leven (Scottish loch), Stephen, Genevan, uneven.

261.114
given, Niven, riven, driven, forgiven, Sullivan, unforgiven.

261.115
Ivan, liven, wyvern (heraldic beast), enliven.

261.116
cloven, woven, Eindhoven (Dutch city), Beethoven, interwoven.

261.117
oven, bhavan (large Indian house), coven, govern, sloven, misgovern.

261.118
scallion, stallion, rapscallion, medallion, Italian, battalion.

261.119 [see also **261.3.9**]

hellion (troublesome person), rebellion, Trevelyan.

261.120 [see also **261.3.11**]

billion, jillion (extremely large number), gillion (one thousand million), million, pillion, trillion, zillion, tourbillion (whirlwind), modillion (architectural ornament), vermilion, nonillion (10^{54}), carillon, quadrillion (10^{24}), decillion (10^{60}), cotillion, octillion (10^{48}), centillion (10^{600}), quintillion (10^{30}), septillion (10^{42}), postilion, sextillion (10^{36}), civilian, pavilion.

261.121

banyan, canyon, fanion (surveyor's small flag), companion.

261.122 [see also **261.3.17**]

minion, pinion, dominion, opinion.

261.123

union, reunion, communion, nonunion, intercommunion.

261.124

blazon, raisin, brazen, emblazon, diapason (organ stop).

261.125

reason, treason, season, unreason.

261.126

mizzen, risen, prison, wizen, malison (a curse), benison, denizen, orison, arisen, imprison, bartizan (small turret), partisan (a spear), citizen.

261.127

greisen (light-coloured rock), horizon, spiegeleisen (type of pig iron).

261.128

foison (plentiful supply), poison, empoison.

261.129

chosen, frozen, lederhosen.

262 -iln

kiln, Milne, limekiln.

263 -ang

bang, bhang (narcotic from Indian hemp), cangue (wooden instrument of punishment), dang, fang, gang, gangue (worthless material in ore), hang, Lang, lang (*Scot* long), clang, slang, pang, spang (*US* exactly), rang, prang, sprang, sang, Shang (Chinese dynasty), Tang (Chinese dynasty), tang, stang (*Dialect* throb with pain), vang (nautical term), whang, twang.

kiang (Tibetan wild ass), shebang, gangbang, Nanchang (Chinese city), padang (Malaysian field), Malang (Indonesian city), boomslang (venomous snake), Penang (Malaysian island and state), trepang (Oriental sea cucumber), linsang (forest-dwelling mammal), satang (Thai coin), mustang, Poyang (Chinese lake), Loyang (Chinese city), Shenyang (Chinese city), Pyongyang (capital of North Korea).

overhang, siamang (large black gibbon), navarin, Mazarin, parasang (Persian unit of distance), burrawang (Australian plant).

Heilungkiang (Chinese province), ylang-ylang (aromatic Asian tree), goreng pisang (Malaysian banana fritters), orang-outang.

263.1

probang (surgical instrument), charabanc, interrobang (punctuation mark).

263.2

harangue, meringue, Serang (Indonesian island), boomerang.

264 -eng

Kaifeng (Chinese city), ronggeng (Malay traditional dance), ginseng.

265 -ing [further rhymes may be created by adding -ing to appropriate verbs]

king, Ching (Chinese dynasty), ding, ling, cling, fling, sling, Ming, ping, wring, ring, bring, spring, string, sing, ting, sting, thing, wing, swing, zing.

gnawing, drawing, webbing, dubbing, rubbing, tubing, backing, blacking, packing, cracking, sacking, whacking, Barking, marking, parking, working, sneaking, Peking, speaking, liking, striking, Viking, smoking, soaking, Woking, ducking, fucking, trucking, sucking, booking, cooking, erlking (mythical malevolent spirit), hulking, Nanking, banking, planking, spanking, ranking, catching, etching, fetching, searching, I Ching (Chinese book of divination), teaching, breeching (harness strap), itching, stitching, witching, coaching, hoatching (*Scot* infested), poaching, scorching, touching, cladding, padding, wording, bidding, sodding, wadding, budding, pudding, gelding, balding, wingding (*US* lively party), surfing, briefing, spiffing, offing, stuffing, roofing, bagging (coarse woven cloth), lagging, flagging, rigging, frigging, wigging, edging, lodging, grudging, swingeing, curling, hurling (Irish game), sterling, Stirling, tiling, hireling, schooling, ruling, tooling, marbling, stabling, sibling, gambling, rambling, brambling (Eurasian finch), crackling, weakling, inkling, sprinkling, twinkling, reedling (Eurasian songbird), seedling, fiddling, middling, piddling, codling (variety of cooking apple), puddling (wrought-iron-making process), worldling (materialist), handling, brandling (small red earthworm), kindling, pindling (*Dialect* peevish), spindling (long and slender), foundling, groundling, rifling (grooves inside gun barrel), trifling, stifling, niggling, juggling, smuggling, angling, gangling, fledgling, changeling, green-ling (Pacific fish), weanling, grappling, sapling, Kipling, crippling, stripling, coupling, dumpling, nestling, wrestling, nursling, brisling (Norwegian sprat), whistling, princeling, unsling, catling (surgical knife), fatling (fattened young animal), Gatling (machine-gun), rattling, footling, scantling (narrow rafter), mantling (heraldic term), firstling (first offspring), earthling, riesling, quisling (collaborator), gosling, gaming, flaming, lemming, Fleming, slimming, trimming, swimming, priming, timing, canning, planning, awning, mourning, morning, warning, browning, Liaoning (Chinese province), nooning (*US* midday break), tuning, lightning, evening, hanging, longing, mapping, wrapping, strapping, Epping, skipping, chipping, clipping, flipping, ripping, dripping, gripping, shipping, whipping, piping, typing, hopping, sopping, shopping, topping, stopping, whopping, coping, sloping, stoping (geology term), grouping, scalping, helping, camping, tamping (*Welsh* very angry), rasping, grasping, barring, sparring, herring, bullring, hairspring, headspring, handspring, offspring, mainspring, drawstring, bowstring, shoestring, hamstring, unstring, passing, nursing, piercing, icing, crossing, coursing (hunting game by sight), dancing, fencing, bouncing, flouncing (material for making flounces), dashing, lashing, flashing, smashing, crashing, thrashing, Pershing, washing, Flushing (Dutch port), bushing (pipe connector), Cushing, pushing, ruching, batting, matting, tatting, parting, skirting, shirting, beating, heating, fleeting, meeting, greeting, seating, sheeting, boating, coating, floating, outing, Scouting, houting (European whitefish), cutting, nutting, putting, footing, fluting, suiting, shooting, belting, felting, lilting, quilting, halting, malting, vaulting, fainting, painting, printing, wanting, daunting, haunting, pointing, bunting, hunting, tempting, costing, frosting, posting, roasting.

plaything, nothing, something, farthing, bathing, scathing, Worthing, breathing, sheathing (material covering ship's hull), teething, loathing, clothing, soothing, carving, starving, diving, driving, loving, moving, shelving, clearwing (moth), forewing, redwing (European thrush), gull-wing, lapwing, lacewing (insect), batwing, waxwing (songbird), beeswing (crust formed in port), boxing, foxing, pleasing, freezing, seizing (nautical term), dowsing, housing, rousing.

dairying, disturbing, absorbing, woodworking, beseeching, bird-watching, unflinching, regarding, forbidding, unyielding, scaffolding, demanding, commanding, intriguing, obliging, unchanging, towelling, gruelling, sanderling (small sandpiper), underling, fingerling (young fish), panelling, ting-a-ling, snivelling, bitterling (European freshwater fish), fosterling (foster child), hostelling, travelling, bloodcurdling, programming, performing, ausforming (steel-strengthening treatment), brainstorming, adjoining, belonging, galloping, walloping, unceasing, refreshing, brainwashing, first-footing, comforting, shoplifting, weightlifting, revolting, imprinting, excepting, blockbusting, disgusting, anything, everything, revolving, underwing.

pony trekking, overcrowding, corresponding, overwhelming, embarrassing, conveyancing, unrelenting, disappointing, multiplepoinding (Scottish legal term).

265.1
Maying (celebration of May Day), saying, bricklaying, soothsaying, surveying.

265.2
being, skiing, seeing, wellbeing, sightseeing.

265.3
dying, dyeing, flying, spying, crying, trying, undying, outlying, underlying.

265.4
owing, bowing, going, knowing, rowing, sewing, showing, seagoing, foregoing, churchgoing, ingoing, ongoing, outgoing, following, unknowing, harrowing, ingrowing, easy-going, thoroughgoing, overflowing.

265.5
doing, blueing (substance that whitens clothes), brewing, viewing, undoing, wrongdoing, canoeing.

265.6
baking, making, taking, waking, haymaking, dressmaking, lovemaking, backbreaking, housebreaking, heartbreaking, earthshaking, stocktaking, breathtaking, painstaking, merrymaking, undertaking.

265.7
licking, ticking, Mafeking, pigsticking (hunting wild boar), politicking (political canvassing).

265.8
smocking, frocking (coarse material), shocking, stocking, bluestocking.

265.9
corking, Dorking, hawking, walking, sleepwalking.

265.10
blinking, pinking, sinking, stinking, thinking, unblinking, freethinking, unthinking, unwinking.

265.11
fading, lading (cargo), braiding, trading, shading, unfading, degrading.

265.12
bedding, heading, leading (printing term), Reading, wedding, subheading, featherbedding.

265.13
beading, leading, bleeding, pleading, reading, reeding (type of moulding), breeding, sheading (Manx region), mispleading (legal term), misleading, sight-reading, preceding, proceeding, exceeding.

265.14
guiding, hiding, sliding, gliding, riding, siding, abiding, confiding, nitriding (metallurgy term), providing, law-abiding.

265.15
boarding, chording (musical term), hoarding, recording, according, rewarding, unrewarding.

265.16
loading, foreboding.

265.17
building, gilding, shipbuilding, outbuilding.

265.18
scolding, holding, moulding, stockholding, roadholding, smallholding.

265.19
landing, standing, crashlanding, freestanding, upstanding, outstanding, understanding, notwithstanding, misunderstanding.

265.20
ending, mending, pending, spending, unbending, unending, impending, heart-rending, moneylending, condescending.

265.21
binding, finding, blinding, winding, bookbinding.

265.22
grounding, sounding, surrounding, astounding, resounding.

265.23
jogging, logging (lumberjacking), flogging, nogging (building term), frogging (decoration on uniform), pettifogging.

265.24
ageing, staging, engaging.

265.25
bridging, packaging, managing.

265.26
carling (ship's supporting beam), darling, sparling (a fish), starling, rosemaling (Scandinavian decoration).

265.27
ailing, failing, paling, railing, grayling (freshwater fish), sailing, tailing (part of a beam), whaling, unfailing, prevailing, unveiling, unavailing.

265.28
spelling, telling, dwelling, swelling, compelling, misspelling, fortune-telling.

265.29
Ealing, feeling, peeling, ceiling, shieling (*Scot* shepherd's hut), stealing, unfeeling, Darjeeling, revealing, freewheeling.

265.30
billing, killing, skilling (former Scandinavian coin), filling, milling, thrilling, shilling, schilling (Austrian currency), willing, spine-chilling, atheling (Anglo-Saxon prince), unwilling.

265.31
calling, galling, crawling, sprawling, snowballing, appalling, enthralling.

265.32
bowling, polling, rolling, potholing.

265.33
cowling (metal covering), fowling, howling, antifouling (protective paint).

265.34
buckling (bloater), duckling, swashbuckling.

265.35
charming, farming, alarming, disarming.

265.36
scheming, seeming, teeming, redeeming, daydreaming.

265.37
combing, coaming (frame around ship's hatches), homing, gloaming, Wyoming.

265.38
coming, plumbing, becoming, homecoming, incoming, oncoming, shortcoming, forthcoming, unbecoming.

265.39
blooming, grooming, assuming, unassuming.

265.40
caning, graining, training, veining, remaining, entertaining.

265.41
burning, churning, learning, turning, discerning, concerning.

265.42
leaning, cleaning, meaning, greening (variety of cooking apple), Sining (Chinese city), dry-cleaning, demeaning, overweening.

265.43
inning, spinning, winning, beginning, underpinning.

265.44
fining (process of clarifying liquid), lining, mining, refining, divining, designing, interlining.

265.45
cunning, gunning, running, stunning, gunrunning.

265.46
ironing, reckoning, sickening, thickening, questioning, maddening, gardening, happening, opening, fastening, christening, sweetening, frightening, shortening, ravening (voracious), reasoning, seasoning, conditioning.

265.47
springing (architectural term), singing, swinging, mudslinging, upbringing, bell-ringing.

265.48
mapping, wrapping, strapping, overlapping.

265.49
keeping, weeping, sweeping, safekeeping, book-keeping, housekeeping.

265.50
chumping (*Dialect* collecting bonfire wood), thumping, showjumping.

265.51
furring, purring, shirring, stirring, recurring, unerring.

265.52
airing, bearing, daring, fairing, glaring, paring, sparing, raring, tearing, wearing, uncaring, seafaring, unsparing, cheeseparing, overbearing.

265.53
earring, earing (nautical term), gearing, hearing, clearing, searing, steering, endearing, god-fearing, veneering, sheepshearing, engineering, mountaineering, electioneering, orienteering.

265.54
firing, tiring, wiring, aspiring, inspiring, inquiring, retiring, untiring, uninspiring.

265.55
boring, flooring, roaring, warring, skijoring (snow sport), outpouring.

265.56
mooring, during, alluring, enduring, reassuring.

265.57
flowering, towering, overpowering.

265.58
layering (method of plant propagation), neighbouring, timbering, lumbering, doddering, rendering, wandering, thundering, offering, suffering, staggering, fingering, conjuring, colouring, ashlaring (building material), murmuring, scattering, flattering, smattering, catering, Kettering, lettering, guttering, shuttering (wooden mould for con-

crete), factoring (business term), sweltering, plastering, gathering, feathering (plumage), weathering (erosion), blithering, Havering (Greater London borough).

considering, self-catering, woolgathering (daydreaming), manufacturing, mouthwatering.

265.58.1
flavouring, unwavering.

265.59
casing, facing, lacing, placing, spacing, racing, bracing, tracing, interfacing.

265.60
blessing, dressing, pressing, hairdressing, depressing, distressing, prepossessing, unprepossessing.

265.61
kissing, missing, promising, Nipissing (Canadian lake).

265.62
mincing, convincing, unconvincing.

265.63
fishing, furnishing, perishing, brattishing (architectural term), ravishing, astonishing.

265.64
skating, plating, slating, rating, grating, weighting, vacillating, calculating, fulgurating (piercingly painful), penetrating, excruciating, accommodating, unhesitating.

265.64.1
fascinating, discriminating.

265.65
netting, petting, setting, blood-letting, typesetting, upsetting, vignetting (photography term), thermosetting (hardening after heating).

265.66
fitting, splitting, knitting, sitting, bracketing, marketing, spirketting (nautical term), picketing, pipefitting,

hairsplitting, permitting, carpeting, unwitting, unremitting.

265.67
biting, fighting, lighting, slighting, writing, whiting, backbiting, bullfighting, infighting (boxing term), moonlighting, skywriting, handwriting, typewriting, inviting, exciting, uninviting.

265.68
jotting, knotting, potting, rotting, yachting, train-spotting, globetrotting.

265.69
courting, sporting, Storting (Norwegian parliament), supporting.

265.70
acting, distracting, exacting, overacting.

265.71
affecting, respecting, expecting, self-respecting, unsuspecting.

265.72
slanting, enchanting.

265.73
mounting, accounting.

265.74
casting, lasting, blasting, surfcasting (shore-fishing), contrasting, everlasting.

265.75
nesting, resting, cresting (ornamental ridge on building), testing, arresting.

265.76
listing, consisting, harvesting, interesting.

265.77
caving, paving, raving, craving, saving, shaving, engraving, timesaving.

265.78
Irving, nerving (surgical removal of nerve), serving, unnerving, unswerving, deserving, undeserving.

265.79
sleeving (wire insulation), grieving, thieving, weaving, unbelieving.

265.80
living, forgiving, misgiving, thanksgiving.

265.81
glazing, raising, phrasing, grazing, stargazing, amazing, self-raising, doubleglazing.

265.82
rising, uprising, surprising, enterprising, appetizing, advertising, uncompromising.

265.83
closing, nosing (projecting edge). supposing, imposing.

265.84
losing, bruising, confusing, amusing.

266 -ong
bong, Caen, dong, gong, hong (Chinese factory), long, flong (printing term), nong (*Austral* stupid person), pong, wrong, prong, strong, throng, song, tong, thong.

Mekong, Hong Kong, quandong (Australian fruit tree), ding-dong, bogong (Australian moth), dugong, mahjong, kalong (fruit bat), élan, daylong, furlong, belong, Shillon (Indian city), oolong, oblong, headlong, sidelong, endlong, lifelong, nightlong, livelong, chaise longue, kampong (Malaysian village), ping-pong (*Trademark*), barong (Philippine knife), headstrong, Armstrong, croissant, plainsong, singsong, souchong (black tea), penchant, diphthong, triphong (composite vowel sound), morwong (Australian fish), foo yong (Chinese omelette), Qui Nhong (Vietnamese port), bouffant, Kyongsong (former name for Seoul, capital of South Korea).

billabong, aide-de-camp, Vietcong, wobbegong (shark), Chittagong (Bangladeshi port), Wollongong (Australian city), kurrajong (Australian tree), denouement, scuppernong (US wine),

binturong (Asian mammal), cradlesong, evensong, contretemps, monophthong (simple vowel), currawong (Australian songbird).

266.1
along, prolong, overlong.

266.2
sarong, restaurant.

267 -ung
bung, dung, hung, lung, clung, flung, slung, mung (Australian bean), pung (*US* horse-drawn sleigh), wrung, rung, sprung, strung, sung, tongue, stung, swung, young, among, unstrung, unsung, bluetongue (Australian lizard), Nantung (Chinese city), Shantung (Chinese province), shantung (heavy silk fabric), underhung (protruding from beneath), overhung, aqualung, highly-strung

268 -ap
bap, cap, chap, dap, gap, Jap, Lapp, lap, clap, flap, slap, map, nap, knap (*Dialect* crest of hill), nappe (rock fold), snap, pap, rap, wrap, crap, scrap, frap (nautical term), trap, strap, sap, tap, yap, zap.

kneecap, recap, snowcap, toecap, mobcap, hubcap, blackcap (European bird), madcap, skullcap, uncap, icecap, nightcap, whitecap (white-crested wave), foolscap, stopgap mishap, burlap (coarse fabric), dewlap, carflap, genappe (worsted yarn), kidnap, unsnap, catnap, enwrap, unwrap, flytrap, firetrap (building susceptible to burning), giftwrap, mantrap, entrap, suntrap, claptrap, mousetrap, watchstrap, bootstrap, rattrap, deathtrap, jockstrap, heeltap, lagniappe (*US* small gift).

handicap, overlap, thunderclap, photomap (map from from aerial photograph), genipap (West Indian tree), rattletrap (broken-down car), wentletrap (marine mollusc), Tonle Sap (Cambodian lake).

269 -arp

carp, scarp, jarp (*Dialect* to smash), harp, sharp, tarp (*Austral* tarpaulin), syncarp (fleshy multiple fruit), escarp (side of fortification ditch), alap (Indian music), cardsharp, watap (American Indian sewing thread), archicarp (fungal reproductive structure), Polycarp (Christian saint), epicarp (outer skin of fruit), pericarp (part of a fruit), ascocarp (part of a fungus), endocarp (inner part of fruit), mesocarp (fleshy part of fruit), cystocarp (reproductive structure of algae), counterscarp (side of fortification ditch), vibraharp (percussion instrument).

270 -ape

ape, cape, scape (leafless stalk bearing flowers), chape (scabbard mounting), gape, jape, nape, rape, crepe, scrape, drape, grape, shape, tape, seascape, escape, cloudscape, landscape, inscape (person's inner nature), townscape, agape, broomrape (plant parasite), reshape, shipshape, misshape, nametape, waterscape, Sellotape (*Trademark*).

271 -ep

kep (*Dialect* to catch), skep (beehive), hep, schlep (*US* to drag), pep, rep, prep, cep (edible fungus), step, steppe, Dieppe, salep (dried orchid tuber), doorstep, sidestep, instep, footstep, quickstep, overstep, Amenhotep (Egyptian pharaoh), Gaziantep (Turkish city).

272 -erp

Earp, burp, chirp, slurp, twerp, Antwerp, usurp.

273 -eep

beep, keep, cheep, cheap, deep, jeep, heap, leap, bleep, sleep, neap, neep (*Dialect* turnip), peep, reap, creep, threap (*Dialect* to scold), seep, sheep, steep, weep, sweep, upkeep, scrapheap, asleep, upsweep, oversleep, cassareep

(juice of cassava root), Lakshadweep (islands in Arabian Sea).

274 -ip

kip, skip, chip, dip, gyp, hip, lip, blip, clip, flip, slip, nip, snip, pip, quip, rip, scrip (written certificate), drip, grip, grippe (influenza), trip, strip, sip, ship, tip, whip, zip.

rosehip, harelip, fillip, Philip, polyp, julep (sweet drink), tulip, cowslip, sideslip, gymslip, nonslip, oxlip (woodland plant), genip (West Indian tree), turnip, parsnip, equip, hairgrip, handgrip, unrip, atrip (nautical term), cantrip (magic spell), airstrip, outstrip, gossip, worship, airship, heirship, mayorship, warship, hardship, headship, midship, Lordship, wardship, friendship, flagship, judgeship, steamship, kinship, township, unship, kingship, longship, troopship, spaceship, transship, lightship, courtship, bullwhip (long rawhide whip), horsewhip, bunyip (*Austral* legendary monster), unzip.

paperclip, pillowslip, trusteeship, Ladyship, fellowship, comradeship, battleship. internship, studentship, fingertip, apprenticeship.

274.1

membership, leadership, lectureship, readership, scholarship, ownership, partnership, censorship, sponsorship, authorship, premiership, chancellorship, councillorship, governorship, dictatorship, directorship, receivership (legal term), ambassadorship.

274.2

seamanship, showmanship, workmanship, brinkmanship, penmanship, horsemanship, marksmanship, swordsmanship, salesmanship, gamesmanship, statesmanship, sportsmanship, guardianship, championship, one-upmanship, relationship, musicianship, companionship, citizenship, librarianship.

275 -ipe

hype, clype (*Scot* tell tales), slype (covered passageway in cathedral), snipe, pipe, ripe, gripe, tripe, stripe, type, stipe (plant's reproductive stalk), wipe, swipe.

jacksnipe (Eurasian bird), blowpipe, standpipe, windpipe, bagpipe, tailpipe, drainpipe, hornpipe, downpipe, stovepipe, hawsepipe (nautical term), rareripe (*US* ripening early), unripe, pinstripe, subtype, ectype (a copy), tintype (photographic print), sideswipe.

guttersnipe, liripipe (tip of graduate's hood), underripe, overripe, archetype, Teletype (*Trademark*), antitype (something represented by symbol), antetype (earlier form).

275.1

biotype (biology term), ecotype (ecology term), logotype, collotype (printing process), holotype (original biological type specimen), genotype (organism's genetic constitution), phenotype (biology term), Linotype (*Trademark*), monotype (single print), cerotype (printing process), autotype (photographic process), phototype (photographically-produced printing plate), prototype, countertype (opposite type), heliotype (printing process), karyotype (appearance of organism's chromosomes), stereotype, cyanotype (blueprint), daguerreotype, electrotype (electroplated printing plate), somatotype (classification of physique).

276 -op

bop, cop, kop (prominent isolated African hill), scop (Anglo-Saxon minstrel), chop, fop, hop, lop, clop (sound like horse's hooves), flop, plop, slop, mop, pop, crop, drop, prop, strop, sop, shop, top, stop, whop (to hit), swap.

coop, bebop, Cu-bop (jazz music), Boskop (prehistoric African race), car-

hop (drive-in restaurant waiter), hedgehop (fly near ground level), bellhop, orlop (nautical term), Dunlop, clipclop, flip-flop (type of sandal), slipslop (weak drink), rollmop, coin-op, joypop (*Slang* take drugs), sharecrop (*US* cultivate farmland), stonecrop (fleshy-leaved plant), airdrop (delivery by parachute), eardrop (pendant earring), snowdrop, dewdrop, gumdrop, raindrop, eavesdrop, Aesop, soursop (West Indian tree), sweetsop (West Indian tree), Worksop, milksop, teashop, workshop, bookshop, pawnshop, sweatshop, sweetshop, foretop (platform on ship's foremast), blacktop (*US* bitumen for pavements), hardtop, maintop (platform on ship's mainmast), tiptop, estop (legal term), doorstop, housetop, nonstop, unstop, flattop.

escalope, lollipop, overcrop (cultivate excessively), paradrop (delivery by parachute), turboprop, agitprop (Russian propaganda bureau), barbershop.

276.1

atop, overtop.

277 -orp

scaup (diving duck), dorp (small South African village), gawp, Thorpe, warp, whaup (*Scot* curlew), Scunthorpe, mouldwarp (*Dialect* mole), Krugersdorp (South African city), Australorp (domestic fowl).

278 -ope

cope, scope, dope, hope, lope, slope, mope, nope, pope, rope, roup (*Dialect* auction off), grope, trope (word used figuratively), soap, tope, taupe (brownish-grey colour), stope (mine excavation).

myope, pyrope (yellowish-red garnet), towrope, dragrope, manrope (rope railing on ship), tightrope, sandsoap (gritty soap), metope (architectural term).

radarscope, telescope, episcope (optical projector), periscope, interlope, envelope, antipope, phalarope (aquatic shore bird), lycanthrope (werewolf), misanthrope, isotope, radioisotope.

278.1

stroboscope, bronchoscope, endoscope, thermoscope (temperature-change indicator), seismoscope, chronoscope, snooperscope (US military instrument), baroscope (atmospheric-pressure measurer), gyroscope, horoscope, stauroscope (optical instrument), fluoroscope (x-ray instrument), dichroscope (optical instrument), microscope, hydroscope (instrument for underwater observation), hygroscope (humidity indicator), gastroscope, statoscope (aircraft instrument), otoscope, stethoscope, stereoscope, kaleidoscope, pharyngoscope, laryngoscope, ophthalmoscope, galvanoscope (electric-current detector), urethroscope, tachistoscope (instrument displaying images momentarily).

278.1.1

bioscope (early film projector), skiascope (eye-examining instrument), diascope (optical projector), epidiascope (optical projector).

278.1.2

spectroscope (spectrum-producing instrument), electroscope (electric-charge detector).

278.2

elope, antelope.

278.3

allotrope (chemistry term), thaumatrope (optical illusion toy), heliotrope, azeotrope (chemistry term).

279 -up

up, cup, scup (Atlantic fish), dup (*Dialect* to open), pup, sup, tup, yup, backup, make-up, checkup, teacup, hiccup, eyecup, cockup, kingcup,

roundup, close-up, lash-up (temporary connection of equipment), wickiup (American Indian hut), giddy-up, buttercup.

280 -oop

coop, coupe (shallow glass), scoop, goop (*US* rude person), whoop, hoop, loop, loupe (jeweller's magnifying glass), sloop, snoop, poop, roup (respiratory disease of birds), croup, scroop (*Dialect* make grating sound), droop, drupe (fleshy fruit), group, troupe, troop, soup, stoop, stoup (basin for holy water), swoop, dupe, stupe (hot medicated compress).

recoup, hencoop, regroup, subgroup, Woop Woop (*Austral* backward remote town), nincompoop.

280.1

saloop (infusion of aromatic herbs), Guadeloupe, cantaloupe.

281 -'p

ketchup, gallop, Gallup, galop (19th-century dance), jalap (Mexican plant), Salop, shallop (rowing boat), stanhope (one-seater carriage), larrup (*Dialect* to beat), chirrup, syrup, stirrup, Europe, satrap (Persian governor), caltrop (tropical plant), hyssop (aromatic herb), catsup (*US* ketchup), bishop, tittup (*US* prance), archbishop.

281.1

develop, envelop, redevelop, underdevelop, overdevelop.

281.2

collop (*Dialect* slice of meat), scallop, dollop, gollop (to eat greedily), lollop, trollop, Trollope (British novelist), wallop, codswallop.

282 -alp

alp, scalp, palp, pedipalp (zoology term).

283 -elp
kelp, skelp (*Dialect* to slap), chelp (*Dialect* to chatter), help, whelp, yelp.

284 -ulp
gulp, pulp.

285 -amp
amp, camp, scamp, champ, damp, gamp (umbrella), lamp, clamp, ramp, cramp, tramp, tamp (pat down firmly), stamp, vamp, decamp, encamp, firedamp, blackdamp (gas in mines), whitedamp (gas in mines), blowlamp, revamp, afterdamp (gas in mines).

286 -emp
hemp, temp.

287 -imp
imp, skimp, chimp, gimp (stiffened fabric trimming), guimpe (short blouse), limp, blimp (small airship), pimp, crimp, scrimp, primp, shrimp, simp (*US short for* simpleton).

288 -omp
comp, chomp, clomp, pomp, romp, trompe (apparatus in a forge), stomp, swamp.

289 -ump
bump, chump, dump, jump, hump, lump, clump, plump, slump, pump, rump, crump (to thud), scrump, frump, grump, trump, sump, tump (*Dialect* small mound), stump, thump, mugwump (politically neutral person), gazump, undertrump, overtrump.

290 -asp
gasp, hasp, clasp, rasp, grasp, handclasp, enclasp, unclasp.

291 -isp
lisp, crisp, wisp, will-o'-the-wisp.

292 -osp
wasp, galliwasp (American lizard).

293 -ass
ass, as (ancient Roman unit), bass, gas, lass, mass, wrasse (marine fish), crass, frass (insect excrement), trass (volcanic rock), strass (glass for imitation gemstones), sass, tass (*Dialect* goblet), Tass.

Troas (region of Asia Minor), jackass, ACAS, degas, bagasse (pulp from sugar cane), megass (type of paper), alas, camass (US plant), amass, admass (people susceptible to advertising), landmass, groundmass, en masse, vinasse (residue in a still), Aras (river on Russian border), cuirass, morass, Patras, Mithras (Persian god), Alsace, crevasse.

anabas (freshwater fish), Caiaphas, distringas (legal term), Ladislas (Hungarian saint and king), biomass (biology term), Maecenas (Roman statesman), hippocras (spiced wine), sassafras, demitasse (small coffee cup), tarantass (Russian horse-drawn carriage).

Leonidas (king of Sparta), Epaminondas (ancient Greek general).

293.1
Phidias (Greek sculptor), galleass (type of warship), palliasse, capias (legal term), Lysias (Athenian orator), Herodias (mother of Salome), Asturias (former Spanish kingdom), materfamilias (female head of family), paterfamilias (male head of family).

294 -arse
arse, carse (*Scot* low-lying land), farce, class, glass, pass, sparse, brass, grass, kvass (Russian alcoholic drink).

Donbass (Russian industrial region), volte-face, springhaas (African rodent), declass, subclass, outclass, eyeglass, spyglass, hourglass, wineglass, sunglass (burning glass), surpass, bypass, impasse, Madras, deergrass (bog plant), bluegrass (folk music), eelgrass (marine plant), goosegrass, knotgrass (weedy plant).

superclass (group in classification system), Plexiglass (*Trademark*), galloglass (Irish chieftain's military retainer), fibreglass, weatherglass (barometer), isinglass, underpass, overpass, sparrowgrass (*Dialect* asparagus), peppergrass (flowering plant).

295 -ace

ace, base, bass, case, chase, dace, face, lace, place, plaice, mace, pace, space, race, brace, grace, trace, Thrace.

surbase (architectural term), debase, subbass (organ stop), subbase (base of pedestal), wheelbase, staircase, bookcase, crankcase (part of car engine), watchcase, seedcase, briefcase, encase, slipcase (protective case for books), typecase, notecase, nutcase, suitcase, enchase (engrave metal), vendace (white fish), wheyface (pale face), reface, pigface (*Austral* creeping plant), coalface, typeface, outface, shoelace, enlace, unlace, replace, fireplace, showplace, emplace (put in position), someplace, displace, misplace, birthplace, bootlace, Lovelace (English poet), grimace, tenace (bridge term), airspace, footpace (platform before altar), backspace, vambrace (piece of armour), embrace, mainbrace, unbrace (relax), headrace, landrace (breed of pig), scapegrace, disgrace, tailrace, millrace, retrace, rosace (rose window), ambsace (lowest throw at dice).

steeplechase, interface, interlace, periclase (mineral), orthoclase (mineral), commonplace, marketplace, hyper-

space, aerospace, interspace, Samothrace (Greek island).

plagioclase (mineral), oligoclase (mineral).

295.1

abase, rheobase (minimum nerve impulse), diabase (type of rock), contrabass.

295.2

showcase, pillowcase.

295.3

efface, deface, Boniface (Anglo-Saxon saint).

295.4

apace, carapace.

296 -ess

Bess, Bes (ancient Egyptian god), chess, fesse (heraldic term), guess, jess (falconry term), Hesse (West German state), less, bless, mess, Ness, cress, dress, press, tress, stress, cess, Tess, yes.

profess, confess, largess, noblesse, unless, Sheerness, Foulness, Caithness, liquesce, fluoresce, duress, redress, address, headdress, undress, sundress, nightdress, egress, regress, digress, progress, aggress, ingress, congress, transgress, depress, repress, impress, compress, winepress, express, prestress, distress, recess, precess, process, assess, abscess, obsess, princess, access, excess, success, possess.

acquiesce, S.O.S., bouillabaisse, recrudesce, incandesce, otherguess (different), intumesce, deliquesce, effloresce, pennycress (flowering plant), watercress, maladdress, retrogress, decompress, politesse, effervesce, repossess, prepossess, dispossess.

296.1

coalesce, recalesce (physics term), nonetheless, obsolesce, convalesce, nevertheless.

296.2
finesse, luminesce.

296.3
Lyonnesse (place in Arthurian legend), Dungeness, pythoness, evanesce, Inverness, rejuvenesce.

296.4
caress, phosphoresce, manageress.

296.5
oppress, suppress, letterpress.

297 -erse
Erse, burse (*Scot* student allowance), curse, hearse, Merse (Scottish lowland area), nurse, purse, perse (dark greyish-blue), terse, thyrse (type of inflorescence), verse, worse.

coerce, disburse, rehearse, immerse, commerce, disperse, cutpurse, sesterce (Roman coin), traverse, diverse, covers (maths term), averse, perverse, obverse, adverse, inverse, converse, transverse, reimburse.

297.1
asperse, intersperse.

297.2
reverse, universe.

298 -eece
geese, lease, fleece, niece, Nice, peace, piece, crease, Greece, grease, cease.

obese, pelisse (fur-trimmed cloak), release, coulisse, police, sublease, hairpiece, earpiece, eyepiece, showpiece, headpiece, codpiece, fieldpiece (field gun), tailpiece, timepiece, crownpiece (part of horse's bridle), crosspiece, mouthpiece, decrease, increase, Dumfries, degrease, caprice, cassis, decease, Métis (person of mixed parentage).

chimneypiece, battlepiece (painting commemorating a battle), mantelpiece, frontispiece, ambergris, predecease.

298.1
chersonese (peninsula), Peloponnese.

298.2
apiece, altarpiece, centrepiece, masterpiece.

299 -eerse
fierce, pierce, tierce (fencing position), transpierce.

300 -iss [further rhymes may be created by adding *-less* to appropriate verbs or *-ness* to appropriate adjectives]
kiss, Dis (Roman god), hiss, bliss, miss, piss, cuisse (piece of armour), Riss (European glaciation period), kris (Malayan knife), sis, this, Swiss.

dais, Saïs (ancient Egyptian city), Thaïs (Athenian courtesan), Powys, prowess, Jewess, Lewes, Lewis, brewis (*Dialect* gravy-soaked bread), abbess, ibis, rachis (biology term), orchis (orchid), Colchis (ancient Asian country), purchase, duchess, caddis, Sardis (ancient Asian city), jaundice, aphis (aphid), preface, surface, office, Memphis, haggis, Burgess, burgess (citizen of borough), dehisce (burst open), Alice, chalice, malice, palace, Tallis, starless, Ellis, trellis, airless, heirless, careless, hairless, Perlis (Malaysian state), Elis (ancient Olympic Games site), treeless, cheerless, fearless, peerless, tearless, eyeless, tireless, wireless, Aulis (ancient Greek town), lawless, flawless, shoreless, joyless, jobless, tubeless, backless, trackless, feckless, necklace, reckless, smokeless, luckless, thankless, matchless, speechless, headless, wordless, heedless, needless, seedless, beardless, lidless, godless, cloudless, cordless, bloodless, childless, endless, friendless, kindless (heartless), mindless, boundless, groundless, soundless, lifeless, selfless, legless, ageless, changeless, guileless, soulless, goalless, armless, harmless, aimless, blameless, nameless, frameless, shameless, dreamless, seamless, limbless, timeless, homeless, formless, gormless, anlace (medieval dagger), painless, brainless, stainless, skinless, chinless, sinless, spineless, boneless, toneless, stoneless, sunless, moonless, tuneless, hapless, strapless, shapeless, surplice, sleepless, topless, hopeless, helpless, classless, baseless, faceless, graceless, ceaseless, creaseless, priceless, voiceless, useless, hatless, artless, heartless, stateless, weightless, flightless, sightless, spotless, thoughtless, doubtless, gutless, bootless, rootless, fruitless, tactless, thriftless, shiftless, guiltless, faultless, dauntless, pointless, countless, tasteless, waistless, restless, listless, faithless, breathless, mirthless, worthless, ruthless, toothless, sleeveless, nerveless, loveless, sexless, noiseless, amice (part of priest's vestment), Amis, premiss, Themis (Greek goddess), commis (agent), promise, pumice, pomace, kumiss (drink of fermented milk), submiss (docile), dismiss, anise (Mediterranean plant), greyness, Tanis (ancient Egyptian city), Ennis (Irish town), Denis, menace, tennis, Venice, furnace, Furness, lenis (linguistics term), penis, dearness, clearness, nearness, Highness, slyness, dryness, shyness, coyness, sourness, blueness, newness, Tunis, drabness, blackness, darkness, bleakness, sleekness, meekness, weakness, likeness, frankness, brusqueness, richness, muchness, badness, gladness, madness, sadness, hardness, staidness, deadness, redness, weirdness, oddness, loudness, goodness, lewdness, rudeness, shrewdness, mildness, wildness, baldness, oldness, boldness, coldness, fondness, roundness, soundness, Daphnis (Greek mythological character), deafness, stiffness, roughness, gruffness, toughness, Agnes, vagueness, smugness, strangeness, paleness, staleness, illness, stillness, vileness, smallness, tallness, foulness, dullness, fullness, coolness, calmness, lameness, sameness, tameness, firmness, dimness, slimness, grim-

ness, warmness, dumbness, glumness, numbness, plainness, sternness, keenness, cleanness, meanness, greenness, thinness, fineness, proneness, oneness, sharpness, cheapness, steepness, ripeness, dampness, plumpness, crispness, sparseness, baseness, coarseness, hoarseness, closeness, looseness, rashness, harshness, freshness, fatness, flatness, smartness, lateness, greatness, straightness, wetness, hotness, shortness, stoutness, strictness, deftness, swiftness, softness, scantness, faintness, quaintness, gauntness, bluntness, aptness, promptness, smoothness, braveness, business, lapis, Apis (ancient Egyptian sacred bull), coppice, Puppis (constellation), Thespis (Greek poet), hospice, auspice, marquess, marquis, arris (sharp edge), Harris, Paris, Eris (Greek goddess), derris (Asian climbing plant), Ferris, peeress, orris (iris plant), Boris, Doris, Horace, Maurice, Morris, hubris, indris (large Madagascan mammal), laundress, Negress, Tigris, tigress, ogress, empress, mattress, waitress, traitress, fortress, portress (female porter), buttress, temptress, mistress, seamstress, Persis (ancient Iranian region), cercis (woody plant), tussis (a cough), Francis, apsis (point in planet's orbit), lattice, brattice (mining term), gratis, lettuce, Thetis (Greek goddess), glottis, cutis, poultice, countess, hostess, justice, solstice, pavis (large square shield), Jarvis, parvis (church porch), Davis, Mavis, service, novice, Clovis (Frankish king), pelvis, unguis (claw or hoof), lexis (complete vocabulary), deixis (linguistics term), Zeuxis (ancient Greek painter).

nereis (marine worm), archduchess, druidess, prejudice, Charybdis, edifice, benefice, orifice, artifice, flowerless, powerless, regardless, bottomless, fathomless, accomplice, remorseless, purposeless, effortless, comfortless, relentless, grotesqueness, forwardness, backwardness, awkwardness, aloofness, handsomeness, remoteness, quietness, exactness, pleasantness, abruptness, earnestness, precipice, Serapis (Graeco-Egyptian god), Polaris, ex libris, dentifrice, verdigris, arbitress, monitress, heritress, cockatrice (legendary monster), seductress, conductress, instructress, enchantress, schoolmistress, housemistress, catharsis, pertussis (whooping cough), proglottis (segment of tapeworm), abatis (fortifications term), clematis, apprentice, viscountess, interstice, armistice, injustice, Glenrothes (Scottish town), self-service, disservice.

unpleasantness, ambassadress, Nunc Dimittis (canticle), epiglottis, amphimixis (sexual reproduction), apomixis (type of asexual reproduction), anaptyxis (linguistics term), stylostixis (acupuncture), amanuensis.

300.1
loess, Powys (English writer), allantois (embryology term).

300.2
pubis, Anubis.

300.3
abyss, cannabis.

300.4
bodice, goddess, demigoddess.

300.5
stewardess, cowardice, leopardess, hendiadys (rhetorical device).

300.6
aegis, Lyme Regis, Bognor Regis, Curia Regis (Norman king's court).

300.7
rayless, lumbricalis (worm-like muscle), digitalis, Corona Australis (constellation), aurora australis, Corona Borealis (constellation), aurora borealis.

300.8
cilice (haircloth), bodiless, syphilis, penniless, weariless, merciless, pitiless, amaryllis.

300.9
polis (ancient Greek city-state), solace, Wallace, Cornwallis (British general), torticollis.

300.10
cullis (gutter), Dulles (US statesman), portcullis.

300.11
bullace (damson tree), valueless.

300.12
clueless, viewless, parulis (gumboil).

300.13
Aeolis (Greek god), numberless, featureless, riderless, odourless, Argolis (region of ancient Greece), colourless, humourless, mannerless, chrysalis, pleasureless, measureless, fortalice (small fort), fatherless, motherless, flavourless, driverless, oxalis (flowering plant), corydalis (climbing plant), Persepolis, Hermoupolis (Greek port), Camelopardalis (constellation).

300.13.1
Annapolis (capital of Maryland), Minneapolis, Indianapolis.

300.13.2
propolis (substance collected by bees), cosmopolis, necropolis (burial ground), Acropolis, metropolis, Heliopolis (ancient Egyptian city), megalopolis (complex of adjacent towns).

300.14
questionless, passionless, motionless, expressionless.

300.15
wingless, meaningless.

300.16
senseless, defenceless.

300.17
witless, profitless, limitless, spiritless.

300.18

kermis (Dutch carnival), dermis, vermis (part of brain), epidermis, endodermis (botany term), hypodermis (biology term).

300.19

remiss, Artemis, epididymis (anatomy term).

300.20

amiss, Salamis (Greek island), Semiramis (legendary Assyrian queen).

300.21

harness, unharness, Kiwanis (US community service organization).

300.22

bareness, fairness, unfairness, awareness.

300.23

finis (the end), Guinness, pinnace (small boat).

shabbiness, flabbiness, grubbiness, tubbiness, stickiness, cockiness, silkiness, sulkiness, hardiness, sturdiness, neediness, greediness, giddiness, tidiness, moodiness, rowdiness, dauphiness, fluffiness, stuffiness, earliness, burliness, curliness, surliness, silliness, holiness, lowliness, godliness, worldliness, friendliness, kindliness, ugliness, cleanliness, loneliness, stateliness, ghostliness, liveliness, loveliness, reminisce, gloominess, happiness, sleepiness, sloppiness, airiness, wariness, dreariness, weariness, hungriness, iciness, spiciness, bossiness, sauciness, fussiness, dirtiness, prettiness, naughtiness, daintiness, emptiness, nastiness, thirstiness, healthiness, filthiness, heaviness, laziness, easiness, dizziness, noisiness, cosiness, drowsiness, clumsiness.

foolhardiness, untidiness, orderliness, scholarliness, ungodliness, cowardliness, unworldliness, unfriendliness, unhappiness, unhealthiness.

300.23.1

readiness, steadiness, unsteadiness.

300.24

cornice, rawness, soreness, notornis (rare flightless bird), archaeornis (extinct bird), aepyornis (extinct flightless bird), ichthyornis (extinct sea bird).

300.25

lowness, slowness, Adonis, callowness, shallowness, hollowness, narrowness, lex talionis (law of retaliation).

300.26 [see also **300.31**]

lioness, soberness, deaconess, wilderness, slenderness, tenderness, eagerness, villainess, Romanes (language of gypsies), canoness, baroness, thoroughness, patroness, marchioness, bitterness, otherness, cleverness, governess, togetherness.

300.27

lychnis (flowering plant), sickness, thickness, airsickness, seasickness, homesickness, chromaticness (physics term).

300.28

Widnes, nakedness, wickedness, crookedness, wretchedness, sordidness, raggedness, doggedness, ruggedness, hurriedness, sacredness, cussedness, vividness.

clear-headedness, bigheadedness, pigheadedness, light-headedness, hotheadedness, cold-bloodedness, broadmindedness, kind-heartedness, halfheartedness, downheartedness, lightheartedness, softheartedness, belatedness, quick-wittedness, far-sightedness, near-sightedness, long-sightedness, short-sightedness, sure-footedness, flatfootedness.

level-headedness, narrow-mindedness, feeble-mindedness, single-mindedness, open-mindedness, absent-mindedness, unexpectedness.

300.28.1
candidness, left-handedness, offhandedness, underhandedness.

300.29
kindness, blindness, unkindness.

300.30
feebleness, nimbleness, fickleness, idleness, carefulness, cheerfulness, awfulness, thankfulness, dreadfulness, painfulness, scornfulness, hopefulness, helpfulness, gracefulness, peacefulness, usefulness, gratefulness, spitefulness, thoughtfulness, doubtfulness, boastfulness, faithfulness, truthfulness, suppleness, brittleness, gentleness, evilness.

forgetfulness, unfaithfulness, untruthfulness.

300.31 [see also **300.26**]
stubbornness, drunkenness, suddenness, sullenness, commonness, openness, barrenness, rottenness, evenness, unevenness.

300.32
willingness, nothingness, unwillingness.

300.33
carelessness, cheerlessness, fearlessness, tirelessness, lawlessness, joblessness, recklessness, lucklessness, thanklessness, heedlessness, godlessness, childlessness, friendlessness, mindlessness, lifelessness, selflessness, changelessness, harmlessness, aimlessness, shamelessness, timelessness, homelessness, painlessness, tunelessness, shapelessness, sleeplessness, hopelessness, helplessness, classlessness, pricelessness, uselessness, artlessness, heartlessness, weightlessness, sightlessness, spotlessness, thoughtlessness, fruitlessness, tactlessness, thriftlessness, faultlessness, pointlessness, tastelessness, restlessness, listlessness, breathlessness, worthlessness, ruthlessness.

mercilessness, pitilessness, powerlessness, meaninglessness, remorselessness,

purposelessness, limitlessness, spiritlessness, effortlessness, relentlessness.

300.33.1
senselessness, defencelessness.

300.34
joyousness, righteousness, callousness, zealousness, pompousness, monstrousness, spaciousness, graciousness, preciousness, cautiousness, consciousness, nervousness, biliousness, hazardousness, contagiousness, scrupulousness, dangerousness, boisterousness, facetiousness, infectiousness, subconsciousness, unconsciousness, covetousness, mischievousness, unscrupulousness, semiconsciousness.

300.34.1
dubiousness, tediousness, studiousness, seriousness, deviousness, fastidiousness, melodiousness, lasciviousness.

300.34.2
sensuousness, sumptuousness, conspicuousness, impetuousness, voluptuousness.

300.34.3
viciousness, officiousness, capriciousness, surreptitiousness.

300.34.4
pretentiousness, conscientiousness.

300.35
snobbishness, childishness, selfishness, foolishness, ticklishness, squeamishness, sheepishness, lavishness, peevishness, unselfishness, feverishness.

300.36
curtness, pertness, alertness.

300.37
neatness, sweetness, completeness, incompleteness.

300.38
fitness, witness, unfitness, eyewitness, appropriateness, inappropriateness.

300.39

lightness, rightness, brightness, triteness, tightness, whiteness, politeness, uprightness, impoliteness.

300.40

cuteness, acuteness, astuteness.

300.41

directness, correctness, indirectness, incorrectness.

300.42

fastness, vastness, steadfastness.

300.43

forgiveness, furtiveness, activeness, plaintiveness, impressiveness, possessiveness, decisiveness, explosiveness, impulsiveness, offensiveness, talkativeness, effectiveness, inventiveness, inquisitiveness.

300.44

heiress, mayoress, Seferis (Greek poet), millionairess, Apollinaris (mineral water).

300.45

iris, Iris, Osiris (Egyptian god).

300.46

loris, cantoris (musical term).

300.47

prioress, berberis (cultivated shrub), Sybaris (ancient Greek colony), liquorice, eucharis (South American plant), murderess, sorceress, clitoris, avarice, ephemeris (astronomical table), mons veneris, sui generis (unique), angina pectoris.

300.48

actress, benefactress.

300.49

classis (governing body of church), glacis (a slope), Onassis.

300.50

Acis (Greek mythological character), basis, crasis (linguistics term), stasis, oasis, cataclasis (geology term), haemostasis.

300.51

tmesis (linguistics term), thesis, noesis (functioning of intellect), mimesis, ecesis (ecology term), ascesis (self-discipline), anthesis (flowering process), exegesis, epiclesis (invocation of Holy Spirit), anamnesis (recollection), diuresis, anuresis, enuresis, catachresis (incorrect use of words), erotesis (rhetorical question), leucopoiesis (white blood cell formation), biopoiesis (biology term), diapedesis (medical term), psychokinesis (parapsychology term), cytokinesis (division of cytoplasm), photokinesis (movement towards light), telekinesis, erythropoiesis (red blood cell formation), haematopoiesis (formation of blood), amniocentesis.

300.51.1

paresis (muscular weakness), hysteresis (physics term), diaphoresis, cataphoresis (analytical technique), electrophoresis (analytical technique), iontophoresis (biochemical technique).

300.52

diesis (printing term), ecdysis (shedding of outer layer), symphysis, synesis (linguistics term), synthesis, prosthesis, diaphysis (shaft of long bone), epiphysis (end of long bone), hypophysis (pituitary gland), apophysis (outgrowth), dieresis, aphaeresis (linguistics term), syneresis (contraction of two vowels), haemoptysis (coughing up of blood), diathesis (hereditary susceptibility to disease), metathesis (linguistics term), antithesis, epenthesis (linguistics term), parenthesis, photosynthesis, biosynthesis (biology term), parasynthesis (linguistics term).

300.52.1

dialysis, analysis, paralysis, catalysis, urinalysis, cryptanalysis (study of codes), haemodialysis, psychoanalysis, microanalysis, electrodialysis, electroanalysis.

300.52.2

biolysis (disintegration of organic matter), glycolysis (breakdown of glucose), thermolysis (loss of body heat), haemolysis (red blood cell disintegration), hydrolysis, cytolysis (disintegration of cells), autolysis (self-destruction of cells), histolysis (disintegration of tissues), electrolysis, pneumatolysis (geology term), bacteriolysis (disintegration of bacteria).

300.52.3

emesis, Nemesis, haematemesis (vomiting of blood).

300.52.4

genesis, agenesis (imperfect development), pangenesis (former heredity theory), biogenesis (biological principle), oogenesis (formation of ova), psychogenesis, morphogenesis (development of organism's form), thermogenesis (heat production), sporogenesis (spore formation), histogenesis (tissue and organ formation), pathogenesis (development of a disease), osteogenesis (bone formation), abiogenesis (biological theory), anthropogenesis (study of man's origin), haematogenesis (formation of blood), spermatogenesis (sperm formation).

300.52.5

prothesis (linguistics term), hypothesis.

300.53

Isis, lysis, crisis, epicrisis (pathology term).

300.54

proboscis, salpiglossis (flowering plant).

300.55

Phocis (district in ancient Greece), gnosis (knowledge of spiritual things), ptosis (drooping of the eyelid).

thrombosis, narcosis, mycosis (disease caused by fungus), psychosis, sycosis (inflammation of hair follicles), lordosis, kyphosis, morphosis (biology term), alphosis (absence of skin pigmentation), phimosis (tightness of foreskin), zymosis (any infectious disease), osmosis, prognosis, hypnosis, pyrosis (heartburn), neurosis, fibrosis, necrosis, hidrosis (sweat), nephrosis (kidney disease), mitosis, ostosis (formation of bone).

silicosis, varicosis, toxicosis, psittacosis, acidosis, ankylosis (abnormal immobility of joint), brucellosis (disease of cattle), ecchymosis (skin discoloration through bruising), syndesmosis (type of joint), cyanosis, melanosis (skin condition), telegnosis (parapsychology term), diagnosis, siderosis (lung disease), diarthrosis (freely movable joint), enarthrosis (ball-and-socket joint), synarthrosis (immovable joint), asbestosis.

metempsychosis (migration of soul), Winnipegosis (Canadian lake), anastomosis, autohypnosis, osteoporosis (loss of bony tissue).

300.55.1

symbiosis, scoliosis, ichthyosis, coccidiosis (disease of domestic animals), apotheosis, mononucleosis, pneumoconiosis, endometriosis (pathology term).

300.55.2

meiosis, miosis (constriction of pupil), pyosis (pus formation), abiosis (absence of life), antibiosis, necrobiosis (normal death of cells), anabiosis (resuscitation), parabiosis (union of two individuals).

300.55.3

tuberculosis, pediculosis (infestation with lice), furunculosis (skin condition), diverticulosis.

300.55.4

kenosis (theology term), stenosis, trichinosis (parasitic disease), pollinosis (hay fever), byssinosis (industrial lung disease), hallucinosis (mental disorder), avitaminosis, hypervitaminosis.

300.55.5

sclerosis, cirrhosis, xerosis (abnormal dryness of tissues), phlebosclerosis (hardening of veins), atherosclerosis (disease of arteries), arteriosclerosis.

300.55.6

ketosis (pathology term), halitosis, amitosis (form of cell division), spirochaetosis (disease).

300.55.7

dermatosis, haematosis (oxygenation of blood), keratosis (skin condition), myxomatosis, carcinomatosis.

300.56

Eleusis (Greek town), anacrusis.

300.57

emphasis, protasis (conditional clause), entasis (architectural term), anabasis (ancient Persian military expedition), parabasis (speech of Greek chorus), catabasis (descent), apodosis (main clause), apophasis (rhetorical device), periphrasis, antiphrasis (rhetorical device), diastasis (separation of joined parts), metastasis (spreading of disease), osteoclasis (surgical fracture of bone), bronchiectasis (dilation of bronchial tubes), atelectasis (lung collapse).

300.57.1

diocese, myiasis (infestation by fly larvae), trichiasis (inversion of eyelashes), archdiocese, taeniasis (tapeworm infestation), phthiriasis (infestation with lice), psoriasis, mydriasis (abnormal pupil dilation). lithiasis, amoebiasis (parasitic infection), leishmaniasis (parasitic infection), satyriasis, acariasis (hair infestation), ascariasis (roundworm infestation), filariasis (tropical disease), bilharziasis (tropical disease), schistosomiasis (tropical disease), elephantiasis, trypanosomiasis (sleeping sickness).

300.57.2

paedomorphosis (zoology term), anamorphosis (distorted image), metamorphosis, anthropomorphosis.

300.58

Chalcis (Greek city), peristalsis, diastalsis (medical term).

300.59

sepsis, syllepsis (linguistics term), prolepsis (rhetorical device), asepsis, antisepsis.

300.60

stypsis (medical term), ellipsis.

300.61

synopsis, caryopsis (one-seeded fruit), stereopsis (stereoscopic vision), coreopsis (tropical plant), ampelopsis (tropical vine), thanatopsis (meditation on death).

300.62

mitis (malleable iron), phlebitis, orchitis, rachitis (rickets), bronchitis, carditis, mephitis (foul stench), colitis, typhlitis (intestinal disorder), rhinitis, scleritis (inflammation of eyeball membrane), iritis, neuritis, nephritis, metritis (inflammation of womb), gastritis, arthritis, bursitis, glossitis (inflammation of tongue), otitis, mastitis, cystitis, vulvitis.

tracheitis, ileitis (intestinal disorder), osteitis, uveitis (eye disorder), thyroiditis, mastoiditis (inflammation in ear), meningitis, pharyngitis, laryngitis, ophthalmitis, pneumonitis, urethritis, sinusitis, fibrositis, dermatitis, hepatitis, parotitis (mumps), keratitis (inflammation of cornea), prostatitis, synovitis (inflammation in a joint).

encephalitis, appendicitis, osteoarthritis.

300.62.1

myelitis (inflammation of spinal cord), spondylitis (inflammation of vertebrae), tonsillitis, pyelitis (inflammation of kidney), osteomyelitis (inflammation of bone marrow), poliomyelitis.

300.62.2
cellulitis (inflammation of body tissues), uvulitis, valvulitis (inflammation of heart valve), utriculitis (inflammation of inner ear), diverticulitis.

300.62.3
splenitis, adenitis (inflammation of a gland), vaginitis, retinitis, duodenitis.

300.62.4
colonitis, tympanitis, peritonitis.

300.62.5
blepharitis (inflammation of eyelids), arteritis, enteritis, ovaritis, gastroenteritis.

300.62.6
gingivitis, conjunctivitis.

300.63
fortis (phonetics term), mortise, rigor mortis.

300.64
notice, stephanotis, myosotis.

300.65
factice (soft rubbery material), practice, practise, malpractice.

300.66
mantis, Atlantis.

300.67
pastis, hydrastis (flowering plant).

300.68
testis, Alcestis (Greek mythological queen), ovotestis (snail's reproductive organ).

300.69
clevis (coupling device), crevice, Ben Nevis.

300.70
axis, praxis (practice), taxis (movement), pseudaxis (botany term), prophylaxis, parapraxis (psychology term), geotaxis (biology term), thermotaxis (movement towards heat), photo-

taxis (movement towards light), epistaxis (nosebleed), anaphylaxis.

301 -ice
ice, bice (medium blue colour), dice, lice, splice, slice, mice, gneiss, nice, pice (former Indian coin), spice, speiss (compound formed after smelting), rice, price, trice, thrice, syce (Indian servant), vice, twice.

de-ice, choc-ice, suffice, allspice, half-price, precise, concise, entice, device, advice.

paradise, merchandise, sacrifice, over-nice, underprice, Haltemprice (English township), imprecise, edelweiss, self-sacrifice.

302 -oss
os, boss, coss (Indian unit of distance), Kos (Greek island), cos (variety of lettuce), doss, fosse (ditch), joss (Chinese deity), Jos (Nigerian city), loss, floss, gloss, moss, Ross, cross, crosse (lacrosse stick), dross, toss, stoss (geology term).

chaos, Keos (Greek island), Eos (Greek goddess), speos (ancient Egyptian temple), Chios (Greek island), emboss, Lesbos (Greek island), reredos, kudos, Paphos (village in Cyprus), Argos (ancient Greek city), Lagos, logos (reason), Carlos, Delos (Greek island), Melos (Greek island), tholos (ancient Greek tomb), siglos (ancient Persian coin), bugloss, Amos, Samos (Greek island), demos (nation as political unit), Patmos (Greek island), cosmos, Minos, Lemnos (Greek island), epos (body of poetry), tripos, topos (basic concept), saros (cycle of eclipses), Pharos (ancient Greek lighthouse), Páros (Greek island), Skyros (Greek island), Eros, kaross (African garment), back-cross (genetics term), incross (inbreed), uncross, crisscross, outcross, Andros (Greek island), Kinross, non-pros (legal term), Thásos (Greek island), custos (superior in Franciscan order), bathos, pathos, ethos, pithos (ceramic oil container), mythos (beliefs of specific group), Naxos (Greek island), Hyksos (Asian nomad).

Barbados, intrados (inner curve of arch), extrados (outer curve of arch), Tenedos (Greek island), parados (bank behind fortification), Calvados, omphalos (sacred conical object), candyfloss, isogloss (line on map), rallycross, double-cross, Charing Cross, albatross, Thanatos (Greek personification of death), Hephaistos (Greek god).

exophthalmos (abnormal protrusion of eyeball), metanephros (part of kidney).

302.1
Phobos (satellite of Mars), Villa-Lobos (Brazilian composer).

302.2
across, lacrosse, autocross, motocross, intercross (crossbreed).

302.3
Sestos (ancient Turkish town), asbestos.

303 -orse
coarse, course, force, gorse, horse, hoarse, Morse, morse (cloak fastening), Norse, source, sauce.

recourse, forecourse (boat's sail), concourse, dampcourse, racecourse, discourse, endorse, deforce (withhold wrongfully), drayhorse, sawhorse, warhorse, packhorse, workhorse, cockhorse, studhorse, unhorse, racehorse, carthorse, clotheshorse, remorse, premorse (biology term), retrorse (pointing backwards), antrorse (directed upwards), introrse (turned inwards), extrorse (turned outwards), dextrorse (spiralling left to right), divorce, resource.

watercourse, intercourse, hobbyhorse, sinistrorse (spiralling right to left).

303.1
perforce, Wilberforce.

303.2
enforce, reinforce.

304 -oice
Boyce, choice, Joyce, voice, rejoice, Rolls Royce (*Trademark*), devoice (phonetics term), revoice (to echo), invoice, unvoice (phonetics term).

305 -oce
Bose (Indian physicist), kos (Indian unit of distance), dose, close, gross, chausses (medieval garment).

verbose, globose (spherical), thrombose, arkose (type of sandstone), floccose (covered with woolly tufts), jocose, viscose, nodose, strigose (biology term), rugose (wrinkled), filose (thread-like), pilose (covered with fine hairs), ramose (having branches), rimose (having a cracked surface), cymose (botany term), osmose (undergo osmosis), venose, spinose, squarrose (having a rough surface), erose (uneven), Tiros (US weather satellite), torose (biology term), necrose, Negros (Philippine island), engross, setose (bristly).

bellicose, varicose, ventricose (biology term), verrucose (covered with warts), overdose, surculose (bearing suckers), cellulose, squamulose (covered with small scales), ramulose (having small branches), tumulose (mound-like), annulose (segmented), lachrymose (tearful), racemose (botany term), pruinose (covered with waxy bloom), farinose (flour-like), anthracnose (fungal disease), adipose, caespitose (growing in tufts), comatose, keratose (having a horny skeleton), sarmentose (botany term), chaparejos (cowboy's leather overalls).

305.1
grandiose, foliose (leafy), otiose (futile), religiose (sanctimonious).

305.2
morose, suberose (relating to cork), tuberose, acerose (needle-shaped).

306 -ouse
scouse, douse, gauss (unit in physics), house, louse, mouse, nous, spouse, grouse, Strauss, souse, shouse (*Austral* lavatory).

lobscouse, degauss (demagnetize), playhouse, warehouse, teahouse, whorehouse, storehouse, poorhouse, Bauhaus, clubhouse, bakehouse, steakhouse, workhouse, cookhouse, madhouse, guardhouse, birdhouse, roadhouse, Wodehouse, roundhouse, doghouse, alehouse, jailhouse, tollhouse, schoolhouse, farmhouse, henhouse, greenhouse, glasshouse, dosshouse, gatehouse, Statehouse (*US* state capitol), lighthouse, hothouse, pothouse (small pub), courthouse, boathouse, outhouse, penthouse, guesthouse, bathhouse, almshouse, delouse, Nicklaus, booklouse (small wingless insect), woodlouse, reremouse (*Dialect* bat), dormouse, fieldmouse, titmouse, woodgrouse, sandgrouse.

bawdyhouse, powerhouse, summerhouse, Charterhouse, slaughterhouse, porterhouse, chapterhouse (building attached to cathedral), flittermouse (*Dialect* bat).

307 -uss
us, bus, cuss, fuss, Gus, jus (legal right), huss (dogfish), plus, muss (*US* rumple), pus, Russ, crus (lower leg), truss, suss, thus, wus (*Welsh* term of address).

airbus, debus, embus (military term), succuss, percuss, concuss, discuss, cuscus (Australasian marsupial), nonplus, untruss.

minibus, omnibus, blunderbuss, motorbus, overplus.

308 -oos
puss, Grus (constellation), schuss, Tungus (member of Mongoloid people), Anschluss (political or economic union), sourpuss, Vilnius (Russian city), ceteris paribus (other things being equal).

309 -uce
douce (*Scot* sedate), goose, juice, loose, sluice, moose, mousse, noose, Bruce, crouse (*Dialect* saucy), spruce, truce, Sousse (Tunisian port), use, deuce, puce, Zeus.

cayuse (*US* small pony), caboose, camboose (lumberjack's cabin), couscous (North African spicy dish), mongoose, wayzgoose (printing works' annual outing), verjuice (juice of unripe grapes), recluse, unloose, footloose, vamoose, burnoose (Arab's hooded cloak), slipnoose, papoose, ceruse (white lead), Elbrus (Russian mountain), abstruse, abuse, excuse, educe (logic term), deduce, reduce, seduce, produce, induce, conduce, refuse, effuse (spreading out), diffuse, profuse, ill-use, almuce (monk's fur-lined cape), prepuce, disuse, misuse, retuse (botany term), obtuse.

charlotte russe, superinduce (introduce as additional factor).

309.1
adduce (cite as proof), produce, traduce (speak badly of), reproduce, introduce.

310 -'s
joyous, psoas (muscle in loin), Phoebus, rebus, bulbous, nimbus, rhombus, thrombus, Orcus (Roman god), caucus, Dorcas, glaucous (covered with waxy bloom), raucous, ruckus, sulcus (linear groove), incus, rhonchus (rattling breathing sound), bronchus, righteous, gradus (book of musical exercises), nodus (problematic situation), Judas, In-

dus, Pindus (Greek mountain range), fundus (anatomy term), Dreyfus, scyphus (ancient Greek drinking cup), typhus, Rufus, rufous (reddish brown), Argus, negus (port and lemon drink), bogus, valgus (medical term), Angus, fungus, fungous, gorgeous, balas (red gemstone), Callas, callous, callus, Dallas, phallus, gallous (containing gallium), thallous (containing thallium), thallus (botany term), parlous (dangerous or difficult), talus, Troilus, bolus (ball of chewed food), troublous, windlass, Douglas, surplus, atlas, cutlass, Lammas, spermous (relating to sperm whale), Thermos (*Trademark*), Remus, Mimas (satellite of Saturn), primus, timeous (*Scot* timely), thymus, Thomas, Comus (Roman god), Momus (Greek god), chromous (containing chromium), houmous (Middle Eastern creamy dip), grumous (consisting of granular tissue), humus, dolmas (stuffed vine leaves), isthmus, Christmas, litmus, Xmas, stannous (containing tin), magnus, carpus (wrist), purpose, lupus (skin disease), upas (Javan tree), pompous, trespass, charas (hashish), varus (medical term), scabrous, glabrous (smooth-skinned), cribrous (sieve-like), fibrous, hydrous, Hydrus (constellation), wondrous, walrus, leprous, Cyprus, cypress, cuprous, citrus, nitrous, oestrus, lustrous, monstrous, dextrous, thyrsus (Bacchus' staff), versus, rhesus, Croesus, lapsus (error), Thapsus (ancient town near Carthage), precious, luscious, factious, fractious, noxious, anxious, conscious, captious, bumptious, scrumptious, Plautus (Roman dramatist), tortoise, cactus, Saktas (Hindu sect), ictus (poetry term), rictus (gap of open mouth), Sanctus (hymn in Eucharist), linctus, cantus (medieval church singing), Faustus, favus (fungal skin disease), nervous, fulvous (dull brownish-yellow), canvas, canvass, plexus, nexus, Texas, Jesus, Kansas.

Barabbas, jacobus (former English gold coin), succubus (female demon), incubus (male demon), syllabus, colobus (monkey), Barnabas, Damascus, self-righteous, unrighteous, solidus, Lepidus (ancient Roman statesman), iodous (containing iodine), tremendous, stupendous, horrendous, Josephus (Jewish historian), Sisyphus (Greek mythological king), pemphigus (blistering skin disease), azygous (developing singly), egregious, Tibullus (Roman poet), Lucullus (Roman general), Agulhas (South African headland), Catullus (Roman lyric poet), Wenceslas, enormous, posthumous, nystagmus, Michaelmas, Candlemas, Martinmas, chiasmus (rhetoric term), Erasmus, marasmus (wasting away), alumnus, Vertumnus (Roman god), acarpous (producing no fruit), syncarpous (botany term), Olympus, tenebrous, ludicrous, anhydrous (containing no water), chivalrous, disastrous, excursus (digression from main story), Caucasus, Pegasus, Confucius, infectious, innoxious (harmless), obnoxious, rambunctious, preconscious, subconscious, self-conscious, unconscious, singultus, Hephaestus (Greek god), Augustus, lecythus (ancient Greek vase), calathus (ancient Greek decorative symbol), Oireachtas (Irish parliament), Gustavus (Swedish king), mischievous, abraxas (ancient magic charm).

Menelaus (Greek mythological king), diadelphous (botany term), philadelphus (fragrant shrub), monadelphous (botany term), homozygous (genetics term), creophagous (flesh-eating), zoophagous (feeding on animals), sarcophagus, monophagous (feeding on one food), carpophagous (feeding on fruit), saprophagous (feeding on decaying matter), coprophagous (feeding on dung), oesophagus, analogous, homologous, isologous (chemistry term), Galápagos, asparagus, cunnilingus, gladiolus, nucleolus (part of cell nucleus), alveolus (small cavity), modiolus (part of inner ear), variolous (relating to smallpox), Nostradamus, borborygmus, acrocarpous (botany term), rhizocarpous (producing subterranean flowers), apocarpous (botany term), metacarpus (bones of the hand), multipurpose, idolatrous, ambidextrous, Dionysus (Greek god), Paracelsus (Swiss physician), semiprecious, semiconscious, microdontous (having unusually small teeth), Pocahontas (American Indian woman).

cumulonimbus, Camelopardus (constellation).

310.1
Dias (Portuguese navigator), Aeneas, Linnaeus, Piraeus, uraeus (ancient Egyptian sacred serpent), gluteus (muscle in buttock), scarabaeus (scarab), Manichaeus (Persian prophet), coryphaeus (ancient Greek chorus leader), Ptolemaeus (crater on moon).

310.2
scabious, rubious (dark red), dubious, plumbeous (relating to lead), Roscius (ancient Roman actor), sardius (Old Testament precious stone), radius, tedious, Claudius, studious, Orpheus, Morpheus (Greek god), congius (unit of liquid measure), malleus, Peleus (father of Achilles), pileus (part of mushroom), pileous (relating to hair), coleus, nucleus, nauplius (larva of crustacean), Ennius (Roman poet), corneous (horny), igneous, ligneous, clypeus (part of insect's head), copious, Gropius (US architect), impious, aqueous, ferreous (relating to iron), nacreous, pancreas, cupreous (relating to copper), citreous (greenish-yellow), vitreous, gaseous, caseous, Theseus, osseous, Celsius, Mencius (Chinese philosopher), courteous, piteous, Grotius (Dutch statesman), Proteus (Greek god), luteous (light greenish-yellow),

beauteous, duteous, plenteous, bounteous, struthious (relating to the ostrich), pervious, devious, previous, obvious, envious, nauseous.

Eusebius (early Christian bishop), triphibious, amphibious, Polybius (ancient Greek historian), compendious, dupondius (ancient Roman coin), Pelagius (British monk), rebellious, Equuleus (constellation), aculeus (prickle), abstemious, calumnious, Asclepius (Greek god), subaqueous, obsequious, opprobrious, lugubrious, salubrious, industrious, illustrious, caduceus (Hermes' staff), Lucretius (Roman poet), Helvétius (French philosopher), discourteous, rumbustious, Boethius (Roman philosopher), impervious, trapezius.

impecunious, Aesculapius (Roman god), Belisarius (Byzantine general), Stradivarius.

310.2.1
hideous, perfidious, chlamydeous (having sepals and petals), insidious, fastidious, invidious.

310.2.2
odious, melodious, commodious, Asmodeus (Jewish prince of demons), incommodious.

310.2.3
alias, Sibelius, Vesalius (Flemish anatomist).

310.2.4
Delius, Aurelius (Roman emperor), Berzelius (Swedish chemist), contumelious (insolent).

310.2.5
ileus (obstruction of intestine), bilious, Marsilius (Italian political philosopher), Lucilius (Roman satirist), punctilious, supercilious.

310.2.6
calcaneus (heel bone), Comenius (Czech educational reformer), extra-

neous, Pausanias (Greek geographer and historian), cutaneous, spontaneous, miscellaneous, percutaneous, subcutaneous, simultaneous, instantaneous, contemporaneous, extemporaneous.

310.2.7
genius, splenius (neck muscle), ingenious, arsenious (relating to arsenic), homogeneous, heterogeneous.

310.2.8
Arminius (Dutch theologian), vimineous (producing long flexible shoots), Flaminius (Roman general), gramineous (relating to grasses), sanguineous (relating to blood), ignominious.

310.2.9
euphonious, felonious, harmonious, erroneous, Petronius (Roman satirist), Suetonius (Roman historian), inharmonious.

310.2.9.1
ceremonious, acrimonious, parsimonious, sanctimonious, unceremonious.

310.2.10
Arius (Greek Christian theologian), carious, scarious (botany term), Marius (Roman general), various, Briareus (Greek giant), precarious, vicarious, calcareous, bifarious (botany term), gregarious, hilarious, denarius, Aquarius, retiarius (Roman gladiator), Sagittarius.

310.2.10.1
nefarious, omnifarious (of all sorts), multifarious.

310.2.11
serious, cereus (large cactus), Tiberius, cinereous (greyish), imperious, mysterious, deleterious.

310.2.12
Sirius, delirious.

310.2.13
aureus (Roman coin), Boreas (Greek god), glorious, arboreous (thickly wooded), laborious, inglorious, uproarious, censorious, sartorius, Sertorius (Roman soldier), notorious, victorious, Nestorius (Syrian churchman), uxorious, meritorious.

310.2.14
curious, furious, spurious, injurious, usurious, incurious, penurious, luxurious.

310.2.15
Nicias (Athenian statesman), piceous (relating to pitch), griseous (streaked with grey), Odysseus, Dionysius.

310.2.16
Statius (Roman poet), Ignatius (early Christian saint), fieri facias (legal term).

310.2.17
niveous (resembling snow), oblivious, lascivious.

310.2.18
pluvious, Vesuvius.

310.3
eyas (nestling hawk or falcon), bias, Gaius (Roman jurist), lias (blue limestone rock), pious, Pius, bacchius (metrical foot), Elias, Matthias, Ananias, Zacharias, hamadryas (type of baboon), nisi prius (former legal term).

310.4
congruous, menstruous, vacuous, nocuous, arduous, cernuous (drooping), sensuous, fatuous, virtuous, tortuous, fructuous, unctuous, flexuous.

superfluous, mellifluous, circumfluous (surrounded by water), incongruous, innocuous, promiscuous, deciduous, assiduous, ambiguous, contiguous, exiguous (scanty), impetuous, spirituous (containing alcohol), anfractuous (convoluted), tumultuous, voluptuous, contemptuous, tempestuous, incestuous.

310.4.1
perspicuous, transpicuous (transparent), conspicuous, inconspicuous.

310.4.2

strenuous, tenuous, ingenuous, disingenuous.

310.4.3

sinuous, continuous, discontinuous.

310.4.4

sumptuous, presumptuous.

310.5

gibbous, arquebus (long-barrelled gun), Erebus (Greek god), circumbendibus (circumlocution).

310.6

plumbous (containing lead), Columbus.

310.7

Bacchus, Gracchus (Roman tribune), Caracas.

310.8

carcass, sarcous (muscular or fleshy), Hipparchus (Greek astronomer), Aristarchus (crater on moon).

310.9

circus, cercus (zoology term), cysticercus (tapeworm larva).

310.10

muticous (botany term), distichous (arranged in two rows), tristichous (arranged in three rows), Cyzicus (ancient Greek colony), umbilicus, Autolycus, Copernicus, ulotrichous (having curly hair), Leviticus.

310.11

coccus (spherical bacterium), floccus (downy covering on birds), diplococcus (type of bacterium), pneumococcus, gonococcus, micrococcus, streptococcus.

310.12

focus, locus, crocus, hocus-pocus.

310.13

fucus (brown seaweed), mucous, mucus, Seleucus (Macedonian general), caducous (biology term), Ophiuchus (constellation).

310.14

abacus, Spartacus, Antiochus (Syrian king), diplodocus (herbivorous dinosaur), Telemachus (son of Odysseus), Callimachus (Greek poet), Lysimachus (king of Thrace), Caratacus (ancient British chieftain).

310.15

discus, viscous, viscus (large internal organ), hibiscus, meniscus, lemniscus (nerve fibres in brain).

310.16

Midas, Cnidus (ancient Greek city), nidus (insect's nest), Abydos (ancient Egyptian town), Nabonidus (Old Testament character).

310.17

exodus, hazardous, Enceladus (Greek mythological giant), ceratodus (extinct fish).

310.18

dimorphous (chemistry term), amorphous, polymorphous, rhizomorphous (resembling a root), anthropomorphous.

310.19

magus (Zoroastrian priest), tragus (projection in ear), Tagus (European river), vagus, choragus (ancient Greek chorus leader), Las Vegas.

310.20

courageous, umbrageous (shady), outrageous, contagious, advantageous, disadvantageous.

310.21

prodigious, religious, litigious, prestigious, irreligious, sacrilegious.

310.22

jealous, Hellas (ancient name for Greece), zealous, Marcellus (Roman general), ocellus (insect's simple eye), nucellus (botany term), entellus (monkey).

310.23

villus, villous (covered with long hairs), obelus (symbol in text), strobilus (plant cone), trochilus (humming-bird), Aeschylus, aphyllous (having no leaves), Angelus, lapillus (small piece of lava), perilous, scurrilous, bacillus, nautilus, pulvillus (pad on insect's leg), Theophilus (crater on moon), zoophilous (pollinated by animals), Herophilus (Greek anatomist), xerophilous (living in dry conditions), hydrophilous (growing in water), hygrophilous (growing in wet places), coprophilous (growing on dung), stenophyllous (having narrow leaves), aspergillus, adactylous (without fingers or toes), erysipelas, hectocotylus (zoology term).

310.24

hilus (anatomy term), stylus, monostylous (botany term).

310.25

garrulous, fabulous, sabulous (gritty), nebulous, bibulous (addicted to alcohol), tubulous (tube-shaped), flocculus (marking on sun's surface), calculus, modulus, pendulous, scrofulous, Regulus (Roman general), regulus (impure metal), famulus (sorcerer's attendant), hamulus (hooklike projection), emulous (competitive), tremulous, limulus (type of crab), stimulus, Romulus, annulus, populace, populous, scrupulous, patulous (spreading widely), volvulus (abnormal twisting of intestine).

edentulous (toothless), miraculous, tuberculous, homunculus (miniature man), ranunculus (plant genus), unscrupulous, convolvulus.

310.25.1

querulous, glomerulus (anatomy term).

310.25.2

ridiculous, funiculus (anatomy term), ventriculus (bird's gizzard), meticulous, canaliculus (small channel).

310.25.3

credulous, sedulous, incredulous.

310.25.4

stridulous, acidulous.

310.25.5

cumulus, tumulus, cirrocumulus, stratocumulus, altocumulus.

310.26

libellous, embolus, Daedalus, scandalous, carolus (former English coin), Tantalus (Greek mythological king), marvellous, frivolous, malleolus (bony projection on ankle), photophilous (growing in strong light), astragalus (anklebone), anomalous, asepalous (having no sepals), synsepalous (having joined sepals), apetalous (having no petals), sympetalous (having joined petals), Sardanapalus (Assyrian king), Papadopoulos.

310.26.1

obolus (Greek unit of weight), discobolus (discus thrower).

310.26.2

Nicholas, nickelous (relating to nickel), nidicolous (ornithology term), limicolous (living in mud), terricolous (living in soil), saxicolous (living on rocks), arenicolous (living in sandy places), stercoricolous (living in dung).

310.26.3

bicephalous (having two heads), Bucephalus, acephalous (headless), hydrocephalus.

310.27

famous, squamous (biology term), ramus (biology term), mandamus (legal term), uniramous (undivided), ignoramus.

310.28

didymous (in pairs), blasphemous, ginglymus (hinge joint), minimus, mittimus (legal term), maximus, Triptolemus (Greek mythological character).

310.28.1

animus, unanimous, magnanimous, pusillanimous.

310.28.2

onymous (bearing author's name), euonymus (cultivated tree), pseudonymous, synonymous, anonymous, eponymous, antonymous, polyonymous (having several names), Hieronymus, heteronymous (spelt alike).

310.29

infamous, venomous, Pyramus, monogamous, didynamous (botany term), autonomous, anadromous (migrating up river), catadromous (migrating down river), physostomous (zoology term).

310.29.1

bigamous, polygamous.

310.29.2

calamus (Asian palm), thalamus, hypothalamus.

310.29.3

xylotomous (boring into wood), hippopotamus.

310.30

trismus (lockjaw), strabismus, vaginismus (painful vaginal spasm).

310.31

anus, Janus, heinous, manus (wrist and hand), pandanus (palm-like plant), Uranus, Silvanus (Roman god), Coriolanus.

310.32

genus, venous, Venus, Albinus (English scholar), subgenus, Silenus (Greek satyr), scalenus (muscle in neck), Comnenus (Byzantine family), Campinas (Brazilian city), intravenous, arteriovenous.

310.33

ruinous, tendinous (relating to tendons), terminus, verminous, ominous, urinous (relating to urine), gangrenous,

acinus (biology term), Circinus (constellation), mountainous, resinous.

libidinous, rubiginous (rust-coloured), indigenous, fuliginous (smoky or sooty), epigenous (growing on the surface), terrigenous (of the earth), perigynous (botany term), vertiginous, vortiginous (whirling), endogenous, homogenous, hypogenous (growing on undersurface), erogenous, urogenous (producing urine), hydrogenous, androgenous (producing only male offspring), nitrogenous, misogynous, autogenous (originating within the body), ferruginous (containing iron), gelatinous.

multitudinous, oleaginous (resembling oil), cartilaginous.

310.33.1

luminous, numinous (awe-inspiring), aluminous (resembling aluminium), voluminous, albuminous (containing albumin), leguminous, bituminous.

310.33.2

glutinous, mutinous, velutinous.

310.34

Minas, minus, Ninus (Assyrian king), spinous (resembling a thorn), sinus, vinous (relating to wine), echinus (sea urchin), Delphinus (constellation), Longinus (Greek writer), Aquinas, Quirinus (Roman god), uncinus (small hooked structure), Plotinus (Roman philosopher), pulvinus (botany term), botulinus (bacterium), matriclinous (resembling female parent), patriclinous (resembling male parent), monoclinous (botany term), Flamininus (Roman general), Antoninus (Roman emperor), laurustinus (flowering shrub).

310.35

onus, bonus, Jonas, clonus (type of convulsion), Cronus, tonus (muscle tone), Tithonus (Greek mythological character), Amazonas (Brazilian state).

310.36

Dardanus (mythological founder of Troy), villainous, uranous (relating to uranium), membranous, synchronous, tetanus, gluttonous, cavernous, ravenous, poisonous, Eridanus (constellation), diaphanous, cacophonous, homophonous (pronounced the same), Telegonus (son of Odysseus), Antigonus (Macedonian king), athermanous (opaque to radiant heat), monotonous, phototonus (botany term), allochthonous (geology term), autochthonous (geology term), diplostemonous (botany term).

310.37

Oedipus, polypus, Lysippus (Greek sculptor), Leucippus (Greek philosopher), platypus, eohippus, Aristippus (Greek philosopher).

310.38

corpus, porpoise, habeas corpus.

310.39

opus, Scopas (Greek sculptor), Canopus.

310.40

octopus, amphitropous (botany term), orthotropous (botany term), pithecanthropus.

310.41

campus, lampas (swelling in horse's mouth), pampas, grampus, hippocampus.

310.42

compass, rumpus, encompass, gyrocompass, astrocompass.

310.43

arras, Arras (French town), harass, embarrass, nonparous (never having given birth), disembarrass.

310.44

ferrous, terrace, nonferrous.

310.45

sclerous (hard or bony), serous, Severus (Roman emperor), Ahasuerus (Old Testament king).

310.46

Pyrrhus, cirrus, scirrhus (cancerous growth), scirrhous (firm), Algeciras (Spanish port).

310.47

gyrus (fold on brain surface), Cyrus, virus, papyrus, Epirus (region of Greece), desirous, echovirus, ultravirus.

310.48

aurous (containing gold), chorus, Horus (Egyptian sun god), chlorous (relating to chlorine), porous, sorus (plant's spore-producing structure), Taurus, torus, pelorus (type of gyrocompass), pylorus (opening in stomach), thesaurus, Centaurus (constellation), Epidaurus (ancient Greek port), Matamoros (Mexican port), Cassiodorus (Roman writer), tubuliflorous (having tubular flowers).

310.48.1

brontosaurus, brachiosaurus, tyrannosaurus.

310.49

Eurus (Greek mythological wind), Honduras, anurous (tailless), coenurus (larva of tapeworm), Arcturus (star), mercurous, Epicurus.

310.50

barbarous, Cerberus (three-headed dog), tuberous, slumberous, acarus (non-parasitic mite), decorous, Icarus, lecherous, treacherous, rapturous, murderous, odorous, Pandarus (Greek mythological character), slanderous, ponderous, chunderous (*Austral* nauseating), thunderous, Zephyrus (Greek god), sulphurous, phosphorus, phosphorous, rigorous, vigorous, languorous, dangerous, valorous, dolorous, amorous, clamorous, glamorous, timorous, humorous, humerus, numerous, generous, onerous, sonorous, vaporous, viperous (relating to a viper), copperas (chemical compound), Hesperus, Bosporus (Turkish strait), prosperous, ulcerous, cancerous, traitorous, tartarous (consisting of tartar), Tartarus (Greek mythological place), stertorous (characterized by heavy snoring), uterus, icterus (jaundice), apterous (wingless), dipterous (having two wings), boisterous, flavorous, Lazarus.

indecorous, adventurous, malodorous, inodorous, Pythagoras, monomerous (botany term), isomerous (botany term), obstreperous, uniparous, multiparous, viviparous, oviparous, dinoceras (extinct mammal), rhinoceros, Monoceros (constellation), adulterous, homopterous (entomology term), macropterous (having large wings), preposterous, cadaverous.

adiaphorous (medical term), electrophorus (apparatus generating static electricity).

310.50.1
cankerous, rancorous, cantankerous.

310.50.2
splendiferous, stelliferous (full of stars), melliferous (producing honey), mammiferous (having breasts), auriferous, ossiferous (containing bones), vociferous, calciferous, lactiferous, fructiferous, umbelliferous, fossiliferous, metalliferous, seminiferous (transporting semen), uriniferous (transporting urine), odoriferous, sudoriferous (producing sweat).

310.50.2.1
coniferous, carboniferous.

310.50.3
herbivorous, frugivorous (fruit-eating), vermivorous (worm-eating), granivorous (grain-eating), carnivorous, omnivorous, apivorous (bee-eating), piscivorous, baccivorous (berry-eating),

graminivorous (grass-eating), insectivorous.

310.51
Lassus (Flemish composer), passus (part of medieval narrative), Crassus, Parnassus, Manassas (US town), Halicarnassus (ancient Greek city).

310.52
Tarsus, tarsus, metatarsus.

310.53
Issus (ancient Turkish battle site), byssus (zoology term), Ephesus, narcissus.

310.54
Knossos, colossus.

310.55
census, consensus.

310.56
spacious, gracious.

herbaceous, sebaceous, bulbaceous (bulb-shaped), audacious, mordacious (bitingly sarcastic), rudaceous (geology term), mendacious, fugacious (passing quickly away), fagaceous (botany term), sagacious, pugnacious, capacious, rapacious, sequacious (following in regular sequence), loquacious, veracious, ceraceous (waxy), voracious, flirtatious, cretaceous (relating to chalk), crustaceous (having a shell), curvaceous, vivacious, vexatious, rosaceous.

alliaceous, liliaceous, tiliaceous (botany term), oleaceous (botany term), foliaceous (resembling a leaf), coriaceous (relating to leather), contumacious (obstinate), saponaceous, carbonaceous, solanaceous (botany term), Athanasius (saint), furfuraceous (relating to bran), arboraceous (resembling a tree), stercoraceous (relating to dung), disputatious, ostentatious, ranunculaceous (botany term).

310.56.1
efficacious, perspicacious, ericaceous (botany term), urticaceous (botany term), inefficacious.

310.56.2

edacious (greedy), predacious (predatory), orchidaceous, iridaceous, hamamelidaceous (botany term), amaryllidaceous.

310.56.3

fallacious, salacious, corollaceous (relating to petals), santalaceous (botany term), polygalaceous (botany term).

310.56.4

minacious (threatening), tenacious, gallinaceous (ornithology term), arenaceous (geology term), farinaceous, erinaceous (relating to hedgehogs), pertinacious.

310.57

specious, synoecious (botany term), facetious, autoecious (botany term), heteroecious (botany term).

310.58

vicious, ambitious, spadiceous (botany term), judicious, officious, flagitious (utterly wicked), delicious, siliceous (relating to silica), malicious, pernicious, propitious, auspicious, suspicious, sericeous (covered with silky hairs), lubricious, capricious, nutritious, factitious, fictitious, injudicious, inofficious (contrary to moral duty), inauspicious, meretricious, repetitious, adscititious (additional), adventitious, surreptitious, superstitious, supposititious.

310.58.1

seditious, expeditious.

310.58.2

Mauritius, avaricious.

310.59

cautious, tortious (legal term), incautious.

310.60

stotious (*Irish* drunk), precocious, ferocious, atrocious.

310.61

Prudentius (Latin Christian poet), tendentious, dissentious, licentious, pretentious, sententious, contentious, conscientious.

310.62

flatus, stratus, status, meatus, hiatus, afflatus (creative power), conatus (striving of natural impulse), saleratus (sodium bicarbonate), apparatus, nimbostratus, cirrostratus, altostratus, cumulostratus.

310.63

fetus, Cetus (constellation), quietus, boletus (brownish fungus), Admetus (Greek mythological king), Servetus (Spanish theologian), Epictetus (Greek philosopher).

310.64

coitus, habitus (physical state), fremitus (medical term), vomitus (vomited matter), crepitus (medical term), impetus, spiritous, acetous (resembling vinegar), Tacitus, covetous, circuitous, fortuitous, gratuitous, Hippolytus (Greek mythological character), calamitous, precipitous, ubiquitous, iniquitous, emeritus, Theocritus (Greek poet), Democritus (Greek philosopher), necessitous, felicitous, solicitous, propositus (legal term).

310.65

situs (location of body part), Titus, tinnitus (ringing in ears), pruritus, detritus, Saint Vitus, Polyclitus (Greek sculptor), Heraclitus (Greek philosopher).

310.66

lotus, Notus (Greek mythological wind), Duns Scotus (Scottish theologian), Polygnotus (Greek painter).

310.67

Brutus, arbutus.

310.68

riotous, Herodotus, eczematous, sclerodermatous (having hard scaly covering), microstomatous (having unusually small mouth).

310.69
rectus (straight muscle), prospectus, conspectus (overall view).

310.70
argentous (relating to silver), momentous, portentous, sedimentous, ligamentous.

310.71
Aegyptus (mythological Egyptian king), eucalyptus.

310.72
canthus (corner of the eye), Xanthus (ancient Asian city), acanthus, acanthous (resembling a thorn), strophanthus (tropical tree), ailanthus (deciduous tree), ananthous (having no flowers), monanthous (one-flowered), helianthus (sunflower), polyanthus, amianthus (variety of asbestos), Erymanthus (Greek mountain), agapanthus (African lily).

310.73
naevus, grievous, longevous (long-lived).

311 -ilse
fils (Middle Eastern coin), grilse.

312 -orlse
false, waltz.

313 -ulse
dulse (red seaweed), pulse, repulse, appulse (astronomy term), impulse, convulse.

314 -ance
hance (architectural term), Hanse (medieval guild of merchants), manse, stance, askance, romance, finance, expanse, Penzance.

315 -arnce
chance, dance, lance, glance, rance (red marble), France, prance, trance, seance, faïence, nuance, perchance, mumchance (dumbstruck), mischance, enhance, freelance, entrance, advance, Afrikaans, contredanse (Continental dance), fer-de-lance (venomous snake), vraisemblance.

316 -ence
dense, fence, hence, flense (strip blubber from whale), pence, spence (*Dialect* larder), cense (burn incense), sense, tense, thence, whence, condense, defence, offence, immense, commence, prepense (premeditated), dispense, suspense, expense, incense, pretence, intense, self-defence, recommence, recompense, frankincense.

317 -ince
mince, quince, rinse, prince, since, wince, evince, province, convince.

318 -once
bonce, sconce, nonce, ponce, ensconce, response.

319 -ounce
ounce, bounce, jounce (jolt), flounce, pounce, trounce, enounce, denounce, renounce, announce, pronounce, mispronounce.

320 -unce
once, dunce, punce (*Dialect* kick or hit).

321 -'nce [further rhymes may be derived from **420**]
cadence, voidance (annulment), prudence, vengeance, parlance, silence, penance, ordnance, fourpence, sixpence, sequence, Clarence, cumbrance, hindrance, fragrance, entrance, monstrance (receptacle for consecrated Host), license, licence, absence, nonsense, patience, sentience (awareness), conscience, substance, instance, Constance, grievance, brilliance, pleasance

(secluded part of garden), presence, usance (commerce term).

abeyance, purveyance, conveyance, flamboyance, annoyance, clairvoyance, allowance, pursuance, disturbance, accordance, concordance, discordance, avoidance, impudence, decadence, abundance, elegance, emergence, resurgence, insurgence, divergence, convergence, allegiance, indulgence, vigilance, pestilence, condolence, virulence, turbulence, ambulance, opulence, corpulence, flatulence, petulance, performance, transhumance (seasonal migration of livestock), ordonnance (systematic arrangement), remanence (physics term), permanence, assonance, dissonance, consonance (agreement), sustenance, governance, resonance, repugnance, subsequence, consequence, eloquence, forbearance, recurrence, occurrence, incurrence, concurrence, remembrance, encumbrance, remonstrance, obeisance, renaissance, innocence, impatience, advertence, importance, inductance (electrical property), conductance (electrical property), reluctance, acquaintance, susceptance (magnetic property), acceptance, circumstance, observance, relevance, connivance, contrivance, ebullience, complaisance, cognizance.

significance, jurisprudence, correspondence, inadvertence, inobservance, omnipresence, recognizance.

overabundance, overindulgence.

321.1
ambience, radiance, audience, permeance, variance, prurience, miscreance, nescience, prescience, transience, irradiance, obedience, clairaudience (psychology term), resilience, convenience, recipience, experience, omniscience, disobedience, inconvenience, inexperience.

321.1.1
dalliance, mésalliance (marriage with social inferior).

321.2
science, defiance, affiance (betroth), reliance, alliance, appliance, compliance, misalliance.

321.3
affluence, effluence, influence, confluence, congruence, issuance, continuance.

321.4
credence, impedance (physics term), antecedence.

321.5
riddance, forbiddance, diffidence, confidence, precedence, incidence, evidence, providence, accidence (linguistics term), residence, self-confidence, coincidence.

321.6
guidance, subsidence.

321.7
resplendence, dependence, attendance, intendance (French public department), independence, condescendence (Scottish legal term).

321.8
arrogance, extravagance.

321.9
diligence, negligence, intelligence, intransigence, counterintelligence.

321.10
balance, valance, imbalance, unbalance, counterbalance.

321.11
valence (chemistry term), surveillance.

321.12
violence, indolence, somnolence, insolence, excellence, nonviolence, ambivalence, equivalence.

321.12.1
prevalence, malevolence, benevolence.

321.13
semblance, resemblance.

321.14
ordinance, eminence, dominance, prominence, chrominance (colour quality of light), luminance (brightness of light), desinence (ending of a word), pertinence, maintenance, countenance, abstinence, provenance, pre-eminence, illuminance (brightness of illumination), appurtenance, impertinence, discountenance, incontinence.

321.15
twopence, comeuppance.

321.16
Terence, aberrance, deterrence.

321.17
clearance, coherence, adherence, inherence, appearance, interference, incoherence, reappearance, nonappearance, disappearance, perseverance.

321.18
Lawrence, Florence, Torrance (Californian city), abhorrence.

321.19
durance (imprisonment), assurance, insurance, endurance, reassurance, coinsurance.

321.20
furtherance, deference, reference, preference, difference, sufferance, inference, conference, transference, tolerance, ignorance, temperance, utterance, protuberance, exuberance, indifference, circumference, belligerence, intolerance, deliverance.

321.20.1
reverence, severance, irreverence.

321.21
essence, quiescence, pubescence, frondescence (leaf-producing process), tumescence, senescence, virescence (process of becoming green), florescence (flowering process), excrescence, vitres-cence (glass-producing process), quintessence.

acquiescence, erubescence (process of becoming red), iridescence, incandescence, decalescence (heat absorption by metal), recalescence (heat emission by metal), adolescence, opalescence, obsolescence, convalescence, detumescence, intumescence, luminescence, juvenescence, deliquescence, efflorescence, inflorescence, fluorescence, phosphorescence, vaporescence (production of vapour), delitescence (disappearance of disease symptoms), effervescence.

321.22
reticence, beneficence, munificence, magnificence, reminiscence, reconnaissance, resipiscence (acknowledgment of error), concupiscence, reviviscence (revival).

321.23
nuisance, translucence.

321.24
pittance, quittance, remittance, admittance, transmittance, penitence, appetence, competence, acquittance, exitance (measure of radiation emission), concomitance, impenitence, incompetence, inheritance, capacitance (electrical property).

321.25
impotence, omnipotence.

321.26
sentence, repentance.

321.27
distance, outdistance, assistance, persistence, subsistence, insistence, resistance, existence, coexistence.

321.28
brisance (shattering effect of explosion), defeasance (annulment), malfeasance (illegal act), nonfeasance (legal term), misfeasance (legal term).

322 -aps [also **268** + -*s*]
apse, lapse, schnapps, craps, traps (belongings), taps, perhaps, elapse, relapse, prolapse, collapse, synapse.

323 -apes [also **270** + -*s*]
gapes (disease of domestic fowl), drapes, traipse, jackanapes.

324 -eps [also **271** + -*s*]
Steppes, biceps, triceps, anableps (tropical fish), quadriceps, editio princeps (first printed edition).

325 -erps [also **272** + -*s*]
turps, stirps (line of descendants).

326 -eeps [also **273** + -*s*]
Pepys, creeps.

327 -ips [also **274** + -*s*]
snips (small metal-cutting shears), Cripps (British Labour statesman), thrips, Mendips, ellipse, Phillips, eclipse, forceps, midships, amidships, apocalypse.

328 -ipes [also **275** + -*s*]
cripes, swipes (*Slang* weak beer), bagpipes, panpipes, stovepipes (tight trousers).

329 -ops [also **276** + -*s*]
Ops (Roman goddess), copse, chops, drops, tops, stops (card game), Cheops (ancient Egyptian king), Pelops (Greek mythological character), stylops (parasitic insect), Cyclops, Cecrops (Greek mythological character), eardrops, muttonchops (side-whiskers), triceratops (rhinoceros-like dinosaur).

330 -orps [also **277** + -*s*]
corpse, Cleethorpes.

331 -imps [also **287** + -*s*]
timps (*short for* timpani), glimpse.

332 -umps [also **289** + -*s*]
dumps, mumps, trumps.

333 -ats [also **365** + -*s*]
flats, rats, swats (*Dialect* freshly brewed beer), dingbats (*Austral* delirium tremens), congrats, ersatz.

334 -arts [also **366** + -*s*]
arts, darts, Ghats (Indian mountain range), Harz (German mountain range), clarts (*Dialect* lumps of mud).

335 -aits [also **367** + -*s*]
Bates, Fates (Greek goddesses controlling destiny), rates, Greats (course at Oxford University), annates (revenue paid to pope), othergates (otherwise).

336 -ets [also **368** + -*s*]
let's, Metz (French city), Donets (Russian river), assets, pantalets, chervonets (Russian coin), solonetz (salt-rich soil), castanets.

337 -erts [also **369** + -*s*]
hertz, outskirts, kilohertz.

338 -eets [also **370** + -*s*]
eats, Keats.

339 -its [also **371** + -*s*]
its, it's, blitz, splits, spitz (breed of dog), quits, grits (coarsely ground grain), wits, blewits (edible fungus), kibitz (*US* interfere), rackets (game resembling squash), rickets, Saint Kitts (West Indian island), credits, giblets, minutes, Leibnitz, Biarritz, Auschwitz, Austerlitz (Napoleonic battle site), applesnits (Canadian apple dish), Saint Moritz, separates, Horowitz (Russian pianist), slivovitz, Massachusetts.

340 -ites [also **372** + -*s*]
lights, nights, brights (*US* car headlights), tights, whites, daylights, footlights, Dolomites.

341 -ots [also **373** + -*s*]
bots (digestive disease of horses), Scots, lots, Notts., culottes, fleshpots.

342 -orts [also **374** + -*s*]
orts (*Dialect* scraps), sports, quartz, shorts.

343 -oats [also **376** + -*s*]
Oates, groats (crushed cereal grain), John o'Groats.

344 -outs [also **377** + -*s*]
grouts, thereabouts, whereabouts, hereabouts.

345 -oots [also **379** + -*s*]
foots (dregs), toots (term of endearment), kibbutz.

346 -utes [also **380** + -*s*]
boots, hoots, gumboots, cahoots.

347 -ants [also **407** + -*s*]
Hants., pants, Northants., Konstanz (West German city), underpants.

348 -ints [also **412** + -*s*]
chintz, Linz (Austrian port), blintz (thin filled pancake).

349 -ash
ash, bash, cash, cache, dash, fash (*Scot* worry), gash, hash, lash, clash, flash, plash (splash), splash, slash, mash, smash, gnash, Nash, pash (*Slang* infatuation), rash, brash, crash, trash, thrash, sash, tache (*short for* moustache), stash.

earbash (*Austral* talk incessantly), Wabash (US river), encash, czardas (Hungarian national dance), slapdash, rehash, eyelash, goulash, calash (horse-drawn carriage), backlash, unlash, whiplash, throatlash (bridle strap), Shamash (Assyrian sun god), quamash (US plant), mishmash, panache, gatecrash, midrash (Jewish biblical commentaries), potash, soutache (narrow braid).

balderdash, pebble-dash, synchroflash (camera mechanism), photoflash (flash bulb), callipash (edible part of turtle), sabretache (cavalryman's leather case), succotash (*US* cooked mixed vegetables).

349.1
abash, calabash (US tropical tree).

350 -arsh
harsh, marsh, gouache (art term), apache (Parisian gangster), moustache, Chuvash (Russian people).

351 -esh
flesh, mesh, nesh, crèche, fresh, thresh, tête-bêche (philately term), parfleche (dried rawhide), horseflesh, enmesh, Mureş (European river), refresh, afresh, Marrakech, Bangladesh, synchromesh, Gilgamesh (legendary Sumerian king), Andhra Pradesh (Indian state), Uttar Pradesh (Indian state), Madhya Pradesh (Indian state).

352 -eesh
quiche, fiche (*short for* microfiche), leash, niche, Niš (Yugoslavian town), babiche (rawhide thongs), unleash, hashish, maxixe (Brazilian dance), baksheesh, potiche (tall vase), schottische (19th-century German dance), pastiche, postiche (architectural term), microfiche, ouananiche (Atlantic salmon), nouveau riche.

353 -ish [further rhymes may be created by adding -*ish* to appropriate adjectives and nouns]
bish (*Slang* mistake), kish (carbon-rich graphite), dish, fish, Flysch (Alpine

rock deposits), knish (stuffed dumpling), squish, wish, whish, swish.

Laoighis (Irish county), greyish, boyish, Jewish, bluish, shrewish, newish, furbish, snobbish, rubbish, blackish, brackish, rakish, peckish, Turkish, freakish, stockish (stupid), mawkish, bookish, Frankish, pinkish, monkish, reddish, Kurdish (language group), Swedish, modish, loudish, rudish, prudish, childish, Wendish (language group), fiendish, roundish, raffish, garfish, starfish, crayfish, offish, oarfish, crawfish, sawfish, oafish, blowfish, roughish, jewfish, bluefish, rockfish, stockfish, monkfish, trunkfish, codfish, swordfish, goldfish, dogfish, hogfish, frogfish, batfish, catfish, flatfish, ratfish, whitefish, saltfish, waggish, biggish, piggish, priggish, doggish, hoggish, roguish, sluggish, largish, Salish (American Indian language), churlish, girlish, stylish, Gaulish, smallish, Polish, owlish, bullish, foolish, ghoulish, mulish, publish, ticklish, English, purplish, famish, rammish, blemish, Flemish, skirmish, squeamish, Rhemish (relating to Rheims), warmish, banish, clannish, planish (produce smooth surface on), mannish, Spanish, vanish, garnish, tarnish, varnish, Danish, greenish, burnish, furnish, swinish, Cornish, corniche (coastal road), clownish, brownish, Hunnish (barbarous), punish, longish, apish, sheepish, foppish, popish, uppish, impish, lumpish (clumsy), frumpish, waspish, vanquish, parish, cherish, perish, currish (rude), Irish, boarish, moreish, boorish, Moorish, flattish, rattish, latish, fetish, Lettish, pettish, skittish, British, rightish, whitish, Scottish, goatish, loutish, sluttish, ruttish, Jutish (ancient dialect of Kent), brutish, coltish, Kentish, lavish, ravish, slavish, knavish, dervish, peevish, elvish, anguish, languish, unwish.

babyish, tomboyish, refurbish, Cavendish, jellyfish, killifish, standoffish,

silverfish, angelfish, cuttlefish, damselfish, devilish, establish, accomplish, schoolmarmish, Carchemish (ancient Syrian city), womanish, kittenish, heathenish, relinquish, tovarisch (Russian term of address), distinguish, extinguish, disestablish.

353.1
caddish, Kaddish (ancient Jewish prayer), faddish, radish, horseradish.

353.2
blandish, brandish, standish (inkstand), outlandish.

353.3
elfish, selfish, shellfish, unselfish.

353.4
hellish, relish, embellish, disrelish (dislike).

353.5
polish, abolish, demolish.

353.6
Rhenish, replenish.

353.7
finish, Finnish, diminish.

353.8
donnish, admonish, astonish.

353.9
bearish, fairish, garish, squarish, nightmarish.

353.10
flourish, nourish, undernourish.

353.11
gibberish, lickerish, feverish, liverish, amateurish, impoverish.

354 -osh
bosh, Bosch (Dutch painter), cosh, gosh, josh (US to tease), cloche, slosh, nosh, posh, quash, squash, tosh, wash, swash (splash noisily).

brioche, kibosh, cohosh (US plant), guilloche (ornamental architectural border), backwash, musquash, caroche (ceremonial carriage), eyewash, siwash

(Canadian knitted sweater), awash, hogwash, brainwash, whitewash, outwash (glacial deposit), mouthwash.

tokoloshe (Bantu mythical malevolent creature), mackintosh.

355 -oshe
gauche, troche (lozenge).

356 -ush
Cush (biblical character), gush, hush, lush, blush, flush, plush, slush, mush, rush, brush, crush, thrush, tush, airbrush (atomizer), hairbrush, sagebrush (US shrub), nailbrush, paintbrush, toothbrush, woodrush (a plant), bulrush, inrush, onrush, uprush, outrush, underbrush (*US* undergrowth), bottlebrush (Australian shrub).

357 -oosh
bush, Cluj (Rumanian city), mush (*Slang* face), push, shush, tusche (substance used in lithography), whoosh, swoosh, shadbush (US shrub), ambush, spicebush (US shrub), saltbush (desert shrub), Hindu Kush (Asian mountain range).

358 -ushe
douche, louche (shifty), ruche, tarboosh (brimless Muslim cap), Ingush (Russian people), capuche (friar's large hood), barouche (horse-drawn carriage), cartouche, Kiddush (Jewish traditional blessing).

359 -arzh
plage (mark on sun's surface), bocage (French wooded countryside), sondage (archaeological trench), collage, ménage, barrage, garage, mirage, massage, dressage, corsage, frottage (rubbing), montage, gavage (forced feeding).

fuselage, persiflage, camouflage, badinage, decoupage (decoration with cutouts), entourage, arbitrage (stock exchange term), vernissage (opening of art exhibition), repechage (contest for runners-up), curettage (surgical process), reportage, cabotage (coastal navigation), sabotage, décolletage.

espionage, photomontage, counterespionage.

360 -azhe
beige, greige (undyed), Liège, manège (riding school), cortège.

361 -erzh
concierge, demivierge.

362 -eezh
prestige, noblesse oblige.

363 -ozhe
loge (theatre box), Limoges.

364 -uzhe
luge, rouge, Bruges, vouge (medieval weapon).

365 -at
at, bat, batt (quilt wadding), cat, kat (evergreen shrub), scat, skat (card game), chat, fat, hat, lat (former Latvian currency), blat (*US* bleat), flat, plait, Platte (US river system), plat (small plot), splat, slat, mat, matt, gnat, pat, Pat, spat, rat, brat, drat, prat, sprat, sat, tat, that, vat, VAT, twat.

Croat, sabbat (period of rest), brickbat, bullbat (American nightjar), combat, wombat, numbat (small Australian marsupial), dingbat, meerkat (South African mongoose), Sno-Cat (*Trademark*), mudcat (US catfish), wildcat, hellcat, polecat, hepcat, tipcat (a game), muscat, backchat, woodchat, whinchat, stonechat, chitchat, Sadat, SOGAT, sunhat, doormat, format, cowpat, thereat, whereat, hereat, jurat (legal term), firebrat (small wingless insect), muskrat, comsat (*short for* communications satellite), Hallstatt (archaeology term), Darmstadt (West German city), Dumyat (Egyptian town).

Uniat (denoting Eastern Church group), caveat, acrobat, concordat (treaty), butterfat, marrowfat, Astolat (town in Arthurian legend), cervelat (smoked sausage), diplomat, achromat (type of lens), Laundromat (*Trademark*), automat, assignat (former French paper money), pitapat, ziggurat, Ballarat (Australian town), Ararat, dandiprat (16th-century English coin), Intelsat (communications satellite), habitat, aegrotat, ratatat, rheostat (electrical component), chemostat (apparatus for bacteria culture), haemostat (device to stop bleeding), thermostat, clinostat (apparatus for studying plants), barostat (device maintaining constant pressure), aerostat (lighter-than-air craft), pyrostat (fire-alarm activating device), hydrostat (water-detection device), Photostat (*Trademark*), rubáiyát.

Magnificat, requiescat, anastigmat (type of lens), ratatat-tat.

365.1
begat, Kattegat.

365.2 [further rhymes may be derived from 16.307.5]
democrat, Eurocrat, bureaucrat, autocrat, plutocrat, aristocrat.

365.3
cravat, savate (form of boxing), avadavat (Asian weaverbird).

366 -art
art, baht (Thai currency), cart, chart, dart, fart, ghat (steps leading to river), Jat (Indo-European people), heart, hart, mart, smart, part, tart, start, wat (Thai Buddhist monastery).

kyat (Burmese currency), kiaat (African tree), tuart (eucalyptus tree), Hobart, Rabat (capital of Morocco), jam-

bart (piece of armour), Descartes, teacart, go-kart, handcart, dogcart, dustcart, Bogart, Earhart (US aviatrix), blackheart (darkening of woody stems), Bernhardt, greenheart (tropical tree), sweetheart, Eilat (Israeli port), Kalat (division of Pakistan), outsmart, depart, forepart, rampart, impart, mouthpart, Mozart, diktat (imposed decree), redstart, upstart, kick-start.

à la carte, undercart (undercarriage), applecart, Bundesrat (West German federal council).

366.1
apart, Bonaparte, counterpart.

367 -ait
eight, ait (*Dialect* islet), bate, bait, skate, date, fate, fête, gait, gate, hate, late, plate, slate, mate, pate, spate, rate, crate, freight, great, grate, prate, trait, straight, strait, sate, Tate, state, weight, wait.

striate, debate, rebate, tubate (tubular), whitebait, baccate (berry-like), furcate (to fork), plicate (pleated), spicate (having spikes), falcate (sickle-shaped), truncate, cheapskate, predate, chordate (zoology term), caudate (having a tail), cordate (heart-shaped), backdate, mandate, update, misdate, outdate, postdate, sulphate, phosphate, Margate, ligate (constrict with ligature), jugate (having paired parts), floodgate, tailgate, tollgate, Vulgate, sluicegate, Ramsgate, alate (having wings), chelate (having claws), dilate, prolate (spheroidal), bullate (blistered or puckered), ablate, oblate (spheroidal), deflate, reflate, inflate, conflate (combine), drawplate (plate for extruding wire), endplate, nameplate, hotplate, footplate, breastplate, translate, playmate, squamate (scale-like), primate, comate (hairy), bromate, chromate, plumate (having feathers), checkmate, stalemate, schoolmate, roommate, inmate, shipmate, helpmate, classmate, messmate, flatmate, pennate (having feathers or wings), enate (related on mother's side), crenate (having a scalloped edge), binate (occurring in pairs), quinate (composed of five parts), connate (congenital), ornate, phonate (utter speech sounds), pronate, zonate (arranged in zones), lunate (crescent-shaped), agnate (having common male ancestor), magnate, stagnate, cognate (related), pupate, baldpate, palpate, makeweight, ferrate (chemical compound), serrate, aerate, irate, gyrate, orate, borate (chemical compound), chlorate, urate, prorate, librate (to waver), vibrate, third-rate, hydrate, quadrate (make square), migrate, ingrate, disrate (reduce to lower rank), tartrate, nitrate, titrate, filtrate, castrate, first-rate, prostrate, lustrate (purify through religious rituals), frustrate, substrate, clathrate (net-like), pulsate, ansate (having a handle), scutate (covered with bony plates), mutate, lactate, tractate (short tract), dictate, punctate (marked with spots), hastate (botany term), restate, estate, cristate (crested), downstate, upstate, misstate, ovate, flyweight, Kuwait, catchweight, lightweight, fixate, luxate (dislocate).

inchoate (just beginning), benzoate (chemical compound), incubate, intubate (medical term), demarcate, educate, manducate (eat or chew), confiscate, obfuscate (to obscure), infuscate (tinged with brown), coruscate (to sparkle), inundate, fecundate, caliphate, bisulphate, abrogate, subjugate, conjugate, corrugate, promulgate, elongate, Billingsgate, insufflate (blow into), numberplate, boilerplate, copperplate, contemplate, legislate, impregnate, designate, syncopate, extirpate, inculpate, exculpate, lucubrate (to study), adumbrate, dehydrate, second-rate, transmigrate, deflagrate (burn fiercely), infiltrate, concentrate, seques-

trate, illustrate, demonstrate, remonstrate, commutate (reverse electric current), amputate, auscultate, understate, intrastate, interstate, devastate, overstate, reinstate, excavate, enervate, renovate, innovate, aggravate, pennyweight (unit of weight), heavyweight, hundredweight, middleweight, bantamweight, Bassenthwaite.

circumvallate (surround with defensive fortification), interpellate, variolate (inoculate with smallpox virus), capreolate (having tendrils), lanceolate (narrow and tapering), electroplate, carbohydrate, extravasate (exude), tergiversate, methotrexate (a drug).

367.1
create, labiate (aromatic plant), brachiate (swing through trees), radiate, mediate, ideate (imagine), cochleate (shaped like snail's shell), permeate, expiate, re-create, procreate, miscreate (create badly), aviate, obviate, nauseate, roseate.

irradiate, dimidiate (to halve), repudiate, enucleate, delineate, laciniate (jagged), calumniate, excoriate, infuriate, luxuriate, inebriate, appropriate, impropriate (transfer to laity), expropriate, repatriate, expatriate, enunciate, denunciate, annunciate (announce), depreciate, appreciate, excruciate, lixiviate (chemistry term), exuviate (shed outer covering), asphyxiate.

367.1.1
maleate (chemical compound), retaliate.

367.1.2
filiate (fix legal paternity of), affiliate, humiliate, conciliate, disaffiliate.

367.1.3
oleate (chemical compound), spoliate (despoil), defoliate, bifoliate (having two leaves), exfoliate (flake off), linoleate (chemical compound).

367.1.4
caseate (become cheese-like), glaciate, emaciate.

367.1.5
satiate, expatiate, ingratiate.

367.1.6
vitiate, officiate, initiate, propitiate (appease).

367.1.7
negotiate, dissociate, associate, consociate (enter into friendly association), disassociate.

367.1.8
substantiate, instantiate (represent by an example), transubstantiate, circumstantiate.

367.1.9
potentiate (make potent), differentiate.

367.1.10
deviate, alleviate, abbreviate.

367.2
actuate, menstruate, graduate, valuate (*US* value), toluate (chemical compound), fluctuate, punctuate, eventuate (to result), accentuate, evacuate, evaluate, attenuate, extenuate, insinuate, infatuate, perpetuate, effectuate (bring about), individuate (give individuality to), disambiguate, superannuate.

367.2.1
situate, habituate.

367.3
lobate, globate, probate, bilobate, trilobate, conglobate (form into ball).

367.4
abate, cohobate (redistil), stylobate (architectural term), approbate (Scottish legal term), reprobate, acerbate (embitter), masturbate, stereobate (foundation of building), exacerbate.

367.5
dedicate, medicate, predicate, abdicate, indicate, syndicate, vindicate, defecate, spiflicate (*Slang* destroy), triplicate,

supplicate, implicate, complicate, explicate (make explicit), fornicate, muricate (having a roughened surface), suricate (South African mongoose), fabricate, lubricate, rubricate (mark with red), imbricate (decorate with overlapping pattern), deprecate, imprecate, metricate, extricate, desiccate, vesicate (to blister), rusticate, exsiccate (dry up).

eradicate, adjudicate, nidificate (build a nest), certificate, pontificate, canonicate (office of canon), communicate, prevaricate, divaricate (diverge at wide angle), prefabricate, decorticate, authenticate, domesticate, sophisticate, prognosticate, hypothecate (legal term), detoxicate (to rid of poison), intoxicate, excommunicate.

367.5.1
duplicate, quadruplicate, reduplicate, centuplicate, quintuplicate.

367.5.2
masticate, elasticate, scholasticate (Jesuit's probation period).

367.6
locate, placate, vacate, bifurcate, suffocate, allocate, collocate, dislocate, translocate (displace), embrocate, altercate, advocate, reciprocate, equivocate.

367.7
sulcate (marked with parallel grooves), inculcate, bisulcate (cleft or cloven).

367.8
sedate, candidate, validate, chlamydate (zoology term), lapidate (pelt with stones), liquidate, fluoridate, depredate, antedate, oxidate, invalidate, consolidate, intimidate, dilapidate, elucidate.

367.9
gradate, vanadate (chemical compound), accommodate.

367.10
negate, delegate, relegate, colligate (join together), obligate, fumigate, ab-

negate, variegate, irrigate, aggregate, segregate, congregate, litigate, mitigate, castigate, instigate, navigate, levigate (grind into powder), suffumigate (fumigate from below), desegregate, investigate, circumnavigate.

367.11
objurgate (scold), propagate, expurgate, arrogate (claim without justification), subrogate (legal term), Watergate, homologate (ratify).

367.11.1
derogate (disparage), interrogate.

367.12
elate, delate (denounce), relate, barbellate (covered with bristles), sibilate (speak with hissing sound), flagellate, mamillate (having nipples), crenellate, depilate, oppilate (to block), correlate, vacillate, tessellate, oscillate, titillate, mutilate, cantillate (to chant), ventilate, scintillate, constellate (form into clusters), ethylate (chemistry term), methylate (chemistry term), assibilate (phonetics term), invigilate, dissimilate, assimilate, interrelate, salicylate (chemical compound), carboxylate (chemical compound).

367.12.1
jubilate, obnubilate (to darken).

367.13
tubulate (form into a tube), ambulate, peculate (embezzle), speculate, circulate, calculate, osculate (to kiss), adulate, modulate, undulate, regulate, lingulate (tongue-shaped), pullulate, ululate, emulate, formulate, cumulate, cannulate (medical term), granulate, cupulate (cup-shaped), sporulate (produce spores), insulate, capsulate (within a capsule), postulate, pustulate, ovulate.

somnambulate, perambulate, ejaculate, miscalculate, emasculate, acidulate (make slightly acid), coagulate, accu-mulate, encapsulate, congratulate, capitulate, absquatulate (decamp), expostulate.

discombobulate (throw into confusion), circumambulate, recapitulate.

367.13.1
tabulate, confabulate.

367.13.2
vermiculate (decorate with wavy markings), corniculate (having horns), matriculate, articulate, reticulate (covered with a network), gesticulate, disarticulate.

367.13.3
flocculate (form into aggregated mass), deflocculate, inoculate.

367.13.4
angulate, strangulate, triangulate.

367.13.5
simulate, stimulate, dissimulate.

367.13.6
stipulate, manipulate.

367.13.7
copulate, populate, depopulate.

367.14
collate, decollate, cucullate (hood-shaped), escalate, immolate, phenolate (disinfect), desolate, isolate, insolate (expose to sunlight), oxalate (chemical compound), faveolate (honeycombed), machicolate (fortifications term), de-escalate, cardinalate, extrapolate, interpolate.

367.14.1
violate, annihilate.

367.14.2
percolate, intercalate.

367.15
cremate, collimate (adjust optical instrument), sublimate, animate, decimate, intimate, estimate, guesstimate, legitimate, approximate, underestimate.

367.16

carbamate (chemical compound), cyclamate, diplomate (holder of a diploma), desquamate (scale off), consummate, automate, glutamate, meprobamate (tranquillizer), amalgamate.

367.17

innate, pinnate.

cachinnate (laugh loudly), machinate, echinate (covered with spines), pollinate, declinate (drooping), reclinate (bent backwards), culminate, fulminate, supinate, carinate (keel-shaped), marinate, chlorinate, fluorinate, urinate, circinate (botany term), lancinate, pepsinate (medical term), catenate (arrange in rings), Latinate, pectinate (comb-shaped), pulvinate (cushionlike), vaccinate, succinate (chemical compound), resinate.

subordinate, coordinate, originate, oxygenate, hydrogenate, desalinate, disseminate, inseminate, eliminate, recriminate, incriminate, discriminate, peregrinate, indoctrinate, hallucinate, agglutinate, deglutinate (extract gluten from), conglutinate (join together during healing), procrastinate, rejuvenate, ratiocinate (argue logically).

367.17.1

raffinate (chemistry term), decaffeinate.

367.17.2

paginate, evaginate (turn inside out), invaginate.

367.17.3

laminate, deaminate (biochemistry term), delaminate (divide into thin layers), contaminate, interlaminate, decontaminate.

367.17.4

germinate, terminate, exterminate.

367.17.5

dominate, nominate, abominate, predominate, denominate.

367.17.6

ruminate, illuminate, aluminate (chemical compound), acuminate (make pointed).

367.17.7

fascinate, deracinate (uproot), assassinate.

367.18

donate, neonate, carbonate, hibernate, cybernate (control with mechanism), hyphenate, sulphonate (chemistry term), manganate (chemical compound), ammonate (compound containing ammonia), emanate, personate (act the part of), fractionate (separate into constituents), detonate, alternate, sultanate, intonate, consternate, alienate, resonate, decarbonate, permanganate, impersonate.

367.19

constipate, emancipate.

367.19.1

dissipate, participate, anticipate.

367.20

equate, liquate (separate by melting), antiquate.

367.21

berate, cirrate (biology term), aspirate, butyrate (chemical compound).

367.22

mercurate (treat with mercury), pandurate (botany term), sulphurate, fulgurate, depurate (purify), suppurate, maturate, saturate, triturate (grind into fine powder), obturate (block up), micturate, inaugurate.

367.23

narrate, liberate, decorate, federate, moderate, underrate, perforate, biforate (having two openings), camphorate, tolerate, separate, operate, perorate, sororate (marriage custom), acerate (needle-shaped), lacerate, macerate, susurrate (make whispering sound), ulcerate, overrate, exarate (entomology term).

elaborate, collaborate, reverberate, deliberate, corroborate, redecorate, edulcorate (purify by washing), acculturate (assimilate another group's culture), confederate, desiderate (long for), preponderate, proliferate, vociferate, invigorate, exaggerate, refrigerate, decelerate, accelerate, exhilarate, commemorate, agglomerate, conglomerate, enumerate, incinerate, itinerate (travel about), exonerate, remunerate, evaporate, cooperate, incorporate, recuperate, vituperate, exasperate, incarcerate, chelicerate (spider-like animal), eviscerate, expectorate, adulterate, coelenterate, exenterate (remove by surgery), asseverate (declare emphatically), commiserate.

ameliorate, deteriorate, equiponderate (to counterbalance).

367.23.1
generate, venerate, degenerate, regenerate, intenerate (make tender).

367.23.2
iterate, reiterate, alliterate, obliterate, transliterate.

367.24
calibrate, celebrate, cerebrate, concelebrate (celebrate mass together), equilibrate, decerebrate (remove brain).

367.25
picrate (chemical compound), desecrate, consecrate, execrate, deconsecrate.

367.26
regrate (buy up anticipating profit), emigrate, immigrate, denigrate, integrate, redintegrate (make whole again), disintegrate.

367.27
citrate, arbitrate, penetrate, perpetrate, impetrate (obtain by prayer).

367.28
orchestrate, magistrate, administrate.

367.29
sensate, condensate (substance formed by condensation), compensate, insensate.

367.30
hebetate (having a blunt point), meditate, agitate, sagittate (arrow-shaped), vegetate, digitate, cogitate, imitate, capitate (headlike), crepitate (to crackle), palpitate, irritate, nictitate (to blink), gravitate, levitate, hesitate, premeditate, revegetate (grow again), regurgitate, ingurgitate (to gorge), excogitate (devise), decapitate, decrepitate (crackle on heating), precipitate, necessitate, felicitate, resuscitate.

367.30.1
militate, debilitate, habilitate (*US* equip and finance), facilitate, rehabilitate.

367.30.2
acetate, subacetate (crystalline compound), capacitate (make legally competent), incapacitate.

367.31
notate, rotate, annotate, dissertate, tête-à-tête.

367.32
dentate, edentate, bidentate, tridentate, commentate, potentate, orientate, disorientate.

367.33
gestate, testate, intestate.

367.34
costate (having ribs), prostate, apostate.

367.35
nervate (having veins), incurvate (curve inwards), innervate (supply nerves to).

367.36
salivate, elevate, titivate, motivate, activate, cultivate, captivate, aestivate, insalivate (saturate food with saliva), de-

activate, reactivate, inactivate, radioactivate.

367.37
excavate, enervate, renovate, innovate, aggravate.

367.38
await, underweight, paperweight, welterweight, counterweight, featherweight, overweight.

368 -et
ate, bet, sket (*Welsh* to splash), debt, get, jet, het, Lett, let, blet (decay in overripe fruit), met, net, pet, ret (soak textile fibre), fret, tret (commerce term), threat, set, sett (small paving slab), stet, vet, whet, wet, sweat, yet.

layette, barbette (gun platform inside parapet), maquette (sculptor's preliminary model), snackette (snack bar), moquette, coquette, coquet (behave flirtatiously), croquette, banquette, vedette, mofette (opening in volcano), Tophet (Old Testament place), baguette, beget, forget, georgette, ramjet (type of jet engine), fanjet (type of jet engine), Colette, toilette, roulette, inlet, outlet, armet (medieval helmet), Kamet (Indian mountain), roomette (*US* railway sleeping compartment), palmette (ornament resembling palm leaf), kismet, hairnet, dinette, nonet, cornett (old woodwind instrument), lunette, brunette, dragnet, fishnet, pipette, Siret (European river), fleurette (flower-shaped ornament), curet, burette, soubrette (pert girl), aigrette (long feather on hat), regret, chevrette (skin of young goat), asset, cassette, placet (vote of assent), tacet (musical term), reset, fossette (small depression in bone), poussette (country dancing figure), subset, headset, wadset (*Scot* mortgage), handset, offset, filmset, inset, onset, boneset (flowering plant), unset, sunset, typeset, upset, outset, ashet (*Dialect* dish), fléchette (missile

dropped from aircraft), brochette, fourchette (anatomy term), couchette, planchette (board for spirit messages), courgette, quartet, motet, octet, quintet, septet, sestet (six-line verse), sextet, curvet (dressage term), revet (face with stones), corvette (small escort ship), cuvette (shallow dish), quickset (type of hedge), thickset, paillette (sequin), vignette, lorgnette, noisette, rosette.

oubliette (type of dungeon), winceyette, serviette, turbojet, suffragette, superhet (radio receiver), aiguillette (ornament on military uniform), landaulet (small horse-drawn carriage), briolette (pear-shaped jewel), triolet (verse form), rondelet (type of poem), flageolet, flannelette, epaulet, mantelet, novelette, calumet (peace pipe), Antoinette, bobbinet (netted fabric), stockinet, kitchenette, midinette (Parisian salesgirl), clarinet, bassinet, satinet, martinet, alkanet (flowering plant), falconet (small falcon), lansquenet (gambling game), luncheonette (*US* café), wagonette (horse-drawn vehicle), burgonet (16th-century helmet), ballonet (gas compartment in balloon), maisonette, canzonet (short lively song), salopette, imaret (Turkish hospice for pilgrims), vinaigrette, photoset, underset (ocean undercurrent), letterset, avocet, overset (disturb), trebuchet (medieval weapon), epithet, minivet (Asian songbird), vilayet (Turkish administrative division), marquisette (type of fabric), chemisette (underbodice), anisette.

Tafilalet (Moroccan oasis), marionette.

368.1
duet, silhouette, pirouette, minuet, statuette.

368.2
Tibet, quodlibet.

368.3
abet, alphabet.

368.4
piquet (card game), briquette (brick of compressed fuel), etiquette.

368.5
cadet, Bernadette.

368.6
barrette (hair clasp), Leatherette (*Trademark*), Launderette (*Trademark*), cigarette, majorette, cellaret (compartment for wine bottles), collarette, solleret (part of armour), swimmeret (zoology term), bannerette, lanneret (large male falcon), minaret, spinneret, usherette.

368.7
beset, salicet (organ stop), scilicet (that is), videlicet (namely).

368.8
musette (type of bagpipe), crêpe suzette.

368.9
gazette, marmoset.

369 -ert
curt, skirt, chert (variety of quartz), dirt, girt, hurt, blurt, flirt, pert, spurt, quirt (whip with leather thong), squirt, cert, shirt, Sturt (English explorer), vert (former legal term), wort.

seagirt, alert, inert, unhurt, expert, milkwort (flowering plant), assert, insert, concert, outsert (printing term), Blackshirt, nightshirt, pervert, terreverte (painting pigment), divert, overt, obvert (logic term), subvert, advert, invert, convert, stitchwort, woundwort, ragwort, stonewort (green alga), pipewort, soapwort, exsert (protrude), desert, dessert, exert.

miniskirt, underskirt, malapert (saucy), inexpert, navicert (neutral ship's cargo certificate), disconcert, undershirt, reconvert, pennywort, moneywort, gipsywort, bladderwort, slipperwort, liverwort, animadvert (criticize strongly).

369.1
evert, revert, ambivert (psychology term), antevert (displace by tilting forwards).

369.2
avert, pervert, introvert, controvert, extrovert.

370 -eet
eat, beet, beat, skeet, cheat, feet, feat, heat, leet (former manorial court), leat (trench conveying water), bleat, cleat, fleet, gleet (gonorrhoeal discharge), pleat, sleet, meet, meat, mete, neat, peat, Crete, greet, treat, street, seat, cete (group of badgers), sheet, teat, wheat, sweet, suite, tweet.

browbeat, deadbeat, offbeat, drumbeat, downbeat, upbeat, heartbeat, mesquite (small tropical tree), escheat (legal term), dustsheet, effete, defeat, reheat, elite, delete, deplete, replete, complete, athlete, gamete, pigmeat, unmeet (unsuitable), forcemeat, mincemeat, sweetmeat, repeat, compete, buckwheat, terete (cylindrical and tapering), secrete, accrete, concrete, discreet, discrete, excrete, afreet (Arabian mythological monster), retreat, maltreat, entreat, estreat (legal term), mistreat, bystreet, backstreet, reseat, deceit, receipt, unseat, conceit, freesheet (free newspaper), foresheet, broadsheet, groundsheet, mainsheet (nautical term), slipsheet (printing term), petite, aesthete.

polychaete (marine worm), lorikeet (small parrot), parakeet, spirochaete (bacterium), exegete (interpreter of biblical text), superheat (heat above boiling point), overheat, obsolete, paraclete (mediator), incomplete, marguerite, Masorete (Hebrew scholar or rabbi), overeat, indiscreet, meadowsweet, bittersweet.

371 -it

it, bit, bitt (mooring post), kit, skit, chit, dit (short sound in code), fit, git, hit, lit, flit, split, slit, mitt, smit (*Dialect* infection), Schmidt, nit, knit, pit, Pitt, spit, quit, squit (*Slang* insignificant person), writ, Brit, brit (young herring), frit (glaze-making material), grit, sprit (nautical term), sit, shit, tit, wit, Whit, whit, twit.

striate, poet, debit, rarebit, obit (*short for* obituary), Cobbett (English journalist), gobbet (chunk of raw meat), orbit, sorbet, cubit, ambit, gambit, titbit, becket (nautical term), Beckett, banket (gold-bearing rock), blanket, trinket, junket, gasket, lasket (nautical term), basket, casket, flasket (long shallow basket), biscuit, brisket, frisket (printing term), bosket (thicket), musket, hatchet, ratchet, rochet (bishop's white surplice), crotchet, adit, audit, plaudit, bandit, Chindit (World War II soldier), conduit, pundit, surfeit, prophet, profit, soffit (architectural term), forfeit, buffet, tuffet (architectural term), forfeit, buffet, tuffet, nymphet, comfit, unfit, outfit, agate, garget (inflammation of cow's udder), target, legate (envoy), Reigate, nugget, drugget (floor-covering fabric), Newgate, Tlingit (American Indian), ringgit (Malaysian currency), gadget, parget (plaster or mortar), pledget (pad used in bandaging), digit, fidget, midget, Bridget, widget, budget, legit, mallet, palate, palette, sallet (15th-century helmet), valet, scarlet, starlet, varlet, playlet, raylet, murrelet (small diving bird), sterlet (small sturgeon), islet, eyelet, stylet (wire in surgical instrument), twilit, collet (claw in jewellery setting), Smollett (Scottish novelist), wallet, toilet, owlet, cullet (waste glass), gullet, mullet, tablet, cablet (small cable), gablet (small gable), driblet (small amount), triblet (spindle used in ringmaking), boblet (two-man bobsleigh), goblet, doublet, circlet, pikelet, spikelet (small grass flower), booklet, brooklet, anklet, cloudlet, leaflet, pamphlet, eaglet, piglet, singlet, camlet (tough waterproof cloth), hamlet, armlet, gimlet, omelette, veinlet, unlit, sunlit, moonlit, kinglet (small warbler), ringlet, springlet, winglet, chaplet (wreath for head), ripplet (small ripple), triplet, droplet, couplet, drupelet (small fruit), duplet (chemistry term), template, bracelet, corselet (foundation garment), flatlet, Bartlett, martlet (heraldic symbol resembling swallow), partlet (16th-century shawl), tartlet, platelet, notelet, cutlet, nutlet (part of fruit), gauntlet, wristlet (bracelet), wavelet, valvelet, Hazlitt, haslet (meat loaf), emmet (*Dialect* ant), hermit, permit, cermet (high-temperature-resistant material), climate, omit, plummet, summit, submit, admit, helmet, pelmet, transmit, Barnet, garnet, genet (catlike mammal), jennet (female donkey), rennet, senate, sennet (fanfare), sennit (braided cordage), tenet, unit, magnet, unknit, close-knit, tightknit, Capet, lappet (small hanging flap), tappet, carpet, fleapit, skippet (box for preserving document), snippet, pipit, frippet (frivolous young woman), sippet (small piece), tippet (fur cape), whippet, moppet, poppet, puppet, cockpit, chalkpit, sandpit, pulpit, armpit, limpet, crumpet, trumpet, strumpet, respite, acquit, banquet, barret (small cap), caret (symbol indicating insertion), garret, pirate, lyrate (lyre-shaped), floret, curate, turret, worrit (*Dialect* tease), secret, Sanskrit, quadrate (cube), pomfret (liquorice sweet), egret, culprit, bowsprit, portrait, basset, facet, tacit, tasset (piece of armour), tercet (three lines of verse), resit, cosset, posset, corset, Dorset, faucet, gusset, russet, dulcet, transit, lancet, Consett, sculpsit (inscription on sculpture), whatsit, freshet (sudden overflowing of river), bullshit, horseshit, bluetit, tomtit, davit (crane-like device), brevet, rivet, grivet (African monkey), privet, trivet, civet, swivet (*Dialect* state of excitement), private, covet, velvet, peewit, godwit (large shore bird), halfwit, dimwit, nitwit, outwit, exit, Tilsit (Russian town).

sobeit, howbeit, albeit, cucurbit (plant of cucumber family), post-obit (legal term), advocate, retrofit (equip with extra parts), Photofit (*Trademark*), counterfeit, discomfit, conjugate, corrugate (wrinkled), Harrogate, surrogate, quadruplet. quintuplet, sextuplet, manumit (free from slavery), decrepit, adequate, priorate (office of prior), floweret, vertebrate, hypocrite, interpret, self-portrait, non licet (unlawful), Somerset, aquavit, margravate, nimblewit (*US* clever person), thimblewit (*US* dunce).

lickety-split (*US* very quickly), predestinate (foreordained), inadequate, invertebrate, haematocrit (medical term), misinterpret, Narraganset (American Indian), affidavit, electromagnet.

371.1
brachiate (botany term), gladiate (sword-shaped), radiate (radiating), ciliate (biology term), pileate (crested), foliate, nucleate (having a nucleus), craniate (having a skull), lineate (streaked), cuneate (wedge-shaped), opiate, seriate (forming a series), fimbriate (fringed), ocreate (sheathed), prussiate (cyanide), cruciate.

chalybeate (containing iron salts), immediate, dimidiate (divided in halves), collegiate, vicariate (rank of vicar), inebriate, appropriate, repatriate, expatriate, initiate (novice), patriciate (rank of patrician), novitiate, associate, licentiate.

intermediate, unifoliate, multifoliate, multinucleate, inappropriate.

371.1.1
Juliet, aculeate (pointed).

371.1.2
aureate (gilded), laureate, baccalaureate, professoriate.

371.2
arcuate (arc-shaped), graduate, Innuit (Eskimo), sinuate (botany term), Jesuit, postgraduate, attenuate (weakened), undergraduate.

371.3
bluet (flowering plant), cruet, suet, intuit (know instinctively).

371.4
babbitt (line with alloy), habit, rabbit, drabbet (coarse yellowish-brown fabric), cohabit, inhabit.

371.5
gibbet, zibet (Asian catlike mammal), prohibit, inhibit, celibate, exhibit, flibbertigibbet.

371.6
jacket, placket (dressmaking term), packet, racquet, racket, bracket, cracket (*Dialect* three-legged stool), tacket (*Dialect* hobnail), bluejacket, straitjacket, lumberjacket, leatherjacket.

371.7
market, Newmarket, matriarchate, patriarchate, Euromarket, hypermarket, supermarket.

371.8
circuit, bifurcate, trifurcate (having three branches), microcircuit.

371.9
snicket (*Dialect* passageway), picket, cricket, pricket (young male deer), ticket, thicket, wicket, predicate, syndicate, forficate (deeply forked), delicate, silicate (chemical compound), triplicate, tunicate (marine animal), imbricate (overlapping), affricate (speech sound), intricate, corticate (having rind or bark), certificate, pontificate, indelicate, umbilicate (having a navel), divaricate (branching), Identikit (*Trademark*), sophisticate, borosilicate (chemical compound).

371.9.1
duplicate, quadruplicate, reduplicate (repeated), centuplicate.

371.10
docket, locket, pocket, rocket, brocket (small deer), crocket (architectural ornament), Crockett, sprocket, socket, pickpocket, skyrocket, retrorocket.

371.11
bucket, tucket (flourish on trumpet), trebucket (medieval weapon), gutbucket (style of jazz-playing), Nantucket.

371.12
edit, credit, coedit, subedit, accredit, discredit, disaccredit.

371.13
befit, benefit.

371.14
frigate, delegate, profligate, aggregate, congregate (assembled).

371.15
pellet, prelate, stellate, flabellate (fanshaped), appellate (relating to appeals), Marprelate (Puritan author), varicellate (marked with small ridges).

371.16
billet, skillet, fillet, millet, rillet, willet (US shore bird), flagellate (whip-like), distillate, penicillate (having tufts of hairs), verticillate (arranged in whorls).

371.17
bullet, pullet, culet (base of gemstone), tabulate (having a flat surface), undulate, virgulate (rod-shaped), ligulate (strap-shaped), angulate (having angles), ungulate, amulet, cumulate, cumulet (variety of pigeon), annulet (architectural moulding), annulate (having rings), consulate, spatulate, postulate, pustulate, rivulet, vesiculate (biology term), tuberculate (covered with nodules), pedunculate (biology term), avunculate (assigning rights to uncle), coagulate (product of coagulation).

371.17.1
sacculate (biology term), ejaculate (semen), immaculate.

371.17.2
vermiculate (relating to worms), geniculate (bending sharply), auriculate (having ears), articulate, reticulate (in form of network), testiculate (having an oval shape), unguiculate (having claws), inarticulate.

371.18
chocolate, desolate, coverlet, subulate (tapering to a point), amygdalate (relating to almonds), disconsolate, apostolate.

371.18.1
violet, inviolate, ultraviolet.

371.19
emit, limit, remit, delimit, animate, ultimate, intimate, estimate, guesstimate, proximate (nearest or next), inanimate, legitimate, penultimate, approximate, illegitimate, underestimate.

371.20
comet, grommet, vomit, Mahomet.

371.21
commit, permit, recommit, consummate, intermit (suspend activity at intervals).

371.22
Banat (plain in eastern Europe), gannet, Janet, planet, granite, Thanet, pomegranate.

371.23
burnet (flowering plant), gurnet (European marine fish), ternate (consisting of three parts), alternate.

371.24
linnet, minute, spinet, cabinet, rabbinate (office of rabbi), turbinate (scrollshaped), definite, infinite, laminate, staminate (having stamens), nominate, agminate (gathered together), basinet (medieval helmet), uncinate (hookshaped), runcinate (botany term), ob-

stinate, indefinite, effeminate, determinate, discriminate, innominate, denominate (maths term), acuminate (narrowing to sharp point), resupinate (reversed or inverted), predeterminate, indeterminate, indiscriminate.

371.24.1
ordinate, coordinate, subordinate, inordinate, incoordinate, insubordinate.

371.24.2
vaginate (having a sheath), Plantagenet, invaginate (folded back on itself).

371.25
bonnet, sonnet, bluebonnet (Scottish brimless hat), unbonnet, sunbonnet.

371.26
cornet, hornet, bicornate.

371.27
punnet, whodunit.

371.28
bayonet, dragonet (spiny-finned fish), pulmonate (having lungs), baronet, coronet, passionate, bicarbonate, diaconate (office of deacon), compassionate, dispassionate, affectionate, subalternate (botany term), Italianate, companionate.

371.28.1
fortunate, unfortunate, importunate.

371.28.2
proportionate, extortionate, disproportionate.

371.29
cygnet, signet, designate.

371.30
parapet, episcopate.

371.31
ferret, merit, serrate, terret (ring on harness), wherrit (to worry), inherit, demerit, disinherit.

371.32
cerate (hard ointment), emirate, vizierate.

371.33
skirret (plant with edible roots), spirit, aspirate, dispirit, inspirit (fill with vigour), levirate (marrying brother's widow), triumvirate.

371.34
accurate, obdurate, indurate (hardened), figurate (musical term), inaccurate, barbiturate.

371.35
federate, moderate, glomerate, numerate, separate, corporate, temperate, desperate, disparate, literate, doctorate, favourite, leveret.

deliberate, confederate, considerate, immoderate, imperforate, agglomerate, conglomerate, innumerate, degenerate, regenerate (restored), subtemperate, intemperate, commensurate, illiterate, electorate, inspectorate, directorate, protectorate, adulterate (impure).

inconsiderate, unregenerate (unrepentant), incommensurate, semiliterate.

371.35.1
tabaret (upholstery fabric), taboret (low stool), elaborate.

371.35.2
preterite, inveterate.

371.36
licit, deficit, elicit, illicit, solicit, implicit, explicit, inexplicit.

371.37
vervet (South African monkey), incurvate (curved inwards), acervate (growing in clusters), enervate (weakened).

371.38
visit, marquisate, marquessate, requisite, perquisite, exquisite, prerequisite.

371.39
closet, posit (postulate), deposit, reposit (put away).

371.40

apposite, opposite, composite, inapposite.

372 -ite

bite, byte (computer term), bight (indentation of shoreline), kite, skite (*Austral* to boast), fight, height, light, blight, flight, flite (*Scot* to scold), plight, sleight, slight, might, mite, smite, knight, night, spite, quite, rite, right, write, Wright, bright, krait (venomous snake), fright, sprite, trite, sight, cite, site, tight, Wight, white, wite (*Dialect* to blame), twite (European finch).

Shiite, fleabite, backbite, snakebite, albite (mineral), frostbite, trachyte (volcanic rock), trichite (slender crystal), Melchite (Eastern Church member), cheddite (an explosive), cordite (an explosive), Luddite, indict, graphite, psephite (type of rock), ophite (type of rock), cockfight, dogfight, sulphite (salt of sulphurous acid), bullfight, gunfight, phosphite (salt of phosphorous acid), prizefight, augite (mineral), halite (rock salt), marlite (type of marl), starlight, daylight, perlite (volcanic rock), skylight, highlight, stylite (pillar-dwelling recluse), twilight, mullite (mineral), searchlight, deadlight (nautical term), headlight, sidelight, floodlight, halflight, taillight, limelight, fanlight, sunlight, moonlight, aplite (type of rock), hoplite (ancient Greek infantryman), droplight (movable electric light), stoplight, gaslight, flashlight, streetlight, spotlight, Hamite (member of African people), samite (heavy silk fabric), Marmite (*Trademark*), Boehmite (mineral), termite, Semite, chromite (mineral), somite (embryology term), stannite (mineral), kainite (mineral), finite, crinite (covered with soft hairs), dunnite (an explosive), dunite (type of rock), Sunnite (orthodox Muslim), unite, stibnite (mineral), weeknight, ichnite (fos-

silized footprint), midnight, good-night, Samnite (ancient Italian), fortnight, despite, requite, playwright, ferrite, pyrite (mineral), chlorite (mineral), norite (type of rock), thorite (mineral), eyebright (flowering plant), Arkwright, dendrite, chondrite (meteorite), nephrite (mineral), tephrite (type of basalt), affright, wheelwright, millwright, alright, wainwright, downright, shipwright, typewrite, upright, cuprite (mineral), Cartwright, outright, contrite, ghostwrite, birthright, forthright, eyesight, foresight, leucite (mineral), hindsight, calcite (mineral), felsite (type of rock), bombsight, insight, incite, quartzite (type of rock), kunzite (gemstone), ratite (flightless bird), partite (divided), airtight, sticktight (plant having barbed fruit), skintight, uptight, proustite (mineral), troostite (mineral), gnathite (zoology term), Levite, cleveite (mineral), sylvite (mineral), invite, bobwhite (US quail), lintwhite (*Scot* linnet), excite, bauxite.

Trotskyite, Karaite (member of Jewish sect), Moabite, coenobite (member of religious order), Jacobite, Rechabite (teetotaller), trilobite, malachite (mineral), blatherskite (foolish talkative person), erudite, recondite (abstruse), heulandite (mineral), pentlandite (mineral), Wycliffite, epiphyte (plant growing on another), geophyte (botany term), neophyte (novice), bryophyte (botany term), cryophyte (plant growing on snow), eclogite (type of rock), Fahrenheit, apartheid, spherulite (crystalline mass in rock), nummulite (fossil), granulite, lazulite, overflight, candlelight, eremite (Christian hermit), Adamite (member of nudist sect), sodomite, calamite (extinct treelike plant), dolomite, dynamite, wolframite (mineral), hellgrammite (US insect larva), catamite, stalagmite, alunite (mineral), disunite, reunite, belemnite, copyright, azurite (gemstone), lazurite (lapis lazuli), achondrite (meteorite), erythrite (mineral), second-sight, bipartite, tripartite, stalactite, transvestite, celestite (mineral), Muscovite, moldavite (natural green glass), Hepplewhite, andesite (volcanic rock), adamsite (poisonous crystalline solid), martensite (metallurgy term).

osteophyte (small bony outgrowth), annabergite (mineral), heteroclite (irregularly formed word), archimandrite (Greek Orthodox monastery head), alexandrite (gemstone), multipartite.

anthropophagite (cannibal), itacolumite (type of sandstone).

372.1
lyddite (an explosive), expedite.

372.2
troglodyte, andradite (gemstone), extradite, hermaphrodite.

372.3
delight, phyllite (type of rock), rubellite (gemstone), tachylyte (black glassy basalt), triphylite (mineral), argillite (type of rock), propylite (geology term), proselyte, apophyllite (mineral), toxophilite (archer), pyrophyllite (mineral), Mutazilite (8th-century liberal Muslim).

372.4
alight, polite.

hyalite (variety of opal), rhyolite (type of rock), cryolite (mineral), zeolite (mineral), oolite (sedimentary rock), kimberlite (rock often containing diamonds), acolyte, Bakelite (*Trademark*), niccolite (mineral), sodalite (mineral), stylolite (geology term), Carmelite, phonolite (volcanic rock), scapolite (mineral), impolite, corallite (fossil coral), uralite (mineral), microlight, coprolite, natrolite (mineral), chrysolite (gemstone), socialite, quarterlight, tantalite (mineral), graptolite (fossil), crystallite (minute crystal in rock).

variolite (type of rock), Israelite, metabolite (substance produced in metabolism), amphibolite (type of rock), lepidolite (mineral), crocidolite (variety of asbestos), theodolite, Pre-Raphaelite, electrolyte, chiastolite (mineral), topazolite (variety of garnet).

372.4.1
satellite, stromatolite (type of rock).

372.5
pinite (mineral), melinite (an explosive), selenite (variety of gypsum), ilmenite (mineral), encrinite (fossil), retinite (resin), nephelinite (type of rock), kaolinite (mineral), gadolinite (mineral), uraninite (mineral).

372.6
tonight, syenite (type of rock), cyanite (mineral), urbanite (*US* city dweller), aconite (poisonous plant), taconite (type of rock), vulcanite (hard rubber), rhodonite (mineral), wulfenite (mineral), morganite (gemstone), melanite (black variety of garnet), ammonite, limonite (mineral), Canaanite, arenite (sandstone), Maronite (Syrian Christian), uranite (mineral), smithsonite (mineral), autunite (mineral), bentonite (clay), austenite (metallurgy term), overnight, sylvanite (mineral), monzonite (type of rock), Midianite, strontianite (mineral), suburbanite, amazonite (gemstone).

372.7
ignite, lignite, gelignite.

372.8
aright, Labourite, sybarite, anchorite, siderite (mineral), underwrite, phosphorite (mineral), margarite (mineral), dolerite (type of rock), tenorite (mineral), Minorite (Franciscan friar), laterite (clay), overwrite, Nazarite (Old Testament ascetic), kieserite (mineral), geyserite (mineral), cordierite (mineral), garnierite (mineral), meteorite, ozocerite (wax), grossularite (gemstone), evaporite (type of rock).

372.9

recite, lewisite (poisonous liquid), plebiscite, scolecite (mineral), magnesite (mineral), variscite (mineral).

372.10

oocyte (immature female germ cell), marcasite, leucocyte, chalcocite (mineral), lymphocyte (type of blood cell), kamacite (iron–nickel alloy), haemocyte (any blood cell), jarosite (mineral), parasite, macrocyte (large red blood cell), microcyte (small red blood cell), anthracite, outasight, oversight, erythrocyte, spermatocyte (immature male germ cell), anorthosite (type of rock).

372.11

Hittite, mimetite (mineral), granitite (type of granite), magnetite (mineral), appetite.

372.12

steatite (variety of talc), biotite (dark-coloured mica), albertite (variety of bitumen), haematite (mineral), apatite (mineral), pyrrhotite (mineral), spessartite (variety of garnet), watertight, goniatite (fossil), peridotite (type of rock).

373 -ot

bot (larva of botfly), cot, Scot, Scott, dot, phot (unit of illumination), got, jot, hot, lot, blot, clot, plot, slot, motte, knot, not, snot, pot, spot, squat, rot, grot (grotto), trot, sot, shott (salt lake in desert), shot, tot, stot (*Scot* to bounce), what, watt, swot, swat, yacht.

robot, boycott, cocotte, dovecot, begot, forgot, inkblot, feedlot (place for fattening livestock), diglot (bilingual), subplot, motmot (tropical bird), cannot, bowknot (decorative knot), slipknot, topknot, whatnot, repot, teapot, jackpot, crackpot, stockpot, stinkpot, hotchpot (legal term), tinpot, despot, tosspot, fusspot, sunspot, nightspot,

cachepot (container for flowerpot), dashpot (mechanism for damping vibration), hotpot, sexpot, Pequot (American Indian), loquat (Oriental fruit tree), kumquat, garotte, dogtrot (gentle trot), foxtrot, earshot, eyeshot, bowshot, buckshot, bloodshot, gunshot, moonshot, slingshot (*US* catapult), slapshot (ice hockey shot), snapshot, grapeshot, upshot, gavotte, abwatt (electrical unit), somewhat.

Candiot (Cretan), carrycot, apricot, massicot (mineral), Sialkot (Pakistani city), peridot (gemstone), microdot, Wyandotte (breed of domestic fowl), Huhehot (Chinese town), melilot (flowering plant), Camelot, ocelot, sans-culotte, polyglot, underplot (subsidiary plot in story), counterplot, guillemot, bergamot, Arbuthnot, monkeypot (tropical tree), coffeepot, gallipot (earthenware pot for ointments), galipot (pine resin), talipot (palm tree), chimneypot, flowerpot, aliquot (maths term), Paraquat (*Trademark*), tommyrot, Aldershot, undershot, overshot, Hottentot, kilowatt, megawatt, forget-me-not.

373.1

allot, calotte (Catholic priest's skullcap), shallot, cachalot (sperm whale), eschalot (shallot).

374 -ort

ought, aught, bought, bort (inferior diamond), caught, court, fought, fort, mort (call on hunting horn), nought, naught, snort, port, sport, quart, rort (*Austral* noisy party), wrought, brought, fraught, sought, sort, short, tort, taut, taught, torte (rich cake), thought, wart, thwart.

abort, forecourt, escort, hillfort, cohort, onslaught, fearnought (heavy woollen fabric), Connaught, dreadnought, carport, purport, airport, seaport, Newport, Stockport, Coalport, import, comport, passport, spaceport, disport (enjoy oneself), Gosport, spoilsport, transport, jetport, outport, Southport, export, inwrought (woven into material), distraught, re-sort, assort, consort, retort, self-taught, untaught, contort, bistort (Eurasian plant), distort, extort, methought, forethought, cavort, athwart, resort, exhort.

Agincourt, Argonaut, juggernaut, cosmonaut, aquanaut, aeronaut, astronaut, reimport, davenport, re-export, overwrought, ultrashort (having very short wavelength), aforethought, afterthought, worrywart (habitual worrier).

374.1
deport, report, heliport, misreport.

374.2
support, hoverport.

375 -oit
coit (*Austral* buttocks), quoit, doit (former Dutch coin), droit, dacoit (armed robber), exploit, adroit, Detroit, maladroit, Massasoit (American Indian chief).

376 -oat
oat, boat, coat, cote, dote, goat, bloat, float, gloat, ploat (*Dialect* thrash), mote, moat, smote, note, quote, rote, wrote, groat, troat (to bellow), throat, shoat (recently-weaned piglet), tote, stoat, vote.

rowboat, showboat, speedboat, lifeboat, whaleboat, steamboat, gunboat, swingboat, longboat, houseboat, surcoat (medieval knight's tunic), redcoat, Rajkot (Indian city), raincoat, turncoat, sheepcote, topcoat, waistcoat, housecoat, greatcoat, dovecote, zygote (fertilized egg cell), afloat, bobfloat (small fishing float), emote, demote, gemot (Anglo-Saxon legal assembly), remote, promote, keynote, denote, connote, woodnote (natural song), footnote, capote (long hooded cloak), com-

pote, unquote, misquote, bluethroat (songbird), whitethroat (songbird), cutthroat, devote, outvote.

powerboat, motorboat, petticoat, undercoat, overcoat, epidote (mineral), lepidote (covered with scaly leaves), antidote, anecdote, table d'hôte, redingote (overcoat), pardalote (Australian songbird), Fomalhaut (star), papillote (paper frill around cutlet), matelote (fish with wine sauce), underquote, creosote, asymptote.

377 -out
out, owt, bout, scout, doubt, gout, lout, clout, flout, nowt, knout (strong whip), snout, pout, spout, rout, drought, grout, sprout, trout, shout, tout, stout.

throughout, blackout, stakeout (*US* police surveillance), lockout, knockout, cookout (*US* barbecue), lookout, redoubt, dugout, mahout (elephant keeper), fallout, ablaut (linguistics term), breechclout (loincloth), umlaut, amaut (Eskimo woman's hood), rainout (radioactive fall-out), brownout (*US* power reduction), dropout, eelpout (marine fish), downspout, without, devout.

waterspout, sauerkraut.

377.1
about, layabout, walkabout, gadabout, roundabout, turnabout, runabout.

378 -ut
butt, but, cut, scut, phut, gut, jut, hut, glut, slut, mutt, smut, nut, putt, rut, strut, shut, tut.

rebut, abut, hackbut (long-barrelled gun), blackbutt (eucalyptus tree), sackbut, haircut, woodcut, uncut, crosscut, foregut, midgut, hindgut, catgut, rotgut, englut (devour ravenously), peanut, doughnut, cobnut, beechnut, groundnut, gallnut (plant gall), walnut, chestnut, half-shut.

scuttlebutt (ship's drinking fountain), Calicut (Indian port), linocut, uppercut, coconut, bladdernut (European shrub), bitternut, butternut, candlenut, hazelnut, sinciput (part of skull), occiput.

379 -oot

foot, put, soot, barefoot, crowfoot (flowering plant), webfoot, Blackfoot (American Indian), finfoot (aquatic bird), goosefoot (weedy plant), coltsfoot (European plant), flatfoot, hotfoot, outfoot (sail faster than), cocksfoot (Eurasian grass), kaput, throughput, Rajput (Hindu military caste member), input, output, pussyfoot, Dasht-i-Lut (Iranian desert plateau), autoput (Yugoslavian motorway), cajuput (Australian shrub).

379.1

afoot, tenderfoot, underfoot.

380 -ute

boot, coot, scoot, jute, hoot, lute, loot, flute, sloot (South African irrigation ditch), moot, snoot (*Slang* nose), root, route, brute, brut, bruit (*US* to report), croute (small piece of toast), fruit, suit, chute, shoot, toot, Ute (American Indian), Bute, beaut, butte (steep-sided hill), cute, scute (zoology term), mute, newt.

freeboot, crowboot (Eskimo boot), jackboot, elute (chemistry term), dilute, Hakluyt (English geographer), folkmoot (medieval district assembly), Beirut, cheroot, snakeroot (US plant), recruit, redroot (bog plant), breadroot (US plant), jackfruit (Asian fruit tree), breadfruit, grapefruit, enroot, en route, unroot, taproot, uproot, beetroot, birthroot (US plant), playsuit, lawsuit, tracksuit, swimsuit, sunsuit, spacesuit, pantsuit, offshoot, outshoot, refute, confute, Salyut, solute, volute, commute, permute, deafmute, transmute, minute, cornute (hornlike), Canute, im-

pute, compute, dispute, Asyut (ancient Egyptian city), hirsute, pursuit, statute, astute.

overboot (protective boot), bandicoot, malamute (Eskimo dog), puttyroot (US orchid), briarroot (wood for tobacco pipes), arrowroot, crinkleroot (flowering plant), coralroot (leafless orchid), Hatshepsut (ancient Egyptian queen), undershoot, parachute, overshoot, persecute, prosecute, execute, comminute (reduce to small fragments).

380.1

galoot (*US* clumsy person), pollute, salute, dissolute, absolute, consolute (chemistry term), evolute (geometric curve), revolute (botany term), involute (intricate), convolute, resolute, irresolute.

380.2

tribute, attribute, contribute, distribute.

380.3

acute, subacute (medical term), electrocute.

380.4

depute, repute, disrepute.

380.5

destitute, prostitute, substitute, institute, constitute, reconstitute.

381 -'t

Fiat (*Trademark*), Stuart, abbot, burbot (freshwater fish), Herbert, sherbet, turbot, nobbut (*Dialect* nothing but), Robert, Schubert, Egbert, Albert, Talbot, filbert, Gilbert, Lambert, Cuthbert, Urquhart, ducat, Alcott, Ascot, mascot, wainscot, effort, Beaufort, Frankfurt, comfort, faggot, maggot, braggart, ergot (crop disease), bigot, Piggott, spigot (cask stopper), boggart (*Dialect* poltergeist), yogurt, ingot, ballot, harlot, Charlotte, Helot (serf), zealot, pilot, Pilate, gamut, marmot, Connacht (Northern Irish province), donnert (*Scot* stunned), caput, Rupert, carat, carrot, claret, parrot, divot, pivot, covert, lovat (colour mixture in tweeds), culvert, stalwart, Quixote, desert.

halibut, Port Talbot, Ethelbert, discomfort, copilot, electret (material with electrical properties), discovert (legal term).

Connecticut, autopilot.

381.1
idiot, galiot (small galley), Eliot, heriot (medieval death duty), Cypriot, patriot, Cheviot, soviet, exeat, compatriot, commissariat, proletariat, secretariat.

381.1.1
chariot, lariat, Marryat, Iscariot.

381.2
diet, fiat (official permission), quiet, ryot (Indian peasant), riot, Wyatt, unquiet, disquiet.

382 -act [also **32** + *-ed*]
act, fact, pact, bract, tract, tact, swacked (*Slang* intoxicated).

react, hunchbacked, unbacked, humpbacked, redact (prepare for publication), enact, impact, compact, infract (violate), detract, retract, attract, protract, subtract, entr'acte, contract, distract, abstract, extract, intact, contact, exact, transact.

abreact (psychology term), retroact, artefact, re-enact, underact, tesseract (four-dimensional figure), cataract, interact, counteract, overact, precontract, subcontract, inexact.

overreact, autodidact (self-taught person).

382.1
diffract, refract, Pontefract.

383 -arct [also **33** + *-ed*]
gedact (organ pipe), infarct (dead tissue), unmarked.

384 -aked [also **34** + *-ed*]
half-baked, unslaked.

385 -ect [also **35** + *-ed*]
sect, unchecked, pandect (comprehensive treatise), defect, prefect, infect, confect (prepare by combining ingredients), eject, deject, reject, project, abject, object, subject, inject, disject (break apart), collect, deflect, reflect, inflect, neglect, connect, landsknecht (mercenary foot soldier), henpecked, aspect, respect, prospect, suspect, inspect, expect, erect, direct, bisect, trisect, transect, insect, protect, obtect (entomology term), exsect (to cut out).

disinfect, genuflect, disconnect, self-respect, disrespect, retrospect, introspect, circumspect, indirect, misdirect, intersect.

interconnect, overprotect.

385.1
effect, defect, aftereffect.

385.2
affect, perfect, disaffect.

385.3
project, traject (to transport), retroject (throw backwards), introject (psychology term), interject.

385.4
elect, prelect (to lecture), select, intellect.

385.5
collect, dialect, recollect, idiolect (individual's language).

385.6
correct, incorrect, resurrect.

385.7
dissect, resect (remove surgically), quadrisect, vivisect.

385.8
detect, architect.

386 -eeked [also **37** + *-ed*]
beaked, peaked, streaked.

387 -ict [also **38** + *-ed*]
Pict, strict, addict, verdict, edict, predict, perfect, object, subject, relict, afflict, inflict, conflict, depict, district, restrict, constrict, evict, convict, maledict (utter a curse), Benedict, pluperfect, imperfect, derelict, apomict (organism produced asexually), derestrict.

387.1
addict, contradict, interdict.

388 -oct [also **40** + *-ed*]
decoct (extract by boiling), concoct, landlocked, unlocked, ectoproct (aquatic animal).

389 -uct [also **43** + *-ed*]
duct, educt (chemistry term), deduct, product, abduct, subduct (draw downwards), induct, conduct, eruct (to belch), destruct, obstruct, instruct, construct, aqueduct, oviduct, viaduct, misconduct, usufruct, superstruct (build on another structure), reconstruct.

390 -ooked [also **44** + *-ed*]
hooked, uncooked.

391 -anct [also **51** + *-ed*]
unthanked, sacrosanct.

392 -inct [also **52** + *-ed*]
tinct (tinted), precinct, distinct, instinct, extinct, succinct, indistinct.

393 -unct [also **54** + *-ed*]
defunct, adjunct, conjunct.

394 -asked [also **56** + *-ed*]
masked, unasked.

395 -atched [also **62** + *-ed*]
well-matched, detached, unscratched, unattached, semidetached.

396 -aft [also **158** + *-ed*]
aft, daft, haft (knife handle), raft, craft, kraft (strong wrapping-paper), draught, draft, graft, shaft, waft.

abaft, aircraft, witchcraft, woodcraft, handcraft, stagecraft, spacecraft, statecraft, redraft, engraft, jackshaft (shaft transmitting engine power), crankshaft, camshaft.

handicraft, hovercraft, needlecraft, overdraft, homograft, autograft, aftershaft (type of feather), countershaft (intermediate shaft in mechanism), understaffed, overstaffed.

anti-aircraft, heterograft.

397 -eft
eft, deft, heft (assess weight of), left, cleft, klepht (Greek brigand), theft, weft, bereft.

398 -ift [also **163** + *-ed*]
gift, lift, rift, drift, shrift, thrift, sift, shift, swift, airlift, uplift, festschrift (commemorative collection of writings), snowdrift, adrift, spindrift (sea spray), spendthrift, gearshift, makeshift.

399 -oft [also **165** + *-ed*]
oft, loft, croft, soft, toft (homestead), aloft, cockloft, Ashcroft, Lowestoft, undercroft (underground chamber).

400 -uft [also **168** + *-ed*]
chuffed, tuft, stuffed, candytuft (flowering plant).

401 -alt
alt (high in pitch), shalt, asphalt, gestalt (overall structure).

402 -elt
belt, Celt, kelt (recently spawned salmon), dealt, felt, gelt (*Slang* money), melt, smelt, knelt, pelt, spelt, celt (ancient axe-like instrument), Scheldt (Eu-

ropean river), veldt, svelte, welt, dwelt, unbelt, backveld (remote rural area), heartfelt, Danegelt, jacksmelt (marine fish), underfelt, Tafilelt (largest oasis in Sahara), Roosevelt.

403 -ilt
built, kilt, guilt, gilt, jilt, hilt, lilt, milt, spilt, quilt, silt, tilt, stilt, wilt, rebuilt, well-built, atilt (tilted), uptilt, Vanderbilt.

404 -orlt
Balt (person from Baltic States), fault, halt, malt, smalt (dark blue glass), salt, vault, cobalt, default, stringhalt (veterinary science term), basalt, persalt (chemical compound), exalt, oxysalt (chemical compound).

404.1
assault, somersault.

405 -oalt
bolt, Boult, colt, dolt, jolt, holt (woodland), moult, smolt (young salmon), poult (young domestic fowl), volt, Humboldt, unbolt, kingbolt (steering bolt on carriage), ringbolt (bolt with ring attached), fishbolt (bolt in railway track), revolt, abvolt (electrical unit), thunderbolt, kilovolt, electronvolt.

406 -ult
cult, occult, adult, indult (Catholic dispensation), tumult, penult (penultimate syllable), insult, consult, result, exult, difficult, catapult, jurisconsult.

407 -ant
ant, bant (*Dialect* string), Kant, cant, scant, pant, rant, Brabant (Belgian province), decant, recant, descant, gallant, Rembrandt, enceinte (enclosure), extant, confidant, commandant, sycophant, hierophant (ancient Greek high priest).

407.1
levant (patterned leather), gallivant.

408 -arnt
aunt, aren't, can't, chant, plant, slant, grant, shan't, plainchant, enchant, supplant, eggplant, implant, transplant, ashplant, waxplant (flowering plant), explant (biology term), aslant, courante (musical term), détente, disenchant, debutante.

409 -aint
ain't, feint, faint, plaint (legal term), paint, quaint, saint, taint, complaint, repaint, greasepaint, acquaint, distraint (legal term), restraint, constraint.

410 -ent
bent, Kent, dent, Ghent, gent, lent, leant, Lent, meant, pent, spent, rent, Brent, brent (small goose), Trent, cent, sent, scent, tent, vent, went, Gwent.

hellbent, unbent, indent, relent, ament (mentally deficient person), fragment, comment, torment, loment (plant pod), augment, unmeant, anent (*Scot* concerning), repent, well-spent, frequent, besprent (sprinkled over), descent, dissent, docent (US lecturer), assent, ascent, per cent, absent, consent, detent (locking device in machine), portent, intent, content, extent, sirvente (Provençal verse form), advent, invent, forwent, forewent, accent.

orient, document, overspent, malcontent, discontent, circumvent, underwent, disorient.

410.1
dement, cement, regiment, aliment, supplement, implement, complement, compliment, experiment, fibrocement.

410.2
foment, ferment, lament, ornament.

410.3
event, prevent, nonevent.

410.4
resent, present, represent, re-present, misrepresent.

411 -ernt

burnt, learnt, weren't, mowburnt (agricultural term), sunburnt, unlearnt.

412 -int

bint (*Slang* girl), skint, dint, hint, lint, flint, Flint, glint, splint, mint, squint, print, sprint, tint, stint.

suint (substance in sheep's wool), skinflint, gunflint, varmint, spearmint, horsemint (European plant), catmint, asquint (glancing furtively), surprint (overprint), reprint, blueprint, woodprint (print from woodcut), offprint (separate reprint of article), imprint, thumbprint, misprint, voiceprint, footprint, newsprint.

calamint (Eurasian plant), peppermint, microprint, fingerprint, mezzotint, undertint (delicate tint), monotint (painting technique), aquatint (copperetching technique), Septuagint.

413 -ynt

pint, cuckoopint.

414 -ont

font, pont (South African river ferry), quant (pole used for punting), want, diplont (biology term), Vermont, Beaumont, piedmont (at foot of mountain), Piedmont (region of Italy), Egmont, schizont (zoology term), symbiont, Negropont (Greek island), Hellespont, halobiont (salt-water organism), Dandie Dinmont.

415 -ornt

daunt, gaunt, jaunt, haunt, flaunt, taunt, vaunt, Broederbond (South African secret society).

416 -oint

joint, point, adjoint (maths term), conjoint, disjoint, anoint, repoint, pourpoint (medieval doublet), viewpoint, breakpoint, checkpoint, knickpoint (break in river profile), midpoint,

standpoint, ballpoint, pinpoint, gunpoint, outpoint (nautical term), needlepoint.

416.1

appoint, disappoint, counterpoint, silverpoint (drawing technique).

417 -oant

don't, wont, won't.

418 -ount

count, fount, mount, re-count, recount, viscount, account, discount, miscount, surmount, demount (remove from mounting), seamount (underwater mountain), dismount.

418.1

amount, paramount, catamount (feline animal), tantamount.

419 -unt

bunt, cunt, dunt (*Dialect* a blow), hunt, blunt, punt, runt, brunt, front, grunt, shunt, stunt, manhunt, seafront, forefront, breakfront (having projecting central section), confront, exeunt.

419.1

affront, waterfront.

420 -'nt [further rhymes may be created by adding -ment to appropriate verbs]

mayn't, lambent, bacchant (drunken reveller), vacant, clinquant (tinsel), etchant (acid used for etching), merchant, couchant (heraldic term), trenchant, hadn't, cadent (rhythmic), pedant, verdant, trident, strident, rodent, scandent (climbing), infant, pageant, argent (silver), sergeant, Sargent, agent, regent, sejant (heraldic term), cogent, pungent, sealant, silent, Solent, volant (heraldic term), coolant, ament (catkin), garment, clement, moment, parchment, oddment, fragment, segment, figment, pigment, lodgment, judgment, scarcement (ledge in wall), treatment, vestment, pavement, stagnant, regnant (prevalent), pregnant, remnant, serpent, dopant (chemistry term), rampant, parent, spirant (phonetics term), tyrant, vibrant, hydrant, quadrant, flagrant, fragrant, vagrant, migrant, titrant (chemistry term), entrant, nascent, absent, quotient, Ushant (French island), ancient, potent, octant (eighth part of circle), saltant (biology term), instant, constant, sextant, Havant, haven't, savant, solvent, convent, Derwent, unguent, valiant, brilliant, poignant, hasn't, wisent (European bison), isn't, wasn't.

absorbent, adsorbent, decumbent (lying flat), recumbent, incumbent, impeccant (free from sin), decadent, elephant, triumphant, reagent, newsagent, sibilant, jubilant, flagellant, vigilant, sterilant, pestilent, inclement, deferment, preferment, interment, agreement, requirement, retirement, endowment, embankment, impeachment, enrichment, debouchment (outlet), embranchment, retrenchment, entrenchment, bombardment, débridement (removal of dead tissue), commandment, amendment, intendment (legal term), secondment, enlargement, engagement, infringement, concealment, fulfilment, instalment, enrolment, annulment, enjambment (poetry term), adjournment, discernment, internment, refinement, confinement, alignment, assignment, consignment, adornment, postponement, atonement, escarpment, escapement, encampment, impressment (conscription into government service), assessment, enticement, inducement, advancement, commencement, announcement, pronouncement, refreshment, department, apartment, compartment, revetment (protective facing of stones), maltreatment, indictment, incitement, excitement, allotment, ballottement (medical term), deportment, comportment, assortment, abutment,

recruitment, enactment, enchantment, contentment, resentment, presentment, investment, adjustment, achievement, bereavement, amazement, appeasement, chastisement, amusement, complainant, alternant, indignant, malignant, benignant, repugnant, oppugnant, discrepant, occupant, erumpent (bursting out), delinquent, godparent, grandparent, step-parent, aspirant, figurant, fulgurant, celebrant, emigrant, immigrant, transmigrant, integrant (part of a whole), re-entrant, registrant (person who registers trademark), ministrant, remonstrant, renascent, adjacent, subjacent (forming a foundation), complacent, innocent, dissentient, presentient, consentient (being in agreement), excitant, important, prepotent (greater in power), reactant, surfactant, attractant, reluctant, consultant, resultant, exultant, repentant, accountant, acceptant, inconstant, relevant, pursuivant, connivent, adjuvant (helping), insolvent, dissolvent, resolvent, emollient, ebullient, complaisant, cognizant, recusant (insubordinate).

equipollent (equal in effect), undergarment, overgarment, disagreement, disengagement, development, divertissement, advertisement, disenchantment, maladjustment, misdemeanant, inadvertent, unimportant, idempotent (maths term), executant, irrelevant, incognizant, redevelopment.

420.1
ambient, radiant, gradient, salient, suppliant, fainéant, sapient, variant, orient, miscreant, nutrient, transeunt (philosophy term), sentient, deviant, transient.

resilient, defoliant, recipient, percipient, incipient, excipient (medical term), invariant (maths term), aperient, inebriant, omniscient, insouciant, officiant, negotiant, assentient (approving), insentient, subservient, asphyxiant.

420 -'nt

420.1.1
mediant, obedient, submediant (musical term), expedient, ingredient, disobedient, inexpedient.

420.1.2
lenient, prevenient (preceding), convenient, inconvenient.

420.1.3
prurient, esurient (greedy), parturient (relating to childbirth), luxuriant.

420.2
giant, client, pliant, defiant, affiant (US legal term), reliant, compliant, eobiont (biology term), supergiant, incompliant.

420.3
buoyant, flamboyant, foudroyant (sudden and severe), chatoyant (changing in lustre), clairvoyant.

420.4
affluent, effluent, profluent (flowing smoothly), influent (flowing in), confluent, congruent, obstruent (causing obstruction), diluent, issuant, fluctuant, interfluent (flowing together), evacuant (promoting bowel evacuation), attenuant, continuant, substituent, constituent.

420.5
fluent, truant, eluent (chemistry term), pursuant.

420.6
piquant, secant, cosecant.

420.7
predicant (relating to preaching), mendicant, indicant, applicant, supplicant, lubricant, desiccant, vesicant (blistering substance), toxicant (a poison), significant, communicant, intoxicant, insignificant.

420.8
ardent, guardant (heraldic term), regardant (heraldic term), retardant.

420.9
needn't, credent, decedent (deceased person), antecedent.

420.10
didn't, diffident, confident, precedent, dissident, incident, evident, provident, accident, oxidant, occident, self-confident, coincident, improvident, overconfident, antioxidant.

420.10.1
resident, president, nonresident.

420.11
mordant, mordent (melodic ornament), accordant, concordant, discordant.

420.12
couldn't, shouldn't, wouldn't, impudent.

420.13
prudent, student, imprudent, jurisprudent.

420.14
pendant, pendent (dangling), defendant, resplendent, dependant, dependent, appendant (attached), descendant, ascendant, transcendent, attendant, intendant (provincial official), independent, interdependent, superintendent.

420.15
fondant, despondent, respondent (legal term), correspondent, co-respondent.

420.16
abundant, redundant, superabundant.

420.17
elegant, fumigant, congregant, litigant, inelegant.

420.18
termagant, arrogant, extravagant.

420.19
urgent, emergent, resurgent, assurgent (curving upwards), insurgent, detergent, abstergent (cleansing), divergent, convergent.

420.20
indigent, diligent, negligent, exigent (urgent), intelligent, intransigent, unintelligent.

420.21
fulgent (resplendent), indulgent, effulgent (radiant), refulgent (shining), self-indulgent.

420.22
plangent (resonant or plaintive), tangent, cotangent, subtangent.

420.23
ringent (botany term), stringent, refringent (refractive), astringent, contingent.

420.24
gallant, talent, topgallant (ship's mast).

420.25
inhalant, exhalant (emitting a vapour), assailant, bivalent, divalent, trivalent, polyvalent, univalent, monovalent.

420.26
repellent, appellant (person who appeals), propellant, expellant, interpellant (interrupting with question).

420.27
virulent, purulent, turbulent, ambulant, feculent (filthy), flocculent (fleecy), truculent, succulent, esculent (edible), osculant (biology term), fraudulent, undulant, tremulant, simulant, stimulant, crapulent, opulent, corpulent, flatulent, petulant, postulant, pustulant, pulverulent (consisting of dust), avirulent, coagulant, puberulent (covered with down), anticoagulant.

420.28
violent, libellant, redolent, indolent, somnolent, insolent, nonchalant, excellent, nonviolent, sanguinolent (containing blood), equivalent.

420.28.1
prevalent, malevolent, benevolent.

420.29
claimant, clamant (noisy), payment, raiment, repayment.

420.30
cerement (burial clothes), endearment.

420.31
vehement, rudiment, condiment, regiment, aliment, element, supplement, implement, compliment, complement, liniment, muniment, orpiment (mineral), diriment (invalidating), worriment, decrement (diminution), recrement (waste matter), increment, excrement, detriment, nutriment, sentiment, embodiment, habiliment (dress), dissepiment (dividing membrane), presentiment, accompaniment.

420.31.1
pediment, sediment, impediment.

420.31.2
merriment, experiment.

420.32
dormant, informant.

420.33
enjoyment, deployment, employment, redeployment, unemployment.

420.34
document, argument, monument, integument (outer protective layer), emolument.

420.35
adamant, fundament (buttocks), wonderment, parliament, filament, armament, firmament, tenement, ornament, tournament, parament (ecclesiastical vestment), sacrament, instrument, measurement, betterment, testament, lineament, medicament, predicament, bewilderment, disarmament, temperament, arbitrament, accoutrement, hereditament (legal term).

420.35.1
ligament, disfigurement.

420.36
catchment, hatchment (heraldic term), detachment, attachment.

420.37
management, abridgment, acknowledgment, disparagement, encouragement, discouragement.

420.38
derangement, arrangement, estrangement, rearrangement.

420.39
ailment, bailment (legal term), derailment, curtailment.

420.40
battlement, settlement, devilment, puzzlement, entablement (platform supporting statue), entanglement, accouplement (supporting beam), entitlement, embezzlement.

420.41
attainment, containment, entertainment.

420.42
government, abandonment, environment, apportionment, enlightenment, imprisonment.

420.43
shipment, equipment.

420.44
basement, casement, placement, subbasement, replacement, emplacement, displacement.

420.45
endorsement, enforcement, reinforcement.

420.46
harassment, embarrassment.

420.47
garnishment (legal notice), punishment, nourishment, embellishment, establishment, accomplishment, astonishment.

420.48
statement, abatement, affreightment (contract hiring cargo ship), understatement, reinstatement.

420.49
fitment, commitment.

420.50
ointment, anointment, appointment, disappointment.

420.51
movement, improvement.

420.52
pennant, tenant, cotenant, subtenant, lieutenant, sublieutenant.

420.53
eminent, imminent, culminant, fulminant (sudden and violent), urinant (heraldic term), pertinent, continent, revenant, disciplinant (member of Catholic sect), pre-eminent, appurtenant, impertinent, conglutinant (adhesive), subcontinent, incontinent.

420.53.1
germinant, determinant.

420.53.2
dominant, prominent, predominant, subdominant.

420.53.3
ruminant, illuminant.

420.54
sonant (phonetics term), deponent (linguistics term), opponent, proponent, imponent (person imposing a duty), component, exponent.

420.55
permanent, immanent (existing within), assonant, dissonant, consonant, covenant, resonant, impermanent, inconsonant.

420.56
flippant, participant, anticipant.

420.57
frequent, sequent, infrequent.

420.58
aliquant (maths term), subsequent, consequent, inconsequent.

420.59
eloquent, ineloquent, grandiloquent, magniloquent (lofty in style).

420.60
arrant, apparent, transparent.

420.61
errant, gerent (ruler or manager), aberrant, vicegerent, deterrent.

420.62
coherent, adherent, inherent, incoherent.

420.63
torrent, warrant, abhorrent.

420.64
currant, current, decurrent (botany term), recurrent, blackcurrant, redcurrant, incurrent (flowing inwards), concurrent, crosscurrent, excurrent (flowing outwards), transcurrent (running across), photocurrent (current produced by light), undercurrent, intercurrent (occurring between).

420.65
roborant (fortifying), saturant (chemistry term), afferent (conducting inwards), efferent (conducting outwards), deferent, referent, different, tolerant, colorant, cormorant, sonorant (phonetics term), ignorant, operant, lacerant (painfully distressing), cauterant (caustic), reverent.

corroborant, protuberant, exuberant, deodorant, preponderant, indifferent, belligerent, refrigerant, accelerant, exhilarant, intolerant, decolorant, itinerant, expectorant, adulterant, irreverent, antiperspirant.

420.66
penetrant, recalcitrant.

420.67
crescent, quiescent, rubescent, pubescent, tabescent (wasting away), albescent (becoming white), confessant, turgescent, spumescent (producing froth), tumescent, liquescent, decrescent (decreasing in size), increscent (increasing in size), excrescent, nigrescent (blackish), depressant, vitrescent (turning in-

to glass), putrescent, acescent (turning sour), incessant, frutescent, lactescent.

acquiescent, iridescent, viridescent (becoming green), incandescent, adolescent, opalescent, obsolescent, convalescent, deliquescent, fluorescent, arborescent (treelike), phosphorescent, antidepressant.

420.67.1
senescent, juvenescent.

420.67.2
canescent (becoming hoary), evanescent.

420.67.3
flavescent (turning yellow), effervescent, ingravescent (becoming worse).

420.68
versant (mountain side), dispersant, conversant.

420.69
decent, recent, indecent.

420.70
dehiscent, reticent, Stuyvesant (Dutch colonial administrator), maleficent, beneficent, munificent, magnificent, omnificent, indehiscent, reminiscent.

420.71
lucent, translucent, abducent (anatomy term).

420.72
demulcent (soothing), convulsant, anticonvulsant.

420.73
patient, impatient, inpatient, outpatient, sorbefacient (causing absorption), calefacient (causing warmth), stupefacient, liquefacient, abortifacient.

420.74
efficient, deficient, proficient, sufficient, coefficient, inefficient, self-sufficient, insufficient, extinguishant.

420.75
latent, blatant, natant (floating on water), patent, statant (heraldic term),

dilatant, supernatant (floating on the surface).

420.76
militant, volitant (moving rapidly), remittent, penitent, competent, equitant (botany term), irritant, hesitant, visitant, annuitant (person receiving annuity), inhabitant, exorbitant, concomitant, intermittent, impenitent, precipitant, incompetent, abirritant (relieving irritation), omnicompetent, counterirritant.

420.77
mutant, nutant (botany term), pollutant, disputant.

420.78
combatant, adjutant, impotent, noncombatant, coadjutant, armipotent (strong in battle), plenipotent (having full authority), omnipotent, totipotent (zoology term).

420.79
humectant, expectant, disinfectant.

420.80
digestant, contestant, decongestant.

420.81
distant, assistant, persistent, insistent, consistent, Protestant, resistant, existent, equidistant, inconsistent, nonresistant, coexistent, nonexistent.

420.82
fervent, servant, maidservant, bondservant, manservant, observant.

420.83
accent, relaxant.

420.84
bezant (Byzantine gold coin), pheasant, pleasant, peasant, present, unpleasant, omnipresent.

421 -apt [also **268** + *-ed*]
apt, rapt, snowcapped, adapt, inapt, unapt, periapt (amulet).

422 -ept [also **271** + *-ed*]
kept, leapt, slept, crept, sept (clan), wept, swept, adept, inept, percept (object of perception), recept (psychology term), precept, transept, incept (ingest), concept, unwept, windswept, backswept, except, accept, nympholept, overslept, intercept.

423 -erpt [also **272** + *-ed*]
excerpt, usurped.

424 -ipt [also **274** + *-ed*]
crypt, script, Egypt, decrypt (decode), prescript, subscript, transcript, conscript, typescript, postscript, nondescript, telescript (script for television), manuscript, superscript.

425 -opt [also **276** + *-ed*]
opt, Copt, coopt, adopt, unstopped.

426 -upt [also **279** + *-ed*]
erupt, irrupt, abrupt, bankrupt, disrupt.

426.1
corrupt, incorrupt, interrupt.

427 -ulpt
sculpt, gulped, pulped.

428 -empt
empt (*Dialect* to empty), kempt (tidy), tempt, pre-empt, unkempt, attempt, contempt, exempt.

429 -ompt [also **288** + *-ed*]
prompt, swamped.

430 -ast [also **293** + *-ed*]
bast (plant tissue), hast, bombast, dicast (Athenian juror), gymnast, peltast (ancient Greek foot soldier), fantast (visionary), trophoblast (embryonic membrane), lymphoblast (immature white blood cell), neuroblast (embryonic nerve cell), mesoblast (embryonic tissue), chloroplast (chlorophyll-con-

taining structure), leucoplast (structure in plant cell), pederast, erythroblast (cell in bone marrow), osteoblast (bone-forming cell), osteoclast (surgical instrument), iconoclast (opponent of established beliefs).

430.1
scholiast (medieval annotator), cineaste (film enthusiast), encomiast (writer of eulogies), gymnasiast (European secondary school student), ecdysiast (striptease artist), enthusiast.

431 -arst [also **294** + *-ed*]
cast, caste, karst, fast, last, blast, mast, past, vast.

precast, die-cast, forecast, broadcast, half-caste, roughcast, wormcast, downcast, typecast, upcast (ventilation shaft in mine), miscast, sportscast, outcast, newscast, makefast (support for securing boat), headfast (ship's mooring rope), holdfast (hook or clamp), Belfast, sunfast (not fading in sunlight), sitfast (sore on horse's back), oblast (Russian administrative division), sandblast, outlast, durmast (oak tree), foremast, half-mast, mainmast, topmast, repast, contrast, avast.

telecast, overcast, simulcast (simultaneous radio–television broadcast), opencast, colourfast, counterblast, jiggermast (small ship's mast), mizzenmast, Elastoplast (*Trademark*).

431.1
aghast, flabbergast.

432 -aste [also **295** + *-ed*]
baste, chaste, haste, paste, taste, waste, waist, lambaste (*Slang* beat severely), barefaced, two-faced, shamefaced, posthaste, unplaced, impaste (apply paint thickly), toothpaste, foretaste, distaste, aftertaste, pantywaist (*US* childish person).

433 -est [also **296** + *-ed*]
best, chest, guest, jest, lest, blest, nest, pest, quest, wrest, rest, Brest, breast, crest, dressed, test, vest, west, zest.

Trieste, gabfest (*US* gathering for conversation), infest, egest (excrete), digest, suggest, ingest, congest, behest, celeste, molest, unblessed, bequest, request, inquest, conquest, abreast, redbreast, goldcrest (small warbler), headrest, well-dressed, kniferest, armrest, unrest, depressed, appressed (pressed closely against), impressed, footrest, unstressed, incest, detest, attest, protest, contest, revest (restore power), divest, invest, northwest, southwest, possessed.

second-best, manifest, disinfest, predigest, Almagest (Ptolemy's treatise on astronomy), alkahest (universal solvent in alchemy), Budapest, rinderpest (disease of cattle), anapaest (metrical foot), overdressed, unimpressed, unexpressed, undervest, self-possessed.

433.1
arrest, Bucharest.

434 -erst [also **297** + *-ed*]
burst, durst, first, Hearst, thirst, versed, worst, wurst, airburst (explosion in the air), cloudburst, sunburst, outburst, headfirst, Pankhurst, Sandhurst, knackwurst (type of sausage), athirst (longing), bratwurst (type of sausage), liverwurst.

435 -eest [also **298** + *-ed*]
east, beast, feast, geest (German heathland), least, piste, priest, yeast, modiste (fashionable milliner or dressmaker), beanfeast, archpriest, deceased, batiste (cotton fabric), artiste, northeast, southeast, wildebeest, hartebeest, arriviste (unscrupulously ambitious person).

436 -ist [Also **300** + *-ed*. Further rhymes may be derived from **242.35** or by adding *-ist* to appropriate adjectives.]

kist (*Dialect* large coffer), fist, gist, hist, list, Liszt, mist, quist (*Dialect* wood pigeon), wrist, grist, tryst, cyst, cist (box holding ritual objects), schist, whist, twist, xyst (long portico).

deist, Maoist, cubist, cambist (foreign-exchange dealer), stockist, Yorkist, sadist, modest, feudist (person involved in feud), nudist, eldest, damnedest, sophist, druggist, fuguist (composer of fugues), Hengist (Jute settler in Britain), legist, cellist, stylist, Gaullist, blacklist, cyclist, enlist, chemist, demist, tanist (heir of Celtic chieftain), earnest, honest, hymnist, Trappist, typist, tempest, Marist (member of Christian sect), aurist (ear specialist), Maurist (16th-century French monk), centrist (person with moderate views), bassist (double bass player), subsist, encyst (biology term), insist, consist, fascist, latticed, artist, chartist, latest, greatest, statist (supporter of state power), rightist, flautist, leftist, dentist, Baptist, farthest, furthest, harvest, linguist, Marxist, sexist, desist, resist, exist.

lobbyist, copyist, atheist, oboist, egoist, soloist, altruist, casuist, Sinarquist (Mexican fascist), anarchist, monarchist, masochist, immodest, pacifist, strategist, violist, extremist, conformist, hygienist, machinist, dishonest, trombonist, communist, columnist, unwitnessed, Decembrist (former Russian revolutionary), Septembrist (former French revolutionary), xenocryst (type of crystal), phenocryst (large crystal), exorcist, defeatist, unpractised, scientist, amethyst, reservist, archivist, Bolshevist, activist, coexist.

propagandist, gymnosophist (member of Indian sect), motorcyclist, biochem-

ist, taxidermist, nonconformist, ventriloquist, equilibrist (person performing balancing acts), optometrist (person treating eye defects), psychiatrist, parachutist, orthodontist, Anabaptist (16th-century Protestant).

encyclopedist, audiotypist.

436.1
Judaist, épéeist, Hebraist (student of Hebrew culture), essayist, Ptolemaist, algebraist.

436.2
Buddhist, Talmudist (Jewish scholar), unprejudiced.

436.3
melodist, rhapsodist, Methodist, chiropodist.

436.4 [further rhymes may be derived from **16.108.4**]
agist (legal term), synergist (medical term), suffragist, liturgist, biologist, zoologist, psychologist, graphologist, technologist, apologist (person defending by argument), archaeologist, radiologist, sociologist, gynaecologist, ornithologist, meteorologist.

436.4.1
allergist, dialogist (contributor to dialogue), metallurgist, genealogist.

436.5
idyllist, pugilist, Familist (member of Christian sect), evangelist.

436.6
fabulist, oculist, Populist (member of People's Party), funambulist, somnambulist.

436.7
loyalist, royalist, arbalest (medieval crossbow), herbalist, verbalist, symbolist, vocalist, medallist, journalist, finalist, moralist, racialist, specialist, socialist, fatalist, metallist (advocate of metal currency), novelist.

minimalist (advocate of minimal policy), maximalist (person favouring direct action), immoralist, generalist (person with broad knowledge), naturalist, capitalist, medievalist, revivalist, removalist (*Austral* furniture remover).

semifinalist, bibliopolist (dealer in rare books), universalist, existentialist.

436.7.1
realist, idealist, surrealist.

436.7.2
aerialist (trapeze artist), glacialist (person studying ice effects), imperialist, materialist, memorialist (writer of memoirs), industrialist.

436.7.3
sensualist, spiritualist, individualist.

436.7.4
analyst, panellist, psychoanalyst.

436.7.5
nationalist, rationalist, sensationalist, educationalist, Congregationalist, conversationalist.

436.7.6
catalyst, philatelist, anticatalyst, biocatalyst (enzyme).

436.7.7
instrumentalist, environmentalist.

436.8
palmist, psalmist, alarmist.

436.9
pessimist, optimist, legitimist (supporter of legitimate ruler).

436.10
alchemist, monogamist, economist, anatomist.

436.10.1
bigamist, polygamist.

436.11
Hellenist (devotee of Greek civilization), feminist, alpinist, Latinist, lutenist (lute player), chauvinist, violinist, determinist.

436.12
balloonist, bassoonist, cartoonist, opportunist.

436.13
hedonist, symphonist, organist, colonist, harmonist, Romanist (supporter of Catholicism), timpanist, Satanist, botanist, alienist (type of psychiatrist), unionist, tobacconist, telephonist, saxophonist, misogynist, accompanist, impressionist, excursionist, abortionist, contortionist, percussionist, destructionist, obstructionist, receptionist, illusionist, exclusionist, coreligionist (adherent of same religion), evolutionist, interventionist.

436.13.1
pianist, Orleanist.

436.13.2
agonist (type of muscle), protagonist, antagonist, deuteragonist (character in Greek drama).

436.13.3
humanist, phillumenist (collector of matchbox labels).

436.13.4
vacationist (*US* holidaymaker), salvationist, segregationist, revelationist (believer in divine revelation), conservationist.

436.13.5
nutritionist, prohibitionist, exhibitionist, abolitionist.

436.13.6
perfectionist, projectionist, protectionist, resurrectionist (body-snatcher), vivisectionist.

436.14
papist, rapist, escapist, landscapist.

436.15
therapist, philanthropist, misanthropist, psychotherapist, radiotherapist, physiotherapist.

436.16
tsarist, guitarist.

436.17
dearest, querist (questioner), careerist.

436.18
forest, florist, deforest, afforest, rainforest, reafforest, disafforest.

436.19
jurist, tourist, purist, manicurist, caricaturist.

436.20
aorist (linguistics term), theorist, diarist, arborist (specialist in tree-cultivation), labourist (supporter of workers' rights), Eucharist, naturist, plagiarist, amorist, humorist, aquarist (aquarium curator), terrorist, satirist, motorist, interest, Everest, apiarist, miniaturist, ocularist (artificial-eye manufacturer), militarist, disinterest, Redemptorist (Catholic missionary), behaviourist, lepidopterist.

436.21
Biblicist (biblical scholar), publicist, Anglicist, lyricist, classicist, physicist, geneticist.

436.22
assist, persist, trichocyst (zoology term), pharmacist, sporocyst (zoology term), macrocyst, statocyst (organ of balance), blastocyst, supremacist, nematocyst (animal's stinging organ).

436.23
cornetist, librettist, clarinetist.

436.24
Semitist (student of Semitic culture), phonetist, portraitist, hereditist (supporter of heredity's influence).

436.25
protist (microscopic organism), unnoticed.

436.26
egotist, dramatist, pragmatist, dogmatist, Donatist (Christian heretic), hypnotist, systematist, numismatist, separatist, anaesthetist.

436.27
dentist, apprenticed, Adventist (member of Christian sect), irredentist.

437 -iced [also **301** + *-ed*]
heist, Kleist (German dramatist), Christ, Zeist (Dutch city), unpriced, poltergeist, Antichrist.

438 -ost [also **302** + *-ed*]
cost, lost, frost, accost, alecost (Asian plant), volost (Russian peasant community), riposte, compost, defrost, hoarfrost, Bifrost (Norse mythological rainbow bridge), teleost (type of fish), Pentecost, permafrost.

439 -orst [also **303** + *-ed*]
horst (ridge of land), exhaust, holocaust, hypocaust (Roman heating system).

440 -oist [also **304** + *-ed*]
foist, joist, hoist, moist, unvoiced.

441 -oast [also **305** + *-ed*]
oast, boast, coast, ghost, host, most, post, roast, toast.

seacoast, rearmost, foremost, backmost, midmost (in the middle), endmost, hindmost, almost, topmost, utmost, doorpost, bedpost, guidepost, soundpost, milepost, impost (customs duty), signpost, lamppost, gatepost, outpost, milquetoast (*US* timid person).

undermost, innermost, uppermost, outermost, farthermost, nethermost, furthermost, bottommost, northernmost, southernmost, westernmost, easternmost.

442 -oust [also **306** + *-ed*]
oust, Faust, joust, roust (rout out), frowst (stuffy atmosphere).

443 -ust [also **307** + *-ed*]
bust, dust, gust, just, lust, must, rust, crust, trust, thrust, robust, combust, stardust, sawdust, august, disgust, adjust, unjust, piecrust, encrust, entrust, distrust, mistrust, upthrust, readjust, wanderlust, underthrust (geological fault), overthrust (geological fault).

444 -oost [also **309** + *-ed*]
boost, roost, Proust, langouste (spiny lobster).

445 -'st [also **310** + *-ed*]
locust, breakfast, steadfast, August, ballast, Sallust (Roman historian), dynast, Bathurst (Australian city), provost, unbiased.

446 -idst
didst, midst.

447 -enst [also **316** + *-ed*]
unfenced, against, fornenst (*Scot* situated against).

448 -'nst [also **321** + *-ed*]
unlicensed, inexperienced.

449 -ished [also **353** + *-ed*]
unfurnished, unfinished, malnourished, unaccomplished, undernourished, undistinguished.

450 -ext [also **496** + *-ed*]
next, sext (Catholic prayer time), text, pretext, context, undersexed, oversexed.

451 -ixt [also **498** + *-ed*]
mixed, sixte (fencing position), betwixt.

452 -ath
Gath (biblical city), hath, Plath (US poet), snath (scythe handle), strath (*Scot* glen), isobath (line on map), polymath, aftermath, chaetognath (wormlike marine animal), plectognath

(spiny-finned fish), psychopath, neuropath (person with nervous disorder), allopath (orthodox medical practitioner), sociopath (psychiatric term), osteopath, naturopath.

453 -arth
bath, Bath, garth (cloistered courtyard), hearth, lath, path, eyebath, birdbath, Hogarth, bypath (little-used track), warpath, towpath, footpath.

454 -aith
faith, wraith, saithe (food fish), Galbraith.

455 -eth
Beth, death, breath, Seth, Macbeth, Japheth (biblical character), megadeath (death of million people), shibboleth, isopleth (line on map), Ashtoreth (biblical character).

456 -erth
earth, berth, birth, dearth, firth, girth, mirth, Perth, worth, rebirth, childbirth, stillbirth, inearth (bury), unearth, afterbirth, pennyworth.

457 -eeth
heath, Leith, Meath, neath, wreath, Reith, sheath, teeth, beneath, B'nai B'rith (Jewish fraternal society), monteith (bowl for cooling wineglasses), underneath.

458 -ith
kith, myth, Smith, pith, grith (place of safety), withe (twig used for binding).

Hadith (Mohammedan tradition), Judith, Griffith, tallith (Jewish prayer shawl), Lilith (biblical demon), goldsmith, gunsmith, tunesmith, whitesmith (metal polisher), blacksmith, locksmith, zenith, turpeth (plant yielding purgative), Asquith, Penrith.

sixtieth, eightieth, thirtieth, fortieth, fiftieth, twentieth, ninetieth, Meredith, eolith (stone tool), neolith (stone tool), laccolith (geology term), coccolith (geology term), megalith, regolith (earth's mantle rock), granolith (paving material), xenolith (geology term), monolith, urolith (stone in urinary tract), acrolith (type of sculpture), microlith (flint tool), gastrolith (stone in the stomach), statolith (biology term), batholith (large mass of granite), Ladysmith, Hammersmith, silversmith.

seventieth, Aberystwyth.

459 -oth
Goth, cloth, moth, wrath, broth, froth, Naboth (biblical character), haircloth, cerecloth (waxed waterproof cloth), backcloth, sackcloth, neckcloth, broadcloth (closely woven fabric), sailcloth, oilcloth, loincloth, dishcloth, cheesecloth, azoth (mercury), Visigoth, Ostrogoth, tablecloth, saddlecloth, behemoth (biblical monster).

460 -orth
Forth, forth, fourth, north, swath (strip of cut grass), henceforth.

461 -oath
oath, both, loath, sloth, quoth, wroth (angry), growth, troth, Thoth (ancient Egyptian deity), Arbroath, ingrowth, upgrowth, outgrowth, undergrowth, overgrowth.

462 -outh
Louth (Irish county), mouth, south, loudmouth, bigmouth, goalmouth, blabbermouth.

463 -ooth
couth, sleuth, Ruth, crwth (ancient stringed instrument), truth, strewth, sooth, tooth, youth, uncouth, Duluth (US port), Redruth, untruth, forsooth, eyetooth, foretooth (front tooth), bucktooth, dogtooth.

464 -'th
Sabbath, Lambeth, mammoth, Yarmouth, Weymouth, vermouth, Plymouth, Falmouth, Monmouth, Bournemouth, Portsmouth, Dartmouth, bismuth, ha'p'orth, Hepworth, Bosworth, Wordsworth, Wandsworth, Goliath, azimuth, Nazareth, Kenilworth, Elizabeth, altazimuth (astronomy instrument).

465 -elth
health, stealth, wealth, Commonwealth.

466 -ilth
filth, tilth (process of tilling land).

467 -anth
hydranth (type of polyp), perianth (part of flower), tragacanth (Asian plant), coelacanth (primitive bony fish), amaranth (flowering plant).

468 -enth
nth, tenth.

469 -eenth
eighteenth, thirteenth, fourteenth, fifteenth, nineteenth, umpteenth, sixteenth, seventeenth.

470 -inth
plinth, helminth (parasitic worm), Corinth, jacinth (gemstone), absinthe, terebinth (small Mediterranean tree), labyrinth, hyacinth, colocynth (climbing plant).

471 -'nth
millionth, billionth, trillionth, thousandth, dozenth.

471.1
seventh, eleventh.

472 -ength
length, strength, wavelength.

473 -athe
bathe, scathe, lathe, spathe (botany term), rathe (blossoming early), swathe, sunbathe, enswathe.

474 -edh
edh (runic character), Gwynedd, Gorsedd (Welsh bardic institution).

475 -eethe
wreathe, breathe, seethe, sheathe, teethe, Westmeath (Irish county), bequeath, enwreath, unsheathe, Pontypridd.

476 -idh
with, therewith, wherewith, herewith, forthwith.

477 -ithe
lithe, blithe, Blyth, writhe, scythe, tithe.

478 -othe
loathe, clothe, reclothe, unclothe, betroth.

479 -oothe
booth, smooth, soothe, tollbooth.

480 -av
have, lav (*short for* lavatory), grav (unit of acceleration).

481 -arve
carve, calve, halve, Slav, Graves (type of wine), starve, varve (geology term), suave, Zouave (French infantryman), Yugoslav.

482 -ave
cave, gave, slave, nave, knave, pave, rave, brave, crave, grave, trave (cage for shoeing horses), save, shave, stave, they've, waive, wave.

concave, forgave, behave, enclave, conclave, exclave, enslave, outbrave, margrave, burgrave (medieval German governor), Redgrave, waldgrave (medieval German forest officer), landgrave, engrave, deprave, spokeshave, palstave (archaeology term).

biconcave, misbehave, autoclave (pressurized container), architrave (moulding), aftershave, microwave, photoengrave.

483 -erve
curve, derv, MIRV (type of missile), nerve, perv (*short for* pervert), serve, verve, swerve, recurve, innerve (stimulate), unnerve, subserve (be helpful), conserve, deserve, reserve, preserve, observe.

484 -eve
Eve, eve, heave, leave, cleave, sleeve, sleave (tangled thread), nieve (*Dialect* fist), peeve, reeve, breve, grieve, greave (piece of armour), sheave, steeve (spar for stowing cargo), thieve, we've, weave.

naive, achieve, khedive (viceroy of Egypt), upheave, shirtsleeve, bereave, aggrieve, Congreve (English dramatist), reprieve, retrieve, perceive, conceive, qui vive, inweave.

interleave, semibreve, apperceive (psychology term), preconceive, misconceive, Genevieve, Tel Aviv, interweave.

underachieve, overachieve, recitative.

484.1
believe, relieve, disbelieve.

484.2
deceive, receive, undeceive.

485 -iv
chiv (*Slang* knife), div, give, live, spiv, sieve, Tiv (member of African people).

forgive, misgive (be apprehensive), relive, olive, unlive, outlive, plausive (expressing approval), octave, plaintive, captive, costive (constipated).

gerundive, abrasive, pervasive, evasive, invasive, dissuasive, persuasive, cohesive, adhesive, purposive, repulsive, impulsive, compulsive, expulsive, revulsive, convulsive, expansive, responsive, expletive, subjunctive, conjunctive, disjunctive, substantive, descriptive, prescriptive, proscriptive, inscriptive, adoptive, absorptive, irruptive, eruptive, disruptive, pre-emptive, consumptive, presumptive, exhaustive, reflexive.

irresponsive, retributive, attributive, contributive, distributive, consecutive, executive, diminutive, substitutive, institutive, constitutive.

485.1
massive, passive, impassive.

485.2
inessive (linguistics term), regressive, digressive, ingressive (phonetics term), depressive, repressive, oppressive, suppressive, impressive, compressive, expressive, recessive, obsessive, concessive, excessive, successive, possessive, inexpressive.

485.2.1
aggressive, progressive, retrogressive.

485.3
cursive, coercive, incursive, discursive, excursive (tending to digress), dispersive, aversive, perversive, subversive.

485.4
missive, permissive, submissive, admissive, dismissive.

485.5
derisive, decisive, incisive, divisive, indecisive.

485.6
plosive (phonetics term), implosive (phonetics term), explosive, erosive, corrosive.

485.7
jussive (linguistics term), percussive (relating to percussion), antitussive (alleviating coughing).

485.8
elusive, illusive, delusive, allusive, reclusive, seclusive, occlusive (phonetics term), inclusive, conclusive, exclusive, protrusive, obtrusive, intrusive, extrusive, abusive, conducive, effusive, diffusive, inconclusive, unobtrusive.

485.9
pensive, tensive (causing tension), defensive, offensive, suspensive, expensive, intensive, ostensive, extensive, inoffensive, apprehensive, comprehensive, inexpensive, coextensive, counteroffensive.

485.10
dative, native, stative (linguistics term), creative, illative (linguistics term), collative, nonstative (linguistics term), concentrative, gravitative.

485.11
furtive, assertive.

485.12
additive, fugitive, volitive (relating to the will), primitive, genitive, lenitive (soothing pain), unitive, punitive, cognitive, secretive, nutritive, transitive, sensitive, partitive, factitive (linguistics term).

intuitive, prohibitive, exhibitive (illustrative), definitive, infinitive, preterite (linguistics term), interpretive, intransitive, insensitive, repetitive, competitive, acquisitive, inquisitive.

photosensitive, hypersensitive, radiosensitive.

485.12.1
positive, prepositive (linguistics term), appositive (linguistics term), suppositive (involving supposition), postpositive, diapositive, electropositive.

485.13

sportive, abortive, supportive.

485.14

motive, votive, emotive, promotive, locomotive, automotive, electromotive.

485.15 [further rhymes may be derived from **367**]

probative (providing evidence), combative, talkative, sedative, negative, purgative, elative (linguistics term), ablative, conative (linguistics term), calmative, donative (gift), lucrative, portative (portable), optative (expressing a wish), laxative, fixative, causative.

radiative (emitting radiation), rebarbative, reprobative, educative, superlative, contemplative, legislative, affirmative, alternative, imperative, pejorative, restorative, suppurative, illustrative, adversative (linguistics term), appreciative, initiative, associative, consultative, facultative, conservative, preservative, innovative, conciliative, accusative.

continuative (linguistics term), investigative, approximative, administrative, inappreciative.

485.15.1

fricative (phonetics term), siccative (substance causing drying), judicative, indicative, applicative, explicative, affricative (phonetics term), significative, multiplicative, communicative, uncommunicative.

485.15.2

locative, vocative, evocative, provocative.

485.15.3

derogative, prerogative, interrogative.

485.15.4

relative, appellative (name or title), irrelative (unrelated), correlative (mutually related).

485.15.5

speculative, calculative, cumulative, copulative, coagulative, accumulative, manipulative.

485.15.6

formative, normative (establishing a norm), reformative, performative (linguistics term), informative.

485.15.7

combinative, carminative, nominative, ruminative, imaginative, determinative, denominative (naming), agglutinative.

485.15.8

narrative, declarative, preparative, comparative.

485.15.9

curative, durative (linguistics term), depurative (purifying).

485.15.10

decorative, figurative, generative, separative, operative, corporative, ulcerative, alterative (therapeutic drug), deliberative, corroborative, desiderative (expressing desire), alliterative, commemorative, remunerative, cooperative, inoperative, postoperative, vituperative, noncooperative.

485.15.11

demonstrative, remonstrative, undemonstrative.

485.15.12

meditative, vegetative, cogitative, qualitative, imitative, quantitative, authoritative, interpretative.

485.15.13

rotative, denotative.

485.15.14

putative (supposed), commutative (involving substitution).

485.15.15

tentative, augmentative, frequentative (linguistics term), preventative, argumentative, representative.

485.15.16
privative, derivative.

485.16
active, tractive, reactive, inactive, refractive, attractive, subtractive, extractive, retroactive, photoactive (responsive to light), hyperactive, interactive,
overactive, unattractive, radioactive.

485.17
effective, defective, affective (arousing
emotions), perfective, infective, ejective
(phonetics term), projective, objective,
subjective, elective, selective, collective,
reflective, connective, respective, perspective, prospective, directive, corrective, detective, protective, invective, ineffective, imperfective, irrespective,
retrospective, introspective, circumspective.

485.18
fictive, predictive, addictive, vindictive,
adjective, conflictive, restrictive, constrictive, convictive, nonrestrictive.

485.19
deductive, seductive, productive, inductive, conductive, destructive, obstructive, instructive, constructive, reproductive, unproductive, counterproductive.

485.20
distinctive, instinctive, extinctive (serving to extinguish), indistinctive.

485.21
pendentive (architectural term), incentive, retentive, attentive, preventive, inventive, disincentive, irretentive, inattentive.

485.22
captive, adaptive.

485.23
deceptive, receptive, preceptive (didactic), perceptive, inceptive (beginning),
exceptive (forming an exception), nociceptive (causing pain), imperceptive
(lacking in perception), contraceptive.

485.24
festive, restive, digestive, suggestive,
congestive, indigestive.

486 -ive
I've, skive, chive, dive, five, jive, hive,
live, Clive, rive (split asunder), drive,
shrive, strive, thrive, shive (flat cork),
wive.

skydive, endive, spoilfive (card game),
ogive, beehive, alive, connive, derive,
arrive, deprive, contrive, revive, survive, overdrive.

487 -ov
of, Pavlov, thereof, whereof, hereof,
Rostov (Russian port), Baal Shem Tov
(Jewish religious leader).

488 -ove
cove, Jove, Hove, hove, clove, mauve,
rove, drove, grove, shrove, trove,
strove, stove, wove, alcove, behove,
mangrove, Bromsgrove.

489 -uv
dove, guv, love, glove, shove, above,
ringdove, truelove, foxglove, turtledove,
ladylove.

490 -oove
move, groove, prove, you've, remove,
reprove, approve, improve, disprove,
interfluve (land between two rivers),
countermove, microgroove (groove in
record), disapprove.

491 -alve
salve, valve, bivalve, univalve.

492 -elve
delve, helve (handle of tool), shelve,
twelve.

493 -olve
solve, evolve, devolve, revolve, involve,
convolve (to coil), dissolve, resolve, ab-
solve.

494 -ax [also **32** + -s]
axe, Bax (English composer), Sfax
(Tunisian port), jacks, lax, flax, slacks,
pax, sax, tax, wax.

coax, pickaxe, panchax (tropical fish),
addax (large antelope), carfax (crossroads), Fairfax, Ajax, relax, smilax
(climbing shrub), poleaxe (battle-axe),
toadflax, climax, Lomax, larnax (terra-
cotta coffin), Fornax (constellation),
hyrax (herbivorous mammal), styrax
(tropical tree), borax, storax (tropical
plant), thorax, anthrax, surtax, syntax,
earwax, paxwax (*Dialect* ligament in
neck), beeswax.

Halifax, parallax, minimax, subclimax,
disclimax (ecology term), supertax,
overtax.

Adirondacks (US mountain range),
anticlimax, Astyanax (Greek mythological character).

495 -arx [also **33** + -s]
Berks., Marx.

496 -ex [also **35** + -s]
ex, kex (flowering plant), hex, lex
(body of laws), flex, specs, Rex, sex,
vex.

ibex, caudex (woody base of stem), co-
dex (volume of ancient manuscripts),
index, telex, ilex (evergreen tree), silex
(heat-resistant glass), pollex (first digit
on forelimb), scolex (head of tapeworm), culex (type of mosquito), reflex, Triplex (*Trademark*), diplex (electronics term), suplex (wrestling hold),
duplex, perplex, simplex (electronics
term), complex, remex (large flight
feather), cimex (bedbug), annex, annexe, Kleenex (*Trademark*), apex, Perspex (*Trademark*), auspex (Roman
soothsayer), Pyrex (*Trademark*), Lurex
(*Trademark*), Durex (*Trademark*), murex (spiny-shelled mollusc), unsex, latex, vertex, cortex, vortex, dentex

(predatory fish), narthex (portico in
church), convex.

subindex, tubifex (small worm), spinifex (Australian grass), pontifex (senior
Catholic cleric), isolex (linguistics
term), retroflex, circumflex, multiplex
(electronics term), quadruplex (fourfold), googolplex (large number), ha-
ruspex (ancient Roman priest), interrex
(interim ruler), unisex, supersex (genetics term), intersex (zoology term),
Middlesex, biconvex.

497 -erx [also **36** + -s]
fireworks, steelworks, gasworks, glassworks, waterworks, ironworks.

498 -ix [also **38** + -s]
fix, mix, nix, Nyx (Greek goddess),
pix, pyx (container for Eucharist), six,
Styx.

spadix (type of inflorescence), radix,
affix, graphics, prefix, suffix, affix, infix, unfix, transfix, postfix (add to the
end), calyx, helix, kylix (two-handled
drinking vessel), prolix (long and boring), rhythmics, fornix (archlike body
structure), technics, tropics, varix (varicose vein), oryx (African antelope),
rectrix (tail feather), tectrix (small
feather), classics, Essex, Wessex, Sussex, glyptics (engraving precious
stones), optics, chopsticks, ethics, cervix, civics (study of citizens' rights),
coccyx, physics.

heroics, aerobics, fluidics (use of fluid
flow), appendix, superfix (linguistics
term), strategics (military strategy),
anthelix (cartilage in ear), hydraulics,
spondulix, polemics, tagmemics (linguistics term), phonemics (branch of
linguistics), eurhythmics, mechanics,
sardonyx (gemstone), philippics (bitter
invective), subtropics, cicatrix, Bellatrix
(star), dioptrics (branch of optics), kinesics (study of body language), forensics (formal debating), politics, Semit-

ics (study of Semitic languages), orthoptics, ekistics (study of human settlements), logistics, sphragistics (study of document seals), ballistics, floristics (branch of botany), statistics, linguistics, acoustics, fiddlesticks.

logopaedics (speech therapy), orthopaedics, pedagogics, isagogics (introductory studies), bionomics (ecology), economics, ergonomics (study of work), agronomics (land economics), loxodromics (navigation technique), pyrotechnics, zootechnics (animal domestication and breeding), metempirics (branch of philosophy), executrix, semiotics (study of symbols), aeronautics, astronautics, hermeneutics (science of scriptural interpretation), therapeutics, pharmaceutics, dialectics, endodontics (branch of dentistry), orthodontics, exodontics (branch of dentistry), prosthodontics, diagnostics, geophysics, astrophysics, biophysics, metaphysics.

498.1
crucifix, antefix (ornament on roof), hieroglyphics.

498.2
dynamics, ceramics, thermodynamics, aerodynamics, electrodynamics.

498.3
eugenics (selective breeding), dysgenics (reducing quality of race), euthenics (study of environment control), cryogenics, callisthenics.

498.4
phoenix, hygienics, irenics (branch of theology).

498.5
onyx, conics (branch of geometry), phonics (phonetic teaching method), bionics, cryonics (freezing corpses for preservation), hedonics (branch of psychology), harmonics, mnemonics, tectonics, nucleonics (application of nuclear energy), thermionics (branch of

electronics), histrionics, avionics, quadraphonics, eudemonics (art of happiness), geoponics (science of agriculture), hydroponics (method of plant cultivation), electronics, supersonics, ultrasonics, architectonics (science of architecture), microelectronics.

498.6
spherics, hysterics, atmospherics.

498.7
apteryx (kiwi), Vercingetorix (Gallic chieftain), archaeopteryx.

498.8
theatrics, paediatrics, geriatrics, physiatrics (US physiotherapy).

498.9
matrix, testatrix, aviatrix, generatrix (geometry term), separatrix (oblique stroke).

498.10
metrics (use of poetic metre), obstetrics, psychometrics (branch of psychology), isometrics, econometrics (branch of economics).

498.11
statics, chromatics (science of colour), pneumatics (branch of physics), rheumatics, dramatics, dogmatics (study of religious doctrines), aquatics, quadratics (branch of algebra), ecstatics, aerobatics, acrobatics, kinematics (branch of physics), systematics (study of systems), diplomatics, mathematics, numismatics, hydrostatics (study of stationary fluids), biostatics (branch of biology), thermostatics, aerostatics (physics term), electrostatics (branch of physics).

498.12
poetics, athletics, kinetics, genetics, magnetics, aesthetics, prosthetics, exegetics (study of textual interpretation), energetics (science of energy), homiletics (art of preaching sermons), theoretics, dietetics, anaesthetics, apologetics (branch of theology).

498.12.1
phonetics, cybernetics, aerodonetics (study of gliding flight).

498.13
tactics, didactics (science of teaching), syntactics (study of symbol systems), phonotactics (branch of linguistics).

498.14
antics, semantics.

498.15
gymnastics, ceroplastics (wax modelling), onomastics (study of proper names).

499 -ox [also **40** + -s]
ox, box, cox, fox, lox (smoked salmon), phlox, Knox, Nox (Roman goddess), pox, stocks, vox (voice).

gearbox, firebox, jukebox, matchbox, soundbox, snuffbox, mailbox, pillbox, strongbox, soapbox, icebox, horsebox, loosebox, hatbox, paintbox, postbox, redox (chemistry term), boondocks (*US* wild desolate country), outfox, cowpox, smallpox, swinepox, Xerox (*Trademark*), aurochs, volvox (microscopic animal).

tinderbox, chatterbox, gogglebox, goldilocks, badderlocks (brownishgreen seaweed), equinox, chickenpox.

499.1
paradox, orthodox, heterodox, unorthodox.

500 -orx [also **41** + -s]
Fawkes, lawks, Yorks.

501 -oax [also **42** + -s]
coax, hoax.

502 -ux [also **43** + -s]
ducks, dux (*Scot* best pupil), lux (unit of illumination), flux, crux, shucks, de luxe, afflux (flowing towards), efflux (flowing out), reflux, influx, conflux (merging of rivers), Benelux.

503 -'x [also **46** + -s]
hallux (first digit on foot), bollocks, Pollux, lummox (clumsy person), flummox, barracks, Trossachs, Appomattox (US Civil War site).

504 -anx [also **51** + -s]
Manx, thanks, Fairbanks, phalanx.

505 -inx [also **52** + -s]
sphinx, jinx, Lincs., lynx, links, minx, high jinks, salpinx (anatomy term), pharynx, larynx, syrinx (bird's vocal organ), methinks, androsphinx (sphinx representing man's head), pilliwinks (medieval instrument of torture), tiddlywinks, nasopharynx (region behind nasal cavity), hieracosphinx (hawk-headed sphinx).

506 -unx [also **54** + -s]
trunks, quincunx (arrangement of five objects).

507 -az
as, jazz, has, razz (*Slang* deride), Boaz (Old Testament character), Hejaz (Saudi Arabian province), La Paz (Bolivian city), topaz, whereas, Alcatraz, razzmatazz.

508 -arz [also **1** + -s]
Mars, parse, vase, Abkhaz (Russian people), Shiraz (Iranian city), Ahwaz (Iranian town), memoirs, handlebars, churidars (Indian long trousers).

509 -aze [also **2** + -s]
baize, daze, phase, faze (*US* disconcert), gaze, haze, laze, lase (function as laser), blaze, glaze, maze, maize, smaze (*US* smoky haze), Naze (Essex headland), pes (foot), raise, raze, braise, braze (decorate with brass), craze, fraise (neck ruff), phrase, graze, praise, prase (variety of quartz), chaise (horsedrawn carriage), stays.

ukase (tsar's edict), diphase (physics term), prophase (biology term), stargaze, malaise, ablaze, zymase (enzyme mixture), amaze, manes (Roman minor deities), guanase (enzyme), kinase (biochemical agent), lipase (enzyme), erase, mores, sucrase (enzyme), rephrase, upraise, appraise, dispraise, lactase (enzyme), pectase (enzyme), maltase (enzyme), sideways, endways, edgeways, always, longways, leastways, lengthways.

peptidase (enzyme), oxidase (enzyme), nowadays, hollandaise, polyphase (having alternating voltages), telophase (biology term), anaphase (biology term), metaphase (biology term), amylase (enzyme), cellulase (enzyme), Bordelaise (sauce with red wine), Marseillaise, catalase (enzyme), underglaze (ceramics term), overglaze (ceramics term), lyonnaise (cooked with onions), Béarnaise (rich sauce), mayonnaise, Bolognese, polonaise, paraphrase, metaphrase (literal translation), écossaise, invertase (enzyme), phosphatase (enzyme), anatase (mineral).

histaminase (enzyme), tyrosinase (enzyme), lecithinase (enzyme).

broderie anglaise, enterokinase (enzyme).

509.1
liaise, nuclease (enzyme), urease (enzyme), casease (enzyme), protease (enzyme), ribonuclease (enzyme).

510 -ez
fez, Baez (US folk singer), Boulez (French composer), Cortes.

511 -erz [also 3 + -s]
furze, hers, Meuse, chartreuse, masseuse, mitrailleuse (machine gun), Betelgeuse (star), secateurs.

512 -airz [also 4 + -s]
airs, theirs, stairs, wares, affairs, upstairs, backstairs, downstairs, unawares, Armentières.

513 -eeze [also 5 + -s]
ease, bise (cold northerly wind), cheese, feaze (nautical term), feeze (to beat), he's, lees, lease (Dialect open pasture), please, mise (legal term), sneeze, pease (Dialect pea), squeeze, breeze, freeze, frieze, seize, seise (legal term), she's, tease, Tees, these, wheeze, tweeze.

scabies, rabies, tabes (wasting of body organ), soubise (onion sauce), pubes, marquise, headcheese (US brawn), Hades, Andes, Ganges, tales (legal term), Thales (Greek philosopher), displease, Burmese, Hermes, limes (boundary of Roman empire), Manes (Persian prophet), Menes (ancient Egyptian king), Chinese, stapes (bone in ear), herpes, stipes (zoology term), appease, trapeze, torques (zoology term), Tabriz (Iranian city), refreeze, unfreeze, deepfreeze, reprise, fasces (Roman magistrate's insignia), bases, faeces, fauces (anatomy term), disseise (legal term), heartsease, species, bêtise, Maltese, striptease, Dives (New Testament character), axes, Xerxes, disease.

Celebes (Indonesian island), Caribbees (West Indian islands), Maccabees (Jewish patriotic family), gourmandise, Portuguese, meninges, Hercules, Pericles, Sophocles, Damocles, Heracles, Androcles, johannes (Portuguese gold coin), talipes (club foot), antifreeze, indices, helices (plural of helix), Ulysses, Rameses, apices (plural of apex), varices (varicose veins), matrices, vertices, vortices, subspecies, consocies (ecology term), penates (Roman household gods), Jaxartes (Russian river), Laertes, expertise, velites (Roman troops), equites (Roman cavalry), pyrites (mineral), sorites (logic term), barytes (mineral), ascites (medical term), Boötes (constellation), litotes (understatement), atlantes (architectural term), Cervantes, Orontes (Asian river).

Diogenes, cheval-de-frise (barrier of spikes), ecospecies, cacoethes (uncontrollable urge).

513.1
sanies (discharge from wound), caries, paries (wall of body organ), facies (biology term), calvities (baldness).

513.2
Héloïse, Genoese, Faeroese, Averroës (Arab philosopher).

513.3
aedes (type of mosquito), heredes (heirs), Archimedes, Diomedes (Greek mythological king).

513.4
Hebrides, Parmenides (Greek philosopher), Eumenides (Greek Furies), Maimonides (Jewish philosopher), Simonides (Greek poet), Pheidippides (Athenian athlete), Euripides, cantharides (former medicine), Hesperides (Greek mythological characters), Pierides (Greek Muses).

513.5
Hyades (cluster of stars), Pleiades, Cyclades, Sporades, antipodes.

513.6
Achilles, Ramillies (Belgian battle site), Antilles, Los Angeles, isosceles, Praxiteles (Greek sculptor).

513.6.1
anopheles (type of mosquito), Mephistopheles.

513.7
valise, vocalise (vocal exercise), legalese, Sinhalese (language of Sri Lanka), journalese, novelese, officialese.

513.8
camise (medieval loose smock), chemise, Siamese, Assamese, Vietnamese.

513.9
Viennese, Lebanese, Pekinese, manganese, Milanese, Japanese, Pyrenees, Cantonese, Dodecanese, Demosthenes (Athenian statesman), Aristophanes (Greek comic dramatist).

513.10
Aries, Ares (Greek god), lares (Roman household gods), nares (nostrils), Antares (star).

513.11
heres (heir), series, Ceres (Roman goddess), congeries (collection).

513.12
cerise, Kanarese (Indian people).

513.13
Pisces, Cambyses (Persian king), Anchises (Trojan prince), Polynices (Greek mythological character).

513.14
menses, Waldenses (members of Catholic sect), Albigenses (medieval French heretics).

513.15
nates (buttocks), Achates (loyal friend), Euphrates, Mithridates (ancient Greek king).

513.16
D.T.s, Aeëtes (Greek mythological king), Sudetes (European mountain range), diabetes.

513.17
Socrates, Xenocrates (Greek philosopher), Hippocrates, Isocrates (Athenian orator).

513.18
cerastes (venomous snake), Ecclesiastes.

513.19
testes, Thyestes (Greek mythological character), Orestes (Greek mythological character).

514 -eerz [also **6** + *-s*]
cheers, shears, Algiers, Pamirs (Asian mountainous region), arrears, Cordeliers (French political club).

515 -iz [Also **16** + *-s*. Further rhymes may be created by adding *-es* to appropriate nouns and verbs.]
is, fizz, phiz (*Slang* face), his, Ms., quiz, squiz (*Austral* inquisitive glance), frizz, 'tis, whizz, swizz (*Slang* disappointment).

Suez, darbies, showbiz, Rockies, laches (legal term), riches, breeches, clutches, crutches, goodies, Cádiz, Indies, undies, hafiz (Islamic title), Kirghiz (Mongoloid people), ages, wages, wellies, Scillies, willies, kermes (dried insect bodies), Orkneys, Jeffreys, glasses, braces, falsies, rushes (film-making term), treatise, panties, civies, blazes, Moses, Menzies.

damages, obsequies, exequies, Benares (Indian city), eyeglasses (*US* spectacles), sunglasses, galluses (*Dialect* braces), galoshes, equities, assizes.

heebie-jeebies, Buenos Aires, elevenses.

515.1
Stannaries, groceries, Potteries, ivories, preliminaries.

515.2
masses, molasses.

515.3
missis, Mrs., premises.

516 -ize [also **7** + *-s*]
guise, pize (*Dialect* to hit), rise, prize, prise, size, wise.

franchise, disguise, stylize, surmise, cognize (perceive), despise, sunrise, moonrise, uprise, comprise, misprize (undervalue), Graecize (imitate ancient Greeks), abscise (to separate), excise, incise, capsize, outsize, pectize (change into jelly), quantize (physics term), baptize, peptize (chemistry term), chastise, Levis (*Trademark*), advise, crabwise, likewise, clockwise, somewise (in some way), unwise, crosswise, slantwise, widthwise.

Judaize, archaize, catechize, affranchise (release from obligation), enfranchise, disfranchise, fluidize, ruggedize (make durable), liquidize, hybridize (to crossbreed), subsidize, oxidize, iodize (treat with iodine), standardize, melodize, anodize, jeopardize, faradize (treat with electricity), sherardize (metallurgy term), rhapsodize, bastardize, methodize, merchandise, gormandize (eat greedily), aggrandize, exorcise, nebulize (atomize), capsulize, butterflies, manyplies (cow's stomach), immunize, communize (nationalize), recognize, solemnize, sulphurize, symmetrize, cicatrize (heal), exorcise, circumcise, amortize, deputize, supervise, improvise, otherwise.

propagandize, apostrophize, philosophize, anticlockwise, counterclockwise, soliloquize, ventriloquize, panegyrize (extol), anthropomorphize (ascribe human form to).

516.1
elegize, syllogize (reason using syllogisms), eulogize, energize, analogize (draw comparisons), geologize (study geology of), neologize (invent new words), theologize, psychologize (make psychological investigations), homologize (be homologous), apologize, mythologize, anthologize (compile an anthology), entomologize (study insects), demythologize.

516.2
stabilize, mobilize, tranquillize, sterilize, fossilize, fertilize, subtilize (refine), utilize, civilize, demobilize, immobilize, lyophilize (freeze-dry), evangelize, volatilize (change into vapour).

516.3

dialyse, symbolize, localize, vocalize, alkalize, idolize, feudalize, scandalize, vandalize, legalize, thermalize (physics term), formalize, normalize, penalize, finalize, signalize, equalize, paralyse, moralize, pluralize, ruralize, hydrolyse, mongrelize, neutralize, centralize, specialize, socialize, catalyse, metallize, vitalize, totalize, brutalize, tantalize, crystallize, breathalyse, novelize (convert into a novel), nasalize.

parabolize (explain by a parable), metabolize, cannibalize, illegalize, animalize, decimalize, caramelize, communalize, monopolize, demoralize, electrolyse, decentralize, commercialize, initialize (computer term), digitalize (treat with digitalis), capitalize, hospitalize, devitalize, revitalize, immortalize, palatalize (phonetics term), recrystallize (chemistry term).

universalize, Orientalize, Occidentalize, sentimentalize, departmentalize, compartmentalize.

516.3.1

realize, idealize.

516.3.2

bestialize, trivialize, mercurialize, industrialize.

516.3.2.1

serialize, arterialize (medical term), materialize, etherealize, immaterialize, dematerialize.

516.3.2.2

memorialize (commemorate), editorialize, territorialize.

516.3.3

actualize, visualize, ritualize, conceptualize, contextualize (put into context), desexualize (castrate or spay), intellectualize, individualize.

516.3.4

verbalize, hyperbolize (exaggerate).

516.3.5

analyse, canalize (provide with canals), channelize, psychoanalyse.

516.3.6

journalize (record in a journal), vernalize (botany term), internalize, externalize.

516.3.7

personalize, nationalize, rationalize, fictionalize, depersonalize, impersonalize, denationalize, conventionalize, internationalize, institutionalize.

516.3.8

liberalize, federalize, generalize, mineralize, gutturalize, naturalize, demineralize, denaturalize.

516.4

demise, remise (legal term), premise (state as a premiss), euphemize (use euphemisms), minimize, racemize (chemistry term), victimize, optimize, maximize, synonymize, legitimize.

516.5

alchemize (alter by alchemy), randomize, infamize (make infamous), Islamize, compromise, atomize, itemize, customize, macadamize, economize, epitomize, phlebotomize (surgical procedure), dichotomize (divide into two), autotomize (zoology term).

516.6

trichinize (infest with parasitic worms), Hellenize (make like ancient Greeks), feminize, scrutinize, divinize (deify), homogenize, nitrogenize, aluminize (cover with aluminium), bituminize, attitudinize (adopt opinion for effect), platitudinize.

516.6.1

Latinize, platinize (coat with platinum), gelatinize (become jelly-like), keratinize (biology term).

516.7

ionize, kyanize (make timber decay-resistant), lionize, carbonize, ebonize (finish to resemble ebony), urbanize, mechanize, preconize (announce publicly), volcanize (subject to volcanic heat), Balkanize (divide into warring states), vulcanize, cinchonize (treat with quinine), Christianize, modernize, euphonize (make pleasant-sounding), jargonize, paganize, organize, colonize, harmonize, Germanize, sermonize, Romanize, womanize, humanize, canonize, tyrannize, ironize (indulge in irony), synchronize, patronize, opsonize (medical term), Russianize, fractionize (divide into fractions), fraternize, Platonize (use Platonic principles), tetanize (induce tetanus), botanize, Teutonize (make German), westernize, heathenize, galvanize, unionize.

decarbonize, suburbanize, reorganize, disorganize, decolonize, dehumanize, skeletonize (reduce to minimum framework), Italianize.

Europeanize, Australianize, pedestrianize, republicanize, Americanize, Mohammedanize, revolutionize.

516.7.1
agonize, antagonize.

516.8
arise, theorize, barbarize, rubberize, suberize (botany term), moisturize, slenderize, tenderize, aphorize (use aphorisms), vulgarize, plagiarize, grangerize (illustrate with borrowed pictures), valorize (fix artificial price for), polarize, solarize (treat with sun's rays), bowdlerize, burglarize (*US* burgle), glamourize, memorize, summarize, mesmerize, vaporize, pauperize (impoverish), temporize, terrorize, mercerize, pressurize, satirize, cauterize, motorize, notarize (authenticate as notary), factorize, pasteurize, authorize, pulverize.

miniaturize, deodorize, categorize, revalorize (revalue), polymerize (chemistry term), isomerize (chemistry term), containerize, contemporize, extempo-

rize, depressurize, computerize, characterize, transistorize, familiarize.

denuclearize, exteriorize (medical term).

516.8.1
secularize, circularize (distribute circulars to), regularize, singularize, popularize, particularize.

516.8.2
militarize, catheterize, demilitarize.

516.9
apprise, surprise, enterprise.

516.10
laicize (remove ecclesiastical status), Gallicize (make French), publicize, anglicize, plasticize, mythicize, synthesize, italicize, catholicize, Hispanicize (make Spanish), fanaticize, poeticize, romanticize, metathesize (linguistics term), hypothesize, parenthesize, photosynthesize.

516.10.1
criticize, politicize, depoliticize.

516.11
assize, emphasize, ostracize, fantasize, oversize, exercise, metastasize (medical term), apotheosize (glorify).

516.12
digitize, sanitize, monetize (establish as legal tender), magnetize, concretize, syncretize (combine differing beliefs), sensitize, proselytize (convert to another faith), demonetize, remonetize, parasitize, desensitize, hyposensitize (make less sensitive), photosensitize (make sensitive to light), hypersensitize (photography term).

516.13
narcotize, schematize, traumatize, stigmatize, dogmatize, hypnotize, concertize (give concerts), advertise, mediatize (partially annex a state), sovietize, alphabetize, emblematize, acclimatize, automatize, aromatize (make aromatic), achromatize (remove colour from),

demagnetize, dehypnotize, operatize (make into an opera), democratize, bureaucratize, hypostatize (regard as real), apostatize (abandon one's faith), anaesthetize, diazotize (chemistry term).

516.13.1
dramatize, melodramatize, epigrammatize, anagrammatize.

516.13.2
systematize, legitimatize, anathematize (to curse).

516.14
empathize, sympathize, telepathize.

516.15
devise, revise, televise, collectivize.

517 -oz
Oz, Boz (pen name of Dickens), cos, was, 'twas, because, sovkhoz (Russian state farm), Badajoz (Spanish city).

518 -orz [also 9 + -s]
cause, gauze, hawse (nautical term), clause, Mors (Roman god), pause, drawers, tawse, yours, yaws, indoors, outdoors, kolkhoz (Russian collective farm), applause, jackstraws, Azores, Doukhobors (Russian Christian sect), Santa Claus, diapause (period of suspended growth), menopause, mesopause (meteorology term), aeropause (region of upper atmosphere), stratopause (meteorology term).

519 -oize [also 11 + -s]
noise, poise, turquoise, equipoise (equilibrium), centipoise (unit in physics), counterpoise (counterbalancing force), corduroys.

520 -oze [also 12 + -s]
chose, doze, hose, close, nose, pose, rose, brose (*Scot* porridge), croze (recess in barrel), froze, prose, throes, those.

ribose (a sugar), sorbose (a sugar), bilboes (iron bar with shackles), glucose, aldose (a sugar), bulldoze, bellows, xylose (a sugar), parclose (church screen), foreclose, enclose, unclose, disclose, mannose (a sugar), bluenose (*US* puritanical person), hooknose, depose, repose, impose, compose, dispose, transpose, expose, Faeroes, Burroughs, Ambrose, rockrose, sucrose, refroze, unfroze, primrose, Montrose, dextrose, ketose (a sugar), lactose, fructose, maltose, pentose, heptose, hexose.

Berlioz, caseose (biochemical compound), pantihose, ankylose, amylose (component of starch), cellulose, laevulose (a sugar), raffinose (a sugar), dominoes, bladdernose (type of seal), diagnose, bottlenose (type of dolphin), shovelnose (US freshwater sturgeon), decompose, recompose, discompose, predispose, indispose, quelquechose (insignificant thing), pettitoes, galactose (a sugar).

metamorphose, anastomose, superimpose, underexpose, overexpose.

520.1
aloes, gallows, Allhallows, lignaloes (Asian tree).

520.2
appose, oppose, propose, suppose, superpose (maths term), presuppose, interpose, juxtapose.

520.3
arose, tuberose (Mexican plant), saccharose, guelder-rose.

521 -ouze [also 13 + -s]
bouse (nautical term), Cowes, dowse, house, blouse, mouse (hunt mice), rouse, browse, drowse, trouse (close-fitting Irish breeches), rehouse, espouse, arouse, carouse.

522 -uz
buzz, does, fuzz, muzz (make muzzy),
abuzz, Hormuz (Iranian island).

523 -ooze [also 15 + -s]
ooze, Ouse, booze, choose, who's,
whose, lose, blues, flews (bloodhound's
fleshy upper lip), schmooze (US chat),
snooze, ruse, roose (Dialect to praise),
bruise, cruise, cruse, Druse (religious
sect in Lebanon), druse (crystals lining
rock cavity), trews, use, fuse, Hughes,
muse, mews, news.

Toulouse, peruse, abuse, accuse, incuse
(design stamped on coin), excuse, defuse, effuse, diffuse, refuse, infuse, confuse, transfuse, bemuse, amuse, misuse,
contuse (to bruise), enthuse.

Veracruz (Mexican state), Santa Cruz
(Argentine province), St. Andrews, disabuse, circumfuse (pour around), hypotenuse.

523.1
perfuse (permeate through), suffuse,
interfuse (intermingle).

524 -'z [also 17 + -s]
pliers, chequers, sneakers, knickers,
blinkers, bonkers, conkers (children's
game), Yonkers (US city), withers,
waders, glanders, Flanders, rounders,
taggers (tin-coated iron sheet), staggers
(type of vertigo), cobblers, bloomers,
honours, Connors, clippers, jodhpurs,
champers, rompers, vespers, horrors,
Messrs., lancers (type of dance), pincers, bitters, afters, hipsters, cleavers
(goosegrass), peevers (Scot hopscotch),
divers, tweezers, scissors, trousers.

Moluccas, dividers, malanders (horse
disease), pyjamas, Bahamas, head-
quarters, estovers (legal term).

Himalayas, camiknickers, knickerbockers, butterfingers, binoculars, Cordilleras (American mountain range).

525 -ads [also 83 + -s]
adze, scads (US lots).

526 -eeds [also 89 + -s]
Leeds, needs, proceeds.

527 -ides [also 92 + -s]
ides, besides, burnsides (US side-
whiskers), ironsides (person with great
stamina).

528 -ords [also 95 + -s]
cords, Lords, Broads, sideboards, towards.

529 -odes [also 98 + -s]
Rhodes, crossroads.

530 -uds [also 100 + -s]
buds, suds.

531 -'ds [also 103 + -s]
innards, backwards, seawards, forwards, inwards, onwards, downwards,
upwards, outwards, westwards, eastwards, northwards, southwards, billiards, afterwards, heavenwards.

532 -ends [also 131 + -s]
bends, amends, calends (day in Roman calendar).

533 -ounds [also 139 + -s]
bounds, zounds (archaic interjection).

534 -'nds [also 143 + -s]
Highlands, Midlands, Netherlands,
Bury St. Edmunds.

535 -egs [also 181 + -s]
dregs, sheerlegs (lifting device),
spindlelegs.

536 -ales [also **214** + -s]
Dales, tails, Wales, entrails.

537 -els [also **215** + -s]
Wells, Seychelles.

538 -ools [also **227** + -s]
pools, gules (heraldic term).

539 -'ls [also **228** + -s]
Peebles, Gorbals, doubles, shambles, gimbals (device enabling free suspension), hackles, Eccles, oodles, singles, shingles, annals, flannels, finals, Naples, Brussels, nuptials, Beatles, skittles, victuals, bristols, measles, bifocals, spectacles, genitals, incidentals, regimentals (regiment's uniform and insignia), unmentionables.

539.1
cobbles, collywobbles.

539.2
clericals, theatricals, academicals.

539.2.1
Chronicles, canonicals.

540 -arms [also **230** + -s]
arms, alms, Brahms, Psalms.

541 -ems [also **232** + -s]
hems, Thames.

542 -imes [also **236** + -s]
sometimes, betweentimes.

543 -'ms [also **242** + -s]
Adams, doldrums, customs, Williams.

544 -ans [also **245** + -s]
banns, cans (headphones), glans, Volans (constellation), Octans (constellation), Prestonpans (Scottish battle site), Lytham St. Anne's.

545 -ains [also **247** + -s]
pains, reins, Staines, remains, afterpains.

546 -ens [also **248** + -s]
ens (metaphysics term), Fens, gens (Roman aristocratic family), lens, cleanse, Valens (Roman emperor), lis pendens (legal term), impatiens (flowering plant), locum tenens, vas deferens, Homo sapiens, delirium tremens.

547 -eens [also **251** + -s]
jeans, means, greens, teens, Milton Keynes, Grenadines (West Indian islands), Philippines, smithereens.

548 -ins [also **252** + -s]
winze (steeply inclined mining shaft), gubbins (object of little value), Rubens, Dickens, dickens, Hawkins, Wilkins, Jenkins, Hopkins, moleskins, buckskins, Higgins, juggins (silly fellow), muggins, Collins, tenpins, ninepins, matins, Athens, avens (flowering plant), spillikins, candlepins (bowling game), withershins (*Scot* anticlockwise), galligaskins (17th-century men's breeches).

549 -ons [also **254** + -s]
bonze (Buddhist priest), pons (bridge of connecting tissue), bronze, frons (entomology term), long johns, nylons.

550 -oans [also **257** + -s]
Jones, nones, sawbones, crossbones, headphones, lazybones.

551 -'ns [also **261** + -s]
jibbons (*Dialect* spring onions), siemens (unit of electrical conductance), summons, barrens (*US* sparsely-vegetated land), Evans, evens, St. Albans, Gay Gordons, environs, abducens (cranial nerve), munitions, House of Commons.

551.1
relations, Galatians, combinations, congratulations, telecommunications.

552 -ings [also 265 + -s]

doings, makings, takings, tidings, leggings, lodgings, dealings, filings, whittlings (wood shavings), earnings, gleanings (useful crop remnants), screenings (refuse separated by sifting), innings, trappings, droppings, heartstrings, Hastings, beestings (first milk from cow), hustings, shavings, leavings, outgoings, surroundings, chitterlings (cooked intestines of pig), belongings, furnishings.

553 -eves [also 484 + -s and plurals of some nouns in 162]

eaves, heaves (disease of horses), greaves (residue of tallow), Hargreaves, Anne of Cleves.

554 -ives [also 486 + -s and plurals of some nouns in 164]

fives (ball game), hives, St. Ives, archives.

555 -elves [also 492 + -s and plurals of some nouns in 172]

ourselves, themselves.

INDEX

absquatulate
367.13
abstain 247
abstainer 17.227
abstemious 310.2
abstention 261.82
abstergent 420.19
abstinence 321.14
abstract 382
abstraction 261.76
abstractionism
242.35.14
abstruse 309
absurd 87
absurdity 16.333
Abu Dhabi 16.6
abulia 17.3.23
abundance 321
abundant 420.16
abuse 309, 523
abusive 485.8
abut 378
abutilon 261.41
abutment 420
abutter 17.349
abuzz 522
abvolt 405
abwatt 373
Abydos 310.16
abysm 242.35.5
abysmal 228.54
abyss 300.3
abyssal 228.85
Abyssinia 17.3.34
acacia 17.322
academe 234
academia 17.3.26
academic 38.25
academicals 539.2
academician
261.71.4
academicism
242.35.16
academy 16.222
Acadia 17.3.7
Acadian 261.3.3
acajou 15
acanthoid 97
acanthopterygian
261.3.7
acanthous 310.72
acanthus 310.72
Acapulco 12
acariasis 300.57.1
acarid 91.27

acaroid 97.12
acarology
16.108.4.13
acarpous 310
acarus 310.50
ACAS 293
accede 89
accelerant 420.65
accelerate 367.23
acceleration
261.67.22
accelerator
17.338.9
accelerometer
17.342.3.4
accent 410, 420.83
accentor 17.368
accentual 228.9
accentuate 367.2
accentuation
261.67.2
accept 422
acceptable
228.16.58
acceptance 321
acceptant 420
acceptation 261.67
acceptor 17.375
access 296
accessible
228.16.37
accession 261.68
accessory 16.274.34
acciaccatura 17.277
accidence 321.5
accident 420.10
accidental
228.110.1
accidie 16.63
accipiter 17.342
accipitrine 253
acclaim 231
acclamation
261.67.16
acclamatory
16.274.43.5
acclimatize 516.13
acclivity 16.333.35
accolade 85
accommodate
367.9
accommodating
265.64
accommodation
261.67.8

accompaniment
420.31
accompanist
436.13
accompany 16.237
accomplice 300
accomplish 353
accomplishment
420.47
accord 95.3
accordance 321
accordant 420.11
according 265.15
accordingly 16.175
accordion 261.3
accost 438
account 418
accountable
228.16.56
accountancy
16.312
accountant 420
accounting 265.73
accouplement
420.40
accoutre 17.351
accoutrement
420.35
Accra 1
accredit 371.12
accrete 370
accretion 261.70
Accrington 261
accrue 15
acculturate 367.23
accumulate 367.13
accumulation
261.67.13
accumulative
485.15.5
accumulator
17.338.6
accuracy 16.307
accurate 371.34
accursed 91
accusal 228.128
accusation 261.67
accusative 485.15
accusatorial
228.3.12.2
accusatory
16.274.43
accuse 523
accused 156
accuser 17.444

accustom 242.32
accustomed 127
ace 295
acedia 17.3.8
acentric 38.47
acephalous
310.26.3
acerate 367.23
acerbate 367.4
acerbic 38
acerbity 16.333
acerose 305.2
acervate 371.37
acescent 420.67
acetabulum 242.10
acetal 212
acetaldehyde 92
acetanilide 92.2
acetate 367.30.2
acetic 38.51
acetify 7.3
acetone 257.2
acetous 310.64
acetum 242.28
acetyl 218
acetylene 251.2
acetylide 92.2
acey-deucy 16.306
Achaea 17.2
Achaemenid 91.21
Achates 513.15
ache 34
achene 251
Achernar 1
Acheron 254.11
achievable
228.16.61
achieve 484
achievement 420
Achillean 261.2.2
Achilles 513.6
achondrite 372
achondroplasia
17.3.59
achromat 365
achromatic 38.49.2
achromatize 516.13
ach-y-fi 5
acicula 17.174.6
aciculum 242.10.1
acid 91.28
acidic 38
acidify 7.3.1
acidimeter 17.342.2

acidimetry 16.285.1
acidity 16.333.5.1
acidosis 300.55
acidulate 367.13
acidulous 310.25.4
acinus 310.33
Acis 300.50
ack-ack 32
ackee 5
acknowledge 197.2
acknowledgment 420.37
acme 16
acne 16.238
acnode 98
Acol 228.19
acolyte 372.4
aconite 372.6
acorn 255
acotyledon 261.23
acouchi 16.326
acoustic 38
acoustician 261.71
acoustics 498
acquaint 409
acquaintance 321
acquainted 91.45
acquiesce 296
acquiescence 321.21
acquiescent 420.67
acquire 8
acquisition 261.71.8
acquisitive 485.12
acquit 371
acquittal 228.102
acquittance 321.24
acre 17.30
acreage 197
acred 103
acrid 91
acridity 16.333.5
acriflavine 252
Acrilan 245.2
acrimonious 310.2.9.1
acrimony 16.237
acrobat 365
acrobatic 38.49
acrobatics 498.11
acrocarpous 310
acrodrome 239
acrogen 261.39

acrolith 458
acromegaly 16.131.2
acromion 261.3
acronychal 228.23.13
acronym 235
acronymic 38.28
acrophobia 17.3.4
acrophobic 38.3
Acropolis 300.13.2
acrospire 8.2
across 302.2
acrostic 38.71
acroter 17.347
acrylic 38.21
acrylonitrile 219
act 382
actin 252
actinal 228.60
acting 265.70
actinia 17.3.34
actinic 38.34
actinide 92
actinium 242.2.11
actinoid 97.8
actinomere 6.3
actinometer 17.342.3
actinomycin 252.22
actinouranium 242.2.10
action 261.76
actionable 228.16.31
Actium 242.2
activate 367.36
activation 261.67
activator 17.338.11
active 485.16
actively 16.206
activeness 300.43
activism 242.35.22
activist 436
activity 16.333.35.2
Acton 261
actor 17.353
actress 300.48
actual 228.9.4
actuality 16.333.8.2
actualize 516.3.3
actually 16.131.1
actuarial 228.3.10
actuary 16.274.2
actuate 367.2

acuity 16.333.3
aculeate 371.1.1
aculeus 310.2
acumen 248
acuminate 367.17.6, 371.24
acupuncture 17.68
acute 380.3
acuteness 300.40
acyclic 38
acyl 218
ad 83
Ada 17.79
adactylous 310.23
adage 197
adagio 12.3
Adam 242.5
adamant 420.35
adamantine 253.9
Adamite 372
Adams 543
adamsite 372
Adana 17.239
adapt 421
adaptable 228.16
adaptation 261.67
adapter 17.374
adaptive 485.22
adaxial 228.3.18
add 83
addax 494
addend 131
addendum 242.7
adder 17.77
addict 387, 387.1
addiction 261.78.2
addictive 485.18
Addis Ababa 17.21
Addison 261.65
addition 261.71.2
additional 228.63.5
additive 485.12
addle 228.31
address 296
addressee 5.19
Addressograph 158.1
adduce 309.1
adduction 261.79.1
adductor 17.357
Adelaide 85
Aden 261.20
adenectomy 16.222.5

adenitis 300.62.3
adenoid 97.8
adenoidal 228.35
adenoidectomy 16.222.5.1
adenoma 17.215
adenosine 251.9
adept 422
adequacy 16.307
adequate 371
adhere 6
adherence 321.17
adherent 420.62
adhesion 261.90
adhesive 485
ad hoc 40
adiaphorism 242.35.15
adiaphorous 310.50
adieu 15.8
ad infinitum 242.29
adipocere 6.7
adipose 305
Adirondacks 494
adit 371
Adivasi 16.295
adjacent 420
adjectival 228.121
adjective 485.18
adjoin 256
adjoining 265
adjoint 416
adjourn 249
adjournment 420
adjudge 203
adjudicate 367.5
adjudication 261.67.5
adjudicator 17.338.2
adjunct 393
adjure 10
adjust 443
adjustable 228.16.60
adjustment 420
adjutant 420.78
adjuvant 420
Adler 17.183
ad-lib 24
adman 261
admass 293
admeasure 17.333

Admetus 310.63
admin 252
adminicle
 228.23.12
administer
 17.384.1
administrate
 367.28
administration
 261.67.25
administrative
 485.15
administrator
 17.338
admirable
 228.16.35
admiral 228.76
admiralty 16.352
admiration
 261.67.22
admire 8
admirer 17.274
admissible
 228.16.39
admission 261.71
admissive 485.4
admit 371
admittance 321.24
admittedly 16.148
admixture 17.76
admonish 353.8
admonition 261.71
ad nauseam 229
adnominal
 228.60.5
adnoun 258
ado 15.3
adobe 16.12
adolescence 321.21
adolescent 420.67
Adonic 38
Adonis 300.25
adopt 425
adopted 91
adoption 261.86
adoptive 485
adorable 228.16
adoration
 261.67.22
adore 9.4
adorn 255
adornment 420
adrenal 228.59
adrenaline 252.11
adrenergic 38.16

Adrian 261.3
Adriatic 38.49
adrift 398
adroit 375
adscititious 310.58
adsorb 27
adsorbent 420
adsorption 261.87
adularia 17.3.38
adulate 367.13
adulation
 261.67.13
adulatory
 16.274.40.2
adult 406
adulterant 420.65
adulterate 367.23,
 371.35
adulterer 17.279
adulterine 253.7
adulterous 310.50
adultery 16.274
adulthood 101
adumbral 228.77
adumbrate 367
Aduwa 1
ad valorem 242.20
advance 315
advancement 420
advantage 197
advantageous
 310.20
advection 261.77
advent 410
Adventist 436.27
adventitia 17.3.49
adventitious 310.58
adventure 17.70
adventurer 17.279
adventurism
 242.35.15
adventurous 310.50
adverb 22
adverbial 228.3
adversary 16.274
adversative 485.15
adverse 297
adversity 16.333.26
advert 369
advertence 321
advertise 516.13
advertisement 420
advertiser 17.441
advertising 265.82
advice 301

advisable 228.16.64
advise 516
advised 154
advisedly 16.148
adviser 17.441
advisory 16.274.53
advocaat 1
advocacy 16.307
advocate 367.6,
 371
advocation
 261.67.6
adynamia 17.3.24
adze 525
aecidium 242.2.3
aeciospore 9.10
aedes 513.3
aedile 219
Aeëtes 513.16
Aegean 261.2
Aegina 17.232
Aegir 6
aegis 300.6
aegrotat 365
Aegyptus 310.71
Aeneas 310.1
Aeneid 91.1
Aeolian 261.3.12
Aeolic 38.22
aeolipile 219
Aeolis 300.13
aeon 261.2
aeonian 261.3.18
aepyornis 300.24
aerate 367
aerial 228.3.10
aerialist 436.7.2
aeriform 238.1
aerify 7.3
aerobatics 498.11
aerobe 28
aerobic 38.3
aerobics 498
aerobium 242.2
aerodonetics
 498.12.1
aerodrome 239
aerodynamic 38.24
aerodynamics
 498.2
aerodyne 253.2
aerofoil 222.1
aerogel 215
aerogram 229.1
aerology 16.108.4

aeromechanic
 38.31
aerometer 17.342.3
aeronaut 374
aeronautical 228.23
aeronautics 498
aeropause 518
aerophagia 17.3.12
aerophobia 17.3.4
aerophobic 38.3
aeroplane 247
aerosol 220
aerospace 295
aerosphere 6.1
aerostat 365
aerostatics 498.11
aerugo 12.32
aery 16.264
Aeschylus 310.23
Aesculapius 310.2
Aesir 6
Aesop 276
aesthesia 17.3.60
aesthete 370
aesthetic 38.50
aesthetician
 261.71.7
aestheticism
 242.35.16
aesthetics 498.12
aestival 228.121
aestivate 367.36
aestivation 261.67
aetiology
 16.108.4.1
Aetolia 17.3.22
afar 1
afebrile 219
affable 228.16
affair 4.3
affairs 512
affect 385.2
affectation 261.67
affected 91.43
affecting 265.71
affection 261.77
affectionate 371.28
affective 485.17
affenpinscher
 17.331
afferent 420.65
affiance 321.2
affiant 420.2
affidavit 371
affiliate 367.1.2

affiliation
261.67.1.1
affine 253
affined 135
affinity 16.333.17
affirm 233
affirmation
261.67.16
affirmative 485.15
affix 498
affixture 17.76
afflatus 310.62
afflict 387
affliction 261.78
affluence 321.3
affluent 420.4
afflux 502
afford 95
afforest 436.18
affranchise 516
affray 2
affreightment
420.48
affricate 371.9
affricative 485.15.1
affright 372
affront 419.1
affusion 261.93
Afghan 245
afghani 16.224
Afghanistan 246.1
aficionado 12.16
afield 115.1
afire 8.1
aflame 231
afloat 376
afoot 379.1
afore 9.6
aforementioned
143
aforesaid 86
aforethought 374
a fortiori 7.11
afoul 224
afraid 85
afreet 370
afresh 351
Africa 17.34
African 261.13
Africanism
242.35.14.2
Afrikaans 315
Afrikaner 17.226.2
Afro 12
afrormosia 17.3.62

aft 396
after 17.358
afterbirth 456
afterbody 16.65
afterburner 17.229
aftercare 4
afterdamp 285
afterdeck 35
aftereffect 385.1
afterglow 12.46
afterimage 197.3
afterlife 164
aftermath 452
afternoon 260.2
afterpains 545
afters 524
aftersensation
261.67.26
aftershaft 396
aftershave 482
aftershock 40
aftertaste 432
afterthought 374
afterwards 531
afterword 87
afterworld 114
aga 17.124
Agadir 6
again 248
against 447
Aga Khan 246
agalloch 46
agama 17.218
Agamemnon 254
agamic 38.24
agapanthus 310.72
Agape 16.254
agape 270
agar 17.125
agaric 38.44
Agartala 1.9
agate 371
agateware 4.9
agave 16.379
age 193
aged 91
agee 5.7
ageing 265.24
ageless 300
agency 16.312
agenda 17.101
agenesis 300.52.4
agent 420
ageratum 242.27
ages 515

agger 17.144
agglomerate
367.23, 371.35
agglomeration
261.67.22
agglutinate 367.17
agglutination
261.67.18
agglutinative
485.15.7
agglutinin 252.17
aggrade 85.6
aggrandize 516
aggravate 367,
367.37
aggravation 261.67
aggregate 367.10,
371.14
aggress 296
aggression 261.68
aggressive 485.2.1
aggressor 17.300
aggrieve 484
aggro 12
aghast 431.1
agile 219
agility 16.333.9
Agincourt 374
agiotage 197
agist 436.4
agitate 367.30
agitation 261.67.27
agitator 17.338.10
agitprop 276
Aglaia 17.4
agleam 234
agley 2
aglitter 17.342
aglow 12.46
agma 17.220
agminate 371.24
agnate 367
Agnes 300
agnomen 248
agnostic 38.71
agnosticism
242.35.16
ago 12.33
agog 185.2
à gogo 12.31
agon 257
agonist 436.13.2
agonistic 38.70.4
agonize 516.7.1
agony 16.237

agora 1.14, 17.279
agoraphobia 17.3.4
agoraphobic 38.3
agouti 16.343
agraffe 157
agrapha 17.120
agraphia 17.3.10
agrarian 261.3.21
agree 5
agreeable 228.16.1
agreed 89
agreement 420
agrestal 228.113
agrestic 38.69
Agricola 17.176.2
agriculture 17.69
agrimony 16.237
Agrippa 17.253
Agrippina 17.230
agrobiology
16.108.4.2
agrology 16.108.4
agronomics 498
agronomy 16.222.3
aground 139.2
agrypnotic 38.53.2
ague 15
Agulhas 310
ah 1
aha 1.5
Ahab 18
Ahasuerus 310.45
ahead 86.5
ahem 232
Ahmed 86
ahoy 11
Ahwaz 508
ai 16.1
aid 85
Aidan 261.20
aide 85
aide-de-camp 266
aider 17.79
aigrette 368
aiguille 217
aiguillette 368
aikido 12.19
ail 214
ailanthus 310.72
aileron 254.11
ailing 265.27
ailment 420.39
ailurophile 219.1
ailurophilia
17.3.21.2

ailurophobe 28
aim 231
aimless 300
aimlessness 300.33
ain 247
ain't 409
aïoli 16.126
air 4
Aïr 6
airborne 255
airbrick 38
airbrush 356
airburst 434
airbus 307
aircraft 396
aircraftman 261
aircrew 15
airdrop 276
Airedale 214
airfield 115
airflow 12
airfoil 222
airframe 231
airhead 86
airiness 300.23
airing 265.52
airless 300
airlift 398
airline 253
airliner 17.232
airlock 40
airman 261.46
airplane 247
airport 374
airs 512
airscrew 15
airship 274
airsick 38
airsickness 300.27
airspace 295
airspeed 89
airstream 234
airstrip 274
airtight 372
airway 2
airworthy 16.375
airy 16.264
airy-fairy 16.264
Aisha 1
aisle 219
ait 367
aitchbone 257
Ajaccio 12.3
ajar 1
Ajax 494

Ajmer 6
Akbar 1
Akela 17.162
akhara 1
Akhenaten 261.95
akimbo 12.6
akin 252.4
Akkad 83
à la 1.7
ala 17.162
Alabama 17.205
alabaster 17.380
à la carte 366
alack 32
alackaday 2.8
alacrity 16.333
Aladdin 252
Alai 7
alameda 17.79
Alamo 12
à la mode 98
alamode 98.1
Alan 261
Alanbrooke 44
alannah 17.225
alap 269
alar 17.162
Alaric 38.44
alarm 230.1
alarmed 123
alarming 265.35
alarmism 242.35
alarmist 436.8
alary 16.274
alas 293
Alaska 17.47
alate 367
albacore 9.2
Alba Longa 17.142
Albania 17.3.31
Albanian 261.3.15
Albans 551
Albany 16.237
albata 17.338
albatross 302
albeit 371
Albert 381
Alberta 17.340
albertite 372.12
albescent 420.67
Albigenses 513.14
albinic 38.34
albinism 242.35.13
albino 12.54
Albinus 310.32

Albion 261.3
albite 372
album 242
albumen 252
albuminoid 97.8
albuminous
   310.33.1
albuminuria
   17.3.42.1
Albuquerque 16.23
Albury 16.274
Alcaic 38.1
alcaide 85
alcalde 16.73
Alcatraz 507
alcazar 1.19
Alcestis 300.68
alchemic 38.25
alchemist 436.10
alchemize 516.5
alchemy 16.222
alcheringa 17.141
alcidine 253
Alcock 40
alcohol 220
alcoholic 38.22
alcoholicity
   16.333.28
alcoholism 242.35
alcoholometer
   17.342.3
Alcoran 246
Alcott 381
alcove 488
Alcyone 16.237.1
Aldabra 17.280
Aldebaran 261.60
aldehyde 92
alder 17.96
alderman 261.52
aldermanic 38.31
Aldermaston 261
Alderney 16.237
Aldershot 373
aldol 220
aldose 520
aldosterone 257.1
ale 214
aleatory
   16.274.43.1
Alec 38.19
alecost 438
alee 5.9
alegar 17.129
alehouse 306

Alemanni 16.224
Alemannic 38.31
alembic 38
alembicated
   91.34.3
Aleppo 12.58
alert 369
alertness 300.36
alethic 38
aleurone 261.59
alevin 252
alewife 164
Alexander 17.99
Alexander Nevski
   16.43
Alexandra 17.287
Alexandria 17.3
Alexandrian 261.3
Alexandrine 253
alexandrite 372
alexia 17.3.57
alfalfa 17.121
alfilaria 17.3.38
Alfred 91
alfresco 12.14
algae 5
algebra 17.283
algebraic 38.1.1
algebraist 436.1
Algeciras 310.46
Algeria 17.3.39
Algerian 261.3.22
algerine 251.7
algicide 92.7
algid 91
Algiers 514
algoid 97
ALGOL 220
Algol 220
algolagnia 17.3
algology 16.108.4
algometer 17.342.3
Algonquian 261.3
Algonquin 252
algophobia 17.3.4
algor 9
algorism 242.35.15
algorithm 242.33
Alhambra 17.284
Al Hufuf 170
alias 310.2.3
Ali Baba 17.10
alibi 7
Alicante 16.353
Alice 300

alidad 83
alidade 85
alien 261.3.8
alienable 228.16.31
alienate 367.18
alienation
 261.67.19
alienee 5.14
alienist 436.13
alienor 17.239
aliform 238.1
alight 372.4
align 253.3
alignment 420
alike 39
aliment 410.1,
 420.31
alimentary
 16.274.47
alimentation
 261.67.32.1
alimony 16.237
aliped 86.6
aliphatic 38.49
aliquant 420.58
aliquot 373
aliunde 16.80
alive 486
alizarin 252.20
alkahest 433
alkali · 7.7
alkalic 38.19
alkalify 7.3
alkalimeter
 17.342.2
alkalimetry
 16.285.1
alkaline 253.3
alkalinity
 16.333.17.1
alkalize 516.3
alkaloid 97.6
alkane 247
alkanet 368
alkyl 218
alkylation
 261.67.12
alkyne 253
all 221
Allah 17.160
allantoid 97
allantois 300.1
allay 2.12
allegation
 261.67.10

allege 194
alleged 109
allegedly 16.148
allegiance 321
allegoric 38.41
allegorical
 228.23.17
allegory 16.274.9
allegretto 12.75
allegro 12
allele 217
alleluia 17.432
allemande 129
Allen 261
Alleppey 16.254
allergen 261.39
allergenic 38.32.1
allergic 38.16
allergist 436.4.1
allergy 16.108.2
alleviate 367.1.10
alleviation
 261.67.1.6
alley 16.112
alleyway 2
Allhallows 520.1
Allhallowtide 92
allheal 217
alliaceous 310.56
alliance 321.2
allied 92
alligator 17.338.3
alliterate 367.23.2
alliteration
 261.67.22.4
alliterative
 485.15.10
allium 242.2
Alloa 17.6
allocate 367.6
allocation 261.67.6
allochthonous
 310.36
allocution 261.75.2
allodial 228.3
allodium 242.2.4
allograph 158.1
allomerism
 242.35.15
allometry 16.285.2
allomorph 166.1
allomorphism
 242.35.7
allonym 235
allopath 452

allopathic 38.72
allopathy 16.373.1
allopatric 38.45
allophane 247.3
allopurinol 220.3
allot 373.1
allotment 420
allotrope 278.3
allotropic 38.37.2
allotropy 16.254
allottee 5
allow 13
allowable 228.16.5
allowance 321
Alloway 2.28
alloy 11, 11.1
allseed 89
allspice 301
allude 102.1
allure 10.4
alluring 265.56
allusion 261.93
allusive 485.8
alluvial 228.3.17
alluvion 261.3.32
alluvium 242.2
ally 7, 7.7
allyl 218
Almagest 433
alma mater 17.337
almanac 32
almandine 253
Al Marj 192
Alma-Tadema
 17.211
almemar 1
almighty 16.334
Almohade 85
almond 143
almoner 17.239
almonry 16.284
Almoravide 92.13
almost 441
alms 540
almshouse 306
almucantar 17.365
almuce 309
aloe 12.38
aloes 520.1
aloft 399
aloha 17.6
alone 257
along 266.1
alongshore 9
alongside 92

aloof 170
aloofness 300
alopecia 17.325
aloud 99
alow 12.45
alp 282
alpaca 17.28
alpenhorn 255
alpenstock 40
alpestrine 252
alpha 17.121
alphabet 368.3
alphabetic 38.50.2
alphabetical
 228.23.19
alphabetize 516.13
Alpha Centauri
 16.269
alphanumeric
 38.39
alphorn 255
alphosis 300.55
alpine 253
alpinism 242.35.13
alpinist 436.11
already 16.60
alright 372
Alsace 293
Alsatian 261.67
alsike 39
also 12
also-ran 245
alt 401
Altaic 38.1
Altair 4
altar 17.363
altarpiece 298.2
altazimuth 464
alter 17.363
alterable 228.16.35
alteration
 261.67.22
alterative 485.15.10
altercate 367.6
altercation
 261.67.6
alter ego 12.28
alternant 420
alternate 367.18,
 371.23
alternately 16.189
alternation
 261.67.19
alternative 485.15
alternator 17.338.8

althorn 255
although 12
altimeter 17.342.2
altimetry 16.285.1
altitude 102.2
alto 12.82
altocumulus
 310.25.5
altogether 17.402
Altona 17.236
altostratus 310.62
altricial 228.93
Altrincham 242.17
altruism 242.35.4
altruist 436
altruistic 38.70
aludel 215
alula 17.174
alum 242
alumina 17.231
aluminate 367.17.6
aluminium
 242.2.11
aluminize 516.6
aluminothermy
 16.214
aluminous 310.33.1
alumna 17.242
alumnus 310
alunite 372
alveolar 17.176
alveolus 310
always 509
alyssum 242.24
am 229
amadou 15.3
amah 17.206
amalgam 242
amalgamate 367.16
amalgamation
 261.67.16
amanita 17.343
amanuensis 300
amaranth 467
amarelle 215
amaryllidaceous
 310.56.2
amaryllis 300.8
amass 293
amateur 17.352
amateurish 353.11
amatol 220
amatory
 16.274.43.5
amaut 377

amaze 509
amazement 420
amazing 265.81
Amazon 261
Amazonas 310.35
Amazonian
 261.3.18
amazonite 372.6
Ambala 17.161
ambary 16.261
ambassador 17.92
ambassadorial
 228.3.12
ambassadorship
 274.1
ambassadress 300
amber 17.23
ambergris 298
amberjack 32
amberoid 97.12
ambidexterity
 16.333.21
ambidextrous 310
ambience 321.1
ambient 420.1
ambiguity 16.333.3
ambiguous 310.4
ambit 371
ambition 261.71
ambitious 310.58
ambivalence
 321.12
ambivert 369.1
amble 228.17
amblyopia 17.3.37
amboceptor 17.375
Amboina 17.235
amboyna 17.235
Ambrose 520
ambrosia 17.3.62
ambsace 295
ambulance 321
ambulant 420.27
ambulate 367.13
ambulatory
 16.274.40.2
ambuscade 85
ambush 357
ameliorate 367.23
amelioration
 261.67.22
amen 248
amenable 228.16
amend 131.2

amendatory
 16.274.43.2
amendment 420
amends 532
Amenhotep 271
amenity 16.333
amenorrhoea
 17.2.2
Amen-Ra 1
ament 410
ament 420
amentia 17.330
America 17.34.2
American 261.13
Americana
 17.226.2
Americanism
 242.35.14.2
Americanize 516.7
Amerindian 261.3
amethyst 436
amethystine 253.10
Amhara 17.268
Amharic 38.38
amiable 228.16.2
amianthus 310.72
amicable 228.16.10
amice 300
amicus curiae 5.2
amid 91.19
amide 92
amidships 327
amigo 12.28
Amin 251
amino 12.54
amir 6.3
Amis 300
amiss 300.20
amitosis 300.55.6
amity 16.333.11
Amman 246
ammeter 17.341
ammine 251
ammo 12
Ammon 261.44
ammonal 228.63
ammonate 367.18
ammonia 17.3.36
ammoniac 32.1
ammoniacal
 228.28.1
ammonic 38.35.3
ammonite 372.6
ammonium
 242.2.12

ammunition 261.71
amnesia 17.3.60
amnesiac 32.1
amnesty 16.366
amniocentesis
 300.51
amnion 261.3
amniotic 38.53
amoeba 17.13
amoebaean 261.2
amoebiasis
 300.57.1
amoebic 38
amoeboid 97
amok 43
among 267
amontillado 12.16
amoral 228.73
amorality
 16.333.8.9
amoretto 12.75
amorist 436.20
amoroso 12.70
amorous 310.50
amorphous 310.18
amortize 516
Amos 302
amount 418.1
amour 10.1
Amoy 11
amp 285
ampelopsis 300.61
ampere 4
ampersand 128
amphetamine
 252.15
amphiaster 17.379
amphibian 261.3.2
amphibiotic
 38.53.1
amphibious 310.2
amphibole 223
amphibolite 372.4
amphibology
 16.108.4
amphibrach 32
amphichroic 38.2
amphictyon 261.3
amphigory
 16.274.9
amphimixis 300
amphipod 94
amphiprostyle
 219.7

amphisbaena 17.230
amphistylar 17.167
amphitheatre 17.352
amphitricha 17.34
Amphitrite 16.334
amphitropous 310.40
Amphitryon 261.3
amphora 17.279
amphoteric 38.39
ample 228
amplexicaul 221.1
amplifier 17.4.1
amplify 7.3
amplitude 102.2
amply 16.178
ampoule 227
ampulla 17.174
amputate 367
amputation 261.67.29
amputee 5.23
Amravati 16.344
amrita 17.341
Amritsar 17.320
Amsterdam 229
amulet 371.17
Amur 10.1
amuse 523
amused 156
amusement 420
amusing 265.84
Amy 16.212
amygdala 17.176
amygdalate 371.18
amygdale 214
amygdalin 252.11
amygdaloid 97.6
amygdaloidal 228.35
amyl 218
amylase 509
amyloid 97.5
amylose 520
amylum 242
an 245
ana 17.226
anabaena 17.230
anabantid 91
Anabaptist 436
anabas 293
anabasis 300.57
anabiosis 300.55.2

anableps 324
anabolic 38.22
anabolism 242.35.11
anabranch 78
anachorism 242.35.15
anachronic 38.35
anachronism 242.35.14
anachronistic 38.70.4
anaclinal 228.61
anaclitic 38.52
anacoluthia 17.3
anacoluthon 254
anaconda 17.104
anacoustic 38
Anacreon 254.1
anacrusis 300.56
anadem 232
anadromous 310.29
anaemia 17.3.26
anaemic 38.27
anaerobic 38.3
anaesthesia 17.3.60
anaesthetic 38.50
anaesthetics 498.12
anaesthetist 436.26
anaesthetize 516.13
anaglyph 163
anaglypta 17.376
anagoge 16.106
anagram 229.1
anagrammatic 38.49.2
anagrammatize 516.13.1
Anaheim 236
anal 228.56
analemma 17.208
analeptic 38.65
analgesia 17.3.60
analgesic 38
analgia 17.3.16
analogize 516.1
analogous 310
analogue 185
analogy 16.108.2
analphabetic 38.50.2
analysand 128
analyse 516.3.5
analysis 300.52.1

analyst 436.7.4
analytic 38.52.1
analytical 228.23.20
Anambra 17.284
anamnesis 300.51
anamorphosis 300.57.2
Ananias 310.3
ananthous 310.72
anapaest 433
anaphase 509
anaphora 17.279
anaphylactic 38.58
anaphylaxis 300.70
anaplasia 17.3.59
anaplastic 38.68
anaplasty 16.361.1
anaptyxis 300
anarchic 38
anarchism 242.35.6
anarchist 436
anarchy 16.33
anarthria 17.3
anasarca 17.29
Anastasia 17.3.59
anastigmat 365
anastigmatic 38.49.3
anastomose 520
anastomosis 300.55
anastrophe 16.90
anatase 509
anathema 17.218
anathematize 516.13.2
Anatolia 17.3.22
Anatolian 261.3.12
anatomical 228.23.9
anatomist 436.10
anatomy 16.222
Anaximander 17.98
anbury 16.274
ancestor 17.382
ancestral 228.81
ancestry 16.292
Anchises 513.13
anchor 17.43
anchorage 197
anchorite 372.8
anchoveta 17.339
anchovy 16.385
anchusa 17.308

ancient 420
ancillary 16.274.16
and 128
Andalusia 17.3
andante 16.353
andantino 12.54
Andean 261.2
Anderson 261
Andes 513
andesite 372
Andhra Pradesh 351
andiron 261.4
Andorra 17.276
Andover 17.417
andradite 372.2
Andrea 17.3.45
Andrew 15
Andrews 523
Androcles 513
androclinium 242.2.11
androecium 242.2
androgen 261.39
androgenic 38.32.1
androgenous 310.33
androgyne 253
android 97
Andromache 16.33
Andromeda 17.83
Andros 302
androsphinx 505
androsterone 257.1
Andvari 16.261
Andy 16.77
ane 247
anecdotage 197.13
anecdotal 228.106
anecdote 376
anechoic 38.2
anemochore 9.2
anemography 16.90.2.3
anemology 16.108.4.9
anemometer 17.342.3
anemometry 16.285.2
anemone 16.237.6
anent 410
anergic 38.16
anergy 16.108

aneurysm 242.35.15
anew 15
anfractuosity 16.333.30.2
anfractuous 310.4
angary 16.274
angel 228
angelfish 353
angelic 38.20
angelica 17.34
angelical 228.23.6
angelology 16.108.4
Angelus 310.23
anger 17.140
Angevin 252
angina 17.232
angina pectoris 300.47
angioma 17.215
angle 228.49
angler 17.194
Anglesey 16.308
Anglia 17.3
Anglian 261.3
Anglican 261.13
Anglicanism 242.35.14.2
Anglice 16.300
Anglicism 242.35.16
Anglicist 436.21
anglicize 516.10
angling 265
Anglomania 17.3.31.1
Anglophile 219.1
Anglophilia 17.3.21.2
Anglophobe 28
Anglophobia 17.3.4
Anglophone 257
Angola 17.171
angora 17.276
angostura 17.277
angry 16
Anguilla 17.166
anguine 252
anguish 353
angular 17.174
angularity 16.333.20.3

angulate 367.13.4, 371.17
angulation 261.67.13.2
Angus 310
anhedral 228.78
anhinga 17.141
Anhwei 2
anhydride 92
anhydrous 310
ani 16.224
Aniakchak 32
aniconic 38.35
anil 218
anile 219
aniline 252.8
anima 17.211
animadversion 261.69
animadvert 369
animal 228.52
animalcule 227
animalism 242.35.11
animality 16.333.8
animalize 516.3
animate 367.15, 371.19
animation 261.67.15
animatism 242.35.20
animator 17.338
animé 2
animism 242.35
animosity 16.333.30
animus 310.28.1
anion 261.4
anise 300
aniseed 89.2
aniseikonia 17.3.36
anisette 368
anisogamy 16.222.2
anisole 223.4
Ankara 17.279
ankh 51
ankle 228
anklebone 257
anklet 371
ankylosaur 9.11
ankylose 520
ankylosis 300.55
anlace 300

Anna 17.225
Annaba 17.21
annabergite 372
annal 228.55
annals 539
Annam 229
Annapolis 300.13.1
annates 335
annatto 12.72
Anne 245
anneal 217.1
annelid 91
Anne of Cleves 553
annex 496
annexation 261.67.35
annexe 496
Annie 16.223
annihilate 367.14.1
annihilation 261.67.14.1
anniversary 16.274.35
anno Domini 7.10
annotate 367.31
annotation 261.67.28
announce 319
announcement 420
announcer 17.317
annoy 11
annoyance 321
annoyed 97.9
annual 228.9.2
annuitant 420.76
annuity 16.333.3
annul 225
annular 17.174.9
annulate 371.17
annulation 261.67.13
annulet 371.17
annulment 420
annulose 305
annulus 310.25
annunciate 367.1
annunciation 261.67.1.4
annunciator 17.338.1
anoa 17.6
anode 98
anodize 516

anodyne 253.2
anoint 416
anointment 420.50
anole 223
anomalous 310.26
anomaly 16.131
anomie 16.219
anon 254.8
anonym 235
anonymity 16.333.12
anonymous 310.28.2
anopheles 513.6.1
anorak 32.3
anorexia 17.3.57
anorexia nervosa 17.306
anorthosite 372.10
anosmia 17.3
another 17.408
anoxaemia 17.3.26.1
anoxia 17.3
ansate 367
Anschluss 308
Anselm 243
anserine 253.7
Anshan 245
answer 17.313
answerable 228.16.35
ant 407
anta 17.365
antacid 91.28
antagonism 242.35.14
antagonist 436.13.2
antagonistic 38.70.4
antagonize 516.7.1
antalkali 7.7
Antarctic 38.59
Antarctica 17.34
Antares 513.10
ante 16.353
anteater 17.341
antebellum 242.8
antecede 89.2
antecedence 321.4
antecedent 420.9
antechoir 8.3
antedate 367.8
antediluvian 261.3.32

aoudad 83
apace 295.4
Apache 16.46
apache 350
apagoge 16.106
Aparri 16.261
apart 366.1
apartheid 372
apartment 420
apathetic 38.50.6
apathy 16.373
apatite 372.12
ape 270
Apeldoorn 255
apelike 39
apeman 261
aperient 420.1
aperiodic 38.9
apéritif 162
aperture 17.62
apery 16.274
apetalous 310.26
apex 496
aphaeresis 300.52
aphagia 17.3.12
aphasia 17.3.59
aphelion 261.3.10
aphid 91
aphis 300
aphonia 17.3.36
aphonic 38.35.2
aphorism 242.35.15
aphoristic 38.70.5
aphorize 516.8
aphotic 38.53
aphrodisiac 32.1
Aphrodite 16.334
aphtha 17.398
aphyllous 310.23
apian 261.3
apiarian 261.3.21
apiarist 436.20
apiary 16.274.1
apical 228.23
apices 513
apiece 298.2
Apis 300
apish 353
apivorous 310.50.3
aplanatic 38.49.5
aplanospore 9.10
aplasia 17.3.59
aplastic 38.68
aplenty 16.355
aplite 372

aplomb 237
Apo 12.57
apocalypse 327
apocalyptic 38.66
apocarpous 310
apochromatic
    38.49.2
apocope 16.254
apocrine 253
Apocrypha 17.114
apocryphal 228.41
apocynthion
    261.3.28
apodal 228.38
apodosis 300.57
apogee 5.7
apolitical 228.23.20
Apollinaris 300.44
Apollo 12.43
Apollonian
    261.3.18
apologetic 38.50.3
apologetics 498.12
apologia 17.3.15
apologist 436.4
apologize 516.1
apologue 185
apology
    16.108.4.12
apolune 260.1
apomict 387
apomixis 300
apophasis 300.57
apophthegm 232
apophyge 16.103
apophyllite 372.3
apophysis 300.52
apoplectic 38.60
apoplexy 16.387
aposematic 38.49.1
apospory 16.269
apostasy 16.307
apostate 367.34
apostatize 516.13
a posteriori 7.11
apostle 228.86
apostolate 371.18
apostolic 38.22
apostrophe 16.90
apostrophic 38.13
apostrophize 516
apothecary
    16.274.4
apothem 232
apotheosis 300.55.1

apotheosize 516.11
apotropaic 38.1
appal 221
Appalachia 17.3
Appalachian 261.3
appalling 265.31
Appaloosa 17.308
apparatus 310.62
apparel 228.72
apparent 420.60
apparition 261.71
apparitor 17.342
appeal 217
appear 6.6
appearance 321.17
appease 513
appeasement 420
appel 215
appellant 420.26
appellate 371.15
appellation
    261.67.12
appellative
    485.15.4
appellee 5
append 131
appendage 197
appendant 420.14
appendectomy
    16.222.5
appendicectomy
    16.222.5
appendicitis 300.62
appendicular
    17.174.6
appendix 498
apperceive 484
apperception
    261.84.1
appertain 247.10
appetence 321.24
appetite 372.11
appetizer 17.441
appetizing 265.82
applaud 95
applause 518
apple 228.64
applecart 366
applejack 32
applesnits 339
appliance 321.2
applicable
    228.16.10
applicant 420.7

application
    261.67.5
applicative
    485.15.1
applicator 17.338.2
applicatory
    16.274.40.1
applied 92
appliqué 2.6
apply 7.9
appoggiatura
    17.277
appoint 416.1
appointee 5
appointment
    420.50
appointor 17.371
Appomattox 503
apportion 261.72.1
apportionment
    420.42
appose 520.2
apposite 371.40
apposition 261.71.9
appositive 485.12.1
appraisal 228.125
appraise 509
appreciable
    228.16.42
appreciate 367.1
appreciation
    261.67.1
appreciative 485.15
apprehend 131.1
apprehensible
    228.16.40
apprehension
    261.82.1
apprehensive 485.9
apprentice 300
apprenticed 436.27
apprenticeship 274
appressed 433
apprise 516.9
approach 70
approachable
    228.16.13
approbate 367.4
approbation
    261.67.3
appropriate 367.1,
    371.1
appropriateness
    300.38

appropriation 261.67.1
approval 228.122
approve 490
approved 150
approximal 228.52
approximate 367.15, 371.19
approximately 16.189.1
approximation 261.67.15
approximative 485.15
appulse 313
appurtenance 321.14
appurtenant 420.53
apraxia 17.3.56
après-ski 5
apricot 373
April 228
a priori 7.11
apron 261
apropos 12.59
apse 322
apsis 300
apt 421
apteral 228.76
apterous 310.50
apterygial 228.3.3
apteryx 498.7
aptitude 102.2
aptness 300
Apurimac 32
apyretic 38.50
Aqaba 17.21
aquaculture 17.69
aqualung 267
aquamarine 251.7
aquanaut 374
aquaphobia 17.3.4
aquaplane 247
aqua regia 17.3.13
aquarelle 215
aquarist 436.20
aquarium 242.2.14
Aquarius 310.2.10
aquatic 38.49
aquatics 498.11
aquatint 412
aquavit 371
aqua vitae 7.13
aqueduct 389
aqueous 310.2

aquifer 17.114
Aquila 17.166
aquilegia 17.3.13
aquiline 253
Aquinas 310.34
Aquitaine 247.9
Ara 17.268
Arab 31
arabesque 57
Arabia 17.3.1
Arabian 261.3.1
Arabic 38
arable 228.16
Araby 16.15
Arachne 16.238
arachnid 91.22
arachnoid 97
Arad 83
Aragon 261
Araguaia 17.4
Arak 33
Aramaic 38.1
Aran 261
araneid 91.2
Arapaho 12.37
Ararat 365
araroba 17.18
Aras 293
Araucania 17.3.31
araucaria 17.3.38
arbalest 436.7
arbiter 17.342
arbitrage 359
arbitral 228.79
arbitrament 420.35
arbitrary 16.274
arbitrate 367.27
arbitration 261.67
arbitress 300
arboraceous 310.56
arboreal 228.3.12
arboreous 310.2.13
arborescent 420.67
arboretum 242.28
arboriculture 17.69
arborist 436.20
arbor vitae 7.13
arbour 17.10
Arbroath 461
Arbuthnot 373
arbutus 310.67
arc 33
arcade 85
Arcadia 17.3.7
Arcadian 261.3.3

arcana 17.227
arcane 247
arcanum 242
arcature 17.62
arch 63
Archaean 261.2
archaeologist 436.4
archaeology 16.108.4.1
archaeopteryx 498.7
archaeornis 300.24
archaic 38.1
archaism 242.35.2
archaize 516
archangel 228
archbishop 281
archbishopric 38
archdeacon 261.12
archdeaconry 16.284
archdiocesan 261.65
archdiocese 300.57.1
archducal 228
archduchess 300
archduchy 16.52
archduke 45
archegonium 242.2.12
archer 17.51
archery 16.274
archespore 9
archetypal 228.67
archetype 275
archfiend 133
archicarp 269
archimage 193
archimandrite 372
Archimedean 261.3.4
Archimedes 513.3
archine 251
archipelagic 38.15
archipelago 12.33
architect 385.8
architectonic 38.35
architectonics 498.5
architectural 228.76.1
architecture 17.64
architrave 482
archives 554

archivist 436
archpriest 435
archway 2
arcograph 158.1
arctic 38.59
Arcturus 310.49
arcuate 371.2
arcuation 261.67.2
ardeb 21
Arden 261
Ardennes 248
ardent 420.8
ardour 17.78
arduous 310.4
are 1
area 17.3.38
areaway 2.28
areca 17.34
arena 17.230.1
arenaceous 310.56.4
arenicolous 310.26.2
arenite 372.6
aren't 408
areography 16.90.2.1
areola 17.176
Arequipa 17.252
Ares 513.10
arethusa 17.444
Arezzo 12.71
argali 16.131
argent 420
argentic 38.63
Argentina 17.230
Argentine 251
argentine 253
argentous 310.70
argil 218
argillite 372.3
Argo 12.26
argol 220
Argolis 300.13
argon 254
Argonaut 374
argonon 254.8
Argos 302
argosy 16.307
argot 12.26
arguable 228.16.6
argue 15
argufy 7
argument 420.34

argumentation
261.67.32
argumentative
485.15.15
Argus 310
argy-bargy 16.99
Argyll 219
aria 17.3
Arian 261.3.21
Arianism
242.35.14.1.1
arid 91.25
aridity 16.333.5
ariel 228.3.10
Ariel 228.3.10
Aries 513.10
arietta 17.339
aright 372.8
Arimathea 17.2
arise 516.8
arisen 261.126
arista 17.384
Aristarchus 310.8
Aristippus 310.37
aristocracy
16.307.5
aristocrat 365.2
aristocratic 38.49.6
Aristophanes 513.9
Aristotelian
261.3.10
Aristotle 228.104
arithmetic 38.50,
38.57
Arius 310.2.10
Arizona 17.236
ark 33
Arkansas 9
arkose 305
Arkwright 372
Arlington 261
arm 230
armada 17.78
armadillo 12.42
Armageddon
261.21
Armagh 1.10
Armagnac 32
armament 420.35
armamentarium
242.2.14
armature 10.5
armband 128
armchair 4
armed 123

Armenia 17.3.33
Armenian 261.3.i6
Armentières 512
armet 368
armful 226
armhole 223
armiger 17.150
armillary 16.274.16
Arminian 261.3.17
Arminius 310.2.8
armipotent 420.78
armistice 300
armless 300
armlet 371
armoire 1
armorial 228.3.12
armour 17.206
armoured 103
armourer 17.279
armoury 16.274.20
armpit 371
armrest 433
arms 540
Armstrong 266
armure 10
army 16.211
Arne 246
Arnhem 242
arnica 17.34
Arno 12.51
Arnold 122
aroma 17.215
aromatic 38.49.2
aromatize 516.13
arose 520.3
around 139.1
arousal 228.129
arouse 521
Arpád 84
arpeggio 12.3
arquebus 310.5
arrack 46
arraign 247.8
Arran 261
arrange 207
arrangement
420.38
arranger 17.156
arrant 420.60
arras 310.43
Arras 310.43
array 2.19
arrears 514
arrest 433.1

arrestable
228.16.59
arrester 17.382
arresting 265.75
arrhythmia 17.3
Ar Rimal 213
arris 300
arrival 228.121
arrive 486
arriviste 435
arrogance 321.8
arrogant 420.18
arrogate 367.11
arrow 12.60
arrowhead 86.3
arrowroot 380
arse 294
arsenal 228.63
arsenic 38
arsenical 228.23.11
arsenide 92.4
arsenious 310.2.7
arsine 251
ars nova 17.417
arson 261.61
arsphenamine
252.15
arsy-versy 16.298.1
art 366
Art Deco 12.9
artefact 382
artel 215
Artemis 300.19
arterial 228.3.11
arterialize 516.3.2.1
arteriole 223.1
arteriosclerosis
300.55.5
arteriovenous
310.32
arteritis 300.62.5
artery 16.274
artesian 261.3.34
artful 226
arthralgia 17.3.16
arthralgic 38
arthritic 38.52
arthritis 300.62
arthropod 94.1
Arthur 17.397
Arthurian 261.3.24
artichoke 42
article 228.23
articular 17.174.6

articulate 367.13.2,
371.17.2
articulation
261.67.13
articulator 17.338.6
artifice 300
artificer 17.302
artificial 228.93
artificiality
16.333.8.1
artillery 16.274.16
artilleryman 261.48
artisan 245.7
artist 436
artiste 435
artistic 38.70
artistry 16.293
artless 300
artlessness 300.33
arts 334
artwork 36
arty 16.328
Aruba 17.20
arum 242.18
Arundel 228
Aruwimi 16.215
as 293, 507
asafoetida 17.83
Asantehene 16.226
asarum 242.21
asbestos 302.3
asbestosis 300.55
ascariasis 300.57.1
ascarid 91.27
ascend 131
ascendancy
16.312.2
ascendant 420.14
ascender 17.101
ascension 261.82
Ascensiontide
92.12
ascent 410
ascertain 247.10
ascesis 300.51
ascetic 38.50
asceticism
242.35.16
asci 7
ascidian 261.3.5
ascidium 242.2.3
ascites 513
Asclepius 310.2
ascocarp 269

ascogonium 242.2.12
Ascot 381
ascribe 25
ascription 261.85
asdic 38
aseity 16.333.1
asepalous 310.26
asepsis 300.59
aseptic 38.65
asexual 228.9
Asgard 84
ash 349
ashamed 124
ashamedly 16.148
Ashanti 16.353
Ashcroft 399
ashen 261.66
Asher 17.321
ashet 368
Ashkenazi 16.392
ashkey 5
ashlaring 265.58
ashore 9
ashplant 408
ashram 242
Ashton 261
Ashtoreth 455
ashtray 2
Ashurbanipal 212
ashy 16.319
Asia 17.322
Asian 261.67
Asiatic 38.49
aside 92.8
asinine 253.6
asininity 16.333.17
Asir 6
ask 56
askance 314
askew 15
aslant 408
asleep 273
ASLEF 160
Asmara 17.268
Asmodeus 310.2.2
asocial 228.94
Asoka 17.38
asparagus 310
Aspasia 17.3.59
aspect 385
aspectual 228.9.5
aspen 261
asper 17.265
aspergillus 310.23

asperity 16.333.21
asperse 297.1
aspersion 261.69
aspersorium 242.2.17
asphalt 401
asphodel 215.1
asphyxia 17.3.58
asphyxiant 420.1
asphyxiate 367.1
asphyxiation 261.67.1
aspic 38
aspidistra 17.297
aspirant 420
aspirate 367.21, 371.33
aspiration 261.67
aspirator 17.338
aspire 8.2
aspirin 252
aspiring 265.54
asquint 412
Asquith 458
ass 293
assai 7
assail 214
assailant 420.25
Assam 229
Assamese 513.8
assassin 252
assassinate 367.17.7
assassination 261.67.18.8
assault 404.1
assay 2, 2.20
assegai 7.4
assemblage 197
assemble 228.18
assembly 16.138
assent 410
assentation 261.67.32
assentient 420.1
assentor 17.368
assert 369
assertion 261.69
assertive 485.11
assess 296
assessment 420
assessor 17.300
asset 368
assets 336
asseverate 367.23

assibilate 367.12
assiduity 16.333.3
assiduous 310.4
assign 253.8
assignat 365
assignation 261.67
assignee 5.13
assignment 420
assignor 9
assimilate 367.12
assimilation 261.67.12
Assiniboine 256
assist 436.22
assistance 321.27
assistant 420.81
assize 516.11
assizes 515
associate 367.1.7, 371.1
association 261.67.1
associationism 242.35.14.3
associative 485.15
assonance 321
assonant 420.55
assort 374
assorted 91
assortment 420
assuage 193
assume 241
assuming 265.39
assumption 261.89
Assur 17.298
assurance 321.19
assure 10
assured 96
assuredly 16.148
assurgent 420.19
Assyria 17.3.40
Astaire 4
Astarte 16.328
astatic 38.49
astatine 251.11
aster 17.379
asteriated 91.34.1
asterisk 58
asterism 242.35.15
astern 249
asternal 228.58
asteroid 97.12
asthenia 17.3.33
asthenic 38.32
asthenopia 17.3.37

asthma 17
asthmatic 38.49
Asti 16.361
astigmatic 38.49.3
astigmatism 242.35.20
astilbe 16.16
astir 3
Astolat 365
Aston 261
astonish 353.8
astonishing 265.63
astonishment 420.47
Astor 17.379
Astoria 17.3.41
astound 139
astounded 91.14
astounding 265.22
astragalus 310.26
astrakhan 245
astral 228
astraphobia 17.3.4
astray 2
astride 92
astringent 420.23
astrobotany 16.237.7
astrocompass 310.42
astrodome 239
astrogeology 16.108.4.1
astroid 97
astrolabe 20
astrologer 17.154
astrology 16.108.4
astrometry 16.285.2
astronaut 374
astronautic 38.54
astronautics 498
astronomer 17.218.1
astronomic 38.29.1
astronomical 228.23.9
astronomy 16.222.3
astrophotography 16.90.2.6
astrophysics 498
Asturias 293.1
astute 380
astuteness 300.40

Astyanax 494
astylar 17.167
asunder 17.108
Aswan 246
aswarm 238
asylum 242.9
asymmetric 38.46
asymmetry 16.285.1
asymptomatic 38.49.2
asymptote 376
asymptotic 38.53
asynchronism 242.35.14
asyndetic 38.50
Asyut 380
at 365
atactic 38.58
ataman 261.52
ataractic 38.58
ataraxia 17.3.56
ataraxic 38
Atatürk 36
atavism 242.35
ataxia 17.3.56
Atbara 17.279
Ate 16.329
ate 368
atelectasis 300.57
atelier 2
Athabaska 17.47
Athanasius 310.56
atheism 242.35.2
atheist 436
atheistic 38.70
atheling 265.30
athematic 38.49.1
Athena 17.230
athenaeum 242.1
Athenian 261.3.16
Athens 548
athermancy 16.312
athermanous 310.36
atheroma 17.215
atherosclerosis 300.55.5
athirst 434
athlete 370
athletic 38.50
athleticism 242.35.16
athletics 498.12
athodyd 92

athwart 374
atilt 403
Atkinson 261
Atlanta 17.365
Atlantean 261.3
atlantes 513
Atlantic 38.62
Atlantis 300.66
atlas 310
Atli 16.187
atman 261
atmometer 17.342.3
atmosphere 6.1
atmospheric 38.39
atmospherics 498.6
atoll 220
atom 242
atomic 38.29
atomicity 16.333.28
atomism 242.35
atomize 516.5
atomizer 17.441
atonal 228.62
atonality 16.333.8
atone 257.3
atonement 420
atonic 38.35
atony 16.237
atop 276.1
atrial 228.3
atrip 274
atrium 242.2
atrocious 310.60
atrocity 16.333.30
atrophic 38.13
atrophy 16.90
atropine 251
attaboy 11
attach 62
attaché 2.22
attachment 420.36
attack 32.4
attacker 17.28
attain 247.10
attainable 228.16.27
attainder 17.100
attainment 420.41
attar 17.336
attempt 428
attemptable 228.16
attempter 17.378
Attenborough 17.279

attend 131
attendance 321.7
attendant 420.14
attender 17.101
attention 261.82.3
attentive 485.21
attenuant 420.4
attenuate 367.2, 371.2
attenuation 261.67.2
attenuator 17.338
attest 433
attestation 261.67.33
Attic 38.49
attic 38.49
Attica 17.34.3
Atticism 242.35.16.4
Attila 17.166
attire 8
attitude 102.2.1
attitudinize 516.6
Attlee 16.186
attorney 16.227
attract 382
attractant 420
attraction 261.76
attractive 485.16
attributable 228.16.52
attribute 380.2
attribution 261.75
attributive 485
attrition 261.71.6
Attu 15
attune 260.6
atypical 228.23
aubergine 251
aubrietia 17.325
auburn 261
Auckland 143
auction 261
auctioneer 6.5
auctorial 228.3.12
audacious 310.56
audacity 16.333.25
Auden 261.27
audible 228.16.16
audience 321.1
audio 12.3
audiogenic 38.32.1
audiology 16.108.4.1

audiometer 17.342.3.1
audiophile 219.1
audiotypist 436
audiovisual 228.9
audiphone 257
audit 371
audition 261.71
auditor 17.342
auditorium 242.2.17
auditory 16.274.41
au fait 2
Augean 261.2
augend 131
auger 17.132
aught 374
augite 372
augment 410
augmentation 261.67.32
augmentative 485.15.15
augur 17.132
augury 16.273
august 443
August 445
Augusta 17.388
Augustan 261
Augustine 252.27
Augustinian 261.3.17
Augustus 310
auk 41
au lait 2
auld 118
auld lang syne 253
aulic 38.23
Aulis 300
aunt 408
au pair 4
aura 17.276
aural 228.74
aureate 371.1.2
Aurelian 261.3.10
Aurelius 310.2.4
aureole 223.1
aureus 310.2.13
auric 38.42
auricle 228.23
auricula 17.174.6
auriculate 371.17.2
auriferous 310.50.2
Auriga 17.130
aurist 436

axletree 5
Axminster 17.394
axolotl 228.104
axon 254
axseed 89
ay 2, 7
ayah 17.4
ayatollah 17.168
Aycliffe 163
aye 7
aye-aye 7
Aylesbury 16.274
Aymara 1.14
Ayr 4
Ayrshire 6
Ayurveda 17.79
azalea 17.3.18
azan 246
Azbine 251
azedarach 32.3
azeotrope 278.3
Azerbaijan 246
Azerbaijani 16.224
azide 92
azimuth 464
azole 223
Azores 518
azoth 459
azotic 38.53
azotobacter 17.353
Aztec 35
azure 17
azurite 372
azygous 310

B

Ba 1
baa 1
Baal 213
Baalbek 35
Baal Shem Tov 487
baba 1
Babbage 197
babbitt 371.4
babble 228
babe 20
Babel 228.11
Babi 16.6
babiche 352

babirusa 17.308
baboon 260
babul 227
baby 16.7
babyhood 101
babyish 353
Babylon 261.41
Babylonia 17.3.36
Babylonian 261.3.18
baby-snatcher 17.50
baccalaureate 371.1.2
baccarat 1.14
baccate 367
Bacchae 5
bacchanal 228.63.1
bacchanalia 17.3.18.1
bacchanalian 261.3.8
bacchant 420
Bacchic 38.6
bacchius 310.3
Bacchus 310.7
baccivorous 310.50.3
baccy 16.19
Bach 33
Bacharach 32.3
bachelor 17.176
bacillus 310.23
bacitracin 252
back 32
backache 34
backbencher 17.70
backbend 131
backbite 372
backbiting 265.67
backboard 95
backbone 257
backbreaker 17.30
backbreaking 265.6
backchat 365
backcloth 459
backcomb 239
backcross 302
backdate 367
backer 17.28
backfire 8
backgammon 261.44
background 139
backhand 128

backhanded 91.12
backhander 17.98
backing 265
backlash 349
backless 300
backlog 185
backmost 441
backscratcher 17.50
backside 92
backslide 92
backspace 295
backspin 252
backstage 193
backstairs 512
backstay 2
backstitch 67
backstreet 370
backstroke 42
backswept 422
backtrack 32
backup 279
backveld 402
backward 103
backwardation 261.67.8
backwardness 300
backwards 531
backwash 354
backwater 17.345
backwoodsman 261
Bacolod 103.3
bacon 261.11
baconer 17.239
bacteraemia 17.3.26
bacteria 17.3.39
bacterial 228.3.11
bactericide 92.7
bacterin 252.20
bacteriology 16.108.4.1
bacteriolysis 300.52.2
bacteriolytic 38.52.1
bacteriophage 193.1
bacterium 242.2.15
bacteroid 97.12
Bactria 17.3
Bactrian 261.3
baculiform 238.1
bad 83

Badajoz 517
badderlocks 499
baddie 16.57
bade 83
Baden 261
badge 191
badger 17.144
badinage 359
badly 16.146
badman 261
badminton 261.105
badness 300
Baedeker 17.34
bael 228.1
Baez 510
baffle 228
bag 178
bagasse 293
bagatelle 215
bagel 228.44
baggage 197
bagging 265
baggy 16.91
bagh 179
Baghdad 83
bagman 261
bagpipe 275
bagpipes 328
baguette 368
bagwig 184
Bahai 16.1
Bahaism 242.35
Bahamas 524
Bahrain 247
baht 366
bahuvrihi 5
Baikal 213
bail 214
bailable 228.16.22
bailee 5
bailey 16.114
Bailey 16.114
bailie 16.114
bailiff 163.1
bailiwick 38
bailment 420.39
bailor 17.162
bailsman 261
Bairam 229
Baird 88
bairn 250
bait 367
baize 509
bake 34
bakehouse 306

barman 261
Barmecide 92.7
barmy 16.211
barn 246
Barnabas 310
barnacle 228.28
Barnard 84
Barnardo 12.16
barn-brack 32
Barnet 371
barney 16.224
barnstorm 238
Barnum 242
barnyard 84
Baroda 17.88
barogram 229.1
barograph 158.1
barometer
  17.342.3.4
barometric 38.46
baron 261
baronage 197
baroness 300.26
baronet 371.28
baronetage 197.12
baronetcy 16.317
barong 266
baronial 228.3.8
barony 16.237
baroque 40
baroscope 278.1
barostat 365
barouche 358
barque 33
barquentine 251
barrack 46
barracks 503
barracouta 17.351
barracuda 17.91
barrage 359
barramunda 17.108
barranca 17.43
barratry 16.286
barré 2.16
barrel 228.72
barren 261
barrenness 300.31
barrens 551
barret 371
barrette 368.6
barricade 85
Barrie 16.260
barrier 17.3
barring 265
barrister 17.384

barroom 241
barrow 12.60
Barry 16.260
Barrymore 9
Barsac 32
bartender 17.101
barter 17.337
Bartholomew 15
bartizan 261.126
Bartlett 371
Bartók 40
Barton 261.95
barycentre
  17.368.1
barye 16.260
baryon 254.1
barysphere 6
barytes 513
baryton 257.2
basal 228
basalt 404
basaltware 4
bascule 227
base 295
baseball 221
baseborn 255
baseless 300
baseline 253
baseman 261
basement 420.44
baseness 300
bases 513
bash 349
Bashan 245
bashaw 9
bashful 226
bashibazouk 45
Bashkir 6
basic 38
basically 16.142
basicity 16.333.28
basidium 242.2.3
Basie 16.296
basify 7.3
Basil 228.124
basil 228.124
basilar 17.166
Basildon 261
Basilian 261.3.11
basilic 38.21
basilica 17.34
basilisk 58
basin 261.62
basinet 371.24
Basingstoke 42

basion 261.3
basipetal 228.102
basis 300.50
bask 56
Baskerville 218.3
basket 371
basketball 221
basketry 16.285
basketwork 36
Basle 213
Basque 55
bas-relief 162.1
bass 293, 295
Bassein 247
Bassenthwaite 367
basset 371
Basse-Terre 4
bassinet 368
bassist 436
basso 12.68
bassoon 260
bassoonist 436.12
bast 430
bastard 103
bastardize 516
bastardry 16.277
bastardy 16.72
baste 432
Bastille 217
bastinado 12.17
bastion 261.3
bat 365
batch 62
bate 367
bateau 12.72
Bates 335
batfish 353
bath 453
Bath 453
bathe 473
bathetic 38.50.6
bathhouse 306
bathing 265
batholith 458
bathometer
  17.342.3
bathos 302
bathrobe 28
bathroom 241
Bathsheba 17.13
bathtub 29
Bathurst 445
bathyal 228.3
bathymetry
  16.285.1

bathyscaph 157
bathysphere 6
batik 38.49
batiste 435
Batley 16.186
batman 261
baton 254
batrachian 261.3
batsman 261
batt 365
battalion 261.118
batten 261.94
Battenburg 182
batter 17.336
battery 16.274
batting 265
battle 228.97
battledore 9
battlefield 115
battlement 420.40
battlepiece 298
battler 17.200
battleship 274
battue 15
batty 16.327
Batum 241
batwing 265
batwoman 261.50
bauble 228
Bauchi 16.51
baud 95
Bauhaus 306
bauhinia 17.3.34
baulk 41
bauxite 372
Bavaria 17.3.38
Bavarian 261.3.21
bawbee 5
bawd 95
bawdry 16.276
bawdy 16.66
bawdyhouse 306
bawl 221
Bax 494
bay 2
bayadere 6
bayonet 371.28
bayou 15
baywood 101
bazaar 1.19
bazoo 15.10
bazooka 17.41
be 5
beach 66

beachcomber 17.215
Beach-la-Mar 1.12
beacon 261.12
Beaconsfield 115
bead 89
beading 265.13
beadle 228
beady 16.62
beagle 228.45
beak 37
beaked 386
beaker 17.33
beam 234
bean 251
beanbag 178
beanery 16.274.25
beanfeast 435
beanie 16.228
beano 12.54
beanpole 223
beanstalk 41
bear 4
bearable 228.16.33
beard 90
bearded 91
beardless 300
bearer 17.271
bearing 265.52
bearish 353.9
Béarnaise 509
bearskin 252
beast 435
beastly 16.200
beat 370
beatable 228.16.48
beaten 261.98
beater 17.341
beatific 38.12
beatify 7.3.8
beating 265
beatitude 102.2.1
Beatles 539
beatnik 38
Beatty 16.332
beau 12
Beaufort 381
beaujolais 2.12
beau monde 136
Beaumont 414
Beaune 257
beaut 380
beauteous 310.2
beautician 261.71
beautiful 226

beautify 7.3
beauty 16.343
beaux-arts 1
beaver 17.413
Beaverbrook 44.1
Bebington 261
bebop 276
becalmed 123
became 231
because 517
beccafico 12.10
béchamel 215
bêche-de-mer 4.4
Bechuanaland 143.4
beck 35
becket 371
Beckett 371
beckon 261
becloud 99
become 240
becoming 265.38
bed 86
bedaub 27
bedazzle 228.124
bedbug 189
beddable 228.16.14
bedder 17.80
bedding 265.12
Bede 89
bedeck 35
bedevil 228.118
bedew 15.7
bedfellow 12.40
Bedford 103.2
Bedfordshire 6
bedim 235
Bedivere 6.11
bedlam 242
Bedouin 252
bedpan 245
bedpost 441
bedraggle 228.43
bedraggled 122
bedridden 261.24
bedrock 40
bedroll 223
bedroom 241
bedside 92
bedsitter 17.342
bedsore 9
bedspread 86
bedstead 86
bedstraw 9
bedtime 236

bedwarmer 17.214
bee 5
Beeb 23
beebread 86
beech 66
Beecham 242
beechnut 378
beef 162
beefburger 17.127
beefcake 34
beefeater 17.341
beefsteak 34
beefy 16.84
beehive 486
beekeeper 17.252
beeline 253
Beelzebub 29
been 251
beep 273
beer 6
Beerbohm 239
Beersheba 17.13
beery 16.265
beestings 552
beeswax 494
beeswing 265
beet 370
Beethoven 261.116
beetle 228.101
beetroot 380
beezer 17.440
befall 221
befell 215
befit 371.13
befog 185.1
befool 227
before 9.5
beforehand 128
befoul 224
befriend 131
befuddle 228.36
beg 181
began 245
begat 365.1
beget 368
beggar 17.126
beggarly 16.131.2
beggarweed 89
beggary 16.274
begin 252
beginner 17.231
beginning 265.43
begird 87
begone 254.4
begonia 17.3.36

begorra 17.275
begot 373
begotten 261.101
begrime 236
begrudge 203
beguile 219
beguine 251
begum 242
begun 259
behalf 158
Behan 261.2
behave 482
behaviour 17.436
behavioural 228.76
behaviourism 242.35.15
behaviourist 436.20
behaviouristic 38.70.5
behead 86.2
beheld 113
behemoth 459
behest 433
behind 135
behindhand 128
Behistun 260
behold 120.1
beholden 261.28
beholder 17.97
behove 488
beige 360
being 265.2
Beira 17.274
Beirut 380
bejewel 228.10
bel 215
belabour 17.11
belah 1
belated 91.34.5
belatedness 300.28
belay 2.11
belch 75
beleaguer 17.128
belemnite 372
Belfast 431
belfry 16
Belgae 5
Belgian 261
Belgium 242
Belgrade 85
Belgravia 17.3.53
Belial 228.3
belie 7.5
belief 162.1

believable
228.16.61
believe 484.1
believer 17.413
Belisarius 310.2
Belisha 17.325
belittle 228.102
bell 215
belladonna
17.233.1
bellarmine 251
Bellatrix 498
bellboy 11
belle 215
Belleek 37
Bellerophon 254.3
bellhop 276
bellicose 305
bellicosity
16.333.30.3
belligerence 321.20
belligerency 16.312
belligerent 420.65
Belloc 40
Bellona 17.236
bellow 12.40
bellows 520
bell-ringing 265.47
bellwether 17.402
belly 16.115
bellyband 128
bellybutton
261.103
bellyful 226
Belmopan 245.4
belong 266
belonging 265
belongings 552
beloved 91
below 12.42
Bel Paese 16.393
Belsen 261
Belshazzar 17.437
belt 402
Beltane 247
belting 265
beltway 2
beluga 17.136
belvedere 6
bema 17.210
Bemba 17.24
bemire 8
bemoan 257
bemuse 523
bemused 156

ben 248
Ben 248
Benares 515
bench 79
bencher 17.70
bend 131
Bendel 215
bender 17.101
Bendigo 12.29
bends 532
bendy 16.78
beneath 457
benedicite
16.333.29
Benedict 387
benediction
261.78.1
benefaction 261.76
benefactor 17.353
benefactress 300.48
benefic 38
benefice 300
beneficence 321.22
beneficent 420.70
beneficial 228.93
beneficiary
16.274.1.2
benefit 371.13
Benelux 502
Benevento 12.84
benevolence
321.12.1
benevolent
420.28.1
Bengal 221
Bengali 16.123
Benghazi 16.392
Ben-Gurion
261.3.24
benighted 91.39
benign 253.6
benignant 420
benignity 16.333.19
Benin 251
benison 261.126
Benjamin 252.15
benne 16.226
Ben Nevis 300.69
benny 16.226
Benoni 16.233
bent 410
Bentinck 52
Bentley 16.197
bentonite 372.6
bentwood 101

Benue 2.3
benumb 240
benzaldehyde 92
Benzedrine 252
benzene 251
benzoate 367
benzoin 252.1
benzol 220
benzyl 218
Beowulf 175
bequeath 475
bequeather 17.404
bequest 433
Berar 1
berate 367.21
Berber 17.12
Berbera 17.279
berberis 300.47
bereave 484
bereavement 420
bereft 397
beret 2
berg 182
bergamot 373
Bergman 261
beriberi 16.262
berk 36
Berkeley 16.140
berkelium 242.2.5
Berks. 495
Berkshire 6
Berlin 252
Berlioz 520
berm 233
Bermuda 17.91
Bern 249
Bernadette 368.5
Bernardine 252
Bernhardt 366
Bernstein 253
berry 16.262
bersagliere 16.264
berseem 234
berserk 36
berth 456
Berwick 38.39
Berwick-upon-
Tweed 89
beryl 218.2
Beryl 218.2
beryllium 242.2.6
Berzelius 310.2.4
Bes 296
beseech 66
beseeching 265

beset 368.7
beside 92.7
besides 527
besiege 196
besmear 6
besmirch 65
besom 242
besotted 91.40
bespangle 228.49
bespatter 17.336
bespeak 37
bespectacled 122
bespoke 42
bespread 86
besprent 410
besprinkle 228.29
Bess 296
Bessarabia 17.3.1
best 433
bestial 228.3.14
bestiality
16.333.8.1
bestialize 516.3.2
bestiary 16.274.1
bestir 3
bestow 12
bestowal 228.7
bestrew 15
bestride 92
bet 368
beta 17.341
betake 34
betel 228.101
Betelgeuse 511
Beth 455
Bethany 16.237
Bethel 228
Bethlehem 232
Bethsaida 17.79
betide 92
bêtise 513
Betjeman 261.52
betoken 261.14
betony 16.237
betook 44
betray 2
betrayal 228.1
betroth 478
betrothal 228
betrothed 145
betta 17.339
better 17.339
betterment 420.35
between 251
betweentimes 542

betwixt 451
Beulah 17.175
Bevan 261.112
bevel 228.118
beverage 197
Beverly 16.131
Bevin 252.28
bevvy 16.380
bevy 16.380
bewail 214
beware 4.7
Bewick 38
bewilder 17.95
bewilderment
    420.35
bewitch 67
bey 2
beyond 136
bezant 420.84
bezel 228
bezique 37
bezoar 9
Bhagalpur 10
Bhagavad-Gita
    17.341
bhang 263
bhavan 261.117
bhindi 16.79
Bhopal 213
Bhutan 246
biannual 228.9.2
Biarritz 339
bias 310.3
biathlon 261
biaxial 228.3.18
bib 24
bibber 17.14
bibcock 40
bibelot 12
Bible 228
biblical 228.23
Biblicist 436.21
bibliography
    16.90.2.1
bibliolatry
    16.286.2.1
bibliomancy
    16.309
bibliomania
    17.3.31.1
bibliophile 219.1
bibliopole 223
bibliopolist 436.7
bibliotheca 17.33
bibulous 310.25

bicameral 228.76
bicapsular 17.174
bicarb 19
bicarbonate 371.28
bice 301
bicentenary
    16.274.25
bicephalous
    310.26.3
biceps 324
bicipital 228.102
bicker 17.34
biconcave 482
biconvex 496
bicorn 255
bicornate 371.26
bicuspid 91
bicycle 228.23
bicyclic 38
bid 91
bidarka 17.29
bidarkee 5.3
biddable 228.16.15
bidden 261.24
bidder 17.83
bidding 265
biddy 16.63
bide 92
bidentate 367.32
bidet 2
Biedermeier 17.4
Biel 217
bield 115
biennial 228.3
bier 6
bierkeller 17.163
bifarious 310.2.10
biff 163
biffin 252
bifid 91
bifocal 228.26
bifocals 539
bifoliate 367.1.3
biforate 367.23
biform 238
Bifrost 438
bifurcate 367.6,
    371.8
bifurcation
    261.67.6
big 184
bigamist 436.10.1
bigamous 310.29.1
bigamy 16.222.1
bigener 17.231

bigeye 7
biggin 252
biggish 353
bighead 86
bigheaded 91.7
bigheadedness
    300.28
bight 372
bigmouth 462
bignonia 17.3.36
bigot 381
bigoted 91
bigotry 16.286
bigwig 184
Bihar 1.6
Bihari 16.261
bijou 15
bijouterie 16.274
Bikaner 6.5
bike 39
bikini 16.228
bilander 17.109
bilateral 228.76
Bilbao 12
bilberry 16.274
bilboes 520
bile 219
bilestone 257
bilharzia 17.3
bilharziasis
    300.57.1
biliary 16.274.1.1
bilinear 17.3.34
bilingual 228
bilious 310.2.5
biliousness 300.34
bilirubin 252
biliverdin 252
bilk 49
bill 218
billabong 266
billboard 95
billet 371.16
billet-doux 15.2
billfold 120
billhook 44
billiard 103
billiards 531
billing 265.30
Billingsgate 367
billion 261.120
billionaire 4.5
billionth 471
billon 261.41
billow 12.42

billowy 16.3
billposter 17.387
billy 16.120
billycan 245
billyo 12.3.2
bilobate 367.3
Bim 235
bimbo 12.6
bimestrial 228.3.13
bimetallic 38.19.1
bimetallism
    242.35.11
bimonthly 16.205
bimorph 166
bin 252
binal 228.61
binary 16.274.27
binate 367
binaural 228.74
bind 135
binder 17.103
bindi-eye 7.1
binding 265.21
bindweed 89
bine 253
binge 209
bingey 16.110
bingle 228.50
bingo 12.36
binnacle 228.28
binocular 17.174.7
binoculars 524
binomial 228.3
binominal 228.60.5
bint 412
binturong 266
bio-assay 2.20
biocatalyst 436.7.6
biocenology
    16.108.4.10
biochemical 228.23
biochemist 436
biochemistry
    16.293
biocide 92.8
biodegradable
    228.16
biodegradation
    261.67.8
biofeedback 32
bioflavonoid 97.9
biogen 261.39
biogenesis 300.52.4
biogeography
    16.90.2.1

biographer
17.120.1
biographical
228.23.3
biography 16.90.2
biological 228.23.5
biologist 436.4
biology 16.108.4.2
biolysis 300.52.2
biomass 293
biometry 16.285.2
bionic 38.35
bionics 498.5
bionomics 498
biophysics 498
biopoiesis 300.51
biopsy 16.315
bioptic 38.67
bioscope 278.1.1
biosphere 6.1
biostatics 498.11
biostrome 239
biosynthesis 300.52
biota 17.347
biotic 38.53.1
biotin 252
biotite 372.12
biotype 275.1
bipartisan 245.7
bipartite 372
biped 86
biplane 247
bipod 94
bipolar 17.171
biquadratic 38.49
birch 65
bird 87
birdbath 453
birdcage 193
birdhouse 306
birdie 16.61
birdlime 236
birdman 261
birdseed 89
bird-watching 265
bireme 234
biretta 17.339
biriani 16.224
Birkenhead 86
Biro 12.64
birr 3
birth 456
birthday 2
birthmark 33
birthplace 295

birthright 372
birthroot 380
birthstone 257
Biscay 2
biscuit 371
bise 513
bisect 385
bisection 261.77
bisector 17.354
bisexual 228.9
bish 353
bishop 281
bishopric 38
Biskra 1
Bismarck 33
bismuth 464
bison 261
bisque 58
bissextile 219.8
bistort 374
bistoury 16.274.49
bistre 17.384
bistro 12
bisulcate 367.7
bisulphate 367
bisymmetric 38.46
bit 371
bitch 67
bitchy 16.49
bite 372
Bithynia 17.3.34
biting 265.67
bitser 17.320
bitstock 40
bitt 371
bitten 261.99
bitter 17.342
bitterling 265
bittern 261.99
bitterness 300.26
bitternut 378
bitters 524
bittersweet 370
bitterwood 101
bitty 16.333
bitumen 252
bituminize 516.6
bituminous
310.33.1
bivalent 420.25
bivalve 491
bivouac 32
bivvy 16.382
biweekly 16.141
biyearly 16.119

bizarre 1
Bizerte 17.340
Bizet 2.30
blab 18
blabber 17.9
blabbermouth 462
black 32
blackball 221
Blackbeard 90
blackberry 16.274
blackbird 87
blackboard 95
blackbuck 43
Blackburn 249
blackbutt 378
blackcap 268
blackcock 40
blackcurrant
420.64
blackdamp 285
blacken 261
blackfly 7
Blackfoot 379
blackguard 84
blackhead 86
blackheart 366
blacking 265
blackish 353
blackjack 32
blackleg 181
blacklist 436
blackmail 214
blackmailer 17.162
Black Maria 17.4.2
blackness 300
blackout 377
blackpoll 223
Blackpool 227
Blackshirt 369
blacksmith 458
blacksnake 34
blackthorn 255
blacktop 276
Blackwall 221
Blackwood 101
blackwood 101
bladder 17.77
bladder ketmia
17.3
bladdernose 520
bladdernut 378
bladderwort 369
bladderwrack 32.3
blade 85
blah 1

blain 247
Blake 34
blame 231
blameful 226
blameless 300
blameworthy
16.375
blanch 78
bland 128
blandish 353.2
blank 51
blanket 371
blankly 16.144
blare 4
blarney 16.224
blasé 2
blaspheme 234
blasphemer 17.210
blasphemous
310.28
blasphemy 16.216
blast 431
blasted 91.51
blastema 17.210
blasting 265.74
blastocoel 217.2
blastocyst 436.22
blastoderm 233
blastoff 165
blastomere 6.3
blastopore 9
blastula 17.174
blat 365
blatancy 16.312.6
blatant 420.75
blather 17.400
blatherskite 372
blaubok 40
Blaydon 261.20
blaze 509
blazer 17.439
blazes 515
blazon 261.124
blazonry 16.284
bleach 66
bleak 37
bleakness 300
bleary 16.265
bleat 370
bleb 21
bleed 89
bleeder 17.82
bleeding 265.13
bleep 273
blemish 353

blench 79
blend 131
blender 17.101
Blenheim 235
blennioid 97
blenny 16.226
blepharitis
300.62.5
bless 296
blessed 91
blessing 265.60
blest 433
blet 368
blew 15
blewits 339
Blida 17.82
Bligh 7
blight 372
blighter 17.343
Blighty 16.334
blimey 16.217
blimp 287
blind 135
blindage 197
blindfold 120
blinding 265.21
blindly 16.155
blindness 300.29
blindstorey 16.269
blindworm 233
blini 16.229
blink 52
blinker 17.44
blinkers 524
blinking 265.10
blintz 348
blip 274
bliss 300
blissful 226
blister 17.384
blithe 477
blithering 265.58
blithesome 242
blitz 339
blitzkrieg 183
blizzard 103
bloat 376
bloated 91.41
bloater 17.347
blob 26
bloc 40
block 40
blockade 85
blockage 197
blockboard 95

blockbuster 17.388
blockbusting 265
blocker 17.36
blockhead 86
Bloemfontein
247.11
bloke 42
blond 136
blonde 136
blood 100
bloodcurdling 265
blooded 91.11
bloodhound 139
bloodless 300
blood-letting
265.65
bloodshed 86
bloodshot 373
bloodstain 247
bloodstained 130
bloodstock 40
bloodsucker 17.39
bloodthirsty 16.365
bloody 16.69
bloody-minded 91
bloom 241
bloomer 17.217
bloomers 524
bloomery
16.274.22
blooming 265.39
Bloomsbury 16.274
blooper 17.259
blossom 242.25
blot 373
blotch 68
blotchy 16.50
blotter 17.344
blotto 12.77
blouse 521
blouson 254
blow 12
blower 17.6
blowfish 353
blowfly 7
blowhard 84
blowhole 223
blowlamp 285
blown 257
blowpipe 275
blowtorch 69
blowy 16.3
blowzy 16.400
blub 29
blubber 17.19

blubbery 16.274
bludge 203
bludgeon 261.38
blue 15
Bluebeard 90
bluebell 215
blueberry 16.274
bluebill 218
bluebird 87
blue-blooded 91.11
bluebonnet 371.25
bluebook 44
bluebottle 228.104
bluefish 353
bluegrass 294
blueing 265.5
bluejacket 371.6
blueness 300
bluenose 520
blueprint 412
blues 523
bluestocking 265.8
bluet 371.3
bluethroat 376
bluetit 371
bluetongue 267
bluey 16.4
bluff 168
bluffer 17.118
bluish 353
blunder 17.108
blunderbuss 307
blunge 211
blunger 17.159
blunt 419
bluntness 300
blur 3
blurb 22
blurry 16.263
blurt 369
blush 356
blusher 17.329
bluster 17.388
blustery 16.274
Blyth 477
B'nai B'rith 457
boa 17.6
Boadicea 17.2
boar 9
board 95
boarder 17.86
boarding 265.15
boardroom 241
boardwalk 41
boarhound 139

boarish 353
boast 441
boastful 226
boastfulness 300.30
boat 376
boatel 215.4
boater 17.347
boathook 44
boathouse 306
boating 265
boatload 98
boatman 261
boatswain 261
Boaz 507
bob 26
bobbery 16.274.3
bobbin 252
bobbinet 368
bobble 228
bobby 16.11
bobbysoxer 17.428
bobfloat 376
boblet 371
bobolink 52
bobotie 16.342
bobowler 17.172
bobsleigh 2
bobtail 214
bobwhite 372
bocage 359
boccia 17.57
bock 40
bod 94
bode 98
bodega 17.128
bodge 199
bodger 17.152
bodgie 16.104
bodice 300.4
bodiless 300.8
bodily 16.120
bodkin 252
Bodleian 261.3
Bodmin 252
Bodoni 16.233
body 16.65
bodycheck 35
bodyguard 84.1
body-snatcher
17.50
bodywork 36
Boehmite 372
Boeotia 17.328
Boer 10
Boethius 310.2

boeuf Bourguignon 254.12
boffin 252
bog 185
bogan 261
Bogarde 84
Bogart 366
bogey 16.96
bogeyman 261.48
boggart 381
boggle 228.47
boggy 16.94
bogie 16.96
bogle 228
Bognor Regis 300.6
bogong 266
Bogor 9
Bogotá 1
bogus 310
bogwood 101
Bohemia 17.3.26
Bohemian 261.3
Bohol 221
boil 222
boiler 17.170
boilermaker 17.30
boilerplate 367
Boise 16.398
boisterous 310.50
boisterousness 300.34
bokmakierie 16.265
bola 17.171
bold 120
boldness 300
bole 223
bolection 261.77
bolero 12.62
boletus 310.63
Boleyn 252
bolide 92
Bolingbroke 44
bolivar 1
Bolivia 17.3.54
Bolivian 261.3.30
boll 223
bollard 103.3
bollocks 503
bolo 12.44
Bolognese 509
bolometer 17.342.3
Bolshevik 38.74
Bolshevist 436

bolson 257
bolster 17.392
bolt 405
bolter 17.364
Bolton 261
boltonia 17.3.36
bolus 310
bomb 237
bombard 84
bombardier 6
bombardment 420
bombast 430
bombastic 38.68
Bombay 2
bombazine 251
bombé 2
bomber 17.213
bombora 17.276
bombshell 215
bombsight 372
bombycid 91.29
bona fide 16.64
Bonaire 4
bonanza 17.445
Bonaparte 366.1
Bonapartism 242.35.17
bona vacantia 17.3.50
Bonaventura 17.277
bonbon 254
bonce 318
bond 136
bondage 197
bonded 91
bondmaid 85
bondservant 420.82
bone 257
boneblack 32
bonehead 86
boneless 300
boner 17.236
boneset 368
bonesetter 17.339
boneshaker 17.30
boneyard 84
bonfire 8
bong 266
bongo 12
bonhomie 16.222.3
Boniface 295.3
bonism 242.35
bonito 12.76

bonkers 524
Bonn 254
bonnet 371.25
bonny 16.231
bonsai 7
bonsela 17.163
bonspiel 217
bonus 310.35
bony 16.233
bonze 549
boo 15
boob 30
boobialla 17.160
boobook 44
booby 16.14
boodle 228.37
boogie 16.98
boogie-woogie 16.98
boohoo 15
book 44
bookbinder 17.103
bookbindery 16.274.8
bookbinding 265.21
bookcase 295
bookie 16.31
booking 265
bookish 353
book-keeper 17.252
book-keeping 265.49
booklet 371
booklouse 306
bookmaker 17.30
bookmark 33
bookshop 276
bookstall 221
bookworm 233
Boole 227
boom 241
boomer 17.217
boomerang 263.2
boomslang 263
boon 260
boondocks 499
boondoggle 228.47
boor 10
boorish 353
boost 444
booster 17.389
boot 380
bootblack 32

booted 91.42
bootee 5
Boötes 513
booth 479
bootlace 295
Bootle 228.108
bootleg 181
bootlegger 17.126
bootless 300
bootlick 38
bootlicker 17.34
boots 346
bootstrap 268
booty 16.343
booze 523
boozer 17.444
boozy 16.402
bop 276
bora 17.276
Bora Bora 17.276
boracic 38.48
borage 197
borak 46
borane 247
borate 367
borax 494
borazon 254
borborygmus 310
Bordeaux 12
Bordelaise 509
bordello 12.40
border 17.86
bordereau 12
borderer 17.279
borderland 143.4
borderline 253.3
bordure 10
bore 9
boreal 228.3.12
Boreas 310.2.13
boredom 242
boree 5
borer 17.276
Borg 186
Borgia 17.153
boric 38.42
boride 92.5
boring 265.55
Boris 300
born 255
borne 255
Borneo 12.3
borneol 220.1
Borodin 252
Borodino 12.54

boron 254.10
boronia 17.3.36
borosilicate 371.9
borough 17.278
borrow 12.65
borrower 17.6
borstal 228.116
bort 374
borzoi 11
boscage 197
Bosch 354
boschvark 33
Bose 305
bosh 354
bosk 59
bosket 371
Boskop 276
Bosnia 17.3
bosom 242
bosomy 16.222
boson 254
Bosporus 310.50
boss 302
bossa nova 17.417
bossiness 300.23
bossy 16.302
Boston 261
bosun 261
Boswell 228
Bosworth 464
bot 373
botanical 228.23.10
botanist 436.13
botanize 516.7
botany 16.237.7
botargo 12.26
botch 68
botcher 17.57
botchy 16.50
botfly 7
both 461
bother 17.407
botheration 261.67.22
bothersome 242
bothy 16.371
bots 341
Botswana 17.226
bottle 228.104
bottlebrush 356
bottleneck 35
bottlenose 520
bottom 242
bottomless 300
bottommost 441

botulin 252.10
botulinus 310.34
botulism 242.35.10
bouchée 2
bouclé 2
bouclée 2
Boudicca 17.34
boudoir 1
bouffant 266
Bougainville 218
bougainvillea 17.3.21
bough 13
bought 374
boughten 261.102
bougie 5
bouillabaisse 296
bouillon 254
boulder 17.97
boule 227
boulevard 1
boulevardier 2.1
Boulez 510
boulle 227
Boulogne 256
Boult 405
bounce 319
bouncer 17.317
bouncing 265
bound 139
boundary 16.274
bounden 261
bounder 17.107
boundless 300
bounds 533
bounteous 310.2
bountiful 226
bounty 16.359
bouquet 2
bouquet garni 5.10
Bourbon 261
bourbon 261.9
bourdon 261
bourg 187
bourgeois 1
bourgeoisie 5
bourn 255
Bournemouth 464
bourrée 2.18
bouse 521
boustrophedon 261.23
bout 377
boutique 37
boutonniere 4.1

bouzouki 16.32
bovid 91
bovine 253
Bovril 218
bovver 17.416
bow 12, 13
bowdlerism 242.35.15
bowdlerize 516.8
bowel 228.8
bower 14
bowerbird 87
bowfin 252
bowhead 86.3
bowing 265.4
bowknot 373
bowl 223
bow-legged 91
bowler 17.171
bowlful 226
bowline 252.9
bowling 265.32
bowman 261, 261.49
bowsaw 9
bowser 17.443
bowshot 373
bowsprit 371
bowstring 265
bow-wow 13
bowyer 17.431
box 499
boxcar 1
boxer 17.428
boxing 265
boxroom 241
boxwood 101
boy 11
Boyce 304
boycott 373
Boyd 97
boyfriend 131
boyhood 101
boyish 353
boyla 17.170
Boyle 222
Boyne 256
boysenberry 16.274
Boz 517
bra 1
Brabant 407
brace 295
bracelet 371
bracer 17.299
braces 515

brachial 228.3
brachiate 367.1, 371.1
brachiopod 94.1
brachiosaurus 310.48.1
brachium 242.2
brachylogy 16.108.3
brachyuran 261.59
bracing 265.59
bracken 261
bracket 371.6
bracketing 265.66
brackish 353
Bracknell 228
bract 382
brad 83
bradawl 221
Bradford 103
Bradley 16.146
Bradman 261
Bradshaw 9
bradycardia 17.3.6
brae 2
brag 178
braggadocio 12.3
braggart 381
bragger 17.123
Brahma 17.206
Brahman 261
Brahmana 17.239
Brahmanic 38.31
Brahmanism 242.35.14
Brahmaputra 17.294
Brahmin 252
Brahminic 38.34
Brahms 540
Brahui 16.4
braid 85
braided 91.6
braiding 265.11
brail 214
Braille 214
brain 247
brainchild 117
brainless 300
brainpan 245
brainsick 38
brainstorm 238
brainstorming 265
brainwash 354
brainwashing 265

brainy 16.225
braise 509
brake 34
bramble 228.17
brambling 265
bran 245
branch 78
branchia 17.3
branchiopod 94.1
Brancusi 16.402
brand 128
Brandenburg 182
brandish 353.2
brandling 265
Brando 12.23
brandy 16.77
branle 228.55
brash 349
brashy 16.319
Brasilia 17.3.21
brass 294
brassard 84
brassbound 139
brasserie 16.274
brassica 17.34
brassie 16.294
brassiere 17.3.46
brassy 16.295
brat 365
Bratislava 17.409
brattice 300
brattishing 265.63
bratwurst 434
bravado 12.16
brave 482
braveness 300
bravery 16.274.50
bravissimo 12.48
bravo 12
bravura 17.277
braw 9
brawl 221
brawler 17.169
brawn 255
brawny 16.232
braxy 16.386
bray 2
braze 509
brazen 261.124
brazier 17.3.59
Brazil 218
Brazilian 261.3.11
breach 66
bread 86
breadboard 95

breadfruit 380
breadline 253
breadroot 380
breadwinner 17.231
break 34
breakable 228.16.9
breakage 197
breakaway 2.28
breakdown 258
breaker 17.30
breakfast 445
breakfront 419
breakneck 35
breakpoint 416
breakwater 17.345
bream 234
breast 433
breastbone 257
breastpin 252
breastplate 367
breaststroke 42
breastwork 36
breath 455
breathalyse 516.3
Breathalyzer 17.441
breathe 475
breather 17.404
breathing 265
breathless 300
breathlessness 300.33
breathtaking 265.6
breathy 16.369
breccia 17.3
Brecknockshire 6
Brecon 261
Breconshire 6.8
bred 86
Breda 17.82
bree 5
breech 66
breechblock 40
breechclout 377
breeches 515
breeching 265
breed 89
breeder 17.82
breeding 265.13
breeze 513
breezy 16.395
bregma 17.221
Bremen 261.45
Bren 248

Brent 410
brent 410
Brentwood 101
br'er 3
Brest 433
brethren 252
Breton 261.96
breve 484
brevet 371
breviary 16.274.1
brevity 16.333.34
brew 15
brewage 197
brewer 17.8
brewery 16.274
brewing 265.5
brewis 300
Brezhnev 160
Brian 261.4
Brian Boru 15.6
briar 17.4
Briareus 310.2.10
briarroot 380
bribable 228.16.8
bribe 25
briber 17.15
bribery 16.274
bric-a-brac 32
brick 38
brickbat 365
bricklayer 17.1
bricklaying 265.1
brickle 228.23
brickwork 36
brickyard 84
bricole 223
bridal 228.33
bride 92
bridegroom 241
bridesmaid 85
bridewell 215
bridge 197
Bridget 371
bridgework 36
bridging 265.25
Bridgwater 17.345
bridie 16.64
bridle 228.33
bridler 17.187
bridoon 260
Brie 5
brief 162
briefcase 295
briefing 265
briefly 16.158

brig 184
brigade 85.1
brigadier 6
brigalow 12.45
brigand 143
brigandine 251
brigantine 251
bright 372
brighten 261.100
brightness 300.39
Brighton 261.100
brights 340
brightwork 36
Brigid 91.15
brill 218
brilliance 321
brilliant 420
brilliantine 251
brim 235
brimful 226
brimstone 257
brindle 228.40
brindled 122
brine 253
bring 265
brink 52
brinkmanship 274.2
brinny 16.229
briny 16.230
brioche 354
briolette 368
briquette 368.4
brisance 321.28
Brisbane 261
brise-soleil 2.12
brisk 58
brisket 371
brisling 265
bristle 228.85
bristly 16.181
Bristol 228.114
bristols 539
Brit 371
brit 371
Britain 261.99
Britannia 17.3.29
Britannic 38.31
Briticism 242.35.16
British 353
Britisher 17.326
Britishism 242.35
Briton 261.99
Brittany 16.237
Britten 261.99

318

brittle 228.102
brittleness 300.30
broach 70
broad 95
broadbrim 235
broadcast 431
broadcaster 17.380
broadcloth 459
broaden 261.27
broadleaf 162
broadloom 241
broadly 16.150
broad-minded 91
broad-mindedness 300.28
Broadmoor 9
Broads 528
broadsheet 370
broadside 92
broadsword 95
broadtail 214
Broadway 2
brocade 85
brocatelle 215
broccoli 16.131
broch 40
broché 2
brochette 368
brochure 10
brock 40
brocket 371.10
broddle 228.34
broderie anglaise 509
Broederbond 415
brogan 261
brogue 188
broil 222
broiler 17.170
broke 42
broken 261.14
brokenhearted 91.33
broker 17.38
brokerage 197
brolga 17.138
brolly 16.122
bromate 367
brome 239
bromeliad 83.1
bromic 38
bromide 92
bromidic 38
bromine 251
bromism 242.35

bromoform 238.2
Bromsgrove 488
bronchi 7
bronchia 17.3
bronchial 228.3
bronchiectasis 300.57
bronchiole 223.1
bronchitic 38.52
bronchitis 300.62
bronchopneumonia 17.3.36
bronchoscope 278.1
bronchus 310
bronco 12
broncobuster 17.388
Brontë 16.357
brontosaurus 310.48.1
bronze 549
brooch 70
brood 102
brooder 17.91
broody 16.71
brook 44
brooklet 371
brooklime 236
Brooklyn 252
broom 241
broomrape 270
broomstick 38
brose 520
broth 459
brothel 228
brother 17.408
brotherhood 101
brother-in-law 9
brotherly 16.131
brougham 242
brought 374
brouhaha 1.5
brow 13
browband 128
browbeat 370
brown 258
brownie 16.234
browning 265
brownish 353
brownout 377
browse 521
browser 17.443
Brubeck 35
Bruce 309

brucellosis 300.55
Bruges 364
bruin 252
bruise 523
bruised 156
bruiser 17.444
bruising 265.84
bruit 380
Brummagem 242
Brummell 228
Brummie 16.220
brunch 82
Brunei 7
Brunel 215
brunette 368
Brunhild 116
Brunswick 38
brunt 419
brush 356
brushoff 165
brushwood 101
brushwork 36
brusque 60
brusqueness 300
Brussels 539
brut 380
brutal 228.108
brutality 16.333.8
brutalize 516.3
brute 380
brutify 7.3
brutish 353
Brutus 310.67
bryology 16.108.4.2
bryony 16.237.1
bryophyte 372
bryozoan 261.6
Brythonic 38.35
bubal 228
bubble 228.14
bubbly 16.136
bubo 12
bubonic 38.35
bubonocele 217.2
buccal 228.27
buccaneer 6.5
buccinator 17.338.7
bucentaur 9.12
Bucephalus 310.26.3
Buchanan 261.55
Bucharest 433.1
buck 43
buckaroo 15.6

buckbean 251
buckboard 95
bucket 371.11
buckeye 7
Buckingham 242.17
Buckinghamshire 6
buckjumper 17.264
buckle 228.27
buckling 265.34
bucko 12
buckram 242
bucksaw 9
buckshee 5
buckshot 373
buckskin 252
buckskins 548
buckthorn 255
bucktooth 463
buckwheat 370
bucolic 38.22
bud 100
Budapest 433
Buddha 17
Buddhism 242.35
Buddhist 436.2
budding 265
buddle 228.36
buddleia 17.3
buddy 16.69
budge 203
budgerigar 1.4
budget 371
budgie 16.107
buds 530
Buenos Aires 515
buff 168
buffalo 12.45
buffer 17.118
buffet 2, 371
bufflehead 86
buffoon 260
buffoonery 16.274.28
bug 189
bugaboo 15.1
Buganda 17.98
bugbane 247
bugger 17.134
buggery 16.274.10
buggy 16.97
bugle 228.48
bugleweed 89.7
bugloss 302
build 116

builder 17.95
building 265.17
built 403
Bukhara 17.268
Bukovina 17.230
Bulawayo 12.1
bulbaceous 310.56
bulbil 218
bulbous 310
bulbul 226
Bulgaria 17.3.38
Bulgarian 261.3.21
bulge 205
bulimia 17.3.27
bulk 50
bulkhead 86
bulky 16.35
bull 226
bulla 17.174
bullace 300.11
bullate 367
bullbat 365
bulldog 185
bulldoze 520
bulldozer 17.442
bullet 371.17
bulletin 252.23
bulletproof 170
bullfight 372
bullfighter 17.343
bullfighting 265.67
bullfinch 80
bullfrog 185
bullhead 86
bullion 261
bullish 353
bullock 46
bullpen 248
bullring 265
bullshit 371
bullwhip 274
bully 16.129
bullyrag 178
bulrush 356
bulwark 46
bum 240
bumbailiff 163.1
bumble 228
bumblebee 5
bumbler 17.180
bummalo 12.45
bummer 17.216
bump 289
bumper 17.264
bumph 177

bumpkin 252
bumptious 310
bumpy 16.257
bun 259
bunch 82
bunchy 16.56
bund 140
Bund 141
Bundaberg 182
Bundelkhand 140
Bundesrat 366
Bundestag 179
bundh 140
bundle 228
bung 267
bungalow 12.45
bungle 228
bunion 261
bunk 54
bunker 17.46
bunkum 242
bunny 16.235
bunraku 15
Bunsen 261
bunt 419
buntal 228.112
bunting 265
Bunyan 261
bunyip 274
buoy 11
buoyage 197
buoyancy 16.312
buoyant 420.3
buprestid 91.52
bur 3
buran 246
Burbage 197
Burberry 16.274
burble 228
burbot 381
burden 261.22
burdensome 242
burdock 40
bureau 12.66
bureaucracy
  16.307.5
bureaucrat 365.2
bureaucratic
  38.49.6
bureaucratize
  516.13
burette 368
burg 182
burgee 5
burgeon 261.35

burger 17.127
burgess 300
Burgess 300
burgher 17.127
Burghley 16.116
burglar 17
burglarize 516.8
burglary 16.274
burgle 228
burgonet 368
burgrave 482
Burgundy 16.81
burial 228.3
burin 252
burka 17.32
burke 36
burl 216
burlap 268
burlesque 57
burley 16.116
burliness 300.23
Burlington 261
burly 16.116
Burma 17.209
Burmese 513
burn 249
burner 17.229
burnet 371.23
Burnham 242.13
burning 265.41
burnish 353
burnoose 309
burnsides 527
burnt 411
buroo 15.6
burp 272
burr 3
burrawang 263
Burroughs 520
burrow 12
burry 16.263
bursa 17.301
bursar 17.301
bursarial
  228.3.10
bursary 16.274.35
burse 297
bursitis 300.62
burst 434
burton 261.97
Burton 261.97
bury 16.262
Bury 16.262
bus 307
busbar 1

busby 16
busera 17.269
bush 357
bushbaby 16.7
bushbuck 43
bushel 228
Bushido 12.19
bushing 265
Bushire 8
bushman 261
bushpig 184
bushranger 17.156
bushwhack 32
bushwhacker 17.28
bushy 16.325
business 300
businesslike 39.1
businessman 261
busk 60
busker 17.49
buskin 252
bust 443
bustard 103
buster 17.388
bustle 228.87
bustler 17.199
busty 16.368
busuuti 16.343
busy 16.396
busybody 16.65
busy Lizzie 16.396
but 378
butane 247
butanone 257
butch 73
butcher 17
butcherbird 87
butchery 16.274
Bute 380
butler 17.202
butlery 16.274
butt 378
butte 380
butter 17.349
butterbur 3
buttercup 279
butterfat 365
butterfingered 103
butterfingers 524
butterflies 516
butterfly 7
butterine 251.7
Buttermere 6.3
buttermilk 49
butternut 378

butterscotch 68
buttery 16.274
buttock 46
button 261.103
buttonhole 223
buttonhook 44
buttonmould 120
buttonwood 101
buttress 300
butty 16.341
butyl 218
butyrate 367.21
buxom 242
Buxton 261
buy 7
buyer 17.4
buzz 522
buzzard 103
bwana 17.226
by 7
bye 7
Byelorussian
  261.74
bygone 254
bylaw 9
bypass 294
bypath 453
Byrd 87
byre 8
byrnie 16.227
byroad 98
Byron 261.58
Byronic 38.35
byssinosis 300.55.4
byssus 310.53
bystander 17.98
bystreet 370
byte 372
byway 2.26
byword 87
Byzantine 253.9
Byzantium 242.2

C

cab 18
cabal 212
caballero 12.62
cabaret 2.19
cabbage 197
cabbagetown 258

cabbala 17.161
cabby 16.5
caber 17.11
cabezon 254
cabin 252
cabinet 371.24
cable 228.11
cablegram 229
cablet 371
cableway 2
cabman 261
cabochon 254
caboodle 228.37
caboose 309
Cabora Bassa
  17.298
cabotage 359
cabretta 17.339
cabriole 223.1
cabriolet 2.12
cacao 12
cacciatore 16.269
cachalot 373.1
cache 349
cachepot 373
cachet 2.22
cachexia 17.3.57
cachinnate 367.17
cachou 15
cachucha 17.61
cacique 37
cack-handed 91.12
cackle 228.19
cacodemon 261.47
cacodyl 218
cacoepy 16.245
cacoethes 513
cacography 16.90.2
cacology 16.108.4.6
cacomistle 228.85
cacophonous
  310.36
cacophony
  16.237.3
cactus 310
cacuminal 228.60
cad 83
cadaster 17.379
cadaver 17.410
cadaverous 310.50
caddie 16.57
caddis 300
caddish 353.1
Caddoan 261.6
caddy 16.57

cade 85
cadelle 215.1
cadence 321
cadency 16.312
cadent 420
cadenza 17.446
cadet 368.5
cadge 191
cadger 17.144
cadi 16.58
Cadillac 32
Cádiz 515
cadmium 242.2
cadre 17.78
caduceus 310.2
caducity 16.333
caducous 310.13
caecilian 261.3.11
caecum 242
Caelian 261.3.10
Caelum 242
Caen 266
Caerleon 261.3
Caernarvon
  261.110
Caernarvonshire
  6.8
Caerphilly 16.120
Caesar 17.440
Caesarea 17.2.2
Caesarean 261.3.21
Caesarism
  242.35.15
caesium 242.2.20
caespitose 305
caesura 17.277
café 2
cafeteria 17.3.39
caff 157
caffeine 251
cage 193
cagey 16.100
Cagliari 16.261
cagmag 178
cagoule 227
cahoots 346
Caiaphas 293
Cain 247
caïque 37
cairn 250
Cairngorm 238
cairngorm 238
Cairo 12.64
caisson 261.62
Caithness 296

caitiff 163
cajole 223
cajolery 16.274.17
cajuput 379
cake 34
cakewalk 41
Calabar 1.2
calabash 349.1
Calabria 17.3
caladium 242.2.1
Calais 2
calalu 15.5
calamander 17.98
calamine 253
calamint 412
calamite 372
calamitous 310.64
calamity 16.333.11
calamondin 252
calamus 310.29.2
calandria 17.3.45
calash 349
calathus 310
calcaneus 310.2.6
calcar 1
calcareous 310.2.10
calceolaria
  17.3.38.1
calcic 38
calciferol 220.4
calciferous
  310.50.2
calcific 38.12
calcifuge 204
calcify 7.3
calcimine 253
calcine 253
calcite 372
calcium 242.2
calcsinter 17.369
calculable
  228.16.25
calculate 367.13
calculated 91.34
calculating 265.64
calculation
  261.67.13
calculative 485.15.5
calculator 17.338.6
calculus 310.25
Calcutta 17.349
caldarium 242.2.14
caldera 17.271
Caldwell 215
Caledonia 17.3.36

Caledonian
261.3.18
calefacient 420.73
calefactory
16.274.44
calendar 17.102
calender 17.102
calends 532
calendula 17.174
calenture 10
calf 158
calfskin 252
Calgary 16.274
calibrate 367.24
calibration
261.67.23
calibre 17.14
calico 12.11
Calicut 378
California 17.3.35
californium 242.2
Caligula 17.174
calipee 5
caliph 163.1
caliphate 367
calk 41
call 221
calla 17.160
Callaghan 245
callais 2
Callas 310
callboy 11
caller 17.160,
17.169
calligraphy 16.90
Callimachus 310.14
calling 265.31
calliope 16.254
callipash 349
calliper 17.253
callipygian 261.3.7
callisthenic 38.32
callisthenics 498.3
callosity 16.333.30
callous 310
callousness 300.34
callow 12.38
callowness 300.25
callus 310
calm 230
calmative 485.15
calmness 300
calomel 215
caloric 38.41
calorie 16.274.15

calorific 38.12.1
calorimeter
17.342.2.1
calotte 373.1
caloyer 17.5
calpac 32
calque 47
caltrop 281
calumet 368
calumniate 367.1
calumnious 310.2
calumny 16
Calvados 302
calvaria 17.3.38
Calvary 16.274
calve 481
Calvin 252
Calvinism
242.35.13
calvities 513.1
calycle 228.23
calypso 12
calyx 498
Cam 229
cam 229
Camagüey 2
camail 214
camaraderie
16.274.6
camarilla 17.166.3
camass 293
camber 17.23
Camberwell 215
cambist 436
cambium 242.2
Cambodia 17.3
cambogia 17.3.15
camboose 309
Cambria 17.3.43
Cambrian 261.3
cambric 38
Cambridge 197
Cambridgeshire 6
Cambyses 513.13
Camden 261
came 231
camel 228.51
cameleer 6
camellia 17.3.20
camelopard 84
Camelopardalis
300.13
Camelopardus 310
Camelot 373
cameo 12.3

camera 17.279
cameral 228.76
camera lucida
17.83
cameraman 261.52
camera obscura
17.277
Cameroon 260.3
camiknickers 524
camion 261.3
camise 513.8
camisole 223.4
camlet 371
camomile 219
camoodi 16.71
Camorra 17.275
camouflage 359
camp 285
campaign 247.7
campaigner 17.227
Campania 17.3.31
campanile 16.118
campanology
16.108.4.11
campanula
17.174.9
Campbell 228.17
camper 17.261
campestral 228.81
camphire 8
camphor 17.122
camphorate 367.23
camphoric 38.41
Campinas 310.32
camping 265
campion 261.3
camporee 5.17
campus 310.41
camshaft 396
can 245
Cana 17.227
Canaan 261
Canaanite 372.6
Canada 17.92
Canadian 261.3.3
Canadianism
242.35.14.1
canaigre 17.130
canal 212
canaliculus
310.25.2
canalize 516.3.5
canapé 16.254
canard 84
canary 16.264

canasta 17.379
canaster 17.390
Canaveral 228.76
Canberra 17.279
cancan 245
cancel 228
cancellation
261.67.12
Cancer 17.312
cancer 17.312
cancerous 310.50
cancroid 97
candela 17.165
candelabrum 242
candid 91.12
candidacy 16.307
candidate 367.8
candidness
300.28.1
candied 91.12
Candiot 373
candle 228.39
candlelight 372
Candlemas 310
candlenut 378
candlepins 548
candlestick 38
candlewick 38
candlewood 101
candour 17.98
candy 16.77
candyfloss 302
candytuft 400
cane 247
canebrake 34
canella 17.163
canescent 420.67.2
canfield 115
cangue 263
canine 253
caning 265.40
canister 17.384
canker 17.43
cankerous 310.50.1
canna 17.225
cannabin 252
cannabis 300.3
Cannae 5
canned 128
cannel 228.55
cannelloni 16.233
cannelure 10.4
canner 17.225
cannery 16.274
Cannes 245

cannibal 228.12
cannibalism 242.35.11
cannibalistic 38.70.2
cannibalize 516.3
cannikin 252.3
canning 265
Cannock 46
cannon 261.55
cannonade 85.3
cannonball 221
cannoneer 6.5
cannonry 16.284
cannot 373
cannula 17.174.9
cannulate 367.13
canny 16.223
canoe 15
canoeing 265.5
canon 261.55
canoness 300.26
canonical 228.23.13
canonicals 539.2.1
canonicate 367.5
canonize 516.7
canonry 16.284
canoodle 228.37
Canopus 310.39
canopy 16.254
Canossa 17.304
cans 544
cant 407
can't 408
Cantab. 18
cantabile 16.120
Cantabrigian 261.3.7
cantala 17.161
cantaloupe 280.1
cantankerous 310.50.1
cantata 17.337
canteen 251
canter 17.365
Canterbury 16.274
cantharides 513.4
canthus 310.72
canticle 228.23
cantilena 17.227
cantilever 17.413
cantillate 367.12
cantina 17.230
cantle 228.109

canto 12.83
canton 254
Canton 254
Cantonese 513.9
cantor 9
cantoris 300.46
cantrip 274
Cantuar. 1
cantus 310
canty 16.353
Canute 380
canvas 310
canvasback 32
canvass 310
canvasser 17.309
canyon 261.121
canzona 17.236
canzone 16.233
canzonet 368
caoutchouc 45
cap 268
capability 16.333.9.2
capable 228.16.32
capacious 310.56
capacitance 321.24
capacitate 367.30.2
capacitor 17.342
capacity 16.333.25.1
cap-a-pie 5
caparison 261.65.1
cape 270
capelin 252.11
Capella 17.163
caper 17.249
Capernaum 242.2
Cape Roca 17.38
Capet 371
Capetian 261.70
capias 293.1
capillarity 16.333.20.2
capillary 16.274.16
capital 228.102
capitalism 242.35.11
capitalist 436.7
capitalistic 38.70.2
capitalize 516.3
capitate 367.30
capitation 261.67.27
Capitol 228.102
Capitoline 253.3

capitular 17.174.12
capitulate 367.13
capitulation 261.67.13
capitulum 242.10
capo 12
capon 261.57
Capone 257
caporal 213
capote 376
Cappadocia 17.3
cappie 16.243
cappuccino 12.54
capreolate 367
Capri 5
capriccio 12.3
capriccioso 12.70
caprice 298
capricious 310.58
capriciousness 300.34.3
Capricorn 255.2
caprifig 184
caprine 253
capriole 223.1
capsaicin 252.21
capsicum 242.4
capsid 91.31
capsize 516
capstan 261
capsulate 367.13
capsule 227
capsulize 516
captain 252.25
captaincy 16.311
caption 261.83
captious 310
captivate 367.36
captivation 261.67
captive 485, 485.22
captivity 16.333.35
captor 17.374
capture 17.72
Capua 17.7
capuche 358
capuchin 252
caput 381
capybara 17.268
car 1
carabao 12.1
carabid 91.4
carabineer 6.4
caracal 212
Caracalla 17.160
caracara 17.268

Caracas 310.7
caracole 223
caracul 225
carafe 157
caramba 17.23
caramel 228
caramelize 516.3
carangid 91
carapace 295.4
carat 381
Caratacus 310.14
caravan 245
caravanserai 7.12
caravel 215
caraway 2.28
carbamate 367.16
carbazole 223
carbide 92
carbine 253
carbohydrate 367
carbolic 38.22
carbon 261.8
carbonaceous 310.56
carbonade 85.3
carbonado 12.17
Carbonari 16.261
carbonate 367.18
carbonation 261.67.19
carbonic 38.35
carboniferous 310.50.2.1
carbonize 516.7
carboxyl 218
carboxylate 367.12
carboy 11
carbuncle 228.30
carbuncular 17.174
carburation 261.67.21
carburettor 17.339
carby 16.6
carcass 310.8
Carchemish 353
carcinogen 261.39
carcinogenic 38.32.1.1
carcinoma 17.215
carcinomatosis 300.55.7
card 84
cardamom 242
cardboard 95
cardiac 32.1

cardialgia 17.3.16
Cardiff 163
cardigan 261.32
Cardiganshire 6.8
cardinal 228.60
cardinalate 367.14
cardiogram 229.1.1
cardiograph 158.1.1
cardiography 16.90.2.1
cardiomegaly 16.131.2
carditis 300.62
cardoon 260
cardsharp 269
cardsharper 17.248
care 4
careen 251.7
career 6
careerist 436.17
carefree 5
careful 226
carefulness 300.30
careless 300
carelessness 300.33
caress 296.4
caret 371
caretaker 17.30
careworn 255
Carey 16.264
carfare 4.2
carfax 494
cargo 12.26
carhop 276
Caria 17.3.38
Carib 24
Caribbean 261.2
Caribbees 513
caribou 15
caricature 10.5
caricaturist 436.19
caries 513.1
CARIFTA 17.359
carillon 261.120
carillonneur 3
Carina 17.230.1
carinate 367.17
Carinthia 17.3.52
carioca 17.38
cariogenic 38.32.1
cariole 223.1
carious 310.2.10
Carl 213
carline 252

carling 265.26
Carlisle 219
Carlos 302
Carlow 12.39
Carlton 261
Carlyle 219
carmagnole 223
carman 261
Carmarthen 261
Carmarthenshire 6.8
Carmelite 372.4
carminative 485.15.7
carmine 253
carnage 197
carnal 228
carnassial 228.3
Carnatic 38.49
carnation 261.67.17
carnelian 261.3.10
carnet 2.14
carnify 7.3
Carniola 17.171
carnival 228.120
carnivore 9.13
carnivorous 310.50.3
Carnot 12.51
carny 16.224
carob 31
caroche 354
carol 228.72
Carol 228.72
Carolina 17.232
Caroline 253.3
Carolingian 261.3
carolus 310.26
carom 242
carotene 251.11
carotenoid 97.8
carotid 91.40
carousal 228.129
carouse 521
carousel 215.2
carouser 17.443
carp 269
carpal 228
Carpathian 261.3
carpel 228
Carpentaria 17.3.38
carpenter 17.369
carpentry 16.289

carpet 371
carpetbag 178.1
carpetbagger 17.123
carpeting 265.66
carpogonium 242.2.12
carpology 16.108.4
carpophagous 310
carpophore 9.6
carport 374
carpus 310
carrack 46
carrageen 251
Carrara 17.268
carrefour 9.6
carrel 228.72
carriage 197.9
carriageway 2.29
carrier 17.3
carrion 261.3.20
carronade 85.3
carrot 381
carroty 16.344
carry 16.260
carryall 221
carrycot 373
carse 294
carsick 38
Carson 261.61
cart 366
cartage 197
carte blanche 78
cartel 215
Carter 17.337
Cartesian 261.3.34
cartful 226
Carthage 197
Carthaginian 261.3.17
carthorse 303
Carthusian 261.3
cartilage 197.1
cartilaginous 310.33
cartload 98
cartogram 229.1
cartography 16.90.2
cartomancy 16.309
carton 261.95
cartoon 260
cartoonist 436.12
cartouche 358
cartridge 197

cartulary 16.274.18
cartwheel 217
Cartwright 372
caruncle 228.30
carve 481
carven 261.110
carver 17.409
carvery 16.274
carving 265
caryatid 91.32
caryopsis 300.61
carzey 16.392
casaba 17.10
Casablanca 17.43
Casanova 17.417
cascade 85
cascara 17.268
cascarilla 17.166.3
case 295
casease 509.1
caseate 367.1.4
caseation 261.67.1.3
casebound 139
casefy 7.3
casein 252
casement 420.44
caseose 520
caseous 310.2
casern 249
casework 36
cash 349
cashew 15
cashier 6
cashmere 6
casing 265.59
casino 12.54
cask 56
casket 371
Caspar 17.265
Caspian 261.3
casque 55
cassareep 273
cassata 17.337
cassation 261.67
cassava 17.409
casserole 223.3
cassette 368
cassia 17.3.46
cassimere 6.2
Cassiodorus 310.48
Cassiopeia 17.2.1
cassis 298
cassock 46
cassoulet 2

cassowary 16.264
cast 431
castanets 336
castaway 2.28
caste 431
castellan 261.41
castellated 91.34.5
caster 17.380
castigate 367.10
castigation
   261.67.10
Castile 217
Castilian 261.3.11
casting 265.74
castle 228.83
Castlereagh 2
castor 17.380
castrate 367
castration 261.67
castrato 12.73
Castro 12
casual 228.9
casualty 16.352
casuarina 17.232
casuist 436
casuistic 38.70
casuistry 16.293
cat 365
catabasis 300.57
catabolic 38.22
catabolism
   242.35.11
catachresis 300.51
cataclasis 300.50
cataclinal 228.61
cataclysm 242.35
cataclysmic 38
catacomb 241
catadromous
   310.29
catafalque 47
Catalan 245
catalase 509
catalectic 38.60
catalepsy 16.313
catalogue 185
Catalonia 17.3.36.2
catalyse 516.3
catalysis 300.52.1
catalyst 436.7.6
catalytic 38.52.1
catamaran 245.5
catamenia 17.3.33
catamite 372
catamount 418.1

cataphoresis
   300.51.1
catapult 406
cataract 382
catarrhal 228
catastrophe 16.90
catastrophic 38.13
catastrophism
   242.35
catatonia 17.3.36
Catawba 17.17
catcall 221
catch 62
catcher 17.50
catchfly 7
catching 265
catchment 420.36
catchpenny 16.226
catchpole 223
catchweight 367
catchword 87
catchy 16.46
catechetical
   228.23.19
catechin 252.4
catechism 242.35
catechize 516
catecholamine
   251.4
catechumen 248.3
categoric 38.41
categorical
   228.23.17
categorize 516.8
category 16.274.9
catena 17.230
catenane 247.6
catenary 16.274.25
catenate 367.17
cater 17.338
cateran 261.60
caterer 17.279
catering 265.58
caterpillar 17.166.2
caterwaul 221
catfall 221
catfish 353
catgut 378
catharsis 300
cathartic 38
Cathay 2
cathead 86
cathectic 38.60
cathedral 228.78
Catherine 252.20

catheter 17.342
catheterize 516.8.2
cathode 98
Catholic 38
catholic 38
Catholicism
   242.35.16.2
Catholicity
   16.333.28
catholicity
   16.333.28
catholicize 516.10
catholicon 261.13
cation 261.4
catkin 252
catlike 39
catling 265
catmint 412
catnap 268
Cato 12.74
catsup 281
cattalo 12.45
cattery 16.274
cattle 228.97
cattleman 261
cattleya 17.3
catty 16.327
Catullus 310
catwalk 41
Caucasia 17.3.59
Caucasian 261.3.33
Caucasoid 97
Caucasus 310
caucus 310
caudad 83
caudal 228
caudate 367
caudex 496
caught 374
caul 221
cauldron 261
caulicle 228.23
cauliflower 14
caulk 41
causal 228
causalgia 17.3.16
causality 16.333.8
causation 261.67
causative 485.15
cause 518
cause célèbre
   17.282
causerie 16.274
causeway 2
caustic 38

cauterant 420.65
cauterize 516.8
cautery 16.274
caution 261.72
cautionary
   16.274.29
cautious 310.59
cautiousness
   300.34
cavalcade 85
cavalier 6
cavalla 17.160
cavalry 16.283
cavalryman 261.48
cavatina 17.230
cave 16.379, 482
caveat 365
caveat emptor 9
caveator 17.338.1
caveman 261
Cavendish 353
cavern 261
cavernous 310.36
cavesson 261.65
cavetto 12.75
caviar 1
cavicorn 255.2
cavie 16.379
cavil 228.117
caving 265.77
cavitation
   261.67.27
Cavite 16.332
cavity 16.333.33
cavort 374
cavy 16.379
caw 9
Cawdrey 16.276
Cawnpore 9
Caxton 261
cay 2
cayenne 248
cayman 261.45
cayuse 309
cease 298
ceaseless 300
Cecil 228
Cecilia 17.3.21
cecity 16.333.27
Cecrops 329
cedar 17.82
cede 89
cedi 16.59
cedilla 17.166
ceiba 17.11

ceilidh 16.114
ceiling 265.29
celadon 254
celandine 253
Celebes 513
celebrant 420
celebrate 367.24
celebrated 91.34
celebration
261.67.23
celebratory
16.274.40
celebrity 16.333.24
celeriac 32.1
celerity 16.333.21
celery 16.274
celesta 17.382
celeste 433
celestial 228.3.14
celestite 372
celibacy 16.307
celibate 371.5
cell 215
cella 17.163
cellar 17.163
cellarage 197
cellarer 17.279
cellaret 368.6
Cellini 16.228.1
cellist 436
cello 12.40
cellophane 247.3
cellular 17.174
cellulase 509
cellule 227
cellulitis 300.62.2
Celluloid 97
cellulose 305, 520
Celsius 310.2
celt 402
Celt 402
Celtic 38
cembalo 12.45
cement 410.1
cementation
261.67.32
cementum 242
cemetery 16.274.41
cenacle 228.28
cenotaph 158
cenote 2.24
Cenozoic 38.2
cense 316
censer 17.314
censor 17.314

censorious 310.2.13
censorship 274.1
censure 17.330
census 310.55
cent 410
cental 228.110
centaur 9.12
Centaurus 310.48
centaury 16.269
centenarian
261.3.21.1
centenary
16.274.25
centennial 228.3
centesimal 228.52.1
centesimo 12.48
centigrade 85.5
centigram 229
centilitre 17.341
centillion 261.120
centime 234
centimetre 17.341
centipede 89.1
centipoise 519
cento 12.84
central 228.80
centralism
242.35.11
centrality 16.333.8
centralization
261.67.36
centralize 516.3
centre 17.368
centreboard 95.1
centrefold 120
centrepiece 298.2
centric 38.47
centrifugal 228.48
centrifuge 204
centriole 223.1
centripetal 228.101
centrist 436
centrobaric 38.38
centroid 97
centromere 6.3
centrosome 239
centrosphere 6.1
centuplicate
367.5.1, 371.9.1
centurion 261.3.24
century 16.274
cep 271
cephalad 83
cephalalgia 17.3.16
cephalic 38.19

cephalin 252.11
cephalometer
17.342.3
Cephalonia
17.3.36.2
cephalopod 94.1
ceraceous 310.56
Ceram 229
ceramic 38.24
ceramics 498.2
cerastes 513.18
cerate 371.32
cerated 91.34
ceratodus 310.17
Cerberus 310.50
cercaria 17.3.38
cercis 300
cercopithecoid 97.3
cercus 310.9
cere 6
cereal 228.3.11
cerebellum 242.8
cerebral 228
cerebrate 367.24
cerebration
261.67.23
cerebrospinal
228.61
cerebrum 242
cerecloth 459
cerement 420.30
ceremonial 228.3.8
ceremonious
310.2.9.1
ceremony 16.237
Ceres 513.11
ceresin 252.21
cereus 310.2.11
ceria 17.3.39
cerise 513.12
cerium 242.2.15
cermet 371
cernuous 310.4
cero 12.63
cerography 16.90.2
ceroplastic 38.68
ceroplastics 498.15
cerotype 275.1
cert 369
certain 261.97
certainly 16.174
certainty 16.360
certifiable
228.16.3.1

certificate 367.5,
371.9
certified 92.1
certify 7.3
certiorari 7
certitude 102.2
cerulean 261.3
cerumen 248.3
ceruse 309
Cervantes 513
cervelat 365
cervical 228.23
cervid 91.55
cervine 253
cervix 498
cess 296
cessation 261.67
cesser 17.300
cession 261.68
cessionary
16.274.29.2
cesspool 227
cestode 98
cestoid 97
cetacean 261.67.27
cete 370
ceteris paribus 308
cetology 16.108.4
Cetus 310.63
Ceylon 254.6
chablis 16.132
cha-cha 1
chacma 17.219
chaconne 254
Chad 83
Chadic 38.7
chaeta 17.341
chaetognath 452
chaetopod 94.1
chafe 159
chafer 17.111
chaff 158
chaffer 17.110
chaffinch 80
chagrin 252
chain 247
chair 4
chairborne 255
chairman 261.46
chaise 509
chaise longue 266
chalaza 17.439
chalcedony 16.237
chalcid 91
Chalcidice 16.300

cheerleader 17.82
cheerless 300
cheerlessness
    300.33
cheers 514
cheery 16.265
cheese 513
cheeseboard 95
cheesecake 34
cheesecloth 459
cheeseparing
    265.52
cheesy 16.395
cheetah 17.341
chef 160
Chekhov 165
chela 17.162,
    17.165
chelate 367
chelicera 17.279.2
chelicerate 367.23
cheliform 238.1
Chelmsford 103
chelonian 261.3.18
chelp 283
Chelsea 16
Cheltenham 242.16
chemical 228.23
chemin de fer 4.3
chemise 513.8
chemisette 368
chemisorb 27
chemisorption
    261.87
chemist 436
chemistry 16.293
chemostat 365
chemotherapy
    16.254
chempaduk 43
chemurgy 16.102
Chenab 18
Chengteh 2
chenille 217.1
chenopod 94.1
cheongsam 229
Cheops 329
cheque 35
chequebook 44
chequer 17.31
chequerboard 95.1
chequered 103
chequers 524
Cherbourg 187
cherish 353

chernozem 232
Cherokee 5
cheroot 380
cherry 16.262
chersonese 298.1
chert 369
Chertsey 16.316
cherub 31
cherubic 38.4
cherubim 235
Cherubini 16.228
chervil 218
chervonets 336
Chesapeake 37
Cheshire 6
chess 296
chessboard 95
chessel 228
chessman 261.53
chest 433
Chester 17.382
chesterfield 115.1
Chesterfield 115.1
Chesterton 261
chestnut 378
chesty 16.364
Chetnik 38
cheval-de-frise 513
chevet 2
Cheviot 381.1
chevrette 368
chevron 261
chevrotain 247.10
chevy 16.380
chew 15
chewy 16.4
Cheyenne 245
chiack 32
Chiang Kai-shek
    35
chianti 16.353
chiaroscuro 12.66
chiasma 17.223
chiasmus 310
chiastolite 372.4
chibouk 45
chic 37
Chicago 12.26
chicalote 2.24
chicane 247.1
chicanery 16.274
Chichester 17.384
chichi 5
chick 38
chickabiddy 16.63

chickadee 5.4
chickaree 5.17
Chickasaw 9.11
chicken 252.3
chicken-hearted
    91.33
chickenpox 499
chickpea 5
chickweed 89.6
chicle 228.23
chico 12.10
chicory 16.274.4
chide 92
chief 162
chiefly 16.158
chieftain 261
chiffchaff 157
chiffon 254
chiffonier 6.5
chigetai 7
chigger 17.129
chignon 254.12
chigoe 12.29
chihuahua 1
chilblain 247
child 117
childbed 86
childbirth 456
childhood 101
childish 353
childishness 300.35
childless 300
childlessness
    300.33
childlike 39
children 261
Chile 16.120
chiliad 83.1
chiliasm 242.34
chill 218
chilli 16.120
chilli con carne
    16.224
Chillon 254.6
chilly 16.120
chilopod 94.1
Chiltern 261
chime 236
chimera 17.272
chimere 6.2
chimerical
    228.23.15
chimney 16
chimneypiece 298
chimneypot 373

chimp 287
chimpanzee 5
chin 252
china 17.232
China 17.232
chinaberry 16.274
Chinagraph 158.1
Chinaman 261.52
Chinatown 258
chinaware 4.8
chinch 80
chincherinchee 5
chinchilla 17.166
Chindit 371
chiné 2
chine 253
Chinee 5.13
Chinese 513
Ching 265
chink 52
chinless 300
chino 12.54
chinoiserie 5.17
Chinook 45
Chinookan 261.15
chinquapin 252
chintz 348
chinwag 178
chionodoxa 17.428
Chios 302
chip 274
chipboard 95
chipmunk 54
chipolata 17.337.1
Chippendale 214
chipper 17.253
chipping 265
chippy 16.248
chirm 233
chiromancy 16.309
Chiron 254
chiropodist 436.3
chiropody 16.72
chiropractic 38.58
chiropractor
    17.353
chiropteran 261.60
chirp 272
chirper 17.251
chirpy 16.246
chirr 3
chirrup 281
chisel 228
chiselled 122
chit 371

chital 228.101
chitarrone 16.233
chitchat 365
chitin 252
chiton 261.100
Chittagong 266
chitter 17.342
chitterlings 552
chiv 485
chivalrous 310
chivalry 16.283
chive 486
chivy 16.382
chlamydate 367.8
chlamydeous 310.2.1
chlamydospore 9.10
Chloe 16.3
chloracne 16.238
chloral 228.74
chloramphenicol 220
chlorate 367
chlorella 17.163
chloric 38.42
chloride 92.5
chlorinate 367.17
chlorination 261.67.18
chlorine 251.6
chlorite 372
chlorobenzene 251
chloroform 238.2
chlorophyll 218.1
chloroplast 430
chlorothiazide 92
chlorous 310.48
chlorpropamide 92.3
choc-ice 301
chock 40
chocker 17.36
chocolate 371.18
chocolaty 16.344
Choctaw 9
Chogyal 213
choice 304
choir 8
choirboy 11
choirmaster 17.380
choke 42
chokebore 9
chokecherry 16.262
choker 17.38

cholecystectomy 16.222.5
choler 17.168
cholera 17.279
choleric 38.44
cholesterol 220.4
choli 16.126
choline 251
cholinergic 38.16
cholla 1
Cholon 259
chomp 288
chon 257
chondrify 7.3
chondrite 372
chondrule 227
choose 523
choosy 16.402
chop 276
Chopin 245
chopine 251
choplogic 38.18
chopper 17.255
choppy 16.250
chops 329
chopsticks 498
choragus 310.19
choral 228.74
chorale 213
chord 95
chordate 367
chording 265.15
chordophone 257
chore 9
chorea 17.2
choreograph 158.1.1
choreographer 17.120.1
choreography 16.90.2.1
choric 38.41
chorion 261.3.23
chorister 17.384
Chorley 16.123
chorography 16.90.2
choroid 97
chorology 16.108.4.13
chortle 228.105
chorus 310.48
chose 520
chosen 261.129
Chota Nagpur 10

Chou 12
chou 15
chough 168
choux 15
chow 13
chowder 17.89
chow mein 247
chrematistic 38.70.6
chrism 242.35
chrismatory 16.274.43
chrisom 242.35
Christ 437
Christadelphian 261.3
Christchurch 65
christen 261.65
Christendom 242
christening 265.46
Christian 261
Christiania 17.3.30
Christianity 16.333.14
Christianize 516.7
christianly 16.174
Christie 16.366
Christina 17.230
Christine 251
Christlike 39
Christmas 310
Christmastide 92
Christology 16.108.4
Christopher 17.120
chromate 367
chromatic 38.49.2
chromaticity 16.333.28
chromaticness 300.27
chromatics 498.11
chromatid 91
chromatin 252
chromatography 16.90.2.6
chromatophore 9.6
chrome 239
chromic 38
chrominance 321.14
chromite 372
chromium 242.2.9
chromogen 261.39

chromogenic 38.32.1
chromolithography 16.90.2
chromonema 17.210
chromosomal 228
chromosome 239
chromous 310
chronaxie 16.386
chronic 38.35
chronicle 228.23.13
chronicler 17.181
Chronicles 539.2.1
chronogram 229.1
chronograph 158.1
chronological 228.23.5
chronology 16.108.4.11
chronometer 17.342.3.3
chronometry 16.285.2.2
chronon 254
chronoscope 278.1
chrysalis 300.13
chrysanthemum 242.12
chrysolite 372.4
Chrysostom 242
chthonian 261.3.18
chub 29
chubby 16.13
chuck 43
chuckle 228.27
chuddar 17.90
chufa 17.118
chuff 168
chuffed 400
chuffy 16.88
chug 189
chukar 1
chukker 17.39
chum 240
chummy 16.220
chump 289
chumping 265.50
chunder 17.108
chunderous 310.50
chunk 54
chunky 16.39
Chunnel 228
chunter 17.373
church 65

churchgoer 17.6
churchgoing 265.4
Churchill 218
churchman 261
churchwarden 261.27
churchwoman 261.50
churchyard 84
churidars 508
churinga 17.141
churl 216
churlish 353
churn 249
churning 265.41
chute 380
chutney 16
chuttie 16.341
Chuvash 350
chyle 219
chyme 236
ciao 13
ciborium 242.2.17
cicada 17.78
cicatrix 498
cicatrize 516
cicely 16.131
Cicero 12
cicerone 16.233
Ciceronian 261.3.18
cichlid 91
cider 17.84
cig 184
cigar 1.4
cigarette 368.6
cigarillo 12.42
ciggy 16.93
cilia 17.3.21
ciliary 16.274.1.1
ciliate 371.1
cilice 300.8
cilium 242.2.6
cimbalom 242.11
cimex 496
Cimmerian 261.3.22
Cimon 261
cinch 80
cinchona 17.236
cinchonize 516.7
Cincinnati 16.327
cincture 17.67
cinder 17.102
Cinderella 17.163

cine 16.229
cineaste 430.1
cinema 17.211
cinematic 38.49.1
cinematograph 158.1
cinematography 16.90.2.6
Cinerama 17.206
cineraria 17.3.38
cinerarium 242.2.14
cinerator 17.338.9
cinereous 310.2.11
cingulum 242.10
Cinna 17.231
cinnabar 1.2
cinnamon 261.52
cinquain 247
cinquefoil 222
Cinzano 12.51
cipher 17.115
cipolin 252.11
circa 17.32
circadian 261.3.3
Circassia 17.3.46
Circassian 261.3
Circe 16.298
circinate 367.17
Circinus 310.33
circle 228.22
circlet 371
circuit 371.8
circuitous 310.64
circuitry 16.285
circuity 16.333.3
circular 17.174.5
circularize 516.8.1
circulate 367.13
circulation 261.67.13
circulatory 16.274.40.2
circumambulate 367.13
circumbendibus 310.5
circumcise 516
circumcision 261.91
circumference 321.20
circumflex 496
circumfluous 310.4
circumfuse 523

circumlocution 261.75.2
circumlocutory 16.274.42
circumlunar 17.238
circumnavigable 228.16.19
circumnavigate 367.10
circumnavigation 261.67.10
circumscissile 219.2
circumscribe 25
circumscription 261.85
circumspect 385
circumspective 485.17
circumstance 321
circumstantial 228.95
circumstantiate 367.1.8
circumvallate 367
circumvent 410
circumvention 261.82
circumvolution 261.75.1
circus 310.9
ciré 2
Cirencester 17.382
cirque 36
cirrate 367.21
cirrhosis 300.55.5
cirrhotic 38.53
cirripede 89.1
cirrocumulus 310.25.5
cirrostratus 310.62
cirrus 310.46
cisalpine 253
cisco 12.15
cislunar 17.238
cissoid 97
cist 436
Cistercian 261.69
cistern 261.107
cisterna 17.229
citadel 228.38
citation 261.67
cite 372
cithara 17.279
citified 92.1

citify 7.3
citizen 261.126
citizenry 16.284
citizenship 274.2
Citlaltépetl 228.100
citral 228.79
citrate 367.27
citreous 310.2
citric 38
citrin 252
citrine 252
citron 261
citronella 17.163
citronellal 212
citrulline 251.3
citrus 310
cittern 249.1
city 16.333
civet 371
civic 38.74
civics 498
civies 515
civil 228.120
civilian 261.120
civility 16.333.9
civilization 261.67.36
civilize 516.2
civilized 154
civvy 16.382
clack 32
Clackmannan 261.55
Clacton 261
clad 83
cladding 265
cladoceran 261.60
cladode 98
cladophyll 218.1
claim 231
claimant 420.29
clairaudience 321.1
clair-obscure 10
clairvoyance 321
clairvoyant 420.3
clam 229
clamant 420.29
clamatorial 228.3.12.2
clambake 34
clamber 17.23
clammy 16.210
clamorous 310.50
clamour 17.205
clamp 285

clamper 17.261
clan 245
clandestine 252.26
clang 263
clanger 17.245
clangour 17.140
clank 51
clannish 353
clansman 261
clap 268
Clapham 242
clapper 17.247
clapperboard 95.1
Clapton 261
claptrap 268
claque 32
clarabella 17.163.1
Clare 4
Clarence 321
Clarendon 261
claret 381
clarify 7.3.4
clarinet 368
clarinetist 436.23
clarion 261.3.20
clarity 16.333.20
Clark 33
clarkia 17.3
claro 12.61
clarts 334
clary 16.264
clash 349
clasp 290
class 294
classic 38.48
classical 228.23
classicalism
    242.35.11
classicism
    242.35.16
classicist 436.21
classics 498
classifiable
    228.16.3.1
classification
    261.67.5.1
classified 92.1
classify 7.3.6
classis 300.49
classless 300
classlessness
    300.33
classmate 367
classroom 241
classy 16.295

clastic 38.68
clathrate 367
clatter 17.336
claudication
    261.67.5
Claudius 310.2
clause 518
claustrophobia
    17.3.4
claustrophobic
    38.3
claver 17.410
clavichord 95.2
clavicle 228.23
clavicorn 255.2
clavier 17.3
claw 9
clay 2
claybank 51
claymore 9
claypan 245
claytonia 17.3.36
clean 251
cleaner 17.230
cleaning 265.42
cleanliness 300.23
cleanly 16.171,
    16.172
cleanness 300
cleanse 546
cleanser 17.446
clean-shaven
    261.111
clear 6
clearance 321.17
clearcole 223
clear-headedness
    300.28
clearing 265.53
clearness 300
clear-sighted 91.39
clearway 2
clearwing 265
cleat 370
cleavage 197
cleave 484
cleaver 17.413
cleavers 524
cleck 35
cleek 37
Cleethorpes 330
clef 160
cleft 397
cleg 181
clem 232

clematis 300
clemency 16.312
clement 420
clementine 251
clench 79
Cleo 12.2
cleome 16.219
Cleopatra 17.291
clerestory 16.269
clergy 16.102
clergyman 261.48
cleric 38.39
clerical 228.23.15
clericalism
    242.35.11
clericals 539.2
clerihew 15
clerk 33
clerkly 16.140
cleruchy 16.31
cleveite 372
Cleveland 143
clever 17.411
cleverness 300.26
clevis 300.69
clew 15
cliché 2
cliché'd 85
Clichy 5
click 38
clicker 17.34
client 420.2
clientele 215
cliff 163
cliffhanger 17.245
climacteric 38.44
climactic 38.58
climate 371
climatic 38.49
climatology
    16.108.4.15.1
climax 494
climb 236
climber 17.212
clime 236
clinch 80
clincher 17.71
cline 253
cling 265
clinger 17.246
clinic 38.34
clinical 228.23.12
clinician 261.71.5
clink 52
clinker 17.44

clinometer 17.342.3
clinostat 365
clinquant 420
clip 274
clipboard 95
clip-clop 276
clipper 17.253
clippers 524
clippie 16.248
clipping 265
clique 37
cliquey 16.24
clishmaclaver
    17.410
clitellum 242.8
clitic 38.52
clitoris 300.47
Clive 486
cloaca 17.30
cloak 42
cloakroom 241
clobber 17.16
cloche 354
clock 40
clockmaker 17.30
clockwise 516
clockwork 36
clod 94
clodhopper 17.255
clog 185
cloisonné 2
cloister 17.386
cloistered 103
cloistral 228
clomp 288
clone 257
clonic 38.35
clonk 53
clonus 310.35
clop 276
close 305, 520
closed 155
close-grained 130
close-hauled 118
close-knit 371
closely 16.182
closeness 300
closer 17.442
close-stool 227
closet 371.39
close-up 279
closing 265.83
clostridium 242.2.3
closure 17.335
clot 373

coffee 16.86
coffeepot 373
coffer 17.116
cofferdam 229
coffin 252
coffle 228
cog 185
cogent 420
cogitate 367.30
cogitative
485.15.12
Cognac 32
cognate 367
cognition 261.71
cognitive 485.12
cognizable
228.16.63
cognizance 321
cognizant 420
cognize 516
cognomen 248
cognoscenti 16.355
cogon 257
cogwheel 217
cohabit 371.4
cohabitation
261.67.27
cohere 6
coherence 321.17
coherent 420.62
cohesion 261.90
cohesive 485
coho 12
cohobate 367.4
cohort 374
cohosh 354
cohune 260
coiffeur 3
coil 222
coin 256
coincide 92.9
coincidence 321.5
coincident 420.10
coincidental
228.110.1
coin-op 276
coinsurance 321.19
coinsure 10.2
Cointreau 12
coir 17.5
coit 375
coition 261.71
coitus 310.64
coke 42
col 220

cola 17.171
colander 17.109
colatitude 102.2.1
colcannon 261.55
Colchester 17.384
colchicine 251.8
colchicum 242.4
Colchis 300
colcothar 1
cold 120
cold-blooded 91.11
cold-bloodedness
300.28
cold-hearted 91.33
coldness 300
cole 223
colectomy 16.222.5
coleoptile 219
coleorhiza 17.441.1
Coleridge 197
coleslaw 9
Colette 368
coleus 310.2
coley 16.126
colic 38.22
colicweed 89.6
colitis 300.62
collaborate 367.23
collaboration
261.67,22.1
collaborator
17.338.9
collage 359
collagen 261.39
collapsar 1
collapse 322
collapsible 228.16
collar 17.168
collarbone 257
collard 103.3
collarette 368.6
collate 367.14
collateral 228.76
collation 261.67
collative 485.10
collator 17.338
colleague 183
collect 385, 385.5
collectanea 17.3.31
collected 91.43
collection 261.77
collective 485.17
collectivism
242.35.22

collectivity
16.333.35
collectivize 516.15
collector 17.354
colleen 251
college 197.2
collegian 261.36
collegiate 371.1
collet 371
collide 92
collie 16.122
collier 17.3
colliery 16.274
colligate 367.10
collimate 367.15
collimator 17.338
collinear 17.3.34
Collins 548
collinsia 17.3
collision 261.91
collocate 367.6
collocation
261.67.6
collocutor 17.351
collodion 261.3.6
collogue 188
colloid 97
collop 281.2
colloquial 228.3
colloquialism
242.35.11.2
colloquium 242.2
colloquy 16.259
collotype 275.1
collude 102.1
collusion 261.93
colluvium 242.2
colly 16.122
collyrium 242.2.16
collywobbles 539.1
colobus 310
colocynth 470
Cologne 257
cologne 257
Colombia 17.3
Colombo 12.7
colon 254.7, 257,
261.43
colonel 228.58
colonial 228.3.8
colonialism
242.35.11.2
colonic 38.35
colonist 436.13
colonitis 300.62.4

colonize 516.7
colonnade 85.3
colonnaded 91.6
Colonsay 2
colony 16.237
colophon 254.3
colophony 16.237.3
Colorado 12.16
colorant 420.65
coloration
261.67.22
coloratura 17.277
colorific 38.12.1
colorimeter
17.342.2.1
colossal 228.86
colosseum 242.1
colossus 310.54
colostomy 16.222.6
colostrum 242.23
colotomy 16.222.4
colour 17.173
colourable
228.16.35
coloured 103.4
colourfast 431
colourful 226
colouring 265.58
colourless 300.13
colourman 261.52
coloury 16.274
colporteur 17.345
colt 405
coltish 353
coltsfoot 379
colubrid 91
colubrine 253
colugo 12.32
Columba 17.27
columbarium
242.2.14
Columbia 17.3
Columbian 261.3
columbine 253.1
Columbus 310.6
columella 17.163
column 242
columnar 17.242
columniation
261.67.1
columnist 436
colure 10.4
Colwyn 252
coly 16.126
coma 17.215

compeer 6
compel 215
compelling 265.28
compendious 310.2
compendium 242.2
compensate 367.29
compensation
261.67.26
compensatory
16.274.40
compere 4
compete 370
competence 321.24
competent 420.76
competition
261.71.7
competitive 485.12
competitor 17.342
compilation
261.67.12
compile 219
compiler 17.167
complacency
16.312
complacent 420
complain 247
complainant 420
complaint 409
complaisance 321
complaisant 420
complement 410.1,
420.31
complementary
16.274.47
complete 370
completeness
300.37
completion 261.70
complex 496
complexion 261.77
complexity 16.333
compliance 321.2
compliant 420.2
complicate 367.5
complicated
91.34.3
complication
261.67.5
complicity
16.333.28
compliment 410.1,
420.31
complimentary
16.274.47
comply 7

component 420.54
compony 16.233
comport 374
comportment 420
compose 520
composed 155
composer 17.442
composite 371.40
composition
261.71.9
compositor
17.342.5
compost 438
composure 17.335
compote 376
compound 139
comprador 9.4
comprehend 131.1
comprehensible
228.16.40
comprehension
261.82.1
comprehensive
485.9
compress 296
compression
261.68
compressive 485.2
compressor 17.300
comprise 516
compromise 516.5
Comptometer
17.342.3
compulsion 261
compulsive 485
compulsory 16.274
compunction
261.80
computation
261.67.29
compute 380
computer 17.351
computerize 516.8
comrade 85
comradeship 274
comsat 365
comstockery
16.274.5
Comus 310
con 254
con amore 16.269
conation 261.67.19
conative 485.15
conatus 310.62
con brio 12.2

concatenation
261.67.18
concave 482
concavity
16.333.33
conceal 217
concealment 420
concede 89.5
conceit 370
conceited 91.37
conceivable
228.16.61
conceive 484
concelebrate
367.24
concentrate 367
concentration
261.67
concentrative
485.10
concentre 17.368
concentric 38.47
concentricity
16.333.28
concept 422
conceptacle 228.28
conception 261.84
conceptual 228.9
conceptualism
242.35.11.3
conceptualize
516.3.3
concern 249
concerned 132
concernedly 16.148
concerning 265.41
concert 369
concertante 16.353
concerted 91.36
concertgoer 17.6
concertina 17.230
concertino 12.54
concertize 516.13
concerto 12
concession 261.68
concessionaire 4.5
concessionary
16.274.29.2
concessive 485.2
conch 53
concha 17.45
conchoid 97
conchoidal 228.35
conchology
16.108.4

concierge 361
conciliar 17.3.21
conciliate 367.1.2
conciliation
261.67.1.1
conciliative 485.15
conciliatory
16.274.43.1
concise 301
concision 261.91
conclave 482
conclude 102
conclusion 261.93
conclusive 485.8
concoct 388
concoction 261
concomitance
321.24
concomitant
420.76
concord 95
concordance 321
concordant 420.11
concordat 365
Concorde 95
concourse 303
concrete 370
concretion 261.70
concretize 516.12
concubinage 197.7
concubine 253
concupiscence
321.22
concur 3
concurrence 321
concurrent 420.64
concuss 307
concussion 261.74
condemn 232
condemnation
261.67
condemnatory
16.274.40
condensate 367.29
condensation
261.67.26
condense 316
condenser 17.314
condescend 131
condescendence
321.7
condescending
265.20
condescension
261.82.2

condign 253
condiment 420.31
condition 261.71
conditional 228.63.5
conditioned 143.5
conditioner 17.239.2
conditioning 265.46
condole 223.2
condolence 321
condom 242
condominium 242.2.11
condonation 261.67.19
condone 257
condor 9
condottiere 16.264
conduce 309
conducive 485.8
conduct 389
conductance 321
conduction 261.79
conductive 485.19
conductivity 16.333.35.3
conductor 17.357
conductress 300
conduit 371
condyle 218
condyloid 97.5
condyloma 17.215
cone 257
confab 18
confabulate 367.13.1
confabulation 261.67.13.1
confect 385
confection 261.77
confectioner 17.239
confectionery 16.274.29.4
confederacy 16.307.4
confederate 367.23, 371.35
confederation 261.67.22
confer 3
conferee 5
conference 321.20

conferrer 17.270
conferva 17.412
confess 296
confessant 420.67
confessedly 16.148
confession 261.68
confessional 228.63.4
confessor 17.300
confetti 16.330
confidant 407
confide 92
confidence 321.5
confident 420.10
confidential 228.96.1
confidentiality 16.333.8.1.1
confiding 265.14
configuration 261.67.21
confine 253
confinement 420
confirm 233
confirmand 128
confirmation 261.67.16
confiscate 367
Confiteor 9.1
confiture 10
conflagration 261.67
conflate 367
conflict 387
conflictive 485.18
confluence 321.3
confluent 420.4
conflux 502 ·
conform 238
conformable 228.16
conformal 228.53
conformation 261.67
conformist 436
conformity 16.333.13
confound 139
confounded 91.14
confraternity 16.333.16
confrère 4
confront 419
confrontation 261.67

Confucian 261.75
Confucianism 242.35.14
Confucius 310
con fuoco 12.12
confuse 523
confusedly 16.148
confusing 265.84
confusion 261.93
confute 380
conga 17.142
congé 2
congeal 217
congelation 261.67.12
congener 17.230
congenial 228.3.6
congeniality 16.333.8.1
congenital 228.102
conger 17.142
congeries 513.11
congest 433
congestion 261.18
congestive 485.24
congius 310.2
conglobate 367.3
conglomerate 367.23, 371.35
conglomeration 261.67.22
conglutinant 420.53
conglutinate 367.17
Congo 12
congrats 333
congratulate 367.13
congratulations 551.1
congratulatory 16.274.40.2
congregant 420.17
congregate 367.10, 371.14
congregation 261.67.10
congregational 228.63.3
Congregationalism 242.35.11.5.2
Congregationalist 436.7.5
congress 296

congressional 228.63.4
Congressman 261.53
Congreve 484
congruence 321.3
congruent 420.4
congruity 16.333.3
congruous 310.4
conic 38.35
conical 228.23.13
conics 498.5
conidium 242.2.3
conifer 17.114
coniferous 310.50.2.1
Coniston 261.107
conium 242.2.12
conjectural 228.76.1
conjecture 17.64
conjoin 256
conjoint 416
conjugal 228
conjugate 367, 371
conjugation 261.67
conjunct 393
conjunction 261.80
conjunctiva 17.415
conjunctive 485
conjunctivitis 300.62.6
conjuncture 17.68
conjuration 261.67.21
conjure 10, 17.159
conjurer 17.279
conjuring 265.58
conk 53
conker 17.45
conkers 524
con moto 12.79
Connacht 381
connate 367
Connaught 374
connect 385
Connecticut 381
connection 261.77
connective 485.17
connector 17.354
Connemara 17.268
conniption 261.85
connivance 321
connive 486
connivent 420

connoisseur 3
Connors 524
connotation
261.67.28
connote 376
connubial 228.3
conoid 97
conquer 17.45
conqueror 17.279
conquest 433
conquistador 9.4
Conrad 83
consanguinity
16.333.17
conscience 321
conscientious
310.61
conscientiousness
300.34.4
conscionable
228.16.31
conscious 310
consciousness
300.34
conscript 424
conscription
261.85
consecrate 367.25
consecration
261.67
consecution 261.75
consecutive 485
consensual 228.9
consensus 310.55
consent 410
consentient 420
consequence 321
consequent 420.58
consequential
228.96
consequently
16.198
conservancy 16.312
conservation
261.67
conservationist
436.13.4
conservatism
242.35.20
conservative 485.15
conservatoire 1.17
conservator 17.338
conservatory
16.274.43
conserve 483

Consett 371
consider 17.83
considerable
228.16.35
considerate 371.35
consideration
261.67.22
considering 265.58
consign 253
consignee 5.13
consignment 420
consignor 17.232
consist 436
consistency 16.312
consistent 420.81
consisting 265.76
consistory
16.274.49
consociate 367.1.7
consocies 513
consolation
261.67.14
consolatory
16.274.43
console 223
consolidate 367.8
consolidation
261.67.7
consolute 380.1
consommé 2
consonance 321
consonant 420.55
consonantal
228.109
consort 374
consortium 242.2
conspecific 38.12
conspectus 310.69
conspicuous
310.4.1
conspicuousness
300.34.2
conspiracy 16.307
conspirator 17.352
conspiratorial
228.3.12.2
conspire 8
constable 228.16
constabulary
16.274.18
Constance 321
constancy 16.312
constant 420
constantan 245
Constantine 253

Constantinople
228.69
constantly 16.198
constatation
261.67.30
constellate 367.12
constellation
261.67.12
consternate 367.18
consternation
261.67.19
constipate 367.19
constipated 91.34
constipation
261.67.20
constituency
16.312
constituent 420.4
constitute 380.5
constitution 261.75
constitutional
228.63.7
constitutionalism
242.35.11.5
constitutionality
16.333.8.7
constitutive 485
constrain 247
constraint 409
constrict 387
constriction 261.78
constrictive 485.18
constrictor 17.355
construct 389
construction
261.79
constructional
228.63
constructive 485.19
constructivism
242.35.22
construe 15
consubstantiation
261.67.1
consuetude 102.2
consul 228.89
consular 17.174
consulate 371.17
consult 406
consultancy 16.312
consultant 420
consultation 261.67
consultative 485.15
consumable 228.16
consume 241

consumer 17.217
consumerism
242.35.15
consummate
367.16, 371.21
consummation
261.67.16
consumption
261.89
consumptive 485
contact 382
contactor 17.353
contagion 261.34
contagious 310.20
contagiousness
300.34
contagium 242.2
contain 247
container 17.227
containerize 516.8
containment
420.41
contaminate
367.17.3
contamination
261.67.18.3
contango 12.35
conté 2
contemn 232
contemplate 367
contemplation
261.67
contemplative
485.15
contemporaneous
310.2.6
contemporary
16.274.32
contemporize 516.8
contempt 428
contemptible
228.16
contemptuous
310.4
contend 131
content 410
contented 91.46
contention 261.82
contentious 310.61
contentment 420
contest 433
contestable
228.16.59
contestant 420.80
context 450

337

contextual

contextual 228.9
contextualize
  516.3.3
contexture 17.75
contiguity 16.333.3
contiguous 310.4
continent 420.53
continental
  228.110
contingency
  16.312.4
contingent 420.23
continual 228.9
continuance 321.3
continuant 420.4
continuation
  261.67.2
continuative
  485.15
continuator 17.338
continue 15.9
continuity
  16.333.3.1
continuo 12
continuous 310.4.3
continuum 242.3
conto 12.85
contort 374
contortion 261.72
contortionist
  436.13
contour 10
contraband 128
contrabass 295.1
contraception
  261.84.1
contraceptive
  485.23
contract 382
contractile 219.4
contraction 261.76
contractor 17.353
contractual 228.9.4
contracture 17.63
contradict 387.1
contradiction
  261.78.2
contradictory
  16.274.46
contrail 214
contralto 12.82
contraption 261.83
contrapuntal
  228.112

contrariety
  16.333.2.1
contrary 16.274
contrast 431
contrasting 265.74
contrasty 16.362
contravallation
  261.67.14
contravene 251.12
contravention
  261.82
contrayerva 17.412
contredanse 315
contretemps 266
contribute 380.2
contribution
  261.75
contributive 485
contributor 17.350
contributory
  16.274.42
contrite 372
contrition 261.71
contrivance 321
contrive 486
contrived 149
control 223
controllable
  228.16.24
controller 17.171
controversial
  228.92
controversy 16.298
controvert 369.2
contumacious
  310.56
contumacy 16.307
contumelious
  310.2.4
contuse 523
contusion 261.93
conundrum 242
conurbation 261.67
conure 10
convalesce 296.1
convalescence
  321.21
convalescent
  420.67
convection 261.77
convector 17.354
convene 251
convener 17.230
convenience 321.1
convenient 420.1.2

convent 420
conventicle
  228.23.23
convention 261.82
conventional
  228.63.9
conventionalism
  242.35.11.5
conventionality
  16.333.8.7
conventionalize
  516.3.7
conventual 228.9
converge 195
convergence 321
convergent 420.19
conversable
  228.16.38
conversant 420.68
conversation
  261.67
conversational
  228.63.3
conversationalist
  436.7.5
converse 297
conversion 261.69
convert 369
converter 17.340
convertible
  228.16.47
convex 496
convexity 16.333
convey 2
conveyance 321
conveyancing 265
conveyor 17.1
convict 387
conviction 261.78
convictive 485.18
convince 317
convincible
  228.16.41
convincing 265.62
convivial 228.3.15
conviviality
  16.333.8.1.2
convocation
  261.67.6
convoke 42
convolute 380.1
convoluted 91.42
convolution
  261.75.1
convolve 493

convolvulus 310.25
convoy 11
convulsant 420.72
convulse 313
convulsion 261
convulsive 485
Conway 2
cony 16.233
coo 15
Cooch Behar 1.6
cooee 5
cook 44
cookbook 44
cooker 17.40
cookery 16.274
cookhouse 306
cookie 16.31
cooking 265
cookout 377
cool 227
coolabah 1.2
coolant 420
cooler 17.175
Coolidge 197
coolie 16.130
coolness 300
coomb 241
coon 260
cooncan 245
coop 276, 280
cooper 17.259
Cooper 17.259
cooperate 367.23
cooperation
  261.67.22.3
cooperative
  485.15.10
coopery 16.274
coopt 425
coordinate 367.17,
  371.24.1
coordination
  261.67.18.1
coordinator
  17.338.7
Coorg 187
coot 380
cootch 73
cootie 16.343
cop 276
copaiba 17.15
copal 228.69
copalm 230
coparcenary
  16.274.26

338

coparceny 16.229.4
cope 278
Copenhagen
261.31
copepod 94
coper 17.257
Copernicus 310.10
copestone 257
copier 17.3
copilot 381
coping 265
copious 310.2
coplanar 17.227
copper 17.255
copperas 310.50
copperhead 86.5
copperplate 367
coppice 300
copra 17.290
coprolite 372.4
coprophagous 310
coprophilia
17.3.21.2
coprophilous
310.23
copse 329
Copt 425
copter 17.377
Coptic 38.67
copula 17.174.10
copulate 367.13.7
copulation
261.67.13
copulative 485.15.5
copy 16.250
copybook 44
copyhold 120.1
copyist 436
copyread 89
copyright 372
copywriter 17.343
coquelicot 12.11
coquet 368
coquetry 16.285
coquette 368
coquina 17.230
coquito 12.76
Cora 17.276
coracle 228.28
coracoid 97
coral 228.73
coralline 253.3
corallite 372.4
coralloid 97.6
coralroot 380

cor anglais 2
corban 261
corbel 228
corbicula 17.174.6
cor blimey 16.217
cord 95
cordage 197
cordate 367
corded 91.9
Cordelier 6
Cordeliers 514
cordial 228.3.2
cordiality
16.333.8.1
cordierite 372.8
cordiform 238.1
cordillera 17.271
Cordilleras 524
cordite 372
cordless 300
cordoba 17.21
cordon 261.27
cordovan 261
cords 528
corduroy 11
corduroys 519
core 9
coreligionist 436.13
coreopsis 300.61
corer 17.276
co-respondent
420.15
corf 166
Corfam 229
Corfu 15
corgi 16.95
coriaceous 310.56
coriander 17.98.1
Corinth 470
Corinthian
261.3.28
Coriolanus 310.31
corium 242.2.17
cork 41
Cork 41
corkage 197
corkboard 95
corker 17.37
corking 265.9
corkscrew 15
corm 238
cormel 228.53
cormorant 420.65
corn 255
corncob 26

corncockle 228.25
corncrake 34
corncrib 24
cornea 17.3.35
corneal 228.2
corned 137
corneous 310.2
corner 17.234
cornerstone 257
cornet 371.26
cornetist 436.23
cornett 368
cornfield 115
cornflour 14
cornflower 14
cornhusk 60
cornice 300.24
corniche 353
corniculate
367.13.2
Cornish 353
cornstalk 41
cornstarch 63
cornucopia 17.3.37
cornute 380
Cornwall 221
Cornwallis 300.9
corny 16.232
corolla 17.168
corollaceous
310.56.3
corollary 16.274
corona 17.236
Corona Australis
300.7
Corona Borealis
300.7
coronach 46
coronagraph
158.1.2
coronal 228.62,
228.63
coronary 16.274.29
coronation
261.67.19
coroner 17.239
coronet 371.28
coroneted 91.35
corpora 17.279
corporal 228.76
corporate 371.35
corporation
261.67.22
corporative
485.15.10

corporator
17.338.9
corporeal 228.3.12
corporeity 16.333.1
corps 9
corpse 330
corpulence 321
corpulent 420.27
corpus 310.38
Corpus Christi
16.366
corpuscle 228.87
corpuscular
17.174.8
corpus delicti 7
corpus luteum
242.2
corpus striatum
242.27
corpus vile 16.121
corrade 85
corral 213
correct 385.6
correction 261.77.4
correctitude 102.2
corrective 485.17
correctly 16.195
correctness 300.41
Corregidor 9.3
correlate 367.12
correlation
261.67.12
correlative 485.15.4
correspond 136
correspondence
321
correspondent
420.15
corresponding 265
corridor 9.3
corrie 16.268
Corriedale 214
corrigendum 242.7
corrigible
228.16.20
corroborant 420.65
corroborate 367.23
corroborative
485.15.10
corroboree
16.274.3
corrode 98
corrosion 261.92
corrosive 485.6
corrugate 367, 371

corrugator
17.338.4
corrupt 426.1
corruptible 228.16
corruption 261.88
corsac 32
corsage 359
corsair 4
corselet 371
corset 371
corsetier 6
corsetry 16.285
Corsica 17.34
Corsican 261.13
cortège 360
Cortes 510
cortex 496
corticate 371.9
corticosteroid
97.10
cortisol 220
cortisone 257
corundum 242
Corunna 17.237
coruscate 367
coruscation 261.67
corvée 2
corvette 368
corvine 253
corydalis 300.13
coryphaeus 310.1
coryphée 2
coryza 17.441.1
cos 302, 517
cosecant 420.6
cosh 354
cosher 17.327
cosignatory
16.274.43
cosine 253
cosiness 300.23
cosmetic 38.50
cosmetician
261.71.7
cosmic 38
cosmodrome 239
cosmogony
16.237.4
cosmography
16.90.2
cosmology 16.108.4
cosmonaut 374
cosmopolis
300.13.2

cosmopolitan
261.99
cosmos 302
COSPAR 1
coss 302
Cossack 32
cosset 371
cost 438
costa 17.385
Costa Brava
17.409
costal 228.115
Costa Rica 17.33
costate 367.34
costermonger
17.143
costing 265
costive 485
costly 16
costmary 16.264
costume 241
costumier 17.3
cosy 16.399
cot 373
cotangent 420.22
cote 376
cotenant 420.52
coterie 16.274
cotillion 261.120
cotinga 17.141
cotoneaster 17.379
Cotswold 120
cotta 17.344
cottage 197
cottager 17.150
cotter 17.344
cottier 17.3
cotton 261.101
cottonade 85.3
cottonseed 89.5
cottontail 214
cottonweed 89
cottonwood 101
cottony 16.237.7
cotyledon 261.23
cotyloid 97.5
coucal 212
couch 71
couchant 420
couchette 368
coudé 2
cougar 17.136
cough 165
could 101
couldn't 420.12

coulee 2
coulisse 298
couloir 1
coulomb 237
coulometer
17.342.3
coulter 17.364
coumarin 252.20
coumarone 257.1
council 228
councillor 17.176
councillorship
274.1
counsel 228
counsellor 17.176
count 418
countdown 258
countenance
321.14
counter 17.372
counteract 382
counterattack 32.4
counterbalance
321.10
counterblast 431
counterchange 207
countercharge 192
counterclaim 231
counterclockwise
516
counterculture
17.69
counterespionage
359
counterfeit 371
counterfeiter
17.342
counterfoil 222.1
counterglow 12.46
counterinsurgency
16.312.3
counterintelligence
321.9
counterirritant
420.76
countermand 129
countermarch 63
countermeasure
17.333
countermove 490
counteroffensive
485.9
counterpane 247
counterpart 366.1
counterplot 373

counterpoint 416.1
counterpoise 519
counterproductive
485.19
counterproof 170
counterproposal
228.127
counter-revolution
261.75.1
counterscarp 269
countershaft 396
countersign 253.8
countersink 52
counterspy 7
countertenor
17.228
countertype 275.1
countervail 214
counterweigh 2.28
counterweight
367.38
counterwork 36
countess 300
countless 300
countrified 92.1
countrify 7.3
country 16.290
countryman 261.48
countryside 92.7
county 16.359
coup 15
coup d'état 1
coupé 2
coupe 280
couple 228
couplet 371
coupling 265
coupon 254
courage 197.10
courageous 310.20
courante 408
courgette 368
courier 17.3.42
courlan 261
Courland 143
course 303
courser 17.305
coursing 265
court 374
Courtelle 215.3
courteous 310.2
courtesan 245.7
courtesy 16.300
courthouse 306
courtier 17.3

courting 265.69
courtly 16.192
courtroom 241
courtship 274
courtyard 84
couscous 309
cousin 261
couteau 12.80
couth 463
couthie 16.372
couture 10
couturier 2.1
cove 488
coven 261.117
covenant 420.55
covenantee 5.24
Coventry 16.291
cover 17.418
coverage 197
coverlet 371.18
covers 297
covert 381
coverture 17.62
covet 371
covetous 310.64
covetousness
  300.34
covey 16.383
cow 13
cowage 197
coward 103
cowardice 300.5
cowardliness
  300.23
cowardly 16.152
cowbane 247
cowbell 215
cowbind 135
cowboy 11
cower 14
Cowes 521
cowgirl 216
cowherb 22
cowherd 87
cowhide 92
cowitch 67
cowl 224
cowlick 38
cowling 265.33
cowman 261
cowpat 365
cowpea 5
cowpox 499
cowry 16.271
cowslip 274

cox 499
coxa 17.428
coxalgia 17.3.16
coxswain 261
coy 11
coyness 300
coyote 16.339
coypu 15
cozen 261
crab 18
crab-apple 228.64
crabbed 91
crabber 17.9
crabby 16.5
crabstick 38
crabwise 516
crack 32
crackbrain 247
crackbrained 130
cracker 17.28
crackerjack 32
cracket 371.6
cracking 265
crackjaw 9
crackle 228.19
crackling 265
cracknel 228
crackpot 373
Cracow 13
cradle 228
cradle-snatcher
  17.50
cradlesong 266
craft 396
craftsman 261
crafty 16.345
crag 178
cragged 91
craggy 16.91
Craig 180
crake 34
cram 229
crambo 12
crammer 17.205
cramoisy 16.398
cramp 285
crampon 261
cran 245
cranage 197
cranberry 16.274
crane 247
cranesbill 218
cranial 228.3.5
craniate 371.1

craniology
  16.108.4.1
craniometer
  17.342.3.1
craniometry
  16.285.2.1
craniotomy
  16.222.4.1
cranium 242.2.10
crank 51
crankcase 295
crankpin 252
crankshaft 396
cranky 16.36
cranny 16.223
crap 268
crappie 16.243
craps 322
crapshooter 17.351
crapulent 420.27
craquelure 10.4
crash 349
crashing 265
crashlanding
  265.19
crasis 300.50
crass 293
Crassus 310.51
cratch 62
crate 367
crater 17.338
craunch 81
cravat 365.3
crave 482
craven 261.111
craving 265.77
craw 9
crawfish 353
crawl 221
crawler 17.169
Crawley 16.123
crawling 265.31
cray 2
crayfish 353
crayon 261.1
craze 509
crazed 152
crazy 16.393
creak 37
creaky 16.24
cream 234
creamer 17.210
creamery 16.274
creamlaid 85
creamy 16.215

crease 298
creaseless 300
create 367.1
creatine 251.11
creation 261.67.1
creationism
  242.35.14.3
creative 485.10
creativity 16.333.35
creator 17.338.1
creature 17.55
crèche 351
Crécy 16.297
credence 321.4
credendum 242.7
credent 420.9
credential 228.96.1
credenza 17.446
credibility
  16.333.9.2
credible 228.16.14
credit 371.12
creditable
  228.16.49
creditor 17.342.1
credits 339
credo 12.18
credulity 16.333
credulous 310.25.3
Cree 5
creed 89
creek 37
creel 217
creep 273
creeper 17.252
creepie 16.247
creeps 326
creepy 16.247
creepy-crawly
  16.123
cremate 367.15
cremation
  261.67.15
crematorium
  242.2.17
crème 232
Cremona 17.236
crenate 367
crenation 261.67.18
crenature 10.5
crenel 228.57
crenellate 367.12
creole 223
creolized 154
Creon 254

creophagous 310
creosol 220
creosote 376
creosotic 38.53
crepe 270
crepe de Chine 251.10
crêpe suzette 368.8
crepitate 367.30
crepitus 310.64
crept 422
crepuscular 17.174.8
crescendo 12.24
crescent 420.67
crescentic 38.63
cresol 220
cress 296
Cressida 17.83
crest 433
crested 91.52
crestfallen 261
cresting 265.75
cresylic 38.21
cretaceous 310.56
Cretan 261.98
Crete 370
cretic 38.51
cretin 252
cretinism 242.35.13
cretonne 254
crevasse 293
crevice 300.69
crew 15
Crewe 15
crewel 228.10
crew-neck 35
crib 24
cribbage 197
cribellum 242.8
cribriform 238.1
cribrous 310
cribwork 36
Crichton 261.100
crick 38
cricket 371.9
cricketer 17.342
cricoid 97
crier 17.4
crikey 16.26
crim 235
crime 236
Crimea 17.2
Crimean 261.2
criminal 228.60.4

criminality 16.333.8.6
criminology 16.108.4.10
crimp 287
crimper 17.263
crimple 228
Crimplene 251
crimson 261
cringe 209
cringle 228.50
crinite 372
crinkle 228.29
crinkleroot 380
crinkly 16.145
crinkum-crankum 242
crinoid 97.8
crinoline 252.11
crinum 242.15
criollo 12.44
cripes 328
Crippen 261
cripple 228.66
crippling 265
Cripps 327
crisis 300.53
crisp 291
crispation 261.67
crispbread 86
crisper 17.266
Crispin 252
crispness 300
crispy 16.258
crisscross 302
crissum 242.24
crista 17.384
cristate 367
criterion 261.3.22
critic 38.52
critical 228.23.20
criticism 242.35.16
criticize 516.10.1
critique 37
critter 17.342
croak 42
croaker 17.38
croaky 16.29
Croat 365
Croatia 17.322
Croatian 261.67
crocein 252
crochet 2
crocidolite 372.4
crock 40

crockery 16.274.5
crocket 371.10
Crockett 371.10
Crockford 103
crocodile 219
crocodilian 261.3.11
crocus 310.12
Croesus 310
croft 399
crofter 17.360
croissant 266
Cro-Magnon 254
crombec 35
cromlech 35
Cromwell 215, 228
Cromwellian 261.3.9
crone 257
cronk 53
Cronus 310.35
crony 16.233
crook 44
crooked 91
crookedness 300.28
croon 260
crooner 17.238
crop 276
cropper 17.255
croquet 2
croquette 368
crosier 17.3.62
cross 302
crossbar 1
crossbeam 234
crossbones 550
crossbow 12
crossbred 86
crossbreed 89
crosscheck 35
crosscurrent 420.64
crosscut 378
crosse 302
cross-examination 261.67.18.3
cross-eyed 92
crossfire 8
crosshatch 62
crosshead 86
crossing 265
crossjack 32
cross-legged 91
crossopterygian 261.3.7
crossover 17.417

crosspatch 62
crosspiece 298
crossroads 529
crossruff 168
crosstalk 41
crosstree 5
crosswalk 41
crosswind 134
crosswise 516
crossword 87
crotch 68
crotchet 371
crotchety 16.333
croton 261
crouch 71
croup 280
croupier 17.3
crouse 309
croute 380
crouton 254
crow 12
crowbar 1
crowberry 16.274
crowboot 380
crowd 99
crowded 91
crowfoot 379
crown 258
crownpiece 298
crownwork 36
Croydon 261
croze 520
cru 15
crucial 228
crucian 261.75
cruciate 371.1
crucible 228.12
crucifer 17.114
crucifix 498.1
crucifixion 261.78
cruciform 238.1
crucify 7.3
cruck 43
crud 100
crude 102
crudity 16.333
cruel 228.10
cruelty 16.352
cruet 371.3
Cruickshank 51
cruise 523
cruiser 17.444
cruiseway 2
cruller 17.173
crumb 240

crumble 228
crumbly 16.139
crumby 16.220
crumhorn 255
crummy 16.220
crump 289
crumpet 371
crumple 228
crunch 82
crunchy 16.56
crunode 98
crupper 17.258
crura 17.277
crural 228.75
crus 307
crusade 85
crusader 17.79
cruse 523
crush 356
crusher 17.329
crust 443
crustacean 261.67
crustaceous 310.56
crusted 91.54
crusty 16.368
crutch 72
crutches 515
crux 502
crux ansata 17.338
cruzeiro 12.62
crwth 463
cry 7
crybaby 16.7
crying 265.3
cryobiology
 16.108.4.2
cryogen 261.39
cryogenics 498.3
cryolite 372.4
cryometer 17.342.3
cryonics 498.5
cryophilic 38.21
cryophyte 372
cryoscopy 16.254.2
cryosurgery
 16.274.13
cryotherapy 16.254
crypt 424
cryptaesthesia
 17.3.60
cryptanalysis
 300.52.1
cryptic 38.66
cryptogam 229
cryptogenic 38.32.1

cryptogram 229.1
cryptograph 158.1
cryptography
 16.90.2
cryptology
 16.108.4.17
cryptomeria
 17.3.39
cryptozoic 38.2
crystal 228.114
crystalline 253.3
crystallite 372.4
crystallize 516.3
crystallography
 16.90.2.2
crystalloid 97.6
ctenidium 242.2.3
ctenoid 97.7
ctenophore 9.6
cub 29
Cuba 17.20
cubage 197
Cuban 261
cubane 247
cubature 17.62
cubbyhole 223
cube 2, 30
cubeb 21
cubic 38.4
cubical 228.23
cubicle 228.23
cubiculum 242.10.1
cubiform 238.1
cubism 242.35
cubist 436
cubit 371
cubital 228.102
cuboid 97
Cu-bop 276
cuckold 122
cuckoldry 16.278
cuckoo 15
cuckoopint 413
cuculiform 238.1
cucullate 367.14
cucumber 17.27
cucurbit 371
cud 100
cuddle 228.36
cuddlesome 242
cuddly 16.151
cuddy 16.69
cudgel 228
cudgerie 16.274
cue 15

cuesta 17.382
cuff 168
cuirass 293
cuirassier 6.7
cuir-bouilli 5
cuisine 251
cuisse 300
culch 77
cul-de-sac 32
culet 371.17
culex 496
culicid 91.29
culinary 16.274.26
cull 225
cullet 371
cullis 300.10
Culloden 261.26
cully 16.128
culminant 420.53
culminate 367.17
culmination
 261.67.18
culottes 341
culpa 1
culpable 228.16
culprit 371
cult 406
cultigen 261.37
cultivar 1
cultivate 367.36
cultivated 91.34
cultivation 261.67
cultivator
 17.338.11
cultural 228.76
culture 17.69
cultured 103
culver 17.424
culverin 252.20
culvert 381
cumber 17.27
Cumberland
 143.4.1
Cumbernauld 118
cumbersome 242
cumbrance 321
Cumbria 17.3.44
Cumbrian 261.3.25
cumin 252
cummerbund 140
cumshaw 9
cumulate 367.13,
 371.17
cumulation
 261.67.13

cumulative
 485.15.5
cumulet 371.17
cumuliform 238.1
cumulonimbus 310
cumulostratus
 310.62
cumulus 310.25.5
cuneal 228.3
cuneate 371.1
cuneiform 238.1
cunjevoi 11
cunnilingus 310
cunning 265.45
cunt 419
cup 279
cupbearer 17.271
cupboard 103
cupcake 34
cupel 228
cupellation
 261.67.12
Cupid 91
cupidity 16.333.5
cupola 17.176
cuppa 17.258
cupreous 310.2
cupric 38
cuprite 372
cupronickel 228.23
cuprous 310
cupulate 367.13
cupule 227
cur 3
curable 228.16.34
Curacao 12
curacy 16.307
curare 16.261
curarine 251.7
curate 371
curative 485.15.9
curator 17.338
curb 22
curd 87
curdle 228
curdler 17.185
cure 10
curet 368
curettage 359
curfew 15
curia 17.3.42
Curia Regis 300.6
Curie 16.270
curio 12.3

curiosity
16.333.30.1
curious 310.2.14
curl 216
curler 17.164
curlew 15
curlicue 15
curliness 300.23
curling 265
curly 16.116
curmudgeon
261.38
currant 420.64
currawong 266
currency 16.312
current 420.64
curricle 228.23
curriculum
242.10.1
curriculum vitae
7.13
currier 17.3
curriery 16.274.1
currish 353
curry 16.272
currycomb 239
curse 297
cursed 91
cursive 485.3
cursor 17.301
cursorial 228.3.12
cursory 16.274.35
curt 369
curtail 214
curtailment 420.39
curtain 261.97
curtana 17.226
curtilage 197.1
curtness 300.36
curtsy 16.316
curvaceous 310.56
curvature 17.62
curve 483
curvet 368
curvilinear 17.3.34
curvy 16.381
cuscus 307
cusec 35
Cush 356
Cushing 265
cushion 261
Cushitic 38.52
cushy 16.325
CUSO 12
cuspid 91

cuspidation
261.67.7
cuspidor 9.3
cuss 307
cussed 91
cussedness 300.28
custard 103
Custer 17.388
custodial 228.3
custodian 261.3.6
custody 16.72
custom 242.32
customary 16.274
customer 17.218
customize 516.5
customs 543
custos 302
cut 378
cutaneous 310.2.6
cutaway 2.28
cutback 32
cutch 72
cute 380
cuteness 300.40
Cuthbert 381
cuticle 228.23.21
cuticula 17.174.6
cutie 16.343
cutin 252.24
cutis 300
cutlass 310
cutler 17.202
cutlery 16.274
cutlet 371
cutpurse 297
Cuttack 32
cutter 17.349
cutthroat 376
cutting 265
cuttle 228.107
cuttlebone 257
cuttlefish 353
cutty 16.341
cuvette 368
Cuxhaven 261.110
cwm 241
Cwmbran 246
cyan 245
cyanamide 92.3
cyanide 92.4
cyanine 251
cyanite 372.6
cyanocobalamin
252.15
cyanosis 300.55

cyanotype 275.1
Cybele 16.120
cybernate 367.18
cybernetic 38.50.5
cybernetics
498.12.1
cycad 83
Cyclades 513.5
cyclamate 367.16
cyclamen 261.52
cycle 228.24
cyclic 38
cyclist 436
cycloalkane 247
cyclohexane 247
cycloid 97
cyclometer
17.342.3
cyclone 257
cyclonic 38.35
Cyclopean 261.2
cyclopedia 17.3.8
cycloplegia 17.3.13
Cyclops 329
cyclorama 17.206
cyclostome 239
cyclostyle 219.7
cyclotron 254
cygnet 371.29
cylinder 17.102
cylindrical 228.23
cylindroid 97
cymar 1.11
cymatium 242.2
cymbal 228
cymbalo 12.45
cyme 236
cymoid 97
cymophane 247.3
cymose 305
Cymric 38
Cynewulf 175
cynic 38.34
cynical 228.23.12
cynicism 242.35.16
cynosure 10
Cynthia 17.3.52
cy pres 2
cypress 310
Cyprian 261.3
cyprinid 91
cyprinoid 97.8
Cypriot 381.1
cypripedium
242.2.2

Cyprus 310
Cyrenaica 17.33
Cyril 228
Cyrillic 38.21
Cyrus 310.47
cyst 436
cystectomy
16.222.5
cystic 38.70
cysticercoid 97.2
cysticercus 310.9
cystine 251
cystitis 300.62
cystocarp 269
cystocele 217.2
cystoid 97
cystotomy 16.222.4
Cythera 17.272
cytokinesis 300.51
cytology
16.108.4.14
cytolysis 300.52.2
cytoplasm 242.34
cytotaxonomy
16.222.3
Cyzicus 310.10
czardas 349
Czech 35
Czechoslovak 32
Czechoslovakia
17.3
Czechoslovakian
261.3

D

dab 18
dabber 17.9
dabble 228
dabbler 17.177
dabchick 38
da capo 12.57
Dacca 17.28
dace 295
dacha 17.50
dachshund 141
dacoit 375
dacoity 16.338
Dacron 254
dactyl 218
dactylic 38.21

dactylogram 229.1.2
dactylography 16.90.2.2
dactylology 16.108.4.8
dad 83
Dada 1
Dadaism 242.35
daddy 16.57
dado 12.17
Daedalus 310.26
daff 157
daffodil 218
daffy 16.82
daft 396
Dagan 261
Dagenham 242.16
dagger 17.123
daglock 40
dagoba 17.21
daguerreotype 275.1
dah 1
dahlia 17.3.18
Dahna 1
Dahomey 16.219
daily 16.114
daintiness 300.23
dainty 16.354
daiquiri 16.266
dairy 16.264
dairying 265
dairyman 261.48
dais 300
daisy 16.393
daisycutter 17.349
Dakar 17.28
Dakota 17.347
dal 213
Dalai Lama 17.206
dalasi 16.295
dale 214
Dales 536
dalesman 261
Dalhousie 16.400
Dali 16.113
Dallas 310
dalliance 321.1.1
dally 16.112
Dalmatia 17.322
Dalmatian 261.67
dalmatic 38.49
Dalton 261

daltonism 242.35.14
dam 229
damage 197
damages 515
Damanhûr 10
Damara 17.268
damascene 251.9
Damascus 310
damask 61
dame 231
Damietta 17.339
dammar 17.205
damn 229
damnable 228.16
damnation 261.67
damnatory 16.274.43
damnedest 436
damnify 7.3
Damocles 513
damp 285
dampcourse 303
dampen 261
damper 17.261
damply 16.178
dampness 300
damsel 228
damselfish 353
damselfly 7
damson 261
dan 245
Dan 245
Danaë 5.1
dance 315
dancer 17.313
dancing 265
dandelion 261.4
dander 17.98
Dandie Dinmont 414
dandify 7.3
dandiprat 365
dandle 228.39
dandruff 171
dandruffy 16.88
dandy 16.77
Dane 247
Danegeld 113
Danegelt 402
Danelaw 9
dang 263
danger 17.156
dangerous 310.50

dangerousness 300.34
dangle 228.49
Daniel 228.123
Danish 353
dank 51
Danny 16.223
Dante 16.353
Danton 261
Danube 30
Danzig 184
dap 268
daphnia 17.3
Daphnis 300
dapper 17.247
dapple 228.64
daraf 171
darbies 515
Dardan 261
Dardanus 310.36
Dardic 38
dare 4
daredevil 228.118
Dar es Salaam 230.1
Darfur 10
darg 179
daric 38.38
Darien 261.3.21
daring 265.52
dariole 223.1
Darjeeling 265.29
dark 33
darken 261.10
darkle 228.20
darkly 16.140
darkness 300
darkroom 241
darksome 242
darling 265.26
Darlington 261
Darmstadt 365
darn 246
darned 129
darnel 228
dart 366
dartboard 95
darter 17.337
Dartford 103
Dartmoor 10
Dartmouth 464
darts 334
Darwin 252
Darwinian 261.3.17

Darwinism 242.35.13
dash 349
dashboard 95
dasheen 251
dasher 17.321
dashiki 16.24
dashing 265
dashpot 373
Dasht-i-Lut 379
dassie 16.294
dastard 103
dastardly 16.152
dasyure 10
data 17.338
date 367
dated 91.34
dateline 253
dative 485.10
dato 12.73
datum 242.27
datura 17.277
daub 27
daube 28
dauber 17.17
daubery 16.274
daughter 17.345
daughter-in-law 9
daunt 415
daunting 265
dauntless 300
dauphin 252
dauphine 251
dauphiness 300.23
davenport 374
David 91
Davis 300
davit 371
Davy 16.379
daw 9
dawdle 228
dawn 255
Dawson 261
day 2
Dayan 246
daybook 44
dayboy 11
daybreak 34
daydream 234
daydreamer 17.210
daydreaming 265.36
daylight 372
daylights 340
daylong 266

daystar

daystar 1
daytime 236
Dayton 261
Daytona 17.236
day-tripper 17.253
daze 509
dazzle 228.124
deacon 261.12
deaconess 300.26
deaconry 16.284
deactivate 367.36
dead 86
deadbeat 370
deaden 261.21
deadeye 7
deadhead 86
deadlight 372
deadline 253
deadlock 40
deadly 16.147
deadness 300
deadpan 245
deadwood 101
deaf 160
deafen 261
deafmute 380
deafness 300
deal 217
dealer 17.165
dealings 552
dealt 402
deaminate 367.17.3
dean 251
deanery 16.274.25
dear 6
dearest 436.17
dearly 16.119
dearness 300
dearth 456
deary 16.265
death 455
deathbed 86
deathblow 12
deathly 16.203
deathtrap 268
deathwatch 68
Deauville 217
deb 21
debacle 228.20
debag 178
debar 1.1
debark 33
debase 295
debatable
    228.16.45

debate 367
debater 17.338
debauch 69
debauchee 5
debauchery 16.274
debenture 17.70
debilitate 367.30.1
debility 16.333.9.2
debit 371
debonair 4.5
Deborah 17.279
debouch 71
debouchment 420
Debrecen 248
débridement 420
debrief 162
debris 16
debt 368
debtor 17.339
debug 189
debunk 54
debus 307
Debussy 16.306
debut 15
debutante 408
decade 85
decadence 321
decadent 420
decaffeinate
    367.17.1
decagon 254.5
decahedron 261
decal 212
decalcomania
    17.3.31.1
decalescence
    321.21
Decalogue 185
decamp 285
decanal 228.56
decane 247
decani 7
decant 407
decanter 17.365
decapitate 367.30
decapitation
    261.67.27
decapod 94.1
decarbonate 367.18
decarbonize 516.7
decathlon 261
decay 2.7
Deccan 261
decease 298
deceased 435

decedent 420.9
deceit 370
deceitful 226
deceive 484.2
deceiver 17.413
decelerate 367.23
deceleration
    261.67.22
decelerometer
    17.342.3.4
December 17.24
Decembrist 436
decency 16.312
decennary
    16.274.23
decennium 242.2
decent 420.69
decentralize 516.3
deception 261.84
deceptive 485.23
decerebrate 367.24
decern 249
decibel 215
decide 92.7
decided 91.8
decidedly 16.148
decider 17.84
decidua 17.7
deciduous 310.4
decillion 261.120
decimal 228.52.1
decimalize 516.3
decimate 367.15
decimation
    261.67.15
decipher 17.115
decision 261.91.1
decisive 485.5
decisiveness 300.43
deck 35
deckle 228.21
declaim 231
declamation
    261.67.16
declamatory
    16.274.43.5
declaration
    261.67.22
declarative
    485.15.8
declarator 17.352
declaratory
    16.274.43
declare 4
declarer 17.271

declass 294
declassify 7.3.6
declension 261.82
declinate 367.17
declination
    261.67.18
decline 253.4
declivity 16.333.35
declutch 72
decoct 388
decoction 261
decode 98
decoder 17.88
decoke 42
decollate 367.14
décolletage 359
décolleté 2
decolonize 516.7
decolorant 420.65
decompose 520
decomposer 17.442
decomposition
    261.71.9
decompound 139
decompress 296
decompression
    261.68
decongestant
    420.80
deconsecrate
    367.25
decontaminate
    367.17.3
decontamination
    261.67.18.3
decontrol 223
décor 9
decorate 367.23
decoration
    261.67.22
decorative
    485.15.10
decorator 17.338.9
decorous 310.50
decorticate 367.5
decorum 242.20
decoupage 359
decoy 11
decrease 298
decreasingly 16.175
decree 5
decree nisi 7
decrement 420.31
decrepit 371
decrepitate 367.30

decrepitude 102.2
decrescent 420.67
decretal 228.101
decry 7
decrypt 424
decumbent 420
decurion 261.3.24
decurrent 420.64
decurved 147
decury 16.270
Dedéagach 63
dedicate 367.5
dedicated 91.34.3
dedication 261.67.5
deduce 309
deduct 389
deductible
 228.16.54
deduction 261.79
deductive 485.19
Dee 5
deed 89
deejay 2
deek 37
deem 234
deemster 17.393
deep 273
deepen 261
deepfreeze 513
deer 6
deergrass 294
deerhound 139
deerskin 252
deerstalker 17.37
de-escalate 367.14
de-escalation
 261.67.14
deface 295.3
de facto 12
defamation
 261.67.16
defamatory
 16.274.43.5
defame 231
default 404
defaulter 17.363
defeasance 321.28
defeat 370
defeatism 242.35
defeatist 436
defecate 367.5
defecation
 261.67.5
defect 385, 385.1
defection 261.77

defective 485.17
defector 17.354
defence 316
defenceless 300.16
defencelessness
 300.33.1
defend 131
defendant 420.14
defender 17.101
defenestration
 261.67.25
defensible
 228.16.40
defensive 485.9
defer 3
deference 321.20
deferent 420.65
deferential
 228.96.2
deferment 420
deferral 228
defiance 321.2
defiant 420.2
defibrillator
 17.338.5
deficiency 16.312.5
deficient 420.74
deficit 371.36
defilade 85
defile 219
definable 228.16.30
define 253
definiendum 242.7
definite 371.24
definitely 16.189
definition 261.71.5
definitive 485.12
deflagrate 367
deflate 367
deflation 261.67
deflect 385
deflection 261.77
deflocculate
 367.13.3
deflower 14
Defoe 12
defoliant 420.1
defoliate 367.1.3
defoliation
 261.67.1.2
deforce 303
deforest 436.18
deform 238.1
deformation 261.67
deformed 125

deformity
 16.333.13
defraud 95
defray 2
defrock 40
defrost 438
defroster 17.385
deft 397
deftness 300
defunct 393
defuse 523
defy 7.3
Degas 1
degas 293
de Gaulle 223
degauss 306
degeneracy
 16.307.4
degenerate
 367.23.1, 371.35
degeneration
 261.67.22.2
deglutinate 367.17
deglutition 261.71
degradable 228.16
degradation
 261.67.8
degrade 85:5
degrading 265.11
degrease 298
degree 5.18
degression 261.68
dehisce 300
dehiscent 420.70
dehorn 255
Dehra Dun 260
dehumanize 516.7
dehumidifier 17.4.1
dehumidify 7.3.1
dehydrate 367
dehydration 261.67
dehypnotize 516.13
de-ice 301
de-icer 17.303
deicide 92.7
deictic 38
deific 38.12
deiform 238.1
deify 7.3
deign 247
deil 217
deism 242.35.1
deist 436
deity 16.333.1
deixis 300

deject 385
dejecta 17.354
dejected 91.43
dejection 261.77
de jure 2.18
dekko 12.9
delaine 247.4
De la Mare 4
delaminate
 367.17.3
delate 367.12
Delaware 4.8
delay 2.11
dele 16.118
delectable 228.16
delectation 261.67
delegacy 16.307
delegate 367.10,
 371.14
delegation
 261.67.10
delete 370
deleterious
 310.2.11
deletion 261.70
Delhi 16.115
deli 16.115
deliberate 367.23,
 371.35
deliberation
 261.67.22
deliberative
 485.15.10
delicacy 16.307.1
delicate 371.9
delicatessen 261.63
delicious 310.58
delight 372.3
delighted 91.39
delightful 226.9
Delilah 17.167
delimit 371.19
delineate 367.1
delineation
 261.67.1
delineator 17.338.1
delinquency 16.312
delinquent 420
deliquesce 296
deliquescence
 321.21
deliquescent 420.67
delirious 310.2.12
delirium 242.2.16

delirium tremens
546
delitescence 321.21
Delius 310.2.4
deliver 17.414
deliverance 321.20
deliverer 17.279
delivery 16.274.51
dell 215
Delmarva 17.409
Delos 302
delouse 306
Delphic 38
delphinium
242.2.11
Delphinus 310.34
delta 17.361
deltiology
16.108.4.1
deltoid 97
delude 102
deluge 204
delusion 261.93.1
delusive 485.8
de luxe 502
delve 492
demagnetize
516.13
demagogic 38
demagogue 185.2
demagoguery
16.274.12
demagogy 16.94
demand 129
demanding 265
demarcate 367
demarcation
261.67.4
dematerialize
516.3.2.1
Demavend 131
deme 234
demean 251
demeaning 265.42
demeanour 17.230
dement 410.1
demented 91.46
dementia 17.330
demerara 17.271
demerit 371.31
demersal 228.84
demesne 247
Demeter 17.341
demibastion 261.3
demicanton 254

demigod 94
demigoddess 300.4
demijohn 254
demilitarize 516.8.2
De Mille 218
demilune 260
demimondaine 247
demimonde 136
demineralize
516.3.8
demirelief 162.1
demise 516.4
demission 261.71
demist 436
demitasse 293
demiurge 195
demivierge 361
demo 12
demob 26
demobilize 516.2
democracy
16.307.5
democrat 365.2
democratic 38.49.6
democratize 516.13
Democritus 310.64
demodulation
261.67.13
Demogorgon
261.33
demography
16.90.2.3
demoiselle 215
demolish 353.5
demolition
261.71.3
demon 261.47
demonetize 516.12
demoniac 32.1
demonic 38.35
demonism
242.35.14
demonolatry
16.286.2
demonology
16.108.4.11
demonstrable
228.16
demonstrate 367
demonstration
261.67
demonstrative
485.15.11
demonstrator
17.338

demoralize 516.3
demos 302
Demosthenes 513.9
demote 376
demotic 38.53
demotion 261.73
demount 418
demulcent 420.72
demulsify 7.3.7
demur 3
demure 10
demurrage 197.10
demurrer 17.278
demy 7
demystify 7.3
demythologize
516.1
den 248
denarius 310.2.10
denary 16.274.25
denationalize
516.3.7
denaturalize
516.3.8
denature 17.52
denazify 7.3
Denbighshire 6
dendriform 238.1
dendrite 372
dendrochronology
16.108.4.11
dendroid 97
dendrology
16.108.4
dene 251
Deneb 21
denegation
261.67.10
deniable 228.16.3
denial 228.4
denier 17.3
denigrate 367.26
denim 235
Denis 300
denizen 261.126
Denmark 33
denominate
367.17.5, 371.24
denomination
261.67.18.6
denominational
228.63.3
denominationalism
242.35.11.5.2

denominative
485.15.7
denominator
17.338.7
denotation
261.67.28
denotative
485.15.13
denote 376
denouement 266
denounce 319
denouncer 17.317
dense 316
densimeter
17.342.2
densitometer
17.342.3
density 16.333.31
dent 410
dental 228.110
dentalium 242.2
dentate 367.32
dentation
261.67.32
dentex 496
denticle 228.23.23
denticulation
261.67.13
dentiform 238.1
dentifrice 300
dentil 218
dentine 251
dentist 436, 436.27
dentistry 16.293
dentition 261.71
dentoid 97
Denton 261
denture 17.70
denuclearize 516.8
denudation 261.67
denude 102
denunciate 367.1
denunciation
261.67.1.4
deny 7.10
deodand 128
deodar 1
deodorant 420.65
deodorize 516.8
deontic 38.64
deontology
16.108.4.16
deoxyribonucleic
38.1
depart 366

dessertspoon 260
dessiatine 251.11
destination
261.67.18
destine 252.26
destined 134
destiny 16.229
destitute 380.5
destitution 261.75
destroy 11
destroyer 17.5
destruct 389
destructible
228.16.54
destruction 261.79
destructionist
436.13
destructive 485.19
destructor 17.357
desuetude 102.2
desultory 16.274
detach 62
detachable 228.16
detached 395
detachment 420.36
detail 214
detailed 112
detain 247.9
detainee 5.11
detainer 17.227
detect 385.8
detectable 228.16
detection 261.77
detective 485.17
detector 17.354
detent 410
détente 408
detention 261.82
deter 3
deterge 195
detergency
16.312.3
detergent 420.19
deteriorate 367.23
deterioration
261.67.22
determinable
228.16.29
determinant
420.53.1
determinate 371.24
determination
261.67.18.4
determinative
485.15.7

determine 252.13
determined 134
determiner 17.231
determinism
242.35.13
determinist 436.11
deterrence 321.16
deterrent 420.61
detest 433
detestable
228.16.59
detestation
261.67.33
dethrone 257
detinue 15.9
Detmold 120
detonate 367.18
detonation
261.67.19
detonator 17.338.8
detour 10
detoxicate 367.5
detoxify 7.3
detract 382
detraction 261.76
detrain 247
detriment 420.31
detrimental
228.110.2
detrition 261.71
detritus 310.65
Detroit 375
de trop 12
detrude 102
detumescence
321.21
Deucalion 261.3.8
deuce 309
deuced 91.30
deuteragonist
436.13.2
deuteranopia
17.3.37.2
deuteride 92.6
deuterium 242.2.15
Deuteronomy
16.222.3
deutzia 17.3
deva 17.410
devaluation
261.67.2
devalue 15
Devanagari 16.274
devastate 367
devastation 261.67

develop 281.1
developer 17.260
development 420
developmental
228.110
deviant 420.1
deviate 367.1.10
deviation
261.67.1.6
deviationism
242.35.14.3
device 301
devil 228.118
devilish 353
devilment 420.40
devilry 16.283
devious 310.2
deviousness
300.34.1
devisable 228.16.64
devisal 228
devise 516.15
devisee 5
devisor 17.441
devitalize 516.3
devoice 304
devoid 97
devoirs 1.18
devolution
261.75.1
devolve 493
Devon 261.112
Devonian 261.3.18
devote 376
devoted 91.41
devotee 5
devotion 261.73
devotional 228.63.6
devour 14
devout 377
dew 15
dewan 246
Dewar 17.8
dewberry 16.274
dewclaw 9
dewdrop 276
Dewey 16.4
dewlap 268
Dewsbury 16.274
dewy 16.4
dexterity 16.333.21
dextrorotation
261.67.28
dextrorse 303
dextrose 520

dextrous 310
dey 2
dhak 33
dhal 213
dharma 17.206
dharna 17.237
Dhaulagiri 16.265
dhobi 16.12
dhole 223
dhoti 16.339
dhow 13
diabase 295.1
diabetes 513.16
diabetic 38.50.2
diablerie 16.274
diabolic 38.22
diabolical 228.23.8
diabolism
242.35.11
diabolo 12.45
diachronic 38.35
diaconal 228.63.1
diaconate 371.28
diacritic 38.52
diacritical
228.23.20
diactinic 38.34
diadelphous 310
diadem 232
diagnose 520
diagnosis 300.55
diagnostic 38.71
diagnostician
261.71
diagnostics 498
diagonal 228.63
diagram 229.1
diagrammatic
38.49.2
dial 228.4
dialect 385.5
dialectic 38.60
dialectical 228.23
dialectics 498
dialectology
16.108.4
diallage 197
dialler 17.176.1
dialogism 242.35.8
dialogist 436.4.1
dialogue 185
dialyse 516.3
dialyser 17.441
dialysis 300.52.1

diamagnetism 242.35.18
diamanté 16.353
diamantine 253.9
diameter 17.342
diametral 228.79
diametric 38.46
diametrically 16.142
diamond 143
diamondback 32
Diana 17.225
dianoetic 38.50.1
dianoia 17.5
diapason 261.124
diapause 518
diapedesis 300.51
diaphanous 310.36
diaphonic 38.35.2
diaphony 16.237
diaphoresis 300.51.1
diaphoretic 38.50
diaphragm 229
diaphysis 300.52
diapir 6.6
diapositive 485.12.1
diarch 33
diarchy 16.20
diarist 436.20
diarrhoea 17.2.2
diarthrosis 300.55
diary 16.274
Dias 310.1
diascope 278.1.1
Diaspora 17.279
diaspore 9.10
diastalsis 300.58
diastasis 300.57
diastema 17.210
diaster 17.379
diastole 16.131
diastolic 38.22
diastrophism 242.35
diatessaron 254.11
diathermancy 16.312
diathermic 38.26
diathermy 16.214
diathesis 300.52
diatomic 38.29
diatonic 38.35.5
diatribe 25

diazotize 516.13
dib 24
dibble 228.12
dicast 430
dice 301
dicey 16.301
dichasium 242.2.19
dichloride 92.5
dichogamy 16.222.2
dichotomize 516.5
dichotomy 16.222.4
dichroism 242.35.3
dichromatic 38.49.2
dichromaticism 242.35.16.4
dichroscope 278.1
Dick 38
Dickens 548
dickens 548
Dickensian 261.3
dicker 17.34
Dickinson 261
dicky 16.25
dicotyledon 261.23
dicrotic 38.53
dicta 17.355
Dictaphone 257
dictate 367
dictation 261.67
dictator 17.338
dictatorial 228.3.12.2
dictatorship 274.1
diction 261.78
dictionary 16.274.29
dictum 242
did 91
Didache 5
didactic 38.58
didactics 498.13
diddle 228.32
Diderot 12
didgeridoo 15.2
didicoy 11
didn't 420.10
Dido 12.20
didst 446
didymous 310.28
didynamous 310.29
die 7
dieback 32

die-cast 431
die-hard 84
dielectric 38
Dien Bien Phu 15
Dieppe 271
dieresis 300.52
diesel 228
diesis 300.52
diestock 40
diet 381.2
dietary 16.274.43
dieter 17.352.1
dietetic 38.50
dietetics 498.12
dietitian 261.71.7
differ 17.114
difference 321.20
different 420.65
differentia 17.3
differentiable 228.16.2
differential 228.96.2
differentiate 367.1.9
differentiation 261.67.1
difficult 406
difficulty 16.352
diffidence 321.5
diffident 420.10
diffract 382.1
diffraction 261.76
diffuse 309, 523
diffuser 17.444
diffusion 261.93
diffusive 485.8
dig 184
digamy 16.222.1
digastric 38
digest 433
digestant 420.80
digester 17.382
digestible 228.16.59
digestion 261.18
digestive 485.24
digger 17.129
digit 371
digital 228.102
digitalin 252
digitalis 300.7
digitalism 242.35.11
digitalize 516.3

digitate 367.30
digitiform 238.1
digitigrade 85.5
digitize 516.12
digitoxin 252.29
diglot 373
dignified 92.1
dignify 7.3.3
dignitary 16.274.41
dignity 16.333.19
digraph 158
digress 296
digression 261.68
digressive 485.2
dihedral 228.78
dihybrid 91
dik-dik 38
diktat 366
dilapidate 367.8
dilapidated 91.34
dilapidation 261.67.7
dilatancy 16.312.6
dilatant 420.75
dilatation 261.67.30
dilate 367
dilation 261.67
dilatometer 17.342.3
dilator 17.338
dilatory 16.274.43.4
dildo 12
dilemma 17.208
dilemmatic 38.49.1
dilettante 16.353
diligence 321.9
diligent 420.20
dill 218
dilly 16.120
dilly-dally 16.112
diluent 420.4
dilute 380
dilution 261.75
diluvial 228.3.17
diluvium 242.2
dim 235
dime 236
dimension 261.82
dimer 17.212
dimercaprol 220
dimeter 17.342.2
dimethylsulphoxide 92.14

dimetric 38.46
dimidiate 367.1
dimidiate 371.1
diminish 353.7
diminuendo 12.24
diminution 261.75
diminutive 485
dimissory 16.274.36
dimity 16.333.12
dimmer 17.211
dimness 300
dimorph 166
dimorphous 310.18
dimple 228
dimwit 371
dim-witted 91.38
din 252
Dinah 17.232
dinar 1
dine 253
diner 17.232
dineric 38.39
dinette 368
ding 265
dingbat 365
dingbats 333
ding-dong 266
dinge 209
dinghy 16.242
dingle 228.50
dingo 12.36
dingy 16.110
dink 52
Dinka 17.44
dinkum 242
dinky 16.37
dinner 17.231
dinoceras 310.50
dinosaur 9.11
dinothere 6.10
dint 412
diocesan 261.65
diocese 300.57.1
Diocletian 261.70
diode 98
Diogenes 513
Diomedes 513.3
Dionysia 17.3.61
Dionysiac 32.1
Dionysian 261.3.35
Dionysius 310.2.15
Dionysus 310
diopside 92.10
dioptre 17.377

dioptric 38
dioptrics 498
Dior 9.1
diorama 17.206
dioxide 92.14
dip 274
dipeptide 92
diphase 509
diphtheria 17.3.39
diphtherial 228.3.11
diphthong 266
diplegia 17.3.13
diplex 496
diplococcus 310.11
diplodocus 310.14
diploë 5
diploid 97
diploma 17.215
diplomacy 16.307
diplomat 365
diplomate 367.16
diplomatic 38.49.2
diplomatics 498.11
diplont 414
diplopia 17.3.37
diplopod 94.1
diplostemonous 310.36
dipnoan 261.6
dipody 16.72
dipole 223
dipper 17.253
dippy 16.248
dipsomania 17.3.31.1
dipsomaniac 32.1
dipstick 38
dipteral 228.76
dipterous 310.50
diptych 38.66
Dirac 32
dire 8
direct 385
direction 261.77.3
directional 228.63.8
directive 485.17
directly 16.195
directness 300.41
director 17.354
directorate 371.35
directorial 228.3.12
directorship 274.1
directory 16.274.45

dirge 195
dirham 229
dirigible 228.16.20
diriment 420.31
dirk 36
dirndl 228
dirt 369
dirtiness 300.23
dirty 16.331
Dis 300
disability 16.333.9.2
disable 228.11
disabuse 523
disaccharide 92.6
disaccord 95.3
disaccredit 371.12
disaccustom 242.32
disadvantage 197
disadvantaged 110
disadvantageous 310.20
disaffect 385.2
disaffiliate 367.1.2
disaffiliation 261.67.1.1
disaffirm 233
disafforest 436.18
disagree 5
disagreeable 228.16.1
disagreement 420
disallow 13
disambiguate 367.2
disannul 225
disappear 6.6
disappearance 321.17
disappoint 416.1
disappointed 91.48
disappointing 265
disappointment 420.50
disapprobation 261.67.3
disapproval 228.122
disapprove 490
disarm 230
disarmament 420.35
disarming 265.35
disarrange 207
disarray 2.19

disarticulate 367.13.2
disassemble 228.18
disassociate 367.1.7
disaster 17.380
disastrous 310
disavow 13
disavowal 228.8
disband 128
disbar 1
disbelief 162.1
disbelieve 484.1
disbranch 78
disbud 100
disburden 261.22
disburse 297
disc 58
discard 84
discern 249
discernible 228.16.28
discerning 265.41
discernment 420
discharge 192
disciple 228.67
disciplinant 420.53
disciplinarian 261.3.21.1
disciplinary 16.274.26
discipline 252
discipular 17.174
disclaim 231
disclaimer 17.207
disclimax 494
disclose 520
disclosure 17.335
disco 12.15
discobolus 310.26.1
discography 16.90.2
discoid 97
discoloration 261.67.22
discolour 17.173
discombobulate 367.13
discomfit 371
discomfiture 17.56
discomfort 381
discommend 131.2
discommode 98.1
discommodity 16.333.6
discommon 261

discompose 520
discomposure 17.335
disconcert 369
disconcerted 91.36
disconnect 385
disconsolate 371.18
discontent 410
discontented 91.46
discontinue 15.9
discontinuity 16.333.3.1
discontinuous 310.4.3
discophile 219.1
discord 95
discordance 321
discordant 420.11
discotheque 35
discount 418
discountenance 321.14
discourage 197.10
discouragement 420.37
discourse 303
discourteous 310.2
discourtesy 16.300
discover 17.418
discoverer 17.279
discovert 381
discovery 16.274
discredit 371.12
discreditable 228.16.49
discreet 370
discrepancy 16.312
discrepant 420
discrete 370
discretion 261.68
discretionary 16.274.29.2
discriminate 367.17, 371.24
discriminating 265.64.1
discrimination 261.67.18.5
discriminator 17.338.7
discriminatory 16.274.43.6
discursive 485.3
discus 310.15
discuss 307

discussion 261.74
disdain 247
disdainful 226.4
disease 513
diseased 153
disembark 33
disembarkation 261.67.4
disembarrass 310.43
disembodied 91
disembody 16.65
disembogue 188
disembowel 228.8
disembroil 222
disenable 228.11
disenchant 408
disenchantment 420
disencumber 17.27
disendow 13
disengage 193
disengagement 420
disentangle 228.49
disenthral 221
disentitle 228.103
disentomb 241
disentwine 253
disequilibrium 242.2
disestablish 353
disesteem 234
disfavour 17.410
disfigure 17.129
disfigurement 420.35.1
disfranchise 516
disgorge 200
disgrace 295
disgraceful 226
disgruntle 228.112
disgruntled 122
disguise 516
disgust 443
disgusted 91.54
disgusting 265
dish 353
dishabille 217
disharmony 16.237
dishcloth 459
dishearten 261.95
dishevel 228.118
dishevelled 122
dishonest 436
dishonesty 16.366

dishonour 17.233
dishonourable 228.16.35
dishwasher 17.327
dishwater 17.345
dishy 16.322
disillusion 261.93.1
disincentive 485.21
disinclination 261.67.18
disincline 253.5
disinfect 385
disinfectant 420.79
disinfection 261.77
disinfest 433
disingenuous 310.4.2
disinherit 371.31
disintegrate 367.26
disintegration 261.67.24
disinter 3
disinterest 436.20
disinterested 91.53
disject 385
disjoin 256
disjoint 416
disjointed 91.48
disjunction 261.80
disjunctive 485
disk 58
dislikable 228.16
dislike 39.1
dislimn 235
dislocate 367.6
dislocation 261.67.6
dislodge 199
disloyal 228.6
disloyalty 16.352.1
dismal 228.54
dismantle 228.109
dismantler 17.203
dismay 2
dismember 17.24
dismiss 300
dismissal 228.85
dismissive 485.4
dismount 418
Disneyland 143.2
disobedience 321.1
disobedient 420.1.1
disobey 2.4
disoblige 198

disoperation 261.67.22.3
disorder 17.86
disorderly 16.131
disorganize 516.7
disorganized 154
disorient 410
disorientate 367.32
disown 257
disparage 197.9
disparagement 420.37
disparate 371.35
disparity 16.333.20
dispassion 261.66
dispassionate 371.28
dispatch 62
dispel 215
dispensable 228.16.40
dispensary 16.274.38
dispensation 261.67.26
dispensatory 16.274.43
dispense 316
dispenser 17.314
dispersal 228.84
dispersant 420.68
disperse 297
dispersion 261.69
dispersive 485.3
dispirit 371.33
dispirited 91.38
displace 295
displacement 420.44
display 2
displease 513
displeasure 17.333
disport 374
disposable 228.16
disposal 228.127
dispose 520
disposed 155
disposition 261.71.9
dispossess 296
dispossession 261.68
dispraise 509
disproof 170

disproportion
261.72.1
disproportionate
371.28.2
disprove 490
disputable
228.16.53
disputant 420.77
disputation
261.67.29
disputatious 310.56
dispute 380
disqualifier 17.4.1
disqualify 7.3.2
disquiet 381.2
disquietude 102.2
disquisition
261.71.8
Disraeli 16.114
disrate 367
disregard 84.1
disrelish 353.4
disrepair 4.6
disreputable
228.16.52
disrepute 380.4
disrespect 385
disrespectful
226.10
disrobe 28
disrupt 426
disruption 261.88
disruptive 485
dissatisfaction
261.76
dissatisfied 92
dissatisfy 7
dissect 385.7
dissection 261.77.5
disseise 513
dissemble 228.18
disseminate 367.17
dissension 261.82.2
dissent 410
dissenter 17.368.1
dissentient 420
dissentious 310.61
dissepiment 420.31
dissertate 367.31
dissertation
261.67.30
disservice 300
dissever 17.411
dissident 420.10
dissimilar 17.166

dissimilarity
16.333.20.2
dissimilate 367.12
dissimilation
261.67.12
dissimilitude 102.2
dissimulate
367.13.5
dissimulation
261.67.13.3
dissipate 367.19.1
dissipated 91.34
dissipation
261.67.20.1
dissociable
228.16.44
dissociate 367.1.7
dissociation
261.67.1
dissolute 380.1
dissolution
261.75.1
dissolve 493
dissolvent 420
dissonance 321
dissonant 420.55
dissuade 85
dissuasion 261
dissuasive 485
dissymmetry
16.285.1
distaff 158
distal 228.114
distance 321.27
distant 420.81
distaste 432
distasteful 226.12
distemper 17.262
distend 131
distich 38.70
distichous 310.10
distil 218
distillate 371.16
distillation
261.67.12
distiller 17.166
distillery 16.274.16
distinct 392
distinction 261
distinctive 485.20
distinguish 353
distinguishable
228.16.43
distort 374
distortion 261.72

distract 382
distracting 265.70
distraction 261.76
distrain 247
distrainee 5.11
distraint 409
distrait 2
distraught 374
distress 296
distressing 265.60
distributary
16.274.42
distribute 380.2
distributee 5.23
distribution 261.75
distributive 485
distributor 17.350
district 387
distringas 293
distrust 443
distrustful 226.13
disturb 22
disturbance 321
disturbing 265
disulfiram 242.19
disulphide 92
disunite 372
disunity 16.333.18
disuse 309
disused 156
dit 371
dita 17.341
ditch 67
ditheism 242.35.2
dither 17.405
dithyramb 229
dithyrambic 38.5
dittander 17.98
dittany 16.237
ditto 12
dittography
16.90.2.5
ditty 16.333
diuresis 300.51
diuretic 38.50
diurnal 228.58
div 485
diva 17.413
divalent 420.25
divan 245
divaricate 367.5,
371.9
divaricator
17.338.2
dive 486

diver 17.415
diverge 195
divergence 321
divergent 420.19
divers 524
diverse 297
diversiform 238.1
diversify 7.3
diversion 261.69
diversity 16.333.26
divert 369
diverticulitis
300.62.2
diverticulosis
300.55.3
diverticulum
242.10.1
divertimento 12.84
divertissement 420
Dives 513
divest 433
divide 92
dividend 131
divider 17.84
dividers 524
divi-divi 16.382
divination
261.67.18
divine 253
diviner 17.232
diving 265
divining 265.44
divinity 16.333.17
divinize 516.6
divisibility
16.333.9.2.2
divisible 228.16.63
division 261.91.2
divisional 228.63
divisionism
242.35.14
divisive 485.5
divisor 17.441
divorcé 2
divorce 303
divorcee 5.21
divot 381
divulge 205
divulsion 261
divvy 16.382
Dixie 16.388
dixie 16.388
Dixieland 143.2
Diyarbakir 6
dizziness 300.23

dizzy 16.396
Djaja 17.145
Djajapura 17.277
Djakarta 17.337
Djambi 16.17
Djerba 17.12
Djibouti 16.343
Dnieper 17.252
Dniester 17.383
do 15
doab 19
doable 228.16.7
dobbin 252
dobby 16.11
Doberman pinscher 17.331
dobla 1
dobsonfly 7
doc 40
docent 410
Docetism 242.35.18
docile 219
docility 16.333.9
dock 40
dockage 197
docker 17.36
docket 371.10
dockland 143
dockyard 84
doctor 17.356
doctoral 228.76
doctorate 371.35
doctrinaire 4
doctrinal 228.61
doctrine 252
document 410, 420.34
documentary 16.274.47
documentation 261.67.32
dodder 17.85
doddering 265.58
doddery 16.274
doddle 228.34
dodecagon 254.5
Dodecanese 513.9
dodecaphonic 38.35.2
dodge 199
Dodgem 242
dodger 17.152
dodgy 16.104
dodo 12.21

Dodona 17.236
doe 12
doek 44
doer 17.8
does 522
doeskin 252
doff 165
dog 185
dogberry 16.274
dogcart 366
doge 201
dogfight 372
dogfish 353
dogged 91
doggedness 300.28
Dogger 17.131
dogger 17.131
doggerel 228.76
doggery 16.274.12
doggish 353
doggo 12
doggone 254
doggy 16.94
doghouse 306
dogie 16.96
dogleg 181
dogma 17
dogman 261
dogmatic 38.49
dogmatics 498.11
dogmatism 242.35.20
dogmatist 436.26
dogmatize 516.13
dogsbody 16.65
dogtooth 463
dogtrot 373
dogvane 247
dogwatch 68
dogwood 101
doh 12
Doha 1
doily 16.125
doing 265.5
doings 552
doit 375
dol 220
dolabriform 238.1
doldrums 543
dole 223
doleful 226
dolerite 372.8
dolina 17.230
doll 220
dollar 17.168

dollarbird 87
dollop 281.2
dolly 16.122
dolman 261
dolmas 310
dolmen 248
Dolmetsch 64
dolomite 372
Dolomites 340
dolorimetry 16.285.1
doloroso 12.70
dolorous 310.50
dolour 17.168
dolphin 252
dolt 405
dom 237
domain 247.5
dome 239
domestic 38.69
domesticate 367.5
domestication 261.67.5
domesticity 16.333.28
domicile 219.2
domiciliary 16.274.1.1
dominance 321.14
dominant 420.53.2
dominate 367.17.5
domination 261.67.18.6
domineer 6.4
Dominic 38.34
Dominica 17.33
dominical 228.23.12
Dominican 261.13
dominie 16.229
dominion 261.122
dominium 242.2.11
domino 12.55
dominoes 520
Domitian 261.71.4
don 254
Don 254
Donar 1
donate 367.18
donation 261.67.19
Donatist 436.26
donative 485.15
Donbass 294
Doncaster 17.390
done 259

donee 5
Donegal 221
Donets 336
dong 266
Donizetti 16.330
Don Juan 261
donkey 16.38
Donna 17.233
donned 136
donnert 381
donnish 353.8
donnybrook 44
donor 17.236
Donovan 261
Don Quixote 16.339
don't 417
doodah 1.3
doodle 228.37
doodlebug 189
Doolittle 228.102
doom 241
doomsday 2
door 9
doorbell 215
doorframe 231
doorjamb 229
doorkeeper 17.252
doorman 261
doormat 365
doornail 214
doorpost 441
doorsill 218
doorstep 271
doorstop 276
doorway 2
dooryard 84
dopant 420
dope 278
dopey 16.251
Doppelgänger 17.245
Dopper 17.255
Doppler 17.195
dor 9
Dora 17.276
Dorado 12.16
Dorcas 310
Dorchester 17.384
Dorian 261.3.23
Doric 38.41
Doris 300
Dorking 265.9
dorm 238
dormant 420.32

dormer 17.214
dormie 16.218
dormitory
  16.274.41
Dormobile 217
dormouse 306
dornick 38
doronicum 242.4
dorp 277
dorsad 83
dorsal 228
Dorset 371
dorsoventral
  228.80
dorsum 242
Dortmund 143
dorty 16.336
dory 16.269
dosage 197
dose 305
do-si-do 12.19
dosimeter 17.342.2
doss 302
dossal 228.86
dosser 17.304
dosshouse 306
dossier 2.1
Dostoevsky 16.43
dot 373
dotage 197.13
dotard 103
dotation 261.67.28
dote 376
dotted 91.40
dottle 228.104
dotty 16.335
Dou 13
Douai 2.2
double 228.14
double-breasted
  91.52
double-cross 302
double-decker
  17.31
double entendre
  17.287
double-glazing
  265.81
double-jointed
  91.48
doubles 539
doublet 371
doublethink 52
doubleton 261
doubletree 5

doubloon 260
doublure 10
doubly 16.136
doubt 377
doubter 17.348
doubtful 226
doubtfulness
  300.30
doubtless 300
douc 45
douce 309
douceur 3
douche 358
dough 12
doughboy 11
doughnut 378
doughty 16.340
doughy 16.3
Douglas 310
Doukhobors 518
dour 10
dourine 251
Douro 12.66
douroucouli 16.130
douse 306
douser 17.307
dove 489
dovecot 373
dovecote 376
Dover 17.417
dovetail 214
dowable 228.16.5
dowager 17.154
dowdy 16.68
dowel 228.8
dower 14
dowitcher 17.56
Dowland 143
down 258
downbeat 370
downcast 431
downfall 221
downfallen 261
downgrade 85
downhaul 221
downhearted 91.33
downheartedness
  300.28
downhill 218
Downpatrick 38.45
downpipe 275
downpour 9
downright 372
downspout 377
downstage 193

downstairs 512
downstate 367
downstream 234
downtown 258
downtrodden
  261.26
downward 103
downwards 531
downwind 134
downy 16.234
dowry 16.271
dowse 521
dowser 17.443
dowsing 265
doxastic 38.68
doxology 16.108.4
doxy 16.389
doyen 261.5
doyenne 248
Doyle 222
doze 520
dozen 261
dozenth 471
dozer 17.442
dozy 16.399
drab 18
drabbet 371.4
drabble 228
drably 16.132
drabness 300
dracaena 17.230
drachma 17.219
dracone 257
Draconian
  261.3.18
draconic 38.35
draff 157
draft 396
draftee 5
drag 178
dragée 2
draggle 228.43
draghound 139
dragnet 368
dragoman 261.49
dragon 261.30
dragonet 371.28
dragonfly 7
dragonhead 86
dragonnade 85.3
dragoon 260
dragrope 278
drail 214
drain 247
drainage 197

drainer 17.227
drainpipe 275
drake 34
Drakensberg 182
dram 229
drama 17.206
Dramamine 251.4
dramatic 38.49.2
dramatically
  16.142
dramatics 498.11
dramatis personae
  7
dramatist 436.26
dramatization
  261.67.36
dramatize 516.13.1
dramaturge 195
dramaturgy 16.102
Drambuie 16.4
drank 51
drape 270
draper 17.249
drapery 16.274
drapes 323
drastic 38.68
drastically 16.142
drat 365
dratted 91.32
draught 396
draughtboard 95
draught-excluder
  17.91
draughtsman 261
draughty 16.345
Drava 17.409
Dravidian 261.3.5
draw 9
drawback 32
drawbar 1
drawbridge 197
drawee 5
drawer 9
drawers 518
drawing 265
drawknife 164
drawl 221
drawn 255
drawplate 367
drawstring 265
drawtube 30
dray 2
drayhorse 303
dread 86
dreadful 226

dreadfully 16.129
dreadfulness 300.30
dreadnought 374
dream 234
dreamer 17.210
dreamless 300
dreamlike 39
dreamy 16.215
dreariness 300.23
dreary 16.265
dredge 194
dredger 17.147
dree 5
dreg 181
dreggy 16.92
dregs 535
drench 79
Dresden 261
dress 296
dressage 359
dressed 433
dresser 17.300
dressing 265.60
dressmaker 17.30
dressmaking 265.6
dressy 16.297
drew 15
Dreyfus 310
dribble 228.12
driblet 371
drift 398
drifter 17.359
driftwood 101
drill 218
drillstock 40
drink 52
drinkable 228.16.11
drinker 17.44
drip 274
dripping 265
drippy 16.248
drive 486
drivel 228.120
driven 261.114
driver 17.415
driverless 300.13
driveway 2
driving 265
drizzle 228
drizzly 16.209
drogue 188
droit 375
droll 223

drollery 16.274.17
dromedary 16.274.7
dromond 143
drone 257
drongo 12
drool 227
droop 280
droopy 16.253
drop 276
droplet 371
droplight 372
dropout 377
dropper 17.255
droppings 552
drops 329
dropsical 228.23
dropsonde 136
dropsy 16.315
drosophila 17.166
dross 302
drought 377
drove 488
drover 17.417
drown 258
drowse 521
drowsiness 300.23
drowsy 16.400
drub 29
drudge 203
drudgery 16.274
druffen 261
drug 189
drugget 371
druggist 436
drugstore 9
druid 91.3
druidess 300
druidic 38
drum 240
drumbeat 370
drumhead 86
drumlin 252
drummer 17.216
drumstick 38
drunk 54
drunkard 103
drunken 261
drunkenness 300.31
drupe 280
drupelet 371
Drury 16.270
druse 523
Druse 523

dry 7
dryad 83.2
dryadic 38.7
dry-cleaning 265.42
Dryden 261.25
dryer 17.4
dryness 300
Drysdale 214
D.T.s 513.16
dual 228.10
dualism 242.35.11
duality 16.333.8.2
dub 29
Dubai 7
dubbin 252
dubbing 265
dubiety 16.333.2
dubious 310.2
dubiousness 300.34.1
dubitable 228.16.49
dubitation 261.67.27
Dublin 252
Dubonnet 2
Dubrovnik 38
ducal 228
ducat 381
duce 16.53
duchess 300
duchy 16.52
duck 43
duckboard 95
ducking 265
duckling 265.34
ducks 502
duckweed 89
ducky 16.30
duct 389
ductile 219
dud 100
dude 102
dudeen 251
dudgeon 261.38
Dudley 16.151
due 15
duel 228.10
dueller 17.176
duello 12.40
duenna 17.228
duet 368.1
duff 168
duffel 228.42

duffer 17.118
dug 189
dugong 266
dugout 377
duiker 17.35
duke 45
dukedom 242
dulcet 371
dulciana 17.226.1
dulcify 7.3.7
dulcimer 17.211
dulia 17.3.23
dull 225
dullard 103.4
Dulles 300.10
dullness 300
dullsville 218
dulse 313
Duluth 463
duly 16.130
Du Maurier 2.1
dumb 240
Dumbarton 261.95
dumbbell 215
dumbfound 139
dumbness 300
dumbstruck 43
dumbwaiter 17.338
dumdum 240
Dumfries 298
dummy 16.220
dump 289
dumper 17.264
dumpling 265
dumps 332
dumpy 16.257
Dumyat 365
dun 259
Dunbar 1
Duncan 261
dunce 320
Dundalk 41
Dundee 5
dunderhead 86.5
dune 260
Dunedin 252
Dunfermline 252
dung 267
dungaree 5.17
Dungeness 296.3
dungeon 261
dunghill 218
dunite 372
dunk 54

Dun Laoghaire
17.271
dunlin 252
Dunlop 276
dunnage 197
dunnakin 252.4
dunnite 372
dunno 12
dunnock 46
dunny 16.235
Dunoon 260.2
Dunsany 16.225
Dunsinane 247.6
Duns Scotus
310.66
Dunstable 228.16
Dunstan 261
dunt 419
duo 12
duodecimal
228.52.1
duodenal 228.59
duodenary
16.274.25
duodenitis 300.62.3
duodenum 242
duologue 185
duomo 12.49
duotone 257.3
dup 279
dupe 280
dupery 16.274
duple 228
duplet 371
duplex 496
duplicate 367.5.1
duplicate 371.9.1
duplication
261.67.5
duplicator 17.338.2
duplicity 16.333.28
dupondius 310.2
durable 228.16.34
dura mater 17.338
duramen 248.2
durance 321.19
Durango 12.35
duration 261.67.21
durative 485.15.9
Durban 261.9
durbar 1
duress 296
Durex 496
durgah 1
Durham 242

durian 261.3.24
during 265.56
durmast 431
duro 12.66
Duroc 40
durra 17.278
durst 434
durum 242
dusk 60
dusky 16.42
Düsseldorf 166
dust 443
dustbin 252
dustcart 366
duster 17.388
dustman 261
dustpan 245
dustsheet 370
dusty 16.368
Dutch 72
Dutchman 261
duteous 310.2
dutiable 228.16.2
dutiful 226
duty 16.343
duvet 2
duvetyn 251.11
dux 502
dvandva 1
Dvořák 32
dwale 214
dwarf 166
dwarfism 242.35.7
dwell 215
dweller 17.163
dwelling 265.28
dwelt 402
dwindle 228.40
dyad 83.2
dyadic 38.7
Dyak 32
dye 7
dyed 92
dyeing 265.3
dyeline 253
dyer 17.4
dyestuff 168
dyewood 101
Dyfed 86
dying 265.3
dyke 39
Dylan 261.41
dynamic 38.24
dynamics 498.2
dynamism 242.35

dynamite 372
dynamo 12
dynamometer
17.342.3.2
dynamometry
16.285.2
dynamotor 17.347
dynast 445
dynastic 38.68
dynasty 16
dyne 253
dynode 98
dysentery
16.274.48
dysfunction 261.80
dysgenics 498.3
dysgraphia 17.3.10
dyslectic 38.60
dyslexia 17.3.57
dyslexic 38
dysmenorrhoea
17.2.2
dyspepsia 17.3
dyspeptic 38.65
dysphagia 17.3.12
dysphasia 17.3.59
dysphemism
242.35
dysphonia 17.3.36
dysphoria 17.3.41
dysplasia 17.3.59
dyspnoea 17.2
dysteleology
16.108.4.1
dystopia 17.3.37
dystrophia 17.3.11
dystrophy 16.90.3
dysuria 17.3.42
dytiscid 91.29
Dzongka 17.45
Dzungaria 17.3.38

E

each 66
eager 17.128
eagerness 300.26
eagle 228.45
eaglet 371
eaglewood 101
eagre 17.125

ealdorman 261.52
Ealing 265.29
ear 6
earache 34
earbash 349
eardrop 276
eardrops 329
eardrum 240
eared 90
earflap 268
earful 226
Earhart 366
earing 265.53
earl 216
earldom 242
earliness 300.23
early 16.116
earmark 33
earmuff 168
earn 249
earner 17.229
earnest 436
earnestness 300
earnings 552
Earp 272
earphone 257
earpiece 298
earplug 189
earring 265.53
earshot 373
earth 456
earthborn 255
earthbound 139
earthen 261
earthenware 4
earthling 265
earthly 16.204
earthquake 34
earthshaking 265.6
earthstar 1
earthwork 36
earthworm 233
earthy 16
earwax 494
earwig 184
ease 513
easeful 226
easel 228
easiness 300.23
east 435
East Anglia 17.3
eastbound 139
Eastbourne 255
Easter 17.383
easterly 16.131

eastern 261
Easterner 17.239
easternmost 441
Eastertide 92.11
East Kilbride 92
Eastleigh 5
eastward 103
eastwards 531
easy 16.395
easy-going 265.4
eat 370
eatable 228.16.48
eatage 197
eaten 261.98
eater 17.341
eats 338
eau de Javelle 215
eau de nil 217.1
eau de vie 5
eaves 553
eavesdrop 276
eavesdropper
17.255
ebb 21
ebbed 104
Ebbw Vale 214
Ebenezer 17.440
ebon 261
ebonize 516.7
ebony 16.237
Eboracum 242
ebullience 321
ebullient 420
ebullition 261.71.3
eburnation
261.67.19
ecad 83
écarté 2.23
Ecbatana 17.239
ecbolic 38.22
eccentric 38.47
eccentricity
16.333.28
ecchymosis 300.55
Eccles 539
ecclesia 17.3.60
Ecclesiastes 513.18
ecclesiastic 38.68.1
ecclesiastical
228.23
ecclesiasticism
242.35.16.6
ecclesiolatry
16.286.2.1

ecclesiology
16.108.4.1
eccrine 253
ecdysiast 430.1
ecdysis 300.52
ecdysone 257
ecesis 300.51
echelon 254.7
echeveria 17.3.39
echidna 17.241
echinate 367.17
echinoid 97
echinus 310.34
echo 12.9
echoic 38.2
echoism 242.35.3
echolalia 17.3.18
echopraxia 17.3.56
echovirus 310.47
éclair 4
eclampsia 17.3
éclat 1
eclectic 38.60
eclipse 327
ecliptic 38.66
eclogite 372
eclogue 185
eclosion 261.92
ecocide 92.8
ecological 228.23.5
ecology 16.108.4
econometrics
498.10
economic 38.29.1
economical
228.23.9
economics 498
economist 436.10
economize 516.5
economy 16.222.3
écorché 2
ecospecies 513
ecosphere 6.1
écossaise 509
ecosystem 242
ecotone 257.3
ecotype 275.1
écraseur 3
ecru 15
ecstasy 16.307
ecstatic 38.49
ecstatics 498.11
ecthyma 17.211
ectoderm 233
ectomorph 166.1

ectomorphic 38.14
ectopia 17.3.37
ectopic 38.37
ectoplasm 242.34
ectoproct 388
ectosarc 33
ectype 275
Ecuador 9.4
ecumenical
228.23.11
eczema 17.211
eczematous 310.68
edacious 310.56.2
Edam 229
edaphic 38.11
Edda 17.80
eddo 12
eddy 16.60
Eddystone 261.107
Ede 17.79
edelweiss 301
Eden 261.23
edentate 367.32
edentulous 310.25
Edgar 17
edge 194
Edgehill 218
edgeways 509
edging 265
edgy 16.101
edh 474
edible 228.16.14
edict 387
edifice 300
edify 7.3
Edinburgh 17.279
Edison 261.65
edit 371.12
edition 261.71.1
editio princeps 324
editor 17.342.1
editorial 228.3.12.1
editorialize
516.3.2.2
Edmonton 261
Edmund 143
Edmunds 534
Edom 242
educable 228.16
educate 367
educated 91.34
education 261.67
educational
228.63.3

educationalist
436.7.5
educative 485.15
educator 17.338
educatory
16.274.43
educe 309
educt 389
eduction 261.79
edulcorate 367.23
Edward 103
Edwardian 261.3
Edwin 252
eel 217
eelgrass 294
eelpout 377
e'er 4
eerie 16.265
eff 160
effable 228.16
efface 295.3
effaceable
228.16.36
effect 385.1
effective 485.17
effectively 16.206
effectiveness
300.43
effector 17.354
effectual 228.9.5
effectually 16.131.1
effectuate 367.2
effeminate 371.24
effendi 16.78
efferent 420.65
effervesce 296
effervescence
321.21
effervescent
420.67.3
effete 370
efficacious 310.56.1
efficacy 16.307.1
efficiency 16.312.5
efficient 420.74
effigial 228.3.3
effigy 16.103
effloresce 296
efflorescence
321.21
effluence 321.3
effluent 420.4
effluvium 242.2
efflux 502
effort 381

effortless 300
effortlessness
   300.33
effrontery 16.274
effulgent 420.21
effuse 309, 523
effusion 261.93
effusive 485.8
eft 397
egad 83
egalitarian
   261.3.21.2
Egbert 381
Egeria 17.3.39
egest 433
egesta 17.382
egg 181
eggbeater 17.341
egger 17.126
egghead 86
eggnog 185
eggplant 408
eggshell 215
Egham 242
eglantine 253
Egmont 414
ego 12.28
egocentric 38.47
egocentrism 242.35
egoism 242.35.3
egoist 436
egoistic 38.70
egomania 17.3.31.1
egomaniac 32.1
egotism 242.35.20
egotist 436.26
egotistic 38.70.6
egotistical
   228.23.24
egregious 310
egress 296
egret 371
Egypt 424
Egyptian 261.85
Egyptology
   16.108.4.17
eh 2
eider 17.84
eiderdown 258
eidetic 38.50
eidolon 254
Eiffel 228
eigenfrequency
   16.312
Eiger 17.130

eight 367
eighteen 251
eighteenth 469
eightfold 120
eightieth 458
eightsome 242
eighty 16.329
Eilat 366
Eindhoven 261.116
einkorn 255
Einstein 253
Eire 17.271
Eisenhower 14
Eisenstein 253
eisteddfod 103.2
either 17.406
ejaculate 367.13,
   371.17.1
ejaculation
   261.67.13
eject 385
ejecta 17.354
ejection 261.77
ejective 485.17
ejector 17.354
eke 37
ekistics 498
elaborate 367.23,
   371.35.1
Elaine 247
El Alamein 247.5
Elam 242
élan 266
eland 143.1
elapid 91
elapse 322
elasmosaur 9.11
elastic 38.68
elasticate 367.5.2
elasticity
   16.333.28.2
elastomer 17.218
Elastoplast 431
elate 367.12
elater 17.352
elaterid 91.27
elaterium 242.2.15
elation 261.67.12
elative 485.15
Elba 17.22
elbow 12
elbowroom 241
Elbrus 309
El Cid 91
elder 17.93

elderberry 16.274
elderly 16.131
eldest 436
El Dorado 12.16
eldritch 67
Eleanor 17.231
Eleatic 38.49
elecampane 247.7
elect 385.4
election 261.77.2
electioneer 6.5
electioneering
   265.53
elective 485.17
elector 17.354
electoral 228.76.3
electorate 371.35
Electra 17.295
electret 381
electric 38
electrical 228.23
electrician 261.71
electricity
   16.333.28
electrification
   261.67.5.1
electrify 7.3
electroanalysis
   300.52.1
electrocardiogram
   229.1.1
electrocardiograph
   158.1.1
electrocardiography
   16.90.2.1
electrocute 380.3
electrocution
   261.75.2
electrode 98
electrodialysis
   300.52.1
electrodynamics
   498.2
electroencephalo-
   gram 229.1
electroencephalo-
   graph 158.1
electroform 238.2
electrograph
   158.1.3
electrolyse 516.3
electrolysis
   300.52.2
electrolyte 372.4
electrolytic 38.52.1

electromagnet 371
electromagnetic
   38.50
electromagnetism
   242.35.18
electrometallurgy
   16.108.2
electrometer
   17.342.3.5
electromotive
   485.14
electron 254
electronic 38.35
electronics 498.5
electronvolt 405
electrophoresis
   300.51.1
electrophorus
   310.50
electroplate 367
electropositive
   485.12.1
electroscope
   278.1.2
electrostatic
   38.49.7
electrostatics
   498.11
electrosurgery
   16.274.13
electrotype 275.1
electrovalency
   16.312
electrum 242.22
electuary 16.274.2
eleemosynary
   16.274.26
elegance 321
elegant 420.17
elegiac 46
elegize 516.1
elegy 16.103
element 420.31
elemental
   228.110.2
elementary
   16.274.47
elemi 16.216
elenctic 38
elephant 420
elephantiasis
   300.57.1
elephantine 253.9
Eleusis 300.56
elevate 367.36

elevated 91.34
elevation 261.67
elevator 17.338.11
eleven 261.112
elevenses 515
eleventh 471.1
elevon 254
elf 172
El Faiyum 241
elfish 353.3
elflock 40
Elgar 1
Elgin 252
El Greco 12.9
Eli 7
Elia 17.3.20
Elias 310.3
elicit 371.36
elide 92.2
eligible 228.16.20.1
Elijah 17.151
eliminate 367.17
elimination
    261.67.18.5
Eliot 381.1
Elis 300
elision 261.91
elite 370
elitism 242.35
elixir 17.427
Elizabeth 464
Elizabethan 261
elk 48
elkhound 139
ell 215
Ellington 261
ellipse 327
ellipsis 300.60
ellipsoid 97
elliptic 38.66
elliptical 228.23
Ellis 300
elm 243
El Mansura 17.277
El Misti 5
El Obeid 85
clocution 261.75.2
elongate 367
elongation 261.67
elope 278.2
eloquence 321
eloquent 420.59
El Paso 12.68
El Salvador 9.4
elsewhere 4

Elsinore 9
elucidate 367.8
elucidation
    261.67.7
elude 102
eluent 420.5
elusive 485.8
elute 380
eluvium 242.2
elver 17.421
elvish 353
Ely 16.118
Elysian 261.3.35
Elysium 242.2
elytron 254
em 232
'em 242
emaciate 367.1.4
emaciation
    261.67.1.3
emanate 367.18
emanation
    261.67.19
emancipate 367.19
emancipation
    261.67.20
emasculate 367.13
emasculation
    261.67.13
embalm 230
embalmer 17.206
embank 51
embankment 420
embargo 12.26
embark 33
embarkation
    261.67.4
embarrass 310.43
embarrassing 265
embarrassment
    420.46
embassy 16.307
embattle 228.97
embed 86
embellish 353.4
embellishment
    420.47
ember 17.24
embezzle 228
embezzlement
    420.40
embitter 17.342
emblazon 261.124
emblem 242
emblematic 38.49.2

emblematize
    516.13
embodiment
    420.31
embody 16.65
embolden 261.28
embolic 38.22
embolism
    242.35.11
embolus 310.26
emboly 16.131
emboss 302
embouchure 10
embowel 228.8
embower 14
embrace 295
embraceor 17.299
embracery
    16.274.33
embranchment 420
embrasure 17.332
embrectomy
    16.222.5
embrocate 367.6
embrocation
    261.67.6
embroider 17.87
embroidery 16.274
embroil 222
embryo 12.3
embryogeny
    16.229.2
embryology
    16.108.4.1
embryonic 38.35.1
embus 307
emcee 5
emend 131
emendation
    261.67.9
emerald 122
emerge 195
emergence 321
emergency
    16.312.3
emergent 420.19
emeritus 310.64
emersion 261.69
Emerson 261
emery 16.274
emesis 300.52.3
emetic 38.50
emigrant 420
emigrate 367.26

emigration
    261.67.24
émigré 2
eminence 321.14
eminent 420.53
emir 6
emirate 371.32
emissary 16.274.36
emission 261.71
emit 371.19
emitter 17.342.2
Emmanuel 228.9.2
Emmen 261
emmenagogue
    185.2
Emmenthal 213
emmer 17.208
emmet 371
Emmy 16.213
emollient 420
emolument 420.34
emote 376
emotion 261.73
emotional 228.63.6
emotionalism
    242.35.11.5
emotive 485.14
empanel 228.55
empathetic 38.50.6
empathic 38.72
empathize 516.14
empathy 16.373
empennage 197.6
emperor 17.279
empery 16.274.31
emphasis 300.57
emphasize 516.11
emphatic 38.49
emphatically
    16.142
emphysema 17.210
empire 8
empiric 38.40
empirical 228.23.16
empiricism
    242.35.16.3
emplace 295
emplacement
    420.44
emplane 247
employ 11
employable
    228.16.4
employee 5
employer 17.5

enlightenment 420.42
enlist 436
enliven 261.115
en masse 293
enmesh 351
enmity 16.333
ennage 197.6
ennead 83.1
Ennis 300
Enniskillen 252.8
Ennius 310.2
ennoble 228.13
ennui 5
Enoch 40
enol 220
enormity 16.333.13
enormous 310
enough 168
enounce 319
enquire 8
enquirer 17.274
enquiry 16.267
enrage 193
enrapture 17.72
enrich 67
enrichment 420
enrobe 28
enrol 223
enrolment 420
enroot 380
en route 380
ens 546
ensconce 318
ensemble 228
enshrine 253
enshroud 99
ensign 253
ensilage 197.1
ensile 219.3
enslave 482
ensnare 4
ensphere 6
ensue 15
ensure 10.2
enswathe 473
enswathed 144
entablement 420.40
entail 214
entamoeba 17.13
entangle 228.49
entanglement 420.40
entasis 300.57
Entebbe 16.8

entelechy 16.25
entellus 310.22
enter 17.368
enteral 228.76
enteric 38.39
enteritis 300.62.5
enterogastrone 257
enterokinase 509
enteron 254.11
enterotomy 16.222.4
enterprise 516.9
enterprising 265.82
entertain 247.10
entertainer 17.227
entertaining 265.40
entertainment 420.41
enthetic 38.50
enthral 221
enthralling 265.31
enthrone 257
enthuse 523
enthusiasm 242.34
enthusiast 430.1
enthusiastic 38.68.1
entice 301
enticement 420
entire 8
entirety 16.333
entitle 228.103
entitlement 420.40
entity 16.333.32
entomb 241
entomic 38.29
entomologize 516.1
entomology 16.108.4
entopic 38.37
entourage 359
entozoic 38.2
entozoon 254.2
entr'acte 382
entrails 536
entrain 247
entrammel 228.51
entrance 315, 321
entrant 420
entrap 268
entreat 370
entreaty 16.332
entrée 2
entrench 79
entrenchment 420

entrepreneur 3
entrepreneurial 228.3
entresol 220
entropy 16.254
entrust 443
entry 16.288
entwine 253
enucleate 367.1
enumerate 367.23
enumeration 261.67.22
enumerator 17.338.9
enunciate 367.1
enunciation 261.67.1.4
enuresis 300.51
envelop 281.1
envelope 278
envenom 242
envenomed 127
enviable 228.16.2
envious 310.2
environ 261.58
environment 420.42
environmental 228.110.4
environmentalism 242.35.11.6
environmentalist 436.7.7
environs 551
envisage 197
envision 261.91
envoy 11
envy 16
enwind 135
enwomb 241
enwrap 268
enwreath 475
Enzed 86
enzootic 38.53
enzyme 236
enzymology 16.108.4
eobiont 420.2
Eocene 251.9
eohippus 310.37
eolith 458
Eolithic 38.73
eonism 242.35.14
Eos 302
eosin 252

eosinophil 218.1
Eozoic 38.2
Epaminondas 293
eparch 33
eparchy 16.20
epaulet 368
épée 2
épéeist 436.1
epeiric 38
epeirogeny 16.229.2
epenthesis 300.52
epergne 249
ephah 17.113
ephebe 23
ephedrine 252
ephemera 17.279.1
ephemeral 228.76.2
ephemerality 16.333.8.9
ephemerid 91.27
ephemeris 300.47
ephemeron 254.11
Ephesian 261.90
Ephesus 310.53
ephod 94
ephor 9
Ephraim 235
epiboly 16.131
epic 38
epicardium 242.2
epicarp 269
epicene 251.8
epicentre 17.368.1
epiclesis 300.51
epicrisis 300.53
Epictetus 310.63
epicure 10.3
epicurean 261.2
Epicurus 310.49
epicycloid 97
Epidaurus 310.48
epidemic 38.25
epidemiology 16.108.4.1
epidermis 300.18
epidiascope 278.1.1
epididymis 300.19
epidote 376
epidural 228.75
epigastrium 242.2
epigeal 228.2
epigene 251
epigenous 310.33
epiglottis 300

epigram 229
epigrammatic 38.49.2
epigrammatize 516.13.1
epigraph 158
epigraphic 38.11
epigraphy 16.90
epilepsy 16.313
epileptic 38.65
epileptoid 97
epilimnion 261.3
epilogue 185
epimere 6.2
epinasty 16.361
epiphany 16.237.2
epiphragm 229
epiphysis 300.52
epiphyte 372
Epirus 310.47
episcopacy 16.307
episcopal 228
episcopalian 261.3.8
episcopate 371.30
episcope 278
episematic 38.49.1
episiotomy 16.222.4.1
episode 98
episodic 38.9
epispastic 38.68
epistaxis 300.70
epistemic 38.27
epistemology 16.108.4.9
episternum 242.13
epistle 228.85
epistolary 16.274.19
epistoler 17.176
epistrophe 16.90.3
epistyle 219
epitaph 158
epitaphic 38.11
epitaxial 228.3.18
epitaxy 16.386
epithelium 242.2.5
epithet 368
epitome 16.222
epitomize 516.5
epizoic 38.2
epizootic 38.53
epoch 40
epode 98

eponym 235
eponymous 310.28.2
eponymy 16.216
épopée 5.16
epopoeia 17.2.1
epos 302
epoxide 92.14
epoxy 16.389
Epping 265
epsilon 254.6
Epsom 242
Epstein 253
epyllion 261.3.11
equable 228.16
equal 228.71
equality 16.333.10
equalize 516.3
equalizer 17.441
equally 16.131
equanimity 16.333.12
equate 367.20
equation 261
equator 17.338
equatorial 228.3.12.2
equerry 16.262
equestrian 261.3
equestrienne 248.1
equiangular 17.174
equidistant 420.81
equilateral 228.76
equilibrate 367.24
equilibration 261.67.23
equilibrist 436
equilibrium 242.2
equine 253
equinoctial 228
equinox 499
equip 274
equipage 197.8
equipartition 261.71
equipment 420.43
equipoise 519
equipollent 420
equiponderate 367.23
equisetum 242.28
equitable 228.16.49
equitant 420.76
equitation 261.67.27

equites 513
equities 515
equity 16.333
equivalence 321.12
equivalent 420.28
equivocal 228.28
equivocate 367.6
equivocation 261.67.6
Equuleus 310.2
era 17.272
eradicable 228.16.10
eradicate 367.5
eradication 261.67.5
erasable 228.16
erase 509
eraser 17.439
Erasmus 310
Erastianism 242.35.14.1
erasure 17.332
Erbil 218
erbium 242.2
ere 4
Erebus 310.5
Erechtheion 261.3
Erechtheum 242.2
erect 385
erectile 219.5
erection 261.77.3
erector 17.354
eremite 372
erethism 242.35
erg 182
ergo 12
ergonomics 498
ergosterol 220.4
ergot 381
ergotism 242.35.20
Eric 38.39
Erica 17.34.2
ericaceous 310.56.1
Eridanus 310.36
Erie 16.265
erigeron 261.60
Erin 252
erinaceous 310.56.4
Eris 300
eristic 38.70
Eritrea 17.1
erk 36
erlking 265
Ermanaric 38.44

ermine 252.13
erne 249
Ernie 16.227
erode 98
erogeneity 16.333.1
erogenous 310.33
Eros 302
erose 305
erosion 261.92
erosive 485.6
erotema 17.210
erotesis 300.51
erotic 38.53
erotica 17.34
eroticism 242.35.16.5
erotogenic 38.32.1
erotology 16.108.4.15
erotomania 17.3.31.1
err 3
errancy 16.312
errand 143
errant 420.61
errantry 16.291
errata 17.337
erratic 38.49
erratum 242.26
Er Rif 163
erroneous 310.2.9
error 17.269
ersatz 333
Erse 297
erstwhile 219
erubescence 321.21
eruct 389
eructation 261.67
erudite 372
erudition 261.71
erumpent 420
erupt 426
eruption 261.88
eruptive 485
Erymanthus 310.72
eryngo 12.36
erysipelas 310.23
erysipeloid 97.5
erythema 17.210
erythrism 242.35
erythrite 372
erythroblast 430
erythrocyte 372.10
erythrocytic 38.52.3

erythropoiesis
300.51
Esau 9
escadrille 218
escalade 85
escalate 367.14
escalation
261.67.14
escalator 17.338
escallonia 17.3.36.2
escalope 276
escapade 85
escape 270
escapee 5.15
escapement 420
escapism 242.35
escapist 436.14
escapology
16.108.4.12
escarp 269
escarpment 420
eschalot 373.1
eschar 1
eschatology
16.108.4.15
escheat 370
eschew 15
escolar 1.9
Escorial 213
escort 374
escritoire 1
escrow 12
escudo 12.22
esculent 420.27
escutcheon 261
Esdraelon 254
esemplastic 38.68
Esher 17.325
Eskimo 12.48
esoteric 38.39
espadrille 218
esparto 12.73
especial 228
especially 16.131
Esperanto 12.83
espial 228.4
espionage 359
Espíritu Santo
12.83
esplanade 85.3
espousal 228.129
espouse 521
esprit 5
esprit de corps 9.2
espy 7

esquire 8
essay 2
essayist 436.1
essence 321.21
Essene 251
essential 228.96
Essequibo 12.5
Essex 498
establish 353
establishment
420.47
estancia 17.3.48
estate 367
esteem 234
ester 17.382
esterify 7.3.5
Esther 17.382
estimable 228.16
estimate 367.15,
371.19
estimation
261.67.15
Estonian 261.3.18
estop 276
estoppel 228.68
estovers 524
estrade 84
estragon 254.5
estrange 207
estranged 111
estrangement
420.38
estray 2
estreat 370
estuarial 228.3.10
estuarine 253.7
estuary 16.274.2
esurient 420.1.3
eta 17.338
etaerio 12.3
etalon 254.7
etamin 252.15
et cetera 17.293
etch 64
etchant 420
etching 265
eternal 228.58
eternity
16.333.16.1
etesian 261.3
ethane 247
ethanol 220
Ethelbert 381
Ethelred 86
ether 17

ethereal 228.3.11
etherealize
516.3.2.1
ethic 38
ethical 228.23
ethics 498
Ethiopia 17.3.37
Ethiopian 261.3.19
Ethiopic 38.37
ethmoid 97
ethnarch 33
ethnic 38
ethnocentrism
242.35
ethnogeny 16.229.2
ethnography
16.90.2
ethnology 16.108.4
ethology 16.108.4
ethonone 257
ethos 302
ethoxide 92.14
ethyl 218
ethylate 367.12
ethylene 251.2
ethylic 38.21
etiquette 368.4
Etna 17.244
Eton 261.98
Etonian 261.3.18
Etruria 17.3.42
Etruscan 261.17
étude 102
étui 5
etymology
16.108.4.9
etymon 254
Etzel 228
Euboea 17.2
eucalyptol 220
eucalyptus 310.71
eucharis 300.47
Eucharist 436.20
euchlorine 251.6
euchre 17.41
Euclid 91
eudemon 261.47
eudemonia 17.3.36
eudemonics 498.5
eudemonism
242.35.14
eudiometer
17.342.3.1
eugenic 38.32
eugenics 498.3

eugenol 220.3
euglena 17.230
euhemerism
242.35.15
eulogistic 38.70.1
eulogize 516.1
eulogy 16.108
Eumenides 513.4
eunuch 46
euonymus 310.28.2
eupatorium
242.2.17
eupatrid 91
eupepsia 17.3
euphausiid 91.2
euphemism 242.35
euphemistic
38.70.3
euphemize 516.4
euphonic 38.35
euphonious 310.2.9
euphonium
242.2.12
euphonize 516.7
euphony 16.237
euphorbia 17.3
euphoria 17.3.41
euphoric 38.41
euphotic 38.55
euphrasy 16.307
Euphrates 513.15
Euphrosyne 5.12
euphuism 242.35.4
euplastic 38.68
euploid 97
eupnoea 17.2
Eurasia 17.322
Eurasian 261.67.21
eureka 17.33
eurhythmic 38.30
eurhythmics 498
Euripides 513.4
Eurocommunism
242.35
Eurocrat 365.2
Eurodollar 17.168
Euromarket 371.7
Europa 17.257
Europe 281
European 261.2
Europeanize 516.7
europium 242.2.13
Eurovision
261.91.3
Eurus 310.49

Eurydice 16.300
eurypterid 91.27
eurytropic 38.37
Eusebius 310.2
eustatic 38.49
eutectic 38.60
Euterpe 16.246
euthanasia 17.3.59
euthenics 498.3
eutherian 261.3.22
eutrophic 38.13
evacuant 420.4
evacuate 367.2
evacuation
  261.67.2
evacuee 5
evade 85
evaginate 367.17.2
evaluate 367.2
evaluation 261.67.2
evanesce 296.3
evanescent
  420.67.2
evangelical
  228.23.6
evangelism
  242.35.9
evangelist 436.5
evangelistic 38.70
evangelize 516.2
Evans 551
evaporate 367.23
evaporation
  261.67.22
evaporite 372.8
evasion 261
evasive 485
eve 484
Eve 484
evection 261.77
Evelyn 252
even 261.113
evening 265
evenness 300.31
evens 551
evensong 266
event 410.3
eventful 226.11
eventide 92.12
eventual 228.9
eventuality
  16.333.8.2
eventually 16.131.1
eventuate 367.2
ever 17.411

Everest 436.20
evergreen 251
everlasting 265.74
evermore 9.9
evert 369.1
evertor 17.340
every 16.274
everybody 16.65
everyday 2
Everyman 261.48
everyone 259
everything 265
everywhere 4.7
Evesham 242
evict 387
eviction 261.78
evidence 321.5
evident 420.10
evidential 228.96.1
evidently 16.198
evil 228.119
evildoer 17.8
evilness 300.30
evince 317
eviscerate 367.23
evocation 261.67.6
evocative 485.15.2
evocator 17.338
evoke 42
evolute 380.1
evolution 261.75.1
evolutionary
  16.274.29
evolutionist 436.13
evolve 493
evzone 257
ewe 15
ewer 17.8
ex 496
exacerbate 367.4
exacerbation
  261.67.3
exact 382
exacting 265.70
exaction 261.76
exactitude 102.2
exactly 16.194
exactness 300
exaggerate 367.23
exaggerated
  91.34.7
exaggeration
  261.67.22
exalt 404
exaltation 261.67

exalted 91.44
exam 229
examen 248.2
examination
  261.67.18.3
examine 252.12
examinee 5.12
examiner 17.231.1
example 228.70
exanthema 17.210
exarate 367.23
exarch 33
exasperate 367.23
exasperation
  261.67.22
Excalibur 17.14
ex cathedra 17.286
excavate 367,
  367.37
excavation 261.67
excavator 17.338
exceed 89
exceeding 265.13
exceedingly 16.175
excel 215
excellence 321.12
Excellency 16.312
excellent 420.28
excelsior 9.1
except 422
excepting 265
exception 261.84
exceptional 228.63
exceptive 485.23
excerpt 423
excess 296
excessive 485.2
exchange 207
exchequer 17.31
excipient 420.1
excise 516
exciseman 261
excision 261.91
excitable 228.16.50
excitant 420
excitation
  261.67.27
excite 372
excited 91.39
excitement 420
exciter 17.343
exciting 265.67
excitor 17.343
exclaim 231

exclamation
  261.67.16
exclamatory
  16.274.43.5
exclave 482
exclosure 17.335
exclude 102
exclusion 261.93
exclusionist 436.13
exclusive 485.8
excogitate 367.30
excommunicate
  367.5
excommunication
  261.67.5
excoriate 367.1
excrement 420.31
excrescence 321.21
excrescent 420.67
excreta 17.341
excrete 370
excretion 261.70
excruciate 367.1
excruciating 265.64
exculpate 367
excurrent 420.64
excursion 261.69
excursionist 436.13
excursive 485.3
excursus 310
excusable
  228.16.65
excusatory
  16.274.43
excuse 309, 523
exeat 381.1
execrable 228.16
execrate 367.25
executant 420
execute 380
execution 261.75
executioner 17.239
executive 485
executor 17.350
executory
  16.274.42
executrix 498
exegesis 300.51
exegete 370
exegetic 38.50
exegetics 498.12
exemplar 17.196
exemplary 16.274
exemplify 7.3
exemplum 242

extemporaneous
310.2.6
extempore
16.274.31
extemporize 516.8
extend 131
extender 17.101
extendible
228.16.18
extensible
228.16.40
extension 261.82
extensity 16.333.31
extensive 485.9
extensor 17.314
extent 410
extenuate 367.2
exterior 17.3.39
exteriorize 516.8
exterminate
367.17.4
extermination
261.67.18.4
exterminator
17.338.7
extern 249
external 228.58
externalism
242.35.11.4
externality
16.333.8
externalize 516.3.6
extinct 392
extinction 261
extinctive 485.20
extinguish 353
extinguishable
228.16.43
extinguishant
420.74
extinguisher 17.326
extirpate 367
extol 223
extort 374
extortion 261.72
extortionate
371.28.2
extra 17
extract 382
extraction 261.76
extractive 485.16
extractor 17.353
extracurricular
17.174.6

extraditable
228.16.50
extradite 372.2
extradition
261.71.2
extrados 302
extragalactic 38.58
extramarital
228.102
extramural 228.75
extraneous 310.2.6
extranuclear 17.3
extraordinary
16.274.26
extrapolate 367.14
extrapolation
261.67.14
extrasensory
16.274.38
extraterrestrial
228.3.13
extraterritorial
228.3.12.1
extraterritoriality
16.333.8.1
extrauterine 253.7
extravagance 321.8
extravagant 420.18
extravaganza
17.445
extravasate 367
extravehicular
17.174.6
extreme 234
extremely 16.166
extremism 242.35
extremist 436
extremity 16.333
extricable
228.16.10
extricate 367.5
extrinsic 38
extrorse 303
extroversion
261.69.1
extrovert 369.2
extrude 102
extrusion 261.93
extrusive 485.8
exuberance 321.20
exuberant 420.65
exudation 261.67
exude 102
exult 406
exultant 420

exultation 261.67
exurbia 17.3.2
exuviae 5.2
exuviate 367.1
eyas 310.3
eye 7
eyeball 221
eyebath 453
eyebright 372
eyebrow 13
eyecup 279
eyed 92
eyeful 226
eyeglass 294
eyeglasses 515
eyehole 223
eyelash 349
eyeless 300
eyelet 371
eyelid 91
eyeliner 17.232
eyepiece 298
eyeshade 85
eyeshot 373
eyesight 372
eyesore 9
eyestrain 247
eyetooth 463
eyewash 354
eyewitness 300.38
eyra 17.271
eyrie 16.265
eyrir 6
Ezekiel 228.3

F

fa 1
fab 18
Fabergé 2
Fabian 261.3.1
Fabianism
242.35.14.1
fable 228.11
fabled 122
fabric 38
fabricate 367.5
fabrication
261.67.5
fabulist 436.6
fabulous 310.25

facade 84
face 295
facebar 1
faceless 300
facer 17.299
facet 371
facetiae 5.2
facetious 310.57
facetiousness
300.34
facial 228.91
facies 513.1
facile 219
facilitate 367.30.1
facility 16.333.9
facing 265.59
facsimile 16.120
fact 382
factice 300.65
faction 261.76
factional 228.63
factious 310
factitious 310.58
factitive 485.12
factor 17.353
factorial 228.3.12
factoring 265.58
factorize 516.8
factory 16.274.44
factotum 242.31
factual 228.9.4
facula 17.174.3
facultative 485.15
faculty 16.352
fad 83
faddish 353.1
fade 85
faded 91.6
fadge 191
fading 265.11
faecal 228
faeces 513
Faeroes 520
Faeroese 513.2
faff 157
fag 178
fagaceous 310.56
faggot 381
fahlband 128
Fahrenheit 372
faïence 315
fail 214
failing 265.27
faille 214
failure 17.433

fain 247
fainéant 420.1
faint 409
fainter 17.367
fainting 265
faintly 16.196
faintness 300
fair 4
Fairbanks 504
Fairfax 494
fairground 139
fairing 265.52
fairish 353.9
fairlead 89
fairly 16.117
fairness 300.22
fairway 2
fairy 16.264
fairyland 143.2
Faisal 228
faith 454
faithful 226
faithfulness 300.30
faithless 300
fake 34
faker 17.30
fakir 6
fa-la 1.7
Falange 206
falbala 17.176
falcate 367
falciform 238.1
falcon 261.16
falconer 17.239
falconet 368
falconine 253
falconry 16.284
falderal 212
faldstool 227
Falerii 7.1
Faliscan 261
Falkirk 36
Falkland 143
fall 221
fallacious 310.56.3
fallacy 16.307
fallal 212
fallen 261
faller 17.169
fallibility
  16.333.9.2
fallible 228.16
Fallopian 261.3.19
fallout 377
fallow 12.38

Falmouth 464
false 312
false-card 84
falsehood 101
falsetto 12.75
falsework 36
falsies 515
falsify 7.3
falsity 16.333
falter 17.363
Falun 259
Famagusta 17.388
fame 231
familial 228.3.4
familiar 17.3.21
familiarity
  16.333.20.1
familiarize 516.8
Familist 436.5
family 16.120
famine 252.12
famish 353
famous 310.27
famulus 310.25
fan 245
fanatic 38.49.5
fanatical 228.23.18
fanaticism
  242.35.16.4
fanaticize 516.10
fancied 91
fancier 17.3.48
fanciful 226
fancy 16.309
fancywork 36
fandangle 228.49
fandango 12.35
fanfare 4
fang 263
fanion 261.121
fanjet 368
fankle 228
fanlight 372
fanny 16.223
fanon 261.55
fantail 214
fan-tailed 112
fantasia 17.3.59
fantasize 516.11
fantast 430
fantastic 38.68
fantasy 16.307
Fanti 16.353
fantoccini 16.228
far 1

farad 103
Faraday 2.8
faradic 38.7
faradism 242.35
faradize 516
farandole 223.2
faraway 2.28
farce 294
farci 5
farcical 228.23
farcy 16.295
fardel 228
fare 4
Fareham 242.18
farewell 215
farina 17.230.1
farinaceous
  310.56.4
farinose 305
farl 213
farm 230
farmer 17.206
farmhouse 306
farming 265.35
farmland 143
farmstead 86
farmyard 84
Farnborough
  17.279
Farnham 242
faro 12.62
Farouk 45
farrago 12.26
farrier 17.3
farriery 16.274.1
farrow 12.60
far-sighted 91.39
far-sightedness
  300.28
fart 366
farther 17.401
farthermost 441
farthest 436
farthing 265
farthingale 214
fartlek 35
fasces 513
fascia 17.322
fasciation 261.67.1
fascicle 228.23
fascicule 227.1
fascinate 367.17.7
fascinating
  265.64.1

fascination
  261.67.18.8
fascine 251
fascism 242.35
fascist 436
fash 349
fashion 261.66
fashionable
  228.16.31
Fashoda 17.88
fast 431
fastback 32
fasten 261.61
fastener 17.239
fastening 265.46
fastidious 310.2.1
fastidiousness
  300.34.1
fastness 300.42
fat 365
fatal 228.99
fatalism 242.35.11
fatalist 436.7
fatalistic 38.70.2
fatality 16.333.8
fatback 32
fate 367
fated 91.34
fateful 226.7
Fates 335
fathead 86
father 17.401
fatherhood 101
father-in-law 9
fatherland 143.4
fatherless 300.13
fatherly 16.131
fathom 242
fathomable 228.16
fathomless 300
fatidic 38
fatigue 183
Fatima 17.211
fatling 265
fatness 300
fatso 12
fatted 91.32
fatten 261.94
fatty 16.327
fatuity 16.333.3
fatuous 310.4
faubourg 187
faucal 228
fauces 513
faucet 371

fault 404
faultless 300
faultlessness 300.33
faulty 16.351
faun 255
fauna 17.234
Fauré 2
Faust 442
Faustus 310
faux pas 1
faveolate 367.14
favonian 261.3.18
favour 17.410
favourable
228.16.35
favourite 371.35
favouritism
242.35.18
favus 310
Fawkes 500
fawn 255
fay 2
faze 509
fealty 16.352
fear 6
fearful 226
fearfully 16.129
fearless 300
fearlessness 300.33
fearnought 374
fearsome 242
feasible 228.16
feast 435
feat 370
feather 17.402
featherbedding
265.12
featherbrain 247
featherbrained 130
featheredge 194
feathering 265.58
featherstitch 67
featherweight
367.38
feathery 16.274
feature 17.55
featureless 300.13
feaze 513
febrific 38.12
febrifuge 204
febrile 219
febrility 16.333.9
February 16.274.2
feckless 300
fecula 17.174.4

feculent 420.27
fecund 143
fecundate 367
fecundity 16.333.7
fed 86
fedayee 5
federal 228.76
federalize 516.3.8
federate 367.23,
371.35
federation
261.67.22
fedora 17.276
fee 5
feeble 228
feeble-minded 91
feeble-mindedness
300.28
feebleness 300.30
feed 89
feedback 32
feedbag 178
feeder 17.82
feedlot 373
feel 217
feeler 17.165
feeling 265.29
feet 370
feeze 513
feign 247
feint 409
feldspar 1
felicitate 367.30
felicitation
261.67.27
felicitous 310.64
felicity 16.333.28
feline 253
fell 215
fellah 17.163
fellatio 12.3.6
feller 17.163
Fellini 16.228.1
fellmonger 17.143
felloe 12.40
fellow 12.40
fellowship 274
felo de se 5.20
felon 261.40
felonious 310.2.9
felonry 16.284
felony 16.237.5
felsite 372
felt 402
felting 265

felucca 17.39
female 214
feme 232
feminine 252.17
femininity
16.333.17
feminism 242.35.13
feminist 436.11
feminize 516.6
femoral 228.76.2
femur 17.210
fen 248
fence 316
fencer 17.314
fencing 265
fend 131
fender 17.101
fenestella 17.163
fenestrated 91.34
fenestration
261.67.25
Fenian 261.3.16
fennec 35
fennel 228.57
fenny 16.226
Fenrir 6
Fenriswolf 175
Fens 546
fenugreek 37
feral 228
ferbam 229
fer-de-lance 315
Ferdinand 128
feretory 16.274.41
Fergana 17.226
feria 17.3.39
ferial 228.3.11
ferity 16.333.21
Fermanagh 17.225
ferment 410.2
fermentation
261.67.32
Fermi 16.214
fermium 242.2
fern 249
fernery 16.274.24
ferocious 310.60
ferocity 16.333.30.5
Ferrara 17.268
Ferrari 16.261
ferrate 367
ferreous 310.2
ferret 371.31
ferriage 197
ferric 38.39

Ferris 300
ferrite 372
ferritin 252.23
ferrocene 251.9
ferrochromium
242.2.9
ferrocyanide 92.4
ferromagnetism
242.35.18
ferrosilicon 261.13
ferrous 310.44
ferruginous 310.33
ferrule 227
ferry 16.262
fertile 219
fertility 16.333.9
fertilization
261.67.36
fertilize 516.2
fertilizer 17.441
ferula 17.174
ferule 227
fervent 420.82
fervid 91.55
fervour 17.412
fescue 15
fesse 296
festal 228.113
fester 17.382
festival 228.120
festive 485.24
festivity 16.333.35
festoon 260
festoonery
16.274.28
festschrift 398
feta 17.339
fetal 228.101
fetation 261.67
fetch 64
fetching 265
fête 367
feticide 92.7
fetid 91.35
fetish 353
fetishism 242.35
fetlock 40
fetor 17.341
fetter 17.339
fettle 228.100
fettucine 16.228
fetus 310.63
feud 102
feudal 228.37

feudalism 242.35.11
feudality 16.333.8
feudalize 516.3
feudatory 16.274.43
feudist 436
feuilleton 254
fever 17.413
fevered 103
feverfew 15
feverish 353.11
feverishness 300.35
few 15
fey 2
fez 510
Fezzan 246
fiancé 2
Fianna fail 222.1
fiasco 12
Fiat 381
fiat 381.2
fib 24
fibber 17.14
fibre 17.15
fibreboard 95.1
fibreglass 294
fibriform 238.1
fibril 218
fibrillation 261.67.12
fibrinogen 261.39
fibrinolysin 252.21
fibrocement 410.1
fibroid 97
fibroin 252.1
fibroma 17.215
fibrosis 300.55
fibrositis 300.62
fibrous 310
fibula 17.174.2
fiche 352
fichu 15
fickle 228.23
fickleness 300.30
fictile 219
fiction 261.78
fictional 228.63
fictionalize 516.3.7
fictitious 310.58
fictive 485.18
fid 91
fiddle 228.32
fiddle-de-dee 5

fiddle-faddle 228.31
fiddlehead 86
fiddler 17.186
fiddlestick 38
fiddlesticks 498
fiddling 265
fideicommissum 242.24
fideism 242.35
fidelity 16.333
fidget 371
fidgety 16.333
fiduciary 16.274.1
fie 7
fief 162
field 115
fielder 17.94
fieldfare 4
fieldmouse 306
fieldpiece 298
fieldwork 36
fiend 133
fiendish 353
fierce 299
fieri facias 310.2.16
fiery 16.267
fiesta 17.382.1
FIFA 17.113
Fife 164
fife 164
fifteen 251
fifteenth 469
fiftieth 458
fifty 16.347
fig 184
fight 372
fighter 17.343
fighting 265.67
figment 420
figurant 420
figurate 371.34
figuration 261.67.22
figurative 485.15.10
figure 17.129
figurehead 86.5
figurine 251.7
Fijian 261.2
filament 420.35
filar 17.167
filaria 17.3.38
filariasis 300.57.1
filature 17.62

filbert 381
filch 76
file 219
filecard 84
filet mignon 254.12
filial 228.3.4
filiate 367.1.2
filiation 261.67.1.1
filibeg 181
filibuster 17.388
filicide 92.7
filiform 238.1
filigree 5.18
filings 552
Filipino 12.54
fill 218
filler 17.166
fillet 371.16
filling 265.30
fillip 274
fillister 17.384
filly 16.120
film 244
filmography 16.90.2
filmset 368
filoplume 241
filose 305
filoselle 215
fils 311
filter 17.362
filth 466
filthiness 300.23
filthy 16
filtrate 367
filtration 261.67
filum 242.9
fimble 228
fimbria 17.3
fimbriate 371.1
fin 252
finable 228.16.30
finagle 228.44
final 228.61
finale 16.113
finalism 242.35.11
finalist 436.7
finality 16.333.8
finalize 516.3
finally 16.131
finals 539
finance 314
financial 228.95
financier 17.3.48

finch 80
find 135
finder 17.103
finding 265.21
fine 2
fine 253
Fine Gael 214
fineness 300
finery 16.274.27
finespun 259
finesse 296.2
finfoot 379
finger 17.141
fingerboard 95.1
fingering 265.58
fingerling 265
fingermark 33
fingernail 214
fingerprint 412
fingerstall 221
fingertip 274
finicky 16.25
fining 265.44
finis 300.23
finish 353.7
finisher 17.326
Finistère 4
Finisterre 4
finite 372
fink 52
Finland 143
Finn 252
finnan 261.56
finnan haddie 16.57
finned 134
finner 17.231
Finnic 38.34
Finnish 353.7
Finnmark 33
finny 16.229
fino 12.54
Finsteraarhorn 255
fiorin 252.20
fipple 228.66
fir 3
Firdausi 16.304
fire 8
firearm 230
fireball 221
firebird 87
firebomb 237
firebox 499
firebrand 128
firebrat 365

371

firebreak

firebreak 34
firebrick 38
firebug 189
firecracker 17.28
firedamp 285
firedog 185
firedrake 34
firefly 7
fireguard 84
fireman 261
fireplace 295
fireproof 170
fireside 92
firetrap 268
firewarden 261.27
firewater 17.345
fireweed 89
firewood 101
firework 36
fireworks 497
firing 265.54
firkin 252
firm 233
firmament 420.35
firmness 300
firmware 4
firry 16.263
first 434
first-born 255
first-footer 17.350
first-footing 265
firstling 265
first-rate 367
firth 456
fiscal 228
fish 353
fishbolt 405
fishbowl 223
fisher 17.326
fisherman 261.52.1
fishery 16.274
fishfinger 17.141
fishgig 184
fishing 265.63
fishmonger 17.143
fishnet 368
fishtail 214
fishwife 164
fishy 16.322
fissile 219.2
fission 261.71
fissiped 86.6
fissure 17.326
fist 436
fistic 38.70

fistmele 217
fistula 17.174
fit 371
fitch 67
fitful 226
fitly 16.189
fitment 420.49
fitness 300.38
fitted 91.38
fitter 17.342
fitting 265.66
Fittipaldi 16.73
Fitzgerald 122.1
five 486
fivefold 120
fivepenny 16.237
fiver 17.415
fives 554
fix 498
fixate 367
fixation 261.67
fixative 485.15
fixedly 16.148
fixer 17.427
fixity 16.333
fixture 17.76
fizz 515
fizzle 228
fizzy 16.396
fjeld 113
fjord 95
flab 18
flabbergast 431.1
flabbergasted 91.51
flabbiness 300.23
flabby 16.5
flabellate 371.15
flabellum 242.8
flaccid 91.28
flag 178
flagellant 420
flagellate 367.12, 371.16
flagellation 261.67.12
flagellum 242.8
flageolet 368
flagging 265
flaggy 16.91
flagitious 310.58
flagman 261
flagon 261.30
flagpole 223
flagrancy 16.312
flagrant 420

flagship 274
flagstaff 158
flagstone 257
flail 214
flair 4
flak 32
flake 34
flaky 16.21
flam 229
flambé 2.5
flambeau 12
Flamborough 17.279
flamboyance 321
flamboyant 420.3
flame 231
flamen 248.2
flamenco 12.13
flameproof 170
flaming 265
flamingo 12.36
Flamininus 310.34
Flaminius 310.2.8
flammable 228.16.26
Flamsteed 89
flan 245
Flanders 524
flange 206
flank 51
flanker 17.43
flannel 228.55
flannelette 368
flannels 539
flap 268
flapdoodle 228.37
flapjack 32
flapper 17.247
flare 4
flash 349
flashback 32
flashboard 95
flashcube 30
flasher 17.321
flashing 265
flashlight 372
flashover 17.417
flashy 16.319
flask 56
flasket 371
flat 365
flatfish 353
flatfoot 379
flat-footed 91

flat-footedness 300.28
flathead 86
flatiron 261.4
flatlet 371
flatly 16.186
flatmate 367
flatness 300
flats 333
flatten 261.94
flatter 17.336
flatterer 17.279
flattering 265.58
flattery 16.274
flattish 353
flattop 276
flatulence 321
flatulent 420.27
flatus 310.62
flatworm 233
Flaubert 4
flaunch 81
flaunt 415
flaunty 16.358
flautist 436
flavescent 420.67.3
flavine 252
flavone 257
flavorous 310.50
flavour 17.410
flavourful 226
flavouring 265.58.1
flavourless 300.13
flaw 9
flawless 300
flax 494
flaxen 261
flaxseed 89
flay 2
flea 5
fleabag 178
fleabane 247
fleabite 372
fleam 234
fleapit 371
fléchette 368
fleck 35
fled 86
fledge 194
fledgling 265
fledgy 16.101
flee 5
fleece 298
fleecy 16.299
fleet 370

372

fleeting 265
Fleetwood 101
Fleming 265
Flemish 353
flense 316
flesh 351
flesher 17.323
fleshly 16.185
fleshpots 341
fleshy 16.321
fletch 64
Fletcher 17.53
fletcher 17.53
fleur-de-lis 5.9
fleurette 368
fleuron 254
flew 15
flews 523
flex 496
flexibility
16.333.9.2
flexible 228.16
flexion 261.77
flexitime 236
flexor 17.426
flexuous 310.4
fley 2
flibbertigibbet
371.5
flick 38
flicker 17.34
flight 372
flightless 300
flighty 16.334
flimflam 229
flimsy 16.403
flinch 80
flincher 17.71
fling 265
Flint 412
flint 412
Flintshire 6
flinty 16.356
flip 274
flip-flop 276
flippant 420.56
flipper 17.253
flipping 265
flirt 369
flirtation 261.67
flirtatious 310.56
flit 371
flitch 67
flite 372
flitter 17.342

flittermouse 306
flivver 17.414
float 376
floater 17.347
floating 265
floaty 16.339
floccose 305
flocculate 367.13.3
floccule 227
flocculent 420.27
flocculus 310.25
floccus 310.11
flock 40
Flodden 261.26
floe 12
flog 185
flogging 265.23
flong 266
flood 100
floodgate 367
floodlight 372
floor 9
floorage 197
floorboard 95
flooring 265.55
floozy 16.402
flop 276
floppy 16.250
Flora 17.276
flora 17.276
floral 228.74
Florence 321.18
Florentine 253
florescence 321.21
floret 371
floriated 91.34.1
floribunda 17.108
florid 91.26
Florida 17.83
florigen 261.37
florin 252.18
florist 436.18
floristic 38.70
floristics 498
flory 16.269
flos ferri 16.262
floss 302
flossy 16.302
flotage 197.13
flotation 261.67.28
flotilla 17.166
flotsam 242
flounce 319
flouncing 265
flounder 17.107

flour 14
flourish 353.10
floury 16.274
flout 377
flow 12
flowage 197
flower 14
flowerbed 86.1
floweret 371
flowering 265.57
flowerless 300
flowerpot 373
flowery 16.274
flown 257
flu 15
fluctuant 420.4
fluctuate 367.2
fluctuation
261.67.2
flue 15
fluency 16.312
fluent 420.5
fluff 168
fluffiness 300.23
fluffy 16.88
flugelhorn 255
fluid 91.3
fluidics 498
fluidity 16.333.5
fluidize 516
fluke 45
fluky 16.32
flume 241
flummery 16.274
flummox 503
flung 267
flunk 54
flunky 16.39
fluoresce 296
fluorescence 321.21
fluorescent 420.67
fluoric 38.42
fluoridate 367.8
fluoridation
261.67.7
fluoride 92
fluorinate 367.17
fluorine 251
fluorometer
17.342.3
fluoroscope 278.1
fluorspar 1
flurry 16.272
flush 356
Flushing 265

fluster 17.388
flute 380
fluted 91.42
fluter 17.351
fluting 265
flutter 17.349
fluvial 228.3.17
flux 502
fluxion 261.79
fly 7
flyaway 2.28
flyblown 257
flybook 44
flyby 7
flyer 17.4
flying 265.3
flyleaf 162
flyover 17.417
flypaper 17.249
Flysch 353
flyspeck 35
flytrap 268
flyweight 367
flywheel 217
foal 223
foam 239
foamy 16.219
fob 26
focal 228.26
focus 310.12
fodder 17.85
foe 12
foeman 261.49
fog 185
fogbound 139
fogdog 185
fogged 106
foggy 16.94
foghorn 255
fogy 16.96
föhn 249
foible 228
foil 222
Foism 242.35.3
foison 261.128
foist 440
Fokker 17.36
fold 120
foldaway 2.28
folder 17.97
foliaceous 310.56
foliage 197
foliar 17.3.22
foliate 371.1
foliated 91.34.1

foliation 261.67.1.2
folio 12.3.3
foliose 305.1
folium 242.2.7
folk 42
Folkestone 261
folklore 9
folkloric 38.41
folkmoot 380
follicle 228.23.8
follicular 17.174.6
folliculin 252.10
follow 12.43
follower 17.6
following 265.4
folly 16.122
Fomalhaut 376
foment 410.2
fomentation
261.67.32
fond 136
Fonda 17.104
fondant 420.15
fondle 228
fondness 300
fondue 15
font 414
Fontainebleau 12
fontanelle 215
Fonteyn 247.11
Foochow 13
food 102
foodstuff 168
fool 227
foolery 16.274
foolhardiness
300.23
foolhardy 16.58
foolish 353
foolishness 300.35
foolproof 170
foolscap 268
foot 379
footage 197
football 221
footballer 17.169
footboard 95
footboy 11
footbridge 197
footfall 221
footgear 6
foothill 218
foothold 120
footing 265
footle 228.108

footlights 340
footling 265
footloose 309
footman 261
footmark 33
footnote 376
footpace 295
footpad 83
footpath 453
footplate 367
footprint 412
footrest 433
foots 345
footsie 16.318
footslog 185
footsore 9
footstall 221
footstep 271
footstool 227
footway 2
footwear 4
footwork 36
footy 16.342
foo yong 266
foozle 228.128
fop 276
foppery 16.274
foppish 353
for 9
forage 197
foramen 248.2
forasmuch 72
foray 2
forbade 83
forbear 4
forbearance 321
forbid 91.4
forbiddance 321.5
forbidden 261.24
forbidding 265
forbore 9
forby 7
force 303
forceful 226.6
force majeure 3
forcemeat 370
forceps 327
forcible 228.16
ford 95
fordable 228.16.16
fore 9
forearm 230
forebear 4
forebode 98
foreboding 265.16

forebrain 247
forecast 431
forecaster 17.380
foreclose 520
foreclosure 17.335
forecourse 303
forecourt 374
foredeck 35
foredoom 241
forefather 17.401
forefinger 17.141
forefront 419
forego 12
foregoing 265.4
foregone 254
foreground 139
foregut 378
forehand 128
forehanded 91.12
forehead 91.26
forehock 40
foreign 252.18
foreigner 17.231
foreignism
242.35.13
forejudge 203
foreknew 15
foreknow 12
foreknowledge
197.2
foreland 143
foreleg 181
forelimb 235
forelock 40
foreman 261
foremast 431
foremost 441
forename 231
forenamed 124
forenoon 260
forensic 38
forensics 498
foreordain 247
forepart 366
forepaw 9
forepeak 37
foreplay 2
forequarter 17.345
forereach 66
forerun 259
forerunner 17.237
foresail 214
foresaw 9
foresee 5.21

foreseeable
228.16.1
foreseen 251
foreshadow 12
foresheet 370
foreshock 40
foreshore 9
foreshorten
261.102
foresight 372
foreskin 252
forest 436.18
forestall 221
forestation 261.67
forested 91.53
forester 17.384
forestry 16.293
foretaste 432
foretell 215.3
forethought 374
foretime 236
foretold 120
foretooth 463
foretop 276
forever 17.411
forevermore 9.9
forewarn 255
forewent 410
forewind 134
forewing 265
foreword 87
foreyard 84
forfeit 371
forfeiture 17.56
forfend 131
forficate 371.9
forgather 17.400
forgave 482
forge 200
forger 17.153
forgery 16.274
forget 368
forgetful 226.8
forgetfulness
300.30
forget-me-not 373
forgettable
228.16.46
forgivable 228.16
forgive 485
forgiven 261.114
forgiveness 300.43
forgiving 265.80
forgot 373
forgotten 261.101

forjudge 203
fork 41
forlorn 255
form 238
formal 212
formal 228.53
formaldehyde 92
formalin 252.11
formalism
242.35.11
formality
16.333.8.5
formalize 516.3
format 365
formation 261.67
formative 485.15.6
forme 238
former 17.214
formerly 16.131
formic 38
Formica 17.35
formicary 16.274.4
formication
261.67.5
formidable
228.16.15
formless 300
Formosa 17.306
formula 17.174
formulaic 38.1
formulary
16.274.18
formulate 367.13
formulation
261.67.13
formulism
242.35.10
formwork 36
Fornax 494
fornenst 447
fornicate 367.5
fornication
261.67.5
fornix 498
forsake 34
forsaken 261.11
forsook 44
forsooth 463
forswear 4
forsworn 255
forsythia 17.3
fort 374
fortalice 300.13
forte 16.336
fortepiano 12

forth 460
Forth 460
forthcoming 265.38
forthright 372
forthwith 476
fortieth 458
fortification
261.67.5.1
fortify 7.3
fortis 300.63
fortissimo 12.48
fortitude 102.2
fortnight 372
fortnightly 16.190
FORTRAN 245
fortress 300
fortuitism
242.35.18
fortuitous 310.64
fortuity 16.333.3
Fortuna 17.238
fortunate 371.28.1
fortunately 16.189
fortune 260.5
fortune-teller
17.163
fortune-telling
265.28
forty 16.336
forum 242.20
forward 103.8
forwarder 17.92
forwardness 300
forwards 531
forwent 410
fossa 17.304
fosse 302
fossette 368
fossil 228.86
fossiliferous
310.50.2
fossilize 516.2
fossorial 228.3.12
foster 17.385
fosterage 197
fosterling 265
Fotheringhay 2.10
foudroyant 420.3
fought 374
foul 224
foulard 84
Foulness 296
foulness 300
found 139
foundation 261.67

founder 17.107
foundling 265
foundry 16
fount 418
fountain 252
fountainhead 86.4
four 9
fourchette 368
Fourdrinier 17.3.34
fourfold 120
Fourier 2.1
fourpence 321
fourpenny 16.237
four-poster 17.387
fourragère 4
fourscore 9
foursome 242
foursquare 4
fourteen 251
fourteenth 469
fourth 460
fovea 17.3.55
Fowey 11
fowl 224
Fowler 17.172
fowling 265.33
fox 499
foxfire 8
foxglove 489
foxhole 223
foxhound 139
foxing 265
foxtail 214
foxtrot 373
foxy 16.389
foyer 2
Fra 1
fracas 1
fraction 261.76
fractional 228.63
fractionate 367.18
fractionize 516.7
fractious 310
fracture 17.63
frae 2
frag 178
fragile 219
fragility 16.333.9
fragment 410
fragment 420
fragmental 228.110
fragmentary
16.274.48
fragmentation
261.67.32

fragrance 321
fragrant 420
frail 214
fraise 509
framboesia 17.3.60
frame 231
frameless 300
framer 17.207
framework 36
franc 51
France 315
franchise 516
Francis 300
Franciscan 261
francium 242.2
francolin 252.9
Franconian
261.3.18
Francophile 219.1
Francophobe 28
Francophobia
17.3.4
Francophone 257
franger 17.245
frangible 228.16.21
frangipane 247
frangipani 16.224
frank 51
Frank 51
frankalmoign 256
Frankenstein 253
Frankfurt 381
frankfurter 17.340
frankincense 316
Frankish 353
franklin 252
frankly 16.144
frankness 300
frankpledge 194
frantic 38.62
frap 268
frappé 2
Fraser 17.439
frass 293
fratchy 16.46
frater 17.338
fraternal 228.58
fraternity
16.333.16
fraternize 516.7
fratricide 92.7
Frau 13
fraud 95
fraudulent 420.27
fraught 374

fudge 203
fuel 228.10
fug 189
fugacious 310.56
fugacity 16.333.25
fugal 228.48
fugitive 485.12
fugue 190
fuguist 436
Fuji 5
Fukien 248
Fukuoka 17.38
Fula 17.175
fulcrum 242
fulfil 218
fulfilment 420
fulgent 420.21
fulgurant 420
fulgurate 367.22
fulgurating 265.64
fulguration 261.67.21
Fulham 242.10
fuliginous 310.33
full 226
fullback 32
full-blooded 91.11
full-blown 257
fuller 17.174
full-frontal 228.112
fullness 300
full-time 236
full-timer 17.212
fully 16.129
fully-fledged 109
fulminant 420.53
fulminate 367.17
fulmination 261.67.18
fulsome 242
fulvous 310
fumarole 223.3
fumatorium 242.2.17
fumatory 16.274.43
fumble 228
fumbler 17.180
fume 241
fumigant 420.17
fumigate 367.10
fumigation 261.67.10
fumitory 16.274.41
fun 259
funambulist 436.6

function 261.80
functional 228.63
functionalism 242.35.11.5
functionary 16.274.29
fund 140
fundament 420.35
fundamental 228.110.3
fundamentalism 242.35.11.6
fundi 5
fundus 310
Fundy 16.80
funeral 228.76
funerary 16.274.32
funereal 228.3.11
funfair 4
fungal 228
fungi 7
fungicide 92.7
fungiform 238.1
fungoid 97
fungous 310
fungus 310
funicle 228.23
funicular 17.174.6
funiculus 310.25.2
funk 54
funky 16.39
funnel 228
funny 16.235
fur 3
furan 245
furbelow 12.42
furbish 353
furcate 367
furcula 17.174.5
furfuraceous 310.56
furious 310.2.14
furl 216
furlong 266
furlough 12
furnace 300
Furness 300
furnish 353
furnisher 17.326
furnishing 265.63
furnishings 552
furniture 17.56
furor 9
furore 16.269
furphy 16.83

furred 87
furrier 17.3
furriery 16.274.1
furring 265.51
furrow 12
furry 16.263
further 17.403
furtherance 321.20
furthermore 9.9
furthermost 441
furthest 436
furtive 485.11
furtiveness 300.43
furuncle 228.30
furunculosis 300.55.3
fury 16.270
furze 511
fusain 247
fuse 523
fusee 5
fusel 228.128
fuselage 359
Fushun 259
fusible 228.16.65
fusiform 238.1
fusile 219
fusilier 6
fusillade 85
fusion 261.93
fuss 307
fussiness 300.23
fusspot 373
fussy 16.305
fustanella 17.163
fustian 261.3.27
fustic 38
fusty 16.368
futhark 33
futile 219
futilitarian 261.3.21.2
futility 16.333.9
futtock 46
future 17.61
futurism 242.35.15
futuristic 38.70.5
futurity 16.333.23
futurology 16.108.4.13
fuzz 522
fuzzy 16.401
fyke 39
Fylde 117
fyrd 90

G

Ga 1
gab 18
gabble 228
gabbler 17.177
gabby 16.5
gabelle 215
gaberdine 251.1
gabfest 433
gabion 261.3.1
gabionade 85.3
gable 228.11
gabled 122
gablet 371
Gabon 254
Gabor 9
Gaborone 16.233
Gabriel 228.3
gaby 16.7
gad 83
gadabout 377.1
gadfly 7
gadget 371
gadgeteer 6
gadgetry 16.285
Gadhelic 38.20
gadid 91.6
gadoid 97
gadolinite 372.5
gadolinium 242.2.11
gadroon 260
Gael 214
Gaelic 38
gaff 157
gaffe 157
gaffer 17.110
gag 178
gaga 1
Gagauzi 16.397
gage 193
gagger 17.123
gaggle 228.43
gaiety 16.344
gaillardia 17.3.6
gaily 16.114
gain 247
gainer 17.227
gainful 226.4
gainly 16.170
gainsay 2

Gainsborough 17.279
gait 367
gaiter 17.338
Gaitskell 218
Gaius 310.3
gal 212
gala 17.161
galactagogue 185.2
galactic 38.58
galactopoietic 38.50
galactose 520
galago 12.26
galah 1.9
Galahad 83
galangal 228.49
galantine 251
Galápagos 310
galatea 17.2
Galatia 17.322
Galatians 551.1
galaxy 16.390
galbanum 242.16
Galbraith 454
gale 214
galea 17.3.18
Galen 261
galena 17.230
galenical 228.23.11
Galenism 242.35.13
Galibi 16.10
Galilean 261.2.2
Galilee 5.8
galilee 5.8
Galileo 12.1
galingale 214
galiot 381.1
galipot 373
gall 221
gallant 407, 420.24
gallantry 16.291
Galle 17.161
galleass 293.1
galleon 261.3
gallery 16.274.15
galley 16.112
gallfly 7
galliambic 38.5
galliard 103
Gallic 38.19
Gallicanism 242.35.14.2
Gallice 16.300

Gallicism 242.35.16.1
Gallicize 516.10
galligaskins 548
gallimaufry 16.280
gallinaceous 310.56.4
galling 265.31
gallinule 227
Gallipoli 16.131.5
gallipot 373
gallium 242.2
gallivant 407.1
galliwasp 292
gallnut 378
galloglass 294
gallon 261
gallonage 197
galloon 260.1
gallop 281
galloping 265
gallous 310
Galloway 2.28
gallows 520.1
gallstone 257
Gallup 281
galluses 515
galoot 380.1
galop 281
galore 9.8
galoshes 515
Galsworthy 16.375
galumph 177
galvanic 38.31
galvanism 242.35.14
galvanize 516.7
galvanometer 17.342.3.3
galvanoscope 278.1
galvo 12
Galway 2
galyak 32
gam 229
gambado 12.17
gambeson 261.65
Gambetta 17.339
Gambia 17.3.5
gambier 6
gambit 371
gamble 228.17
gambler 17.179
gambling 265
gamboge 201
gambol 228.17

game 231
gamecock 40
gamekeeper 17.252
gamelan 245.2
gamely 16.165
gamesmanship 274.2
gamesome 242
gamete 370
gametophore 9.6
gamic 38.24
gamin 252.12
gamine 251
gaming 265
gamma 17.205
gammadion 261.3.3
gammer 17.205
gammon 261.44
gammy 16.210
gamp 285
gamut 381
gamy 16.212
gan 245
gander 17.98
Gandhi 16.77
Gandhiism 242.35.2
ganef 171
gang 263
gangbang 263
ganger 17.245
Ganges 513
gangland 143
gangling 265
ganglion 261.3
gangplank 51
gangrene 251
gangrenous 310.33
gangster 17
Gangtok 40
gangue 263
gangway 2
ganister 17.384
gannet 371.22
gansey 16.404
gantry 16.287
Ganymede 89
gaol 214
gap 268
gape 270
gapes 323
gar 1
garage 359
Garamond 136

garb 19
garbage 197
garble 228
Garbo 12
Garda 17.78
garden 261
gardener 17.240
gardenia 17.3.33
gardening 265.46
Gardiner 17.240
garfish 353
garganey 16.237
Gargantua 17.7.2
gargantuan 261.7
garget 371
gargle 228
gargoyle 222
Garibaldi 16.75
garibaldi 16.75
garish 353.9
garland 143
garlic 38
garlicky 16.25
garment 420
garner 17.226
garnet 371
garnierite 372.8
garnish 353
garnishee 5
garnishment 420.47
garniture 17.56
garotte 373
garpike 39
garret 371
Garrick 38.38
garrison 261.65.1
garrulous 310.25
garrya 17.3
garter 17.337
garth 453
Gary 16.260
gas 293
gasbag 178
gasconade 85.3
Gascony 16.237
gaseous 310.2
gash 349
gasholder 17.97
gasiform 238.1
gasify 7.3.6
Gaskell 228
gasket 371
gaskin 252
gaslight 372

gasman 261
gasolier 6
gasoline 251.3
gasometer 17.342.3
gasp 290
Gaspé 2
gasser 17.298
gassy 16.294
gastralgia 17.3.16
gastralgic 38
gastrectomy
16.222.5
gastric 38
gastritis 300.62
gastroenteric 38.39
gastroenteritis
300.62.5
gastroenterology
16.108.4.13
gastroenterostomy
16.222.6
gastrolith 458
gastrology 16.108.4
gastronome 239
gastronomer
17.218.1
gastronomic
38.29.1
gastronomical
228.23.9
gastronomy
16.222.3
gastropod 94.1
gastroscope 278.1
gastrostomy
16.222.6
gastrotomy
16.222.4
gastrotrich 38
gastrula 17.174
gastrulation
261.67.13
gasworks 497
gate 367
gateau 12.72
gate-crash 349
gate-crasher 17.321
gatefold 120
gatehouse 306
gatekeeper 17.252
gatepost 441
Gateshead 86
gateway 2
Gath 452
gather 17.400

gathering 265.58
Gatling 265
gauche 355
gaucherie 5.17
gaucho 12
gaud 95
gaudery 16.274
Gaudi 16.68
gaudy 16.66
gauge 193
gauger 17.146
Gauhati 16.328
Gaul 221
Gauleiter 17.343
Gaulish 353
Gaullism 242.35
Gaullist 436
gaultheria 17.3.39
gaunt 415
gauntlet 371
gauntness 300
gaur 14
gauss 306
Gautama 17.218
gauze 518
gauzy 16.397
gavage 359
gave 482
gavel 228.117
gavelkind 135
gavial 228.3
gavotte 373
gawk 41
gawky 16.28
gawp 277
gay 2
Gay Gordons 551
Gay-Lussac 32
Gaynor 17.227
Gaza 17.438
Gazankulu 15.4
gaze 509
gazebo 12.5
gazelle 215
gazctte 368.9
gazetteer 6
Gaziantep 271
gazpacho 12
gazump 289
gean 251
geanticline 253.4
gear 6
gearbox 499
gearing 265.53
gearshift 398

gearwheel 217
gecko 12.9
gedact 383
gee 5
gee-gee 5
geek 37
geepound 139
geese 298
geest 435
geezer 17.440
gegenschein 253
Gehenna 17.228
Geiger 17.130
geisha 17.322
gel 215
gelada 17.92
gelatin 252
gelatine 251.11
gelatinize 516.6.1
gelatinoid 97.8.1
gelatinous 310.33
gelation 261.67.12
geld 113
Gelderland 143.4
gelding 265
gelid 91.17
gelignite 372.7
gelsemium 242.2.8
gelt 402
gem 232
Gemini 7.10
gemma 17.208
gemmulation
261.67.13
gemology 16.108.4
gemot 376
gemsbok 40
gemstone 257
gen 248
genappe 268
gendarme 230
gendarmerie
16.274.20
gender 17.101
gene 251
genealogist 436.4.1
genealogy 16.108.2
genera 17.279
generable
228.16.35
general 228.76
generalissimo 12.48
generalist 436.7
generality
16.333.8.9

generalization
261.67.36
generalize 516.3.8
generally 16.131
generate 367.23.1
generation
261.67.22.2
generative
485.15.10
generator 17.338.9
generatrix 498.9
generic 38.39
generosity
16.333.30.5
generous 310.50
genesis 300.52.4
genet 371
genetic 38.50.4
geneticist 436.21
genetics 498.12
Geneva 17.413
Genevan 261.113
Genevieve 484
Genghis Khan 246
genial 228.2,
228.3.6
geniality 16.333.8.1
genic 38.32
geniculate 371.17.2
genie 16.228
genii 7.1
genip 274
genipap 268
genital 228.102
genitalia 17.3.18
genitalic 38.19.1
genitals 539
genitive 485.12
genitor 17.342
genitourinary
16.274.26
genius 310.2.7
genizah 17.440
Genoa 17.6
genoa 17.6
genocide 92.8
Genoese 513.2
genome 239
genotype 275.1
gens 546
gent 410
genteel 217
gentian 261.82
gentianella 17.163
Gentile 219.6

gentility 16.333.9
gentle 228.110
gentlefolk 42
gentleman 261
gentlemanly 16.174
gentleness 300.30
gentlewoman
   261.50
gently 16.197
gentry 16.288
genu 15
genuflect 385
genuflection 261.77
genuine 252
genus 310.32
geocentric 38.47
geochronology
   16.108.4.11
geode 98
geodesic 38
geodesy 16.300.1
geodetic 38.50
geognosy 16.307.3
geographical
   228.23.3
geography
   16.90.2.1
geoid 97.1
geological 228.23.5
geologize 516.1
geology 16.108.4.1
geomagnetism
   242.35.18
geomancy 16.309
geometer
   17.342.3.1
geometric 38.46
geometrid 91
geometry
   16.285.2.1
geomorphic 38.14
geomorphology
   16.108.4
geophagism
   242.35.8
geophagy 16.108.1
geophysics 498
geophyte 372
geoponic 38.35
geoponics 498.5
Geordie 16.66
George 200
georgette 368
Georgia 17.153
Georgian 261

georgic 38
Georgie 16.105
geostatic 38.49.7
geostrophic 38.13
geosyncline 253.5
geotaxis 300.70
geotectonic 38.35
gerah 17.272
Gerald 122.1
geranial 228.3.5
geraniol 220.1
geranium 242.2.10
geratology
   16.108.4.15
gerbil 218
gerent 420.61
gerenuk 44
geriatric 38.45
geriatrician
   261.71.6
geriatrics 498.8
germ 233
German 261
germander 17.98
germane 247
Germanic 38.31
Germanism
   242.35.14
germanium
   242.2.10
Germanize 516.7
Germanophile
   219.1
Germanophilia
   17.3.21.2
Germanophobe 28
Germanophobia
   17.3.4
Germany 16.237
germicide 92.7
germinal 228.60
germinant 420.53.1
germinate 367.17.4
germination
   261.67.18.4
Germiston 261.107
Geronimo 12.48
gerontocracy
   16.307.5
gerontology
   16.108.4.16
gerrymander 17.98
Gershwin 252
gerund 143
gerundive 485

gesso 12.69
gestalt 401
Gestapo 12.57
gestate 367.33
gestation 261.67.33
gesticulate 367.13.2
gesticulation
   261.67.13
gesture 17.73
get 368
Gethsemane
   16.237.6
getter 17.339
Getty 16.330
Gettysburg 182
geum 242.1
gewgaw 9
geyser 17.440
geyserite 372.8
Gezira 17.272
Ghana 17.226
Ghanaian 261.1
gharry 16.260
ghastly 16.199
ghat 366
Ghats 334
ghazi 16.392
ghee 5
Ghent 410
gherkin 252
ghetto 12.75
ghibli 16.134
ghillie 16.120
ghost 441
ghostlike 39
ghostliness 300.23
ghostly 16.202
ghostwrite 372
ghostwriter 17.343
ghoul 227
ghoulish 353
giant 420.2
gib 24
gibber 17.14
gibberellin 252.7
gibberish 353.11
gibbet 371.5
gibbon 261
gibbous 310.5
gibe 25
Gibeon 261.3.2
giblets 339
Gibraltar 17.363
Gibson 261
gid 91

giddiness 300.23
giddy 16.63
giddy-up 279
Gideon 261.3.5
gidgee 5.6
gie 5
Gielgud 101
gift 398
gifted 91
giftwrap 268
gig 184
gigantic 38.62
gigantism 242.35
gigantomachy
   16.33
giggle 228.46
giggly 16.160
gigolo 12.45
gigot 12.28
gigue 183
Gijón 255
Gilbert 381
Gilbertian 261.3
gild 116
gilding 265.17
Gilead 83.1
gilet 2.11
gilgai 7
Gilgamesh 351
gill 218
Gillian 261.3.11
gillie 16.120
Gillingham 242.17
gillion 261.120
gillyflower 14
gilt 403
gilthead 86
gimbals 539
gimcrack 32
gimlet 371
gimmal 228.52
gimme 5
gimmick 38.28
gimmickry 16.275
gimmicky 16.25
gimp 287
gin 252
ginger 17.157
gingerbread 86
gingerly 16.131
gingery 16.274.14
gingham 242.17
gingili 16.120
gingiva 17.414
gingivitis 300.62.6

ginglymus 310.28
gink 52
ginnel 228.60
ginseng 264
Giotto 12.77
gippy 16.248
gipsywort 369
giraffe 158
girandole 223.2
girasol 220
gird 87
girder 17.81
girdle 228
girl 216
girlfriend 131
girlhood 101
girlie 16.116
girlish 353
giro 12.64
giron 254
gironny 16.231
girt 369
girth 456
gisarme 230
Gisborne 261
gist 436
git 371
gittern 249.1
give 485
given 261.114
giver 17.414
gizzard 103
glabella 17.163.1
glabrous 310
glacé 16.294
glacial 228.91
glacialist 436.7.2
glaciate 367.1.4
glaciation
  261.67.1.3
glacier 17.3.46
glaciology
  16.108.4.1
glacis 300.49
glad 83
gladden 261.19
glade 85
gladiate 371.1
gladiator 17.338.1
gladiatorial
  228.3.12
gladiolus 310
gladly 16.146
gladness 300
gladsome 242

Gladstone 261
glair 4
Glamorgan 261.33
glamorous 310.50
glamour 17.205
glamourize 516.8
glance 315
gland 128
glanders 524
glandular 17.174
glans 544
glare 4
glaring 265.52
glary 16.264
Glasgow 12
glass 294
glass-blower 17.6
glasses 515
glasshouse 306
glassine 251
glasslike 39
glassware 4
glasswork 36
glassworks 497
glassy 16.295
Glastonbury
  16.274
Glaswegian 261.36
Glauce 16.303
glaucoma 17.215
glaucous 310
glaze 509
glazier 17.3.59
glazing 265.81
gleam 234
glean 251
gleanings 552
glebe 23
glee 5
gleeful 226
gleet 370
glen 248
Glencoe 12
Glendower 14
glengarry 16.260
glenoid 97.7
Glenrothes 300
gley 2
gliadin 252
glib 24
glibly 16.134
glide 92
glider 17.84
gliding 265.14
glim 235

glimmer 17.211
glimpse 331
glint 412
glioma 17.215
glissade 84
glissando 12.23
glisten 261.65
glister 17.384
glitter 17.342
glittery 16.274.41
gloaming 265.37
gloat 376
glob 26
global 228.13
globate 367.3
globe 28
globetrotter 17.344
globetrotting
  265.68
globigerina 17.232
globoid 97
globose 305
globular 17.174
globule 227
globulin 252.10
glochidium 242.2.3
glockenspiel 217
glogg 185
glomerate 371.35
glomeration
  261.67.22
glomerulus
  310.25.1
gloom 241
gloominess 300.23
gloomy 16.221
Gloria 17.3.41
gloria 17.3.41
glorify 7.3
glorious 310.2.13
glory 16.269
gloss 302
glossa 17.304
glossary 16.274
glossator 17.338
glossectomy
  16.222.5
glosseme 234
glossitis 300.62
glossolalia 17.3.18
glossy 16.302
glottal 228.104
glottic 38.53
glottis 300
Gloucester 17.385

Gloucestershire 6
glove 489
glover 17.418
glow 12
glower 14
gloxinia 17.3.34
glucagon 254.5
glucinum 242.15
glucose 520
glue 15
gluey 16.4
glum 240
glume 241
glumly 16.168
glumness 300
gluon 254
glut 378
glutamate 367.16
glutamine 251.4
glutelin 252.8
gluten 261.104
gluteus 310.1
glutinous 310.33.2
glutton 261.103
gluttonous 310.36
gluttony 16.237
glyceric 38.39
glyceride 92.6
glycerine 252.20
glycerol 220.4
glycogen 261.39
glycol 220
glycolysis 300.52.2
glycoside 92.8
glycosuria
  17.3.42.2
glyph 163
glyphography
  16.90.2
glyptic 38.66
glyptics 498
glyptography
  16.90.2
gnarl 213
gnash 349
gnat 365
gnathic 38.72
gnathion 254.1
gnathite 372
gnathonic 38.35
gnaw 9
gnawing 265
gneiss 301
gnocchi 16.27
gnome 239

gnomic 38
gnomon 254
gnosis 300.55
gnostic 38.71
Gnosticism
   242.35.16
gnu 15
go 12
Goa 17.6
goa 17.6
goad 98
go-ahead 86.5
goal 223
goalie 16.126
goalkeeper 17.252
goalless 300
goalmouth 462
goanna 17.225
goat 376
goatee 5
goatherd 87
goatish 353
goatsbeard 90
goatskin 252
goatsucker 17.39
gob 26
gobbet 371
gobble 228
gobbledegook 45
gobbler 17.178
Gobelin 252.11
go-between 251
Gobi 16.12
gobioid 97
goblet 371
goblin 252
gobstopper 17.255
goby 16.12
god 94
godchild 117
goddamn 229
Goddard 84
goddaughter
   17.345
goddess 300.4
godetia 17.325
godfather 17.401
god-fearing 265.53
godforsaken 261.11
Godhead 86
godhood 101
Godiva 17.415
godless 300
godlessness 300.33
godlike 39

godliness 300.23
godly 16.149
godmother 17.408
Godolphin 252
godown 258
godparent 420
godsend 131
godson 259
Godspeed 89
Godunov 165
Godwin 252
godwit 371
goer 17.6
goffer 17.117
Gog 185
go-getter 17.339
goggle 228.47
gogglebox 499
Gogol 220
Goiânia 17.3.30
Goidel 228.35
Goidelic 38.20
going 265.4
goitre 17.346
go-kart 366
Golconda 17.104
gold 120
goldarn 246
goldcrest 433
golden 261.28
goldeneye 7
goldenrod 94
goldeye 7
goldfinch 80
goldfish 353
goldilocks 499
goldsmith 458
goldthread 86
golem 232
golf 173
goliard 103
goliardery 16.274.6
Goliath 464
golliwog 185
gollop 281.2
golly 16.122
Gomberg 182
gombroon 260
Gomorrah 17.275
gomuti 16.343
gonad 83.3
Gond 136
Gondar 1
gondola 17.176
gondolier 6

Gondwanaland
   143.4
gone 254
goner 17.233
gonfalon 261
gonfalonier 6.5
gong 266
Gongola 17.171
Gongorism
   242.35.15
goniatite 372.12
gonidium 242.2.3
goniometer
   17.342.3.1
gonion 261.3.18
gonk 53
gonna 17.233
gonococcus 310.11
gonophore 9.6
gonorrhoea 17.2.2
goo 15
goober 17.20
good 101
goodbye 7
good-humoured
   103.5
goodies 515
goodman 261
good-natured 103
goodness 300
good-night 372
goodwife 164
goodwill 218
Goodwin 252
goody 16.70
Goodyear 6
goody-goody 16.70
gooey 16.4
goof 170
goofy 16.89
googly 16.162
googol 220
googolplex 496
Goole 227
goon 260
goop 280
goosander 17.98
goose 309
gooseberry 16.274
goosefoot 379
goosegog 185
goosegrass 294
gooseneck 35
goosy 16.306
gopak 32

gopher 17.117
goral 228.74
Gorbals 539
gorcock 40
Gordon 261.27
gore 9
goreng pisang 263
gorge 200
gorgeous 310
gorger 17.153
gorgerin 252.20
Gorgon 261.33
gorgonian 261.3.18
Gorgonzola 17.171
gorilla 17.166.3
Gorky 16.28
gormandize 516
gormless 300
gorse 303
Gorsedd 474
gory 16.269
gosh 354
goshawk 41
Goshen 261.73
gosling 265
gospel 228
gospeller 17.176
Gosplan 245
Gosport 374
gossamer 17.218
gossip 274
gossipy 16.248
gossoon 260
goster 17.385
got 373
Goth 459
Gothenburg 182
Gothic 38
Gothicism
   242.35.16
Gotland 143
gotta 17.344
gotten 261.101
gouache 350
Gouda 17.89
gouge 202
goulash 349
Gould 121
Gounod 12
gourami 16.222
gourd 96
gourmand 143
gourmandise 513
gourmet 2
gout 377

goutweed 89
govern 261.117
governable
  228.16.31
governance 321
governess 300.26
government 420.42
governmental
  228.110.4
governor 17.239
governorship 274.1
Gower 14
gown 258
Goya 17.5
grab 18
grabble 228
graben 261.8
Gracchus 310.7
grace 295
graceful 226
gracefulness 300.30
graceless 300
gracile 219
gracility 16.333.9
gracious 310.56
graciousness
  300.34
grackle 228.19
grad 83
gradate 367.9
gradation 261.67.8
grade 85
grader 17.79
gradient 420.1
gradine 251.1
gradual 228.9
gradualism
  242.35.11.3
graduand 128
graduate 367.2,
  371.2
graduation
  261.67.2
gradus 310
Graecism 242.35
Graecize 516
graffiti 16.332
graffito 12.76
graft 396
grafter 17.358
Graham 242
Grail 214
grain 247
graining 265.40
grainy 16.225

grallatorial
  228.3.12.2
gram 229, 230
grama 17.206
gramarye 16.274
gramercy 16.298
gramineous 310.2.8
graminivorous
  310.50.3
grammar 17.205
grammarian
  261.3.21
grammatical
  228.23.18
grammatology
  16.108.4.15
gramophone 257
Grampian 261.3
grampus 310.41
Granada 17.78.1
granadilla 17.166
granary 16.274
grand 128
grandchild 117
Grand Coulee
  16.130
granddad 83
granddaughter
  17.345
grandee 5
grandeur 17.155
grandfather 17.401
grandiloquent
  420.59
grandiose 305.1
grandiosity
  16.333.30.1
grandioso 12.70
grandma 1
grand mal 212
grandmama 1.12
grandmaster
  17.380
grandmother
  17.408
grandpa 1
grandpapa 1
grandparent 420
grandson 259
grandstand 128
grange 207
grangerize 516.8
granite 371.22
graniteware 4.9
granitic 38.52

granitite 372.11
granivorous
  310.50.3
granny 16.223
granolith 458
granophyre 8.1
grant 408
Granta 17.365
grantee 5
grantor 9
gran turismo 12.50
granular 17.174.9
granulate 367.13
granulation
  261.67.13
granule 227
granulite 372
grape 270
grapefruit 380
grapeshot 373
grapevine 253
graph 158
grapheme 234
graphic 38.11
graphical 228.23.3
graphics 498
graphite 372
graphitic 38.52
graphologist 436.4
graphology
  16.108.4
grapnel 228
grappa 17.247
Grappelli 16.115
grapple 228.64
grappling 265
graptolite 372.4
Grasmere 6
grasp 290
grasping 265
grass 294
grassfinch 80
grasshook 44
grasshopper 17.255
grassland 143
grassy 16.295
grate 367
grateful 226.7
gratefulness 300.30
grater 17.338
Gratian 261.3
graticule 227.1
gratify 7.3.8
grating 265.64
gratis 300

gratitude 102.2.1
Grattan 261.94
gratuitous 310.64
gratuity 16.333.3
grav 480
gravamen 248.2
grave 16.378, 482
gravel 228.117
gravelly 16.131
graven 261.111
graver 17.410
Graves 481
Gravesend 131
gravestone 257
graveyard 84
gravid 91
gravitate 367.30
gravitation
  261.67.27
gravitational
  228.63.3
gravitative 485.10
gravity 16.333.33
gravure 10
gravy 16.379
Gray 2
grayling 265.27
graze 509
grazier 17.3.59
grazing 265.81
grease 298
greasepaint 409
greasy 16.299
great 367
greatcoat 376
greatest 436
greatness 300
Greats 335
greave 484
greaves 553
grebe 23
Grecian 261.70
Greece 298
greed 89
greediness 300.23
greedy 16.62
Greek 37
Greeley 16.118
green 251
greenback 32
greenbottle
  228.104
greenbrier 17.4
greenery 16.274.25
greenfinch 80

greenfly 7
greengage 193
greengrocer 17.306
greengrocery 16.274
greenhead 86
greenheart 366
greenhorn 255
greenhouse 306
greening 265.42
greenish 353
Greenland 143
Greenlander 17.109
greenling 265
greenness 300
Greenock 46
greenroom 241
greens 547
greensand 128
Greensboro 17.279
greenshank 51
greenstick 38
greenstuff 168
greensward 95
Greenwich 197.7
greenwood 101
greet 370
greeting 265
gregarine 251.7
gregarious 310.2.10
Gregorian 261.3.23
Gregory 16.274
greige 360
greisen 261.127
gremlin 252
Grenada 17.79
grenade 85.2
grenadier 6
grenadine 251.1
Grenadines 547
Grendel 228
Grenoble 228.13
Gresham 242
gressorial 228.3.12
Gretna 17.244
grew 15
grey 2
greyback 32
greybeard 90
greyhen 248
greyhound 139
greyish 353
greylag 178
greyness 300

greywacke 17.28
gribble 228.12
grid 91
griddle 228.32
griddlecake 34
gride 92
gridiron 261.4
grief 162
Grieg 183
grievance 321
grieve 484
grieving 265.79
grievous 310.73
griffe 163
griffin 252
Griffith 458
griffon 261.29
grig 184
grigri 5
grill 218
grillage 197.1
grille 218
grillroom 241
grilse 311
grim 235
grimace 295
Grimaldi 16.75
grimalkin 252
grime 236
Grimm 235
grimness 300
Grimsby 16
grimy 16.217
grin 252
grind 135
grindelia 17.3.20
grinder 17.103
grindery 16.274.8
grindstone 257
gringo 12.36
grip 274
gripe 275
grippe 274
gripping 265
grisaille 214
griseous 310.2.15
griskin 252
grisly 16.209
grison 261
grist 436
gristle 228.85
gristly 16.181
gristmill 218
grit 371
grith 458

grits 339
gritty 16.333
grivet 371
grizzle 228
grizzled 122
grizzly 16.209
groan 257
groat 376
groats 343
grocer 17.306
groceries 515.1
grocery 16.274
grockle 228.25
grog 185
groggy 16.94
grogram 242
groin 256
Grolier 17.3.22
grommet 371.20
gromwell 228
groom 241
grooming 265.39
groove 490
groovy 16.384
grope 278
groper 17.257
Gropius 310.2
grosbeak 37
groschen 261.73
grosgrain 247
gross 305
grossularite 372.8
grot 373
grotesque 57
grotesqueness 300
grotesquery 16.274
Grotius 310.2
grotto 12.77
grouch 71
grouchy 16.51
ground 139
groundage 197
grounding 265.22
groundless 300
groundling 265
groundmass 293
groundnut 378
groundsel 228
groundsheet 370
groundsill 218
groundsman 261
groundspeed 89
groundwork 36
group 280
grouper 17.259

groupie 16.253
grouping 265
grouse 306
grout 377
grouts 344
grouty 16.340
grove 488
grovel 228
grow 12
grower 17.6
growl 224
growler 17.172
grown 257
growth 461
groyne 256
grub 29
grubber 17.19
grubbiness 300.23
grubby 16.13
grudge 203
grudging 265
gruel 228.10
gruelling 265
gruesome 242
gruff 168
gruffness 300
grumble 228
grumbler 17.180
grumbly 16.139
grumous 310
grump 289
grumpy 16.257
Grundy 16.80
grunion 261
grunt 419
grunter 17.373
gruntled 122
Grus 308
Gruyère 4
grysbok 40
guacamole 16.126
Guadalcanal 212
Guadalquivir 6.11
Guadeloupe 280.1
guaiacol 220
Guam 230
guan 246
guanase 509
guano 12.51
guarani 16.237
Guarani 5.14
guarantee 5.24
guarantor 9
guaranty 16.360
guard 84

guardant 420.8
guarded 91.5
guardhouse 306
guardian 261.3
guardianship 274.2
guardrail 214
guardroom 241
guardsman 261
Guarneri 16.265
Guatemala
  17.161.1
guava 17.409
guayule 16.130
gubbins 548
gubernatorial
  228.3.12.2
guck 43
gudgeon 261.38
Gudrun 260
guelder-rose 520.3
Guelph 172
guenon 254.8
guerdon 261.22
Guernica 17.33
guerrilla 17.166.3
guess 296
guesstimate 367.15,
  371.19
guesswork 36
guest 433
guesthouse 306
Guevara 17.268
guff 168
guffaw 9
guidance 321.6
guide 92
guideline 253
guidepost 441
guider 17.84
guiding 265.14
guidon 261.25
Guienne 248
guild 116
guilder 17.95
Guildford 103
guildhall 221
guile 219
guileful 226
guileless 300
guillemot 373
guilloche 354
guillotine 251.11
guilt 403
guiltless 300

guilty 16.350
guimpe 287
Guinea 16.229
guinea 16.229
guinea pig 184
Guinevere 6.11
Guinness 300.23
guipure 10
guise 516
guitar 1
guitarist 436.16
Gujarati 16.328.1
Gujranwala 17.173
Gulag 178
gular 17.175
Gulbenkian 261.3
gulch 77
gules 538
gulf 174
gulfweed 89
gull 225
gullet 371
gullibility
  16.333.9.2
gullible 228.16
gull-wing 265
gully 16.128
gulp 284
gulped 427
gum 240
gumbo 12.7
gumboil 222
gumboots 346
gumdrop 276
gumma 17.216
gummy 16.220
gumption 261.89
gumshield 115
gumshoe 15
gumtree 5
gun 259
gunboat 376
guncotton 261.101
gunfight 372
gunfighter 17.343
gunfire 8
gunflint 412
gunge 211
gungy 16.111
gunk 54
gunlock 40
gunman 261
gunmetal 228.100

gunnel 228
gunner 17.237
gunnery 16.274
gunning 265.45
gunny 16.235
gunplay 2
gunpoint 416
gunpowder 17.89
gunrunner 17.237
gunrunning 265.45
gunshot 373
gunslinger 17.246
gunsmith 458
gunstock 40
Guntur 10
gunwale 228
gunyah 1
guppy 16.252
Gur 10
gurdwara 17.268
gurgitation
  261.67.27
gurgle 228
gurjun 261.35
Gurkha 17.32
Gurkhali 16.113
Gurmukhi 16.31
gurnard 103
gurnet 371.23
guru 15
Gus 307
gush 356
gusher 17.329
gushy 16.324
gusset 371
gust 443
gustation 261.67
Gustavus 310
gusto 12
gusty 16.368
gut 378
gutbucket 371.11
Gutenberg 182
gutless 300
gutta 17.349
gutta-percha 17.54
gutter 17.349
guttering 265.58
guttersnipe 275
guttural 228.76
gutturalize 516.3.8
gutty 16.341
guv 489

guy 7
Guyana 17.225
guyot 12.2
guzzle 228
guzzler 17.204
Gwalior 9.1
Gwelo 12
Gwent 410
Gwyn 252
Gwynedd 474
gwyniad 83.1
gybe 25
gym 235
gymkhana 17.226
gymnasiarch 33.1
gymnasiast 430.1
gymnasium
  242.2.19
gymnast 430
gymnastic 38.68
gymnastics 498.15
gymnosophist 436
gymnosperm 233
gymslip 274
gynaeceum 242.1
gynaecocracy
  16.307.5
gynaecoid 97.3
gynaecologist 436.4
gynaecology
  16.108.4.4
gynaecomastia 17.3
gynandromorph
  166.1
gynarchy 16.20
gynoecium 242.2
gyp 274
gypsophila 17.166
gypsum 242
gypsy 16.314
gyral 228
gyrate 367
gyration 261.67
gyratory 16.274.40
gyre 8
gyrfalcon 261.16
gyrocompass
  310.42
gyromagnetic 38.50
gyroplane 247
gyroscope 278.1
gyrostatic 38.49.7
gyrus 310.47

H

ha 1
haaf 158
haar 1
Habakkuk 46
habanera 17.271
habeas corpus
  310.38
haberdasher 17.321
haberdashery
  16.274
habergeon 261.39
habiliment 420.31
habilitate 367.30.1
habit 371.4
habitable 228.16.49
habitat 365
habitation
  261.67.27
habitual 228.9.3
habituate 367.2.1
habitué 2.3
habitus 310.64
háček 35
hachure 10
hacienda 17.101
hack 32
hackamore 9.9
hackberry 16.274
hackbut 378
hackle 228.19
hackles 539
Hackney 16.238
hackney 16.238
hackneyed 91.22
hacksaw 9
had 83
hadal 228
haddock 46
hade 85
Hades 513
Hadith 458
hadn't 420
Hadrian 261.3
hadrosaur 9.11
hae 2
haecceity 16.333.1
haem 234
haemagogue 185.2
haematemesis
  300.52.3
haematic 38.49

haematin 252
haematinic 38.34
haematite 372.12
haematocele 217.2
haematocrit 371
haematogenesis
  300.52.4
haematoid 97
haematology
  16.108.4.15
haematoma 17.215
haematopoiesis
  300.51
haematosis
  300.55.7
haematoxylon
  254.6
haematozoon 254.2
haematuria 17.3.42
haemic 38.27
haemochrome 239
haemocoel 217.2
haemocyte 372.10
haemodialysis
  300.52.1
haemoglobin 252
haemoglobinuria
  17.3.42.1
haemolysin 252.21
haemolysis
  300.52.2
haemophilia
  17.3.21.2
haemophiliac
  32.1.1
haemophilic 38.21
haemoptysis
  300.52
haemorrhage 197
haemorrhagic
  38.15
haemorrhoid 97.12
haemorrhoidectomy
  16.222.5.1
haemostasis 300.50
haemostat 365
haemostatic
  38.49.7
haeremai 7
hafiz 515
hafnium 242.2
haft 396
hag 178
Hagar 1
hagedena 17.230

Hagen 261
Haggadah 17.78
Haggai 7
haggard 103
haggis 300
haggle 228.43
haggler 17.192
hagiarchy 16.20
hagiocracy
  16.307.5.1
Hagiographa
  17.120.1
hagiography
  16.90.2.1
hagiolatry
  16.286.2.1
hagiology
  16.108.4.1
Hague 180
ha-ha 1.5
Haida 17.84
Haifa 17.115
Haig 180
haik 39
hail 214
Haile Selassie
  16.294
hailstone 257
hailstorm 238
Hainan 245
hair 4
hairball 221
hairbrush 356
haircloth 459
haircut 378
hairdo 15
hairdresser 17.300
hairdressing 265.60
hairgrip 274
hairif 163
hairless 300
hairlike 39
hairline 253
hairnet 368
hairpiece 298
hairpin 252
hairsplitting 265.66
hairspring 265
hairstreak 37
hairstyle 219
hairtail 214
hairy 16.264
Haiti 16.329
Haitian 261.3
Haitink 52

hajj 191
hake 34
hakea 17.3
hakim 234
Hakluyt 380
Hakodate 2.23
Halakah 1
halal 213
halation 261.67.14
halberd 103
halcyon 261.3
hale 214
Haleakala 1.7
haler 17.161
Halesowen 252.1
half 158
halfback 32
half-baked 384
halfbeak 37
half-caste 431
half-day 2
half-hearted 91.33
half-heartedness
  300.28
half-life 164
half-light 372
half-mast 431
half-naked 91
half-open 261
half-price 301
half-shut 378
half-time 236
halftone 257
halfway 2
halfwit 371
halfwitted 91.38
halibut 381
Halicarnassus
  310.51
halide 92
Halifax 494
halite 372
halitosis 300.55.6
hall 221
Hallel 214
Halley 16.112
hallmark 33
hallo 12.45
halloo 15.5
hallow 12.38
hallowed 98
Hallowe'en 251
Hallstatt 365
hallucinate 367.17

hallucination 261.67.18
hallucinatory 16.274.43.6
hallucinogen 261.39
hallucinogenic 38.32.1.1
hallucinosis 300.55.4
hallux 503
hallway 2
halo 12
halobiont 414
halogen 261.39
halothane 247
halt 404
Haltemprice 301
halter 17.363
haltere 6
halting 265
halvah 1
halve 481
halyard 103
ham 229
Hama 1.10
hamadryad 83.2
hamadryas 310.3
hamal 213
hamamelidaceous 310.56.2
Hambletonian 261.3.18
Hamburg 182
hamburger 17.127
hame 231
Hamilcar Barca 17.29
Hamilton 261
Hamite 372
Hamitic 38.52
hamlet 371
Hammarskjöld 120
hammer 17.205
hammerhead 86.5
Hammersmith 458
Hammerstein 253
hammertoe 12
hammock 46
Hammond 143
Hammurabi 16.6
hammy 16.210
Hampden 261
hamper 17.261
Hampshire 6

Hampstead 91
Hampton 261
hamshackle 228.19
hamster 17
hamstring 265
hamulus 310.25
Han 245, 246
hanaper 17.260
hance 314
Hancock 40
hand 128
handbag 178
handball 221
handbarrow 12.60
handbell 215
handbill 218
handbook 44
handbrake 34
handcart 366
handclasp 290
handcraft 396
handcuff 168
Handel 228.39
handfeed 89
handful 226
handgrip 274
handgun 259
handhold 120
handicap 268
handicapper 17.247
handicraft 396
handiwork 36
handkerchief 163
handle 228.39
handlebar 1
handlebars 508
handled 122
handler 17
handling 265
handmade 85
handmaiden 261.20
hand-me-down 258
handrail 214
handsaw 9
handsel 228
handset 368
handshake 34
handsome 242
handsomeness 300
handspike 39
handspring 265
handstand 128

handstroke 42
handwriting 265.67
handwritten 261.99
handy 16.77
handyman 261.48
hang 263
hangar 17.245
Hangchow 13
hangdog 185
hanger 17.245
hanging 265
hangman 261
hangnail 214
hangover 17.417
hank 51
hanker 17.43
hanky 16.36
hanky-panky 16.36
Hannah 17.225
Hannibal 228.12
Hanoi 11
Hanover 17.417
Hanoverian 261.3.22
Hanratty 16.327
Hansard 84
Hanse 314
Hanseatic 38.49
hansom 242
Hants. 347
Hanukkah 17.42
Hanuman 246
haphazard 103
hapless 300
haploid 97
haplology 16.108.4
ha'p'orth 464
happen 261
happening 265.46
happiness 300.23
happy 16.243
Hapsburg 182
hapten 261
hapteron 254.11
haptic 38
harakiri 16.266
harambee 2.5
harangue 263.2
Harappa 17.247
Harar 17.268
harass 310.43
harassment 420.46
Harbin 252
harbinger 17.157
harbour 17.10

harbourage 197
hard 84
hardback 32
hardbake 34
hardboard 95
harden 261
hardened 143
hardener 17.240
hardhack 32
hardhearted 91.33
hardihood 101
hardiness 300.23
hardly 16
hardness 300
hardship 274
hardtack 32
hardtop 276
hardware 4
hardwood 101
hardy 16.58
hare 4
harebell 215
harebrained 130
harelip 274
harem 234
Hargeisa 17.299
Hargreaves 553
haricot 12.11
Harijan 261.37
Haringey 2.10
hark 33
Harlem 242
harlequin 252
harlequinade 85.2
harlot 381
Harlow 12.39
harm 230
harmattan 261.94
harmful 226
harmless 300
harmlessness 300.33
harmonic 38.35
harmonica 17.34.1
harmonics 498.5
harmonious 310.2.9
harmonist 436.13
harmonium 242.2.12
harmonize 516.7
harmony 16.237
harness 300.21
Harold 122
harp 269

heated 91.37
heater 17.341
heath 457
heathen 261
heathendom 242
heathenish 353
heathenize 516.7
heather 17.402
heating 265
heatstroke 42
heaume 239
heave 484
heaven 261.112
heavenly 16.174
heavenwards 531
heaves 553
heaviness 300.23
Heaviside 92.7
heavy 16.380
heavy-handed
  91.12
heavyweight 367
hebdomadal 228.38
hebdomadary
  16.274.7
Hebe 16.10
hebephrenia
  17.3.33
hebetate 367.30
hebetic 38.50
Hebraic 38.1.1
Hebraism 242.35
Hebraist 436.1
Hebrew 15
Hebridean 261.2
Hebrides 513.4
Hebron 254
Hecate 16.344
hecatomb 241
heck 35
heckelphone 257
heckle 228.21
hectare 1
hectic 38.60
hectocotylus
  310.23
hectogram 229.1
hectograph 158.1
hector 17.354
he'd 89
heddle 228
hedge 194
hedgehog 185
hedgehop 276
hedgerow 12

hedonics 498.5
hedonism
  242.35.14
hedonist 436.13
heebie-jeebies 515
heed 89
heedful 226
heedless 300
heedlessness
  300.33
heehaw 9
heel 217
heeled 115
heeltap 268
heft 397
hefty 16.346
Hegel 228.44
hegemony 16.237.6
Hegira 17.272
hegumen 248.3
Heidelberg 182
heifer 17.112
heigh-ho 12
height 372
heighten 261.100
Heilungkiang 263
Heimdall 213
heinous 310.31
heir 4
heirdom 242
heiress 300.44
heirless 300
heirloom 241
heirship 274
heist 437
heitiki 5
Hejaz 507
Hel 215
held 113
Helen 252.7
Helena 17.239
helianthus 310.72
helical 228.23.6
helices 513
helichrysum 242.35
heliclinc 253.4
helicoid 97.3
Helicon 261.13
helicon 261.13
helicopter 17.377
Heligoland 143.3
heliograph 158.1.1
heliolatry
  16.286.2.1
heliolithic 38.73

heliometer
  17.342.3.1
Heliopolis 300.13.2
heliotactic 38.58
heliotherapy
  16.254
heliotrope 278.3
heliotropic 38.37.2
heliotype 275.1
heliport 374.1
helium 242.2.5
helix 498
hell 215
he'll 217
Hellas 310.22
hellbent 410
hellcat 365
helldiver 17.415
hellebore 9
helleborine 251.6
Hellene 251
Hellenic 38.32
Hellenism
  242.35.13
Hellenist 436.11
Hellenistic 38.70
Hellenize 516.6
heller 17.163
hellery 16.274
Hellespont 414
hellfire 8
hellgrammite 372
hellhole 223
hellhound 139
hellion 261.119
hellish 353.4
hello 12.40
helm 243
helmet 371
helmeted 91.38
helminth 470
helminthic 38
helminthology
  16.108.4
Héloïse 513.2
Helot 381
helotism 242.35.20
helotry 16.286
help 283
helpful 226
helpfulness 300.30
helping 265
helpless 300
helplessness 300.33
Helpmann 261

helpmate 367
Helsinki 16.37
helter-skelter
  17.361
helve 492
Helvellyn 252.7
Helvetia 17.325
Helvetian 261.70
Helvetic 38.50
Helvetii 7.1
Helvétius 310.2
hem 232
he-man 261.47
Hemel Hempstead
  91
hemeralopia
  17.3.37.1
hemialgia 17.3.16
hemianopsia 17.3
hemihedral 228.78
Hemingway 2
hemiola 17.171
hemiplegia 17.3.13
hemiplegic 38.17
hemipode 98
hemipteran 261.60
hemisphere 6
hemispheric 38.39
hemispheroid 97.10
hemistich 38.70
hemline 253
hemlock 40
hemmer 17.208
hemp 286
hempen 261
hems 541
hemstitch 67
hen 248
henbane 247
hence 316
henceforth 460
henceforward
  103.8
henchman 261
hencoop 280
hendiadys 300.5
henequen 252.3
henge 208
Hengist 436
henhouse 306
Henley 16.171
henna 17.228
hennery 16.274.23
henpeck 35
henpecked 385

hideaway 2.28
hidebound 139
hideous 310.2.1
hiding 265.14
hidrosis 300.55
hie 7
hieland 143.1
hieracosphinx 505
hierarch 33
hierarchical 228.23
hierarchy 16.20
hieratic 38.49
hierocracy 16.307.5
hierodule 227
hieroglyph 163
hieroglyphic 38.12
hieroglyphics 498.1
hierogram 229.1
hierology 16.108.4
Hieronymus
    310.28.2
hierophant 407
hi-fi 7
Higgins 548
high 7
highball 221
highborn 255
highboy 11
highbrow 13
highchair 4
highfalutin 252.24
high-flown 257
high-handed 91.12
high jinks 505
highland 143
Highlander 17.109
Highlands 534
highlife 164
highlight 372
highly 16.121
highly-strung 267
high-minded 91
Highness 300
highroad 98
high-spirited 91.38
hightail 214
highway 2.26
highwayman
    261.45
High Wycombe
    242.4
hijack 32
hijacker 17.28
hike 39
hiker 17.35

hilarious 310.2.10
hilarity 16.333.20.2
Hilary 16.274.16
Hilda 17.95
hill 218
Hillary 16.274.16
hillbilly 16.120
hillfort 374
Hillingdon 261
hillock 46
hillside 92
hilly 16.120
hilt 403
hilum 242.9
hilus 310.24
Hilversum 242
him 235
Himalayas 524
himation 254.1
Himeji 5.5
himself 172
Himyaritic 38.52.2
hin 252
Hinayana 17.226
Hinckley 16.145
hind 135
hindbrain 247
Hindenburg 182
hinder 17.102
hinder 17.103
hindgut 378
Hindi 16.79
hindmost 441
hindquarter 17.345
hindrance 321
hindsight 372
Hindu 15
Hinduism 242.35.4
Hindu Kush 357
Hindustan 246
Hindustani 16.224
hinge 209
hinny 16.229
hint 412
hinterland 143.4
hip 274
hipbone 257
hipparch 33
Hipparchus 310.8
hippeastrum 242
hippie 16.248
hippo 12
hippocampus
    310.41
hippocras 293

Hippocrates 513.17
Hippocratic
    38.49.6
Hippocrene 251
hippodrome 239
hippogriff 163
Hippolyta 17.342
Hippolyte 5.22
Hippolytus 310.64
hippopotamus
    310.29.3
hipster 17.396
hipsters 524
hiragana 17.226
hircine 253
hire 8
hireling 265
hirer 17.274
Hirohito 12.76
Hiroshige 2
Hiroshima 17.210
hirsute 380
hirundine 253
his 515
Hispania 17.3.29
Hispanic 38.31
Hispanicism
    242.35.16
Hispanicize 516.10
Hispaniola 17.171
hispid 91
hiss 300
hist 436
histaminase 509
histamine 252.15
histaminic 38.34
histogen 261.39
histogenesis
    300.52.4
histogram 229.1
histoid 97
histology 16.108.4
histolysis 300.52.2
historian 261.3.23
historic 38.41
historical 228.23.17
historicism
    242.35.16
historicity
    16.333.28
historiographer
    17.120.1
historiography
    16.90.2.1
history 16.274.49

histrionic 38.35.1
histrionics 498.5
hit 371
hitch 67
Hitchcock 40
hitchhike 39
hitchhiker 17.35
hither 17.405
hitherto 15
Hitler 17.201
Hitlerism
    242.35.15
hitter 17.342
Hittite 372.11
hive 486
hives 554
ho 12
hoar 9
hoard 95
hoarder 17.86
hoarding 265.15
hoarfrost 438
hoarse 303
hoarsen 261
hoarseness 300
hoary 16.269
hoatching 265
hoatzin 252
hoax 501
hoaxer 17.429
hob 26
Hobart 366
hobble 228
hobbledehoy 11
hobby 16.11
hobbyhorse 303
hobgoblin 252
hobnail 214
hobnailed 112
hobnob 26
hobo 12
Hoboken 261.14
hobson-jobson 261
Ho Chi Minh 252
hock 40
hockey 16.27
Hockney 16.239
Hocktide 92
hocus-pocus 310.12
hod 94
hodden 261.26
hodgepodge 199
hoe 12
hoedown 258
Hofei 2

hog 185
hogan 261
Hogarth 453
hogback 32
hogfish 353
Hogg 185
hogged 106
hoggish 353
Hogmanay 2
hogshead 86
hogtie 7
hogwash 354
hogweed 89
Hohenzollern
261.42
hoi polloi 11.1
hoist 440
hoity-toity 16.338
hoke 42
hokey cokey 16.29
Hokkaido 12.20
hokum 242
Hokusai 7
Holarctic 38.59
hold 120
holdall 221
holder 17.97
holdfast 431
holding 265.18
hole 223
holey 16.126
holiday 2
holiness 300.23
Holinshed 86
holism 242.35
Holland 143
holland 143
hollandaise 509
Hollandia 17.3
holler 17.168
hollow 12.43
hollowness 300.25
holly 16.122
hollyhock 40
Hollywood 101
holm 239
holmium 242.2
holocaust 439
Holocene 251.9
holocrine 253
hologram 229.1
holograph 158.1
holography 16.90.2
holophytic 38.52

holothurian
261.3.24
holotype 275.1
holozoic 38.2
Holstein 253
holster 17.392
holt 405
holy 16.126
Holyhead 86.2
holystone 257
hom 237
homa 17.213
homage 197.4
hombre 2
homburg 182
home 239
homebred 86
homecoming
265.38
homeland 143
homeless 300
homelessness
300.33
homely 16
homeopathic 38.72
homeopathy
16.373.1.1
homeotypic 38.36
Homer 17.215
homer 17.215
Homeric 38.39
homesick 38
homesickness
300.27
homespun 259
homestead 86
homesteader 17.80
homeward 103
homework 36
homicidal 228.33
homicide 92.7
homiletic 38.50
homiletics 498.12
homily 16.120
homing 265.37
hominid 91
hominoid 97.8
hominy 16.229
homo 12.49
homocentric 38.47
homocercal 228.22
homogamy
16.222.2
homogeneity
16.333.1

homogeneous
310.2.7
homogenize 516.6
homogenous
310.33
homogeny 16.229.2
homogony 16.237.4
homograft 396
homograph 158.1
homologate 367.11
homologize 516.1
homologous 310
homologue 185
homology 16.108.4
homonym 235
homophone 257
homophonic
38.35.2
homophonous
310.36
homophony
16.237.3
homopterous
310.50
homorganic 38.31
Homo sapiens 546
homoscedasticity
16.333.28.2
homosexual 228.9
homosexuality
16.333.8.2
homozygous 310
homunculus 310.25
homy 16.219
honan 245
Honda 17.104
Honduras 310.49
hone 257
Honegger 17.129
honest 436
honestly 16.201
honesty 16.366
honey 16.235
honeybee 5
honeybunch 82
honeycomb 239
honeydew 15.7
honey-eater 17.341
honeyed 91
honeymoon 260
honeymooner
17.238
honeysucker 17.39
honeysuckle 228.27
hong 266

Hong Kong 266
Honiara 17.268.1
Honiton 261.99
honk 53
honky-tonk 53
Honolulu 15.4
honorarium
242.2.14
honorary 16.274.32
honorific 38.12.1
honour 17.233
honourable
228.16.35
honours 524
Honshu 15
hooch 74
hood 101
hooded 91
hoodlum 242
hoodoo 15
hoodwink 52
hooey 16.4
hoof 170
hoofbound 139
Hooghly 16.162
hoo-ha 1
hook 44
hookah 17.40
hooked 390
hooker 17.40
hooknose 520
hookworm 233
hooky 16.31
hooligan 261.32
hooliganism
242.35.14
hoop 280
hoopla 1
hoopoe 15
hoorah 1.13
hooray 2
hoosegow 13
hoot 380
hootenanny 16.223
hooter 17.351
hoots 346
Hoover 17.419
hop 276
hope 278
hopeful 226
hopefully 16.129
hopefulness 300.30
Hopeh 2
hopeless 300

Hughes 523
Hugo 12.32
Huguenot 12
Huhehot 373
hula 17.175
hulk 50
hulking 265
Hull 225
hull 225
hullabaloo 15.5
hum 240
human 261.51
humane 247
humanism
    242.35.14
humanist 436.13.3
humanitarian
    261.3.21.2
humanitarianism
    242.35.14.1.1
humanity
    16.333.14
humanize 516.7
humankind 135
humanly 16.174
humanoid 97.9
Humber 17.27
Humberside 92.8
humble 228
humbly 16.139
Humboldt 405
humbug 189
humdinger 17.246
humdrum 240
Hume 241
humectant 420.79
humeral 228.76
humerus 310.50
humid 91
humidifier 17.4.1
humidify 7.3.1
humidity 16.333.5
humidor 9.3
humiliate 367.1.2
humiliation
    261.67.1.1
humility 16.333.9
hummel 228
hummingbird 87
hummock 46
humoresque 57
humorist 436.20
humoristic 38.70.5
humorous 310.50
humour 17.217

humourless 300.13
humoursome 242
hump 289
humpback 32
humpbacked 382
humph 177
Humphrey 16.281
humpy 16.257
humus 310
Hun 259
Hunan 245
hunch 82
hunchback 32
hunchbacked 382
hundred 103
hundredweight
    367
hung 267
Hungarian
    261.3.21
Hungary
    16.274.11
hunger 17.143
Hungnam 229
hungriness 300.23
hungry 16
hunk 54
hunky-dory
    16.269
Hunnish 353
hunt 419
hunted 91
hunter 17.373
hunting 265
Huntingdon 261
Huntingdonshire
    6.8
huntsman 261
Huon 254
Hupeh 2
hurdle 228
hurdler 17.185
hurdy-gurdy 16.61
hurl 216
hurley 16.116
hurling 265
hurly-burly 16.116
Huron 261.59
hurrah 1
hurricane 247.1,
    261.13
hurried 91
hurriedness 300.28
hurry 16.272
hurt 369

hurter 17.340
hurtful 226
hurtle 228
husband 143
husbandman 261
husbandry 16.279
hush 356
husk 60
husky 16.42
huss 307
hussar 1
Hussein 247
hussy 16.305
hustings 552
hustle 228.87
hustler 17.199
hut 378
hutch 72
Hutu 15
hyacinth 470
hyacinthine 253
Hyades 513.5
hyaline 252.11
hyalite 372.4
hyaloid 97.6
hybrid 91
hybridize 516
hydantoin 252.1
hydathode 98
hydatid 91
Hyde 92
hydrangea 17.156
hydrant 420
hydranth 467
hydrargyrum 242
hydrastis 300.67
hydrate 367
hydrated 91.34
hydraulic 38.23
hydraulics 498
hydric 38
hydride 92
hydro 12
hydrocarbon 261.8
hydrocele 217.2
hydrocephalus
    310.26.3
hydrocephaly
    16.131
hydrochloric 38.42
hydrochloride 92.5
hydrodynamic
    38.24
hydroelectric 38

hydroelectricity
    16.333.28
hydrofoil 222.1
hydrogen 261.39
hydrogenate
    367.17
hydrogenous
    310.33
hydrography
    16.90.2
hydrokinetic
    38.50.4
hydrology
    16.108.4
hydrolyse 516.3
hydrolysis
    300.52.2
hydrolytic 38.52.1
hydromancy
    16.309
hydrometeor 17.3
hydrometer
    17.342.3
hydropathy
    16.373.1
hydrophane 247.3
hydrophilic 38.21
hydrophilous
    310.23
hydrophobia
    17.3.4
hydrophobic 38.3
hydrophone 257
hydroplane 247
hydroponics 498.5
hydropower 14
hydroscope 278.1
hydroski 5
hydrosphere 6.1
hydrostat 365
hydrostatic
    38.49.7
hydrostatics
    498.11
hydrosulphide 92
hydrotherapy
    16.254
hydrotropic
    38.37.2
hydrous 310
hydroxide 92.14
hydroxy 16.389
hydrozoan 261.6
Hydrus 310
hyena 17.230

hyetograph 158.1
hyetography
16.90.2.5
Hygeia 17.2
hygiene 251
hygienic 38.33
hygienics 498.4
hygienist 436
hygrograph 158.1
hygrometer
17.342.3
hygrophilous
310.23
hygroscope 278.1
hygroscopic
38.37.1
Hyksos 302
hyla 17.167
hylozoism
242.35.3
hymen 248
hymenium 242.2
hymn 235
hymnal 228
hymnist 436
hymnody 16.72
hymnology
16.108.4
hyoid 97
hypaesthesia
17.3.60
hype 275
hyperacidity
16.333.5.1
hyperactive 485.16
hyperactivity
16.333.35.2
hyperaemia
17.3.26
hyperaesthesia
17.3.60
hyperbaric 38.38
hyperbaton 254
hyperbola 17.176
hyperbole 16.131
hyperbolic 38.22
hyperbolize
516.3.4
hyperboloid 97.6
Hyperborean
261.3.23
hypercritical
228.23.20
hyperdulia 17.3.23

hyperglycaemia
17.3.26
hypergolic 38.22
hypericum 242.4
hyperinsulinism
242.35.13
Hyperion 261.3.22
hyperkinesia
17.3.60
hypermarket 371.7
hypermeter
17.342
hypermnesia
17.3.60
hyperon 254.11
hyperplasia
17.3.59
hyperpnoea 17.2
hyperpyrexia
17.3.57
hypersensitive
485.12
hypersensitize
516.12
hyperspace 295
hypertension
261.82.3
hyperthermia
17.3.25
hyperthyroidism
242.35
hypertonic 38.35.5
hypertrophy 16.90
hyperventilation
261.67.12
hypervitaminosis
300.55.4
hypha 17.115
hyphen 261
hyphenate 367.18
hyphenated
91.34.6
hyphenation
261.67.19
hypnagogic 38.18
hypnoid 97
hypnology
16.108.4
hypnopaedia
17.3.8
hypnosis 300.55
hypnotherapy
16.254
hypnotic 38.53.2

hypnotism
242.35.20
hypnotist 436.26
hypnotize 516.13
hypo 12
hypoacidity
16.333.5.1
hypocaust 439
hypocentre 17.368
hypochondria 17.3
hypochondriac
32.1
hypochondrium
242.2
hypocorism
242.35.15
hypocrisy 16.307.5
hypocrite 371
hypocritical
228.23.20
hypocycloid 97
hypodermic 38.26
hypodermis
300.18
Hypodorian
261.3.23
hypogastrium
242.2
hypogeal 228.2
hypogene 251
hypogenous
310.33
hypogeum 242.1
hypoglossal
228.86
hypoglycaemia
17.3.26
hypolimnion 261.3
hypomania
17.3.31.1
hyponasty 16.361
hypophysis 300.52
hypoplasia 17.3.59
hyposensitize
516.12
hypostatic 38.49.7
hypostatize 516.13
hypostyle 219.7
hypotension
261.82
hypotenuse 523
hypothalamus
310.29.2

hypothecate 367.5
hypothermia
17.3.25
hypothesis
300.52.5
hypothesize
516.10
hypothetical
228.23.19
hypothyroidism
242.35
hypotonic 38.35.5
hypoxic 38.75
hypsometry
16.285.2
hyrax 494
hyson 261
hyssop 281
hysterectomy
16.222.5.2
hysteresis 300.51.1
hysteria 17.3.39
hysteric 38.39
hysterical
228.23.15
hysterics 498.6
hysterogenic
38.32.1
hysteroid 97.12
hysterotomy
16.222.4
hystricomorph
166.1

I

I 7
iamb 229
iambic 38.5
Ian 261.2, 261.3
iatric 38.45
Ibadan 261.19
Iberia 17.3.39
Iberian 261.3.22
ibex 496
ibis 300
ibn-Saud 99
Ibo 12.5

Ibsen 261
Icaria 17.3.38
Icarian 261.3.21
Icarus 310.50
ice 301
iceberg 182
iceblink 52
icebound 139
icebox 499
icebreaker 17.30
icecap 268
ice cream 234
Iceland 143
Icelandic 38.10
Iceni 7
I Ching 265
Ichinomiya 17.3
ichneumon 261.51
ichnite 372
ichnology 16.108.4
ichor 9
ichthyic 38
ichthyoid 97
ichthyology
16.108.4.1
ichthyornis 300.24
ichthyosaur 9.11
ichthyosis 300.55.1
icicle 228.23
iciness 300.23
icing 265
icon 254
iconic 38.35
iconoclasm 242.34
iconoclast 430
iconoclastic 38.68
iconography
16.90.2
iconolatry 16.286.2
iconology 16.108.4
iconomatic 38.49.2
icterus 310.50
ictus 310
icy 16.301
id 91
I'd 92
Ida 17.84
Idaho 12.37
ide 92
idea 17.2
ideal 228.2
idealism
242.35.11.1
idealist 436.7.1
idealistic 38.70.2.1

ideality 16.333.8.1
idealize 516.3.1
ideate 367.1
ideatum 242.27
idempotent 420
identical 228.23.23
identifiable
228.16.3.1
identification
261.67.5.1
identify 7.3
Identikit 371.9
identity 16.333.32
ideogram 229.1.1
ideography
16.90.2.1
ideology 16.108.4.1
ides 527
idiocy 16.307
idiolect 385.5
idiom 242.2.3
idiomatic 38.49.2
idiopathic 38.72
idiopathy
16.373.1.1
idiosyncrasy
16.307
idiosyncratic 38.49
idiot 381.1
idiotic 38.53
idle 228.33
idleness 300.30
idler 17.187
idol 228.33
idolater 17.352
idolatrous 310
idolatry 16.286.2
idolize 516.3
idyll 218
idyllic 38.21
idyllist 436.5
if 163
Ife 16.84
igloo 15
Ignatius 310.2.16
igneous 310.2
ignite 372.7
igniter 17.343
ignition 261.71
ignoble 228.13
ignominious
310.2.8
ignominy 16.229
ignoramus 310.27
ignorance 321.20

ignorant 420.65
ignore 9
Igraine 247
iguana 17.226
ihram 230
ikebana 17.226
ILEA 17.3.21
ileac 32.1.1
ileitis 300.62
ileostomy 16.222.6
Ilesha 17.322
ileum 242.2.6
ileus 310.2.5
ilex 496
iliac 32.1.1
Iliad 83.1
Ilion 261.3.11
Ilium 242.2.6
ilium 242.2.6
ilk 49
Ilkeston 261.107
ill 218
I'll 219
ill-advised 154
ill-assorted 91
illative 485.10
Illawarra 17.275
illegal 228.45
illegality 16.333.8.4
illegalize 516.3
illegible 228.16
illegitimacy
16.307.2
illegitimate 371.19
ill-gotten 261.101
illiberal 228.76
illicit 371.36
illimitable
228.16.49
illinium 242.2.11
Illinois 11
Illinoisan 261.5
illiquid 91
illiteracy 16.307.4
illiterate 371.35
illness 300
illocution 261.75.2
illogical 228.23.5
illogicality
16.333.8.3
ill-starred 84
illude 102
illume 241
illuminance 321.14
illuminant 420.53.3

illuminate 367.17.6
illuminati 16.328
illumination
261.67.18.7
illumine 252
illuminism
242.35.13
ill-use 309
illusion 261.93.1
illusionism
242.35.14
illusionist 436.13
illusive 485.8
illusory 16.274
illustrate 367
illustration 261.67
illustrative 485.15
illustrator 17.338
illustrious 310.2
Illyria 17.3.40
Illyricum 242.4
ilmenite 372.5
Iloilo 12.41
Ilorin 252.18
I'm 236
image 197.3
imagery 16.282
imaginable
228.16.29
imaginal 228.60.2
imaginary
16.274.26
imagination
261.67.18.2
imaginative
485.15.7
imagine 252
imagism 242.35
imago 12.27
imam 230
imaret 368
imbalance 321.10
imbecile 217
imbecility 16.333.9
imbibe 25
imbibition 261.71
imbricate 367.5,
371.9
imbroglio 12.3.3
imbue 15
imine 251
imitate 367.30
imitation 261.67.27
imitative 485.15.12
imitator 17.338.10

immaculate
371.17.1
immanent 420.55
immanentism
242.35.21
immaterial
228.3.11
immaterialism
242.35.11.2.1
immaterialize
516.3.2.1
immature 10.5
immaturity
16.333.23
immeasurable
228.16.35.2
immediate 371.1
immediately 16.189
immemorial
228.3.12
immense 316
immensity
16.333.31
immensurable
228.16.35
immerse 297
immersion 261.69
immersionism
242.35.14
immethodical
228.23.2
immigrant 420
immigrate 367.26
immigration
261.67.24
imminent 420.53
Immingham 242.17
immiscible
228.16.39
immobile 219
immobilism
242.35.9
immobility
16.333.9.1
immobilize 516.2
immoderate 371.35
immodest 436
immodesty 16.366
immolate 367.14
immolation
261.67.14
immoral 228.73
immoralist 436.7
immorality
16.333.8.9

immortal 228.105
immortality
16.333.8
immortalize 516.3
immortelle 215.3
immovable
228.16.62
immune 260
immunity
16.333.18
immunize 516
immunoassay 2.20
immunogenic
38.32.1
immunoglobulin
252.10
immunology
16.108.4
immunotherapy
16.254
immure 10
immutable
228.16.53
Imo 12.47
imp 287
impact 382
impacted 91
impair 4
impala 17.161
impale 214
impalpable 228.16
impart 366
impartial 228.90
impartiality
16.333.8.1
impassable 228.16
impasse 294
impassion 261.66
impassioned 143
impassive 485.1
impaste 432
impatience 321
impatiens 546
impatient 420.73
impeach 66
impeachable
228.16.12
impeachment 420
impearl 216
impeccable 228.16
impeccant 420
impecunious 310.2
impedance 321.4
impede 89

impediment
420.31.1
impedimenta
17.368
impel 215
impend 131
impending 265.20
impenetrable
228.16
impenitence 321.24
impenitent 420.76
imperative 485.15
imperator 9
imperceptible
228.16.58
imperceptive
485.23
imperfect 387
imperfection
261.77
imperfective 485.17
imperforate 371.35
imperial 228.3.11
imperialism
242.35.11.2.1
imperialist 436.7.2
imperil 218.2
imperious 310.2.11
imperishable
228.16.43
imperium 242.2.15
impermanent
420.55
impermeable
228.16.2
impermissible
228.16.39
impersonal 228.63
impersonality
16.333.8.7
impersonalize
516.3.7
impersonate 367.18
impersonation
261.67.19
impersonator
17.338.8
impertinence
321.14
impertinent 420.53
imperturbable
228.16
impervious 310.2
impetigo 12.30
impetrate 367.27

impetuosity
16.333.30.2
impetuous 310.4
impetuousness
300.34.2
impetus 310.64
Imphal 213
impi 16.255
impiety 16.333.2
impinge 209
impious 310.2
impish 353
implacable 228.16
implant 408
implantation
261.67
implausible 228.16
implement 410.1,
420.31
implementation
261.67.32.1
implicate 367.5
implication
261.67.5
implicit 371.36
implode 98
implore 9
implosion 261.92
implosive 485.6
imply 7
impolicy 16.300
impolite 372.4
impoliteness
300.39
impolitic 38.52
imponderabilia
17.3.21.1
imponderable
228.16.35
imponent 420.54
import 374
importance 321
important 420
importation 261.67
importer 17.345
importunate
371.28.1
importune 260.5
importunity
16.333.18
impose 520
imposing 265.83
imposition
261.71.9

impossibility
16.333.9.2
impossible 228.16
impost 441
impostor 17.385
imposture 17.74
impotence 321.25
impotent 420.78
impound 139
impoverish 353.11
impracticable
228.16.10
impractical
228.23.22
impracticality
16.333.8.3
imprecate 367.5
imprecation
261.67.5
imprecise 301
imprecision
261.91.1
impregnable
228.16
impregnate 367
impresa 17.439
impresario 12.3.5
impress 296
impressed 433
impression 261.68
impressionable
228.16.31
impressionism
242.35.14.4
impressionist
436.13
impressionistic
38.70.4
impressive 485.2
impressiveness
300.43
impressment 420
imprimatur 17.338
imprint 412
imprinting 265
imprison 261.126
imprisonment
420.42
improbability
16.333.9.2
improbable 228.16
improbity 16.333
impromptu 15
improper 17.255
impropriate 367.1

impropriety
16.333.2
improvable
228.16.62
improve 490
improvement
420.51
improvident 420.10
improvisation
261.67.36
improvise 516
imprudent 420.13
impudence 321
impudent 420.12
impugn 260
impulse 313
impulsion 261
impulsive 485
impulsiveness
300.43
impunity 16.333.18
impure 10
impurity 16.333.23
imputable
228.16.53
imputation
261.67.29
impute 380
in 252
inability 16.333.9.2
inaccessible
228.16.37
inaccuracy 16.307
inaccurate 371.34
inaction 261.76
inactivate 367.36
inactive 485.16
inactivity
16.333.35.2
inadequacy 16.307
inadequate 371
inadmissible
228.16.39
inadvertence 321
inadvertent 420
inadvisable
228.16.64
inalienable
228.16.31
inalterable
228.16.35
inamorata 17.337.2
inamorato 12.73
inane 247.6
inanimate 371.19

inanition 261.71
inanity 16.333.14
inapplicable
228.16.10
inapposite 371.40
inappreciable
228.16.42
inappreciative
485.15
inappropriate
371.1
inappropriateness
300.38
inapt 421
inarticulate
371.17.2
inartistic 38.70
inasmuch 72
inattention
261.82.3
inattentive 485.21
inaudible 228.16.16
inaugural 228.76
inaugurate 367.22
inauguration
261.67.21
inauspicious
310.58
inboard 95
inborn 255
inbound 139
inbred 86
inbreed 89
Inca 17.44
incalculable
228.16.25
in camera 17.279
incandesce 296
incandescence
321.21
incandescent
420.67
incantation
261.67.31
incapable
228.16.32
incapacitate
367.30.2
incapacity
16.333.25.1
Incaparina
17.230.1
incarcerate 367.23
incarnation
261.67.17

incautious 310.59
incendiary 16.274.1
incense 316
incensory
16.274.38
incentive 485.21
incept 422
inception 261.84
inceptive 485.23
incertitude 102.2
incessant 420.67
incest 433
incestuous 310.4
inch 80
inchmeal 217
inchoate 367
inchworm 233
incidence 321.5
incident 420.10
incidental
228.110.1
incidentally 16.131
incidentals 539
incinerate 367.23
incineration
261.67.22
incinerator
17.338.9
incipient 420.1
incise 516
incision 261.91
incisive 485.5
incisor 17.441
incite 372
incitement 420
incivility 16.333.9
inclemency 16.312
inclement 420
inclinable
228.16.30
inclination
261.67.18
incline 253.5
inclined 135
inclinometer
17.342.3
include 102
included 91
inclusion 261.93
inclusive 485.8
incoercible
228.16.38
incognito 12.76
incognizant 420
incoherence 321.17

incoherent 420.62
incombustible
228.16.60
income 240
incoming 265.38
incommensurate
371.35
incommode 98.1
incommodious
310.2.2
incommodity
16.333.6
incommunicable
228.16.10
incommunicado
12.16
incommutable
228.16.53
incomparable
228.16.35
incompatibility
16.333.9.2
incompatible
228.16
incompetence
321.24
incompetent
420.76
incomplete 370
incompleteness
300.37
incompliant 420.2
incomprehensible
228.16.40
incomprehension
261.82.1
incomputable
228.16.53
inconceivable
228.16.61
inconclusive 485.8
incongruity
16.333.3
incongruous 310.4
inconsequent
420.58
inconsequential
228.96
inconsiderable
228.16.35
inconsiderate
371.35
inconsistency
16.312
inconsistent 420.81

inconsolable
228.16.24
inconsonant 420.55
inconspicuous
310.4.1
inconstant 420
incontestable
228.16.59
incontinence
321.14
incontinent 420.53
incontrovertible
228.16.47
inconvenience
321.1
inconvenient
420.1.2
inconvertible
228.16.47
inconvincible
228.16.41
incoordinate
371.24.1
incoordination
261.67.18.1
incorporate 367.23
incorporated
91.34.7
incorporeal
228.3.12
incorporeity
16.333.1
incorrect 385.6
incorrectness
300.41
incorrigible
228.16.20
incorrupt 426.1
incorruptible
228.16
increase 298
incredible
228.16.14
incredulity 16.333
incredulous
310.25.3
increment 420.31
incremental
228.110.2
increscent 420.67
incretion 261.70
incriminate 367.17
incrimination
261.67.18.5
incross 302

incubate 367
incubation 261.67
incubator 17.338
incubus 310
inculcate 367.7
inculcation 261.67
inculpable 228.16
inculpate 367
incumbency 16.312
incumbent 420
incunabula
17.174.1
incur 3
incurable 228.16.34
incuriosity
16.333.30.1
incurious 310.2.14
incurrence 321
incurrent 420.64
incursion 261.69
incursive 485.3
incurvate 367.35,
371.37
incus 310
incuse 523
Ind 134
indebted 91.35
indecency 16.312
indecent 420.69
indecipherable
228.16.35
indecision 261.91.1
indecisive 485.5
indeclinable
228.16.30
indecorous 310.50
indecorum 242.20
indeed 89
indefatigable
228.16.19
indefensible
228.16.40
indefinable
228.16.30
indefinite 371.24
indehiscent 420.70
indelible 228.16
indelicate 371.9
indemnify 7.3
indemnity 16.333
indemonstrable
228.16
indent 410
indentation
261.67.32

indention 261.82
indenture 17.70
independence
321.7
independent
420.14
indescribable
228.16.8
indestructible
228.16.54
indeterminable
228.16.29
indeterminate
371.24
indeterminism
242.35.13
index 496
indexer 17.426
India 17.3
Indian 261.3
Indiana 17.225.1
Indianapolis
300.13.1
Indic 38
indican 261.13
indicant 420.7
indicate 367.5
indication 261.67.5
indicative 485.15.1
indicator 17.338.2
indices 513
indicia 17.3.49
indict 372
indictable
228.16.50
indictment 420
Indies 515
indifference 321.20
indifferent 420.65
indifferentism
242.35.21
indigene 251
indigenous 310.33
indigent 420.20
indigestible
228.16.59
indigestion 261.18
indigestive 485.24
indign 253
indignant 420
indignation 261.67
indignity 16.333.19
indigo 12.29
indirect 385

indirection
261.77.3
indirectness 300.41
indiscernible
228.16.28
indiscipline 252
indiscreet 370
indiscretion 261.68
indiscriminate
371.24
indispensable
228.16.40
indispose 520
indisposed 155
indisposition
261.71.9
indisputable
228.16.53
indissoluble 228.15
indistinct 392
indistinctive 485.20
indistinguishable
228.16.43
indium 242.2
individual 228.9.1
individualism
242.35.11.3
individualist
436.7.3
individualistic
38.70.2
individuality
16.333.8.2
individualize
516.3.3
individuate 367.2
indivisible
228.16.63
Indochina 17.232
indocile 219
indoctrinate 367.17
indoctrination
261.67.18
indole 223
indolence 321.12
indolent 420.28
indomitable
228.16.49
Indonesia 17.3.60
Indonesian
261.3.34
indoor 9
indoors 518
Indore 9
indrawn 255

indris 300
indubitable
228.16.49
induce 309
inducement 420
induct 389
inductance 321
inductee 5
inductile 219
induction 261.79
inductive 485.19
inductor 17.357
indulge 205
indulgence 321
indulgent 420.21
induline 253
indult 406
indurate 371.34
Indus 310
indusium 242.2
industrial 228.3
industrialism
242.35.11.2
industrialist
436.7.2
industrialize
516.3.2
industrious 310.2
industry 16
indwell 215
inearth 456
inebriant 420.1
inebriate 367.1,
371.1
inebriation
261.67.1
inebriety 16.333.2
inedible 228.16.14
ineducable 228.16
ineffable 228.16
ineffaceable
228.16.36
ineffective 485.17
ineffectual 228.9.5
inefficacious
310.56.1
inefficacy 16.307.1
inefficiency
16.312.5
inefficient 420.74
inelastic 38.68
inelasticity
16.333.28.2
inelegant 420.17

ineligible
228.16.20.1
ineloquent 420.59
ineluctable
228.16.54
inept 422
ineptitude 102.2
inequality
16.333.10
inequitable
228.16.49
inequity 16.333
ineradicable
228.16.10
inert 369
inertia 17.324
inescapable
228.16.32
inescutcheon 261
in esse 16.297
inessential 228.96
inessive 485.2
inestimable 228.16
inevitable
228.16.49
inexact 382
inexactitude 102.2
inexcusable
228.16.65
inexhaustible
228.16
inexorable
228.16.35
inexpedient 420.1.1
inexpensive 485.9
inexperience 321.1
inexperienced 448
inexpert 369
inexplicable
228.16.10
inexplicit 371.36
inexpressible
228.16.37
inexpressive 485.2
inextinguishable
228.16.43
inextricable
228.16.10
infallible 228.16
infamize 516.5
infamous 310.29
infamy 16.222
infancy 16.312
infant 420
infanta 17.365

infante 16.353
infanticide 92.7
infantile 219
infantilism
242.35.9
infantility 16.333.9
infantry 16.291
infantryman
261.48
infarct 383
infarction 261
infare 4
infatuate 367.2
infatuated 91.34.2
infatuation
261.67.2
infect 385
infection 261.77
infectious 310
infectiousness
300.34
infective 485.17
infecund 143
infecundity
16.333.7
infelicity 16.333.28
infer 3
inference 321.20
inferential 228.96.2
inferior 17.3.39
inferiority
16.333.22
infernal 228.58
inferno 12.53
infertile 219
infertility 16.333.9
infest 433
infestation
261.67.33
infidel 228.32
infidelity 16.333
infield 115
infighting 265.67
infiltrate 367
infiltration 261.67
infinite 371.24
infinitesimal
228.52.1
infinitive 485.12
infinity 16.333.17
infirm 233
infirmary 16.274.21
infirmity 16.333
infix 498
inflame 231

inflammable
228.16.26
inflammation
261.67.16
inflammatory
16.274.43.5
inflatable 228.16.45
inflate 367
inflation 261.67
inflationary
16.274.29.1
inflationism
242.35.14.3
inflect 385
inflection 261.77
inflexible 228.16
inflict 387
inflorescence
321.21
inflow 12
influence 321.3
influent 420.4
influential 228.96
influenza 17.446
influx 502
info 12
inform 238
informal 228.53
informality
16.333.8.5
informant 420.32
information
261.67.16
informative
485.15.6
informer 17.214
infract 382
infra dig 184
infralapsarian
261.3.21
infrangible
228.16.21
infrared 86
infrasonic 38.35.4
infrastructure
17.66
infrequency 16.312
infrequent 420.57
infringe 209
infringement 420
infulae 5
infundibulum
242.10
infuriate 367.1
infuscate 367

infuse 523
infuser 17.444
infusible 228.16.65
infusion 261.93
infusionism
242.35.14
ingather 17.400
ingenious 310.2.7
ingénue 15
ingenuity
16.333.3.1
ingenuous 310.4.2
ingest 433
ingesta 17.382
ingestion 261.18
ingle 228.50
inglenook 44
inglorious 310.2.13
ingoing 265.4
ingot 381
ingrain 247
ingrained 130
ingrate 367
ingratiate 367.1.5
ingratiation
261.67.1
ingratitude 102.2.1
ingravescent
420.67.3
ingredient 420.1.1
ingress 296
ingressive 485.2
ingrowing 265.4
ingrown 257
ingrowth 461
inguinal 228.60
ingurgitate 367.30
Ingush 358
inhabit 371.4
inhabitant 420.76
inhalant 420.25
inhalation
261.67.14
inhalator 17.338
inhale 214
inhaler 17.162
inharmonious
310.2.9
inhere 6
inherence 321.17
inherent 420.62
inherit 371.31
inheritance 321.24
inherited 91.38
inheritor 17.342

inhesion 261.90
inhibit 371.5
inhibition 261.71
inhibitor 17.342
inhospitable
228.16.49
inhospitality
16.333.8
inhuman 261.51
inhumane 247
inhumanity
16.333.14
inhume 241
inimical 228.23
inimitable
228.16.49
inion 261.3.17
iniquitous 310.64
iniquity 16.333
initial 228.93
initialize 516.3
initially 16.131
initiate 367.1.6,
371.1
initiation
261.67.1.5
initiative 485.15
inject 385
injection 261.77
injector 17.354
injudicious 310.58
Injun 261
injunction 261.80
injure 17.157
injurious 310.2.14
injury 16.274.14
injustice 300
ink 52
inkblot 373
Inkerman 261.52
inkhorn 255
inkle 228.29
inkling 265
inkstand 128
inkwell 215
inky 16.37
inlaid 85
inland 143
inlay 2
inlet 368
inlier 17.4
inmate 367
in memoriam
242.2.17
inn 252

innards 531
innate 367.17
inner 17.231
innermost 441
innervate 367.35
innerve 483
inning 265.43
innings 552
innkeeper 17.252
innocence 321
innocent 420
innocuous 310.4
innominate 371.24
in nomine 2.15
innovate 367,
367.37
innovation 261.67
innovative 485.15
innoxious 310
Innsbruck 44
innuendo 12.24
Innuit 371.2
innumerable
228.16.35
innumerate 371.35
inobservance 321
inoculable
228.16.25
inoculate 367.13.3
inoculation
261.67.13
inoculum 242.10
inodorous 310.50
inoffensive 485.9
inofficious 310.58
inoperable
228.16.35
inoperative
485.15.10
inopportune 260.6
inordinate 371.24.1
inorganic 38.31
inotropic 38.37.2
inpatient 420.73
in posse 16.302
input 379
inqilab 19
inquest 433
inquietude 102.2
inquire 8
inquiring 265.54
inquiry 16.267
inquisition
261.71.8
inquisitive 485.12

inquisitiveness

inquisitiveness
300.43
inquisitor 17.342.4
inquisitorial
228.3.12.1
in re 2
in rem 232
inroad 98
inrush 356
insalivate 367.36
insane 247
insanitary
16.274.41
insanity 16.333.14
insatiable 228.16
inscape 270
inscribe 25
inscription 261.85
inscriptive 485
inscrutable
228.16.53
insect 385
insectarium
242.2.14
insecticide 92.7
insectivore 9.13
insectivorous
310.50.3
insecure 10.3
insecurity
16.333.23
inselberg 182
inseminate 367.17
insemination
261.67.18
insensate 367.29
insensible
228.16.40
insensitive 485.12
insentient 420.1
inseparable
228.16.35.1
insert 369
insertion 261.69
insessorial 228.3.12
inset 368
inshore 9
inside 92.9
insider 17.84
insidious 310.2.1
insight 372
insignia 17.3
insignificant 420.7
insincere 6

insincerity
16.333.21
insinuate 367.2
insinuation
261.67.2
insipid 91.24
insist 436
insistence 321.27
insistent 420.81
insolate 367.14
insolation 261.67
insole 223
insolence 321.12
insolent 420.28
insoluble 228.15
insolvency 16.312
insolvent 420
insomnia 17.3
insomniac 32.1
insomuch 72
insouciant 420.1
inspect 385
inspection 261.77
inspector 17.354
inspectorate 371.35
inspiration 261.67
inspirational
228.63.3
inspiratory
16.274.43
inspire 8
inspiring 265.54
inspirit 371.33
instability
16.333.9.2
install 221
installation
261.67.14
instalment 420
instance 321
instant 420
instantaneous
310.2.6
instanter 17.365
instantiate 367.1.8
instantly 16.198
instar 1
instead 86
instep 271
instigate 367.10
instigation
261.67.10
instil 218
instinct 392
instinctive 485.20

institute 380.5
institution 261.75
institutional
228.63.7
institutionalism
242.35.11.5
institutionalize
516.3.7
institutive 485
instruct 389
instruction 261.79
instructional
228.63
instructive 485.19
instructor 17.357
instructress 300
instrument 420.35
instrumental
228.110.3
instrumentalism
242.35.11.6
instrumentalist
436.7.7
instrumentation
261.67.32
insubordinate
371.24.1
insubordination
261.67.18.1
insubstantial
228.95
insufferable
228.16.35
insufficiency
16.312.5
insufficient 420.74
insufflate 367
insula 17.174.11
insular 17.174.11
insularity
16.333.20.3
insulate 367.13
insulation
261.67.13
insulator 17.338.6
insulin 252.10
insult 406
insuperable
228.16.35
insupportable
228.16.51
insurable 228.16.34
insurance 321.19
insure 10.2
insured 96

insurer 17.277
insurgence 321
insurgency
16.312.3
insurgent 420.19
insurmountable
228.16.56
insurrection
261.77.4
insurrectionary
16.274.29.4
intact 382
intaglio 12.3
intake 34
intangible
228.16.21
intarsia 17.3.47
integer 17.150
integral 228
integrand 128
integrant 420
integrate 367.26
integration
261.67.24
integrator 17.338
integrity 16.333
integument 420.34
intellect 385.4
intellection
261.77.2
intellectual 228.9.5
intellectualism
242.35.11.3
intellectualize
516.3.3
intelligence 321.9
intelligent 420.20
intelligentsia 17.3
intelligible
228.16.20.1
Intelsat 365
intemperate 371.35
intend 131
intendance 321.7
intendant 420.14
intended 91.13
intendment 420
intenerate 367.23.1
intense 316
intensifier 17.4.1
intensify 7.3
intensity 16.333.31
intensive 485.9
intent 410
intention 261.82

402

intentional
228.63.9
intently 16.197
inter 3
interact 382
interaction 261.76
interactive 485.16
interatomic 38.29
interbedded 91.7
interbreed 89
intercalary
16.274.19
intercalate 367.14.2
intercede 89.3
intercept 422
interceptor 17.375
intercession
261.68.1
interchange 207
interchangeable
228.16
intercity 16.333
intercom 237
intercommunication
261.67.5
intercommunion
261.123
interconnect 385
intercontinental
228.110
intercostal 228.115
intercourse 303
intercross 302.2
intercurrent 420.64
interdependent
420.14
interdict 387.1
interdiction
261.78.2
interdisciplinary
16.274.26
interest 436.20
interested 91.53
interesting 265.76
interface 295
interfacing 265.59
interfere 6
interference 321.17
interferometer
17.342.3.4
interferon 254.9
interfluent 420.4
interfluve 490
interfuse 523.1
intergrade 85.6

interim 235
interior 17.3.39
interject 385.3
interjection
261.77.1
interlace 295
Interlaken 261.10
interlaminate
367.17.3
interlard 84
interlay 2.12
interleaf 162
interleave 484
interline 253.3
interlinear 17.3.34
interlining 265.44
interlink 52
interlock 40
interlocution
261.75.2
interlocutor 17.350
interlocutory
16.274.42
interlope 278
interloper 17.257
interlude 102.1
interlunation
261.67
intermarriage 197.9
intermarry 16.260
intermediary
16.274.1
intermediate 371.1
interment 420
intermezzo 12.71
intermigration
261.67
interminable
228.16.29
intermingle 228.50
intermission
261.71.4
intermit 371.21
intermittent 420.76
intermixture 17.76
intern 249
internal 228.58
internalize 516.3.6
international
228.63.2
internationalism
242.35.11.5.1
internationalize
516.3.7
internecine 253

internee 5
internment 420
internode 98
internship 274
interpage 193
interpellant 420.26
interpellate 367
interphone 257
interplay 2
interplead 89
interpleader 17.82
Interpol 220
interpolate 367.14
interpolation
261.67.14
interpose 520.2
interpret 371
interpretation
261.67.27
interpretative
485.15.12
interpreter 17.342
interpretive 485.12
interregnum 242
interrelate 367.12
interrelation
261.67.12
interrex 496
interrobang 263.1
interrogate
367.11.1
interrogation
261.67.11
interrogative
485.15.3
interrogator
17.338.4
interrogatory
16.274.43.3
interrupt 426.1
interruption 261.88
interscholastic
38.68
intersect 385
intersection 261.77
intersex 496
interspace 295
intersperse 297.1
interstate 367
interstice 300
interstitial 228.93
interstratify 7.3.8
intertrigo 12.30
intertwine 253
interval 228

intervene 251.12
intervention 261.82
interventionist
436.13
interview 15
interviewee 5
interviewer 17.8
intervocalic 38.19
interweave 484
interwoven 261.116
intestate 367.33
intestinal 228.60
intestine 252.26
intima 17.211
intimacy 16.307.2
intimate 367.15.
371.19
intimation
261.67.15
intimidate 367.8
intimidation
261.67.7
intinction 261
into 15
intolerable
228.16.35
intolerance 321.20
intolerant 420.65
intonate 367.18
intonation
261.67.19
intone 257
intorsion 261.72
in toto 12.79
intoxicant 420.7
intoxicate 367.5
intoxication
261.67.5
intra-atomic 38.29
intracranial 228.3.5
intractable 228.16
intrados 302
intramural 228.75
intramuscular
17.174.8
intransigence 321.9
intransigent 420.20
intransitive 485.12
intranuclear 17.3
intrastate 367
intrauterine 253.7
intravenous 310.32
intrepid 91.23
intricacy 16.307.1
intricate 371.9

intrigue 183
intriguing 265
intrinsic 38
intro 12
introduce 309.1
introduction
 261.79.1
introductory
 16.274
introject 385.3
introjection
 261.77.1
intromission
 261.71.4
introrse 303
introspect 385
introspection
 261.77
introspective
 485.17
introversion
 261.69.1
introvert 369.2
intrude 102
intruder 17.91
intrusion 261.93
intrusive 485.8
intubate 367
intuit 371.3
intuition 261.71
intuitive 485.12
intumesce 296
intumescence
 321.21
intussusception
 261.84.1
inulin 252.10
inunction 261.80
inundate 367
inundation 261.67
inure 10
inurn 249
invade 85
invader 17.79
invaginate
 367.17.2, 371.24.2
invagination
 261.67.18.2
invalid 89
invalid 91.16
invalidate 367.8
invalidism 242.35
invalidity 16.333.5
invaluable 228.16.6
invariable 228.16.2

invariant 420.1
invasion 261
invasive 485
invective 485.17
inveigh 2
inveigle 228.45
invent 410
invention 261.82
inventive 485.21
inventiveness
 300.43
inventor 17.368
inventory
 16.274.48
inveracity
 16.333.25
Invercargill 218
Inverness 296.3
inverse 297
inversion 261.69
invert 369
invertase 509
invertebrate 371
inverter 17.340
invest 433
investigate 367.10
investigation
 261.67.10
investigative
 485.15
investigator
 17.338.3
investiture 17.56
investment 420
investor 17.382
inveterate 371.35.2
inviable 228.16.3
invidious 310.2.1
invigilate 367.12
invigilation
 261.67.12
invigilator 17.338.5
invigorate 367.23
invincible
 228.16.41
inviolable 228.16
inviolate 371.18.1
invisibility
 16.333.9.2.2
invisible 228.16.63
invitation
 261.67.27
invitatory
 16.274.43
invite 372

inviting 265.67
in vitro 12
invocation 261.67.6
invoice 304
invoke 42
involucel 215
involucre 17.41
involuntary
 16.274.48
involute 380.1
involution 261.75.1
involve 493
involved 151
invulnerable
 228.16.35
invultuation
 261.67.2
inward ˙103
inwardly 16.152
inwards 531
inweave 484
inwrought 374
Io 12.4
iodic 38.9
iodide 92
iodine 251.1
iodism 242.35
iodize 516
iodoform 238.2
iodometry 16.285.2
iodous 310
ion 261.4
Iona 17.236
Ionesco 12.14
Ionia 17.3.36
Ionian 261.3.18
ionic 38.35
Ionic 38.35
ionize 516.7
ionone 257
ionosphere 6.1
iontophoresis
 300.51.1
iota 17.347
I.O.U 15
Iowa 17.6
ipecac 32
ipecacuanha
 17.225
Ipswich 67
iracund˙ 140
Iran 246
Iranian 261.3.15
Iraq 33
Iraqi 16.20

irascible 228.16
irate 367
Irbid 91
ire 8
Ireland 143
Irene 16.228
irenic 38.33
irenics 498.4
iridaceous 310.56.2
iridescence 321.21
iridescent 420.67
iridium 242.2.3
Iris 300.45
iris 300.45
Irish 353
Irishism 242.35
Irishman 261
iritis 300.62
irk 36
irksome 242
iron 261.4
ironbark 33
ironbound 139
ironclad 83
ironic 38.35
ironical 228.23.13
ironing 265.46
ironize 516.7
ironmonger 17.143
ironmongery
 16.274.11
Ironside 92
ironsides 527
ironware 4
ironwood 101
ironwork 36
ironworks 497
irony 16.237,
 16.237.1
Iroquoian 261.5
Iroquois 11
irradiance 321.1
irradiate 367.1
irradiation
 261.67.1
irrational 228.63.2
irrationality
 16.333.8.7.1
Irrawaddy 16.65
irreconcilable
 228.16
irrecoverable
 228.16.35
irrecusable
 228.16.65

irredeemable
228.16
irredentist 436.27
irreducible 228.16
irrefrangible
228.16.21
irrefutable
228.16.52
irregular 17.174
irregularity
16.333.20.3
irrelative 485.15.4
irrelevant 420
irreligion 261.37
irreligious 310.21
irremediable
228.16.2
irremovable
228.16.62
irreparable
228.16.35.1
irreplaceable
228.16.36
irrepressible
228.16.37
irreproachable
228.16.13
irresistible 228.16
irresoluble 228.15
irresolute 380.1
irresolution
261.75.1
irresolvable 228.16
irrespective 485.17
irresponsible
228.16
irresponsive 485
irretentive 485.21
irretrievable
228.16.61
irreverence
321.20.1
irreverent 420.65
irreversible
228.16.38
irrevocable 228.16
irrigate 367.10
irrigation 261.67.10
irrigational
228.63.3
irritable 228.16.49
irritant 420.76
irritate 367.30
irritation 261.67.27
irrupt 426

irruptive 485
Irvine 252
Irving 265.78
is 515
Isaac 46
Isabel 215
Isabella 17.163.1
isagoge 16.106
isagogics 498
Isaiah 17.4
isallobar 1.2
Isar 1
Iscariot 381.1.1
ischaemia 17.3.26
ischium 242.2
isentropic 38.37
Isherwood 101
Ishmael 228.1
isinglass 294
Isis 300.53
Iskander Bey 2.4
Iskenderun 260.3
Islam 230
Islamic 38.24
Islamize 516.5
island 143
islander 17.109
Islay 2
isle 219
islet 371
Islington 261
ism 242.35
Ismaili 16.118
isn't 420
isobar 1.2
isobaric 38.38
isobath 452
isocheim 236
isochor 9.2
isochronal 228.63
isoclinal 228.61
isocline 253
isocracy 16.307.5
Isocrates 513.17
isocyanide 92.4
isodiaphere 6
isodynamic 38.24
isoelectric 38
isogamy 16.222.2
isogloss 302
isogon 254.5
isogonic 38.35
isolate 367.14
isolation 261.67.14

isolationism
242.35.14.3
isolex 496
isologous 310
isomagnetic 38.50
isomer 17.218
isomerism
242.35.15
isomerize 516.8
isomerous 310.50
isometric 38.46
isometrics 498.10
isometry 16.285.2
isomorph 166.1
isomorphism
242.35.7
isoniazid 91
isonomy 16.222.3
isopiestic 38.69
isopleth 455
isorhythmic 38.30
isosceles 513.6
isostasy 16.307
isosteric 38.39
isothere 6.10
isotherm 233
isotone 257.3
isotonic 38.35.5
isotope 278
isotopic 38.37
Israel 228.1
Israeli 16.114
Israelite 372.4
Israfil 217
issuable 228.16.6
issuance 321.3
issuant 420.4
issue 15
Issus 310.53
Istanbul 226
isthmus 310
istle 16.201
Istria 17.3
it 371
itacolumite 372
Italian 261.118
Italianate 371.28
Italianism
242.35.14
Italianize 516.7
italic 38.19.1
Italicism
242.35.16.1
italicize 516.10
Italy 16.131

itch 67
itching 265
itchy 16.49
item 232, 242.29
itemize 516.5
iterate 367.23.2
iteration
261.67.22.4
Ithaca 17.42
itinerancy 16.312
itinerant 420.65
itinerary 16.274.32
itinerate 367.23
it'll 228.102
it's 339
its 339
itself 172
Ivan 261.115
I've 486
Ives 554
ivied 91
ivories 515.1
ivory 16.274.52
ivy 16
Iwo Jima 17.210
ixia 17.3.58
izard 103
Izmir 6

J

jab 18
Jabalpur 10
jabber 17.9
jabberwocky 16.27
jaborandi 16.77
jabot 12
jacamar 1.12
jacana 1
jacaranda 17.98.2
jacinth 470
Jack 32
jack 32
jackal 221
jackanapes 323
jackass 293
jackboot 380
jackdaw 9
jackeroo 15.6
jacket 371.6
jackfruit 380

jockstrap 268
jocose 305
jocosely 16.182
jocular 17.174.7
jocularity
  16.333.20.3
jocund 143
jocundity 16.333.7
jocundly 16.157
jodhpurs 524
Jodo 12.21
Joe 12
joey 16.3
jog 185
jogger 17.131
jogging 265.23
joggle 228.47
Jogjakarta 1
johannes 513
Johannesburg
  182.1
John 254, 261
John Dory 16.269
Johnny 16.231
John o'Groats 343
Johnson 261
Johnsonian
  261.3.18
Johore 9
join 256
joinder 17.106
joiner 17.235
joinery 16.274
joint 416
jointed 91.48
jointer 17.371
joist 440
joke 42
joker 17.38
jokingly 16.175
jollify 7.3.2
jollity 16.333.10
jolly 16.122
Jolo 12.44
jolt 405
Jonah 17.236
Jonas 310.35
Jonathan 261.109
Jones 550
jonnock 46
jonquil 218
Joplin 252
Joppa 17.255
Jordan 261.27
Jordanian 261.3.15

jorum 242.20
Jos 302
Joseph 163
Josephine 251
Josephus 310
josh 354
Joshua 17.7
Josiah 17.4
joss 302
jostle 228.86
jostler 17.198
jot 373
jotter 17.344
jotting 265.68
joual 213
joule 227
jounce 319
journal 228.58
journalese 513.7
journalism
  242.35.11.4
journalist 436.7
journalistic 38.70.2
journalize 516.3.6
journey 16.227
journeyman 261.48
journo 12.53
joust 442
Jove 488
jovial 228.3.16
joviality 16.333.8.1
Jovian 261.3.31
jowl 224
joy 11
Joyce 304
joyful 226
joyless 300
joyous 310
joyousness 300.34
joypop 276
joyrider 17.84
Juan de Fuca
  17.41
juba 17.20
Jubal 228
jube 16.14, 30
jubilant 420
jubilate 367.12.1
jubilation
  261.67.12
jubilee 5.8
Judaea 17.2
Judaean 261.2
Judah 17.91
Judaic 38.1

Judaica 17.33
Judaism 242.35
Judaist 436.1
Judaize 516
Judas 310
judder 17.90
Jude 102
judge 203
judgeship 274
judgment 420
judicative 485.15.1
judicator 17.338.2
judicatory
  16.274.40.1
judicature 17.62
judicial 228.93
judiciary 16.274.1.2
judicious 310.58
Judith 458
judo 12.22
judogi 16.96
judoka 1
Judy 16.71
jug 189
jugal 228.48
jugate 367
juggernaut 374
juggins 548
juggle 228
juggler 17.193
jugglery 16.274
juggling 265
jugular 17.174
juice 309
juicy 16.306
jujitsu 15
juju 15
jujube 30
jukebox 499
julep 274
Julia 17.3.23
Julian 261
Juliana 17.226.1
Julie 16.130
julienne 248.1
Juliet 371.1.1
Jullundur 17.109
July 7.6
jumble 228
jumbo 12.7
jumbuck 43
Jumna 17.242
jump 289
jumper 17.264
jumpy 16.257

junction 261.80
juncture 17.68
June 260
Jungian 261.3
jungle 228
junior 17
juniper 17.253
junk 54
Junker 17.46
junket 371
junkie 16.39
junkyard 84
Juno 12
Junoesque 57
junta 17.373
Jupiter 17.342
jupon 254
Jura 17.277
jural 228.75
Jurassic 38.48
jurat 365
juratory 16.274.43
jurel 215
juridical 228.23
jurisconsult 406
jurisdiction 261.78
jurisprudence 321
jurisprudent 420.13
jurist 436.19
juristic 38.70
juror 17.277
jury 16.270
juryman 261.48
jus 307
jus civile 16.118
jus divinum 242
jus naturale 16.114
jussive 485.7
jus soli 7
just 443
justice 300
justiciable 228.16.2
justiciar 1
justiciary
  16.274.1.2
justifiable
  228.16.3.1
justification
  261.67.5.1
justificatory
  16.274.40.1
justify 7.3
Justin 252.27
Justinian 261.3.17
justle 228.87

Kettering 265.58
kettle 228.100
kettledrum 240
kevel 228.118
Kew 15
kex 496
key 5
keyboard 95
keyhole 223
keynote 376
keystone 257
keystroke 42
Khachaturian
    261.3.24
khaddar 17.78
khadi 16.58
khaki 16.20
khan 246
kharif 162.2
Khartoum 241
khayal 213
kheda 17.80
khedive 484
Khmer 4
Khoikhoi 11
Khotan 246
Khrushchev 165
Khyber 17.15
kiaat 366
kiang 263
Kiangsi 5
kibble 228.12
kibbutz 345
kibe 25
kibitz 339
kiblah 1
kibosh 354
kick 38
kickback 32
kicker 17.34
kickshaw 9
kicksorter 17.345
kickstand 128
kick-start 366
kid 91
Kidd 91
Kidderminster
    17.394
kiddle 228.32
Kiddush 358
kiddy 16.63
kidnap 268
kidnapper 17.247
kidney 16.240
kidskin 252

Kiel 217
kier 6
Kierkegaard 84
kieselguhr 10
kieserite 372.8
Kiev 160.1
kif 163
kikoi 11
kikumon 254
Kildare 4
Kilimanjaro 12.61
Kilkenny 16.226
kill 218
Killarney 16.224
killdeer 6
killer 17.166
killick 38.21
Killiecrankie 16.36
killifish 353
killing 265.30
Kilmarnock 46
kiln 262
kilo 12.41
kilocalorie
    16.274.15
kilogram 229.1.2
kilohertz 337
kilometre 17.341
kilometric 38.46
kiloton 259
kilovolt 405
kilowatt 373
kilt 403
kilted 91
Kimberley 16.131
kimberlite 372.4
kimono 12.56
kin 252
Kinabalu 15.5
kinaesthesia
    17.3.60
kinase 509
kincob 26
kind 135
kindergarten
    261.95
kind-hearted 91.33
kind-heartedness
    300.28
kindle 228.40
kindler 17.189
kindless 300
kindliness 300.23
kindling 265
kindly 16.155

kindness 300.29
kindred 91
kine 253
kinematics 498.11
kinesics 498
kinetic 38.50.4
kinetics 498.12
king 265
kingbolt 405
kingcup 279
kingdom 242
kingfisher 17.326
kinglet 371
kingpin 252
kingship 274
King's Lynn 252
Kingston 261.108
kingwood 101
kink 52
kinkajou 15
kinky 16.37
kinnikinnick 38.34
kino 12.54
Kinross 302
Kinsey 16.406
kinsfolk 42
Kinshasa 17.438
kinship 274
kinsman 261
kiosk 59
kip 274
Kipling 265
kipper 17.253
Kirghiz 515
kirigami 16.211
kirk 36
Kirkby 16.9
kirkman 261
Kirkpatrick 38.45
Kirkuk 44
Kirman 246
kish 353
kismet 368
kiss 300
kissable 228.16.39
kissel 228.85
kisser 17.302
kissing 265.61
Kissinger 17.157
kist 436
kit 371
kitbag 178.1
kitchen 252
Kitchener 17.231
kitchenette 368

kitchenware 4
kite 372
kith 458
kitsch 67
kitten 261.99
kittenish 353
kittiwake 34
kittle 228.102
kitty 16.333
kiva 17.413
Kiwanis 300.21
klangfarbe 17.10
Klansman 261
klaxon 261
Kleenex 496
Kleist 437
Klemperer 17.279
klepht 397
kleptomania
    17.3.31.1
kleptomaniac 32.1
klipspringer 17.246
Klondike 39
kloof 170
knack 32
knacker 17.28
knackwurst 434
knag 178
knap 268
knapsack 32
knapweed 89
knar 1
knave 482
knavery 16.274.50
knavish 353
knawel 228.5
knead 89
knee 5
kneecap 268
kneehole 223
kneel 217
kneeler 17.165
kneepad 83
kneepan 245
knell 215
knelt 402
knew 15
Knickerbocker
    17.36
knickerbockers 524
knickers 524
knickknack 32
knickpoint 416
knife 164
kniferest 433

knight 372
knighthood 101
knightly 16.190
knish 353
knit 371
knitted 91.38
knitter 17.342
knitting 265.66
knitwear 4.9
knob 26
knobbly 16.135
knobkerrie 16.262
knock 40
knocker 17.36
knock-kneed 89
knockout 377
knoll 223
Knossos 310.54
knot 373
knotgrass 294
knothole 223
knotted 91.40
knotting 265.68
knotty 16.335
knotweed 89
knout 377
know 12
know-how 13
knowing 265.4
knowledge 197.2
knowledgeable
　228.16.20
known 257
Knox 499
knuckle 228.27
knucklebone 257
knuckle-duster
　17.388
knucklehead 86
knur 3
knurl 216
K.O. 12.1
koa 17.6
koala 17.161
koan 245
kob 26
Kobe 16.12
kobold 120
Kochi 5
Kodiak 32.1
Kodok 40
kofta 17.360
koftgar 1
Kohima 1.11
Kohinoor 10

kohl 223
kohlrabi 16.6
Kohoutek 35
koine 5
kokanee 16.223
Koko Nor 9
kolinsky 16.45
kolkhoz 518
Kol Nidre 2
kolo 12.44
Komati 16.328
komatik 38.49
Komi 16.219
Komodo 12.21
Komsomol 220.2
kongoni 16.233
Konstanz 347
Konya 1
kook 45
kookaburra 17.278
kooky 16.32
Kootenay 5.14
kop 276
kopeck 35
kopje 16.250
Koran 246
Kordofan 245
Korea 17.2.2
Korean 261.2.3
korma 17.214
koruna 17.238
Kos 302
kos 305
kosher 17.328
Kota 17.347
koto 12.79
koulibiaca 17.29
kowhai 7
Kowloon 260
kowtow 13
Kozhikode 98
Kra 1
kraal 213
kraft 396
krait 372
Krakatoa 17.6
kraken 261.10
krameria 17.3.39
Krefeld 113
Kremlin 252
kriegspiel 217
krill 218
krimmer 17.211
Krio 12.2
kris 300

Krishna 17.243
Kriss Kringle
　228.50
Kristiansand 128
Kristianstad 84
kromesky 16.40
krone 17.236
Kruger 17.136
Krugersdorp 277
krypton 254
Kuala Lumpur 10
Kublai Khan 246
Kubrick 38
kudos 302
kudu 15
Kufic 38
Ku Klux Klan 245
kula 17.175
kulak 32
Kumamoto 12.79
Kumasi 16.294
kumbaloi 11.1
kumiss 300
kumquat 373
kung fu 15
Kungur 10
kunzite 372
Kura 1
Kurd 87
Kurdish 353
Kurdistan 246.1
Kure 2
kurrajong 266
kursaal 228.126
Kuskokwim 235
Kutch 72
Kuwait 367
kvass 294
Kwa 1
kwacha 1
Kwajalein 247.4
Kwakiutl 228.108
Kwangchowan 246
kwanza 17.445
kwashiorkor 17.37
Kweisui 2
kwela 17.162
kyanize 516.7
kyat 366
kyle 219
kylix 498
kyloe 12
kymograph 158.1
Kyongsong 266
Kyoto 12.79

kyphosis 300.55
kyu 15

L

laager 17.124
lab 18
labarum 242.21
labdanum 242.16
label 228.11
labeller 17.176
labellum 242.8
labia 17.3.1
labial 228.3
labiate 367.1
labile 219
labium 242.2
lablab 18
laboratory
　16.274.43.7
laborious 310.2.13
labour 17.11
labourer 17.279
labourism
　242.35.15
labourist 436.20
Labourite 372.8
Labrador 9.4
labroid 97
labrum 242
Labuan 261
laburnum 242.13
labyrinth 470
labyrinthian
　261.3.28
labyrinthine 253
lac 32
laccolith 458
lace 295
Lacedaemon
　261.47
Lacedaemonian
　261.3.18
lacerant 420.65
lacerate 367.23
laceration
　261.67.22
Lacerta 17.340
lacertilian 261.3.11
lacewing 265
laches 515

lachrymose 305
lacing 265.59
laciniate 367.1
lack 32
lackadaisical
228.23
lackey 16.19
lacklustre 17.388
laconic 38.35
lacquer 17.28
lacrimal 228.52
lacrimation
261.67.15
lacrimator 17.338
lacrimatory
16.274.43
lacrosse 302.2
lactam 229
lactary 16.274.44
lactase 509
lactate 367
lactation 261.67
lacteal 228.3
lactescent 420.67
lactic 38.58
lactiferous 310.50.2
lactogenic 38.32.1
lactone 257
lactose 520
lacuna 17.238
lacunar 17.238
lacy 16.296
lad 83
ladder 17.77
laddie 16.57
lade 85
laden 261.20
la-di-da 1
lading 265.11
ladino 12.54
Ladislas 293
ladle 228
lady 16.59
ladybird 87
ladyfy 7.3
ladylike 39
ladylove 489
Ladyship 274
Ladysmith 458
Laertes 513
laevorotation
261.67.28
laevulose 520
lag 178
lagan 261

lagena 17.230
lager 17.124
laggard 103
lagging 265
lagniappe 268
lagomorph 166.1
lagoon 260
Lagos 302
La Guardia 17.3.6
lah 1
Lahnda 17.99
Lahore 9
laic 38.1
laicize 516.10
laid 85
laik 34
lain 247
lair 4
laird 88
lairy 16.264
laity 16.333
lake 34
Lakeland 143
laker 17.30
lakh 33
Lakshadweep 273
laky 16.21
Lala 1.7
lallation 261.67
lallygag 178
lam 229
lama 17.206
Lamaism 242.35
Lamarckian 261.3
Lamarckism
242.35
lamb 229
lambaste 432
lambent 420
Lambert 381
Lambeth 464
lambkin 252
lambrequin 252.3
lamé 2
lame 231
lamella 17.163
lamellicorn 255.2
lamely 16.165
lameness 300
lament 410.2
lamentable
228.16.57
lamentation
261.67.32
lamented 91.46

lamia 17.3.24
lamina 17.231.1
laminaria 17.3.38
laminate 367.17.3,
371.24
lamination
261.67.18.3
Lammas 310
lammergeier 17.4
lamp 285
lampas 310.41
lampblack 32
Lampedusa 17.444
lampern 261
lampion 261.3
lamplighter 17.343
lampoon 260
lamppost 441
lamprophyre 8.1
Lanai 16.1
lanai 16.1
Lanark 46
Lancashire 6
Lancaster 17.390
Lancastrian
261.3.26
lance 315
lanceolate 367
lancer 17.313
lancers 524
lancet 371
lanceted 91.38
lancinate 367.17
land 128
landammann
261.52
landau 9
landaulet 368
landed 91.12
Landeshauptmann
261
landfall 221
landform 238
landgrave 482
landgravine 251.12
landing 265.19
landlady 16.59
landlocked 388
landloper 17.257
landlord 95
landlubber 17.19
landmark 33
landmass 293
landowner 17.236
landrace 295

landscape 270
landscapist 436.14
Landseer 6
landshark 33
landside 92
landsknecht 385
landslide 92
landsman 261
Landtag 33
landward 103
lane 247
Lang 263
lang 263
Langland 143
langouste 444
language 197
langue de chat 1
languid 91
languish 353
languor 17.140
languorous 310.50
langur 10
laniary 16.274.1
lank 51
lanky 16.36
lanner 17.225
lanneret 368.6
lanolin 252.11
lansquenet 368
lantana 17.227
lantern 261
lanthanide 92.4
lanthanum 242.16
lanugo 12.32
lanyard 103
Lao 13
Laoag 179
Laocoon 254.2
Laodicea 17.2
Laodicean 261.2.4
Laoighis 353
Laotze 2
lap 268
laparotomy
16.222.4
La Paz 507
lapel 215
lapidary 16.274
lapidate 367.8
lapidify 7.3.1
lapillus 310.23
lapis 300
lapis lazuli 7.6
Lapland 143
Laplander 17.109

Lapp

Lapp 268
lappet 371
lapse 322
lapstrake 34
lapsus 310
lapwing 265
larboard 103
larceny 16.229.4
larch 63
lard 84
larder 17.78
lardon 261
lares 513.10
large 192
largen 261
largess 296
largish 353
largo 12.26
lariat 381.1.1
larine 253
Larisa 17.302
lark 33
Larkin 252.2
larkspur 3
larnax 494
La Rochefoucauld 12
larrigan 261.32
larrikin 252.3
larrup 281
Larry 16.260
larva 17.409
larval 228
larvicide 92.7
Larwood 101
laryngeal 228.2
laryngitic 38.52
laryngitis 300.62
laryngology 16.108.4.7
laryngoscope 278.1
laryngotomy 16.222.4
larynx 505
lasagne 17.434
La Salle 212
lascar 17.47
lascivious 310.2.17
lasciviousness 300.34.1
lase 509
laser 17.439
lash 349
lashing 265
Lashio 12.3

lash-up 279
lasket 371
lass 293
lassie 16.294
lassitude 102.2
lasso 15
Lassus 310.51
last 431
lasting 265.74
lastly 16.199
Las Vegas 310.19
lat 365
latch 62
latchkey 5
late 367
latecomer 17.216
lateen 251.11
lately 16.188
lateness 300
latent 420.75
later 17.338
lateral 228.76
Lateran 261.60
laterite 372.8
latest 436
latex 496
lath 453
lathe 473
lather 17.401
lathery 16.274
lathi 16.328
Latimer 17.218
latimeria 17.3.39
Latin 252
Latinate 367.17
Latinism 242.35.13
Latinist 436.11
Latinity 16.333.17
Latinize 516.6.1
Latino 12.54
latish 353
latitude 102.2.1
latitudinal 228.60.1
latitudinarian 261.3.21.1
Latium 242.2
latria 17.4
latrine 251
latten 261.94
latter 17.336
latterly 16.131.7
lattice 300
latticed 436
Latvian 261.3
laud 95

laudable 228.16.16
laudanum 242.16
laudation 261.67
laudatory 16.274.43
Lauder 17.86
laugh 158
laughable 228.16
laughter 17.358
Laughton 261.102
launch 81
launder 17.105
Launderette 368.6
laundress 300
Laundromat 365
laundry 16
laundryman 261.48
Laura 17.276
Laurasia 17.322
laureate 371.1.2
laurel 228.73
laurustinus 310.34
Lausanne 245
lav 480
lava 17.409
lavage 197
Laval 212
lavation 261.67
lavatory 16.274.43
lavender 17.109
laver 17.409, 17.410
laverock 46
lavish 353
lavishness 300.35
law 9
law-abiding 265.14
lawbreaker 17.30
lawful 226.1
lawgiver 17.414
lawks 500
lawless 300
lawlessness 300.33
lawman 261
lawn 255
Lawrence 321.18
Lawrentian 261.82
lawsuit 380
lawyer 17.430
lax 494
laxation 261.67.34
laxative 485.15
laxity 16.333
lay 2
layabout 377.1

layer 17.1
layering 265.58
layette 368
layman 261.45
lazar 17.437
lazaretto 12.75
Lazarus 310.50
laze 509
laziness 300.23
lazulite 372
lazurite 372
lazy 16.393
lazybones 550
L-dopa 17.257
lea 5
leach 66
Leacock 40
lead 86, 89
Leadbelly 16.115
leaded 91.7
leaden 261.21
leader 17.82
leadership 274.1
leading 265.12, 265.13
leaf 162
leafcutter 17.349
leaflet 371
leafstalk 41
leafy 16.84
league 183
Leah 6
leak 37
leakage 197
leaky 16.24
leal 217
Leamington 261
lean 251
Leander 17.98.1
leaning 265.42
leant 410
leap 273
leapfrog 185
leapt 422
Lear 6
learn 249
learned 91
learner 17.229
learning 265.41
learnt 411
lease 298, 513
leaseback 32
leasehold 120
leaseholder 17.97
leash 352

least 435
leastways 509
leat 370
leather 17.402
leatherback 32.2
Leatherette 368.6
Leatherhead 86.5
leatherhead 86.5
leatherjacket 371.6
leatherneck 35
leatherwood 101
leathery 16.274
leave 484
leaved 148
leaven 261.112
leavings 552
Lebanese 513.9
Lebanon 261
leben 261
lebkuchen 261.15
Le Carré 2.16
Lech 35
lech 64
lecher 17.53
lecherous 310.50
lechery 16.274
lecithin 252
lecithinase 509
lectern 261
lection 261.77
lectionary
   16.274.29.4
lector 9
lecture 17.64
lecturer 17.279
lectureship 274.1
lecythus 310
led 86
Leda 17.82
lederhosen 261.129
ledge 194
ledger 17.147
lee 5
leeboard 95
leech 66
Leeds 526
leek 37
leer 6
leery 16.265
lees 513
leet 370
leeward 103
leeway 2
left 397
left-handed 91.12

left-handedness
   300.28.1
left-hander 17.98
leftism 242.35
leftist 436
leftover 17.417
lefty 16.346
leg 181
legacy 16.307
legal 228.45
legalese 513.7
legalism 242.35.11
legality 16.333.8.4
legalize 516.3
legate 371
legatee 5
legation 261.67.10
legato 12.73
legator 9
legend 143
legendary 16.274
legendry 16.279
legerdemain 247.5
leggings 552
leggy 16.92
leghorn 255
legible 228.16
legion 261.36
legionary 16.274.29
legionnaire 4.5
legislate 367
legislation 261.67
legislative 485.15
legislator 17.338
legislatorial
   228.3.12.2
legislature 17.52
legist 436
legit 371
legitimacy 16.307.2
legitimate 367.15,
   371.19
legitimatize
   516.13.2
legitimist 436.9
legitimize 516.4
legless 300
legman 261
legroom 241
legume 241
legumen 252
leguminous
   310.33.1
legwork 36
Lehár 1

lei 5.1
Leibnitz 339
Leicester 17.382
Leicestershire 6
Leiden 261.25
Leigh 5
Leipzig 184
leishmania 17.3.31
leishmaniasis
   300.57.1
leister 17.383
leisure 17.333
leisured 103.6
leisurely 16.131
Leith 457
leitmotiv 162
Leitrim 235
lek 35
Lely 16.118
lemma 17.208
lemming 265
lemniscus 310.15
Lemnos 302
lemon 261
lemonade 85.3
lemony 16.237.6
lempira 17.272
lemur 17.210
lemuroid 97
Len 248
Lena 17.230
lend 131
lender 17.101
length 472
lengthen 261
lengthways 509
lengthy 16
leniency 16.312.1
lenient 420.1.2
Lenin 252.16
Leningrad 83
Leninism 242.35.13
lenis 300
lenitive 485.12
lenity 16.333.15
Lennon 261
leno 12.54
lens 546
Lent 410
lent 410
lentamente 16.355
lenten 261
lentic 38.63
lenticular 17.174.6
lentiform 238.1

lentigo 12.30
lentil 218
lento 12.84
Leo 12.2
Leonidas 293
leonine 253
leopard 103
leopardess 300.5
Leopold 120
leotard 84
leper 17.250
lepidolite 372.4
lepidopterist
   436.20
lepidosiren 261.58
lepidote 376
Lepidus 310
leporid 91.27
leporine 253.7
leprechaun 255
leprosarium
   242.2.14
leprosy 16.307
leprous 310
lepton 254
leptosome 239
lequear 6
Lerwick 38
lesbian 261.3
lesbianism
   242.35.14.1
Lesbos 302
Les Cayes 2
lese-majesty 16.366
lesion 261.90
Lesley 16.208
less 296
lessee 5.19
lessen 261.63
lesser 17.300
lesson 261.63
lessor 9
lest 433
let 368
lethal 228
lethargic 38
lethargy 16.108
Lethbridge 197
Leto 12.76
let's 336
Lett 368
letter 17.339
letterhead 86.5
lettering 265.58
letterpress 296.5

413

Limassol 220
limb 235
limber 17.25
limbless 300
limbo 12.6
Limburg 182
Limburger 17.127
lime 236
limeade 85
limekiln 262
limelight 372
limen 248
Limerick 38.44
limerick 38.44
limes 513
limestone 257
limey 16.217
limicoline 253.3
limicolous 310.26.2
liminal 228.60.4
limit 371.19
limitarian
  261.3.21.2
limitary 16.274.41
limitation
  261.67.27
limited 91.38
limitless 300.17
limitlessness
  300.33
limitrophe 167
limn 235
limnetic 38.50
limnology 16.108.4
Limoges 363
limonite 372.6
limousine 251
limp 287
limpet 371
limpid 91
limpkin 252
Limpopo 12
limulus 310.25
limy 16.217
linchpin 252
Lincoln 261
Lincolnshire 6.8
lincrusta 17.388
Lincs. 505
linctus 310
lindane 247
Lindbergh 182
linden 261
Lindisfarne 246
line 253

lineage 197
lineal 228.3.7
lineament 420.35
linear 17.3.34
lineate 371.1
lineation 261.67.1
linen 252.17
liner 17.232
linesman 261
ling 265
lingcod 94
linger 17.141
lingerie 16.274
lingo 12.36
lingua franca
  17.43
lingual 228
linguiform 238.1
linguini 16.228
linguist 436
linguistic 38.70
linguistics 498
lingulate 367.13
linhay 16.229
liniment 420.31
lining 265.44
link 52
linkage 197
linkboy 11
linkman 261
links 505
linn 252
Linnaeus 310.1
linnet 371.24
Linnhe 16.229
lino 12
linocut 378
linoleate 367.1.3
linoleum 242.2.7
Linotype 275.1
linsang 263
linseed 89.4
linstock 40
lint 412
lintel 228
linter 17.369
lintwhite 372
Linz 348
lion 261.4
lioness 300.26
lion-hearted 91.33
lionize 516.7
lip 274
lipase 509
lipid 91.24

lipoid 97
lipoma 17.215
lipophilic 38.21
Lippe 17.253
Lippizaner 17.226
lippy 16.248
lip-read 89
lip-reader 17.82
lipstick 38
liquate 367.20
liquefacient 420.73
liquefaction 261.76
liquefy 7.3
liquesce 296
liquescent 420.67
liqueur 10.3
liquid 91
liquidambar 17.23
liquidate 367.8
liquidation
  261.67.7
liquidator 17.338
liquidity 16.333.5
liquidize 516
liquidizer 17.441
liquor 17.34
liquorice 300.47
lira 17.272
liripipe 275
Lisbon 261
lisle 219
lisp 291
lis pendens 546
Lissajous 15
lissom 242.24
list 436
listed 91.53
listel 228.114
listen 261.65
Lister 17.384
lister 17.384
listing 265.76
listless 300
listlessness 300.33
Liszt 436
lit 371
litany 16.237
literacy 16.307.4
literal 228.76
literalism 242.35.11
literally 16.131
literary 16.274.32
literate 371.35
literati 16.328.1
literatim 235

literation
  261.67.22.4
literator 17.338.9
literature 17.56
litharge 192
lithe 477
lithesome 242
lithia 17.3.51
lithiasis 300.57.1
lithic 38.73
lithium 242.2
lithograph 158.1
lithography 16.90.2
lithoid 97
lithology
  16.108.4.18
lithomarge 192
lithosol 220
lithosphere 6.1
lithotomy 16.222.4
lithotrity 16.333
Lithuania 17.3.31
Lithuanian
  261.3.15
litigable 228.16.19
litigant 420.17
litigate 367.10
litigation 261.67.10
litigious 310.21
litmus 310
litotes 513
litre 17.341
litter 17.342
littérateur 3.1
litterbug 189
little 228.102
littoral 228.76
liturgical 228.23.4
liturgist 436.4
liturgy 16.108
live 485, 486
livelihood 101
liveliness 300.23
livelong 266
lively 16
liven 261.115
liver 17.414
liveried 91.27
liverish 353.11
Liverpool 227
Liverpudlian 261.3
liverwort 369
liverwurst 434
livery 16.274.51
livestock 40

liveware 4
livid 91
living 265.80
Livingstone
261.108
Livonia 17.3.36
Livy 16.382
lixiviate 367.1
lixivium 242.2
lizard 103
Ljubljana 17.226
llama 17.206
Llandaff 157
Llandudno 12
Llanelli 16.203
llano 12.51
Llano Estacado
12.16
Llewellyn 252.7
Lloyd 97
lo 12
loach 70
load 98
loaded 91.10
loader 17.88
loading 265.16
loaf 167
loafer 17.117
loam 239
loamy 16.219
loan 257
loath 461
loathe 478
loathing 265
loathsome 242
lob 26
lobar 17.18
lobate 367.3
lobby 16.11
lobbyist 436
lobe 28
lobelia 17.3.20
Lobengula 17.175
loblolly 16.122
lobotomy 16.222.4
lobscouse 306
lobster 17.391
lobster thermidor
9.3
lobule 227
local 228.26
locale 213
localism 242.35.11
locality 16.333.8
localize 516.3

locate 367.6
location 261.67.6
locative 485.15.2
loch 40
lochia 17.3
loci 7
lock 40
lockable 228.16
lockage 197
locker 17.36
locket 371.10
lockjaw 9
lockout 377
locksmith 458
loco 12.12
locoism 242.35.3
locoman 261.49
locomotion
261.73.1
locomotive 485.14
locomotor 17.347
locular 17.174.7
locule 227
locum tenens 546
locus 310.12
locus sigilli 7.5
locus standi 7
locust 445
locution 261.75.2
Lod 94
lode 98
loden 261
lodestar 1
lodestone 257
lodge 199
lodger 17.152
lodging 265
lodgings 552
lodgment 420
lodicule 227.1
loess 300.1
loft 399
lofter 17.360
lofty 16.348
log 185
Logan 261
loganberry 16.274
logaoedic 38.8
logarithm 242.33
logarithmic 38.30
logbook 44
loge 363
logger 17.131
loggerhead 86.5
loggia 17.152

logging 265.23
logia 17.3
logic 38.18
logical 228.23.5
logician 261.71
logicism 242.35.16
logion 254.1
logistic 38.70.1
logistician 261.71
logistics 498
loglog 185
logo 12.31
logogram 229.1
logogriph 163
logomachy 16.33
logopaedics 498
logorrhoea 17.2.2
logos 302
logotype 275.1
logwood 101
logy 16.96
Lohengrin 252
loin 256
loincloth 459
loiter 17.346
Loki 16.29
Lola 17.171
loll 220
Lollard 103.3
lollipop 276
lollop 281.2
lolly 16.122
Lomax 494
Lombard 103
Lombardy 16.72
Lombok 40
loment 410
lomentum 242
Lomond 143
London 261
Londonderry
16.262
Londoner 17.239
lone 257
loneliness 300.23
lonely 16.173
loner 17.236
lonesome 242
long 266
longanimity
16.333.12
longboat 376
longbow 12
longeron 261.60
longevity 16.333.34

longevous 310.73
Longfellow 12.40
Longford 103
long-haired 88
longhand 128
longhorn 255
longicorn 255.2
longing 265
Longinus 310.34
longish 353
longitude 102.2
longitudinal
228.60.1
long johns 549
longship 274
longshore 9
long-sighted 91.39
long-sightedness
300.28
longspur 3
longtime 236
Longueuil 214
longways 509
long-winded 91
Longyearbyen 248
lonicera 17.279.2
loo 15
looby 16.14
loofah 17.119
look 44
looker 17.40
lookout 377
loom 241
loon 260
loony 16.236
loop 280
looper 17.259
loophole 223
loopy 16.253
loose 309
loosebox 499
loosely 16.183
loosen 261
looseness 300
loosestrife 164
loot 380
looter 17.351
lop 276
lope 278
lop-eared 90
lophophore 9.6
lopsided 91.8
loquacious 310.56
loquacity 16.333.25
loquat 373

lor 9
lord 95
lordly 16.150
lordosis 300.55
Lords 528
Lordship 274
lordy 16.66
lore 9
Lorelei 7.7
lorgnette 368
lorica 17.35
lorikeet 370
lorimer 17.211
loris 300.46
lorn 255
Lorraine 247
lorry 16.268
lory 16.269
Los Angeles 513.6
lose 523
losel 228.127
loser 17.444
losing 265.84
loss 302
lossy 16.302
lost 438
lot 373
lota 17.347
Lothair 4
Lothario 12.3.5
Lothian 261.3
lotic 38.55
lotion 261.73
lots 341
lottery 16.274
lotto 12.77
lotus 310.66
louche 358
loud 99
louden 261
loud-hailer 17.162
loudish 353
loudmouth 462
loudness 300
loudspeaker 17.33
lough 40
Loughborough
    17.279
Louis 16.4
louis 16.4
Louisburg 182.1
louis d'or 9.3
Louisiana 17.225.1
lounge 210
lounger 17.158

loupe 280
lour 14
louse 306
lousy 16.400
lout 377
Louth 462
loutish 353
louvar 1
louvre 17.419
louvred 103
lovable 228.16
lovage 197
lovat 381
love 489
lovebird 87
Lovelace 295
loveless 300
loveliness 300.23
Lovell 228
lovelock 40
lovelorn 255
lovely 16.207
lovemaking 265.6
lover 17.418
lovesick 38
lovey 16.383
lovey-dovey 16.383
loving 265
low 12
lowan 261.6
lowborn 255
lowboy 11
lowbred 86
lowbrow 13
lowdown 258
lower 17.6
Lowestoft 399
lowland 143
lowliness 300.23
lowly 16.126
lowness 300.25
Lowry 16.271
lox 499
loxodromics 498
loyal 228.6
loyalism 242.35.11
loyalist 436.7
loyalty 16.352.1
Loyang 263
lozenge 209
lozengy 16.110
Lozi 16.399
Luanda 17.98
Luba 17.20
lubber 17.19

Lubbock 46
lubricant 420.7
lubricate 367.5
lubrication
    261.67.5
lubricator 17.338.2
lubricious 310.58
lubricity 16.333.28
Lubumbashi
    16.319
Lucan 261.15
lucarne 246
lucent 420.71
Lucerne 249
lucerne 249
Lucian 261.3
lucid 91.30
lucidity 16.333.5
Lucifer 17.114
luciferin 252.20
Lucilius 310.2.5
Lucina 17.232
luck 43
luckless 300
lucklessness 300.33
lucky 16.30
lucrative 485.15
lucre 17.41
Lucretius 310.2
lucubrate 367
lucubration 261.67
Lucullus 310
Lucy 16.306
Luddite 372
Ludhiana 17.226.1
ludicrous 310
ludo 12.22
luff 168
luffa 17.118
lug 189
luge 364
Luger 17.136
luggage 197
lugger 17.134
lugubrious 310.2
Luke 45
lukewarm 238
lull 225
lullaby 7
Lulu 15.4
lumbago 12.27
lumbar 17.27
lumber 17.27
lumbering 265.58
lumberjack 32

lumberjacket 371.6
lumberyard 84
lumbricalis 300.7
lumbricoid 97.3
lumen 252
luminance 321.14
luminary 16.274.26
luminesce 296.2
luminescence
    321.21
luminosity
    16.333.30.4
luminous 310.33.1
lumme 16.220
lummox 503
lump 289
lumpen 261
lumper 17.264
lumpish 353
lumpy 16.257
Luna 17.238
lunacy 16.307
lunar 17.238
lunate 367
lunatic 38.57
lunation 261.67
lunch 82
luncheon 261
luncheonette 368
Lund 141
Lundy 16.80
lune 260
lunette 368
lung 267
lunge 211
lungi 5
lunula 17.174
Lupercalia 17.3.18
lupin 252
lupine 253
lupulin 252.10
lupus 310
lur 10
lurch 65
lurcher 17.54
lurdan 261.22
lure 10
Lurex 496
lurid 91
lurk 36
Lusaka 17.29
luscious 310
lush 356
Lusitania 17.3.31.2
lust 443

lustful 226.13
lustrate 367
lustre 17.388
lustreware 4.8
lustrous 310
lusty 16.368
lute 380
lutenist 436.11
luteous 310.2
Lutetia 17.325
lutetium 242.2
Lutheran 261.60
Lutherism 242.35.15
luthern 261
Luton 261.104
lux 502
luxate 367
Luxembourg 182
Luxor 9
luxuriant 420.1.3
luxuriate 367.1
luxurious 310.2.14
luxury 16.274
Luzon 254
Lyallpur 10
lycanthrope 278
lycanthropy 16.254
lycée 2
lyceum 242.1
lychee 5
lychnis 300.27
lycopodium 242.2.4
lyddite 372.1
Lydia 17.3.9
lye 7
lyke-wake 34
Lyme Regis 300.6
Lymington 261
lymph 176
lymphangial 228.3
lymphatic 38.49
lymphoblast 430
lymphocyte 372.10
lymphocytic 38.52.3
lymphoid 97
lyncean 261.2
lynch 80
lyncher 17.71
Lynn 252
lynx 505
lyonnaise 509
Lyonnesse 296.3

lyophilic 38.21
lyophilize 516.2
Lyra 17.274
lyrate 371
lyre 8
lyrebird 87
lyric 38.40
lyrical 228.23.16
lyricism 242.35.16.3
lyricist 436.21
Lysander 17.98
Lysenko 12.13
lysergic 38.16
Lysias 293.1
Lysimachus 310.14
lysin 252.22
Lysippus 310.37
lysis 300.53
lysozyme 236
lytic 38.52
lytta 17.342

M

ma 1
ma'am 230
maar 1
Mab 18
mabela 17.163
mac 32
macabre 17.281
macadam 242.5
macadamia 17.3.24
macadamize 516.5
macaque 33
macaroni 16.233
macaronic 38.35
macaroon 260.3
Macaulay 16.123
macaw 9.2
Macbeth 455
Maccabean 261.2.1
Maccabees 513
maccaboy 11
Macclesfield 115
Macdonald 122
mace 295
macebearer 17.271
macedoine 246
Macedon 254

Macedonia 17.3.36
Macedonian 261.3.18
macer 17.299
macerate 367.23
machan 246
machete 16.330
Machiavelli 16.115
Machiavellian 261.3.9
machicolate 367.14
machinate 367.17
machination 261.67.18
machine 251.10
machinery 16.274.25
machinist 436
machismo 12.50
Machmeter 17.341
machree 5
Machu Picchu 15
Macias Nguema 17.207
Mackay 7.2
Mackenzie 16.405
mackerel 228.76
Mackinaw 9
mackintosh 354
mackle 228.19
Maclean 247
Macleod 99.1
Macmillan 261.41
Macpherson 261.64
macramé 16.211
macrencephaly 16.131
macrobiotic 38.53.1
macrocephaly 16.131
macrocosm 242
macrocyst 436.22
macrocyte 372.10
macrograph 158.1
macron 254
macrophage 193.1
macropterous 310.50
macroscopic 38.37.1
macruran 261.59
macula 17.174.3
macula lutea 17.3

maculation 261.67.13
macule 227
mad 83
Madagascar 17.47
madam 242.5
madcap 268
madden 261.19
maddening 265.46
madder 17.77
made 85
Madeira 17.272
madeleine 252.11
mademoiselle 215
madhouse 306
Madhya Pradesh 351
Madison 261.65
madly 16.146
madman 261
madness 300
Madonna 17.233.1
Madras 294
madrepore 9
Madrid 91
madrigal 228.46
madrilène 248
Madura 17.277
Madurai 7
maduro 12.66
Maebashi 5
Maecenas 293
maelstrom 237
maenad 83
maestoso 12.70
maestro 12
Maeterlinck 52
Mafeking 265.7
Mafia 17.3.10
mafioso 12.70
mag 178
magazine 251
magdalen 252.11
Magdalena 17.227
Magdalene 251.3
Magdeburg 182
Magellan 261.40
magenta 17.368
maggot 381
maggoty 16.344
Maghreb 31
magi 7
magic 38.15
magical 228.23
magician 261.71

Maginot 12.55
magisterial
228.3.11
magistery
16.274.49
magistracy 16.307
magistral 228.82
magistrate 367.28
magistrature 10.5
magma 17.220
magmatic 38.49
Magna Carta
17.337
magnanimity
16.333.12
magnanimous
310.28.1
magnate 367
magnesia 17.325
magnesite 372.9
magnesium
242.2.20
magnet 371
magnetic 38.50
magnetics 498.12
magnetism
242.35.18
magnetite 372.11
magnetize 516.12
magneto 12.76
magnetometer
17.342.3
magneton 254
magnetosphere 6.1
magnifiable
228.16.3.1
Magnificat 365
magnificence
321.22
magnificent 420.70
magnifico 12.11
magnifier 17.4.1
magnify 7.3
magniloquent
420.59
magnitude 102.2
magnolia 17.3.22
magnum 242
magnus 310
Magog 185
magot 12.26
magpie 7
maguey 2
magus 310.19
Magyar 1

Mahabharata
17.352
Mahanadi 16.72
maharajah 17.145
maharani 5.10
maharishi 16.322
Mahayana 17.226
Mahdi 16.58
Mahé 2
mahjong 266
Mahler 17.161
mahogany 16.237.4
Mahomet 371.20
Mahometan 261.99
mahonia 17.3.36
mahout 377
mahseer 17.3.47
Maia 17.4
maid 85
maidan 246
maiden 261.20
maidenhair 4
Maidenhead 86
maidenhead 86
maidenhood 101
maidenly 16.174
maidservant 420.82
Maidstone 261
maieutic 38.56
mail 214
mailbag 178
mailbox 499
mailcoach 70
mailer 17.162
mailsack 32
maim 231
Maimonides 513.4
main 247
mainbrace 295
Maine 247
mainland 143
mainly 16.170
mainmast 431
mainsail 214
mainsheet 370
mainspring 265
mainstay 2
mainstream 234
maintain 247
maintenance
321.14
maintop 276
maisonette 368
maître d'hôtel
215.4

maize 509
majestic 38.69
majesty 16.366
major 17.146
Majorca 17.37
major-domo 12.49
majorette 368.6
majority 16.333.22
majuscule 227
Makasar 17.298
make 34
makefast 431
maker 17.30
makeshift 398
make-up 279
makeweight 367
making 265.6
makings 552
Makurdi 16.61
Malabar 1.2
Malacca 17.28
malacca 17.28
Malachi 7.2
malachite 372
malacology
16.108.4.6
malacopterygian
261.3.7
maladdress 296
maladjusted 91.54
maladjustment 420
maladminister
17.384.1
maladministration
261.67.25
maladroit 375
malady 16.72
mala fide 16.64
Malagasy 16.294
malaise 509
malamute 380
malanders 524
Malang 263
malapert 369
malapropism
242.35
malapropos 12.59
malar 17.162
malaria 17.3.38.1
malarial 228.3.10
malarkey 16.20
malassimilation
261.67.12
Malay 2.12
Malaya 17.1

Malayan 261.1
Malaysian 261.3.33
Malcolm 242
malcontent 410
Male 2
male 214
maleate 367.1.1
maledict 387
malediction
261.78.1
malefactor 17.353
malefic 38
maleficent 420.70
malevolence
321.12.1
malevolent
420.28.1
malfeasance 321.28
malformation
261.67
malformed 125
malfunction 261.80
Mali 16.113
malice 300
malicious 310.58
malign 253.3
malignancy 16.312
malignant 420
malignity
16.333.19
malimprinted 91
malines 251.3
malinger 17.141
malingerer 17.279
Malinke 16.37
Malinowski 16.44
malison 261.126
mall 221
mallam 229
mallard 84
malleable 228.16.2
mallee 5
mallemuck 43
malleolus 310.26
mallet 371
malleus 310.2
mallow 12.38
malm 230
Malmö 12
malnourished 449
malnutrition
261.71
malocclusion
261.93
malodorous 310.50

Malory 16.274.15
malposition
261.71.9
malpractice 300.65
malt 404
Malta 17.363
maltase 509
malted 91.44
Maltese 513
Malthusian 261.3
malting 265
maltose 520
maltreat 370
maltreatment 420
malty 16.351
Malvern 261
mam 229
mama 1.12
mamba 17.23
mambo 12
mamelon 261
Mameluke 45
mamey 5
mamilla 17.166
mamillate 367.12
mamma 17.205
mammal 228.51
mammalian
261.3.8
mammalogy
16.108.2
mammary 16.274
mammiferous
310.50.2
mammock 46
mammon 261.44
mammoth 464
mammy 16.210
man 245
mana 17.226
manacle 228.28
manage 197.5
manageable
228.16.20
management
420.37
manager 17.150
manageress 296.4
managerial
228.3.11
managing 265.25
manakin 252.4
Manama 17.206
Manassas 310.51
Manasseh 16.294

manatee 5
Manchester 17.384
manchineel 217
Manchu 15
Manchuria 17.3.42
manciple 228.66
Mancunian 261.3
Mandaean 261.3
Mandalay 2.12
mandamus 310.27
mandarin 252.20
mandate 367
mandatory
16.274.43
Mande 2
mandi 16.80
mandible 228.12
mandibular
17.174.2
mandir 6
mandolin 252.11
mandorla 17.169
mandragora 17.279
mandrake 34
mandrel 228
mandrill 218
manducate 367
mane 247
manège 360
Manes 513
manes 509
manful 226
mangabey 2.4
Mangalore 9.8
manganate 367.18
manganese 513.9
mange 207
mangelwurzel
228.126
manger 17.156
mangle 228.49
mango 12.35
mangonel 215
mangosteen 251
mangrove 488
mangy 16.109
manhandle 228.39
Manhattan 261.94
manhole 223
manhood 101
manhunt 419
Mani 16.224
mania 17.3.31
maniac 32.1
maniacal 228.28.1

manic 38.31
Manichaeus 310.1
manicotti 16.335
manicure 10.3
manicurist 436.19
manifest 433
manifestation
261.67.33
manifesto 12.86
manifold 120
manikin 252.3
Manila 17.166.1
manilla 17.166.1
manille 218
manioc 40
maniple 228.66
manipulability
16.333.9.2
manipular 17.174
manipulate
367.13.6
manipulation
261.67.13.4
manipulative
485.15.5
Manisa 1
Manitoba 17.18
mankind 135
manky 16.36
manlike 39
manly 16.169
manna 17.225
manned 128
mannequin 252.3
manner 17.225
mannered 103
mannerism
242.35.15
mannerless 300.13
mannerly 16.131
Mannheim 236
mannish 353
mannose 520
manoeuvrable
228.16
manoeuvre 17.419
man-of-war 9
manometer
17.342.3.3
manor 17.225
manorial 228.3.12
manpower 14
manrope 278
mansard 84
manse 314

manservant 420.82
Mansfield 115
mansion 261.81
manslaughter
17.345
mansuetude 102.2
manta 17.365
manteau 12.83
mantel 228.109
mantelet 368
mantelletta 17.339
mantelpiece 298
manteltree 5
mantic 38.62
mantilla 17.166
mantis 300.66
mantissa 17.302
mantle 228.109
mantling 265
Mantoux 15
mantra 17.296
mantrap 268
Mantua 17.7.2
mantua 17.7.2
manual 228.9.2
manubrium 242.2
manufacture 17.63
manufacturer
17.279
manufacturing
265.58
manuka 17.41
manumit 371
manure 10
manus 310.31
manuscript 424
Manx 504
Manxman 261
many 16.226
manyplies 516
manzanilla
17.166.1
Maoism 242.35
Maoist 436
Maori 16.271
map 268
maple 228
mapping 265,
265.48
Maputo 12.80
maquette 368
maquis 5.3
mar 1
mara 1.14
marabou 15.1

massotherapy
16.254
massy 16.294
mast 431
mastaba 17.21
mastectomy
16.222.5
master 17.380
masterful 226
masterly 16.131
mastermind 135
masterpiece 298.2
masterstroke 42
mastery 16.274
masthead 86
mastic 38.68
masticate 367.5.2
mastication
261.67.5
masticatory
16.274.43
mastiff 163
mastitis 300.62
mastodon 254
mastoid 97
mastoiditis 300.62
masturbate 367.4
masturbation
261.67.3
Masuria 17.3.42.2
masurium 242.2
mat 365
Matabele 16.118
Matabeleland
143.2
Matadi 16.58
matador 9.4
Mata Hari
16.261.1
Matamoros 310.48
Matapan 245.4
match 62
matchboard 95
matchbox 499
matchless 300
matchmaker 17.30
matchmark 33
matchstick 38
matchwood 101
maté 2.23
mate 367
matelote 376
mater 17.338
materfamilias
293.1

material 228.3.11
materialism
242.35.11.2.1
materialist 436.7.2
materialistic
38.70.2.1
materiality
16.333.8.1
materialize
516.3.2.1
materially 16.131
materia medica
17.34
materiel 215
maternal 228.58
maternity
16.333.16
matey 16.329
mathematical
228.23.18
mathematician
261.71
mathematics
498.11
Mathura 17.277
Matilda 17.95
matin 252
matinée 2.15
matins 548
Matlock 40
matriarch 33.1
matriarchate 371.7
matriarchy 16.20
matrices 513
matricide 92.7
matriclinous
310.34
matriculate
367.13.2
matriculation
261.67.13
matrilineal 228.3.7
matrilocal 228.26
matrimonial
228.3.8
matrimony 16.237
matrix 498.9
matron 261
matronage 197
matronly 16.174
matt 365
mattamore 9.9
matted 91.32
matter 17.336
Matterhorn 255

Matthew 15
Matthias 310.3
matting 265
mattock 46
mattress 300
maturate 367.22
maturation
261.67.21
mature 10.5
maturity 16.333.23
matutinal 228.61
matza 17.319
matzoon 260
Maud 95
maud 95
maudlin 252
Maugham 238
maul 221
mauler 17.169
maulstick 38
Mau Mau 13
Mauna Kea 1
Mauna Loa 1
maund 137
maunder 17.105
Maureen 251.6
Maurice 300
Maurist 436
Mauritania
17.3.31.2
Mauritius 310.58.2
Mauser 17.443
mausoleum 242.1
mauve 488
maverick 38.44
Mavis 300
mavourneen 251
maw 9
mawkish 353
mawsie 16.397
maxi 16.386
maxilla 17.166
maxillary 16.274.16
maxilliped 86.6
maxim 235
maxima 17.211
maximal 228.52
maximalist 436.7
Maximilian
261.3.11
maximin 252.14
maximize 516.4
maximum 242
maximus 310.28
maxixe 352

Maxwell 228
May 2
may 2
maya 17.4
Mayan 261.4
maybe 16.7
Mayday 2
Mayfair 4
Mayflower 14
mayfly 7
mayhem 232
Maying 265.1
mayn't 420
Mayo 12.1
Mayon 255
mayonnaise 509
mayor 4
mayoral 228
mayoralty 16.352
mayoress 300.44
mayorship 274
maypole 223
mayweed 89
Mazarin 263
Mazdaism 242.35
maze 509
mazuma 17.217
mazurka 17.32
mazy 16.393
Mbabane 16.224
McCarthyism
242.35.2
McCoy 11
McQueen 251
me 5
mead 89
meadow 12
meadowlark 33
meadowsweet 370
meagre 17.128
meal 217
mealy 16.118
mean 251
meander 17.98.1
meaning 265.42
meaningful 226
meaningless 300.15
meaninglessness
300.33
meanness 300
means 547
meant 410
meantime 236
meanwhile 219
meany 16.228

measled 122
measles 539
measurable 228.16.35.2
measure 17.333
measured 103.6
measureless 300.13
measurement 420.35
meat 370
meatball 221
Meath 457
meatus 310.62
meaty 16.332
Mecca 17.31
Meccano 12.51
mechanic 38.31
mechanical 228.23.10
mechanician 261.71
mechanics 498
mechanism 242.35.14
mechanistic 38.70.4
mechanize 516.7
mechanotherapy 16.254
meck 35
Mecklenburg 182
meconium 242.2.12
Med 86
medal 228
medallic 38.19
medallion 261.118
medallist 436.7
meddle 228
meddler 17.184
meddlesome 242
Mede 89
Medea 17.2
media 17.3.8
medial 228.3.1
median 261.3.4
mediant 420.1.1
mediastinum 242.15
mediate 367.1
mediation 261.67.1
mediatize 516.13
mediator 17.338.1
medic 38
medicable 228.16.10

Medicaid 85
medical 228.23.1
medicament 420.35
Medicare 4
medicate 367.5
medication 261.67.5
medicinal 228.60.6
medicine 252.21
medick 38
medico 12.11
medieval 228.119
medievalism 242.35.11
medievalist 436.7
Medina 17.230
mediocre 17.38
mediocrity 16.333
meditate 367.30
meditation 261.67.27
meditative 485.15.12
Mediterranean 261.3.15.1
medium 242.2.2
medlar 17.184
medley 16.147
Médoc 40
medulla 17.173
medullated 91.34
medusa 17.444
Medway 2
mee 5
meek 37
meekly 16.141
meekness 300
meerkat 365
meet 370
meeting 265
megadeath 455
megalith 458
megalithic 38.73
megalocardia 17.3.6
megalomania 17.3.31.1
megalomaniac 32.1
megalopolis 300.13.2
megalosaur 9.11
megaphone 257
megaphonic 38.35.2
megapode 98

Megara 17.279
megaron 254.11
megaspore 9.10
megass 293
megathere 6.10
megaton 259
megawatt 373
megillah 17.166
megohm 239
megrim 235
Meiji 5
meiosis 300.55.2
meiotic 38.53.1
Meir 6
Meistersinger 17.246
Mekong 266
mel 215
melaleuca 17.41
melamine 251.4
melancholia 17.3.22
melancholic 38.22
melancholy 16.131
Melanesia 17.334
Melanesian 261.3.34
melanin 252
melanism 242.35.14
melanite 372.6
melanoid 97.9
melanosis 300.55
melaphyre 8.1
Melba 17.22
Melbourne 261
Melchior 9.1
Melchite 372
meld 113
melee 2
melic 38.20
melilot 373
melinite 372.5
melioration 261.67.22
melisma 17.224
melismatic 38.49.4
melliferous 310.50.2
mellifluous 310.4
mellophone 257
mellow 12.40
melodeon 261.3.6
melodic 38.9
melodious 310.2.2

melodiousness 300.34.1
melodist 436.3
melodize 516
melodrama 17.206
melodramatic 38.49.2
melodramatize 516.13.1
melody 16.72
meloid 97.4
melon 261.40
Melos 302
melt 402
Melville 218
member 17.24
membership 274.1
membrane 247
membranous 310.36
memento 12.84
memento mori 7.11
memo 12
memoir 1
memoirs 508
memorabilia 17.3.21.1
memorable 228.16.35
memoranda 17.98.2
memorandum 242.6
memorial 228.3.12
memorialist 436.7.2
memorialize 516.3.2.2
memorize 516.8
memory 16.274
Memphis 300
Memphremagog 185
memsahib 24
men 248
menace 300
ménage 359
menagerie 16.274
Menai 7
Menam 229
Menander 17.98
menarche 16.20
Mencius 310.2
mend 131

mendable
228.16.18
mendacious   310.56
mendacity
16.333.25
Mendel 228
mendelevium   242.2
Mendelism
242.35.11
Mendelssohn 261
mender 17.101
mendicant 420.7
mending 265.20
Mendips 327
Mendoza 17.442
Menelaus 310
Menelik 38.21
Menes 513
menfolk 42
menhaden 261.20
menhir 6
menial 228.3.6
meninges 513
meningitic 38.52
meningitis 300.62
meniscus 310.15
meno 12.52
menology 16.108.4
menopause 518
menorah 17.276
menorrhagia
17.3.12
Menotti 16.335
Mensa 17.314
menses 513.14
Menshevik 38.74
menstrual 228.9
menstruate 367.2
menstruation
261.67.2
menstruous 310.4
menstruum 242.3
mensurable
228.16.35
mensural 228.76
mensuration
261.67.21
menswear 4
mental 228.110
mentalism
242.35.11.6
mentality
16.333.8.10
menthol 220
mentholated 91.34

mention 261.82
mentor 9.12
menu 15
Menuhin 252
Menzies 515
meow 13
Mephistopheles
513.6.1
mephitic 38.52
mephitis 300.62
meprobamate
367.16
mercantile 219
mercantilism
242.35.9
mercaptan 245
mercaptide 92
Mercator 17.338
mercenary
16.274.26
mercer 17.301
mercerize 516.8
merchandise 301,
516
merchant 420
merchantable
228.16.57
merchantman 261
Mercia 17.3
merciful 226
merciless 300.8
mercilessness
300.33
mercurate 367.22
mercurial 228.3
mercurialism
242.35.11.2
mercurialize
516.3.2
mercuric 38.43
mercurous 310.49
mercury 16.273
Mercury 16.274
mercy 16.298
mere 16.262, 6
Meredith 458
merely 16.119
merengue 2
meretricious 310.58
merganser 17.312
merge 195
merger 17.148
meridian 261.3.5
meridional 228.63
meringue 263.2

merino 12.54
Merionethshire 6
meristem 232
meristic 38.70.5
merit 371.31
meritocracy
16.307.5
meritorious
310.2.13
merkin 252
merle 216
Merlin 252
merlin 252
merlon 261
mermaid 85
merman 261
merocrine 253
Meroë 5
Merovingian 261.3
merrily 16.120
merriment 420.31.2
merry 16.262
merry-go-round
139
merrymaker 17.30
merrymaking 265.6
Merse 297
Mersey 16.394
Merseyside 92.7
Merthyr Tydfil
218
Merton 261.97
mesa 17.299
mésalliance 321.1.1
mesarch 33
Mesa Verde 87
mescaline 251.3
mesembryanthemum
242.12
mesenchyme 236
mesenteron 254.11
mesentery
16.274.48
mesh 351
Meshach 32
meshy 16.321
mesial 228.3
mesmeric 38.39
mesmerism
242.35.15
mesmerize 516.8
mesne 251
mesoblast 430
mesocarp 269
mesocratic 38.49.6

mesoderm 233
Mesolithic 38.73
mesomorph 166.1
mesomorphic 38.14
meson 254
mesopause 518
mesophyll 218.1
Mesopotamia
17.3.24
mesosphere 6.1
mesothelium
242.2.5
Mesozoic 38.2
mesquite 370
mess 296
message 197.11
Messalina 17.230
messaline 251.3
Messene 16.228
messenger 17.157
Messiah 17.4
messianic 38.31.1
Messina 17.230
messmate 367
Messrs. 524
messuage 197
messy 16.297
mester 17.382
mestranol 220
met 368
Meta 17.338
metabolic 38.22
metabolism
242.35.11
metabolite 372.4
metabolize 516.3
metacarpal 228
metacarpus 310
metagalaxy 16.390
metage 197
metal 228.100
metalanguage 197
metallic 38.19.1
metalliferous
310.50.2
metalline 253.3
metallist 436.7
metallize 516.3
metallography
16.90.2.2
metalloid 97.6
metallurgical 38.16
metallurgical
228.23.4

metallurgist 436.4.1
metallurgy 16.108.2
metalwork 36
metamer 17.218
metamere 6.3
metamerism 242.35.15
metamorphic 38.14
metamorphism 242.35.7
metamorphose 520
metamorphosis 300.57.2
metanephros 302
metaphase 509
metaphor 17.120
metaphoric 38.41
metaphorical 228.23.17
metaphrase 509
metaphysic 38
metaphysical 228.23.25
metaphysician 261.71.8
metaphysics 498
metapsychology 16.108.4.5
metastasis 300.57
metastasize 516.11
metatarsal 228.83
metatarsus 310.52
metatheory 16.265
metatherian 261.3.22
metathesis 300.52
metathesize 516.10
mete 370
metempirics 498
metempsychosis 300.55
meteor 17.3
meteoric 38.41
meteorite 372.8
meteoritic 38.52.2
meteorograph 158.1
meteoroid 97.12
meteorologist 436.4
meteorology 16.108.4.13
meter 17.341

methadone 257
methane 247
methanol 220
methinks 505
method 103
methodical 228.23.2
Methodism 242.35
Methodist 436.3
methodize 516
methodology 16.108.4
methotrexate 367
methought 374
methoxide 92.14
Methuselah 17.176
methyl 218
methylal 212
methylate 367.12
methyldopa 17.257
methylene 251.2
methylic 38.21
metic 38.50
meticulous 310.25.2
métier 2.1
Métis 298
metol 220
metonym 235
metonymy 16.216
metope 278
metopic 38.37
metralgia 17.3.16
metre 17.341
metric 38.46
metrical 228.23
metricate 367.5
metrication 261.67.5
metrics 498.10
metrify 7.3
metritis 300.62
metro 12
metrology 16.108.4
metronome 239
metronomic 38.29.1
metronymic 38.28
metropolis 300.13.2
metropolitan 261.99
metrorrhagia 17.3.12
mettle 228.100

mettled 122.2
Metz 336
meunière 4
Meuse 511
mew 15
mewl 227
mews 523
Mexicali 16.113
Mexican 261.13
Mexico 12.11
mezereon 261.3.22
mezereum 242.2.15
mezzanine 251
mezzo 12.71
mezzotint 412
mi 5
Miami 16.210
miasma 17.223
mica 17.35
Micah 17.35
Micawber 17.17
mice 301
micella 17.163
Michael 228.24
Michaelmas 310
Michelangelo 12.42
Michigan 261.32
Mick 38
mickery 16.274.4
mickle 228.23
Micmac 32
microanalysis 300.52.1
microbe 28
microbiology 16.108.4.2
microcephaly 16.131
microcircuit 371.8
microclimatology 16.108.4.15.1
microcline 253
micrococcus 310.11
microcopy 16.250
microcosm 242
microcosmic 38
microcyte 372.10
microdontous 310
microdot 373
microelectronic 38.35
microelectronics 498.5
microfiche 352
microfilm 244

micrograph 158.1
micrography 16.90.2
microgroove 490
microlight 372.4
microlith 458
micrometer 17.342.3
micron 254
Micronesia 17.334
microorganism 242.35.14
micropalaeontology 16.108.4.16
microphone 257
microphonic 38.35.2
microphotograph 158.1
microprint 412
microprocessor 17.300
micropyle 219
microscope 278.1
microscopic 38.37.1
microscopy 16.254.2
microsecond 143
microspore 9.10
microstomatous 310.68
microtome 239
microtomy 16.222.4
microwave 482
micrurgy 16.102
micturate 367.22
micturition 261.71
mid 91
midair 4
Midas 310.16
midbrain 247
midday 2
Middelburg 182
midden 261.24
middle 228.32
middlebrow 13
middleman 261
Middlesex 496
Middleton 261
middleweight 367
middling 265
middy 16.63
midfield 115

Midgard 84
midge 197
midget 371
midgut 378
Midheaven 261.112
midi 16.63
Midian 261.3.5
Midianite 372.6
midinette 368
midiron 261.4
midland 143
Midlands 534
Midlothian 261.3
midmost 441
midnight 372
midpoint 416
midrash 349
midrib 24
midriff 163
midsection 261.77
midship 274
midshipman 261
midships 327
midst 446
midsummer 17.216
midterm 233
midtown 258
midway 2
midweek 37
midwife 164
midwifery 16.274
midwinter 17.369
mien 251
Mies van der Rohe
  17.6
miff 163
miffy 16.85
might 372
mighty 16.334
migraine 247
migrant 420
migrate 367
migration 261.67
migratory
  16.274.43
mihrab 18
mikado 12.16
mike 39
mil 218
milady 16.59
Milan 245.2
Milanese 513.9
milch 76
mild 117
mildew 15

mildness 300
mile 219
mileage 197
mileometer
  17.342.3
milepost 441
miler 17.167
milestone 257
milfoil 222
miliaria 17.3.38
miliary 16.274.1.1
milieu 3
militancy 16.312
militant 420.76
militarism
  242.35.15
militarist 436.20
militarize 516.8.2
military 16.274.41
militate 367.30.1
militia 17.326
militiaman
  261.52.1
milium 242.2.6
milk 49
milkmaid 85
milkman 261
milko 12
milksop 276
milkweed 89
milkwort 369
milky 16.34
Milky Way 2
mill 218
Millais 2.11
millboard 95
milldam 229
millefleurs 3
millenarian
  261.3.21.1
millenarianism
  242.35.14.1.1
millenary
  16.274.23
millennial 228.3
millennium 242.2
millepore 9
miller 17.166
millesimal 228.52.1
millet 371.16
milliard 84
millibar 1.1
millieme 232
Milligan 261.32
milligram 229

Millikan 261.13
millilitre 17.341
millimetre 17.341
milliner 17.231
millinery 16.274.26
milling 265.30
million 261.120
millionaire 4.5
millionairess
  300.44
millionth 471
millipede 89.1
millisecond 143
millpond 136
millrace 295
millrun 259
millstone 257
millstream 234
millwheel 217
millwright 372
Milne 262
milord 95
milquetoast 441
milt 403
milter 17.362
Milton 261
Miltonian 261.3.18
Miltonic 38.35
Milton Keynes
  547
Milwaukee 16.28
mim 235
Mimas 310
mime 236
Mimeograph
  158.1.1
mimesis 300.51
mimetic 38.50
mimetite 372.11
mimic 38.28
mimicry 16.275
Mimir 6
mimosa 17.306
Min 252
minacious 310.56.4
Mina Hassan Tani
  16.224
minaret 368.6
Minas 310.34
minatory
  16.274.43.6
mince 317
mincemeat 370
mincer 17.315
Minch 80

mincing 265.62
mind 135
minded 91
Mindel 228.40
minder 17.103
mindful 226
mindless 300
mindlessness
  300.33
Mindszenty 16.355
mine 253
minefield 115
miner 17.232
mineral 228.76
mineralize 516.3.8
mineralocorticoid
  97.3
mineralogy
  16.108.2
Minerva 17.412
minestrone 16.233
minesweeper
  17.252
Ming 265
mingle 228.50
Mingrelian
  261.3.10
mingy 16.110
mini 16.229
miniature 17.56
miniaturist 436.20
miniaturize 516.8
minibus 307
minicab 18
minim 235
minima 17.211
minimal 228.52
minimalist 436.7
minimax 494
minimize 516.4
minimum 242
minimus 310.28
mining 265.44
minion 261.122
minipill 218
miniskirt 369
miniskirted 91.36
minister 17.384.1
ministerial
  228.3.11
ministerium
  242.2.15
ministrant 420
ministration
  261.67.25

misuse 309, 523
misuser 17.444
mitch 67
Mitchell 228
mite 372
Mithraism 242.35
Mithras 293
Mithridates 513.15
miticide 92.7.1
mitigable 228.16.19
mitigate 367.10
mitigation
 261.67.10
mitis 300.62
mitochondrion
 261.3
mitosis 300.55
mitrailleuse 511
mitre 17.343
mitt 371
mitten 261.99
mittimus 310.28
mix 498
mixed 451
mixer 17.427
Mixtec 35
mixture 17.76
Mizar 1
Mizoguchi 16.53
Mizoram 242.20
mizzen 261.126
mizzenmast 431
mizzle 228
m'lud 100
mnemonic 38.35
mnemonics 498.5
Mnemosyne 5.12
mo 12
moa 17.6
Moab 18
Moabite 372
moan 257
moaner 17.236
moat 376
mob 26
mobcap 268
mobile 219
mobility 16.333.9.1
mobilize 516.2
mobocracy
 16.307.5
mobster 17.391
moccasin 252
mocha 17.36
mock 40

mockery 16.274.5
mockingbird 87
mod 94
modal 228
modality 16.333.8
mode 98
model 228.34
modeller 17.176
modem 232
moderate 367.23,
 371.35
moderation
 261.67.22
moderato 12.73
moderator 17.338.9
modern 261.26
moderne 250
modernism
 242.35.14
modernistic 38.70.4
modernity
 16.333.16
modernize 516.7
modest 436
modestly 16.201
modesty 16.366
modge 199
modicum 242.4
modifiable
 228.16.3.1
modification
 261.67.5.1
modifier 17.4.1
modify 7.3
modillion 261.120
modiolus 310
modish 353
modiste 435
modular 17.174
modulate 367.13
modulation
 261.67.13
modulator 17.338.6
module 227
modulus 310.25
mofette 368
mog 185
Mogadishu 15
Mogador 9.4
mogul 228
mohair 4
Mohammed 91
Mohammedan
 261.24

Mohammedanism
 242.35.14
Mohammedanize
 516.7
Mohave 16.378
Mohawk 41
Mohican 261.12
Mohock 40
Mohorovičić 67
moider 17.87
moidore 9
moiety 16.333
moire 1
moiré 2.17
moist 440
moisten 261
moisture 17
moisturize 516.8
moisturizer 17.441
moke 42
mola 17.171
molality 16.333.8
molar 17.171
molarity 16.333.20
molasses 515.2
Moldau 13
Moldavia 17.3.53
moldavite 372
mole 223
molecular 17.174.4
molecule 227.1
molehill 218
moleskin 252
moleskins 548
molest 433
molestation
 261.67.33
molester 17.382
moline 253.3
moll 220
mollify 7.3.2
mollusc 61
Molly 16.122
molly 16.122
mollycoddle 228.34
mollycoddler
 17.188
Molly Maguire 8
Moloch 40
Molokai 16.1
Molotov 165
molten 261
Moluccas 524
moly 16.126

molybdenum
 242.14
mom 237
Mombasa 17.298
moment 420
momentarily
 16.120.1
momentary
 16.274.48
momentous 310.70
momentum 242
momism 242.35
Momus 310
Mona 17.236
mona 17.236
Monacan 261
monachal 228.28
Monaco 12
monad 83.3
monadelphous 310
monadism 242.35
monadnock 40
Monaghan 261
monal 221
Mona Lisa 17.440
monanthous
 310.72
monarch 46
monarchal 228.20
monarchism
 242.35.6
monarchist 436
monarchy 16.33
monarda 17.78
monasterial
 228.3.11
monastery 16.274
monastic 38.68
monasticism
 242.35.16.6
monatomic 38.29
monaural 228.74
Monday 2
mondial 228.3
Monegasque 55
monetary
 16.274.41
monetize 516.12
money 16.235
moneychanger
 17.156
moneyed 91
moneylender
 17.101

moneylending
265.20
moneymaker 17.30
moneywort 369
mongo 12
Mongol 220
mongol 228
Mongolia 17.3.22
Mongolian
261.3.12
Mongolic 38.22
mongolism
242.35.11
mongoloid 97.6
mongoose 309
mongrel 228
mongrelize 516.3
Monica 17.34.1
moniker 17.34.1
monism 242.35
monition 261.71
monitor 17.342
monitory 16.274.41
monitress 300
monk 54
monkey 16.39
monkeypot 373
monkfish 353
monkhood 101
monkish 353
monkshood 101
Monmouth 464
Monmouthshire 6
mono 12
monoacid 91.28
Monoceros 310.50
monochasium
242.2.19
monochord 95.3
monochromatic
38.49.2
monochromatism
242.35.20
monochrome 239
monocle 228.28
monocline 253
monoclinic 38.34
monoclinous
310.34
monocoque 40
monocotyledon
261.23
monocracy
16.307.5

monocular
17.174.7
monoculture 17.69
monody 16.72
monogamist 436.10
monogamous
310.29
monogamy
16.222.2
monogram 229.1
monogrammatic
38.49.2
monograph 158.1
monogyny 16.229.2
monolatry 16.286.2
monolingual 228
monolith 458
monolithic 38.73
monologue 185
monomania
17.3.31.1
monomark 33
monomer 17.218.1
monomerous
310.50
monometallism
242.35.11
monometer
17.342.3
monomial 228.3
monomorphic
38.14
mononuclear 17.3
mononucleosis
300.55.1
monophagous 310
monophobia 17.3.4
monophonic
38.35.2
monophony
16.237.3
monophthong 266
monopodium
242.2.4
monopolize 516.3
monopoly 16.131.6
monorail 214
monosaccharide
92.6
monosemy 16.215
monosome 239
monostich 38
monostome 239
monostrophe 16.90

monostylous
310.24
monosyllabic 38
monosyllable
228.16.23
monotheism
242.35.2
monotint 412
monotone 257.3
monotonous
310.36
monotony 16.237.7
monotreme 234
monotype 275.1
monotypic 38.36
monovalent 420.25
monoxide 92.14
Monroe 12
Monrovia 17.3.55
Monsignor 17.435
monsoon 260
monster 17
monstrance 321
monstrosity
16.333.30
monstrous 310
monstrousness
300.34
mons veneris
300.47
montage 359
Montagnard 84
Montague 15
Montana 17.225
montane 247.11
montbretia 17.325
monte 16.357
Monte Carlo 12.39
Montego 12.28
monteith 457
Montenegro 12.67
Monterey 2.19
montero 12.62
Monterrey 2.19
Montessori 16.269
Montezuma 17.217
montgolfier 17.3
Montgomery
16.274
monthly 16.205
monticule 227.1
Montreal 221
Montrose 520
Monty 16.357
monument 420.34

monumental
228.110
monzonite 372.6
moo 15
mooch 74
mood 102
moodiness 300.23
moody 16.71
Moog 190
moolah 1
moolvie 5
moon 260
moonbeam 234
mooncalf 158
mooneye 7
moonflower 14
moonless 300
moonlight 372
moonlighter 17.343
moonlighting
265.67
moonlit 371
moonquake 34
moonraker 17.30
moonrise 516
moonseed 89
moonshine 253
moonshiner 17.232
moonshot 373
moonstone 257
moonstruck 43
moony 16.236
Moor 10
moor 10
moorage 197
moorcock 40
Moore 10
moorfowl 224
moorhen 248
mooring 265.56
Moorish 353
moorland 143
moose 309
moot 380
mop 276
mope 278
moped 86
mopoke 42
moppet 371
moquette 368
mor 9
moraine 247
moral 228.73
morale 213
moralism 242.35.11

moralist

moralist 436.7
morality 16.333.8.9
moralize 516.3
Morar 17.276
morass 293
moratorium
 242.2.17
Morava 17.409
Moravia 17.3.53
Moravian 261.3.29
moray 2
morbid 91
morbidity 16.333.5
morbific 38.12
morbilli 7.5
morcha 1
mordacious 310.56
mordacity
 16.333.25
mordant 420.11
Mordecai 16.2
mordent 420.11
more 9
Morecambe 242
moreen 251
moreish 353
morel 215
morello 12.40
moreover 17.417
mores 509
Moresque 57
Morgan 261.33
morganatic 38.49.5
morganite 372.6
Morgan le Fay 2.9
morgue 186
moribund 140
morion 261.3.23
Morisco 12.15
Morley 16.123
Mormon 261
Mormonism
 242.35.14
morn 255
mornay 2
morning 265
Moroccan 261
Morocco 12
morocco 12
moron 254.10
moronic 38.35
morose 305.2
morosely 16.182
morph 166
morpheme 234

Morpheus 310.2
morphia 17.3
morphine 251
morphinism
 242.35.13
morphogenesis
 300.52.4
morphology
 16.108.4
morphosis 300.55
Morris 300
Morrison 261.65
morro 12.65
morrow 12.65
Mors 518
Morse 303
morse 303
morsel 228
mort 374
mortal 228.105
mortality 16.333.8
mortar 17.345
mortarboard 95.1
mortgage 197
mortgagee 5.6
mortgagor 17.150
mortician 261.71
mortify 7.3
Mortimer 17.211
mortise 300.63
mortmain 247
Morton 261.102
mortuary 16.274.2
morula 17.174
morwong 266
mosaic 38.1
moschatel 215
Moscow 12
Moselle 215
Moses 515
mosey 16.399
Moslem 242
Moslemic 38.25
mosque 59
mosquito 12.76
moss 302
mossback 32
mossbunker 17.46
Mossi 16.302
mossie 16.302
mosstrooper
 17.259
mossy 16.302
most 441
mostly 16.202

mot 12
mote 376
motel 215.4
motet 368
moth 459
mothball 221
mother 17.408
motherfucker 17.39
motherhood 101
mother-in-law 9
motherland 143.4
motherless 300.13
motherly 16.131
mother-of-pearl
 216
mothproof 170
mothy 16.371
motif 162
motile 219
motility 16.333.9
motion 261.73
motionless 300.14
motivate 367.36
motivation 261.67
motive 485.14
motivity 16.333.35
motley 16.191
motmot 373
motocross 302.2
motor 17.347
motorbike 39
motorboat 376
motorbus 307
motorcade 85
motorcar 1
motorcoach 70
motorcycle 228.24
motorcyclist 436
motorist 436.20
motorize 516.8
motorman 261.52
motorway 2.28
Motown 258
motte 373
mottle 228.104
motto 12.77
mouflon 254
mouillé 2
mould 120
moulder 17.97
moulding 265.18
mouldwarp 277
mouldy 16.76
moulin 252
moult 405

mound 139
mount 418
mountain 252
mountaineer 6.4
mountaineering
 265.53
mountainous
 310.33
Mountbatten
 261.94
mountebank 51
mounted 91.49
Mountie 16.359
mounting 265.73
Mount Rushmore
 9
mourn 255
mourner 17.234
mournful 226
mourning 265
mouse 306, 521
mouser 17.443
mousetrap 268
moussaka 17.29
mousse 309
moustache 350
mousy 16.304
mouth 462
mouthbrooder
 17.91
mouthful 226
mouthpart 366
mouthpiece 298
mouthwash 354
mouthwatering
 265.58
mouton 254
movable 228.16.62
move 490
moved 150
movement 420.51
mover 17.419
movie 16.384
moving 265
Moviola 17.171
mow 12, 13
mowburnt 411
mower 17.6
mown 257
moxa 17.428
moxie 16.389
Mozambique 37
Mozart 366
mozzarella 17.163
mozzetta 17.339

Mr. 17.384
Mrs. 515.3
Ms. 515
much 72
muchness 300
mucid 91.30
mucilage 197.1
muck 43
mucker 17.39
muckle 228.27
muckrake 34
mucky 16.30
mucoid 97
mucosa 17.306
mucous 310.13
mucus 310.13
mud 100
mudcat 365
muddle 228.36
muddleheaded 91.7
muddy 16.69
mudguard 84
mudir 6
mudlark 33
mudpack 32
mudra 1
mudskipper 17.253
mudslinging 265.47
muezzin 252.30
muff 168
muffin 252.5
muffle 228.42
muffler 17.191
Mufti 16.349
mufti 16.349
Mufulira 17.272
mug 189
Mugabe 16.6
mugger 17.134
muggins 548
muggy 16.97
mugwump 289
Muhammad 103
Muhammadan 261
Muir 10
mukluk 43
mulatto 12.72
mulberry 16.274
mulch 77
mule 227
muleta 17.339
muleteer 6
muley 16.130
mulga 17.139

muliebrity
  16.333.24
mulish 353
Mull 225
mull 225
mullah 17.173
mullein 252
muller 17.173
mullet 371
mulley 16.128
mulligan 261.32
mulligatawny
  16.232
mullion 261.3.13
mullite 372
mullock 46
mulloway 2.28
Multan 246
multeity 16.333.1
multicide 92.7
multicollinearity
  16.333.20.1
multicoloured
  103.4
multidisciplinary
  16.274.26
multifaceted 91.38
multifactorial
  228.3.12
multifarious
  310.2.10.1
multifid 91
multifoil 222
multifoliate 371.1
multiform 238.1
multigravida 17.83
multihull 225
multilateral 228.76
multilingual 228
multimedia 17.3.8
multimillionaire
  4.5
multinational
  228.63.2
multinuclear 17.3
multinucleate
  371.1
multipara 17.279
multiparous 310.50
multipartite 372
multiplane 247
multiple 228.66
multiplepoinding
  265
multiplex 496

multiplicand 128.1
multiplication
  261.67.5
multiplicative
  485.15.1
multiplicity
  16.333.28.1
multiplier 17.4
multiply 7.8
multipurpose 310
multiracial 228.91
multirole 223
multiscreen 251
multistage 193
multistorey 16.269
multitude 102.2
multitudinous
  310.33
multure 17.69
mum 240
mumble 228
mumbler 17.180
mumbo jumbo
  12.7
mumchance 315
mummer 17.216
mummery 16.274
mummify 7.3
mummy 16.220
mumps 332
munch 82
mundane 247
mung 267
munga 17.143
Munich 38
municipal 228.66
municipality
  16.333.8.8
munificence 321.22
munificent 420.70
muniment 420.31
munition 261.71
munitions 551
Munster 17.395
muntjac 32
muon 254
mural 228.75
murder 17.81
murderer 17.279
murderess 300.47
murderous 310.50
Murdoch 40
Mures 351
murex 496
muricate 367.5

Murillo 12.42
murine 253
murk 36
murky 16.23
murmur 17.209
murmuring 265.58
Murphy 16.83
murrain 252
Murray 16.272
murre 3
murrelet 371
murrhine 253
Murrumbidgee
  16.103
murther 17.403
Musca 17.49
muscadine 252
muscarine 252.20
muscat 365
muscatel 215
muscid 91
muscle 228.87
muscleman 261
muscovado 12.16
Muscovite 372
Muscovy 16.385
muscular 17.174.8
muscularity
  16.333.20.3
musculature 17.62
muse 523
museology
  16.108.4.1
musette 368.8
museum 242.1
mush 356, 357
mushroom 241
mushy 16.324
music 38
musical 228.23
musician 261.71
musicianship 274.2
musicology
  16.108.4.4
musk 60
muskeg 181
muskellunge 211
musket 371
musketeer 6
musketry 16.285
muskmelon 261.40
muskrat 365
musky 16.42
Muslim 235
Muslimism 242.35

muslin 252
muso 12
musquash 354
muss 307
mussel 228.87
Mussolini 16.228.1
must 443
mustachio 12.3
mustang 263
mustard 103
mustee 5
musteline 253
muster 17.388
musty 16.368
mutable 228.16.53
mutagen 261.39
mutant 420.77
mutate 367
mutation 261.67.29
Mutazilite 372.3
mutch 72
mute 380
muticous 310.10
mutilate 367.12
mutilation
  261.67.12
mutineer 6.4
mutinous 310.33.2
mutiny 16.229
mutism 242.35.19
mutt 378
mutter 17.349
mutton 261.103
muttonchops 329
mutual 228.9
mutuality
  16.333.8.2
Muzak 32
muzhik 38
muzz 522
muzzle 228
muzzler 17.204
muzzy 16.401
my 7
myalgia 17.3.16
myalism 242.35.11
myall 228.4
myasthenia 17.3.33
mycelium 242.2.5
Mycenae 5
mycology
  16.108.4.5
mycorrhiza
  17.441.1
mycosis 300.55

mycotic 38.53
mydriasis 300.57.1
mydriatic 38.49
myelin 252.8
myelitis 300.62.1
myeloid 97.5
myeloma 17.215
myiasis 300.57.1
mynah 17.232
myocardial 228.3
myocardiograph
  158.1.1
myocardium 242.2
myogenic 38.32.1
myoglobin 252
myograph 158.1
myology 16.108.4.2
myoma 17.215
myope 278
myopia 17.3.37
myopic 38.37
myosin 252
myosotis 300.64
myotonia 17.3.36
myriad 103.1
myriapod 94.1
myrica 17.35
myrmecology
  16.108.4.4
myrmecophile
  219.1
Myrmidon 254
Myron 261.58
myrrh 3
myrtle 228
myself 172
Mysore 9
mystagogue 185.2
mysterious
  310.2.11
mystery 16.274.49
mystic 38.70
mystical 228.23.24
mysticism
  242.35.16
mystify 7.3
mystique 37
myth 458
mythical 228.23
mythicize 516.10
mythological
  228.23.5
mythologize 516.1
mythology
  16.108.4.18

mythomania
  17.3.31.1
mythos 302
myxoedema 17.210
myxomatosis
  300.55.7

N

NAAFI 16.82
nab 18
nabob 26
Nabokov 165
Nabonidus 310.16
Naboth 459
nacelle 215.2
nacre 17.30
nacreous 310.2
Na-Dene 16.225
nadir 6
nae 2
naevus 310.73
nag 178
Nagaland 143.4
nagana 17.226
Nagano 12.51
Nagari 16.274
Nagasaki 16.20
nagger 17.123
nagor 9
Nagoya 17.431
Nagpur 10
Nahuatl 228.98
Nahum 242
naiad 83.2
naïf 162
nail 214
nailbrush 356
nailfile 219
nailhead 86
nainsook 44
naira 17.269
Nairn 250
Nairobi 16.12
naive 484
naiveté 2
naked 91
nakedness 300.28
naker 17.30
NALGO 12.34
Nama 17.206

namby-pamby
  16.17
name 231
nameless 300
namely 16.165
nameplate 367
namesake 34
nametape 270
Namhoi 11
Namibia 17.3.3
Namur 10
nan 245
Nanchang 263
Nancy 16.309
nankeen 251
Nanking 265
nanna 17.225
nanny 16.223
nanometre 17.341
Nanook 45
nanosecond 143
Nansen 261
Nan Shan 245
Nantucket 371.11
Nantung 267
Naoise 16.299
Naomi 16.222
nap 268
napalm 230
nape 270
naphtha 17.398
naphthalene 251.3
naphthol 220
Napier 17.3
napiform 238.1
napkin 252
Naples 539
Napoleon 261.3.12
Napoleonic 38.35.1
nappa 17.247
nappe 268
napper 17.247
nappy 16.243
Nara 17.268
Narayanganj 211
narceine 251
narcissism
  242.35.16
narcissistic 38.70
narcissus 310.53
narcolepsy 16.313
narcosis 300.55
narcotic 38.53
narcotism
  242.35.20

narcotize 516.13
nard 84
nares 513.10
narial 228.3.10
nark 33
Narraganset 371
narrate 367.23
narration 261.67.22
narrative 485.15.8
narrator 17.338.9
narrow 12.60
narrow-minded 91
narrow-mindedness
  300.28
narrowness 300.25
narthex 496
Narvik 38
narwhal 228
nary 16.264
NASA 17.298
nasal 228.125
nasalize 516.3
nascent 420
Nash 349
Nashville 218
nasion 261.3.33
nasopharynx 505
Nastase 16.392
nastiness 300.23
nasturtium 242
nasty 16.362
natal 228.99
natality 16.333.8
natant 420.75
natation 261.67.30
natatory 16.274.40
natch 62
nates 513.15
Nathan 261
Nathaniel 228.123
nation 261.67
national 228.63.2
nationalism
  242.35.11.5.1
nationalist 436.7.5
nationalistic
  38.70.2
nationality
  16.333.8.7.1
nationalization
  261.67.36
nationalize 516.3.7
nationwide 92
native 485.10
nativism 242.35.22

nativity 16.333.35.1
NATO 12.74
natrolite 372.4
natron 261
NATSOPA 17.257
natter 17.336
natterjack 32
natty 16.327
natural 228.76
naturalism
  242.35.11
naturalist 436.7
naturalistic 38.70.2
naturalize 516.3.8
naturally 16.131
nature 17.52
naturism 242.35.15
naturist 436.20
naturopath 452
naturopathic 38.72
naturopathy
  16.373.1
naught 374
naughtiness 300.23
naughty 16.336
nauplius 310.2
nausea 17.3
nauseate 367.1
nauseous 310.2
nautch 69
nautical 228.23
nautiloid 97.5
nautilus 310.23
Navaho 12.37
naval 228
navar 1
navarin 263
Navarre 1.15
nave 482
navel 228
navicert 369
navicular 17.174.6
navigable
  228.16.19
navigate 367.10
navigation
  261.67.10
navigational
  228.63.3
navigator 17.338.3
navvy 16.377
navy 16.379
nawab 19
Naxos 302
nay 2

Nazarene 251.7
Nazareth 464
Nazarite 372.8
Naze 509
Nazi 16
Nazify 7.3
Nazism 242.35
Ndjamena 17.227
Ndola 17.171
Neagh 2
Neanderthal 213
neap 273
Neapolitan 261.99
near 6
nearby 7
Nearctic 38.59
nearly 16.119
nearness 300
nearside 92
near-sighted 91.39
near-sightedness
  300.28
neat 370
neaten 261.98
neath 457
neatness 300.37
neb 21
Nebraska 17.47
nebula 17.174
nebulize 516
nebulosity
  16.333.30
nebulous 310.25
necessarily
  16.120.1
necessary
  16.274.36
necessitarianism
  242.35.14.1.1
necessitate 367.30
necessitous 310.64
necessity 16.333
neck 35
Neckar 1
neckband 128
neckcloth 459
neckerchief 163
necklace 300
neckline 253
necktie 7
neckwear 4
necrobiosis
  300.55.2
necrolatry 16.286.2
necrology 16.108.4

necromancy 16.309
necrophilia
  17.3.21.2
necrophilism
  242.35.9
necrophobia 17.3.4
necrophobic 38.3
necropolis 300.13.2
necrose 305
necrosis 300.55
necrotic 38.53
necrotomy
  16.222.4
nectar 17.354
nectarine 252.20
nectary 16.274.45
neddy 16.60
née 2
need 89
needful 226
neediness 300.23
needle 228
needlecord 95
needlecraft 396
needleful 226
needlepoint 416
needless 300
needlewoman
  261.50
needlework 36
needn't 420.9
needs 526
needy 16.62
neep 273
ne'er 4
nefarious
  310.2.10.1
Nefertiti 16.332
negate 367.10
negation 261.67.10
negative 485.15
negativism
  242.35.22
negativity
  16.333.35.1
negator 17.338.3
neglect 385
neglectful 226.10
negligee 2
negligence 321.9
negligent 420.20
negligible
  228.16.20
negotiable
  228.16.44

negotiant 420.1
negotiate 367.1.7
negotiation
261.67.1
negotiator 17.338.1
Negress 300
Negritic 38.52
Negrito 12.76
Negro 12.67
Negroid 97
Negrophile 219.1
Negrophobe 28
Negrophobia
17.3.4
Negropont 414
Negros 305
negus 310
Nehemiah 17.4
Nehru 15
neigh 2
neighbour 17.11
neighbourhood 101
neighbouring
265.58
neighbourly 16.131
Neil 217
Neisse 17.303
neither 17.406
nek 35
nelly 16.115
Nelson 261
nelumbo 12.7
nematic 38.49.1
nematocyst 436.22
nematode 98
Nembutal 213
nemertean 261.3
nemesia 17.334
Nemesis 300.52.3
nene 2
neoanthropic
38.37.3
Neocene 251.9
neoclassicism
242.35.16
neodymium 242.2
neoimpressionism
242.35.14.4
neolith 458
Neolithic 38.73
neologism 242.35.8
neologize 516.1
neomycin 252.22
neon 254
neonate 367.18

neophyte 372
neoplasticism
242.35.16.6
neoplasty 16.361.1
neoteny 16.237.7
Neozoic 38.2
Nepal 221
Nepali 16.123
neper 17.249
nephelinite 372.5
nephew 15
nephogram 229.1
nephograph 158.1
nephology 16.108.4
nephralgia 17.3.16
nephralgic 38
nephrectomy
16.222.5
nephridium 242.2.3
nephrite 372
nephritic 38.52
nephritis 300.62
nephron 254
nephrosis 300.55
nephrotomy
16.222.4
nepotic 38.53
nepotism 242.35.20
Neptune 260
Neptunian 261.3
neral 212
Nereid 91.2
nereis 300
neritic 38.52
Nero 12.63
neroli 16.131
Nerva 17.412
nervate 367.35
nerve 483
nerveless 300
nervine 251
nerving 265.78
nervous 310
nervousness 300.34
nervure 10
nervy 16.381
nescience 321.1
nesh 351
Ness 296
nesselrode 98
nest 433
nesting 265.75
nestle 228
nestler 17.197
nestling 265

Nestor 9
Nestorianism
242.35.14.1
Nestorius 310.2.13
net 368
netball 221
nether 17.402
Netherlands 534
nethermost 441
netting 265.65
nettle 228.100
nettlesome 242
netty 16.330
network 36
neume 241
neural 228.75
neuralgia 17.3.16
neuralgic 38
neurasthenia
17.3.33
neuritis 300.62
neuroblast 430
neurogenic 38.32.1
neurolemma
17.208
neurology 16.108.4
neuromuscular
17.174.8
neuron 254
neurone 257
neuropath 452
neuropathology
16.108.4
neuropathy
16.373.1
neuropsychiatry
16.286.1
neurosis 300.55
neurosurgeon
261.35
neurosurgery
16.274.13
neurosurgical
228.23.4
neurotic 38.53
neuroticism
242.35.16.5
neurotomy
16.222.4
neuter 17.351
neutral 228
neutralism
242.35.11
neutrality 16.333.8
neutralize 516.3

neutralizer 17.441
neutretto 12.75
neutrino 12.54
neutron 254
neutrophil 218.1
Neva 17.413
Nevada 17.78
névé 2
never 17.411
nevermore 9.9
nevertheless 296.1
new 15
Newark 46
newborn 255
Newburg 182
Newbury 16.274
Newcastle 228.83
newcomer 17.216
newel 228.10
newfangled 122
Newfie 16.89
Newfoundland 143
Newgate 371
Newham 242
Newhaven 261.111
newish 353
newly 16.130
newlywed 86
Newman 261.51
Newmarket 371.7
newness 300
Newport 374
news 523
newsagent 420
newscast 431
newscaster 17.380
newshawk 41
newsletter 17.339
newspaper 17.249
newspaperman
261.52
newspeak 37
newsprint 412
newsreel 217
newsstand 128
newsworthy 16.375
newsy 16.402
newt 380
Newton 261.104
Newtonabbey 16.5
Newtonian
261.3.18
New Zealand
143.1

New Zealander
17.109
next 450
nexus 310
ngaio 12.4
ngoma 17.215
Nguni 16.236
ngwee 2
niacin 252
Niagara 17.289
Niamey 2
nib 24
nibble 228.12
niblick 38
Nicaragua 17.7.1
niccolite 372.4
Nice 298
nice 301
nicety 16.333.29
niche 67, 352
Nicholas 310.26.2
Nicholson 261
Nicias 310.2.15
nick 38
nickel 228.23
nickelic 38.20
nickelodeon
261.3.6
nickelous 310.26.2
nicker 17.34
Nicklaus 306
nickname 231
Nicosia 17.2
nicotiana 17.226.1
nicotinamide 92.3
nicotine 251.11
nicotinic 38.34
nicotinism 242.35
nictitate 367.30
niddle-noddle
228.34
nide 92
nidicolous 310.26.2
nidificate 367.5
nidify 7.3.1
nid-nod 94
nidus 310.16
Niebuhr 10
niece 298
niello 12.40
Nietzsche 17.55
nieve 484
niff 163
nifty 16.347
Niger 17.151

Nigeria 17.3.39
Nigerian 261.3.22
niggard 103
niggardly 16.152
niggle 228.46
niggling 265
niggly 16.160
nigh 7
night 372
nightcap 268
nightclub 29
nightdress 296
nightfall 221
nightgown 258
nighthawk 41
nightie 16.334
nightingale 214
nightjar 1
nightlife 164
nightlong 266
nightly 16.190
nightmare 4
nightmarish 353.9
nightrider 17.84
nights 340
nightshade 85
nightshirt 369
nightspot 373
nightwear 4
nigrescent 420.67
nigrosine 251.9
nihilism 242.35.9
Nijinsky 16.45
Nijmegen 261.31
Nikko 12.10
nil 218
nil desperandum
242.6
Nile 219
nilgai 7
Nilotic 38.53
nim 235
nimble 228
nimbleness 300.30
nimblewit 371
nimbostratus
310.62
nimbus 310
niminy-piminy
16.229.3
Nimrod 94
Nina 17.230
nincompoop 280
nine 253
ninefold 120

ninepins 548
nineteen 251
nineteenth 469
ninetieth 458
ninety 16
Nineveh 17.414
ninny 16.229
Ninus 310.34
niobium 242.2
nip 274
nipa 17.252
Nipigon 254.5
Nipissing 265.61
nipper 17.253
nipple 228.66
Nippon 254
Nippur 10
nippy 16.248
nirvana 17.226
Niš 352
Nishapur 10
nisi 7
nisi prius 310.3
Nissen 261.65
nit 371
nitid 91.38
nitrate 367
nitre 17.343
nitric 38
nitride 92
nitriding 265.14
nitrify 7.3
nitrobacteria
17.3.39
nitrobenzene 251
nitrochloroform
238.2
nitrogen 261.39
nitrogenize 516.6
nitrogenous 310.33
nitroglycerin
252.20
nitroglycerine
251.7
nitrometer 17.342.3
nitroso 12.70
nitrosyl 218
nitrous 310
nitty 16.333
nitty-gritty 16.333
nitwit 371
Niue 2.2
nival 228.121
nivation 261.67
Niven 261.114

niveous 310.2.17
nix 498
nixer 17.427
nixie 16.388
Nixon 261
nizam 229
Nizam 230
Njord 95
Nkomo 12.49
Nkrumah 17.217
no 12
Noachian 261.3
Noachic 38.6
Noah 17.6
nob 26
nobble 228
nobbut 381
Nobel 215
nobelium 242.2
nobiliary
16.274.1.1
nobility 16.333.9.1
noble 228.13
nobleman 261
noblesse 296
noblesse oblige
362
nobody 16.72
nociceptive 485.23
nock 40
noctiluca 17.41
noctuid 91
noctule 227
nocturn 249
nocturnal 228.58
nocturne 249
nocuous 310.4
nod 94
nodal 228
noddle 228.34
noddy 16.65
node 98
nodical 228.23
nodose 305
nodular 17.174
nodule 227
nodus 310
Noel 228.7
noesis 300.51
noetic 38.50.1
nog 185
noggin 252
nogging 265.23
noil 222
noise 519

noiseless 300
noisette 368
noisiness 300.23
noisome 242
noisy 16.398
Nolan 261.43
noli-me-tangere
16.274
noma 17.215
nomad 83
nomadic 38.7
nomarch 33
nomarchy 16.20
nombril 218
nom de guerre 4
nom de plume 241
nome 239
nomen 248
nomenclator
17.338
nomenclature
17.62
nominal 228.60.5
nominate 367.17.5,
371.24
nomination
261.67.18.6
nominative
485.15.7
nominee 5.12
nomism 242.35
nomocracy
16.307.5
nomogram 229.1
nomology 16.108.4
nomothetic 38.50.6
nonage 197
nonagenarian
261.3.21.1
nonagon 254.5
nonaligned 135
nonappearance
321.17
nonce 318
nonchalant 420.28
non-com 237
noncombatant
420.78
noncommissioned
143.5
noncommittal
228.102
nonconductor
17.357

nonconformism
242.35.12
nonconformist 436
nonconformity
16.333.13
noncontributory
16.274.42
noncooperation
261.67.22.3
noncooperative
485.15.10
nondescript 424
none 259
nonentity
16.333.32
nones 550
nonessential 228.96
nonesuch 72
nonet 368
nonetheless 296.1
nonevent 410.3
nonexistent 420.81
nonfeasance 321.28
nonferrous 310.44
nonfiction 261.78
nonflammable
228.16.26
nong 266
nonharmonic 38.35
nonillion 261.120
nonjoinder 17.106
nonjuror 17.277
non licet 371
nonmember 17.24
nonmetal 228.100
nonmetallic 38.19.1
nonpareil 228.76
nonparous 310.43
nonpartisan 245.7
nonparty 16.328
nonplus 307
non-pros 302
nonresident
420.10.1
nonresistant 420.81
nonrestrictive
485.18
nonreturnable
228.16.28
nonrigid 91.15
nonsense 321
nonsensical 228.23
non sequitur
17.342
nonslip 274

nonsmoker 17.38
nonstandard 103
nonstarter 17.337
nonstative 485.10
nonstick 38
nonstop 276
nonswimmer
17.211
non-U 15
nonunion 261.123
nonunionism
242.35.14
nonviolence 321.12
nonviolent 420.28
nonvoter 17.347
noodle 228.37
nook 44
noon 260
noonday 2
nooning 265
noontime 236
noose 309
nopal 228.69
nope 278
nor 9
Nora 17.276
noradrenaline
252.11
Nordic 38
Norfolk 46
noria 17.3.41
Noricum 242.4
norite 372
nork 41
norm 238
Norma 17.214
normal 228.53
normality
16.333.8.5
normalize 516.3
normally 16.131
Norman 261
Normandy 16.81
normative 485.15.6
Norn 255
Norse 303
Norseman 261
north 460
Northampton 261
Northamptonshire
6.8
Northants. 347
northbound 139
northeast 435

northeasterly
16.131
northeastward 103
northerly 16.131
northern 261
Northerner 17.239
northernmost 441
Northumberland
143.4.1
Northumbria
17.3.44
Northumbrian
261.3.25
northward 103
northwards 531
northwest 433
northwesterly
16.131
northwestward 103
Northwich 67
Norway 2
Norwegian 261.36
Norwich 197
nose 520
nosebag 178
noseband 128
nosebleed 89
nosegay 2
nosh 354
nosing 265.83
nosography 16.90.2
nosology 16.108.4
nostalgia 17.3.16
nostalgic 38
nostoc 40
Nostradamus 310
nostril 218
nostrum 242.23
nosy 16.399
nosy-parker 17.29
not 373
notability
16.333.9.2
notable 228.16
notarize 516.8
notary 16.274
notate 367.31
notation 261.67.28
notch 68
note 376
notebook 44
notecase 295
noted 91.41
notelet 371
notepaper 17.249

noteworthy 16.375
nothing 265
nothingness 300.32
notice 300.64
noticeable
  228.16.39
notifiable
  228.16.3.1
notification
  261.67.5.1
notify 7.3
notion 261.73
notional 228.63.6
notitia 17.3.49
notochord 95.3
notoriety
  16.333.2.1
notorious 310.2.13
notornis 300.24
nototherium
  242.2.15
notour 17.347
Notre Dame 230
Nottingham 242.17
Nottinghamshire 6
Notts. 341
notum 242.31
Notus 310.66
notwithstanding
  265.19
nougat 1
nought 374
noumenon 261.56
noun 258
nourish 353.10
nourishment
  420.47
nous 306
nouveau riche 352
nova 17.417
Nova Scotia
  17.328
novation 261.67
novel 228
novelese 513.7
novelette 368
novelist 436.7
novelistic 38.70.2
novelize 516.3
novella 17.163
Novello 12.40
novelty 16.352
November 17.24
novena 17.230
novice 300

novitiate 371.1
Novocaine 247.2
now 13
nowadays 509
noway 2.27
Nowell 215
nowhere 4
nowt 377
Nox 499
noxious 310
noyade 84
noyau 12.4
nozzle 228
nth 468
nuance 315
nub 29
Nuba 17.20
nubbin 252
nubble 228.14
nubecula 17.174.4
Nubia 17.3
Nubian 261.3
nubile 219
nucellus 310.22
nucha 17.41
nuclear 17.3
nuclease 509.1
nucleate 371.1
nuclei 7.1
nucleolus 310
nucleon 254.1
nucleonics 498.5
nucleoside 92.8
nucleotide 92.11
nucleus 310.2
nuclide 92
nuddy 16.69
nude 102
nudge 203
nudicaul 221.1
nudism 242.35
nudist 436
nudity 16.333
Nuffield 115
nugatory 16.274.43
nuggar 17.134
nugget 371
nuisance 321.23
nuke 45
null 225
nullah 1
nulla-nulla 17.173
nullifidian 261.3.5
nullify 7.3

nullipara 17.279
nullipore 9
nullity 16.333
Numantia 17.3.50
numb 240
numbat 365
number 17.27
numberless 300.13
numberplate 367
numbness 300
numbskull 225
numdah 1
numen 248.3
numeracy 16.307.4
numeral 228.76
numerary
  16.274.32
numerate 371.35
numeration
  261.67.22
numerator 17.338.9
numeric 38.39
numerical
  228.23.15
numerology
  16.108.4.13
numerous 310.50
Numidia 17.3.9
numinous 310.33.1
numismatic 38.49.4
numismatics
  498.11
numismatist 436.26
nummary 16.274
nummular 17.174
nummulite 372
nun 259
nunatak 32.4
Nunc Dimittis 300
nuncio 12.3
nuncle 228.30
Nuneaton 261.98
nunhood 101
nunnery 16.274
NUPE 16.253
Nupe 2
nuptial 228
nuptials 539
Nuremberg 182
Nuri 16.270
Nuristan 246.1
nurse 297
nursemaid 85
nursery 16.274.35

nurseryman 261.48
nursing 265
nursling 265
nurture 17.54
nut 378
nutant 420.77
nutation 261.67.29
nutbrown 258
nutcase 295
nutcracker 17.28
nuthatch 62
nutlet 371
nutmeg 181
nutria 17.3
nutrient 420.1
nutriment 420.31
nutrition 261.71
nutritional
  228.63.5
nutritionist
  436.13.5
nutritious 310.58
nutritive 485.12
nutshell 215
nutter 17.349
nutting 265
nutty 16.341
nux vomica 17.34
nuzzle 228
nyala 17.161
Nyanja 17.434
Nyasaland 143.4
nyctalopia
  17.3.37.1
nyctinasty 16.361
nyctophobia 17.3.4
nye 7
nylghau 9
nylon 254
nylons 549
nymph 176
nymphalid 91
nymphet 371
nympho 12
nympholepsy
  16.313
nympholept 422
nymphomania
  17.3.31.1
nymphomaniac
  32.1
nystagmus 310
nystatin 252
Nyx 498

O

oaf 167
oafish 353
oak 42
oaken 261.14
oakum 242
oar 9
oared 95
oarfish 353
oarlock 40
oarsman 261
oasis 300.50
oast 441
oat 376
oatcake 34
oaten 261
Oates 343
oath 461
oatmeal 217
oba 1
Obadiah 17.4
Oban 261
obbligato 12.73
obconic 38.35
obdurate 371.34
obeah 17.3.4
obedience 321.1
obedient 420.1.1
obedientiary
  16.274.39
obeisance 321
obelisk 58
obelus 310.23
Oberland 143.4
Oberon 254.11
obese 298
obesity 16.333.27
obey 2.4
obfuscate 367
obi 16.12
obit 371
obituary 16.274.2
object 385, 387
objectify 7.3.9
objection 261.77
objectionable
  228.16.31
objective 485.17
objectivism
  242.35.22
objectivity
  16.333.35

objurgate 367.11
oblast 431
oblate 367
oblation 261.67
obligate 367.10
obligation
  261.67.10
obligatory
  16.274.43
oblige 198
obligee 5.6
obliging 265
obligor 9
oblique 37
obliquity 16.333
obliterate 367.23.2
obliteration
  261.67.22.4
oblivion 261.3.30
oblivious 310.2.17
oblong 266
obloquy 16.259
obnoxious 310
obnubilate
  367.12.1
oboe 12
oboe da caccia
  17.50
oboist 436
obol 220
obolus 310.26.1
Obote 2.24
obovoid 97
obreption 261.84
obscene 251
obscenity
  16.333.15
obscure 10
obscurity 16.333.23
obsequies 515
obsequious 310.2
observable 228.16
observance 321
observant 420.82
observation 261.67
observatory
  16.274.43
observe 483
observer 17.412
obsess 296
obsession 261.68
obsessive 485.2
obsidian 261.3.5
obsolesce 296.1

obsolescence
  321.21
obsolescent 420.67
obsolete 370
obstacle 228.28
obstetric 38.46
obstetrician 261.71
obstetrics 498.10
obstinacy 16.307
obstinate 371.24
obstipation
  261.67.20
obstreperous
  310.50
obstruct 389
obstruction 261.79
obstructionist
  436.13
obstructive 485.19
obstruent 420.4
obtain 247
obtainable
  228.16.27
obtect 385
obtrude 102
obtrusion 261.93
obtrusive 485.8
obtund 140
obturate 367.22
obtuse 309
obverse 297
obvert 369
obviate 367.1
obvious 310.2
obviously 16.184
oca 17.38
ocarina 17.230.1
O'Casey 16.296
occasion 261
occasional 228.63
occasionalism
  242.35.11.5
occasionally
  16.131.4
occident 420.10
Occidental
  228.110.1
Occidentalize 516.3
occipital 228.102
occiput 378
occlude 102
occlusion 261.93
occlusive 485.8
occult 406
occultism 242.35

occupancy 16.312
occupant 420
occupation 261.67
occupational
  228.63.3
occupier 17.4
occupy 7
occur 3
occurrence 321
ocean 261.73
oceanarium
  242.2.14
Oceania 17.3.30
oceanic 38.31.1
oceanid 91.21
oceanography
  16.90.2.4
oceanology
  16.108.4.11
ocellus 310.22
ocelot 373
och 40
ochlocracy
  16.307.5
ochlophobia 17.3.4
ochre 17.38
ocker 17.36
Ockham 242
o'clock 40
O'Connor 17.233
ocreate 371.1
octachord 95.3
octad 83
octagon 254.5
octagonal 228.63
octahedron 261
octane 247
Octans 544
octant 420
octave 485
Octavia 17.3.53
Octavian 261.3.29
octavo 12
octet 368
octillion 261.120
October 17.18
octogenarian
  261.3.21.1
octopod 94.1
octopus 310.40
octoroon 260.3
octroi 1
octuple 228
ocular 17.174.7
ocularist 436.20

oculist 436.6
odalisque 58
odd 94
oddball 221
oddity 16.333.6
oddly 16.149
oddment 420
oddness 300
ode 98
Oder 17.88
Odessa 17.300
odeum 242.2.4
Odin 252
odious 310.2.2
odium 242.2.4
odometer 17.342.3
odontalgia 17.3.16
odontoglossum
 242.25
odontograph 158.1
odoriferous
 310.50.2
odorous 310.50
odour 17.88
odourless 300.13
Odyssean 261.2.4
Odysseus 310.2.15
Odyssey 16.300.1
oedema 17.210
Oedipus 310.37
oeillade 84
oenology 16.108.4
oenomel 215
Oenone 16.233
o'er 9
oersted 86
oesophageal 228.2
oesophagus 310
oestrin 252
oestriol 220.1
oestrogen 261.39
oestrogenic 38.32.1
oestrone 257
oestrus 310
of 487
off 165
Offa 17.116
offal 228
offbeat 370
Offenbach 33
offence 316
offend 131
offender 17.101
offensive 485.9

offensiveness
 300.43
offer 17.116
offering 265.58
offertory 16.274.43
offhand 128
offhandedness
 300.28.1
office 300
officer 17.302
official 228.93
officialdom 242
officialese 513.7
officially 16.131
officiant 420.1
officiary 16.274.1.2
officiate 367.1.6
officiation
 261.67.1.5
officious 310.58
officiousness
 300.34.3
offing 265
offish 353
offprint 412
offset 368
offshoot 380
offshore 9
offside 92
offspring 265
offstage 193
oft 399
often 261
Ogaden 248
ogee 5
ogive 486
ogle 228
Ogooué 2.27
ogre 17.133
ogress 300
Ogygian 261.3.7
oh 12
Ohio 12.4
ohm 239
oidium 242.2.3
oil 222
oilcan 245
oilcloth 459
oiler 17.170
oilfield 115
oilfired 93
oilman 261
oilskin 252
oily 16.125
ointment 420.50

Oireachtas 310
Oita 17.346
oka 17.38
okapi 16.244
okay 2
Okeechobee 16.12
okey-doke 42
okey-dokey 16.29
Oklahoma 17.215
okta 17.356
old 120
Old Bailey 16.114
olden 261.28
Oldenburg 182
older 17.97
oldfangled 122
old-fashioned 143
Oldham 242
oldie 16.76
oldness 300
old-timer 17.212
oldwife 164
olé 2
oleaceous 310.56
oleaginous 310.33
oleander 17.98.1
oleaster 17.379
oleate 367.1.3
olecranon 254.8
oleograph 158.1.1
olfactory 16.274.44
Olga 17.138
olibanum 242.16
olid 91.18
oligarch 33
oligarchy 16.20
Oligocene 251.9
oligoclase 295
oligopoly 16.131.6
oligotrophic 38.13
olio 12.3.3
olivary 16.274.51
olive 485
Oliver 17.414
Olivia 17.3.54
Olivier 2.1
olivine 251
olla 17.168
olla podrida 17.82
ology 16.108.4
oloroso 12.70
Olympia 17.3
Olympiad 83.1
Olympian 261.3
Olympic 38

Olympus 310
Om 239
omadhaun 258
Omagh 1
Omaha 1
Oman 246
Omar Khayyam
 230
omasum 242
Omayyad 83.2
ombre 17.26
ombudsman 261
Omdurman 246
omega 17.129
omelette 371
omen 261.49
omentum 242
omer 17.215
ominous 310.33
omissible 228.16.39
omission 261.71.4
omit 371
ommatophore 9.6
omnibus 307
omnicompetent
 420.76
omnifarious
 310.2.10.1
omnific 38.12
omnificent 420.70
omnipotence
 321.25
omnipotent 420.78
omnipresence 321
omnipresent
 420.84
omnirange 207.1
omniscience 321.1
omniscient 420.1
omnium-gatherum
 242.21
omnivore 9.13
omnivorous
 310.50.3
omophagia 17.3.12
omophagy 16.108.1
Omphale 5.9
omphalos 302
on 254
onager 17.154
onanism 242.35.14
Onassis 300.49
once 320
oncogenic 38.32.1
oncology 16.108.4

oncoming 265.38
ondograph 158.1
one 259
Oneida 17.84
oneiric 38
oneness 300
oner 17.237
onerous 310.50
oneself 172
one-sided 91.8
one-upmanship
274.2
ongoing 265.4
onion 261
onionskin 252
oniony 16.237
Onitsha 17.56
onlooker 17.40
only 16.173
onomastic 38.68
onomastics 498.15
onomatopoeia
17.2.1
onomatopoeic 38
onrush 356
onset 368
onshore 9
onside 92
onslaught 374
Ontario 12.3
onto 15
ontogeny 16.229.2
ontology
16.108.4.16
onus 310.35
onus probandi
16.77
onward 103
onwards 531
onymous 310.28.2
onyx 498.5
oocyte 372.10
oodles 539
oof 170
oogamy 16.222.2
oogenesis 300.52.4
oogonium 242.2.12
ooh 15
oolite 372.4
oolitic 38.52.1
oology 16.108.4.3
oolong 266
oompah 1
oophorectomy
16.222.5.2

ooze 523
opacity 16.333.25
opal 228.69
opalescence 321.21
opalescent 420.67
opaline 253.3
opaque 34
OPEC 35
open 261
opencast 431
opener 17.239
opening 265.46
open-minded 91
open-mindedness
300.28
openness 300.31
openwork 36
opera 17.290
operable 228.16.35
operand 128
operant 420.65
operate 367.23
operatic 38.49
operation
261.67.22.3
operational
228.63.3
operationalism
242.35.11.5.2
operative 485.15.10
operatize 516.13
operator 17.338.9
operculum 242.10
operetta 17.339
operon 254.11
ophicleide 92
ophidian 261.3.5
ophiology
16.108.4.1
Ophir 17.117
ophite 372
Ophiuchus 310.13
ophthalmia 17.3.28
ophthalmic 38
ophthalmitis
300.62
ophthalmology
16.108.4
ophthalmoscope
278.1
ophthalmoscopy
16.254.2
opiate 371.1
opine 253
opinion 261.122

opium 242.2.13
Oporto 12.78
opossum 242.25
Oppenheimer
17.212
oppidan 261.24
oppilate 367.12
opponent 420.54
opportune 260.6
opportunism
242.35
opportunist 436.12
opportunity
16.333.18
opposable 228.16
oppose 520.2
opposite 371.40
opposition
261.71.9
oppress 296.5
oppression 261.68
oppressive 485.2
oppressor 17.300
opprobrious 310.2
opprobrium 242.2
oppugn 260
oppugnant 420
Ops 329
opsonize 516.7
opt 425
optative 485.15
optic 38.67
optical 228.23
optician 261.71
optics 498
optimal 228.52
optimism 242.35
optimist 436.9
optimistic 38.70.3
optimize 516.4
optimum 242
option 261.86
optional 228.63
optometer 17.342.3
optometrist 436
optometry 16.285.2
opulence 321
opulent 420.27
opuntia 17.3
opus 310.39
or 9
orache 67
oracle 228.28
oracular 17.174.3
oracy 16.307

oral 228.74
Oran 245.5
orange 209
orangeade 85
Orangeman 261
orangery 16.274.14
orangewood 101
orang-outang 263
orang-utan 245.6
orate 367
oration 261.67
orator 17.352
oratorical
228.23.17
oratorio 12.3
oratory 16.274.43.7
orb 27
orbicular 17.174.6
orbit 371
orbital 228.102
orc 41
Orcadian 261.3.3
orchard 103
orchestra 17.297
orchestral 228.81
orchestrate 367.28
orchestration
261.67
orchestrina 17.230
orchid 91
orchidaceous
310.56.2
orchis 300
orchitis 300.62
orcinol 220.3
Orcus 310
ordain 247
ordeal 217
order 17.86
orderliness 300.23
orderly 16.131
ordinal 228.60
ordinance 321.14
ordinand 128
ordinarily 16.120.1
ordinary 16.274.26
ordinate 371.24.1
ordination
261.67.18.1
ordnance 321
ordonnance 321
Ordovician 261.71
ordure 10
ore 9
oread 83.1

orectic 38.60
oregano 12.51
Oregon 261.32
Orenburg 182
Orestes 513.19
orfe 166
Orff 166
organ 261.33
organdie 16.81
organelle 215
organic 38.31
organicism
  242.35.16
organism 242.35.14
organist 436.13
organization
  261.67.36
organize 516.7
organizer 17.441
organography
  16.90.2.4
organology
  16.108.4.11
organon 254.8
organotherapy
  16.254
organza 17.445
organzine 251
orgasm 242.34
orgasmic 38
orgeat 1
orgiastic 38.68.1
orgy 16.105
oriel 228.3.12
orient 410
orient 420.1
oriental 228.110
Orientalism
  242.35.11.6
Orientalize 516.3
orientate 367.32
orientation
  261.67.32
Oriente 2
orienteering 265.53
orifice 300
oriflamme 229
origami 16.211
origan 261.32
origin 252.6
original 228.60
originality
  16.333.8.6
originally 16.131.3
originate 367.17

Orinoco 12.12
oriole 223.1
Orion 261.4.1
orison 261.126
Orissa 17.302
Orizaba 17.10
Orkneys 515
Orlando 12.23
orle 221
Orleanist 436.13.1
Orlon 254
orlop 276
Orly 5
Ormandy 16.81
ormer 17.214
ormolu 15.5
ornament 410.2,
  420.35
ornamental
  228.110.3
ornamentation
  261.67.32
ornate 367
ornithic 38.73
ornithine 251
ornithischian 261.3
ornithologist 436.4
ornithology
  16.108.4.18
ornithomancy
  16.309
ornithopod 94.1
ornithopter 17.377
ornithoscopy
  16.254.2
orogeny 16.229.2
orography 16.90.2
oroide 92
orology 16.108.4
Orontes 513
orotund 140
orphan 261
orphanage 197
orpharion 261.3.20
Orphean 261.3
Orpheus 310.2
Orphic 38.14
Orphism 242.35.7
orphrey 16.280
orpiment 420.31
orpine 253
orrery 16.274
orris 300
ortanique 37
orthicon 254

orthocentre 17.368
orthoclase 295
orthodontic 38.64
orthodontics 498
orthodontist 436
orthodox 499.1
orthodoxy 16.389
orthoepy 16.245
orthogenic 38.32.1
orthogonal 228.63
orthography
  16.90.2
orthopaedic 38.8
orthopaedics 498
orthopteran 261.60
orthoptic 38.67
orthoptics 498
orthorhombic 38
orthoscopic 38.37.1
orthostichy 16.25
orthotropous
  310.40
ortolan 261
orts 342
Orwell 228
Orwellian 261.3.9
oryx 498
os 302
Osage 193
Osaka 17.29
Osborne 255
Oscar 17
oscillate 367.12
oscillation
  261.67.12
oscillator 17.338.5
oscillogram 229.1.2
oscillograph 158.1
osculant 420.27
oscular 17.174
osculate 367.13
osculation
  261.67.13
osculum 242.10
Oshawa 17.425
osier 17.3.62
Osiris 300.45
Oslo 12
Osman 261
Osmanli 16.169
osmiridium 242.2.3
osmium 242.2
osmose 305
osmosis 300.55
osmotic 38.53

osmunda 17.108
osnaburg 182
Ossa 17.304
osseous 310.2
Ossetia 17.325
Ossian 261.3
ossicle 228.23
ossiferous 310.50.2
ossify 7.3
ossuary 16.274.2
osteal 228.3
osteitis 300.62
Ostend 131
ostensible
  228.16.40
ostensive 485.9
ostensory
  16.274.38
ostentation
  261.67.32
ostentatious 310.56
osteoarthritic 38.52
osteoarthritis
  300.62
osteoblast 430
osteoclasis 300.57
osteoclast 430
osteogenesis
  300.52.4
osteoid 97
osteology
  16.108.4.1
osteoma 17.215
osteomalacia
  17.322
osteomyelitis
  300.62.1
osteopath 452
osteopathic 38.72
osteopathy
  16.373.1.1
osteophyte 372
osteoplasty
  16.361.1
osteoporosis
  300.55
osteotomy
  16.222.4.1
Ostia 17.3
ostiary 16.274.1
ostinato 12.73
ostiole 223.1
ostium 242.2
ostler 17.198
ostmark 33

overground 139.2
overgrow 12
overgrown 257
overgrowth 461
overhand 128
overhang 263
overhaul 221
overhead 86.5
overhear 6
overheard 87
overheat 370
overhung 267
overindulgence 321
overjoy 11
overkill 218
overland 143.4
overlap 268
overlapping 265.48
overlay 2.12
overleaf 162
overlie 7.7
overload 98
overlong 266.1
overlook 44
overlord 95
overly 16.131
overman 245
overmantel 228.109
overmuch 72
overnice 301
overnight 372.6
overpaid 85
overpass 294
overpay 2
overpitch 67
overplay 2
overplus 307
overpower 14
overpowering 265.57
overprotect 385
overprotection 261.77
overran 245.5
overrate 367.23
overreach 66
overreact 382
override 92.6
overripe 275
overrule 227
overrun 259
overscore 9
oversee 5
overseer 17.2
oversell 215.2

overset 368
oversew 12
oversexed 450
overshadow 12
overshoe 15
overshoot 380
overshot 373
overside 92.8
oversight 372.10
oversimplify 7.3
oversize 516.11
oversized 154
overslaugh 9
oversleep 273
overslept 422
oversoul 223
overspend 131.4
overspent 410
overspill 218
overstaffed 396
overstate 367
overstay 2
oversteer 6
overstep 271
overstuff 168
overt 369
overtake 34
overtaken 261.11
overtask 56
overtax 494
overthrew 15
overthrow 12
overthrown 257
overthrust 443
overtime 236
overtired 93
overtone 257.3
overtook 44
overtop 276.1
overtrade 85
overtrick 38
overtrump 289
overture 10.5
overturn 249
overview 15
overwatch 68
overweening 265.42
overweigh 2.28
overweight 367.38
overwhelm 243
overwhelming 265
overwind 135
overwinter 17.369
overword 87

overwork 36
overwrite 372.8
overwrought 374
Ovid 91
oviduct 389
oviform 238.1
ovine 253
oviparity 16.333.20
oviparous 310.50
ovipositor 17.342.5
ovisac 32
ovoid 97
ovotestis 300.68
ovulate 367.13
ovulation 261.67.13
ovule 227
ovum 242
ow 13
owe 12
owelty 16.352
Owen 252.1
Owerri 16.262
owing 265.4
owl 224
owlet 371
owlish 353
own 257
owner 17.236
ownership 274.1
owt 377
ox 499
oxalate 367.14
oxalis 300.13
oxblood 100
oxbow 12
Oxbridge 197
oxen 261
oxeye 7
Oxford 103
Oxfordshire 6
oxhide 92
oxidant 420.10
oxidase 509
oxidate 367.8
oxidation 261.67.7
oxide 92.14
oxidimetry 16.285.1
oxidize 516
oxime 234
oxlip 274
Oxon. 261
Oxonian 261.3.18
oxpecker 17.31

oxtail 214
oxyacetylene 251.2
oxyacid 91.28
oxygen 261.37
oxygenate 367.17
oxygenic 38.32
oxymoron 254.10
oxysalt 404
oxytocin 252
oyer 17.5
Oyo 12
oyster 17.386
oystercatcher 17.50
Oz 517
Ozalid 91
ozocerite 372.8
ozone 257
ozonic 38.35
ozonosphere 6.1

P

pa 1
paca 17.29
pace 295
pacemaker 17.30
pacer 17.299
pacesetter 17.339
paceway 2
pachisi 16.395
pachyderm 233
Pacific 38.12
pacific 38.12
pacifier 17.4.1
pacifism 242.35
pacifist 436
pacify 7.3.6
pack 32
package 197
packager 17.150
packaging 265.25
packer 17.28
packet 371.6
packhorse 303
packing 265
packsaddle 228.31
packthread 86
pact 382
pad 83
padang 263
padding 265

paddle 228.31
paddler 17.183
paddock 46
Paddy 16.57
paddy 16.57
paddywhack 32
pademelon 261.40
padlock 40
padrone 16.233
Padua 17.7
paduasoy 11
paean 261.2
paediatric 38.45
paediatrician 261.71.6
paediatrics 498.8
paedology 16.108.4
paedomorphosis 300.57.2
paedophile 219.1
paedophilia 17.3.21.2
paella 17.163
paeon 261.2
pagan 261.31
paganism 242.35.14
paganize 516.7
page 193
pageant 420
pageantry 16.291
pageboy 11
paginal 228.60.2
paginate 367.17.2
pagination 261.67.18.2
pagoda 17.88
pagurian 261.3.24
Pahari 16.261.1
Pahlavi 16.385
paid 85
paigle 228.44
Paignton 261
pail 214
paillette 368
pain 247
pained 130
painful 226.4
painfulness 300.30
painkiller 17.166
painless 300
painlessness 300.33
pains 545
painstaking 265.6
paint 409

paintbox 499
paintbrush 356
painter 17.367
painting 265
painty 16.354
pair 4
paisa 1
paisley 16
pakeha 1.6
Pakistan 246.1
Pakistani 16.224
pal 212
palace 300
paladin 252
palaeanthropic 38.37.3
palaeethnology 16.108.4
palaeoanthropology 16.108.4.12
palaeobotany 16.237.7
Palaeocene 251.9
palaeoclimatology 16.108.4.15.1
palaeography 16.90.2.1
Palaeolithic 38.73
palaeontography 16.90.2
palaeontology 16.108.4.16
Palaeozoic 38.2
palaeozoology 16.108.4.3
palais 2
palanquin 251
palatable 228.16
palatal 228
palatalize 516.3
palate 371
palatial 228.91
palaver 17.409
pale 214
paleness 300
palette 371
palindrome 239
paling 265.27
pall 221
palladium 242.2.1
palliasse 293.1
pallid 91.16
pallium 242.2
pallor 17.160
pally 16.112

palm 230
Palmerston 261
palmette 368
palmetto 12.75
palmist 436.8
palmistry 16.293
palmitin 252.23
palmy 16.211
palmyra 17.274
palolo 12.44
Palomar 1.12
palomino 12.54
palooka 17.41
palp 282
palpable 228.16
palpate 367
palpebral 228
palpitate 367.30
palpitation 261.67.27
palsied 91
palstave 482
palter 17.363
paltry 16
paly 16.114
palynology 16.108.4.10
Pamirs 514
pampas 310.41
pampean 261.3
pamper 17.261
pampero 12.62
pamphlet 371
pamphleteer 6
Pamphylia 17.3.21
Pamplona 17.236
Pan 245
pan 245
panacea 17.2
panache 349
panada 17.78.1
Panama 1.12
Panamanian 261.3.15
panatella 17.163.2
Panay 7
pancake 34
panchax 494
pancreas 310.2
pancreatic 38.49
panda 17.98
pandanus 310.31
Pandarus 310.50
Pandean 261.2
pandect 385

pandemic 38.25
pandemonium 242.2.12
pander 17.98
Pandora 17.276
pandour 10
pandowdy 16.68
pandurate 367.22
pandy 16.77
pane 247
panegyric 38.40
panegyrize 516
panel 228.55
panelling 265
panellist 436.7.4
panettone 16.233
pang 263
panga 17.140
pangenesis 300.52.4
pangolin 252.9
panhandle 228.39
panic 38.31
panicky 16.25
panicle 228.23.10
panjandrum 242
Pankhurst 434
pannage 197.5
panne 245
pannier 17.3.29
pannikin 252.3
panocha 17.59
panoply 16
panoptic 38.67
panorama 17.206
panoramic 38.24
panpipes 328
pansophy 16.90
pansy 16.404
pant 407
pantalets 336
pantaloon 260.1
pantechnicon 261.13
pantheism 242.35.2
pantheon 261.3
panther 17.399
panties 515
pantihose 520
pantile 219
pantisocracy 16.307.5
panto 12.83
pantograph 158.1
pantomime 236

pattern 261.94
Patton 261.94
patty 16.327
patulous 310.25
paua 14
paucal 228
paucity 16.333
Paul 221
pauldron 261
Pauline 253
paulownia 17.3.36
paunch 81
paunchy 16.55
pauper 17.256
pauperize 516.8
Pausanias 310.2.6
pause 518
pavage 197
pavane 246
pavé 2
pave 482
pavement 420
pavilion 261.120
paving 265.77
paviour 17.436
pavis 300
Pavlov 487
Pavlova 17.417
pavonine 253
paw 9
pawky 16.28
pawl 221
pawn 255
pawnbroker 17.38
Pawnee 5
pawnshop 276
pawpaw 9
pax 494
Paxton 261
paxwax 494
pay 2
payable 228.16
payday 2
payee 5.1
payer 17.1
payload 98
paymaster 17.380
payment 420.29
paynim 235
payola 17.171
payroll 223
pea 5
peace 298
peaceable 228.16
peaceful 226

peacefulness 300.30
peacemaker 17.30
peacetime 236
peach 66
peacock 40
peafowl 224
peak 37
peaked 386
peaky 16.24
peal 217
pean 251
peanut 378
pear 4
pearl 216
pearler 17.164
pearlized 154
pearly 16.116
pearmain 247
Peary 16.265
peasant 420.84
peasantry 16.291
pease 513
peashooter 17.351
peasouper 17.259
peat 370
peaty 16.332
peau de soie 1
pebble 228
pebble-dash 349
pebbly 16.133
pecan 245
peccable 228.16
peccadillo 12.42
peccary 16.274
peccavi 5
peck 35
pecker 17.31
Peckinpah 1
peckish 353
pectase 509
pectin 252
pectinate 367.17
pectize 516
pectoral 228.76.3
peculate 367.13
peculiar 17.3.23
peculiarity 16.333.20.1
pecuniary 16.274.1
pedagogic 38.18
pedagogics 498
pedagogue 185.2
pedagogy 16.104
pedal 228

pedalfer 17.121
pedalo 12.45
pedant 420
pedantic 38.62
pedantry 16.291
peddle 228
pederast 430
pederasty 16.361
pedestal 228.114
pedestrian 261.3
pedestrianize 516.7
Pedi 16.60
pedicab 18
pedicel 215
pedicle 228.23.1
pedicular 17.174.6
pediculosis 300.55.3
pedicure 10.3
pediform 238.1
pedigree 5.18
pediment 420.31.1
pedipalp 282
pedlar 17.184
pedocal 212
pedology 16.108.4
pedometer 17.342.3
peduncle 228.30
pedunculate 371.17
pee 5
Peebles 539
peek 37
peekaboo 15.1
peel 217
peeler 17.165
peelie-wally 16.112
peeling 265.29
peen 251
peep 273
peeper 17.252
peephole 223
peepshow 12
peepul 228.65
peer 6
peerage 197
peeress 300
peerless 300
peeve 484
peevers 524
peevish 353
peevishness 300.35
peewee 5
peewit 371
peg 181
Pegasus 310

pegboard 95
peignoir 1.16
pejoration 261.67.22
pejorative 485.15
pekan 261
peke 37
Pekin 252
Pekinese 513.9
Peking 265
pekoe 12.10
pelage 197
Pelagianism 242.35.14.1
pelagic 38.15
Pelagius 310.2
pelargonium 242.2.12
Pelé 2
Pelée 2.12
pelerine 251.7
Peleus 310.2
pelf 172
pelham 242.8
pelican 261.13
Pelion 261.3.10
pelisse 298
Pella 17.163
pellagra 17.289
pellet 371.15
pellicle 228.23.6
pellitory 16.274.41
pell-mell 215
pellucid 91.30
pelmanism 242.35.14
pelmet 371
Peloponnese 298.1
Pelops 329
peloria 17.3.41
pelorus 310.48
pelota 17.344
pelt 402
peltast 430
pelvic 38
pelvis 300
Pemba 17.24
Pembroke 44
Pembrokeshire 6
pemmican 261.13
pemphigus 310
pen 248
penal 228.59
penalize 516.3
penalty 16.352

penance 321
Penang 263
penates 513
pence 316
pencel 228.88
penchant 266
Penchi 5
pencil 228.88
pend 131
pendant 420.14
pendent 420.14
pendente lite
16.334
pendentive 485.21
pending 265.20
pendragon 261.30
pendulous 310.25
pendulum 242.10
Penelope 16.254
peneplain 247
penetralia 17.3.18
penetrant 420.66
penetrate 367.27
penetrating 265.64
penetration 261.67
penguin 252
penicillate 371.16
penicillin 252.8
penicillium 242.2.6
penile 219
penillion 261.3.11
peninsula
17.174.11
peninsular
17.174.11
penis 300
penitence 321.24
penitent 420.76
penitential 228.96
penitentiary
16.274.39
penknife 164
penman 261
penmanship 274.2
Penn 248
penna 17.228
pennant 420.52
pennate 367
penned 131
penniless 300.8
Pennine 253
pennon 261
Pennsylvania
17.3.31

Pennsylvanian
261.3.15
penny 16.226
pennycress 296
pennyroyal 228.6
pennyweight 367
pennywort 369
pennyworth 456
penology 16.108.4
Penrith 458
pensile 219.3
pension 261.82
pensionable
228.16.31.1
pensionary
16.274.29
pensioner 17.239
pensive 485.9
penstock 40
pent 410
pentacle 228.28
pentad 83
pentagon 254.5
pentameter 17.342
pentaprism 242.35
pentarchy 16.20
pentastich 38
Pentateuch 45
pentathlon 261
pentatonic 38.35.5
Pentecost 438
Pentecostal
228.115
pentene 251
penthouse 306
pentimento 12.84
pentlandite 372
pentode 98
pentomic 38.29
pentosan 245
pentose 520
pentstemon 261.47
penuche 16.53
penult 406
penultimate 371.19
penumbra 17.285
penurious 310.2.14
penury 16.273
Penzance 314
peon 261.2
peonage 197
peony 16.237
people 228.65
pep 271
peplum 242

pepper 17.250
peppercorn 255
peppergrass 294
peppermint 412
peppery 16.274
peppy 16.245
pepsin 252
pepsinate 367.17
pepsinogen 261.39
peptic 38.65
peptidase 509
peptide 92
peptize 516
peptone 257
Pepys 326
Pequot 373
per 3
peracid 91.28
peradventure 17.70
Peraea 17.2.2
perambulate
367.13
perambulation
261.67.13
perambulator
17.338.6
per annum 242
percale 214
percaline 251.3
per capita 17.342
perceive 484
per cent 410
percentage 197.14
percentile 219.6
percept 422
perceptible
228.16.58
perception
261.84.1
perceptive 485.23
perceptual 228.9
perch 65
perchance 315
Percheron 254.11
percipient 420.1
Percival 228.120
percoid 97.2
percolate 367.14.2
percolator 17.338
percuss 307
percussion 261.74
percussionist
436.13
percussive 485.7

percutaneous
310.2.6
Percy 16.298
per diem 232
perdition 261.71.2
peregrinate 367.17
peregrination
261.67.18
peregrine 252
peremptory 16.274
perennial 228.3
perfect 385.2, 387
perfectible 228.16
perfection 261.77
perfectionism
242.35.14
perfectionist
436.13.6
perfective 485.17
perfecto 12.81
perfervid 91.55
perfidious 310.2.1
perfidy 16.63
perforate 367.23
perforated 91.34.7
perforation
261.67.22
perforce 303.1
perform 238.2
performance 321
performative
485.15.6
performer 17.214
performing 265
perfume 241
perfumer 17.217
perfumery
16.274.22
perfunctory 16.274
perfuse 523.1
Pergamum 242
pergola 17.176
perhaps 322
peri 16.265
perianth 467
periapt 421
periblem 232
pericardium 242.2
pericarp 269
perichondrium
242.2
periclase 295
Pericles 513
periclinal 228.61
pericline 253.4

pericope 16.254.1
pericranium 242.2.10
pericynthion 261.3.28
periderm 233
peridium 242.2.3
peridot 373
peridotite 372.12
perigee 5.6
perigon 261.32
perigynous 310.33
perihelion 261.3.10
peril 218.2
perilous 310.23
perilune 260
perilymph 176
perimeter 17.342.2.1
perimorph 166
perinatal 228.99
perineal 228.2
perinephrium 242.2
perineum 242.1
period 103.1
periodic 38.9
periodical 228.23.2
periodontal 228.111
perionychium 242.2
periosteum 242.2
periotic 38.55
peripatetic 38.50
peripeteia 17.4
peripheral 228.76
periphery 16.274
periphrasis 300.57
periphrastic 38.68
perique 37
perisarc 33
periscope 278
periscopic 38.37
perish 353
perishable 228.16.43
perishing 265.63
perispomenon 254.8
peristalsis 300.58
peristaltic 38.61
peristyle 219
peritoneal 228.2
peritoneum 242.1

peritonitis 300.62.4
peritricha 17.34
periwig 184
periwinkle 228.29
perjure 17.148
perjurer 17.279
perjury 16.274.13
perk 36
perky 16.23
Perlis 300
perlite 372
perlocution 261.75.2
perm 233
permafrost 438
permalloy 11
permanence 321
permanency 16.312
permanent 420.55
permanganate 367.18
permeability 16.333.9.2
permeable 228.16.2
permeance 321.1
permeate 367.1
Permian 261.3
permissible 228.16.39
permission 261.71.4
permissive 485.4
permit 371, 371.21
permitting 265.66
permittivity 16.333.35
permutation 261.67.29
permute 380
pernicious 310.58
pernickety 16.333.4
Pernod 12.53
peroneal 228.2
perorate 367.23
peroration 261.67.22
peroxide 92.14
perpend 131, 143
perpendicular 17.174.6
perpendicularity 16.333.20.3.1
perpetrate 367.27
perpetrator 17.338
perpetual 228.9

perpetuate 367.2
perpetuation 261.67.2
perpetuity 16.333.3
perplex 496
perplexity 16.333
perquisite 371.38
perron 261
perry 16.262
persalt 404
per se 2
perse 297
persecute 380
persecution 261.75
persecutor 17.351
Persephone 16.237
Persepolis 300.13
perseverance 321.17
perseveration 261.67.22
persevere 6.11
Pershing 265
Persia 17.324
Persian 261.69
persicaria 17.3.38
persiflage 359
persimmon 261.48
Persis 300
persist 436.22
persistence 321.27
persistent 420.81
person 261.64
persona 17.236
personable 228.16.31
personage 197
personal 228.63
personalism 242.35.11.5
personality 16.333.8.7
personalize 516.3.7
personally 16.131.4
personalty 16.352
personate 367.18
personify 7.3
personnel 215
perspective 485.17
Perspectivism 242.35.22
Perspex 496
perspicacious 310.56.1

perspicuity 16.333.3
perspicuous 310.4.1
perspiration 261.67.22
perspiratory 16.274.43
perspire 8.2
persuade 85
persuasion 261
persuasive 485
pert 369
pertain 247.10
Perth 456
pertinacious 310.56.4
pertinacity 16.333.25
pertinence 321.14
pertinent 420.53
pertness 300.36
perturb 22
perturbation 261.67.3
pertussis 300
Peru 15.6
peruke 45
perusal 228.128
peruse 523
Peruvian 261.3.32
perv 483
pervade 85
pervasion 261
pervasive 485
perverse 297
perversion 261.69.1
perversity 16.333.26
perversive 485.3
pervert 369, 369.2
perverted 91.36
pervious 310.2
pes 509
Pesach 33
pesade 84
peseta 17.338
pesewa 1
Peshitta 17.341
pesky 16.40
peso 12
pessary 16.274.34
pessimism 242.35
pessimist 436.9
pessimistic 38.70.3

pest 433
pester 17.382
pesticide 92.7
pestilence 321
pestilent 420
pestilential 228.96
pestle 228
pet 368
petal 228.100
petalody 16.67
petaloid 97.6
petard 84
petcock 40
petechia 17.3
Peter 17.341
peter 17.341
Peterborough
17.279
Peterlee 5.9
Peterloo 15.5
peterman 261.52
Petersburg 182
petersham 242
Peterson 261
pethidine 251
petiole 223.1
petit bourgeois 1
petite 370
petit four 9.5
petition 261.71.7
petitioner 17.239.2
petit mal 212
Petra 17.293
Petrarch 33
petrel 228
petrifaction 261.76
petrify 7.3
Petrine 253
petrodollar 17.168
petroglyph 163
Petrograd 83
petrography
16.90.2
petrol 228
petrolatum 242.27
petroleum 242.2.7
petrolic 38.22
petrology 16.108.4
petronel 215
Petronius 310.2.9
petticoat 376
pettifog 185.1
pettifogger 17.131
pettifoggery
16.274.12

pettifogging 265.23
petting 265.65
pettish 353
pettitoes 520
petty 16.330
petulance 321
petulant 420.27
petunia 17.3
pew 15
pewter 17.351
peyote 16.339
pfennig 184
Phaedra 17.286
Phaëthon 261.109
phaeton 261
phage 193
phagomania
17.3.31.1
phagophobia
17.3.4
phalange 206
phalangeal 228.3
phalanger 17.155
phalanx 504
phalarope 278
phallic 38.19
phallicism
242.35.16.1
phallus 310
phantasm 242.34
phantasmagoria
17.3.41
phantasmagoric
38.41
phantom 242
Pharaoh 12.62
Pharaonic 38.35
Pharisaic 38.1
Pharisee 5.20
pharmaceutical
228.23.21
pharmaceutics 498
pharmacist 436.22
pharmacognosy
16.307.3
pharmacology
16.108.4.6
pharmacopoeia
17.2.1
pharmacy 16.307
Pharos 302
pharyngeal 228.2
pharyngitis 300.62
pharyngology
16.108.4.7

pharyngoscope
278.1
pharyngotomy
16.222.4
pharynx 505
phase 509
phasmid 91
phatic 38.49
pheasant 420.84
Pheidippides 513.4
phellem 242.8
phelloderm 233
phellogen 261.39
phenacetin 252.23
phenetic 38.50.4
phenobarbitone
257.2
phenocopy 16.250
phenocryst 436
phenol 220
phenolate 367.14
phenology
16.108.4.10
phenomena 17.231
phenomenal
228.60.5
phenomenalism
242.35.11
phenomenology
16.108.4.10
phenomenon
261.56
phenotype 275.1
phenyl 218
phenylketonuria
17.3.42
pheromone 257
phew 15
phial 228.4
Phi Beta Kappa
17.247
Phidias 293.1
Philadelphia 17.3
philadelphus 310
Philae 5
philander 17.98
philanderer 17.279
philanthropic
38.37.3
philanthropist
436.15
philanthropy
16.254
philatelic 38.20
philatelist 436.7.6

philately 16.131.7
Philby 16.16
philharmonic 38.35
philhellene 251
Philip 274
Philippi 7
philippic 38.36
philippics 498
Philippine 251
Philippines 547
Philistine 253.10
Phillips 327
phillumenist
436.13.3
philodendron 261
philogyny 16.229.2
philology
16.108.4.8
philomel 215
Philomela 17.165
philosopher 17.120
philosophic 38.13
philosophical
228.23
philosophize 516
philosophy 16.90.4
philtre 17.362
phimosis 300.55
phiz 515
phlebitic 38.52
phlebitis 300.62
phlebosclerosis
300.55.5
phlebotomize 516.5
phlebotomy
16.222.4
phlegm 232
phlegmatic 38.49
phloem 232
phlogistic 38.70.1
phlogiston 254
phlox 499
phlyctena 17.230
phobia 17.3.4
phobic 38.3
Phobos 302.1
phocine 253
Phocis 300.55
phocomelia 17.3.20
Phoebe 16.10
phoebe 16.10
Phoebus 310
Phoenicia 17.3.49
Phoenician
261.71.5

phoenix 498.4
phon 254
phonate 367
phone 257
phoneme 234
phonemic 38.27
phonemics 498
phonetic 38.50.5
phonetician
  261.71.7
phonetics 498.12.1
phonetist 436.24
phoney 16.233
phonic 38.35
phonics 498.5
phonogram 229.1
phonograph
  158.1.2
phonography
  16.90.2
phonolite 372.4
phonology
  16.108.4.11
phonometer
  17.342.3.3
phonotactics
  498.13
phonotypy 16.249
phooey 16.4
phosgene 251
phosphatase 509
phosphate 367
phosphatide 92.11
phosphaturia
  17.3.42
phosphene 251
phosphide 92
phosphite 372
phospholipid 91.24
phosphoresce 296.4
phosphorescence
  321.21
phosphorescent
  420.67
phosphoric 38.41
phosphorite 372.8
phosphorous
  310.50
phosphorus 310.50
phot 373
photic 38.55
photo 12.79
photoactive 485.16
photobathic 38.72
photocell 215

photocopier 17.3
photocopy 16.250
photocurrent
  420.64
photoelasticity
  16.333.28.2
photoelectric 38
photoelectricity
  16.333.28
photoengrave 482
Photofit 371
photoflash 349
photoflood 100
photogenic 38.32.1
photogram 229.1
photogrammetry
  16.285
photograph 158.1
photographer
  17.120.1
photographic 38.11
photography
  16.90.2.6
photogravure 10
photokinesis
  300.51
photolithography
  16.90.2
photomap 268
photometry
  16.285.2
photomicrograph
  158.1
photomontage 359
photomultiplier
  17.4
photon 254
photonasty 16.361
photoperiod 103.1
photophilous
  310.26
photophobia 17.3.4
photophore 9.6
photopia 17.3.37
photosensitive
  485.12
photosensitize
  516.12
photoset 368
photosphere 6.1
Photostat 365
photosynthesis
  300.52
photosynthesize
  516.10

photosynthetic
  38.50
phototaxis 300.70
phototelegraphy
  16.90
phototherapy
  16.254
photothermic 38.26
phototonic 38.35.5
phototonus 310.36
phototropic 38.37.2
prototype 275.1
phototypography
  16.90.2
phrasal 228.125
phrase 509
phraseogram
  229.1.1
phraseograph
  158.1.1
phraseology
  16.108.4.1
phrasing 265.81
phrenic 38.32
phrenology
  16.108.4.10
Phrygia 17.3.14
Phrygian 261.3.7
phthalein 251
phthiriasis 300.57.1
phut 378
phycology
  16.108.4.5
phylactery
  16.274.44
phyle 16.121
phyletic 38.50
phyllite 372.3
phylloclade 85
phylloid 97.5
phyllome 239
phylloxera 17.272
phylogeny 16.229.2
phylum 242.9
physiatrics 498.8
physic 38
physical 228.23.25
physicalism
  242.35.11
physically 16.142
physician 261.71.8
physicist 436.21
physics 498
physiognomic
  38.29

physiognomy
  16.222.3.1
physiography
  16.90.2.1
physiology
  16.108.4.1
physiotherapist
  436.15
physiotherapy
  16.254
physique 37
physostigmine 251
physostomous
  310.29
phytogenic 38.32.1
phytology
  16.108.4.14
phytopathology
  16.108.4
phytosociology
  16.108.4.1
phytotoxin 252.29
phytotron 254
pi 7
piacular 17.174.3
piaffe 157
pia mater 17.338
pianism 242.35.14
pianissimo 12.48
pianist 436.13.1
piano 12
pianoforte 16.336
Pianola 17.171
piassava 17.409
piastre 17.379
piazza 17.319
pibroch 40
pica 17.35
picador 9.4
Picardy 16.72
picaresque 57
picaroon 260.3
Picasso 12.68
picayune 260
Piccadilly 16.120
piccalilli 16.120
piccaninny 16.229
piccolo 12.45
pice 301
piceous 310.2.15
pichiciego 12.27
pick 38
pickaback 32.2
pickaxe 494
picker 17.34

pickerel 228.76
pickerelweed 89.7
picket 371.9
picketing 265.66
pickle 228.23
pickled 122
picklock 40
pickpocket 371.10
Pickwickian 261.3
picnic 38
picnicker 17.34
picot 12.10
picotee 5
picrate 367.25
Pict 387
pictograph 158.1
pictorial 228.3.12
picture 17.65
picturesque 57
picul 228.23
piddle 228.32
piddling 265
piddock 46
pidgin 252.6
pie 7
piebald 118
piece 298
piecemeal 217
piecework 36
piecrust 443
pied 92
Piedmont 414
piedmont 414
pieman 261
pier 6
pierce 299
piercing 265
Pierian 261.3.22
Pierides 513.4
Pierrot 12.63
pietà 1
Pietermaritzburg 182.2
piety 16.333.2
piezometer 17.342.3
piffle 228.41
pig 184
pigeon 261.37
pigeonhole 223
pigface 295
piggery 16.274.9
piggin 252
piggish 353
Piggott 381

piggy 16.93
piggyback 32
pig-headedness 300.28
piglet 371
pigmeat 370
pigment 420
pigmentation 261.67.32
pigskin 252
pigstick 38
pigsticking 265.7
pigsty 7
pigswill 218
pigtail 214
pigtailed 112
pigweed 89
pika 17.35
pike 39
pikelet 371
pikeperch 65
piker 17.35
pikestaff 158
pilaster 17.379
Pilate 381
pilau 13
pilch 76
pilchard 103
pile 219
pileate 371.1
pileous 310.2
pileum 242.2
pileus 310.2
pilfer 17
pilferage 197
pilgarlic 38
pilgrim 235
pilgrimage 197.3
pili 5.8
piliform 238.1
pill 218
pillage 197.1
pillar 17.166
pillbox 499
pillion 261.120
pilliwinks 505
pillory 16.274.16
pillow 12.42
pillowcase 295.2
pillowslip 274
pilose 305
pilot 381
pilotage 197
Piltdown 258
pilule 227

pimento 12.84
pimp 287
pimpernel 215
pimple 228
pimpled 122
pimply 16.179
pin 252
pinafore 9.6
pinaster 17.379
pinball 221
pince-nez 2
pincer 17.315
pincers 524
pinch 80
pinchbeck 35
pinchcock 40
pinchpenny 16.226
pincushion 261
Pindar 17.102
Pindaric 38.38
pindling 265
Pindus 310
pine 253
pineal 228.3.7
pineapple 228.64
Pinero 12.63
pinery 16.274.27
pinetum 242.28
pinfold 120
ping 265
pinger 17.246
ping-pong 266
pinguid 91
pinhead 86.4
pinhole 223
pinion 261.122
pinite 372.5
pink 52
Pinkerton 261
pinkeye 7
pinkie 16.37
pinking 265.10
pinkish 353
pinna 17.231
pinnace 300.23
pinnacle 228.28
pinnate 367.17
pinnatiped 86.6
pinner 17.231
pinniped 86.6
pinnula 17.174
pinny 16.229
Pinocchio 12.3
pinochle 228.27
pinole 16.126

pinpoint 416
pinprick 38
pinstripe 275
pint 413
pinta 17.369
pintadera 17.271
pintail 214
Pinter 17.369
pintle 228
pinwheel 217
pinworm 233
piny 16.230
piolet 2
pioneer 6.5
pious 310.3
pip 274
pipa 17.252
pipage 197
pipe 275
pipeclay 2
pipefitting 265.66
pipeline 253
piper 17.254
piperidine 251
piperine 253.7
piperonal 212
pipette 368
pipewort 369
piping 265
pipistrelle 215
pipit 371
pipkin 252
pippin 252
pipsissewa 17.425
pipsqueak 37
piquancy 16.312
piquant 420.6
piqué 2.6
pique 37
piquet 368.4
piracy 16.307
Piraeus 310.1
piranha 17.226
pirate 371
piratic 38.49
pirn 249
pirog 188
pirogue 188
pirouette 368.1
Pisa 17.440
piscary 16.274
piscatorial 228.3.12.2
Pisces 513.13
piscina 17.230

piscine 253
piscivorous
310.50.3
pishogue 188
pisiform 238.1
pismire 8
piss 300
Pissarro 12.61
pistachio 12.3
pistareen 251.7
piste 435
pistil 218
pistol 228.114
pistole 223
pistoleer 6
piston 261.107
pit 371
pita 17.341
pitapat 365
Pitcairn 250
pitch 67
pitchblende 131
pitcher 17.56
pitchfork 41
pitchy 16.49
piteous 310.2
pitfall 221
pith 458
pithead 86
pithecanthropus
310.40
pithos 302
pithy 16.370
pitiable 228.16.2
pitiful 226
pitiless 300.8
pitilessness 300.33
Pitman 261
pitman 261
piton 254
Pitot 12.76
Pitt 371
pitta 17.342
pittance 321.24
pitter-patter 17.336
Pittsburgh 182.2
pituitary 16.274.41
pituri 16.274.41
pity 16.333
Pius 310.3
pivot 381
pivotal 228
pix 498
pixie 16.388
pixilated 91.34.5

Pizarro 12.61
pize 516
pizza 17
pizzeria 17.2.2
pizzicato 12.73
placable 228.16
placard 84
placate 367.6
placatory 16.274.43
place 295
placebo 12.5
placement 420.44
placenta 17.368
placental 228.110
placentation
261.67.32
placer 17.298
placet 368
placid 91.28
placidity 16.333.5.1
placing 265.59
placket 371.6
placoid 97
plagal 228.44
plage 359
plagiarism
242.35.15
plagiarist 436.20
plagiarize 516.8
plagioclase 295
plague 180
plaice 295
plaid 83
plain 247
plainchant 408
plainness 300
plainsong 266
plaint 409
plaintiff 163
plaintive 485
plaintiveness
300.43
plait 365
plan 245
planar 17.227
planarian 261.3.21
planation 261.67
planchette 368
plane 247
planer 17.227
planet 371.22
planetarium
242.2.14
planetary
16.274.41

planform 238
plangent 420.22
planimeter
17.342.2
planimetry
16.285.1
planish 353
plank 51
planking 265
plankton 261
planktonic 38.35
planner 17.225
planning 265
planography
16.90.2.4
planometer
17.342.3
planosol 220
plant 408
Plantagenet
371.24.2
plantain 252
plantar 17.365
plantation
261.67.31
planter 17.366
plantigrade 85.5
planula 17.174.9
plaque 32
plash 349
plashy 16.319
plasm 242.34
plasma 17.223
plasmagel 215
plasmasol 220
plasmin 252
plasmodium
242.2.4
Plassey 16.294
plaster 17.380
plasterboard 95.1
plastered 103
plasterer 17.279
plastering 265.58
plastic 38.68
Plasticine 251.8
plasticity
16.333.28.2
plasticize 516.10
plastid 91
plastometer
17.342.3
plat 365
platan 261.94
plat du jour 10

plate 367
plateau 12.72
plated 91.34
plateful 226.7
platelayer 17.1
platelet 371
platemark 33
platen 261.94
plater 17.338
platform 238
Plath 452
platina 17.231
plating 265.64
platinize 516.6.1
platinocyanide
92.4
platinoid 97.8.1
platinum 242.14
platitude 102.2.1
platitudinize 516.6
Plato 12.74
Platonic 38.35.5
Platonism
242.35.14
Platonize 516.7
platoon 260.4
Platte 365
platter 17.336
platy 16.327,
16.329
platypus 310.37
platyrrhine 253
plaudit 371
plausible 228.16
plausive 485
Plautus 310
play 2
playable 228.16
playback 32
playbill 218
playboy 11
player 17.1
playful 226
playgoer 17.6
playground 139
playhouse 306
playlet 371
playmate 367
playpen 248
playroom 241
playschool 227
playsuit 380
plaything 265
playtime 236
playwright 372

plaza 17.438
plea 5
pleach 66
plead 89
pleader 17.82
pleading 265.13
pleasance 321
pleasant 420.84
pleasantness 300
pleasantry 16.291
please 513
pleased 153
pleasing 265
pleasurable 228.16.35.2
pleasure 17.333
pleasureless 300.13
pleat 370
pleater 17.341
pleb 21
plebby 16.8
plebeian 261.2.1
plebiscite 372.9
plectognath 452
plectron 261
plectrum 242.22
pledge 194
pledgee 5.5
pledget 371
pledgor 9
pleiad 83.2
Pleiades 513.5
plein-air 4
Pleistocene 251.9
plenary 16.274.25
plenipotent 420.78
plenipotentiary 16.274.39
plenitude 102.2
plenteous 310.2
plentiful 226
plenty 16.355
pleonasm 242.34
plesiosaur 9.11
plethora 17.279
pleura 17.277
pleural 228.75
pleurisy 16.300
pleurodynia 17.3
pleuron 254
pleuropneumonia 17.3.36
pleuston 261
plew 15
plexiform 238.1

Plexiglass 294
plexor 17.426
plexus 310
pliable 228.16.3
pliant 420.2
plica 17.35
plicate 367
plication 261.67
plié 2
pliers 524
plight 372
plimsoll 228
plinth 470
Pliny 16.229
Pliocene 251.9
plissé 2
ploat 376
plod 94
plodder 17.85
plodge 199
plonk 53
plonko 12
plop 276
plosion 261.92
plosive 485.6
plot 373
Plotinus 310.34
plotter 17.344
plough 13
ploughboy 11
ploughman 261
ploughshare 4
ploughstaff 158
plover 17.418
ploy 11
pluck 43
plucky 16.30
plug 189
plum 240
plumage 197
plumate 367
plumb 240
plumbago 12.27
plumbeous 310.2
plumber 17.216
plumbery 16.274
plumbing 265.38
plumbism 242.35
plumbous 310.6
plumbum 242
plume 241
plummet 371
plummy 16.220
plump 289
plumper 17.264

plumpness 300
plumy 16.221
plunder 17.108
plunderage 197
plunderer 17.279
plunge 211
plunger 17.159
plunk 54
pluperfect 387
plural 228.75
pluralism 242.35.11
plurality 16.333.8
pluralize 516.3
plus 307
plush 356
Plutarch 33
Pluto 12.80
plutocracy 16.307.5
plutocrat 365.2
plutocratic 38.49.6
pluton 254
Plutonian 261.3.18
plutonic 38.35
plutonium 242.2.12
pluvial 228.3.17
pluvious 310.2.18
ply 7
Plymouth 464
plywood 101
pneuma 17.217
pneumatic 38.49
pneumatics 498.11
pneumatology 16.108.4.15
pneumatolysis 300.52.2
pneumatophore 9.6
pneumococcus 310.11
pneumoconiosis 300.55.1
pneumoencephalo-
gram 229.1
pneumogastric 38
pneumograph 158.1
pneumonectomy 16.222.5
pneumonia 17.3.36
pneumonic 38.35
pneumonitis 300.62
Po 12
po 12
poach 70

poacher 17.59
poaching 265
Pocahontas 310
pochard 103
pock 40
pocket 371.10
pocketbook 44
pocketful 226
pocketknife 164
pockmark 33
poco 12.12
pococurante 16.353
pod 94
podagra 17.289
poddy 16.65
podesta 17.382
podgy 16.104
podiatry 16.286.1
podium 242.2.4
podophyllin 252.8
podzol 220
Poe 12
poem 235
poesy 16.396
poet 371
poetaster 17.379
poetic 38.50.1
poeticize 516.10
poetics 498.12
poetry 16.285
pogge 185
pogonia 17.3.36.1
pogrom 242
Pohai 7
poi 11
poignancy 16.312
poignant 420
poinciana 17.226.1
poinsettia 17.3
point 416
pointed 91.48
pointer 17.371
pointillism 242.35.9
pointing 265
pointless 300
pointlessness 300.33
poise 519
poison 261.128
poisoner 17.239
poisonous 310.36
poke 42
poker 17.38
pokeweed 89

posy 16.399
pot 373
potable 228.16
potamic 38.24
potamology
16.108.4
potash 349
potassium 242.2
potation 261.67.28
potato 12.74
potbellied 91.17
potbelly 16.115
potboy 11
potch 68
poteen 251
Potemkin 252
potency 16.312
potent 420
potentate 367.32
potential 228.96
potentiality
16.333.8.1.1
potentiate 367.1.9
potentiometer
17.342.3.1
potful 226
pothead 86
pother 17.407
potherb 22
pothole 223
potholer 17.171
potholing 265.32
pothook 44
pothouse 306
pothunter 17.373
potiche 352
potion 261.73
Potiphar 17.114
potlatch 62
potluck 43
Potomac 46
potpie 7
potpourri 16.270
Potsdam 229
potsherd 87
pottage 197
potted 91.40
potter 17.344
Potteries 515.1
pottery 16.274
potting 265.68
potto 12.77
potty 16.335
pouch 71
pouffe 170

poulard 84
poult 405
poulterer 17.279
poultice 300
poultry 16
poultryman 261.48
pounce 319
pound 139
poundage 197
poundal 228
pour 9
pourer 17.276
pourpoint 416
poussette 368
pout 377
pouter 17.348
poverty 16.344
pow 13
powder 17.89
powdery 16.274
Powell 228.8
power 14
powerboat 376
powerful 226
powerhouse 306
powerless 300
powerlessness
300.33
powwow 13
Powys 300, 300.1
pox 499
Poyang 263
pozzuolana 17.226
practicability
16.333.9.2
practicable
228.16.10
practical 228.23.22
practicality
16.333.8.3
practice 300.65
practise 300.65
practitioner
17.239.2
praemunire 16.267
praenomen 248
Praesepe 16.247
praetor 17.341
pragmatic 38.49
pragmatism
242.35.20
pragmatist 436.26
Prague 179
prairie 16.264
praise 509

praiseworthy
16.375
praline 251
pralltriller 17.166
pram 229, 230
prance 315
prandial 228.3
prang 263
prank 51
prase 509
praseodymium
242.2
prat 365
prate 367
pratfall 221
pratincole 223
pratique 37
prattle 228.97
prattler 17.200
prawn 255
praxis 300.70
Praxiteles 513.6
prayer 4
prayerful 226
preach 66
preacher 17.55
preachify 7.3
preadaptation
261.67
preamble 228.17
preamplifier 17.4.1
prearranged 111
preaxial 228.3.18
prebend 143
prebendary 16.274
precarious 310.2.10
precast 431
precaution 261.72
precautionary
16.274.29
precede 89.2
precedence 321.5
precedent 420.10
precedential
228.96.1
preceding 265.13
precentor 17.368.1
precept 422
preceptive 485.23
preceptor 17.375
precess 296
precession 261.68
precinct 392
preciosity
16.333.30.1

precious 310
preciousness
300.34
precipice 300
precipitant 420.76
precipitate 367.30
precipitation
261.67.27
precipitin 252.23
precipitous 310.64
precis 5
precise 301
precisian 261.91.1
precision 261.91.1
preclude 102
precocial 228.94
precocious 310.60
precocity
16.333.30.3
precognition
261.71
preconceive 484
preconception
261.84
precondition
261.71
preconize 516.7
preconscious 310
precontract 382
precursor 17.301
precursory
16.274.35
predacious
310.56.2
predate 367
predation 261.67.7
predator 17.352
predatory
16.274.43
predecease 298
predecessor 17.300
predestinarian
261.3.21.1
predestinate 371
predestination
261.67.18
predestine 252.26
predeterminate
371.24
predetermine
252.13
predial 228.3.1
predicable
228.16.10

457

presuppose 520.2
presupposition
261.71.9
pretence 316
pretend 131.5
pretender 17.101
pretension 261.82
pretentious 310.61
pretentiousness
300.34.4
preterite 371.35.2
preterition 261.71
preteritive 485.12
preternatural
228.76
pretext 450
Pretoria 17.3.41
prettify 7.3
prettiness 300.23
pretty 16.333
pretzel 228
Preussen 261
prevail 214
prevailing 265.27
prevalence
321.12.1
prevalent 420.28.1
prevaricate 367.5
prevarication
261.67.5
prevenient 420.1.2
prevent 410.3
preventable
228.16.55
preventative
485.15.15
preventer 17.368
prevention 261.82
preventive 485.21
preview 15
Previn 252.28
previous 310.2
previously 16.184
prevision 261.91.2
prevocalic 38.19
prewar 9
Priam 242
priapism 242.35
price 301
priceless 300
pricelessness
300.33
pricey 16.301
prick 38
pricker 17.34

pricket 371.9
prickle 228.23
prickly 16.142
pride 92
prie-dieu 3
priest 435
priesthood 101
Priestley 16.200
priestly 16.200
prig 184
priggish 353
prim 235
prima 17.210
primacy 16.307
prima donna
17.233.1
primal 228
primarily 16.120.1
primary 16.274
primate 367
primatology
16.108.4.15.1
prime 236
primer 17.212
primero 12.62
primeval 228.119
primigravida 17.83
priming 265
primipara 17.279
primitive 485.12
primitivism
242.35.22
primo 12.47
primogenitor
17.342
primogeniture
17.56
primordial 228.3.2
primp 287
primrose 520
primula 17.174
primus 310
prince 317
princedom 242
princeling 265
princess 296
Princeton 261
principal 228.66
principality
16.333.8.8
Principe 5
principium 242.2
principle 228.66
principled 122
prink 52

print 412
printable 228.16
printer 17.369
printing 265
prior 17.4
priorate 371
prioress 300.47
priority 16.333.22
priory 16.274
prisage 197
Priscilla 17.166
prise 516
prism 242.35
prismatic 38.49.4
prismatoid 97
prison 261.126
prisoner 17.239
prissy 16.300
pristine 251
pristine 253.10
prithee 16.376
privacy 16.307
private 371
privateer 6.9
privation 261.67
privative 485.15.16
privet 371
privilege 197.1
privileged 110
privity 16.333.35
privy 16.382
prize 516
prizefight 372
prizefighter 17.343
pro 12
proa 17.6
pro-am 229
probabilism
242.35.9
probability
16.333.9.2
probable 228.16
probably 16.137
proband 128
probang 263.1
probate 367.3
probation 261.67.3
probationer
17.239.1
probative 485.15
probe 28
probity 16.333
problem 242
problematic
38.49.2

proboscidean
261.3.5
proboscis 300.54
procaine 247
procathedral
228.78
procedure 17.149
proceed 89.3
proceeding 265.13
proceeds 526
proceleusmatic
38.49
process 296
procession 261.68.1
processional
228.63.4
processor 17.300
prochronism
242.35.14
proclaim 231
proclamation
261.67.16
proclamatory
16.274.43.5
proclitic 38.52
proclivity
16.333.35
Procne 16.239
proconsul 228.89
procrastinate
367.17
procrastination
261.67.18
procreate 367.1
procreation
261.67.1
Procrustean
261.3.27
procryptic 38.66
proctology
16.108.4
proctor 17.356
procuration
261.67.21
procurator 17.338
procuratory
16.274.43
procure 10
procurer 17.277
prod 94
prodigal 228.46
prodigality
16.333.8.4
prodigious 310.21
prodigy 16.103

prodrome 239
produce 309, 309.1
producer 17.308
product 389
production 261.79.1
productive 485.19
productivity 16.333.35.3
proem 232
prof 165
profanation 261.67.19
profane 247.3
profanity 16.333.14
profess 296
profession 261.68
professional 228.63.4
professionalism 242.35.11.5
professor 17.300
professorial 228.3.12
professoriate 371.1.2
proffer 17.116
proficiency 16.312.5
proficient 420.74
profile 219
profit 371
profitable 228.16.49
profiteer 6
profiterole 223.3
profitless 300.17
profligacy 16.307
profligate 371.14
profluent 420.4
profound 139
profoundly 16.156
profundity 16.333.7
profuse 309
profusely 16.183
profusion 261.93
prog 185
progenitor 17.342
progeny 16.229.2
progestational 228.63.3
progesterone 257.1
progestin 252.26
proglottis 300

prognosis 300.55
prognostic 38.71
prognosticate 367.5
prognostication 261.67.5
programmable 228.16.26
programmatic 38.49.2
programme 229
programmer 17.205
programming 265
progress 296
progression 261.68
progressive 485.2.1
prohibit 371.5
prohibition 261.71
prohibitionist 436.13.5
prohibitive 485.12
project 385, 385.3
projectile 219.5
projection 261.77.1
projectionist 436.13.6
projective 485.17
projector 17.354
projet 2
Prokofiev 160.1
prolamine 251.4
prolapse 322
prolate 367
prole 223
proleg 181
prolegomenon 261.56
prolepsis 300.59
proletarian 261.3.21.2
proletariat 381.1
proliferate 367.23
proliferation 261.67.22
prolific 38.12
proline 251
prolix 498
prolocutor 17.350
prologue 185
prolong 266.1
prolongation 261.67
prolusion 261.93
prom 237
promenade 84

promenader 17.78.1
Promethean 261.3
promethium 242.2
prominence 321.14
prominent 420.53.2
promiscuity 16.333.3
promiscuous 310.4
promise 300
promisee 5.20
promising 265.61
promisor 9
promissory 16.274.36
promontory 16.274.48
promote 376
promoter 17.347
promotion 261.73.1
promotional 228.63.6
promotive 485.14
prompt 429
promptitude 102.2
promptness 300
promulgate 367
promulgation 261.67
pronate 367
pronator 17.338
prone 257
proneness 300
prong 266
pronghorn 255
pronominal 228.60.5
pronoun 258
pronounce 319
pronounceable 228.16
pronouncement 420
pronto 12.85
pronunciamento 12.84
pronunciation 261.67.1.4
proof 170
proofread 89
proof-reader 17.82
prop 276
propaedeutic 38.56
propaganda 17.98
propagandist 436

propagandize 516
propagate 367.11
propagation 261.67.11
propagator 17.338.4
propane 247
propel 215
propellant 420.26
propeller 17.163
propensity 16.333.31
proper 17.255
properly 16.131.6
propertied 91
property 16.344
prophage 193
prophase 509
prophecy 16.300
prophesy 7
prophet 371
prophetic 38.50
prophylactic 38.58
prophylaxis 300.70
propinquity 16.333
propitiate 367.1.6
propitious 310.58
propolis 300.13.2
proponent 420.54
proportion 261.72.1
proportional 228.63
proportionate 371.28.2
proposal 228.127
propose 520.2
proposer 17.442
proposition 261.71.9
propositus 310.64
propound 139
propraetor 17.341
proprietary 16.274.41
proprietor 17.352.1
propriety 16.333.2
proprioceptor 17.375
propulsion 261
propylaeum 242.1
propylite 372.3
pro rata 17.337
prorate 367
prorogue 188

prosaic 38.1
prosaism 242.35
proscenium 242.2
prosciutto 12.80
proscribe 25
proscription 261.85
proscriptive 485
prose 520
prosector 17.354
prosecute 380
prosecution 261.75
prosecutor 17.351
proselyte 372.3
proselytize 516.12
Proserpina 17.231
prosimian 261.3.14
prosody 16.72
prosopopoeia
17.2.1
prospect 385
prospective 485.17
prospector 17.354
prospectus 310.69
prosper 17.267
prosperity
16.333.21
prosperous 310.50
prostaglandin 252
prostate 367.34
prostatectomy
16.222.5
prostatitis 300.62
prosthesis 300.52
prosthetic 38.50
prosthetics 498.12
prosthodontics 498
prostitute 380.5
prostitution 261.75
prostomium
242.2.9
prostrate 367
prostration 261.67
prostyle 219
prosy 16.399
protactinium
242.2.11
protagonist
436.13.2
protamine 251.4
protanopia
17.3.37.2
protasis 300.57
protea 17.3
protean 261.2
protease 509.1

protect 385
protection 261.77
protectionism
242.35.14
protectionist
436.13.6
protective 485.17
protector 17.354
protectorate 371.35
protectory
16.274.45
protégé 2
protein 251
protest 433
Protestant 420.81
Protestantism
242.35.21
protestation
261.67.33
protester 17.382
Proteus 310.2
prothesis 300.52.5
protist 436.25
protium 242.2
protocol 220
protohistory
16.274.49
protolanguage 197
protolithic 38.73
protomorphic
38.14
proton 254
protoplasm 242.34
Protosemitic 38.52
prototherian
261.3.22
prototrophic 38.13
prototype 275.1
protozoan 261.6
protozoology
16.108.4.3
protozoon 254.2
protract 382
protractile 219.4
protraction 261.76
protractor 17.353
protrude 102
protrusion 261.93
protrusive 485.8
protuberance
321.20
protuberant 420.65
protyle 219
proud 99
Proust 444

proustite 372
provable 228.16.62
prove 490
proven 261
provenance 321.14
Provencal 213
provender 17.102
proverb 22
proverbial 228.3
provide 92.13
providence 321.5
provident 420.10
providential
228.96.1
providing 265.14
province 317
provincial 228
provincialism
242.35.11
provinciality
16.333.8.1
provision 261.91.3
provisional 228.63
proviso 12
provitamin 252.15
Provo 12
provocation
261.67.6
provocative
485.15.2
provoke 42
provolone 16.233.1
provost 445
prow 13
prowess 300
prowl 224
prowler 17.172
Proxima 17.211
proximal 228.52
proximate 371.19
proximity
16.333.12
proximo 12.48
proxy 16.389
prude 102
prudence 321
prudent 420.13
prudential 228.96
Prudentius 310.61
prudish 353
pruinose 305
prune 260
prunella 17.163
prunelle 215
pruner 17.238

prurience 321.1
prurient 420.1.3
prurigo 12.30
pruritus 310.65
Prussia 17.329
Prussian 261.74
prussiate 371.1
pry 7
psalm 230
psalmist 436.8
psalmodic 38.9
psalmody 16.72
Psalms 540
psalter 17.363
psalterium 242.2.15
psaltery 16.274
psephite 372
psephology
16.108.4
pseud 102
pseudaxis 300.70
Pseudepigrapha
17.120
pseudo 12.22
pseudomorph
166.1
pseudomutuality
16.333.8.2
pseudonym 235
pseudonymous
310.28.2
pseudopodium
242.2.4
pshaw 9
psittacine 253.8
psittacosis 300.55
psoas 310
psoralea 17.3.18
psoriasis 300.57.1
psych 39
Psyche 16.26
psyche 16.26
psychedelia 17.3.19
psychedelic 38.20
psychiatric 38.45
psychiatrist 436
psychiatry 16.286.1
psychic 38
psycho 12
psychoanalyse
516.3.5
psychoanalysis
300.52.1
psychoanalyst
436.7.4

quagga

quagga 17.123
quaggy 16.91
quagmire 8
quahog 185
quail 214
quaint 409
quaintness 300
quake 34
Quaker 17.30
Quakerism
242.35.15
quaky 16.21
quale 16.113
qualification
261.67.5.1
qualified 92.1
qualifier 17.4.1
qualify 7.3.2
qualitative
485.15.12
quality 16.333.10
qualm 230
quamash 349
quandary 16.274
quandong 266
quango 12.35
quant 414
quantal 228.111
quantic 38.64
quantifiable
228.16.3.1
quantifier 17.4.1
quantify 7.3
quantitative
485.15.12
quantity 16.333
quantize 516
quantum 242
quaquaversal
228.84
quarantine 251
quare 4
quark 33
quarrel 228.73
quarreller 17.176
quarrelsome 242
quarrian 261.3
quarrier 17.3
quarry 16.268
quarryman 261.48
quart 374
quartan 261.102
quarter 17.345
quarterage 197
quarterback 32.2

quarterdeck 35
quarterfinal 228.61
quarterlight 372.4
quarterly 16.131
quartermaster
17.380
quartern 261.102
quarterstaff 158
quartet 368
quartic 38
quartile 219
quarto 12.78
quartz 342
quartzite 372
quasar 1
quash 354
Quasimodo 12.21
quassia 17.327
quatercentenary
16.274.25
quaternary
16.274.24
quaternion 261.3
quaternity
16.333.16
quatrain 247
quatre 17.291
quatrefoil 222.1
quaver 17.410
quay 5
quayside 92
queasy 16.395
Quebec 35
quebracho 12
queen 251
queencake 34
queenly 16.172
Queensberry
16.274
Queensland 143
queer 6
quell 215
quelquechose 520
quench 79
quenchable 228.16
quenelle 215
quercetin 252.23
quercine 253
querist 436.17
quern 249
querulous 310.25.1
query 16.265
quest 433
question 261.18

questionable
228.16.31
questioner 17.239
questioning 265.46
questionless 300.14
questionnaire 4.5
Quetta 17.339
quetzal 228
Quetzalcoatl
228.97
queue 15
Quezon y Molina
17.230
quibble 228.12
quiche 352
quick 38
quicken 261.13
quickie 16.25
quicklime 236
quickly 16.142
quicksand 128
quickset 368
quicksilver 17.422
quickstep 271
quick-witted 91.38
quick-wittedness
300.28
quid 91
quiddity 16.333.5
quidnunc 54
quid pro quo 12
quiescence 321.21
quiescent 420.67
quiet 381.2
quieten 261
quietism 242.35.20
quietness 300
quietude 102.2
quietus 310.63
quiff 163
quill 218
quillai 7.5
quilt 403
quilting 265
quim 235
quin 252
quinary 16.274.27
quinate 367
quince 317
quincentenary
16.274.25
quincunx 506
Qui Nhong 266
quinine 251
quinol 220.3

quinquagenarian
261.3.21.1
Quinquagesima
17.211
quinquennium
242.2
quinquereme 234
quinsy 16.406
quintal 228
quintan 261.105
quintessence
321.21
quintessential
228.96
quintet 368
quintile 219
Quintilian 261.3.11
quintillion 261.120
quintuple 228
quintuplet 371
quintuplicate
367.5.1
quip 274
quipster 17.396
quire 8
Quirinal 228.60
Quirinus 310.34
quirk 36
quirky 16.23
quirt 369
quisling 265
quist 436
quit 371
quitch 67
quitclaim 231
quite 372
Quito 12.76
quits 339
quittance 321.24
quitter 17.342
quittor 17.342
quiver 17.414
quiverful 226
quivery 16.274.51
qui vive 484
Quixote 381
quixotic 38.53
quiz 515
quizmaster 17.380
quizzical 228.23.25
quod 94
quodlibet 368.2
quoin 256
quoit 375
quokka 17.36

ramble 228.17
rambler 17.179
rambling 265
Rambouillet 2
rambunctious 310
rambutan 261.104
ramekin 252.3
Rameses 513
ramie 16.210
ramification
261.67.5.1
ramiform 238.1
ramify 7.3
Ramillies 513.6
ramjet 368
rammish 353
ramose 305
ramp 285
rampage 193
rampant 420
rampart 366
rampion 261.3
ramrod 94
Ramsgate 367
ramshackle 228.19
ramulose 305
ramus 310.27
ran 245
rance 315
ranch 78
ranchero 12.62
Ranchi 16.54
rancid 91
rancorous 310.50.1
rancour 17.43
rand 128
randan 245
Randolph 173
random 242.6
randomize 516.5
randy 16.77
rang 263
range 207
rangefinder 17.103
ranger 17.156
Rangoon 260
rangy 16.109
rani 16.224
rank 51
ranker 17.43
ranking 265
rankle 228
ransack 32
ransom 242
rant 407

ranunculaceous
310.56
ranunculus 310.25
rap 268
rapacious 310.56
rapacity
16.333.25.1
Rapa Nui 16.4
rape 270
rapeseed 89
Raphael 228.1
raphide 92
rapid 91
rapidity 16.333.5
rapier 17.3
rapine 253
rapist 436.14
rapparee 5.17
rappee 5
rappel 215
rapper 17.247
rapport 9
rapporteur 3
rapscallion 261.118
rapt 421
raptor 17.374
raptorial 228.3.12
rapture 17.72
rapturous 310.50
rare 4
rarebit 371
rarefaction 261.76
rarefied 92.1
rarefy 7.3
rarely 16.117
rareripe 275
raring 265.52
rarity 16.333
Rarotonga 17.142
rasbora 17.276
rascal 228
rascality 16.333.8
rascally 16.131
rash 349
rasher 17.321
rashness 300
rasp 290
raspatory
16.274.43
raspberry 16.274
rasping 265
Rasputin 252.24
rasse 16.294
Rasta 17.379

Rastafarian
261.3.21
raster 17.379
rat 365
rata 17.337
ratafia 17.2
ratal 228.99
ratatat 365
ratatat-tat 365
ratatouille 5
ratbag 178
ratchet 371
rate 367
rateable 228.16.45
ratel 228.99
ratepayer 17.1
rates 335
ratfink 52
ratfish 353
rathe 473
rather 17.401
ratify 7.3.8
ratiné 2.15
ratine 251
rating 265.64
ratio 12.3.6
ratiocinate 367.17
ration 261.66
rational 228.63.2
rationale 213.1
rationalism
242.35.11.5.1
rationalist 436.7.5
rationalistic
38.70.2
rationality
16.333.8.7.1
rationalize 516.3.7
Ratisbon 254
ratite 372
Ratlam 230
ratline 252
ratoon 260
rats 333
ratsbane 247
rattan 245
ratter 17.336
Rattigan 261.32
rattish 353
rattle 228.97
rattler 17.200
rattlesnake 34
rattletrap 268
rattling 265
rattly 16.186

rattrap 268
ratty 16.327
raucous 310
raunchy 16.55
rauwolfia 17.3
ravage 197
rave 482
Ravel 215
ravel 228.117
ravelin 252
raven 261, 261.111
ravening 265.46
Ravenna 17.228
ravenous 310.36
raver 17.410
ravine 251.12
raving 265.77
ravioli 16.126
ravish 353
ravishing 265.63
raw 9
Rawalpindi 16.79
rawboned 138
rawhide 92
rawinsonde 136
rawness 300.24
ray 2
rayless 300.7
raylet 371
rayon 254
raze 509
razee 5
razoo 15.10
razor 17.439
razorback 32.2
razorbill 218
razz 507
razzle-dazzle
228.124
razzmatazz 507
re 2, 5
reach 66
reachable
228.16.12
react 382
reactant 420
reaction 261.76
reactionary
16.274.29
reactivate 367.36
reactive 485.16
reactivity
16.333.35.2
reactor 17.353
read 86, 89

readable 228.16
reader 17.82
readership 274.1
readily 16.120
readiness 300.23.1
Reading 265.12
reading 265.13
readjust 443
ready 16.60
reaffirm 233
reafforest 436.18
Reagan 261.31
reagent 420
real 213, 228.2
realgar 17.137
realism 242.35.11.1
realist 436.7.1
realistic 38.70.2.1
reality 16.333.8.1
realizable
228.16.64
realization
261.67.36
realize 516.3.1
really 16.119
realm 243
realty 16.352
ream 234
reamer 17.210
reap 273
reaper 17.252
reappear 6.6
reappearance
321.17
rear 6
rearguard 84
rearm 230
rearmost 441
rearrange 207
rearrangement
420.38
reason 261.125
reasonable
228.16.31.2
reasoned 143.6
reasoning 265.46
reassurance 321.19
reassure 10
reassuring 265.56
Réaumur 10
reb 21
rebarbative 485.15
rebate 367
rebec 35
Rebecca 17.31

rebel 215, 228
rebellion 261.119
rebellious 310.2
rebirth 456
reborn 255
rebound 139
rebuff 168
rebuild 116
rebuilt 403
rebuke 45
rebus 310
rebut 378
rebuttal 228.107
rebutter 17.349
rec 35
recalcitrant 420.66
recalesce 296.1
recalescence 321.21
recall 221.1
recant 407
recantation
261.67.31
recap 268
recapitulate 367.13
recapitulation
261.67.13
recaption 261.83
recapture 17.72
recce 16.22
recede 89.2
receipt 370
receiptor 17.341
receive 484.2
receiver 17.413
receivership 274.1
recension 261.82.2
recent 420.69
recept 422
receptacle 228.28
reception 261.84
receptionist 436.13
receptive 485.23
receptivity
16.333.35
receptor 17.375
recess 296
recession 261.68
recessional
228.63.4
recessive 485.2
Rechabite 372
recharge 192
recherché 2
recidivism
242.35.22

Recife 17.113
recipe 16.248
recipience 321.1
recipient 420.1
reciprocal 228.28
reciprocate 367.6
reciprocity
16.333.30
recision 261.91.1
recital 228.103
recitation
261.67.27
recitative 484
recite 372.9
reckless 300
recklessness 300.33
reckon 261
reckoner 17.239
reckoning 265.46
reclaim 231
reclamation
261.67.16
reclinable
228.16.30
reclinate 367.17
recline 253.4
recliner 17.232
reclothe 478
recluse 309
reclusive 485.8
recognition 261.71
recognizable
228.16.64
recognizance 321
recognize 516
recognizee 5
recognizor 9
recoil 222
recollect 385.5
recollection 261.77
recombination
261.67.18
recommence 316
recommend 131.2
recommendable
228.16.18
recommendation
261.67.9
recommendatory
16.274.43.2
recommit 371.21
recompense 316
recompose 520
reconcilable 228.16
reconcile 219

reconciliation
261.67.1.1
reconciliatory
16.274.43.1
recondite 372
recondition 261.71
reconnaissance
321.22
reconnoitre 17.346
reconsider 17.83
reconstitute 380.5
reconstruct 389
reconstruction
261.79
reconvert 369
record 95, 95.2
recordable
228.16.16
recorder 17.86
recording 265.15
recount 418
recoup 280
recourse 303
recover 17.418
recovery 16.274
re-create 367.1
recreation 261.67.1
recreational
228.63.3
recrement 420.31
recriminate 367.17
recrimination
261.67.18.5
recrudesce 296
recruit 380
recruitment 420
recrystallize 516.3
recta 17.354
rectal 228
rectangle 228.49
rectangular 17.174
recti 7
rectifiable
228.16.3.1
rectifier 17.4.1
rectify 7.3.9
rectilinear 17.3.34
rectitude 102.2
recto 12.81
rectocele 217.2
rector 17.354
rectory 16.274.45
rectrix 498
rectum 242
rectus 310.69

recumbent 420
recuperate 367.23
recuperation
 261.67.22
recuperator
 17.338.9
recur 3
recurrence 321
recurrent 420.64
recurring 265.51
recursion 261.69
recurve 483
recusant 420
recycle 228.24
red 86
redact 382
redan 245.1
redbreast 433
redbrick 38
redbud 100
redbug 189
redcoat 376
redcurrant 420.64
redd 86
redden 261.21
reddish 353
Redditch 67
redecorate 367.23
redeem 234
redeemable 228.16
redeemer 17.210
redeeming 265.36
redemption 261
redemptioner
 17.239
Redemptorist
 436.20
redeploy 11
redeployment
 420.33
redevelop 281.1
redevelopment 420
redeye 7
redfin 252
Redford 103.2
Redgrave 482
red-handed 91.12
redhead 86
redia 17.3.8
redingote 376
redintegrate 367.26
redintegration
 261.67.24
rediscover 17.418
Redmond 143

redneck 35
redness 300
redo 15
redolent 420.28
redouble 228.14
redoubt 377
redoubtable 228.16
redound 139
redox 499
redpoll 220
redraft 396
redress 296
redroot 380
Redruth 463
redshank 51
redskin 252
redstart 366
reduce 309
reducer 17.308
reducible 228.16
reduction 261.79
redundancy 16.312
redundant 420.16
reduplicate 367.5.1,
 371.9.1
reduplication
 261.67.5
reduviid 91.2
redware 4
redwing 265
redwood 101
re-echo 12.9
reed 89
reedbuck 43
reeding 265.13
reedling 265
reedy 16.62
reef 162
reefer 17.113
reek 37
reel 217
re-election 261.77.2
reen 251
re-enact 382
re-entrant 420
re-entry 16.288
reeve 484
re-examine 252.12
re-export 374
ref 160
reface 295
refection 261.77
refectory 16.274.45
refer 3
referee 5.17

reference 321.20
referendum 242.7
referent 420.65
referral 228
refill 218
refillable 228.16.23
refine 253
refined 135
refinement 420
refiner 17.232
refinery 16.274.27
refining 265.44
reflate 367
reflation 261.67
reflect 385
reflection 261.77
reflective 485.17
reflectivity
 16.333.35
reflector 17.354
reflet 2
reflex 496
reflexive 485
reflux 502
re-form 238, 238.1
reformation
 261.67.16
reformative
 485.15.6
reformatory
 16.274.43
reformed 125
reformer 17.214
reformism
 242.35.12
refract 382.1
refraction 261.76
refractive 485.16
refractometer
 17.342.3
refractor 17.353
refractory
 16.274.44
refrain 247
refrangible
 228.16.21
refreeze 513
refresh 351
refresher 17.323
refreshing 265
refreshment 420
refrigerant 420.65
refrigerate 367.23
refrigeration
 261.67.22

refrigerator
 17.338.9
refringent 420.23
refroze 520
refuel 228.10
refuge 204
refugee 5
refulgent 420.21
re-fund 140
refundable 228.16
refurbish 353
refusal 228.128
refuse 309, 523
refutation
 261.67.29
refute 380
regain 247
regal 228.45
regale 214
regalia 17.3.18
regality 16.333.8.4
regard 84.1
regardant 420.8
regardful 226
regarding 265
regardless 300
regatta 17.336
regency 16.312
regenerate
 367.23.1, 371.35
regeneration
 261.67.22.2
regent 420
reggae 2
regicide 92.7
regime 234
regimen 248
regiment 410.1,
 420.31
regimental
 228.110.2
regimentals 539
regimentation
 261.67.32.1
Regina 17.232
region 261.36
regional 228.63
regionalism
 242.35.11.5
register 17.384
registrant 420
registrar 1
registration
 261.67.25
registry 16.293

Reno 12.54
Renoir 1
renounce 319
renovate 367,
367.37
renovation 261.67
renown 258
renowned 139
rent 410
rental 228.110
rented 91.46
renter 17.368
renunciation
261.67.1.4
renvoi 11
reopen 261
reorganize 516.7
rep 271
repaint 409
repair 4.6
repairable
228.16.33
repairer 17.271
repairman 261.46
repand 128
reparable
228.16.35.1
reparation
261.67.22
repartee 5
repartition 261.71
repast 431
repatriate 367.1,
371.1
repatriation
261.67.1
repay 2
repayment 420.29
repeal 217
repeat 370
repeatable
228.16.48
repeated 91.37
repeatedly 16.148
repeater 17.341
repechage 359
repel 215
repellent 420.26
repent 410
repentance 321.26
repentant 420
repercussion
261.74
repertoire 1.17
repertory 16.274.43

repetend 131.5
repetition 261.71.7
repetitious 310.58
repetitive 485.12
rephrase 509
repine 253
replace 295
replaceable
228.16.36
replacement 420.44
replay 2
replenish 353.6
replete 370
repletion 261.70
replevin 252.28
replevy 16.380
replica 17.34
replication
261.67.5
reply 7.8
repoint 416
repone 257
report 374.1
reportage 359
reportedly 16.148
reporter 17.345
repose 520
reposit 371.39
reposition 261.71.9
repository
16.274.41
repossess 296
repossession
261.68
repot 373
repoussé 2.21
reprehend 131.1
reprehensible
228.16.40
reprehension
261.82.1
represent 410.4
re-present 410.4
representation
261.67.32
representational
228.63.3
representationalism
242.35.11.5.2
representative
485.15.15
repress 296
repression 261.68
repressive 485.2
reprieve 484

reprimand 129
reprint 412
reprisal 228
reprise 513
repro 12
reproach 70
reproachable
228.16.13
reproachful 226
reprobate 367.4
reprobation
261.67.3
reprobative 485.15
reproduce 309.1
reproduction
261.79.1
reproductive
485.19
reprography
16.90.2
reproof 170
reprove 490
reptile 219
reptilian 261.3.11
republic 38
republican 261.13
republicanism
242.35.14.2
republicanize 516.7
repudiate 367.1
repudiation
261.67.1
repugn 260
repugnance 321
repugnant 420
repulse 313
repulsion 261
repulsive 485
reputable
228.16.52
reputation
261.67.29
repute 380.4
reputed 91.42
request 433
requiem 232
requiescat 365
require 8.3
requirement 420
requisite 371.38
requisition
261.71.8
requital 228.103
requite 372
reredos 302

reremouse 306
rerun 259
resale 214
resaleable
228.16.22
rescind 134
rescissible
228.16.39
rescissory
16.274.36
rescue 15
rescuer 17.7
research 65
researcher 17.54
reseat 370
resect 385.7
resection 261.77.5
reseda 17.83
resemblance 321.13
resemble 228.18
resent 410.4
resentful 226.11
resentment 420
reserpine 251
reservation 261.67
reserve 483
reserved 147
reservedly 16.148.1
reservist 436
reservoir 1.18
reset 368
resettle 228.100
reshape 270
reshuffle 228.42
reside 92
residence 321.5
resident 420.10.1
residential 228.96.1
residentiary
16.274.39
residual 228.9.1
residuary 16.274.2
residue 15.7
residuum 242.3
resign 253
resignation 261.67
resignedly 16.148
resile 219
resilience 321.1
resilient 420.1
resin 252.30
resinate 367.17
resinoid 97.8
resinous 310.33
resipiscence 321.22

resist 436
resistance 321.27
resistant 420.81
resistible 228.16
resistivity 16.333.35
resistor 17.384
resit 371
resoluble 228.15
resolute 380.1
resolution 261.75.1
resolve 493
resolved 151
resolvent 420
resonance 321
resonant 420.55
resonate 367.18
resonator 17.338.8
resorb 27
resort 374
resound 139
resounding 265.22
resource 303
resourceful 226.6
respect 385
respectable 228.16
respecter 17.354
respectful 226.10
respecting 265.71
respective 485.17
respectively 16.206
respiration 261.67.22
respirator 17.338.9
respiratory 16.274.43
respire 8
respite 371
resplendence 321.7
resplendent 420.14
respond 136
respondent 420.15
response 318
responser 17.316
responsibility 16.333.9.2
responsible 228.16
responsive 485
respray 2
rest 433
restate 367
restaurant 266.2
restaurateur 3.1
restful 226
restharrow 12.60

resting 265.75
restitution 261.75
restive 485.24
restless 300
restlessness 300.33
restoration 261.67.22
restorationism 242.35.14.3
restorative 485.15
restore 9
restorer 17.276
restrain 247
restrainer 17.227
restraint 409
restrict 387
restriction 261.78
restrictive 485.18
result 406
resultant 420
résumé 2
resume 241
resumption 261.89
resupinate 371.24
resurge 195
resurgence 321
resurgent 420.19
resurrect 385.6
resurrection 261.77.4
resurrectionist 436.13.6
resuscitate 367.30
resuscitation 261.67.27
resuscitator 17.338.10
ret 368
retable 228.11
retail 214
retailer 17.162
retain 247.9
retainer 17.227
retake 34
retaliate 367.1.1
retaliation 261.67.1
retaliatory 16.274.43.1
retard 84
retardant 420.8
retardation 261.67
retarded 91.5
retarder 17.78
retch 64
rete 16.332

retention 261.82
retentive 485.21
rethink 52
retiarius 310.2.10
reticence 321.22
reticent 420.70
reticle 228.23.19
reticulate 367.13.2
reticulate 371.17.2
reticule 227.1
reticulum 242.10.1
retina 17.231
retinite 372.5
retinitis 300.62.3
retinol 220.3
retinoscopy 16.254.2
retinue 15.9
retire 8
retirement 420
retiring 265.54
retorsion 261.72
retort 374
retortion 261.72
retouch 72
retrace 295
retract 382
retractable 228.16
retractile 219.4
retraction 261.76
retractor 17.353
re-tread 86
retreat 370
retrench 79
retrenchment 420
retrial 228.4
retribution 261.75
retributive 485
retrievable 228.16.61
retrieval 228.119
retrieve 484
retriever 17.413
retro 12
retroact 382
retroaction 261.76
retroactive 485.16
retrocede 89.3
retrochoir 8
retrofire 8
retrofit 371
retroflex 496
retroflexion 261.77
retrograde 85.6
retrogress 296

retrogressive 485.2.1
retroject 385.3
retrorocket 371.10
retrorse 303
retrospect 385
retrospection 261.77
retrospective 485.17
retroussé 2.21
retry 7
retsina 17.230
return 249.1
returnable 228.16.28
retuse 309
Reuben 252
reunify 7.3
reunion 261.123
reunite 372
Reuter 17.346
revalorize 516.8
revaluation 261.67.2
revalue 15
revamp 285
reveal 217
revealing 265.29
revegetate 367.30
reveille 16.112
revel 228.118
revelation 261.67.14
revelationist 436.13.4
reveller 17.176
revelry 16.283
revenant 420.53
revenge 208
revengeful 226
revenue 15.9
revenuer 17.8
reverberate 367.23
reverberation 261.67.22
reverberator 17.338.9
reverberatory 16.274.43
revere 6.11
reverence 321.20.1
reverend 143
reverent 420.65
reverential 228.96.2

reverie 16.274
revers 6.11
reversal 228.84
reverse 297.2
reversi 16.298.1
reversible
 228.16.38
reversion 261.69
reversioner 17.239
revert 369.1
revest 433
revet 368
revetment 420
review 15
reviewer 17.8
revile 219
revise 516.15
revision 261.91.2
revisionism
 242.35.14
revisory 16.274.53
revitalize 516.3
revival 228.121
revivalism
 242.35.11
revivalist 436.7
revive 486
revivify 7.3
reviviscence 321.22
revocable 228.16
revocation 261.67.6
revoice 304
revoke 42
revolt 405
revolting 265
revolute 380.1
revolution 261.75.1
revolutionary
 16.274.29
revolutionize 516.7
revolve 493
revolver 17.423
revolving 265
revue 15
revulsion 261
revulsive 485
reward 95
rewardable
 228.16.16
rewarding 265.15
rewind 135
rewinder 17.103
rewire 8
reword 87
rework 36

Rex 496
Reykjavik 38
Reynard 103
rhabdomancy
 16.309
Rhaetian 261.70
Rhaetic 38.51
rhapsodic 38.9
rhapsodist 436.3
rhapsodize 516
rhapsody 16.72
rhatany 16.237
Rhea 17.2
rhea 17.2
Rhemish 353
Rhenish 353.6
rheobase 295.1
rheology 16.108.4.1
rheometer
 17.342.3.1
rheostat 365
rhesus 310
rhetor 17.341
rhetoric 38.44
rhetorical
 228.23.17
rhetorician 261.71
rheum 241
rheumatic 38.49
rheumatics 498.11
rheumatism
 242.35.20
rheumatoid 97
rheumatology
 16.108.4.15
rheumy 16.221
rhinal 228.61
Rhine 253
Rhineland 143
rhinestone 257
rhinitis 300.62
rhino 12
rhinoceros 310.50
rhinology 16.108.4
rhinoplasty
 16.361.1
rhinoscopy
 16.254.2
rhizobium 242.2
rhizocarpous 310
rhizoid 97
rhizome 239
rhizomorph 166.1
rhizomorphous
 310.18

rhizopod 94.1
rhizosphere 6.1
rhodamine 251.4
Rhodes 529
Rhodesia 17.325
Rhodian 261.3.6
rhodinal 212
rhodium 242.2.4
rhododendron 261
rhodonite 372.6
rhombic 38
rhombohedral
 228.78
rhombohedron 261
rhomboid 97
rhombus 310
rhonchus 310
Rhondda 17.104
Rhône 257
rhotic 38.55
rhubarb 19
rhyme 236
rhyolite 372.4
rhythm 242.33
rhythmic 38.30
rhythmical 228.23
rhythmics 498
ria 17.2
rial 228.4
Rialto 12.82
riata 17.337
rib 24
ribald 122
ribaldry 16.278
riband 143
Ribble 228.12
ribbon 261
ribbonwood 101
riboflavin 252
ribonuclease 509.1
ribose 520
ribosome 239
rice 301
ricer 17.303
ricercare 2.17
rich 67
Richard 103
Richardson 261
Richelieu 3
riches 515
Richmond 143
richness 300
ricin 252.22
rick 38
rickets 339

rickettsia 17.3
rickety 16.333.4
rickrack 32
rickshaw 9
ricochet 2
ricotta 17.344
rictus 310
rid 91
riddance 321.5
ridden 261.24
riddle 228.32
ride 92
rider 17.84
riderless 300.13
ridge 197
ridgepole 223
ridgetree 5
ridgeway 2.29
ridicule 227.1
ridiculous 310.25.2
riding 265.14
Ridley 16.148
ridotto 12.77
riesling 265
Rif 163
rife 164
riff 163
riffle 228.41
riffler 17.190
riffraff 157
rifle 228
riflebird 87
rifleman 261
riflery 16.283
rifling 265
rift 398
rig 184
Riga 17.128
rigadoon 260
rigatoni 16.233
rigger 17.129
rigging 265
right 372
righten 261.100
righteous 310
righteousness
 300.34
rightful 226.9
right-handed 91.12
right-hander 17.98
rightish 353
rightism 242.35
rightist 436
rightly 16.190
rightness 300.39

Romulus 310.25
rondeau 12
rondel 228
rondelet 368
rondo 12
rondure 10
rone 257
Roneo 12.3.4
ronggeng 264
roo 15
rood 102
roof 170
roofing 265
rook 44
rookery 16.274
rookie 16.31
room 241
roomette 368
roomful 226
roommate 367
roomy 16.221
roorback 32
roose 523
Roosevelt 402
roost 444
rooster 17.389
root 380
rootle 228.108
rootless 300
rootstock 40
rope 278
ropewalk 41
ropy 16.251
roque 42
Roquefort 9
roquelaure 9.8
rorqual 228
Rorschach 33
rort 374
Rosa 17.442
rosace 295
rosaceous 310.56
rosarian 261.3.21
Rosario 12.3.5
rosarium 242.2.14
rosary 16.274
Roscius 310.2
Roscommon 261
rosé 2.31
rose 520
roseate 367.1
rosebay 2
rosebud 100
rosehip 274
rosella 17.163

rosemaling 265.26
rosemary 16.274
roseola 17.176
rosery 16.274
Rosetta 17.339
rosette 368
rosewood 101
Rosh Hashanah 17.226
Rosicrucian 261.75
Rosie Lee 5.8
rosin 252
Rosinante 16.353
ROSPA 17.267
Ross 302
Ross and Cromarty 16.344
Rossetti 16.330
Rossini 16.228
rostellum 242.8
roster 17.385
Rostock 40
Rostov 487
Rostropovich 67
rostrum 242.23
rosy 16.399
rot 373
rota 17.347
Rotarian 261.3.21
rotary 16.274
rotate 367.31
rotation 261.67.28
rotative 485.15.13
rotator 17.338
rote 376
rotenone 257
rotgut 378
Rotherham 242.21
Rothermere 6.3
Rothschild 117
roti 16.339
rotifer 17.114
rotisserie 16.274.36
rotl 228.104
rotogravure 10
rotor 17.347
Rotorua 17.8
rotten 261.101
rottenness 300.31
rotter 17.344
Rotterdam 229
rotting 265.68
Rottweiler 17.167
rotund 140
rotunda 17.108

Rouault 12
rouble 228
roué 2.2
rouge 364
rouge et noir 1.16
rough 168
roughage 197
roughcast 431
roughen 261
roughish 353
roughly 16.159
roughneck 35
roughness 300
roughshod 94
roulade 84
rouleau 12
roulette 368
round 139
roundabout 377.1
rounded 91.14
roundel 228
roundelay 2.11
rounder 17.107
rounders 524
Roundhead 86
roundhouse 306
roundish 353
roundly 16.156
roundness 300
roundsman 261
roundup 279
roundworm 233
roup 278, 280
rouse 521
rousing 265
Rousseau 12
roust 442
rout 377
route 380
routemarch 63
router 17.348
routine 251
roux 15
rove 488
rover 17.417
row 12, 13
rowan 261.6
rowboat 376
rowdiness 300.23
rowdy 16.68
rowel 228.8
rower 17.6
rowing 265.4
rowlock 46
Roy 11

royal 228.6
royalism 242.35.11
royalist 436.7
royalty 16.352.1
rub 29
rubáiyát 365
Rub' al Khali 16.113
rubato 12.73
rubber 17.19
rubberize 516.8
rubberneck 35
rubbery 16.274
rubbing 265
rubbish 353
rubbishy 16.322
rubble 228.14
rube 30
rubefy 7.3
rubella 17.163
rubellite 372.3
Rubens 548
rubeola 17.176
rubescent 420.67
Rubicon 261.13
rubicund 143
rubidium 242.2.3
rubiginous 310.33
Rubinstein 253
rubious 310.2
rubric 38
rubricate 367.5
ruby 16.14
ruche 358
ruching 265
ruck 43
rucksack 32
ruckus 310
ruction 261.79
rudaceous 310.56
rudbeckia 17.3
rudd 100
rudder 17.90
rudderhead 86.5
ruddle 228.36
ruddock 46
ruddy 16.69
rude 102
rudeness 300
ruderal 228.76
rudiment 420.31
rudimentary 16.274.47
rudish 353
Rudolf 173

rue 15
rueful 226
ruff 168
ruffian 261.3
ruffle 228.42
ruffler 17.191
rufous 310
Rufus 310
rug 189
ruga 17.136
rugby 16
rugged 91
ruggedize 516
ruggedness 300.28
rugger 17.134
rugose 305
Ruhr 10
ruin 252
ruination 261.67.18
ruinous 310.33
Ruisdael 213
rule 227
ruler 17.175
ruling 265
rum 240
Rumania 17.3.31
Rumanian 261.3.15
rumba 17.27
rumble 228
rumbustious 310.2
Rumelia 17.3.20
rumen 248.3
ruminant 420.53.3
ruminate 367.17.6
rumination
  261.67.18.7
ruminative
  485.15.7
rummage 197
rummer 17.216
rummy 16.220
rumour 17.217
rumoured 103.5
rump 289
Rumpelstiltskin
  252
rumple 228
rumpus 310.42
run 259
runabout 377.1
runch 82
runcinate 371.24
Runcorn 255
rundle 228
rune 260

rung 267
runic 38
runnel 228
runner 17.237
running 265.45
runny 16.235
Runnymede 89
runt 419
runway 2
Runyon 261
rupee 5
Rupert 381
rupture 17
rural 228.75
ruralize 516.3
Rurik 38.43
Ruritania 17.3.31.2
Ruse 2.21
ruse 523
rush 356
rushes 515
rushy 16.324
rusk 60
Ruskin 252
Russ 307
Russell 228.87
russet 371
Russia 17.329
Russian 261.74
Russianize 516.7
Russky 16.42
Russophile 219.1
Russophobe 28
rust 443
rustic 38
rusticate 367.5
rustle 228.87
rustler 17.199
rustproof 170
rusty 16.368
rut 378
rutabaga 17.125
Ruth 463
Ruthenia 17.3.33
Ruthenian 261.3.16
ruthenium 242.2
Rutherford 103
ruthful 226.14
ruthless 300
ruthlessness 300.33
rutilated 91.34.5
rutile 219
Rutland 143
ruttish 353
rutty 16.341

Ruwenzori 16.269
Rwanda 17.98
Ryan 261.4
Rydal 228.33
rye 7
ryokan 261.14
ryot 381.2

S

Saab 19
Saar 1
Saba 17.10
sabadilla 17.166
Sabah 1
sabayon 254
sabbat 365
Sabbatarian
  261.3.21
Sabbath 464
sabbatical
  228.23.18
Sabellian 261.3.9
sabin 252
Sabine 253
sable 228.11
sabotage 359
saboteur 3.1
sabra 17.281
sabre 17.11
sabretache 349
sabulous 310.25
sac 32
sacaton 257.3
saccharide 92.6
saccharify 7.3.4
saccharimeter
  17.342.2.1
saccharin 252.20
saccharine 251.7,
  253.7
saccharoid 97.12
saccharose 520.3
sacculate 371.17.1
saccule 227
sacerdotal 228.106
sacerdotalism
  242.35.11
sachet 2.22
sack 32
sackbut 378

sackcloth 459
sacking 265
sacral 228
sacrament 420.35
sacramental
  228.110.3
sacramentalism
  242.35.11.6
Sacramento 12.84
sacrarium 242.2.14
sacred 91
sacredness 300.28
sacrifice 301
sacrificial 228.93
sacrilege 197.1
sacrilegious 310.21
sacristan 261.107
sacristy 16.366
sacroiliac 32.1.1
sacrosanct 391
sacrum 242
sad 83
Sadat 365
sadden 261.19
saddle 228.31
saddlebag 178
saddlecloth 459
saddler 17.183
saddlery 16.274
saddletree 5
Sadducee 5
Sade 84
sadiron 261.4
sadism 242.35
sadist 436
sadistic 38.70
sadly 16.146
sadness 300
sadomasochism
  242.35.6
sadomasochistic
  38.70
Sadowa 17.417
safari 16.261
safe 159
safeguard 84
safekeeping 265.49
safety 16
saffian 261.3
safflower 14
saffron 261
Safid Rud 102
safrole 223
sag 178
saga 17.124

sagacious 310.56
sagacity 16.333.25
sagamore 9.9
sage 193
sagebrush 356
saggar 17.123
Sagitta 17.342
sagittal 228.102
Sagittarius
 310.2.10
sagittate 367.30
sago 12.27
Saguache 62
saguaro 12.61
Sahaptin 252.25
Sahara 17.268
Saharan 261
sahib 24
said 86
Saida 17.83
saiga 17.130
Saigon 254
sail 214
sailable 228.16.22
sailcloth 459
sailing 265.27
sailor 17.162
sailplane 247
sainfoin 256
saint 409
Saint Austell
 228.116
sainted 91.45
Sainte Foy 11
Saint Helena
 17.230
Saint Helier
 17.3.19
sainthood 101
Saint Kilda 17.95
Saint Kitts 339
Saint Leger 17.147
saintly 16.196
Saint Moritz 339
saintpaulia 17.3
Saint Petersburg
 182
Saint-Simonianism
 242.35.14.1
Saint Vitus 310.65
Saipan 245
Saïs 300
saithe 454
Saiva 17.415
Sakai 7

sake 16.20, 34
saker 17.30
Saki 16.20
saki 16.20
Saktas 310
Sakyamuni 16.236
sal 212
salaam 230.1
salacious 310.56.3
salad 103
Saladin 252
salamander 17.98
Salambria 17.3.43
salami 16.211
Salamis 300.20
salaried 91.27
salary 16.274.15
salchow 12
sale 214
saleable 228.16.22
Salem 242
salep 271
saleratus 310.62
saleroom 241
salesclerk 33
salesman 261
salesmanship 274.2
Salford 103
Salian 261.3.8
salic 38.19
salicet 368.7
salicin 252.21
salicional 228.63.5
salicornia 17.3.35
salicylate 367.12
salient 420.1
salientian 261.3
salify 7.3
salina 17.232
saline 253
Salinger 17.157
salinity 16.333.17.1
salinometer
 17.342.3
Salisbury 16.274
Salish 353
saliva 17.415
salivary 16.274.52
salivate 367.36
salivation 261.67
sallee 16.112
sallet 371
sallow 12.38
Sallust 445
Sally 16.112

sally 16.112
salmagundi 16.80
Salmanazar 17.437
salmon 261.44
salmonella 17.163
salmonoid 97.9
salol 220
Salome 16.219
salon 254
Salonika 17.34.1
saloon 260.1
saloop 280.1
Salop 281
salopette 368
salpicon 261.13
salpiglossis 300.54
salpingectomy
 16.222.5
salpinx 505
salsify 16.85
salt 404
saltant 420
saltarello 12.40
saltation 261.67
saltatorial
 228.3.12.2
saltbush 357
saltcellar 17.163
salted 91.44
salter 17.363
saltern 261
saltfish 353
saltigrade 85.5
saltire 8
saltpetre 17.341
saltwater 17.345
salty 16.351
salubrious 310.2
Saluki 16.32
salutary 16.274.42
salutation
 261.67.29
salutatory
 16.274.43
salute 380.1
Salvador 9.4
salvage 197
salvageable
 228.16.20
salvation 261.67
salvationist
 436.13.4
salve 491
salver 17.420
salverform 238.2

salvia 17.3
salvo 12
sal volatile 16.120
salvor 17.420
Salween 251
Salyut 380
samara 17.268
Samaria 17.3.38
Samaritan 261.99
samarium 242.2.14
Samarkand 128
samba 17.23
sambar 17.23
same 231
sameness 300
Samian 261.3
samisen 248
samite 372
samiti 16.333
Samnite 372
Samnium 242.2
Samoa 17.6
Samos 302
Samothrace 295
samovar 1.15
Samoyed 86
sampan 245
samphire 8
sample 228.70
sampler 17
Samson 261
Samuel 228.9
samurai 7
San 246
sanatorium
 242.2.17
sanbenito 12.76
San Bernardino
 12.54
sanctify 7.3
sanctimonious
 310.2.9.1
sanctimony 16.237
sanction 261
sanctitude 102.2
sanctity 16.333
sanctuary 16.274.2
sanctum 242
sanctum sanctorum
 242.20
Sanctus 310
sand 128
sandal 228.39
sandalwood 101
sandarac 32.3

schnozzle 228
Schoenberg 182
schola cantorum
    242.20
scholar 17.168
scholarliness
    300.23
scholarly 16.131
scholarship 274.1
scholastic 38.68
scholasticate
    367.5.2
scholasticism
    242.35.16.6
scholiast 430.1
scholium 242.2.7
school 227
schoolboy 11
schoolhouse 306
schoolie 16.130
schooling 265
schoolmarm 230
schoolmarmish 353
schoolmaster
    17.380
schoolmate 367
schoolmistress 300
schoolteacher
    17.55
schooner 17.238
schorl 221
schottische 352
Schubert 381
Schumann 261.51
schuss 308
schwa 1
Schwaben 261.8
sciaenid 91.20
sciamachy 16.33
sciatic 38.49
sciatica 17.34.3
science 321.2
scienter 17.368
sciential 228.96
scientific 38.12
scientism 242.35.21
scientist 436
Scientology
    16.108.4
sci-fi 7
scilicet 368.7
scilla 17.166
Scillies 515
Scilly 16.120
scimitar 17.342.2

scintigraphy 16.90
scintilla 17.166
scintillate 367.12
scintillation
    261.67.12
scintillator
    17.338.5
sciomancy 16.309
scion 261.4
Scipio 12.3
scirrhous 310.46
scirrhus 310.46
scissel 228.85
scissile 219.2
scission 261.91
scissors 524
sciurine 253
sciuroid 97
sclaff 157
sclera 17.272
sclerenchyma
    17.211
scleritis 300.62
scleroderma 17.209
sclerodermatous
    310.68
scleroid 97.10
scleroma 17.215
sclerometer
    17.342.3
sclerophyll 218.1
sclerosis 300.55.5
sclerotic 38.53
sclerotomy
    16.222.4
sclerous 310.45
scoff 165
scoffer 17.116
scofflaw 9
Scofield 115
scold 120
scolding 265.18
scolecite 372.9
scolex 496
scoliosis 300.55.1
scolopendrid 91
scombroid 97
sconce 318
scone 254, 257
Scone 260
scoop 280
scoot 380
scooter 17.351
scop 276
Scopas 310.39

scope 278
scopula 17.174.10
scorbutic 38.56
scorch 69
scorcher 17.58
scorching 265
score 9
scoreboard 95
scorecard 84
scorer 17.276
scoria 17.3.41
scorify 7.3
scorn 255
scornful 226
scornfulness 300.30
scorpaenid 91.20
scorpaenoid 97.7
scorper 17.256
Scorpio 12.3
scorpioid 97
scorpion 261.3
Scot 373
Scotch 68
scotch 68
Scotchman 261
scoter 17.347
scotia 17.328
Scotland 143
scotoma 17.215
scotopia 17.3.37.3
Scots 341
Scotsman 261
Scott 373
Scotticism
    242.35.16.5
Scottie 16.335
Scottish 353
scoundrel 228
scour 14
scourge 195
scouse 306
scout 377
scouter 17.348
Scouting 265
scoutmaster 17.380
scow 13
scowl 224
scrabble 228
scrag 178
scraggy 16.91
scram 229
scramb 229
scramble 228.17
scrambler 17.179
scran 245

Scranton 261
scrap 268
scrapbook 44
scrape 270
scraper 17.249
scraperboard 95.1
scrapheap 273
scrappy 16.243
scratch 62
scratchy 16.46
scrawl 221
scrawny 16.232
screak 37
scream 234
screamer 17.210
scree 5
screech 66
screed 89
screen 251
screenings 552
screenplay 2
screw 15
screwball 221
screwdriver 17.415
screwy 16.4
Scriabin 252
scribble 228.12
scribbly 16.134
scribe 25
scriber 17.15
scrim 235
scrimmage 197.3
scrimp 287
scrimshank 51
scrimshaw 9
scrip 274
script 424
scriptorium
    242.2.17
scriptural 228,76
scripture 17
scriptwriter 17.343
scrod 94
scrofula 17.174
scrofulous 310.25
scroll 223
Scrooge 204
scroop 280
scrotum 242.31
scrouge 202
scrounge 210
scrounger 17.158
scrub 29
scrubber 17.19
scrubby 16.13

scrubland 143
scruff 168
scruffy 16.88
scrum 240
scrummage 197
scrump 289
scrumptious 310
scrumpy 16.257
scrunch 82
scruple 228
scrupulous 310.25
scrupulousness
  300.34
scrutator 17.338
scrutineer 6.4
scrutinize 516.6
scrutiny 16.229
scry 7
scuba 17.20
scud 100
scuff 168
scuffle 228.42
scull 225
scullery 16.274
scullion 261.3.13
sculpsit 371
sculpt 427
sculptor 17
sculptural 228.76
sculpture 17
sculpturesque 57
scum 240
scumble 228
scuncheon 261
scunge 211
scungy 16.111
scunner 17.237
Scunthorpe 277
scup 279
scupper 17.258
scuppernong 266
scurf 161
scurrilous 310.23
scurry 16.272
scurvy 16.381
scut 378
scutate 367
scutcheon 261
scute 380
scutellation
  261.67.12
scutellum 242.8
scutiform 238.1
scutter 17.349
scuttle 228.107

scuttlebutt 378
scutum 242
Scylla 17.166
scyphiform 238.1
scyphistoma
  17.218
scyphus 310
scythe 477
Scythia 17.3
Scythian 261.3
sea 5
seaboard 95
seaborne 255
seacoast 441
seacock 40
seadog 185
seafarer 17.271
seafaring 265.52
seafood 102
seafront 419
seagirt 369
seagoing 265.4
seal 217
sealant 420
sealer 17.165
sealery 16.274
sealskin 252
Sealyham 242.2.5
seam 234
seaman 261.47
seamanly 16.174
seamanship 274.2
seamark 33
seamless 300
seamount 418
seamstress 300
seamy 16.215
Sean 255
seance 315
seaplane 247
seaport 374
seaquake 34
sear 6
search 65
searcher 17.54
searching 265
searchlight 372
searing 265.53
seascape 270
seashell 215
seashore 9
seasick 38
seasickness 300.27
seaside 92
season 261.125

seasonable
  228.16.31.2
seasonal 228.63
seasoning 265.46
seat 370
seated 91.37
seating 265
Seaton 261.98
Seattle 228.97
seawan 261
seaward 103
seawards 531
seaware 4
seaway 2
seaweed 89
seaworthy 16.375
sebaceous 310.56
Sebastopol 228
sebum 242
sec 35
secant 420.6
secateurs 511
secco 12.9
secede 89.2
secession 261.68
seclude 102
secluded 91
seclusion 261.93
seclusive 485.8
second 136
second 143
secondary 16.274
second-best 433
seconde 136
seconder 17.109
second-hand 128
secondly 16.157
secondment 420
second-rate 367
second-sight 372
secrecy 16.300
secret 371
secretarial 228.3.10
secretariat 381.1
secretary 16.274.43
secrete 370
secretion 261.70
secretive 485.12
secretory 16.274
sect 385
sectarian 261.3.21
sectary 16.274.45
sectile 219.5
section 261.77
sectional 228.63.8

sector 17.354
secular 17.174.4
secularity
  16.333.20.3
secularize 516.8.1
secund 140
secure 10.3
security 16.333.23
sedan 245.1
sedate 367.8
sedation 261.67.7
sedative 485.15
sedentary
  16.274.48
Seder 17.79
sedge 194
Sedgemoor 10
sedilia 17.3
sediment 420.31.1
sedimental
  228.110.2
sedimentary
  16.274.47
sedimentation
  261.67.32.1
sedimentous
  310.70
sedition 261.71.1
seditionary
  16.274.29.3
seditious 310.58.1
seduce 309
seducer 17.308
seduction 261.79
seductive 485.19
seductress 300
sedulous 310.25.3
sedum 242
see 5
Seebeck 35
seed 89
seedbed 86
seedcake 34
seedcase 295
seeder 17.82
seedless 300
seedling 265
seedy 16.62
seeing 265.2
seek 37
seeker 17.33
seel 217
seem 234
seeming 265.36
seemingly 16.175

seemly 16.166
seen 251
seep 273
seepage 197
seer 17.2
seersucker 17.39
seesaw 9
seethe 475
Seferis 300.44
segment 420
segmental 228.110
segmentation
 261.67.32
Segovia 17.3.55
segregate 367.10
segregation
 261.67.10
segregationist
 436.13.4
seigneur 3
Seine 247
seise 513
seisin 252
seism 242
seismic 38
seismograph 158.1
seismography
 16.90.2
seismology
 16.108.4
seismoscope 278.1
seize 513
seizing 265
seizure 17.334
sejant 420
Sejm 231
Sekondi 5
selachian 261.3
Selangor 17.245
seldom 242
select 385.4
selection 261.77.2
selective 485.17
selectivity
 16.333.35
selector 17.354
selenite 372.5
selenium 242.2
selenography
 16.90.2
selenology
 16.108.4.10
Seleucid 91.30
Seleucus 310.13
self 172

self-assured 96
self-catering 265.58
self-centred 103
self-confidence
 321.5
self-confident
 420.10
self-conscious 310
self-contained 130
self-control 223
self-deception
 261.84
self-defence 316
self-denial 228.4
self-esteem 234
selfheal 217
selfhood 101
self-indulgent
 420.21
self-inflicted 91
selfish 353.3
selfishness 300.35
selfless 300
selflessness 300.33
self-made 85
self-opinionated
 91.34
self-pity 16.333
self-portrait 371
self-possessed 433
selfpossession
 261.68
self-propelled 113
self-raising 265.81
self-respect 385
self-respecting
 265.71
self-righteous 310
self-sacrifice 301
selfsame 231
self-service 300
self-sufficient
 420.74
self-taught 374
self-willed 116
Seljuk 45
Selkirk 36
sell 215
seller 17.163
Sellotape 270
selva 17.421
selvage 197
semantic 38.62
semantics 498.14
semaphore 9.6

semaphoric 38.41
sematic 38.49.1
semblance 321.13
semé 2
sememe 234
semen 248
semester 17.382
semi 16.213
semiaquatic 38.49
semiarid 91.25
semiautomatic
 38.49.2
semibold 120
semibreve 484
semicircle 228.22
semicircular
 17.174.5
semicolon 261.43
semiconductor
 17.357
semiconscious 310
semiconsciousness
 300.34
semidetached 395
semidome 239
semifinal 228.61
semifinalist 436.7
semifluid 91.3
semiliterate 371.35
semilunar 17.238
seminal 228.60.3
seminar 1
seminarian
 261.3.21.1
seminary 16.274.26
seminiferous
 310.50.2
Seminole 223
semiotic 38.53
semiotics 498
semiparasitic
 38.52.3
semipermeable
 228.16.2
semiprecious 310
semipro 12
semiprofessional
 228.63.4
semiquaver 17.410
Semiramis 300.20
semirigid 91.15
semiskilled 116
semisolid 91.18
Semite 372
Semitic 38.52

Semitics 498
Semitist 436.24
semitone 257.2
semivowel 228.8
semolina 17.230
sempiternal 228.58
semplice 16.49
sen 248
senary 16.274.25
senate 371
senator 17.352
senatorial
 228.3.12.2
send 131
Sendai 7
sendel 228
sender 17.101
sendoff 165
Seneca 17.34
senega 17.129
Senegal 221
Senegambia 17.3.5
senescence 321.21
senescent 420.67.1
seneschal 228.93
senile 219
senility 16.333.9.3
senior 17.435
seniority 16.333.22
Senlac 32
senna 17.228
Sennacherib 24
Sennar 1
sennet 371
sennit 371
señor 9
señorita 17.341
sensate 367.29
sensation 261.67.26
sensational
 228.63.3
sensationalism
 242.35.11.5.2
sensationalist
 436.7.5
sensationalistic
 38.70.2
sense 316
senseless 300.16
senselessness
 300.33.1
sensibilia 17.3.21
sensibility
 16.333.9.2
sensible 228.16.40

481

sex 496
sexagenarian
261.3.21.1
Sexagesima 17.211
sexism 242.35
sexist 436
sexless 300
sexology 16.108.4
sexpot 373
sext 450
sextant 420
sextet 368
sextile 219.8
sextillion 261.120
sexton 261
sextuple 228
sextuplet 371
sexual 228.9
sexuality 16.333.8.2
sexy 16.387
Seychelles 537
Seymour 9
Sfax 494
sforzando 12.23
sfumato 12.73
shabbiness 300.23
shabby 16.5
shack 32
shackle 228.19
Shackleton 261
shad 83
shadbush 357
shaddock 46
shade 85
shading 265.11
shadoof 170
shadow 12
shadowgraph 158
shadowy 16.3
Shadrach 32
shady 16.59
shaft 396
Shaftesbury 16.274
shag 178
shagbark 33
shaggy 16.91
shagreen 251
shah 1
shake 34
shakedown 258
shaken 261.11
shaker 17.30
Shakespeare 6
Shakespearean
261.3.22

Shakespeareana
17.226.1
shako 12.8
shaky 16.21
shale 214
shall 212
shalloon 260
shallop 281
shallot 373.1
shallow 12.38
shallowness 300.25
shalt 401
sham 229
shaman 261.44
shamanism
242.35.14
Shamash 349
shamble 228.17
shambles 539
shame 231
shamefaced 432
shameful 226
shameless 300
shamelessness
300.33
shammer 17.205
shampoo 15
shamrock 40
Shan 246
shandrydan 245.1
shandy 16.77
shandygaff 157
Shang 263
Shanghai 7
shanghai 7
Shangri-la 1.8
shank 51
Shankar 1
Shannon 261.55
shanny 16.223
Shansi 5
shan't 408
Shantung 267
shantung 267
shanty 16.353
shantytown 258
shape 270
shapeless 300
shapelessness
300.33
shaper 17.249
shard 84
share 4
sharecrop 276

sharecropper
17.255
shareholder 17.97
sharia 17.2.2
shark 33
sharkskin 252
Sharon 261
sharp 269
sharpen 261
sharpener 17.239
sharper 17.248
sharpness 300
sharpshooter
17.351
sharp-sighted 91.39
sharp-witted 91.38
shashlik 38
shatter 17.336
shatterproof 170
shave 482
shaven 261.111
shaver 17.410
Shavian 261.3.29
shaving 265.77
shavings 552
Shaw 9
shawl 221
shawm 238
Shawnee 5
she 5
sheading 265.13
sheaf 162
shear 6
shears 514
shearwater 17.345
sheath 457
sheathe 475
sheathing 265
sheave 484
Sheba 17.13
shebang 263
shebeen 251
Shechem 242
shed 86
she'd 89
shedder 17.80
sheen 251
sheep 273
sheepcote 376
sheepdog 185
sheepfold 120
sheepish 353
sheepishness
300.35
sheep-ked 86

sheepshank 51
sheepshead 86
sheepshearer
17.272
sheepshearing
265.53
sheepskin 252
sheepwalk 41
sheer 6
sheerlegs 535
Sheerness 296
sheet 370
sheeting 265
Sheffield 115
sheik 34
sheikdom 242
Sheila 17.165
shekel 228.21
sheldrake 34
shelduck 43
shelf 172
shell 215
she'll 217
shellac 32
shellback 32
Shelley 16.115
shellfire 8
shellfish 353.3
shell-like 39
shellproof 170
Shelta 17.361
shelter 17.361
shelve 492
shelving 265
Shem 232
Shema 1.12
Shenandoah 17.6
shenanigan 261.32
Shensi 5
Shenyang 263
Sheol 223
shepherd 103
sherardize 516
Sheraton 261
sherbet 381
Sherbrooke 44
Sheridan 261.24
sherif 162
sheriff 163.2
Sherman 261
Sherpa 17.251
sherry 16.262
sherwani 16.224
Sherwood 101
she's 513

shunt 419
shunter 17.373
shunt-wound 139
shush 357
shut 378
shutdown 258
shuteye 7
shutter 17.349
shuttering 265.58
shuttle 228.107
shuttlecock 40
shy 7
Shylock 40
shyness 300
sial 228.4
sialagogue 185.2
Sialkot 373
sialoid 97.6
Siam 229
siamang 263
Siamese 513.8
sib 24
Sibelius 310.2.3
Siberia 17.3.39
Siberian 261.3.22
sibilant 420
sibilate 367.12
sibling 265
sibyl 218
sic 38
siccative 485.15.1
Sicilian 261.3.11
Sicily 16.120
sick 38
sickbay 2
sicken 261.13
sickening 265.46
sickle 228.23
sickly 16.142
sickness 300.27
Sicyon 254.1
Sid 91
Siddhartha 17.337
side 92
sideband 128
sideboard 95
sideboards 528
sidecar 1
sidekick 38
sidelight 372
sideline 253
sidelong 266
sidereal 228.3.11
siderite 372.8
siderosis 300.55

sideshow 12
sideslip 274
sidesman 261
sidestep 271
sidestroke 42
sideswipe 275
sidetrack 32
sidewalk 41
sidewall 221
sideward 103
sideways 509
sidewheel 217
sidewheeler 17.165
sidewinder 17.103
siding 265.14
sidle 228.33
sidler 17.187
Sidney 16.240
Sidon 261.25
siege 196
Siegfried 89
siemens 551
Siena 17.228
sienna 17.228
sierra 17.271
Sierra Leone
    16.233
siesta 17.382.1
sieve 485
sifaka 17.29
sift 398
sigh 7
sight 372
sighted 91.39
sighter 17.343
sightless 300
sightlessness
    300.33
sightly 16.190
sight-read 89
sight-reading
    265.13
sightsee 5
sightseeing 265.2
sightseer 17.2
Sigismund 143
siglos 302
sigma 17.222
sigmoid 97
Sigmund 143
sign 253
signal 228
signalize 516.3
signaller 17.176
signally 16.131

signalman 261
signatory 16.274.43
signature 17.56
signboard 95
signet 371.29
significance 321
significant 420.7
significative
    485.15.1
signify 7.3.3
signor 9
signora 17.276
signori 16.269
signorina 17.230
signpost 441
Sigurd 96
sika 17.33
sike 39
Sikh 37
Sikkim 235
silage 197
sild 116
sile 219
silence 321
silencer 17.318
silent 420
Silenus 310.32
Silesia 17.3.60
silesia 17.3.60
silex 496
silhouette 368.1
silica 17.34
silicate 371.9
siliceous 310.58
silicic 38
silicide 92.7
silicle 228.23.7
silicon 261.13
silicone 257
silicosis 300.55
silk 49
silkaline 251.3
silken 261
silkiness 300.23
silkworm 233
silky 16.34
sill 218
silliness 300.23
silly 16.120
silo 12
silt 403
silty 16.350
Silurian 261.3.24
Silvanus 310.31
silver 17.422

silverfish 353
silverpoint 416.1
silverside 92.8
silversmith 458
silverware 4.8
silverweed 89
silvery 16.274
sima 17.212
simarouba 17.20
Simeon 261.3.14
simian 261.3.14
similar 17.166
similarity
    16.333.20.2
simile 16.120
similitude 102.2
simmer 17.211
simnel 228
Simon 261
simoniac 32.1
Simonides 513.4
simony 16.237
simoom 241
simp 287
simpatico 12.11
simper 17.263
simple 228
simpleton 261
simplex 496
simplicity
    16.333.28
simplify 7.3
simplistic 38.70
simply 16.179
Simpson 261
simulant 420.27
simulate 367.13.5
simulated 91.34
simulation
    261.67.13.3
simulator 17.338.6
simulcast 431
simultaneous
    310.2.6
sin 252
Sinai 7
sinapism 242.35
Sinarquist 436
Sinatra 17.292
since 317
sincere 6
sincerely 16.119
sincerity 16.333.21
sinciput 378
Sinclair 4

skulk 50
skull 225
skullcap 268
skunk 54
sky 7
skydive 486
Skye 7
skyjack 32
Skylab 18
skylark 33
skylight 372
skyline 253
skyrocket 371.10
Skyros 302
skysail 214
skyscraper 17.249
skywriting 265.67
slab 18
slabber 17.9
slack 32
slacken 261
slacker 17.28
slacks 494
slag 178
slain 247
slaister 17.381
slake 34
slalom 242
slam 229
slander 17.99
slanderous 310.50
slang 263
slangy 16.241
slant 408
slanting 265.72
slantwise 516
slap 268
slapdash 349
slaphappy 16.243
slapjack 32
slapshot 373
slapstick 38
slash 349
slat 365
slate 367
slater 17.338
slather 17.401
slating 265.64
slattern 261.94
slaty 16.329
slaughter 17.345
slaughterer 17.279
slaughterhouse 306
slaughterman
　261.52

Slav 481
slave 482
slaver 17.410
slavery 16.274.50
slavey 16.379
Slavic 38
slavish 353
slavocracy 16.307.5
Slavonia 17.3.36
Slavonic 38.35
slay 2
sleave 484
sleazy 16.395
sled 86
sledge 194
sledgehammer
　17.205
sleek 37
sleekness 300
sleep 273
sleeper 17.252
sleepiness 300.23
sleepless 300
sleeplessness
　300.33
sleepwalk 41
sleepwalker 17.37
sleepwalking 265.9
sleepy 16.247
sleepyhead 86.2
sleet 370
sleeve 484
sleeveless 300
sleeving 265.79
sleigh 2
sleight 372
slender 17.101
slenderize 516.8
slenderness 300.26
slept 422
sleuth 463
sleuthhound 139
slew 15
slice 301
slicer 17.303
slick 38
slickenside 92
slicker 17.34
slid 91
slide 92
slider 17.84
sliding 265.14
slight 372
slighting 265.67
slightly 16.190

Sligo 12.30
slim 235
slime 236
slimmer 17.211
slimming 265
slimness 300
slimsy 16.403
slimy 16.217
sling 265
slingback 32
slingshot 373
slink 52
slinky 16.37
slip 274
slipcase 295
slipknot 373
slipnoose 309
slipover 17.417
slippage 197.8
slipper 17.253
slipperwort 369
slippery 16.274.30
slippy 16.248
slipsheet 370
slipshod 94
slipslop 276
slipstream 234
slipway 2
slit 371
slither 17.405
sliver 17.414
slivovitz 339
Sloane 257
slob 26
slobber 17.16
slobbery 16.274.3
sloe 12
slog 185
slogan 261
sloganeer 6.5
sloop 280
sloot 380
slop 276
slope 278
sloping 265
sloppiness 300.23
sloppy 16.250
slopwork 36
slosh 354
slot 373
sloth 461
slothful 226
slouch 71
sloucher 17.60
Slough 13

slough 13, 168
Slovak 32
Slovakia 17.3
sloven 261.117
Slovene 251
Slovenia 17.3.33
slovenly 16.174
slow 12
slowcoach 70
slowdown 258
slowly 16.126
slowness 300.25
slowpoke 42
slub 29
slubberdegullion
　261.3.13
sludge 203
slug 189
slugabed 86.1
sluggard 103
slugger 17.134
sluggish 353
sluice 309
sluicegate 367
slum 240
slumber 17.27
slumberer 17.279
slumberous 310.50
slump 289
slung 267
slunk 54
slur 3
slurp 272
slurry 16.272
slush 356
slushy 16.324
slut 378
sluttish 353
sly 7
slyness 300
slype 275
smack 32
smacker 17.28
small 221
smallboy 11
smallholder 17.97
smallholding
　265.18
smallish 353
smallness 300
smallpox 499
smalt 404
smarm 230
smarmy 16.211
smart 366

487

smart aleck 38.19
smarten 261.95
smartie 16.328
smartness 300
smash 349
smasher 17.321
smashing 265
smatter 17.336
smattering 265.58
smaze 509
smear 6
smectic 38.60
smegma 17.221
smell 215
smelly 16.115
smelt 402
smelter 17.361
smew 15
smidgen 261.37
smilax 494
smile 219
smirch 65
smirk 36
smit 371
smite 372
Smith 458
smithereens 547
Smithsonian
  261.3.18
smithsonite 372.6
smithy 16.376
smitten 261.99
smock 40
smocking 265.8
smog 185
smoke 42
smokejack 32
smokeless 300
smoker 17.38
smokestack 32
smoking 265
smoko 12.12
smoky 16.29
Smollett 371
smolt 405
smooch 74
smoodge 204
smooth 479
smoothbore 9
smoothen 261
smoothness 300
smorgasbord 95
smote 376
smother 17.408
smoulder 17.97

smriti 16.333
smudge 203
smudgy 16.107
smug 189
smuggle 228
smuggler 17.193
smuggling 265
smugly 16.161
smugness 300
smut 378
smutch 72
smutty 16.341
Smyrna 17.229
snack 32
snackette 368
snaffle 228
snafu 15
snag 178
snail 214
snake 34
snakebite 372
snakelike 39
snakeroot 380
snakeskin 252
snaky 16.21
snap 268
snapdragon 261.30
snapper 17.247
snappy 16.243
snapshot 373
snare 4
snarl 213
snatch 62
snatchy 16.46
snath 452
snazzy 16.391
sneak 37
sneakers 524
sneaking 265
sneaky 16.24
sneck 35
sned 86
sneer 6
sneeze 513
snib 24
snick 38
snicker 17.34
snicket 371.9
snide 92
sniff 163
sniffle 228.41
sniffy 16.85
snifter 17.359
snigger 17.129
sniggle 228.46

snip 274
snipe 275
sniper 17.254
snippet 371
snips 327
snitch 67
snivel 228.120
snivelling 265
snob 26
snobbery 16.274.3
snobbish 353
snobbishness
  300.35
Sno-Cat 365
snog 185
snood 102
snook 45
snooker 17.41
snoop 280
snooper 17.259
snooperscope 278.1
snoot 380
snooty 16.343
snooze 523
snore 9
snorer 17.276
snorkel 228
snort 374
snorter 17.345
snot 373
snotty 16.335
snout 377
snow 12
snowball 221
snowballing 265.31
snowberry 16.274
snowbird 87
snowblink 52
snowbound 139
snowcap 268
snowcapped 421
Snowdon 261
Snowdonia 17.3.36
snowdrift 398
snowdrop 276
snowfall 221
snowfield 115
snowflake 34
snowman 261.49
snowmobile 217
snowplough 13
snowshed 86
snowshoe 15
snowstorm 238
snowy 16.3

snub 29
snuff 168
snuffbox 499
snuffer 17.118
snuffle 228.42
snuffly 16.159
snuffy 16.88
snug 189
snuggery 16.274.10
snuggle 228
snye 7
so 12
soak 42
soaking 265
so-and-so 12
soap 278
soapbark 33
soapbox 499
soapolallie 16.112
soapstone 257
soapwort 369
soapy 16.251
soar 9
sob 26
sobeit 371
sober 17.18
soberness 300.26
sobriety 16.333.2
sobriquet 2.7
socage 197
soccer 17.36
sociable 228.16.44
social 228.94
socialism 242.35.11
socialist 436.7
socialistic 38.70.2
socialite 372.4
sociality 16.333.8.1
socialize 516.3
society 16.333.2
Socinian 261.3.17
sociobiology
  16.108.4.2
socioeconomic
  38.29.1
sociologist 436.4
sociology
  16.108.4.1
sociometry
  16.285.2.1
sociopath 452
sock 40
sockdologer 17.154
socket 371.10
sockeye 7

socle 228.25
socman 261
Socrates 513.17
Socratic 38.49
sod 94
soda 17.88
sodalite 372.4
sodality 16.333.8
sodamide 92.3
sodden 261.26
sodding 265
sodium 242.2.4
Sodom 242
sodomite 372
sodomy 16.222
sofa 17.117
sofar 1
soffit 371
Sofia 17.3.11
soft 399
softa 17.360
soften 261
softener 17.239
softhearted 91.33
softheartedness
 300.28
softness 300
software 4
softwood 101
softy 16.348
SOGAT 365
soggy 16.94
soh 12
Soho 12
soignée 2
soil 222
soilage 197
soiree 2.17
sojourn 249
soke 42
sol 223
solace 300.9
solanaceous 310.56
solander 17.98
solanum 242
solar 17.171
solarimeter
 17.342.2.1
solarium 242.2.14
solarize 516.8
sold 120
soldan 261.28
solder 17.97
solderer 17.279
soldier 17

soldierly 16.131
soldiery 16.274
sole 223
solecism
 242.35.16.2
solely 16.164
solemn 242
solemnify 7.3
solemnity 16.333
solemnize 516
solenodon 261
solenoid 97.8
Solent 420
sol-fa 1
solfatara 17.268
solfeggio 12.3
solferino 12.54
soli 16.126
solicit 371.36
solicitor 17.342
solicitous 310.64
solicitude 102.2
solid 91.18
solidago 12.27
solidarity 16.333.20
solidary 16.274
solidify 7.3.1
solidity 16.333.5
solidus 310
solifidian 261.3.5
solifluction 261.79
Solihull 225
soliloquize 516
soliloquy 16.259
solipsism 242.35
solitaire 4
solitary 16.274.41
solitude 102.2
solleret 368.6
sollicitation
 261.67.27
solo 12.44
soloist 436
Solomon 261.52
Solomonic 38.35.3
Solon 261.43
solonchak 32
solonetz 336
solstice 300
solubility 16.333.9
soluble 228.15
solum 242
solute 380
solution 261.75.1
solvation 261.67

solve 493
solvency 16.312
solvent 420
Solway 2
soma 17.215
Somali 16.113,
 17.3.17
Somaliland 143.2
somatic 38.49
somatology
 16.108.4.15
somatopleure 10
somatotype 275.1
sombre 17.26
sombrero 12.62
some 240
somebody 16.72
someday 2
somehow 13
someone 259
someplace 295
somersault 404.1
Somerset 371
something 265
sometime 236
sometimes 542
someway 2
somewhat 373
somewhere 4
somewise 516
somite 372
sommelier 2
somnambulate
 367.13
somnambulism
 242.35.10
somnambulist
 436.6
somniloquy 16.259
somnolence 321.12
somnolent 420.28
son 259
sonant 420.54
sonar 1
sonata 17.337
sonatina 17.230
sondage 359
sonde 136
Sondheim 236
sone 257
son et lumière 4.1
song 266
songbird 87
songful 226
Songhai 7

songwriter 17.343
sonic 38.35
son-in-law 9
sonnet 371.25
sonneteer 6
sonny 16.235
sonobuoy 11
sonorant 420.65
sonority 16.333.22
sonorous 310.50
Soochow 13
sook 44
soon 260
sooner 17.238
soot 379
sooth 463
soothe 479
soothing 265
soothsay 2
soothsayer 17.1
soothsaying 265.1
sooty 16.342
sop 276
Sophie 16.87
sophism 242.35
sophist 436
sophister 17.384
sophistic 38.70
sophisticate 367.5,
 371.9
sophisticated
 91.34.3
sophistication
 261.67.5
sophistry 16.293
Sophocles 513
sophomore 9.9
Sophy 16.87
sopor 17.257
soporific 38.12.1
sopping 265
soppy 16.250
soprano 12.51
sora 17.276
sorb 27
sorbefacient 420.73
sorbet 371
sorbose 520
sorcerer 17.279
sorceress 300.47
sorcery 16.274
sordid 91.9
sordidness 300.28
sore 9
soredium 242.2.2

sorehead 86
sorely 16.123
soreness 300.24
sorghum 242
sorgo 12
sori 7.11
sorites 513
sorn 255
sororate 367.23
sororicide 92.7
sorority 16.333.22
sorption 261.87
sorrel 228.73
Sorrento 12.84
sorrow 12.65
sorrowful 226.2
sorry 16.268
sort 374
sorter 17.345
sortie 16.336
sortilege 197.1
sortition 261.71
sorus 310.48
S.O.S. 296
so-so 12.70
sostenuto 12.80
sot 373
soteriology
   16.108.4.1
Sothic 38
sotto voce 16.50
sou 15
soubise 513
soubrette 368
souchong 266
soufflé 2
sough 13, 168
sought 374
soul 223
soulful 226
soulless 300
sound 139
soundbox 499
sounder 17.107
sounding 265.22
soundless 300
soundly 16.156
soundness 300
soundpost 441
soundproof 170
soundtrack 32
soup 280
soupy 16.253
sour 14
source 303

sourdine 251
sourly 16.127
sourness 300
sourpuss 308
soursop 276
Sousa 17.444
sousaphone 257
souse 306
Sousse 309
soutache 349
soutane 245.6
souter 17.351
souterrain 247.8
south 462
Southampton 261
southbound 139
southeast 435
southeasterly
   16.131
southeastward 103
Southend 131
southerly 16.131
southern 261
Southerner 17.239
southernmost 441
southernwood 101
southpaw 9
Southport 374
southward 103
southwards 531
Southwark 46
southwest 433
southwesterly
   16.131
southwestward 103
souvenir 6.5
sou'wester 17.382
sovereign 252
sovereignty 16.360
soviet 381.1
sovietism 242.35.18
sovietize 516.13
sovkhoz 517
sovran 261
sow 12, 13
sowbread 86
sower 17.6
sown 257
soy 11
soya 17.5
sozzled 122
spa 1
space 295
spaceband 128
spacecraft 396

spaceman 261
spaceport 374
spacer 17.299
spaceship 274
spacesuit 380
spacewalk 41
spacing 265.59
spacious 310.56
spaciousness
   300.34
spade 85
spadework 36
spadiceous 310.58
spadix 498
spae 2
spag 178
spaghetti 16.330
Spain 247
spake 34
spall 221
spallation
   261.67.14
spalpeen 251
Spam 229
span 245
spancel 228
spandrel 228
spang 263
spangle 228.49
Spaniard 103
spaniel 228.123
Spanish 353
spank 51
spanker 17.43
spanking 265
spanner 17.225
spar 1
sparable 228.16
spare 4
sparerib 24
sparge 192
sparid 91.25
sparing 265.52
spark 33
sparkle 228.20
sparling 265.26
sparring 265
sparrow 12.60
sparrowgrass 294
sparrowhawk 41
sparry 16.261
sparse 294
sparsely 16.180
sparseness 300
Sparta 17.337

Spartacus 310.14
Spartan 261.95
spasm 242.34
spasmodic 38.9
spastic 38.68
spat 365
spatchcock 40
spate 367
spathe 473
spathic 38.72
spatial 228.91
spatter 17.336
spatula 17.174
spatulate 371.17
spavin 252
spavined 134
spawn 255
spay 2
speak 37
speakeasy 16.395
speaker 17.33
speaking 265
spear 6
spearhead 86
spearmint 412
spec 35
special 228
specialism
   242.35.11
specialist 436.7
speciality
   16.333.8.1
specialize 516.3
specially 16.131
specialty 16.352
specie 5
species 513
specifiable
   228.16.3.1
specific 38.12
specifically 16.142
specification
   261.67.5.1
specify 7.3
specimen 252.14
speciosity
   16.333.30.1
specious 310.57
speck 35
speckle 228.21
specs 496
spectacle 228.28
spectacled 122
spectacles 539

spectacular
17.174.3
spectator 17.338
spectra 17.295
spectral 228
spectre 17.354
spectrograph
158.1.3
spectroheliograph
158.1.1
spectrometer
17.342.3.5
spectroscope
278.1.2
spectroscopy
16.254.2
spectrum 242.22
specular 17.174.4
speculate 367.13
speculation
261.67.13
speculative
485.15.5
speculator 17.338.6
speculum 242.10
sped 86
speech 66
speechify 7.3
speechless 300
speed 89
speedboat 376
speedo 12.18
speedometer
17.342.3
speedway 2
speedwell 215
speedy 16.62
speel 217
speiss 301
spelaean 261.2.2
speleology
16.108.4.1
spelk 48
spell 215
spellbind 135
spellbound 139
speller 17.163
spelling 265.28
spelt 402
spelter 17.361
spelunker 17.46
spence 316
Spencer 17.314
spend 131
spender 17.101

spending 265.20
spendthrift 398
spent 410
speos 302
sperm 233
spermaceti 16.330
spermary 16.274.21
spermatheca 17.33
spermatic 38.49
spermatid 91
spermatium 242.2
spermatocyte
372.10
spermatogenesis
300.52.4
spermatorrhoea
17.2.2
spermatozoon
254.2
spermic 38.26
spermicidal 228.33
spermicide 92.7
spermogonium
242.2.12
spermophile 219.1
spermous 310
spessartite 372.12
spew 15
Spey 2
sphagnum 242
sphene 251
sphenic 38.32
sphenodon 254
sphenoid 97.7
spheral 228
sphere 6
spherical 228.23.15
sphericity
16.333.28
spherics 498.6
spheroid 97.10
spheroidal 228.35
spherule 227
spherulite 372
sphery 16.265
sphinx 505
sphragistics 498
sphygmic 38
sphygmograph
158.1
sphygmoid 97
Spica 17.33
spica 17.35
spicate 367
spiccato 12.73

spice 301
spiceberry 16.274
spicebush 357
spicery 16.274.37
spiciness 300.23
spick-and-span 245
spicule 227.1
spicy 16.301
spider 17.84
spiderman 261.52
spidery 16.274
spiegeleisen
261.127
spiel 217
spieler 17.165
spiffing 265
spiffy 16.85
spiflicate 367.5
spignel 228
spigot 381
spike 39
spikelet 371
spikenard 84
spiky 16.26
spile 219
spill 218
spillage 197.1
spillikin 252.3
spillikins 548
spillway 2
spilt 403
spin 252
spina bifida 17.83
spinach 197.7
spinal 228.61
spindle 228.40
spindlelegs 535
spindling 265
spindrift 398
spine 253
spine-chiller 17.166
spine-chilling
265.30
spinel 215
spineless 300
spinet 371.24
spinifex 496
spinnaker 17.42
spinner 17.231
spinneret 368.6
spinney 16.229
spinning 265.43
spinose 305
spinous 310.34
Spinoza 17.442

Spinozism 242.35
spinster 17.394
spiny 16.230
spiracle 228.28
spiraea 17.2
spiral 228
spirant 420
spire 8
spireme 234
spirillum 242
spirit 371.33
spirited 91.38
spiritless 300.17
spiritlessness
300.33
spiritous 310.64
spiritual 228.9.3
spiritualism
242.35.11.3
spiritualist 436.7.3
spirituality
16.333.8.2
spirituel 215
spirituous 310.4
spirketting 265.66
spirochaete 370
spirochaetosis
300.55.6
spirograph 158.1
spirogyra 17.274
spiroid 97.11
spirometer
17.342.3
spironolactone 257
spirula 17.174
spiry 16.267
spit 371
spitchcock 40
spite 372
spiteful 226.9
spitefulness 300.30
spitfire 8
Spithead 86
spitsticker 17.34
spittle 228.102
spittlebug 189
spittoon 260
spitz 339
spiv 485
splake 34
splanchnic 38
splash 349
splashback 32
splashboard 95
splashdown 258

splasher

splasher 17.321
splashy 16.319
splat 365
splatter 17.336
splay 2
spleen 251
splendid 91.13
splendiferous
  310.50.2
splendour 17.101
splenectomy
  16.222.5
splenetic 38.50.4
splenic 38.32
splenitis 300.62.3
splenius 310.2.7
splenomegaly
  16.131.2
splice 301
spline 253
splint 412
splinter 17.369
split 371
splits 339
splitting 265.66
splodge 199
splodgy 16.104
splore 9
splotch 68
splurge 195
splutter 17.349
Spock 40
Spode 98
spodumene 251
spoil 222
spoilage 197
spoiler 17.170
spoilfive 486
spoilsport 374
spoke 42
spoken 261.14
spokeshave 482
spokesman 261
spoliate 367.1.3
spoliation
  261.67.1.2
spondee 5
spondulix 498
spondylitis
  300.62.1
sponge 211
sponger 17.159
spongy 16.111
sponsion 261
sponson 261

sponsor 17.316
sponsorship 274.1
spontaneity
  16.333.1
spontaneous
  . 310.2.6
spontoon 260
spoof 170
spook 45
spooky 16.32
spool 227
spoon 260
spoonbill 218
spoonerism
  242.35.15
spoon-feed 89
spoonful 226
spoony 16.236
spoor 10
Sporades 513.5
sporadic 38.7
sporangium 242.2
spore 9
sporocyst 436.22
sporogenesis
  300.52.4
sporogonium
  242.2.12
sporophore 9.6
sporophyll 218.1
sporozoan 261.6
sporran 261
sport 374
sporting 265.69
sportive 485.13
sports 342
sportscast 431
sportsman 261
sportsmanlike 39
sportsmanship
  274.2
sportswear 4
sportswoman
  261.50
sporty 16.336
sporulate 367.13
spot 373
spotless 300
spotlessness 300.33
spotlight 372
spotted 91.40
spotter 17.344
spotty 16.335
spousal 228.129
spouse 306

spout 377
sprag 178
sprain 247
sprang 263
sprat 365
sprawl 221
sprawling 265.31
spray 2
spread 86
spreader 17.80
spree 5
sprig 184
sprightly 16.190
spring 265
springboard 95
springbok 40
springe 209
springer 17.246
Springfield 115
springhaas 294
springhead 86
springing 265.47
springlet 371
springtime 236
springwood 101
springy 16.242
sprinkle 228.29
sprinkler 17.182
sprinkling 265
sprint 412
sprinter 17.369
sprit 371
sprite 372
sprocket 371.10
sprout 377
spruce 309
sprucely 16.183
sprue 15
spruik 38
sprung 267
spry 7
spud 100
spume 241
spumescent 420.67
spumone 16.233
spun 259
spunk 54
spunky 16.39
spur 3
spurge 195
spurious 310.2.14
spurn 249
spurrier 17.3
spurry 16.272
spurt 369

sputnik 38
sputter 17.349
sputum 242
spy 7
spyglass 294
spying 265.3
squab 26
squabble 228
squacco 12.8
squad 94
squadron 261
squalene 251
squalid 91.18
squall 221
squally 16.123
squalor 17.168
squama 17.207
squamate 367
squamation 261.67
squamous 310.27
squamulose 305
squander 17.104
square 4
squarely 16.117
squarish 353.9
squarrose 305
squash 354
squashy 16.323
squat 373
squatter 17.344
squattocracy
  16.307.5
squaw 9
squawk 41
squeak 37
squeaker 17.33
squeaky 16.24
squeal 217
squeamish 353
squeamishness
  300.35
squeegee 5
squeeze 513
squeezer 17.440
squelch 75
squeteague 183
squib 24
squid 91
squiffy 16.85
squiggle 228.46
squill 218
squilla 17.166
squinch 80
squint 412
squire 8

squirearchy 16.20
squirm 233
squirrel 228
squirt 369
squish 353
squit 371
squiz 515
Sri Lanka 17.43
Srinagar 17.134
St. Anne's
    554
stab 18
Stabat Mater
    17.337
stabile 219
stability 16.333.9.2
stabilize 516.2
stabilizer 17.441
stable 228.11
stableboy 11
stableman 261
stabling 265
staccato 12.73
stack 32
stacker 17.28
stacte 5
staddle 228.31
staddlestone 257
stadholder 17.97
stadia 17.3.7
stadium 242.2.1
staff 158
Staffa 17.110
Stafford 103
Staffordshire 6
stag 178
stage 193
stagecoach 70
stagecraft 396
stagehand 128
stager 17.146
stagflation 261.67
staggard 103
stagger 17.123
staggering 265.58
staggers 524
staghound 139
staging 265.24
Stagira 17.274
stagnant 420
stagnate 367
stagy 16.100
staid 85
staidness 300
stain 247

Staines 545
stainless 300
stair 4
staircase 295
stairhead 86
stairs 512
stairway 2
stairwell 215
stake 34
stakeout 377
stalactite 372
stalactitic 38.52
stalag 178
stalagmite 372
stalagmitic 38.52
stale 214
stalemate 367
staleness 300
Stalin 252
Stalingrad 83
Stalinism 242.35.13
stalk 41
stalker 17.37
stalky 16.28
stall 221
stallion 261.118
stalwart 381
Stambul 227
stamen 248.2
stamina 17.231.1
staminate 371.24
staminode 98
staminody 16.67
stammel 228.51
stammer 17.205
stammerer 17.279
stamp 285
stampede 89
stance 314
stanch 78
stanchion 261.81
stand 128
standard 103
standardize 516
standee 5
standing 265.19
standish 353.2
standoffish 353
standpipe 275
standpoint 416
standstill 218
stang 263
stanhope 281
stank 51
Stanley 16.169

Stannaries 515.1
stannary 16.274
stannic 38.31
stannite 372
stannous 310
stanza 17.445
stapelia 17.3.20
stapes 513
staphylorrhaphy
    16.90.1
staple 228
stapler 17
star 1
starboard 103
starch 63
starchy 16.47
stardom 242
stardust 443
stare 4
starfish 353
stargaze 509
stargazer 17.439
stargazing 265.81
stark 33
starless 300
starlet 371
starlight 372
starling 265.26
starry 16.261
start 366
starter 17.337
startle 228.98
starvation 261.67
starve 481
starving 265
stash 349
stasis 300.50
statant 420.75
state 367
statecraft 396
Statehouse 306
stateless 300
stateliness 300.23
stately 16.188
statement 420.48
stater 17.338
stateroom 241
stateside 92
statesman 261
statesmanship
    274.2
static 38.49
statics 498.11
station 261.67

stationary
    16.274.29.1
stationer 17.239.1
stationery
    16.274.29.1
stationmaster
    17.380
statism 242.35
statist 436
statistic 38.70.6
statistical
    228.23.24
statistician 261.71
statistics 498
Statius 310.2.16
stative 485.10
statocyst 436.22
statolith 458
stator 17.338
statoscope 278.1
statuary 16.274.2
statue 15
statuesque 57
statuette 368.1
stature 17.50
status 310.62
status quo 12
statute 380
statutory 16.274.42
staunch 81
stauroscope 278.1
stave 482
stavesacre 17.30
stay 2
stayer 17.1
stays 509
staysail 214
stead 86
steadfast 445
steadfastness
    300.42
steadily 16.120
steadiness 300.23.1
steady 16.60
steak 34
steakhouse 306
steal 217
stealing 265.29
stealth 465
stealthful 226
stealthy 16.374
steam 234
steamboat 376
steamer 17.210
steamie 16.215

493

subaqueous 310.2
subarctic 38.59
subarid 91.25
subassembly 16.138
subatomic 38.29
subbase 295
subbasement 420.44
subbass 295
subception 261.84
subclass 294
subclavian 261.3.29
subclimax 494
subcommittee 16.333
subconscious 310
subconsciousness 300.34
subcontinent 420.53
subcontract 382
subcontractor 17.353
subcutaneous 310.2.6
subdeacon 261.12
subdivide 92
subdivision 261.91.2
subdominant 420.53.2
subduct 389
subdue 15
subdued 102
subedit 371.12
subeditor 17.342.1
subequatorial 228.3.12.2
suberin 252.20
suberize 516.8
suberose 305.2
subfamily 16.120
subfusc 60
subgenus 310.32
subglacial 228.91
subgroup 280
subheading 265.12
subhuman 261.51
subindex 496
subjacent 420
subject 385, 387
subjectify 7.3.9
subjection 261.77
subjective 485.17

subjectivism 242.35.22
subjectivity 16.333.35
subjoin 256
sub judice 16.300
subjugate 367
subjugation 261.67
subjunctive 485
sublease 298
sublieutenant 420.52
sublimate 367.15
sublimation 261.67.15
sublime 236
sublimely 16.167
subliminal 228.60.4
sublimity 16.333.12
sublingual 228
sublunary 16.274.28
submarine 251.7
submariner 17.231
submaxillary 16.274.16
submediant 420.1.1
submental 228.110
submerge 195
submersible 228.16.38
submiss 300
submission 261.71
submissive 485.4
submit 371
submontane 247.11
subnormal 228.53
subnormality 16.333.8.5
suboceanic 38.31.1
suborder 17.86
subordinary 16.274.26
subordinate 367.17
subordinate 371.24.1
subordination 261.67.18.1
suborn 255.1
subornation 261.67
subphylum 242.9
subplot 373
subpoena 17.230
subregion 261.36
subreption 261.84

subrogate 367.11
subrogation 261.67.11
sub rosa 17.442
subroutine 251
subscribe 25
subscriber 17.15
subscript 424
subscription 261.85
subsection 261.77
subsequence 321
subsequent 420.58
subserve 483
subservient 420.1
subset 368
subside 92
subsidence 321.6
subsidiary 16.274.1
subsidize 516
subsidy 16.63
subsist 436
subsistence 321.27
subsoil 222
subsonic 38.35
subspecies 513
substage 193
substance 321
substandard 103
substantial 228.95
substantiate 367.1.8
substantiation 261.67.1
substantive 485
substation 261.67
substituent 420.4
substitute 380.5
substitution 261.75
substitutive 485
substrate 367
substratum 242.26
substructure 17.66
subsume 241
subsumption 261.89
subtangent 420.22
subtemperate 371.35
subtenancy 16.312
subtenant 420.52
subtend 131
subterfuge 204
subterranean 261.3.15.1
subtilize 516.2

subtitle 228.103
subtle 228.107
subtlety 16.352
subtonic 38.35
subtorrid 91.26
subtotal 228.106
subtract 382
subtraction 261.76
subtractive 485.16
subtrahend 131
subtropical 228.23.14
subtropics 498
subtype 275
subulate 371.18
suburb 22
suburban 261.9
suburbanite 372.6
suburbanize 516.7
suburbia 17.3.2
subvene 251
subvention 261.82
subversion 261.69
subversive 485.3
subvert 369
subway 2
subzero 12.63
succedaneum 242.2.10
succeed 89
succentor 17.368
success 296
successful 226.5
succession 261.68
successive 485.2
successor 17.300
succinate 367.17
succinct 392
succinic 38.34
succory 16.274
succotash 349
succour 17.39
succubus 310
succulent 420.27
succumb 240
succursal 228.84
succuss 307
such 72
suchlike 39
suck 43
sucker 17.39
sucking 265
suckle 228.27
sucrase 509
sucrose 520

suction 261.79
Sudan 246
Sudanic 38.31
sudarium 242.2.14
sudatorium
242.2.17
Sudbury 16.274
sudd 100
sudden 261
suddenness 300.31
Sudetenland 143
Sudetes 513.16
sudor 9
sudoriferous
310.50.2
sudorific 38.12.1
suds 530
sue 15
suede 85
suet 371.3
Suetonius 310.2.9
Suez 515
suffer 17.118
sufferance 321.20
sufferer 17.279
suffering 265.58
suffice 301
sufficiency 16.312.5
sufficient 420.74
suffix 498
suffocate 367.6
suffocation
261.67.6
Suffolk 46
suffragan 261
suffrage 197
suffragette 368
suffragist 436.4
suffumigate 367.10
suffuse 523.1
Sufi 16.89
Sufism 242.35
sugar 17.135
sugar daddy 16.57
sugarplum 240
sugary 16.274
suggest 433
suggestibility
16.333.9.2
suggestible
228.16.59
suggestion 261.18
suggestive 485.24
suicidal 228.33
suicide 92.7

sui generis 300.47
suint 412
suit 380
suitability
16.333.9.2
suitable 228.16.53
suitcase 295
suite 370
suiting 265
suitor 17.351
sukiyaki 16.20
Sulawesi 16.296
sulcate 367.7
sulcus 310
Suleiman 246
sulk 50
sulkiness 300.23
sulky 16.35
Sulla 17.173
sullage 197
sullen 261
sullenness 300.31
Sullivan 261.114
sully 16.128
sulphanilamide
92.3
sulphate 367
sulphide 92
sulphite 372
sulphonamide 92.3
sulphonate 367.18
sulphone 257
sulphur 17
sulphurate 367.22
sulphuric 38.43
sulphurize 516
sulphurous 310.50
sultan 261
sultana 17.226
sultanate 367.18
sultanic 38.31
sultry 16
Sulu 15.4
sum 240
sumach 32
Sumatra 17.292
Sumer 17.217
Sumerian 261.3.22
summa 1
summa cum laude
2
summand 128
summarize 516.8
summary 16.274
summation 261.67

summer 17.216
summerhouse 306
summertime 236
summerwood 101
summery 16.274
summit 371
summitry 16.285
summon 261
summons 551
Sumo 12
sump 289
sumptuary
16.274.2
sumptuous 310.4.4
sumptuousness
300.34.2
sun 259
sunbake 34
sunbathe 473
sunbeam 234
sunbird 87
sunbonnet 371.25
sunburn 249
sunburnt 411
sunburst 434
sundae 2
Sunday 2
sunder 17.108
Sunderland 143.4
sundew 15
sundial 228.4
sundog 185
sundown 258
sundress 296
sundry 16
sunfast 431
sunflower 14
sung 267
Sungari 16.274
sunglass 294
sunglasses 515
sungrebe 23
sunhat 365
sunk 54
sunken 261
sunless 300
sunlight 372
sunlit 371
sunn 259
Sunna 17.237
Sunni 16.235
Sunnite 372
sunny 16.235
sunray 2
sunrise 516

sunroof 170
sunset 368
sunshade 85
sunshine 253
sunshiny 16.230
sunspot 373
sunstar 1
sunstroke 42
sunsuit 380
suntan 245
suntanned 128
suntrap 268
Sun Yat-sen 248
sup 279
super 17.259
superable
228.16.35
superabound 139
superabundant
420.16
superadd 83
superannuate 367.2
superannuated
91.34.2
superannuation
261.67.2
superb 22
superbazaar 1.19
supercharge 192
supercharger
17.145
superciliary
16.274.1.1
supercilious
310.2.5
superclass 294
superconductivity
16.333.35.3
supercool 227
super-duper 17.259
superego 12.28
supererogatory
16.274.43.3
superfamily 16.120
superfetation
261.67
superficial 228.93
superficiality
16.333.8.1
superfine 253
superfix 498
superfluid 91.3
superfluidity
16.333.5

superfluity
16.333.3
superfluous 310.4
supergiant 420.2
superheat 370
superhero 12.63
superhet 368
superhighway 2.26
superhuman 261.51
superimpose 520
superinduce 309
superintend 131
superintendency
16.312.2
superintendent
420.14
superior 17.3.39
superiority
16.333.22
superlative 485.15
superman 261.52
supermarket 371.7
supernal 228.58
supernatant 420.75
supernatural
228.76
supernova 17.417
supernumerary
16.274.32
superoxide 92.14
superpose 520.2
superpower 14
supersaturated
91.34.7
superscript 424
supersede 89.3
supersedure 17.149
supersession
261.68.1
supersex 496
supersonic 38.35.4
supersonics 498.5
superstar 1
superstition 261.71
superstitious
310.58
superstratum
242.26
superstruct 389
superstructure
17.66
supertax 494
supertonic 38.35.5
supervene 251.12
supervise 516

supervision
261.91.3
supervisor 17.441
supervisory
16.274.53
supinate 367.17
supinator 17.338.7
supine 253
suplex 496
supper 17.258
supplant 408
supplantation
261.67
supple 228
supplejack 32
supplement 410.1
supplement 420.31
supplementary
16.274.47
suppleness 300.30
suppletion 261.70
suppliant 420.1
supplicant 420.7
supplicate 367.5
supplication
261.67.5
supplier 17.4
supply 7.9
support 374.2
supportable
228.16.51
supporter 17.345
supporting 265.69
supportive 485.13
suppose 520.2
supposed 155.1
supposedly 16.148
supposing 265.83
supposition
261.71.9
suppositious
310.58
suppositive
485.12.1
suppository
16.274.41
suppress 296.5
suppression 261.68
suppressive 485.2
suppurate 367.22
suppuration
261.67.21
suppurative 485.15
supralapsarian
261.3.21

supremacist 436.22
supremacy 16.307
suprematism
242.35.20
supreme 234
supremo 12.47
Surabaya 17.4
surah 17.277
sural 228.75
surbase 295
surcharge 192
surcingle 228.50
surcoat 376
surculose 305
surd 87
sure 10
sure-footed 91
sure-footedness
300.28
surely 16.124
surety 16.337
surf 161
surface 300
surfactant 420
surfboard 95
surfcasting 265.74
surfeit 371
surfie 16.83
surfing 265
surfperch 65
surge 195
surgeon 261.35
surgeoncy 16.312.3
surgery 16.274.13
surgical 228.23.4
suricate 367.5
Surinam 229
surliness 300.23
surly 16.116
surmise 516
surmount 418
surmountable
228.16.56
surname 231
surpass 294
surplice 300
surplus 310
surprint 412
surprise 516.9
surprising 265.82
surprisingly 16.175
surreal 228.2
surrealism
242.35.11.1
surrealist 436.7.1

surrealistic
38.70.2.1
surrender 17.101
surreptitious
310.58
surreptitiousness
300.34.3
Surrey 16.272
surrey 16.272
surrogate 371
surround 139.1
surrounding 265.22
surroundings 552
surtax 494
surveillance 321.11
survey 2
surveying 265.1
surveyor 17.1
survival 228.121
survive 486
survivor 17.415
Susa 17.308
Susanna 17.225
susceptance 321
susceptibility
16.333.9.2
susceptible
228.16.58
sushi 16.326
suslik 38
suspect 385
suspend 131.4
suspender 17.101
suspense 316
suspension 261.82
suspensive 485.9
suspensoid 97
suspensory
16.274.38
suspicion 261.71
suspicious 310.58
suspire 8.2
Susquehanna
17.225
suss 307
Sussex 498
sustain 247
sustainer 17.227
sustenance 321
sustentacular
17.174.3
sustentation
261.67.32
susurrate 367.23
Sutcliffe 163

telescript

tarsier 17.3.47
Tarsus 310.52
tarsus 310.52
tart 366
tartan 261.95
Tartar 17.337
tartar 17.337
tartaric 38.38
tartarous 310.50
Tartarus 310.50
Tartary 16.274
tartlet 371
tartrate 367
Tarzan 261
tasimeter 17.342.2
task 56
taskmaster 17.380
taskwork 36
Tasman 261
Tasmania 17.3.31
Tasmanian
  261.3.15
Tass 293
tass 293
tassel 228
tasset 371
taste 432
tasteful 226.12
tasteless 300
tastelessness
  300.33
taster 17.381
tasty 16.363
tat 365
ta-ta 1
Tate 367
tater 17.338
tatouay 2.3
tatter 17.336
tattersall 221
tatting 265
tattle 228.97
tattler 17.200
tattletale 214
tattoo 15
tatty 16.327
tatty-peelin 252
taught 374
taunt 415
taunter 17.370
Taunton 261
taupe 278
Tauranga 17.245
taurine 251.6, 253
tauromachy 16.33

Taurus 310.48
taut 374
tauten 261.102
tautog 185
tautology 16.108.4
tautomer 17.218
tautomerism
  242.35.15
Tavel 215
tavern 261
taverner 17.239
taw 9
tawdry 16.276
tawny 16.232
tawse 518
tax 494
taxable 228.16
taxation 261.67.34
taxi 16.386
taxidermic 38.26
taxidermist 436
taxidermy 16.214
taximeter 17.341
taxiplane 247
taxis 300.70
taxiway 2
taxon 254
taxonomic 38.29.1
taxonomy 16.222.3
taxpayer 17.1
Tay 2
tay 2
Taylor 17.162
tayra 17.274
Tayside 92
tazza 17.319
Tbilisi 16.299
Tchaikovsky 16.44
te 5
tea 5
tcacake 34
teacart 366
teach 66
teachable
  228.16.12
teacher 17.55
teaching 265
teacup 279
teahouse 306
teak 37
teal 217
team 234
teamster 17.393
teamwork 36
teapot 373

teapoy 11
tear 4, 6
tearable 228.16.33
tearful 226
tearing 265.52
tear-jerker 17.32
tearless 300
tearoom 241
tease 513
teasel 228
teaser 17.440
teashop 276
teaspoon 260
teat 370
technetium 242.2
technical 228.23
technicality
  16.333.8.3
technician 261.71
Technicolor 17.173
technics 498
technique 37
technocracy
  16.307.5
technological
  228.23.5
technologist 436.4
technology
  16.108.4
tectonic 38.35
tectonics 498.5
tectrix 498
ted 86
tedder 17.80
Te Deum 242.1
tedious 310.2
tediousness
  300.34.1
tedium 242.2.2
tee 5
teem 234
teeming 265.36
teen 251
teenage 193
teenager 17.146
teens 547
teeny 16.228
teenybopper
  17.255
Tees 513
Teesside 92
teeter 17.341
teeth 457
teethe 475
teething 265

teetotal 228.106
teetotaller 17.176
teetotum 242.31
tef 160
Teflon 254
teg 181
tegmen 261
Teheran 246
Tehuantepec 35
tela 17.165
telaesthesia 17.3.60
telamon 261.52
Tel Aviv 484
telecast 431
telecommunication
  261.67.5
telecommunications
  551.1
teledu 15.2
telega 17.125
telegenic 38.32
telegnosis 300.55
Telegonus 310.36
telegony 16.237
telegram 229
telegraph 158
telegrapher 17.120
telegraphic 38.11
telegraphy 16.90
telekinesis 300.51
telekinetic 38.50.4
Telemachus 310.14
telemark 33.2
telemeter 17.342
telemetry 16.285
teleology
  16.108.4.1
teleost 438
telepathic 38.72
telepathize 516.14
telepathy 16.373
telephone 257
telephonic 38.35
telephonist 436.13
telephony 16.237
telephoto 12.79
telephotography
  16.90.2.6
teleplay 2
teleprinter 17.369
Teleran 245.5
telescope 278
telescopic 38.37
telescopy 16.254
telescript 424

telestich 38.69
telethon 254
teletranscription
  261.85
teletube 30
Teletype 275
televise 516.15
television 261.91.2
telewriter 17.343
telex 496
Telford 103
telic 38.20
teliospore 9.10
telium 242.2.5
tell 215
Tell el Amarna
  17.226
teller 17.163
telling 265.28
telltale 214
tellurian 261.3.24
telluric 38.43
telluride 92
tellurion 261.3.24
tellurium 242.2
tellurometer
  17.342.3
telly 16.115
telophase 509
telpherage 197
telson 261
Telstar 1
Tema 17.210
temerity 16.333.21
temp 286
temper 17.262
tempera 17.279
temperament
  420.35
temperamental
  228.110.3
temperance 321.20
temperate 371.35
temperature 17.56
tempest 436
tempestuous 310.4
Templar 17.196
template 371
temple 228
tempo 12
temporal 228.76
temporality
  16.333.8.9
temporary
  16.274.32

temporize 516.8
tempt 428
temptation 261.67
tempter 17.378
tempting 265
temptress 300
tempura 1.13
ten 248
tenable 228.16
tenace 295
tenacious 310.56.4
tenacity 16.333.25
tenaculum 242.10
tenaille 214
tenancy 16.312
tenant 420.52
tenantry 16.291
tench 79
tend 131
tendency 16.312.2
tendentious 310.61
tender 17.101
tenderfoot 379.1
tenderhearted
  91.33
tenderize 516.8
tenderizer 17.441.1
tenderloin 256
tenderness 300.26
tendinous 310.33
tendon 261
tendril 218
tenebrism 242.35
tenebrosity
  16.333.30
tenebrous 310
Tenedos 302
tenement 420.35
Tenerife 162.2
tenet 371
tenfold 120
Tengri Nor 9
tenner 17.228
Tennessee 5.20
tennis 300
tenno 12.52
Tennyson 261.65
tenon 261
tenor 17.228
tenorite 372.8
tenorrhaphy
  16.90.1
tenotomy 16.222.4
tenpenny 16.237
tenpin 252

tenpins 548
tenrec 35
tense 316
tensible 228.16.40
tensile 219.3
tensiometer
  17.342.3.1
tension 261.82
tensive 485.9
tensor 17.314
tent 410
tentacle 228.28
tentacular 17.174.3
tentage 197.14
tentation 261.67.32
tentative 485.15.15
tenter 17.368
tenterhook 44
tenth 468
tenuity 16.333.3
tenuous 310.4.2
tenure 10
tenuto 12.80
Tenzing Norgay 2
teocalli 16.112
teosinte 16.356
tepal 228.65
tepee 5
tepefy 7.3
tephrite 372
tepid 91.23
tequila 17.165
Terai 7.12
teraph 171
teratism 242.35.20
teratogenic 38.32.1
teratoid 97
teratology
  16.108.4.15
terbium 242.2
tercel 228.84
tercet 371
terebene 251
terebinth 470
terebinthine 253
teredo 12.18
Terence 321.16
terete 370
tergiversate 367
teriyaki 16.20
term 233
termagant 420.18
terminable
  228.16.29
terminal 228.60

terminate 367.17.4
termination
  261.67.18.4
terminator
  17.338.7
terminology
  16.108.4.10
terminus 310.33
termitarium
  242.2.14
termite 372
termor 17.209
tern 249
ternary 16.274.24
ternate 371.23
terne 249
terpene 251
terpineol 220.1
Terpsichore
  16.274.4
Terpsichorean
  261.2.3
terrace 310.44
terra cotta 17.344
terra firma 17.209
terrain 247
terrane 247
terrapin 252
terrarium 242.2.14
terrene 251
terreplein 247
terrestrial 228.3.13
terret 371.31
terre-verte 369
terrible 228.16
terribly 16.137
terricolous
  310.26.2
terrier 17.3
terrific 38.12.1
terrify 7.3.5
terrigenous 310.33
terrine 251
territorial
  228.3.12.1
territorialism
  242.35.11.2
territoriality
  16.333.8.1
territorialize
  516.3.2.2
territory 16.274.41
terror 17.269
terrorism 242.35.15
terrorist 436.20

terroristic 38.70.5
terrorize 516.8
Terry 16.262
terry 16.262
terse 297
tertial 228.92
tertian 261.69
tertiary 16.274
tertium quid 91
Tertullian 261.3.13
Terylene 251.2
terzetto 12.75
Tess 296
tessellate 367.12
tessellation 261.67.12
tessera 17.279
tesseract 382
tessitura 17.277
test 433
testa 17.382
testament 420.35
testamentary 16.274.47
testate 367.33
testator 17.338
testatrix 498.9
tester 17.382
testes 513.19
testicle 228.23
testiculate 371.17.2
testify 7.3
testimonial 228.3.8
testimony 16.237
testing 265.75
testis 300.68
teston 261.106
testosterone 257.1
testudinal 228.60.1
testudo 12.22
testy 16.364
tetanic 38.31
tetanize 516.7
tetanus 310.36
tetany 16.237
tetchy 16.48
tête-à-tête 367.31
tête-bêche 351
tether 17.402
tetra 17.293
tetrabrach 32
tetrachloride 92.5
tetrachord 95.3
tetracid 91.28
tetracycline 251

tetrad 83
tetragonal 228.63
tetragram 229.1
tetrahedron 261
tetralogy 16.108.2
tetrapod 94.1
tetrapody 16.72
tetrarch 33
tetraspore 9.10
tetrastich 38
tetrode 98
tetter 17.339
Teucer 17.308
Teuton 261.104
Teutonic 38.35
Teutonism 242.35.14
Teutonize 516.7
Tewkesbury 16.274
Texan 261
Texas 310
text 450
textbook 44
textile 219.8
textual 228.9
textualism 242.35.11.3
textuary 16.274.2
texture 17.75
Thackeray 16.274
Thai 7
Thailand 143
Thaïs 300
thalamus 310.29.2
thalassic 38.48
thaler 17.161
Thales 513
thalidomide 92.3
thallium 242.2
thallous 310
thallus 310
thalweg 181
Thames 541
than 245
thanatopsis 300.61
Thanatos 302
thane 247
Thanet 371.22
Thanjavur 10
thank 51
thankful 226
thankfulness 300.30
thankless 300

thanklessness 300.33
thanks 504
thanksgiving 265.80
Thapsus 310
Thásos 302
that 365
thatch 62
Thatcher 17.50
thatcher 17.50
thaumatology 16.108.4.15
thaumatrope 278.3
thaumaturge 195
thaw 9
thearchy 16.20
theatre 17.352
theatrical 228.23
theatricals 539.2
theatrics 498.8
theca 17.33
thee 5
theft 397
their 4
theirs 512
theism 242.35.1
them 232
thematic 38.49.1
theme 234
Themis 300
themselves 555
then 248
thenar 1
thence 316
theocentric 38.47
theocracy 16.307.5.1
theocrasy 16.307.5.1
Theocritus 310.64
theodicy 16.300.1
theodolite 372.4
Theodoric 38.44
theogony 16.237.4
theologian 261.3
theologize 516.1
theology 16.108.4.1
theomachy 16.33
theomancy 16.309
theomania 17.3.31.1
theonomy 16.222.3.1

theopathy 16.373.1.1
theophagy 16.108.1
theophany 16.237.3.1
Theophilus 310.23
theophobia 17.3.4
theorem 242.19
theoretical 228.23.19
theoretician 261.71.7
theoretics 498.12
theorist 436.20
theorize 516.8
theory 16.265
theosophy 16.90.4
therapeutic 38.56
therapeutics 498
therapist 436.15
therapsid 91.31
therapy 16.254
there 4
thereabouts 344
thereafter 17.358
thereat 365
thereby 7
therefore 9
therefrom 237
therein 252
thereinto 15
thereof 487
thereon 254
Theresa 17.440
thereto 15
theretofore 9
thereunder 17.108
thereupon 254
therewith 476
therianthropic 38.37.3
theriomorphic 38.14
therm 233
thermae 5
thermaesthesia 17.3.60
thermal 228
thermalize 516.3
thermion 261.3
thermionic 38.35.1
thermionics 498.5
thermistor 17.384
thermocouple 228

thermodynamic 38.24
thermodynamics 498.2
thermoelectric 38
thermoelectricity 16.333.28
thermogenesis 300.52.4
thermograph 158.1
thermography 16.90.2
thermolysis 300.52.2
thermolytic 38.52.1
thermomagnetic 38.50
thermometer 17.342.3.2
thermometry 16.285.2
thermonuclear 17.3
thermophile 219.1
thermophilic 38.21
thermopile 219
thermoplastic 38.68
Thermopylae 5.9
Thermos 310
thermoscope 278.1
thermosetting 265.65
thermosphere 6.1
thermostat 365
thermostatic 38.49.7
thermostatics 498.11
thermotaxis 300.70
thermotensile 219.3
thermotherapy 16.254
theroid 97.10
theropod 94.1
thesaurus 310.48
these 513
Theseus 310.2
thesis 300.51
Thespian 261.3
Thespis 300
Thessalonian 261.3.18
Thessaly 16.131
theta 17.341

thetic 38.50
Thetis 300
theurgy 16.102
thew 15
they 2
they'd 85
they'll 214
they're 4
they've 482
thiamine 252.15
thiazole 223
thick 38
thick-and-thin 252
thicken 261.13
thickener 17.239
thickening 265.46
thicket 371.9
thickleaf 162
thickly 16.142
thickness 300.27
thickset 368
thick-skinned 134
thief 162
thieve 484
thieving 265.79
thigh 7
thighbone 257
thimble 228
thimbleful 226
thimblerig 184
thimbleweed 89.7
thimblewit 371
thin 252
thine 253
thing 265
thingumabob 26
thingumajig 184
think 52
thinkable 228.16.11
thinker 17.44
thinking 265.10
thinner 17.231
thinness 300
thin-skinned 134
thionic 38.35
thionyl 218
thiophen 248
thiourea 17.3.42
third 87
third-rate 367
thirdstream 234
thirl 216
Thirlmere 6
thirst 434
thirstiness 300.23

thirsty 16.365
thirteen 251
thirteenth 469
thirtieth 458
thirty 16.331
this 300
thistle 228.85
thistledown 258
thistly 16.181
thither 17.405
thitherto 15
thixotropic 38.37.2
thole 223
tholos 302
Thomas 310
Thomism 242.35
Thompson 261
thong 266
Thor 9
thoracic 38.48
thoracotomy 16.222.4
thorax 494
thoria 17.3.41
thorite 372
thorium 242.2.17
thorn 255
thornback 32
thornbill 218
Thorndike 39
thorny 16.232
thoron 254.10
thorough 17.278
thoroughbred 86
thoroughfare 4.3
thoroughgoing 265.4
thoroughly 16.131
thoroughness 300.26
thoroughpin 252
Thorpe 277
those 520
Thoth 461
thou 13
though 12
thought 374
thoughtful 226
thoughtfulness 300.30
thoughtless 300
thoughtlessness 300.33
thousand 143
thousandth 471

Thrace 295
thrall 221
thrash 349
thrasher 17.321
thrashing 265
thrawn 255
thread 86
threadbare 4
threadfin 252
threadworm 233
thready 16.60
threap 273
threat 368
threaten 261.96
three 5
three-dimensional 228.63.9
threefold 120
three-legged 91
threescore 9
threesome 242
threnody 16.72
thresh 351
thresher 17.323
threshold 120
threw 15
thrice 301
thrift 398
thriftless 300
thriftlessness 300.33
thrifty 16.347
thrill 218
thriller 17.166
thrilling 265.30
thrips 327
thrive 486
throat 376
throatlash 349
throaty 16.339
throb 26
throes 520
thromboembolism 242.35.11
thrombogen 261.39
thromboplastic 38.68
thrombose 305
thrombosis 300.55
thrombotic 38.53
thrombus 310
throne 257
throng 266
throstle 228.86
throttle 228.104

tipster 17.396
tipsy 16.314
tiptoe 12
tiptop 276
tirade 85
Tirana 17.226
tire 8
tireless 300
tirelessness 300.33
tiresome 242
Tirich Mir 6
tiring 265.54
Tiros 305
Tirunelveli 16.115
'tis 515
tisane 245.7
tissue 15
tit 371
Titan 261.100
Titania 17.3.30
titanic 38.31
Titanism 242.35.14
titanium 242.2.10
titanosaur 9.11
titanothere 6.10
titbit 371
tithable 228.16
tithe 477
Tithonus 310.35
titi 5
Titian 261.71
titillate 367.12
titillation 261.67.12
titivate 367.36
titivation 261.67
title 228.103
titled 122
titman 261
titmouse 306
Tito 12.76
Titoism 242.35.3
titrant 420
titrate 367
titration 261.67
titre 17.343
titter 17.342
tittle 228.102
tittle-tattle 228.97
tittup 281
titubation 261.67
titular 17.174.12
Titus 310.65
Tiv 485
Tivoli 16.131
tizzy 16.396

Tlingit 371
tmesis 300.51
to 15
toad 98
toadflax 494
toadstone 257
toadstool 227
toady 16.67
toast 441
toaster 17.387
toastmaster 17.380
tobacco 12.8
tobacconist 436.13
Tobago 12.27
toboggan 261
Tobruk 44.1
Toby 16.12
toccata 17.337
Tocharian 261.3
tocology 16.108.4
tocopherol 220.4
tocsin 252.29
tod 94
today 2.8
Todd 94
toddle 228.34
toddler 17.188
toddy 16.65
to-do 15.3
tody 16.67
toe 12
toea 1
toecap 268
toehold 120
toenail 214
toey 16.3
toff 165
toffee 16.86
toft 399
tog 185
toga 17.133
together 17.402
togetherness
   300.26
toggery 16.274.12
toggle 228.47
Togliatti 16.327
Togo 12.31
Togoland 143.3
toil 222
toile 213
toilet 371
toiletry 16.285
toilette 368
toilsome 242

tokay 2
Tokay 7
token 261.14
tokenism 242.35.14
tokoloshe 354
Tokyo 12
tola 17.171
tolan 245
tolbutamide 92.3
told 120
tole 223
Toledo 12.17,
   12.18
tolerable 228.16.35
tolerance 321.20
tolerant 420.65
tolerate 367.23
toleration
   261.67.22
Tolkien 251
toll 223
tollbooth 479
tollgate 367
tollhouse 306
Tolpuddle 228.36
Tolstoy 11
Toltec 35
toluate 367.2
toluene 251
Tom 237
tom 237
tomahawk 41
tomalley 16.112
toman 246
tomato 12.73
tomb 241
tombac 32
tombola 17.171
tomboy 11
tomboyish 353
tombstone 257
tome 239
tomentum 242
tomfool 227
tomfoolery 16.274
tommyrot 373
tomography
   16.90.2
tomorrow 12.65
tomtit 371
ton 259
tonal 228.62
tonality 16.333.8
Tonbridge 197
tone 257

toneless 300
toneme 234
toner 17.236
tonetic 38.50
tong 266
Tonga 17.142
tongue 267
tonic 38.35
tonicity 16.333.28
tonight 372.6
tonk 53
tonka 17.45
Tonle Sap 268
tonnage 197
tonne 259
tonneau 12
tonometer
   17.342.3.3
tonsil 228.89
tonsillectomy
   16.222.5
tonsillitic 38.52
tonsillitis 300.62.1
tonsillotomy
   16.222.4
tonsorial 228.3.12
tonsure 17
tontine 251
tonus 310.35
Tony 16.233
too 15
toodle-oo 15.5
took 44
tool 227
tooling 265
toon 260
toot 380
tooth 463
toothache 34
toothbrush 356
toothful 226.14
toothless 300
toothpaste 432
toothpick 38
toothsome 242
toothy 16.372
tootle 228.108
toots 345
tootsy 16.318
tootsy-wootsy
   16.318
top 276
toparch 33
topaz 507
topazolite 372.4

topcoat 376
tope 278
topee 5.16
toper 17.257
topgallant 420.24
Tophet 368
topiary 16.274.1
topic 38.37
topical 228.23.14
topicality
   16.333.8.3
topknot 373
topless 300
toplofty 16.348
topmast 431
topminnow 12.55
topmost 441
topnotch 68
topnotcher 17.57
topography 16.90.2
topology
   16.108.4.12
toponym 235
toponymy 16.216
topos 302
topper 17.255
topping 265
topple 228.68
tops 329
topsail 214
topside 92.10
topsoil 222
topspin 252
topsy-turvy 16.381
toque 42
tor 9
Torbay 2
torch 69
torchbearer 17.271
torchère 4
torchier 17.3
tore 9
toreador 9.4
torero 12.62
tori 7.11
torii 5.2
torment 410
tormentil 218
tormentor 17.368
torn 255
tornadic 38.7
tornado 12.17
toroid 97
Toronto 12.85
torose 305

torpedo 12.18
torpid 91
torpor 17.256
Torquay 5
torque 41
torques 513
torr 9
Torrance 321.18
torrefy 7.3
torrent 420.63
torrential 228.96.2
torrid 91.26
torsade 85
torsion 261.72
torso 12
tort 374
torte 374
tortellini 16.228.1
torticollis 300.9
tortilla 17.2
tortious 310.59
tortoise 310
tortoiseshell 215
tortoni 16.233
tortricid 91.29
tortuosity
   16.333.30.2
tortuous 310.4
torture 17.58
torturer 17.279
torus 310.48
Tory 16.269
Toscanini 16.228
tosh 354
toss 302
tosspot 373
tot 373
total 228.106
totalitarian
   261.3.21.2
totality 16.333.8
totalizator 17.338
totalize 516.3
totalizer 17.441
tote 376
totem 242.31
totemic 38.25
totemism 242.35
totipotent 420.78
totter 17.344
toucan 261.15
touch 72
touchable 228.16
touchdown 258
touché 2

touching 265
touchline 253
touchmark 33
touchstone 257
touchwood 101
touchy 16.52
tough 168
toughen 261
toughie 16.88
toughness 300
Toulouse 523
toupee 2
tour 10
touraco 12
Tourane 246
tourbillion 261.120
tourer 17.277
tourism 242.35
tourist 436.19
touristic 38.70
touristy 16.366
tourmaline 251.3
tournament 420.35
tournedos 12
tourniquet 2.7
tousle 228.129
tous-les-mois 1
tout 377
tovarisch 353
tow 12
towage 197
toward 95.4
towards 528
towbar 1
towel 228.8
towelling 265
tower 14
towering 265.57
tow-haired 88
towhead 86.3
towline 253
town 258
townee 5
townhall 221
townie 16.234
townscape 270
township 274
townsman 261
townspeople
   228.65
townswoman
   261.50
towpath 453
towrope 278
toxaemia 17.3.26.1

toxaphene 251
toxic 38.75
toxicant 420.7
toxicity 16.333.28
toxicogenic 38.32.1
toxicology
   16.108.4.4
toxicosis 300.55
toxin 252.29
toxoid 97
toxophilite 372.3
toy 11
Toyama 1.10
trabeated 91.34.1
trabecula 17.174.4
Trabzon 255
trace 295
traceable 228.16.36
tracer 17.299
tracery 16.274.33
trachea 17.2
tracheid 91.2
tracheitis 300.62
tracheostomy
   16.222.6
tracheotomy
   16.222.4.1
trachoma 17.215
trachyte 372
trachytic 38.52
tracing 265.59
track 32
tracker 17.28
trackless 300
tracksuit 380
tract 382
tractable 228.16
Tractarianism
   242.35.14.1.1
tractate 367
tractile 219.4
traction 261.76
tractive 485.16
tractor 17.353
Tracy 16.296
trad 83
trade 85
trademark 33
trader 17.79
tradescantia
   17.3.50
tradesfolk 42
tradesman 261
trading 265.11
tradition 261.71.2

treacle 228
treacly 16.141
tread 86
treadle 228
treadmill 218
treason 261.125
treasure 17.333
treasured 103.6
treasurer 17.279
treasury 16.274
treat 370
treatise 515
treatment 420
treaty 16.332
Trebizond 136
treble 228
Treblinka 17.44
trebly 16.133
trebuchet 368
trebucket 371.11
tree 5
treehopper 17.255
treeless 300
treen 251
treenail 214
treenware 4
trefoil 222
trehala 17.161
treillage 197
trek 35
trekker 17.31
trellis 300
trelliswork 36
trematode 98
tremble 228.18
trembly 16.138
tremendous 310
tremolo 12.45
tremor 17.208
tremulant 420.27
tremulous 310.25
trench 79
trenchant 420
trencher 17.70
trencherman
   261.52
trend 131
trendy 16.78
Trent 410
Trenton 261
trepan 245.3
trepang 263
trephine 251
trepidation
   261.67.7

treponema 17.210
trespass 310
trespasser 17.309
tress 296
tressure 17.323
trestle 228
trestletree 5
tret 368
trevally 16.112
Trevelyan 261.119
Trevino 12.54
trews 523
trey 2
triable 228.16.3
triacid 91.28
triad 83.2
triage 197
trial 228.4
triangle 228.49
triangular 17.174
triangulate
   367.13.4
triangulation
   261.67.13.2
Triangulum 242.10
triarchy 16.20
Triassic 38.48
triatomic 38.29
triaxial 228.3.18
tribal 228
tribalism 242.35.11
tribe 25
tribesman 261
triblet 371
tribrach 32
tribulation
   261.67.13
tribunal 228
tribune 260
tributary 16.274.42
tribute 380.2
trice 301
tricentenary
   16.274.25
triceps 324
triceratops 329
trichiasis 300.57.1
trichina 17.232
trichinize 516.6
Trichinopoly
   16.131.6
trichinosis 300.55.4
trichite 372
trichloride 92.5
trichocyst 436.22

trichogyne 253
trichoid 97.3
trichology
   16.108.4.4
trichome 239
trichomonad 83.3
trichotomy
   16.222.4
trichroism 242.35.3
trichromatic
   38.49.2
trick 38
trickery 16.274.4
trickle 228.23
tricksy 16.388
tricky 16.25
triclinic 38.34
triclinium 242.2.11
tricolour 17.176.2
tricorn 255
tricot 12.11
tricotine 251.11
tricrotic 38.53
trictrac 32
tricuspid 91
tricycle 228.23
trident 420
tridentate 367.32
Tridentine 253
triennial 228.3
triennium 242.2
trierarchy 16.20
Trieste 433
trifid 91
trifle 228
trifling 265
trifolium 242.2.7
triforium 242.2.17
trifurcate 371.8
trig 184
trigeminal 228.60.3
trigger 17.129
triglyph 163
trigon 254
trigonometry
   16.285.2.2
trigraph 158
trike 39
trilateral 228.76
trilateration
   261.67.22
trilby 16.16
trilemma 17.208
trilinear 17.3.34
trilingual 228

trilithon 254
trill 218
trillion 261.120
trillionth 471
trillium 242
trilobate 367.3
trilobite 372
trilogy 16.108.3
trim 235
trimaran 245.5
trimer 17.212
trimester 17.382
trimeter 17.342.2
trimetric 38.46
trimetrogon 254.5
trimmer 17.211
trimming 265
trimonthly 16.205
trimorph 166
Trimurti 16.337
trinary 16.274.27
Trincomalee 5.9
trine 253
Trinidad 83
Trinitarian
   261.3.21.2
trinity 16.333.17
trinket 371
trinomial 228.3
trio 12.2
triode 98
triolet 368
trioxide 92.14
trip 274
tripartite 372
tripartition 261.71
tripe 275
triphibious 310.2
triphthong 266
triphylite 372.3
triplane 247
triple 228.66
triplet 371
Triplex 496
triplicate 367.5,
   371.9
triplicity
   16.333.28.1
triploid 97
triply 16.177
tripod 94
tripody 16.72
Tripoli 16.131.5
tripoli 16.131.5

tubule 227
tubuliflorous
310.48
tubulous 310.25
Tucana 17.226
tuchun 260
tuck 43
tucker 17.39
tucket 371.11
Tucson 254
Tudor 17.91
Tuesday 2
tufa 17.119
tuff 168
tuffet 371
tuft 400
tufted 91
tufty 16.349
tug 189
tugrik 37
tui 16.4
Tuileries 16.274
tuition 261.71
tularaemia 17.3.26
tulip 274
Tull 225
tulle 227
Tulsa 17.311
tum 240
tumble 228
tumble-down 258
tumblehome 239
tumbler 17.180
tumbleweed 89.7
tumbrel 228.77
tumefaction 261.76
tumefy 7.3
tumescence 321.21
tumescent 420.67
tumid 91
tummy 16.220
tumour 17.217
tump 289
tumular 17.174
tumulose 305
tumult 406
tumultuous 310.4
tumulus 310.25.5
tun 259
tuna 17.238
tunable 228.16
tundra 17.288
tune 260
tuneful 226
tuneless 300

tunelessness 300.33
tuner 17.238
tunesmith 458
tungsten 261
Tungus 308
Tungusic 38
tunic 38
tunicate 371.9
tunicle 228.23
tuning 265
Tunis 300
Tunisia 17.3.61
tunnel 228
tunny 16.235
tup 279
tupelo 12.42
Tupi 5
tuque 45
turban 261.9
turbary 16.274
turbid 91
turbinate 371.24
turbine 253
turbocar 1
turbocharger
  17.145
turbo-electric 38
turbofan 245
turbojet 368
turboprop 276
turbot 381
turbulence 321
turbulent 420.27
turd 87
turdine 253
tureen 251.7
turf 161
turfy 16.83
turgescent 420.67
turgid 91
turgor 17.127
Turin 252
turion 261.3.24
Turk 36
Turkestan 246.1
Turkey 16.23
turkey 16.23
Turkic 38
Turkish 353
Turkoman 261.52
turmeric 38.44
turmoil 222
turn 249
turnabout 377.1
turnaround 139.1

turnbuckle 228.27
turncoat 376
turncock 40
turner 17.229
turnery 16.274.24
turning 265.41
turnip 274
turnkey 5
turnpike 39
turnsole 223
turnstile 219
turntable 228.11
turpentine 253
turpeth 458
Turpin 252
turpitude 102.2
turps 325
turquoise 519
turret 371
turreted 91.38
turtle 228
turtleback 32
turtledove 489
turtleneck 35
Tuscan 261.17
Tuscany 16.237
Tuscarora 17.276
tusche 357
Tusculum 242.10
tush 356
tusk 60
tusker 17.49
Tussaud 12
tussis 300
tussle 228.87
tussock 46
tussore 9
tut 378
Tutankhamen 261
Tutankhamun 260
tutee 5
tutelage 197.1
tutelary 16.274.16
tutor 17.351
tutorial 228.3.12
tutsan 261
tutti 16.342
tutti-frutti 16.343
tutty 16.341
tutu 15
Tuvalu 15.5
tu-whit tu-whoo
  15
tuxedo 12.18
tuyère 4

twaddle 228.34
Twain 247
twain 247
twang 263
'twas 517
twat 365
twayblade 85
tweak 37
twee 5
Tweed 89
tweed 89
Tweedledee 5
Tweedledum 240
tweedy 16.62
tweet 370
tweeter 17.341
tweeze 513
tweezers 524
Twelfthtide 92
twelve 492
twentieth 458
twenty 16.355
'twere 3
twerp 272
Twi 5
twibill 218
twice 301
Twickenham
  242.16
twiddle 228.32
twig 184
twiggy 16.93
twilight 372
twilit 371
twill 218
twin 252
twine 253
twinge 209
twink 52
twinkle 228.29
twinkler 17.182
twinkling 265
twirl 216
twist 436
twister 17.384
twisty 16.366
twit 371
twitch 67
twitcher 17.56
twite 372
twitter 17.342
two 15
two-dimensional
  228.63.9
two-faced 432

twofold 120
twopence 321.15
twopenny 16.237
two-seater 17.341
twosome 242
Tyburn 249
Tyche 16.26
tychism 242.35
Tycho 12
tycoon 260
tyke 39
Tyler 17.167
tylopod 94.1
tympan 261
tympanic 38.31
tympanitis
  300.62.4
tympanum 242.16
tympany 16.237
Tyndale 228.40
Tyne 253
Tyneside 92
Tynwald 122
type 275
typecase 295
typecast 431
typeface 295
typescript 424
typeset 368
typesetter 17.339
typesetting 265.65
typewrite 372
typewriter 17.343
typewriting 265.67
typhlitis 300.62
typhlology
  16.108.4
typhogenic 38.32.1
typhoid 97
typhonic 38.35
typhoon 260
typhus 310
typical 228.23
typically 16.142
typify 7.3
typing 265
typist 436
typo 12
typographical
  228.23.3
typography 16.90.2
typology 16.108.4
typothetae 5.22
tyrannical
  228.23.10

tyrannicide 92.7
tyrannize 516.7
tyrannosaur 9.11
tyrannosaurus
  310.48.1
tyranny 16.237
tyrant 420
Tyre 8
tyre 8
Tyrian 261.3
tyro 12.64
Tyrol 223
Tyrolienne 248.1
Tyrone 257
tyrosinase 509
tyrosine 251.9
tyrothricin 252.22
Tyrrhenian
  261.3.16
Tzigane 246

U

ubiety 16.333.2
ubiquitarian
  261.3.21.2
ubiquitous 310.64
UCCA 17.39
udal 228.37
udder 17.90
udo 12.22
UFO 12
ufology 16.108.4
Uganda 17.98
Ugandan 261
Ugaritic 38.52.2
ugli 16.161
uglify 7.3
ugliness 300.23
ugly 16.161
Ugric 38
uhlan 246
Uigur 10
uintathere 6.10
Ujjain 247
ukase 509
ukiyoe 2
Ukraine 247
Ukrainian 261.3.15
ukulele 16.114
ulcer 17.311

ulcerate 367.23
ulceration
  261.67.22
ulcerative
  485.15.10
ulcerous 310.50
ulema 17.211
ullage 197
Ullswater 17.345
ulotrichous 310.10
Ulster 17
Ulsterman 261.52
ulterior 17.3.39
ultima 17.211
ultimate 371.19
ultimately 16.189.1
ultimatum 242.27
ultimo 12.48
ultrafilter 17.362
ultrahigh 7
ultraism 242.35
ultramarine 251.7
ultramodern
  261.26
ultramontane
  247.11
ultramontanism
  242.35.13
ultrashort 374
ultrasonic 38.35.4
ultrasonics 498.5
ultrasound 139
ultraviolet 371.18.1
ultravirus 310.47
ululate 367.13
Ulysses 513
umbel 228
umbelliferous
  310.50.2
umber 17.27
umbilical 228.23.7
umbilicate 371.9
umbilicus 310.10
umbo 12.7
umbra 17.285
umbrage 197
umbrageous 310.20
umbrella 17.163
Umbria 17.3.44
Umbrian 261.3.25
Umbriel 228.3
umiak 32.1
umlaut 377
umpire 8
umpteen 251

umpteenth 469
Umtali 16.113
unabated 91.34
unable 228.11
unabridged 110
unacceptable
  228.16.58
unacclaimed 124
unaccompanied
  91.21
unaccomplished
  449
unaccountable
  228.16.56
unaccustomed 127
unacquainted
  91.45
unadopted 91
unadorned 137
unadulterated
  91.34.7
unadvised 154
unadvisedly 16.148
unaffected 91.43
unafraid 85
unaided 91.6
unaimed 124
unaired 88
unalloyed 97.6
unanimity
  16.333.12
unanimous
  310.28.1
unanswerable
  228.16.35
unanswered 103
unapproachable
  228.16.13
unappropriated
  91.34.1
unapt 421
unarm 230
unarmed 123
unary 16.274.28
unashamed 124
unashamedly
  16.148
unasked 394
unassailable
  228.16.22
unassisted 91.53
unassuming 265.39
unatoned 138
unattached 395

underlay

unattainable
228.16.27
unattended 91.13
unattested 91.52
unattractive 485.16
unauthorized 154
unavailable
228.16.22
unavailing 265.27
unavoidable 228.16
unaware 4.8
unawares 512
unbacked 382
unbalance 321.10
unbar 1
unbearable
228.16.33
unbeatable
228.16.48
unbeaten 261.98
unbecoming 265.38
unbeknown 257
unbelief 162.1
unbelievable
228.16.61
unbeliever 17.413
unbelieving 265.79
unbelt 402
unbend 131
unbendable
228.16.18
unbending 265.20
unbent 410
unbiased 445
unbidden 261.24
unbind 135
unbirthday 2
unblessed 433
unblinking 265.10
unbolt 405
unbolted 91
unboned 138
unbonnet 371.25
unborn 255
unbosom 242
unbound 139
unbounded 91.14
unbowed 99
unbrace 295
unbreakable
228.16.9
unbred 86
unbridle 228.33
unbridled 122
unbroken 261.14

unbuckle 228.27
unburden 261.22
unbutton 261.103
uncaged 108
uncanny 16.223
uncap 268
uncaring 265.52
unceasing 265
unceremonious
310.2.9.1
uncertain 261.97
uncertainty 16.360
unchain 247
unchanging 265
unchaperoned 138
uncharted 91.33
unchecked 385
unchristian 261
unchristianly
16.174
unchurch 65
uncial 228.3
unciform 238.1
uncinate 371.24
uncinus 310.34
uncircumcised 154
uncivil 228.120
uncivilized 154
unclad 83
unclasp 290
unclassified 92.1
uncle 228.30
unclean 251
uncleaned 133
uncleanly 16.171
unclear 6
unclog 185
unclose 520
unclothe 478
unclothed 145
uncoil 222
uncomfortable
228.16
uncommercial
228.92
uncommon 261
uncommonly
16.174
uncommunicative
485.15.1
uncompromising
265.82
unconcern 249
unconcerned 132

unconcernedly
16.148
unconditional
228.63.5
unconditioned
143.5
unconformity
16.333.13
unconnected 91.43
unconscionable
228.16.31
unconscious 310
unconsciousness
300.34
unconstitutional
228.63.7
uncontrollable
228.16.24
unconventional
228.63.9
unconventionality
16.333.8.7
unconvincing
265.62
uncooked 390
uncoordinated
91.34.6
uncork 41
uncounted 91.49
uncouple 228
uncouth 463
uncovenanted
91.50
uncover 17.418
uncovered 103.7
uncross 302
uncrowned 139
unction 261.80
unctuous 310.4
uncurbed 105
uncurl 216
uncut 378
undaunted 91.47
undecagon 254.5
undeceive 484.2
undecided 91.8
undefended 91.13
undefiled 117
undemonstrative
485.15.11
undeniable
228.16.3
under 17.108
underachieve 484

underachiever
17.413
underact 382
underage 193
underarm 230
underbelly 16.115
underbid 91.4
underbody 16.65
underbred 86
underbrush 356
undercarriage
197.9
undercart 366
undercharge 192
underclay 2
undercoat 376
undercover 17.418
undercroft 399
undercurrent
420.64
underdevelop
281.1
underdog 185
underdone 259
underemployed 97
underestimate
367.15, 371.19
underestimation
261.67.15
underexpose 520
underexposure
17.335
underfed 86
underfeed 89
underfelt 402
underfloor 9
underfoot 379.1
underfur 3
undergarment 420
undergird 87
underglaze 509
undergo 12.33
undergone 254.5
undergraduate
371.2
underground 139.2
undergrown 257
undergrowth 461
underhand 128
underhanded 91.12
underhandedness
300.28.1
underhung 267
underlaid 85
underlay 2.12

515

unguiculate
371.17.2
unguis 300
ungula 17.174
ungulate 371.17
unguligrade 85.5
unhair 4
unhallowed 98
unhand 128
unhappiness
300.23
unhappy 16.243
unharmed 123
unharness 300.21
unhealthiness
300.23
unhealthy 16.374
unheard 87
unheeded 91
unhelm 243
unhesitating 265.64
unhinge 209
unholy 16.126
unhook 44
unhorse 303
unhurried 91
unhurt 369
uni 16.236
Uniat 365
uniaxial 228.3.18
unicameral 228.76
UNICEF 160
unicorn 255.2
unicycle 228.24
unifoliate 371.1
uniform 238.1
uniformitarianism
242.35.14.1.1
uniformity
16.333.13
unify 7.3
unilateral 228.76
unimaginable
228.16.29
unimpaired 88
unimpeachable
228.16.12
unimportant 420
unimpressed 433
unimproved 150
uninformed 125
uninspired 93
uninspiring 265.54
uninsured 96

unintelligent
420.20
unintelligible
228.16.20.1
unintentional
228.63.9
uninterested 91.53
uninvited 91.39
uninviting 265.67
union 261.123
unionism 242.35.14
unionist 436.13
unionize 516.7
uniparous 310.50
unipod 94
unique 37
uniramous 310.27
unisex 496
unisexual 228.9
unison 261.65
unit 371
unitarian
261.3.21.2
unitarianism
242.35.14.1.1
unitary 16.274.41
unite 372
united 91.39
unitive 485.12
unity 16.333.18
univalent 420.25
univalve 491
universal 228.84
universalism
242.35.11
universalist 436.7
universality
16.333.8
universalize 516.3
universally 16.131
universe 297.2
university
16.333.26
unjust 443
unkempt 428
unkenned 131
unkennel 228.57
unkind 135
unkindness 300.29
unknit 371
unknowable 228.16
unknowing 265.4
unknown 257
unlace 295
unlade 85

unladen 261.20
unlash 349
unlatch 62
unlawful 226.1
unlay 2
unlead 86
unleaded 91.7
unlearn 249
unlearned 91
unlearnt 411
unleash 352
unleavened 143
unless 296
unlicensed 448
unlike 39
unlikely 16.143
unlimited 91.38
unlined 135
unlisted 91.53
unlit 371
unlive 485
unload 98
unlock 40
unlocked 388
unloose 309
unlovely 16.207
unlucky 16.30
unmade 85
unmake 34
unman 245
unmanly 16.169
unmanned 128
unmannerly 16.131
unmarked 383
unmarried 91.25
unmask 56
unmeant 410
unmeasured 103.6
unmeet 370
unmentionable
228.16.31.1
unmentionables
539
unmerited 91.38
unmindful 226
unmistakable
228.16.9
unmitigated
91.34.4
unmolested 91.52
unmoor 10
unmounted 91.49
unmourned 137
unmoved 150
unmusical 228.23

unnamed 124
unnatural 228.76
unnecessary
16.274.36
unnerve 483
unnerving 265.78
unnoticed 436.25
unnumbered 103
unobserved 147
unobtainable
228.16.27
unobtrusive 485.8
unoccupied 92
unofficial 228.93
unopened 143
unopposed 155.1
unorthodox 499.1
unowned 138
unpack 32
unpaged 108
unpaid 85
unpainted 91.45
unparalleled 113
unparliamentary
16.274.47
unpaved 146
unpeg 181
unpeople 228.65
unperceived 148
unperforated
91.34.7
unperson 261.64
unperturbed 105
unpick 38
unpin 252
unplaced 432
unpleasant 420.84
unpleasantness 300
unplug 189
unpolled 120
unpolluted 91.42
unpopular
17.174.10
unpopularity
16.333.20.3
unposed 155
unpractised 436
unprecedented
91.46
unpredictable
228.16
unprejudiced 436.2
unpremeditated
91.34
unprepared 88

unprepossessing 265.60
unpresentable 228.16.55
unpreventable 228.16.55
unpriced 437
unprincipled 122
unprintable 228.16
unproductive 485.19
unprofessional 228.63.4
unprofitable 228.16.49
unpronounceable 228.16
unproved 150
unqualified 92.1
unquestionable 228.16.31
unquestioned 143
unquiet 381.2
unquote 376
unravel 228.117
unread 86
unreadable 228.16
unready 16.60
unreal 228.2
unreality 16.333.8.1
unreason 261.125
unreasonable 228.16.31.2
unrecognizable 228.16.64
unreconstructed 91
unrefined 135
unreflected 91.43
unregenerate 371.35
unrelenting 265
unreliability 16.333.9.2.1
unreliable 228.16.3
unremitting 265.66
unrepaired 88
unrequited 91.39
unreserved 147
unreservedly 16.148.1
unresolved 151
unrest 433
unrestrained 130
unrestricted 91

unrewarded 91.9
unrewarding 265.15
unrhymed 126
unriddle 228.32
unrig 184
unrighteous 310
unrip 274
unripe 275
unrivalled 122
unroll 223
unroot 380
unruffled 122
unruled 121
unruly 16.130
unsaddle 228.31
unsafe 159
unsaid 86
unsaturated 91.34.7
unsaved 146
unsavoury 16.274.50
unsay 2
unscathed 144
unscheduled 121
unschooled 121
unscientific 38.12
unscramble 228.17
unscratched 395
unscreened 133
unscrew 15
unscripted 91
unscrupulous 310.25
unscrupulousness 300.34
unseal 217
unseasonable 228.16.31.2
unseasoned 143.6
unseat 370
unsecured 96
unseeded 91
unseemly 16.166
unseen 251
unselfish 353.3
unselfishness 300.35
unset 368
unsettle 228.100
unsettled 122.2
unsex 496
unshaded 91.6

unshakable 228.16.9
unshaken 261.11
unshapen 261.57
unshaven 261.111
unsheathe 475
unship 274
unsighted 91.39
unsightly 16.190
unsigned 135
unsinkable 228.16.11
unskilful 226.3
unskilled 116
unslaked 384
unsling 265
unsnap 268
unsnarl 213
unsociable 228.16.44
unsocial 228.94
unsold 120
unsolved 151
unsophisticated 91.34.3
unsound 139
unsparing 265.52
unspeakable 228.16
unspoiled 119
unspoken 261.14
unspotted 91.40
unstable 228.11
unsteadiness 300.23.1
unsteady 16.60
unstick 38
unstop 276
unstoppable 228.16
unstopped 425
unstrained 130
unstratified 92.1
unstressed 433
unstring 265
unstructured 103
unstrung 267
unstuck 43
unstudied 91.11
unsubstantiated 91.34.1
unsuitability 16.333.9.2
unsuitable 228.16.53
unsuited 91.42

unsung 267
unsure 10
unsuspected 91.43
unsuspecting 265.71
unswear 4
unswerving 265.78
unsystematic 38.49.1
untamed 124
untangle 228.49
untaught 374
unteach 66
unteachable 228.16.12
untearable 228.16.33
untenable 228.16
unthanked 391
unthink 52
unthinkable 228.16.11
unthinking 265.10
unthread 86
untidiness 300.23
untidy 16.64
untie 7
until 218
untimely 16.167
untiring 265.54
untitled 122
unto 15
untold 120
untouchable 228.16
untoward 95.4
untranslatable 228.16.45
untravelled 122
untried 92
untrodden 261.26
untrue 15
untruss 307
untruth 463
untruthful 226.14
untruthfulness 300.30
untuck 43
unturned 132
untutored 103
unusual 228.9
unutterable 228.16.35
unvalued 102
unveil 214
unveiling 265.27

unvoice 304
unvoiced 440
unwanted 91
unwarrantable 228.16.57
unwarranted 91.50
unwary 16.264
unwavering 265.58.1
unwearable 228.16.33
unwearied 91
unweighed 85
unwelcome 242
unwell 215
unwept 422
unwholesome 242
unwieldy 16.74
unwilled 116
unwilling 265.30
unwillingness 300.32
unwind 135
unwinking 265.10
unwise 516
unwish 353
unwitnessed 436
unwitting 265.66
unwonted 91
unworldliness 300.23
unworldly 16.153
unworthy 16.375
unwound 139
unwrap 268
unwritten 261.99
unyielding 265
unyoke 42
unzip 274
up 279
Upanishad 83
upas 310
upbeat 370
upbraid 85
upbringing 265.47
upbuild 116
upcast 431
upcountry 16.290
update 367
upend 131
upgrade 85
upgrowth 461
upheaval 228.119
upheave 484
upheld 113

uphill 218
uphold 120
upholster 17.392
upholsterer 17.279
upholstery 16.274
upkeep 273
upland 143
uplift 398
upon 254
upper 17.258
uppercut 378
uppermost 441
uppish 353
uppity 16.333
Uppsala 17.161
upraise 509
uprear 6
upright 372
uprightness 300.39
uprise 516
uprising 265.82
uproar 9
uproarious 310.2.13
uproot 380
uprush 356
upset 368
upsetting 265.65
upshot 373
upside 92
upside-down 258
upsilon 254.6
upstage 193
upstairs 512
upstanding 265.19
upstart 366
upstate 367
upstream 234
upstroke 42
upsweep 273
upsy-daisy 16.393
uptake 34
upthrust 443
uptight 372
uptilt 403
uptown 258
upturn 249
upward 103
upwards 531
upwind 134
Ur 3
uracil 218
uraemia 17.3.26
uraeus 310.1
Ural 228.75

Uralic 38.19
uralite 372.4
Uranian 261.3.15
uranic 38.31
uranide 92.4
uraninite 372.5
uranite 372.6
uranium 242.2.10
uranography 16.90.2.4
uranous 310.36
Uranus 310.31
uranyl 218
urate 367
urban 261.9
urbane 247
urbanite 372.6
urbanity 16.333.14
urbanize 516.7
urchin 252
urd 87
urdé 2
Urdu 15
urea 17.3.42
urease 509.1
uredium 242.2.2
ureide 92
ureter 17.341
urethral 228
urethritis 300.62
urethroscope 278.1
uretic 38.50
urge 195
urgency 16.312.3
urgent 420.19
urgently 16.198
Uriah 17.4
uric 38.43
urinal 228.61
urinalysis 300.52.1
urinant 420.53
urinary 16.274.26
urinate 367.17
urination 261.67.18
urine 252
uriniferous 310.50.2
urinous 310.33
Urmia 17.3.25
urn 249
urnfield 115
urochord 95.3
urochrome 239
urodele 217
urogenous 310.33

urolith 458
urology 16.108.4
uroscopy 16.254.2
urostyle 219.7
Urquhart 381
ursine 253
Ursula 17.174
Ursuline 253
urticaceous 310.56.1
urticaria 17.3.38
Uruguay 7
urushiol 220.1
us 307
usable 228.16.65
usage 197
usance 321
use 309, 523
used 156
useful 226
usefulness 300.30
useless 300
uselessness 300.33
user 17.444
Ushant 420
usher 17.329
usherette 368.6
Usk 60
Üsküdar 1.3
usquebaugh 9
Ustashi 16.320
Ustinov 165.1
usual 228.9
usually 16.131
usufruct 389
usurer 17.279
usurious 310.2.14
usurp 272
usurpation 261.67
usurped 423
usurper 17.251
usury 16.274
Utah 9
Utamaro 12.61
Ute 380
utensil 228.88
uterine 253.7
uterus 310.50
Utgard 84
Utica 17.34
utilitarian 261.3.21.2
utilitarianism 242.35.14.1.1
utility 16.333.9

vasculum 242.10
vas deferens 546
vase 508
vasectomy 16.222.5
Vaseline 251.2
vasoconstrictor
17.355
vasodilator 17.338
vasopressin 252
vassal 228
vassalage 197
vast 431
vastness 300.42
vasty 16.362
VAT 365
vat 365
vatic 38.49
Vatican 261.13
Vaticanism
242.35.14.2
Vaud 12
vaudeville 218.3
vaudevillian
261.3.11
Vaughan 255
vault 404
vaulted 91.44
vaulting 265
vaunt 415
vavasor 9.11
vcal 217
vealer 17.165
vector 17.354
Veda 17.79
vedalia 17.3.18
Vedanta 17.365
Vedda 17.80
vedette 368
Vedic 38
veer 6
vccry 16.265
veg 194
Vega 17.128
vegan 261
vegetable 228.16
vegetal 228.102
vegetarian
261.3.21.2
vegetarianism
242.35.14.1.1
vegetate 367.30
vegetation
261.67.27
vegetative
485.15.12

vehement 420.31
vehicle 228.23
vehicular 17.174.6
Veii 7
veil 214
veiled 112
vein 247
veining 265.40
veinlet 371
veiny 16.225
velamen 248.2
velar 17.165
velarium 242.2.14
Velcro 12
veldt 402
veleta 17.341
veliger 17.150
velites 513
velleity 16.333.1
Vellore 9.8
vellum 242.8
veloce 16.50
velocipede 89.1
velocity 16.333.30
velodrome 239
velours 10
velouté 2.25
velum 242
velure 10.4
velutinous 310.33.2
velvet 371
velveteen 251
velvety 16.333
vena 17.230
vena cava 17.410
venal 228.59
venality 16.333.8
venatic 38.49
venation 261.67
vend 131
Venda 17.101
vendace 295
vendee 5
vendetta 17.339
vendible 228.16.18
vendor 9, 17.101
vendue 15
veneer 6.4
veneering 265.53
venerable
228.16.35
venerate 367.23.1
veneration
261.67.22.2
venereal 228.3.11

venereology
16.108.4.1
venery 16.274.23
venesection
261.77.5
Venetia 17.325
Venetian 261.70
Venetic 38.50.4
Venezuela 17.162
vengeance 321
vengeful 226
venial 228.3.6
Venice 300
venin 252.16
venipuncture 17.68
venison 261.65
Venite 16.334
venom 242
venomous 310.29
venose 305
venous 310.32
vent 410
ventage 197.14
ventail 214
venter 17.368
ventilate 367.12
ventilation
261.67.12
ventilator 17.338.5
ventral 228.80
ventricle 228.23
ventricose 305
ventricular
17.174.6
ventriculus
310.25.2
ventriloquism
242.35
ventriloquist 436
ventriloquize 516
ventriloquy 16.259
venture 17.70
venturesome 242
Venturi 16.270
venue 15
venule 227
Venus 310.32
Venusian 261.3
veracious 310.56
veracity 16.333.25
Veracruz 523
veranda 17.98.2
verb 22
verbal 228

verbalism
242.35.11
verbalist 436.7
verbalize 516.3.4
verbatim 235
verbena 17.230
verbiage 197
verbid 91
verbose 305
verbosity 16.333.30
Vercingetorix 498.7
verdant 420
verdict 387
verdigris 300
verdure 17.148
verge 195
verger 17.148
verglas 1
veridical 228.23
verifiable
228.16.3.1
verify 7.3.5
verily 16.120
verisimilar 17.166
verisimilitude
102.2
verism 242.35
verismo 12.50
veritable 228.16.49
verity 16.333.21
verjuice 309
Vermeer 6
vermeil 214
vermicelli 16.115
vermicide 92.7
vermicular
17.174.6
vermiculate
367.13.2, 371.17.2
vermiculation
261.67.13
vermiform 238.1
vermifuge 204
vermilion 261.120
vermin 252.13
vermination
261.67.18.4
verminous 310.33
vermis 300.18
vermivorous
310.50.3
Vermont 414
vermouth 464
vernacular 17.174.3

vintage 197
vintager 17.150
vinyl 218
viol 228.4
viola 17.171,
  17.176.1
viola da gamba
  17.23
viola d'amore
  16.269
violate 367.14.1
violation
  261.67.14.1
violence 321.12
violent 420.28
violet 371.18.1
violin 252.11
violinist 436.11
violist 436
violoncello 12.40
viper 17.254
viperous 310.50
virago 12.26
viral 228
virelay 2.11
virescence 321.21
virga 17.127
Virgil 218
virgin 252
virginal 228.60
Virginia 17.3.34
virginity 16.333.17
virginium 242.2.11
Virgo 12
virgulate 371.17
virgule 227
viridescent 420.67
viridian 261.3.5
viridity 16.333.5
virile 219
virilism 242.35.9
virility 16.333.9
virology 16.108.4
virtual 228.9
virtually 16.131.1
virtue 15
virtuosity
  16.333.30.2
virtuoso 12.70
virtuous 310.4
virulence 321
virulent 420.27
virus 310.47
visa 17.440
visage 197

vis-à-vis 5
viscacha 17.50
viscera 17.279.2
visceral 228.76
viscid 91.29
viscoid 97
viscometer
  17.342.3
viscose 305
viscosity 16.333.30
viscount 418
viscountess 300
viscous 310.15
viscus 310.15
Vishnu 15
visibility
  16.333.9.2.2
visible 228.16.63
Visigoth 459
vision 261.91
visionary 16.274.29
visit 371.38
visitant 420.76
visitation 261.67.27
visitatorial
  228.3.12.2
visitor 17.342.4
visor 17.441
vista 17.384
Vistula 17.174
visual 228.9
visualize 516.3.3
vital 228.103
vitalism 242.35.11
vitality 16.333.8
vitalize 516.3
vitamin 252.15
vitellin 252.7
vitiate 367.1.6
vitiation 261.67.1.5
viticulture 17.69
Vitória 17.3.41
vitrain 247
vitreous 310.2
vitrescence 321.21
vitrescent 420.67
vitric 38
vitriform 238.1
vitrify 7.3
vitrine 251
vitriol 220.1
vitriolic 38.22
vitta 17.342
vituline 253
vituperate 367.23

vituperation
  261.67.22
vituperative
  485.15.10
viva 17.413, 17.415
vivace 16.47
vivacious 310.56
vivacity 16.333.25
Vivaldi 16.73
vivarium 242.2.14
viva voce 16.50
viverrine 253
Vivian 261.3.30
vivid 91
vividness 300.28
vivify 7.3
viviparity
  16.333.20
viviparous 310.50
vivisect 385.7
vivisection 261.77.5
vivisectionist
  436.13.6
vixen 261
Viyella 17.163
vizard 103
vizier 6
vizierate 371.32
Vlach 33
Vladimir 6.2
vocab 18
vocable 228.16
vocabulary
  16.274.18
vocal 228.26
vocalic 38.19
vocalise 513.7
vocalism 242.35.11
vocalist 436.7
vocalize 516.3
vocation 261.67.6
vocational 228.63.3
vocative 485.15.2
vociferate 367.23
vociferous 310.50.2
vodka 17
vogue 188
Vogul 228
voice 304
voiceless 300
voiceprint 412
void 97
voidance 321
voided 91
voile 222

voir dire 6
Volans 544
volant 420
Volapuk 44
volar 17.171
volatile 219
volatilize 516.2
volcanic 38.31
volcanism
  242.35.14
volcanize 516.7
volcano 12
volcanology
  16.108.4.11
vole 223
Volga 17.138
volitant 420.76
volition 261.71.3
volitive 485.12
volley 16.122
volleyball 221
volost 438
volplane 247
Volsci 5
volt 405
Volta 17.364
voltage 197
voltaic 38.1
Voltaire 4
voltameter 17.342
volte-face 294
voluble 228.15
volume 241
volumeter 17.342
voluminosity
  16.333.30.4
voluminous
  310.33.1
voluntarism
  242.35.15
voluntary
  16.274.48
volunteer 6
voluptuary
  16.274.2
voluptuous 310.4
voluptuousness
  300.34.2
volute 380
volution 261.75.1
volva 17.423
Volvo 12
volvox 499
volvulus 310.25
vomer 17.215

vomit 371.20
vomitory 16.274.41
vomitus 310.64
voodoo 15
Voortrekker 17.31
voracious 310.56
voracity 16.333.25
vortex 496
vorticella 17.163
vortices 513
vorticism 242.35.16
vortiginous 310.33
Vostok 40
votary 16.274
vote 376
voter 17.347
votive 485.14
Votyak 32.1
vouch 71
voucher 17.60
vouchsafe 159
vouge 364
voussoir 1
Vouvray 2
vow 13
vowel 228.8
vox 499
vox humana
  17.226
vox populi 7.6
voyage 197
voyager 17.150
voyageur 3
voyeur 3
voyeuristic 38.70.5
vraisemblance 315
vroom 241
vug 189
Vulcan 261
vulcanian 261.3.15
vulcanite 372.6
vulcanize 516.7
vulgar 17.139
vulgarian 261.3.21
vulgarism
  242.35.15
vulgarity 16.333.20
vulgarize 516.8
Vulgate 367
vulnerable
  228.16.35
vulnerary
  16.274.32
Vulpecula 17.174.4
vulpine 253

vulture 17.69
vulturine 253.7
vulva 17.424
vulvitis 300.62

W

WAAF 157
Wabash 349
wacky 16.19
wad 94
wadding 265
waddle 228.34
waddler 17.188
waddy 16.65
wade 85
wader 17.79
waders 524
wadi 16.65
Wadi Halfa 17.121
Wad Medani 5.10
wadset 368
wae 2
wafer 17.111
waff 157
waffle 228
waft 396
wafter 17.358
wag 178
wage 193
wager 17.146
wages 515
wagga 17.131
Wagga Wagga
  17.131
waggish 353
waggle 228.43
Wagner 17
Wagnerian
  261.3.22
wagon 261.30
wagoner 17.239
wagonette 368
wagonload 98
wagtail 214
Wahhabi 16.6
wahine 16.228
waif 159
Waikato 12.73
Waikiki 5
wail 214

wain 247
wainscot 381
wainwright 372
waist 432
waistband 128
waistcoat 376
waisted 91
waistless 300
waistline 253
wait 367
waiter 17.338
waitress 300
waive 482
waiver 17.410
wake 34
Wakefield 115
wakeful 226
waken 261.11
wakerife 164
waking 265.6
Walachia 17.3
Waldemar 1.11
Waldenses 513.14
waldgrave 482
Waldorf 166
wale 214
Waler 17.162
Wales 536
walk 41
walkabout 377.1
walker 17.37
walkie-talkie 16.28
walking 265.9
walkover 17.417
walkway 2
wall 221
wallaby 16.15
Wallace 300.9
wallah 17.168
wallaroo 15.6
Wallasey 16.307
walled 118
wallet 371
walleye 7
walleyed 92
wallflower 14
Walloon 260
wallop 281.2
walloper 17.260
walloping 265
wallow 12.43
wallpaper 17.249
Wallsend 131
wally 16.112,
  16.122

walnut 378
Walpole 223
walrus 310
Walsall 221
Walsingham
  242.17
Walton 261
waltz 312
waltzer 17.310
wame 231
wampum 242
wan 254
wand 136
wander 17.104
wanderer 17.279
wandering 265.58
wanderlust 443
wanderoo 15.6
Wandsworth 464
wane 247
Wanganui 16.4
wangle 228.49
wank 51
Wankel 228
wanna 17.233
want 414
wanting 265
wanton 261
wapentake 34
wapiti 16.333
wappenshaw 9
war 9
waratah 17.352
warb 27
Warbeck 35
warble 228
ward 95
warden 261.27
warder 17.86
wardrobe 28
wardroom 241
wardship 274
ware 4
warehouse 306
warehouseman 261
wares 512
warfare 4
warfarin 252.20
warhead 86
warhorse 303
wariness 300.23
warison 261.65.1
Warley 16.123
warlike 39
warlock 40

warlord 95
warm 238
warm-blooded
91.11
warmer 17.214
warmish 353
warmness 300
warmonger 17.143
warn 255
warning 265
warp 277
warpath 453
warplane 247
warrant 420.63
warrantable
228.16.57
warrantee 5.24
warrantor 9
warranty 16.360
warren 261
warrigal 212
warring 265.55
Warrington 261
warrior 17.3
Warsaw 9
warship 274
warsle 228.83
wart 374
wartime 236
warty 16.336
Warwick 38.41
Warwickshire 6
wary 16.264
was 517
wash 354
washable 228.16
washbasin 261.62
washboard 95
washday 2
washer 17.327
washerwoman
261.50
washery 16.274
washing 265
Washington 261
washrag 178
washroom 241
washstand 128
washtub 29
washy 16.323
wasn't 420
wasp 292
waspish 353
wassail 214
wastage 197

waste 432
wasteful 226.12
wasteland 143
wasteweir 6
wastrel 228
wat 366
watap 269
watch 68
watchcase 295
watchdog 185
watcher 17.57
watchful 226
watchmaker 17.30
watchman 261
watchstrap 268
watchtower 14
watchword 87
water 17.345
waterage 197
waterborne 255.1
waterbuck 43
watercolour 17.173
watercourse 303
watercress 296
waterfall 221
Waterford 103
waterfowl 224
waterfront 419.1
Watergate 367.11
waterlogged 106
Waterloo 15.5
waterman 261.52
watermark 33
watermelon 261.40
waterproof 170
waterscape 270
watershed 86
waterside 92.8
waterspout 377
watertight 372.12
waterway 2.28
waterweed 89
waterworks 497
waterworn 255
watery 16.274
Watford 103
Watson 261
watt 373
wattage 197
Watteau 12.77
wattle 228.104
wattlebird 87
Watusi 16.402
Watutsi 16.318
Waugh 9

waul 221
wave 482
waveband 128
waveform 238
waveguide 92
wavelength 472
wavelet 371
waveoff 165
waver 17.410
wavy 16.379
wax 494
waxbill 218
waxen 261
waxplant 408
waxwing 265
waxwork 36
waxy 16.386
way 2
waybill 218
wayfarer 17.271
Wayland 143
waylay 2
Wayne 247
wayside 92
wayward 103
wayzgoose 309
Waziristan 246.1
we 5
weak 37
weaken 261.12
weakling 265
weakly 16.141
weakness 300
weal 217
Weald 115
wealth 465
wealthy 16.374
wean 251
weaner 17.230
weanling 265
weapon 261
weaponry 16.284
wear 4
Wear 6
wearable 228.16.33
wearer 17.271
weariless 300.8
weariness 300.23
wearing 265.52
wearisome 242.24
wearproof 170
weary 16.265
weasand 143.6
weasel 228
weather 17.402

weather-beaten
261.98
weatherboard 95.1
weathercock 40
weatherglass 294
weathering 265.58
weatherly 16.131
weatherman 261.52
weatherproof 170
weatherworn 255
weave 484
weaver 17.413
weaverbird 87
weaving 265.79
web 21
webbed 104
webbing 265
webby 16.8
Weber 17.11
webfoot 379
wed 86
we'd 89
wedded 91.7
wedding 265.12
wedge 194
Wedgwood 101
wedlock 40
Wednesday 2
wee 5
weed 89
weedkiller 17.166
weedy 16.62
week 37
weekday 2
weekender 17.101
weekly 16.141
weeknight 372
weeny 16.228
weep 273
weeper 17.252
weeping 265.49
weepy 16.247
weever 17.413
weevil 228.119
weft 397
weigela 17.165
weigh 2
weighbridge 197
weight 367
weighting 265.64
weightless 300
weightlessness
300.33
weightlifter 17.359
weightlifting 265

Wisconsin 252
wisdom 242
wise 516
wiseacre 17.30
wisecrack 32
wisent 420
wish 353
wishbone 257
wisher 17.326
wishful 226
wishy-washy
  16.323
wisp 291
wispy 16.258
wisteria 17.3.39
wistful 226
wit 371
witan 261.99
witch 67
witchcraft 396
witchery 16.274
witching 265
wite 372
with 476
withal 221
withdraw 9
withdrawal 228.5
withdrawn 255
withdrew 15
withe 458
wither 17.405
withers 524
withershins 548
withheld 113
withhold 120
within 252
without 377
withstand 128
withstood 101
withy 16.376
witless 300.17
witness 300.38
wits 339
Wittgenstein 253
witticism 242.35.16
witty 16.333
Witwatersrand 128
wive 486
wizard 103
wizardry 16.277
wizen 261.126
wizened 143
woad 98
woaded 91.10
wobbegong 266

wobble 228
wobbly 16.135
Wodehouse 306
Woden 261
wodge 199
woe 12
woebegone 254.4
woeful 226.2
woggle 228.47
wok 40
woke 42
woken 261.14
Woking 265
wold 120
wolf 175
wolfbane 247
Wolfe 175
wolfhound 139
wolfram 242
wolframite 372
Wollongong 266
wolly 16.122
Wolof 165
Wolverhampton
  261
wolverine 251.7
woman 261.50
womanhood 101
womanish 353
womanize 516.7
womanizer 17.441
womankind 135
womanly 16.174
womb 241
wombat 365
women 252.14
womenfolk 42
won 254, 259
wonder 17.108
wonderful 226
wonderland 143.4
wonderment
  420.35
wonderwork 36
wonder-worker
  17.32
wondrous 310
wonky 16.38
Wonsan 245
won't 417
wont 417
wonted 91
won ton 254
woo 15
wood 101

woodbine 253
woodborer 17.276
woodchat 365
woodchuck 43
woodcock 40
woodcraft 396
woodcut 378
woodcutter 17.349
wooded 91
wooden 261
woodenhead 86
woodgrouse 306
woodland 143
woodlander 17.109
woodlark 33
woodlouse 306
woodman 261
woodnote 376
woodpecker 17.31
woodpile 219
woodprint 412
woodruff 168
woodrush 356
woodscrew 15
woodshed 86
woodsia 17.3
woodwind 134
woodwork 36
woodworking 265
woodworm 233
woody 16.70
woof 169, 170
woofer 17.119
wool 226
Woolf 175
woolgathering
  265.58
woollen 261
woolly 16.129
woolpack 32
woolsack 32
Woomera 17.279
woomera 17.279
Woop Woop 280
woozy 16.402
Worcester 17.388
Worcestershire 6
word 87
wordage 197
wordbreak 34
wording 265
wordless 300
wordplay 2
Wordsworth 464
wordy 16.61

wore 9
work 36
workable 228.16
workaday 2.8
workbag 178
workbench 79
workbook 44
workday 2
worker 17.32
workfolk 42
workhorse 303
workhouse 306
working 265
workload 98
workman 261
workmanlike 39
workmanly 16.174
workmanship
  274.2
workroom 241
workshop 276
workshy 7
Worksop 276
worktable 228.11
world 114
worldliness 300.23
worldling 265
worldly 16.153
worldwide 92
worm 233
wormcast 431
wormseed 89
wormwood 101
wormy 16.214
worn 255
worriment 420.31
worrisome 242.24
worrit 371
worry 16.272
worrywart 374
worse 297
worsen 261.64
worship 274
worshipful 226
worshipper 17.253
worst 434
worsted 91
wort 369
worth 456
Worthing 265
worthless 300
worthlessness
  300.33
worthwhile 219
worthy 16.375

Wotan 246
would 101
wouldn't 420.12
wound 139, 142
wounded 91
woundwort 369
wove 488
woven 261.116
wow 13
wowser 17.443
wrack 32
wraith 454
wrangle 228.49
wrangler 17.194
wrap 268
wrapover 17.417
wrapper 17.247
wrapping 265
wrapping 265.48
wrasse 293
wrath 459
wrathful 226
wreak 37
wreath 457
wreathe 475
wreck 35
wrecker 17.31
Wrekin 252
wren 248
wrench 79
wrest 433
wrestle 228
wrestler 17.197
wrestling 265
wretch 64
wretched 91
wretchedness 300.28
Wrexham 242
wriggle 228.46
Wright 372
wring 265
wringer 17.246
wrinkle 228.29
wrinkly 16.145
wrist 436
wristlet 371
wristlock 40
wristwatch 68
writ 371
write 372
writer 17.343
writhe 477
writing 265.67
written 261.99

wrong 266
wrongdoer 17.8
wrongdoing 265.5
wrongful 226
wrongly 16.176
wrote 376
wroth 461
wrought 374
wrung 267
wry 7
wrybill 218
wryneck 35
Wu 15
Wuhu 15
wulfenite 372.6
Wu-lu-mu-ch'i 5
wunderkind 134
wurley 16.116
wurst 434
Württemberg 182
wus 307
Wyandotte 373
Wyatt 381.2
wych-elm 243
Wycherley 16.131
Wycliffe 163
Wycliffite 372
Wye 7
wynd 135
Wyoming 265.37
wyvern 261.115

X

xanthein 252
Xanthippe 16.248
xanthochroism 242.35.3
xanthoma 17.215
xanthophyll 218.1
Xanthus 310.72
Xavier 17.3.53
xebec 35
xenia 17.3.33
Xenocrates 513.17
xenocryst 436
xenolith 458
xenon 254
xenophile 219.1
xenophobe 28
xenophobia 17.3.4

xenophobic 38.3
xerarch 33
xeric 38
xeroderma 17.209
xerography 16.90.2
xerophilous 310.23
xerophthalmia 17.3.28
xerosere 6.7
xerosis 300.55.5
Xerox 499
Xerxes 513
xiphisternum 242.13
xiphoid 97
Xmas 310
x-ray 2
xylem 232
xylograph 158.1
xylography 16.90.2
xyloid 97
xylol 220
xylophone 257
xylophonic 38.35.2
xylose 520
xylotomous 310.29.3
xyst 436
xyster 17.384

Y

yacht 373
yachting 265.68
yachtsman 261
yahoo 15
yak 32
yam 229
yammer 17.205
Yank 51
yank 51
yap 268
yappy 16.243
yard 84
Yarmouth 464
yarn 246
yarrow 12.60
yaw 9
yawl 221
yawn 255
yaws 518

ye 5
yea 2
year 6
yearly 16.119
yearn 249
yeast 435
yell 215
yellow 12.40
yellowhammer 17.205
yelp 283
yen 248
yeoman 261.49
yes 296
yes-man 261.53
yesterday 2.8
yet 368
yeti 16.330
yew 15
yield 115
yippee 5
ylang-ylang 263
yob 26
yodel 228
yoga 17.133
yogi 16.96
yogurt 381
yoke 42
yokel 228.26
yolk 42
yon 254
yonder 17.104
yoni 16.233
Yonkers 524
yonnie 16.231
yoo-hoo 15
yore 9
York 41
yorker 17.37
Yorkist 436
Yorks 500
Yorkshire 6
Yosemite 16.333
you 15
you'd 102
you'll 227
young 267
youngster 17
your 9
you're 10
yours 518
yourself 172
youth 463
youthful 226.14
you've 490

yowl 224
yo-yo 12
Ypsilanti 16.353
Yquem 232
ytterbia 17.3.2
ytterbium 242.2
yttrium 242.2
yuan 245
Yucatán 246
yucca 17.39
Yuga 17.135
Yugoslav 481
Yugoslavia 17.3
Yugoslavian 261.3
yuk 43
yukky 16.30
Yukon 254
yulan 245
yule 227
yuletide 92
Yuman 261.51
yummy 16.220
yup 279

Z

zabaglione 16.233
Zachariah 17.4.2
Zacharias 310.3
Zachary 16.274
zaffer 17.110
Zagazig 184
Zagreb 21
Zaïre 6
Zama 17.206
Zambezi 16.395
Zambia 17.3.5
Zamboanga 17.140
zamia 17.3.24
zamindar 1
zamindari 16.261
Zante 16.353

zany 16.225
Zanzibar 1.1
zap 268
Zapotec 35
zareba 17.13
zarf 158
Zaria 17.3
zarzuela 17.162
zeal 217
Zealand 143.1
zealot 381
zealotry 16.286
zealous 310.22
zealousness 300.34
Zeami 16.211
Zebedee 16.63
zebra 17.282
zebrawood 101
zebu 15
zecchino 12.54
Zechariah 17.4.2
zed 86
Zedekiah 17.4
zedoary 16.274
zee 5
zein 252
Zeist 437
Zen 248
Zena 17.230
zenana 17.226
zenith 458
zeolite 372.4
Zephaniah 17.4
zephyr 17.112
Zephyrus 310.50
zeppelin 252.11
zero 12.63
zest 433
Zeus 309
Zeuxis 300
zibeline 253.3
zibet 371.5
Ziegfeld 113
ziff 163
ziggurat 365

zigzag 178
zigzagger 17.123
zila 1.8
zilch 76
zillion 261.120
zinc 52
zincograph 158.1
zincography
  16.90.2
Zinfandel 215
zing 265
zinnia 17.3.34
Zion 261.4
Zionism 242.35.14
zip 274
zipper 17.253
zippy 16.248
zircon 254
zirconia 17.3.36
zirconium 242.2.12
zither 17.405
zloty 16.335
zo 12
zodiac 32.1
zodiacal 228.28.1
Zoffany 16.237.3
Zohar 1
Zola 17.171
Zomba 17.26
zombie 16.18
zonal 228.62
zonate 367
zonation 261.67
Zond 136
zone 257
zoo 15
zoochore 9.2
zoogeography
  16.90.2.1
zoography 16.90.2
zooid 97
zoolatry 16.286.2
zoological 228.23.5
zoologist 436.4

zoology 16.108.4.3
zoom 241
zoometry 16.285.2
zoophagous 310
zoophile 219.1
zoophilia 17.3.21.2
zoophilic 38.21
zoophilism
  242.35.9
zoophilous 310.23
zoophobia 17.3.4
zooplasty 16.361.1
zoosperm 233
zoospore 9.10
zoosterol 220.4
zootechnics 498
zootomy 16.222.4
zootoxin 252.29
zorilla 17.166.3
Zoroaster 17.379
Zoroastrian
  261.3.26
Zoroastrianism
  242.35.14.1
zoster 17.385
Zouave 481
zounds 533
zoysia 17.3
zucchetto 12.75
zucchini 16.228
Zuider Zee 5
Zulu 15.4
Zululand 143
Zürich 38.43
zwieback 32
zwitterion 261.4.1
zygote 376
zymase 509
zymogen 261.39
zymology 16.108.4
zymosis 300.55
zymotic 38.53
zymurgy 16.102
Zyrian 261.3

FOR THE BEST IN PAPERBACKS, LOOK FOR THE 🐧

In every corner of the world, on every subject under the sun, Penguin represents quality and variety – the very best in publishing today.

For complete information about books available from Penguin – including Puffins, Penguin Classics and Arkana – and how to order them, write to us at the appropriate address below. Please note that for copyright reasons the selection of books varies from country to country.

In the United Kingdom: Please write to *Dept JC, Penguin Books Ltd, FREEPOST, West Drayton, Middlesex, UB7 0BR.*

If you have any difficulty in obtaining a title, please send your order with the correct money, plus ten per cent for postage and packaging, to *PO Box No 11, West Drayton, Middlesex*

In the United States: Please write to *Dept BA, Penguin, 299 Murray Hill Parkway, East Rutherford, New Jersey 07073*

In Canada: Please write to *Penguin Books Canada Ltd, 2801 John Street, Markham, Ontario L3R 1B4*

In Australia: Please write to the *Marketing Department, Penguin Books Australia Ltd, P.O. Box 257, Ringwood, Victoria 3134*

In New Zealand: Please write to the *Marketing Department, Penguin Books (NZ) Ltd, Private Bag, Takapuna, Auckland 9*

In India: Please write to *Penguin Overseas Ltd, 706 Eros Apartments, 56 Nehru Place, New Delhi, 110019*

In the Netherlands: Please write to *Penguin Books Netherlands B.V., Postbus 3507, NL–1001 AH, Amsterdam*

In West Germany: Please write to *Penguin Books Ltd, Friedrichstrasse 10–12, D–6000 Frankfurt/Main 1*

In Spain: Please write to *Alhambra Longman S.A., Fernandez de la Hoz 9, E–28010 Madrid*

In Italy: Please write to *Penguin Italia s.r.l., Via Como 4, I-20096 Pioltello (Milano)*

In France: Please write to *Penguin France S.A., 17 rue Lejeune, F-31000 Toulouse*

In Japan: Please write to *Longman Penguin Japan Co Ltd, Yamaguchi Building, 2–12–9 Kanda Jimbocho, Chiyoda-Ku, Tokyo 101*

FOR THE BEST IN PAPERBACKS, LOOK FOR THE 🐧

PENGUIN REFERENCE BOOKS

The New Penguin English Dictionary

Over 1,000 pages long and with over 68,000 definitions, this cheap, compact and totally up-to-date book is ideal for today's needs. It includes many technical and colloquial terms, guides to pronunciation and common abbreviations.

The Penguin Spelling Dictionary

What are the plurals of *octopus* and *rhinoceros*? What is the difference between *stationary* and *stationery*? And how about *annex* and *annexe*, *agape* and *Agape*? This comprehensive new book, the fullest spelling dictionary now available, provides the answers.

Roget's Thesaurus of English Words and Phrases   Betty Kirkpatrick (ed.)

This new edition of Roget's classic work, now brought up to date for the nineties, will increase anyone's command of the English language. Fully cross-referenced, it includes synonyms of every kind (formal or colloquial, idiomatic and figurative) for almost 900 headings. It is a must for writers and utterly fascinating for any English speaker.

The Penguin Dictionary of Quotations

A treasure-trove of over 12,000 new gems and old favourites, from Aesop and Matthew Arnold to Xenophon and Zola.

The Penguin Wordmaster Dictionary
Martin H. Manser and Nigel D. Turton

This dictionary puts the pleasure back into word-seeking. Every time you look at a page you get a bonus – a panel telling you everything about a particular word or expression. It is, therefore, a dictionary to be read as well as used for its concise and up-to-date definitions.

FOR THE BEST IN PAPERBACKS, LOOK FOR THE 🐧

PENGUIN DICTIONARIES

Abbreviations
Archaeology
Architecture
Art and Artists
Biology
Botany
Building
Business
Chemistry
Civil Engineering
Computers
Curious and Interesting
   Words
Curious and Interesting
   Numbers
Design and Designers
Economics
Electronics
English and European
   History
English Idioms
French
Geography
German

Historical Slang
Human Geography
Literary Terms
Mathematics
Modern History 1789–1945
Modern Quotations
Music
Physical Geography
Physics
Politics
Proverbs
Psychology
Quotations
Religions
Rhyming Dictionary
Saints
Science
Sociology
Spanish
Surnames
Telecommunications
Troublesome Words
Twentieth-Century History